Legal Executions in Nebraska, Kansas and Oklahoma Including the Indian Territory

Also by R. Michael Wilson

Legal Executions After Statehood in Arizona, Colorado, Nevada, New Mexico, and Utah: A Comprehensive Registry
(McFarland, 2012)

Legal Executions After Statehood in North Dakota, South Dakota, Wyoming, Montana, Idaho, Washington and Oregon: A Comprehensive Registry
(McFarland, 2011)

Legal Executions in the Western Territories, 1847–1911: Arizona, Colorado, Idaho, Kansas, Montana, Nebraska, Nevada, New Mexico, North Dakota, Oklahoma, Oregon, South Dakota, Utah, Washington and Wyoming
(McFarland, 2010)

Also of Interest

Wells, Fargo & Co. Stagecoach and Train Robberies, 1870–1884: The Corporate Report of 1885 with Additional Facts About the Crimes and Their Perpetrators, rev. ed. James B. Hume and John N. Thacker. Edited and expanded by R. Michael Wilson (McFarland, 2010).

Legal Executions in Nebraska, Kansas and Oklahoma Including the Indian Territory

A Comprehensive Registry

R. MICHAEL WILSON

McFarland & Company, Inc., Publishers
Jefferson, North Carolina, and London

To those too oft forgotten:
THE VICTIMS

LIBRARY OF CONGRESS CATALOGUING-IN-PUBLICATION DATA

Wilson, R. Michael, 1944–
Legal executions in Nebraska, Kansas and Oklahoma including the Indian Territory : a comprehensive registry / R. Michael Wilson.
p. cm.
Includes bibliographical references and index.

ISBN 978-0-7864-6651-1
softcover : acid free paper ∞

1. Executions and executioners — Nebraska. 2. Capital punishment — Nebraska — History. 3. Criminal justice, Administration of— Nebraska — History. 4. Executions and executioners — Kansas. 5. Capital punishment — Kansas — History. 6. Criminal justice, Administration of— Kansas — History. 7. Executions and executioners — Oklahoma. 8. Capital punishment — Oklahoma — History. 9. Criminal justice, Administration of— Oklahoma — History. I. Title.
HV8699.U6N27 2012 364.660978 — dc23 2012018241

BRITISH LIBRARY CATALOGUING DATA ARE AVAILABLE

Manufactured in the United States of America

McFarland & Company, Inc., Publishers
Box 611, Jefferson, North Carolina 28640
www.mcfarlandpub.com

Table of Contents

Preface

Half the world's countries have abolished the death penalty, but in the United States the administration of the death penalty persists as one of the most controversial ethical and practical issues of American jurisprudence. Capital punishment has been under attack in America for a dozen decades and one day may become a relic, the details only to be found in those literary museums known as historical encyclopedias. I was drawn to a study of America's western case histories of capital punishment because the work of documenting these thrilling events has proven so daunting that few have undertaken the task. Those who have examined capital punishment west of the 98th meridian, however, have limited their efforts to mere lists or to documenting a constrained geographical area and time period. An examination of the death penalty in the West is an important aspect of the debate over capital punishment, and nothing less than 100 percent of the executions in 100 percent of the West through the end of 2010 gives us a basis for drawing meaningful conclusions.

In June 2009 sixteen jurisdictions among the United States had no death penalty statute in effect: Alaska, Hawaii, Iowa, Maine, Massachusetts, Michigan, Minnesota, New Jersey, New Mexico, New York, North Dakota, Rhode Island, Vermont, West Virginia, Wisconsin, and the District of Columbia. Thirty-five states, the federal government, and the military retained the death penalty but Kansas, New York and New Hampshire had not executed a person since 1976 when the U.S. Supreme Court restored the death penalty, while Illinois has had a moratorium on death sentences for a decade, and in early 2011 the state legislature voted to abolish capital punishment in the state. As 2010 came to a close, Colorado, Kansas, Maryland, Montana, Nebraska, and New Hampshire had retained the death penalty after close votes in several states, but these and other jurisdictions continue to consider statutes abolishing the practice due at least in part to economic considerations, but these states have the fewest prisoners on death row. Between 1976 and 2010 there have been one thousand two hundred thirty-four executions in the United States, reaching a high of ninety-eight in 1999 but decreasing to thirty-seven by the end of 2008, then increasing to fifty-two in 2009 and forty-six in 2010, and two-thirds of those put to death were executed in just five states: Florida, Missouri, Oklahoma, Texas, and Virginia.

This work contains all the details of all the crimes resulting in executions by hanging, firing squad, electrocution, and lethal injection in the three midwestern American states: Nebraska, Kansas, and Oklahoma including the Indian Territory. With this information one is able to see practices and patterns which lead to the logical conclusion that the death penalty is no deterrent to murder. Regardless of the number of executions, "cold-blooded, pre-meditated, first-degree murder with malice" proliferated in the West, and if there is a justification for the infliction of death as a punishment it must be to prevent future murders by the same miscreant.

The research for this book relied heavily upon contemporary newspapers and we are truly indebted to those editors who relished in the sordid details of executions to boost subscription rates. Other sources include court records and diaries or personal accounts. The work has been arranged with the researcher in mind, with case histories presented by state, chronologically, and each case history is headed by the name of the condemned and the date of execution with specific sources listed at the end of each case history, and a general bibliography and comprehensive index is provided.

Introduction

The English custom of hanging criminals came to America with the Pilgrims, and the practice of hanging criminals moved west with the pioneers. The sentence of death was imposed exclusively for the crime of "cold blooded, premeditated murder," or murder in the first degree, with only a few exceptions, and during the early years hanging was the most common form of execution. However, many convicted murderers were sentenced to prison terms and others eluded the executioner through suicide, by escaping from imprisonment never to be heard of again, or by obtaining a second trial on appeal and being acquitted or by being convicted of or pleading to a lesser degree of crime. In numerous instances death sentences were commuted to a life term in prison and, even when the evidence clearly showed every element necessary for a conviction of murder in the first degree, juries might bring in a peculiar verdict such as murder in the second degree or manslaughter. When a man was sentenced to death during those early years it was often only hours or days before the sentence was imposed, but as years passed the delay grew from months to years, and finally to decades.

Executions were at first thought to be a deterrent to murderers so gallows were built a distance from the jail, allowing for a solemn procession exhibiting the condemned man on his way to his death. Soon it became apparent that this caused more difficulties than benefits so scaffolds were built closer to the place of confinement. When the law changed to require that gallows be built inside an enclosure, and the hanging be a private affair, scaffolds were consistently built adjacent to the jail. The sheriff of each county was responsible for executions, and he invited at least one physician and might invite the district attorney, other lawmen, a coroner's jury of six to twelve reputable citizens, ministers of the gospel, and a small number of relatives or friends requested by the condemned. The condemned was provided access to religious comfort, and many condemned men chose to be baptized into a religion during their final hours. Before the fatal moment arrived the condemned man was offered a hearty meal; he washed, shaved and dressed in a new dark suit or other attire of his choosing provided by the county, state or federal authority; and the death warrant was read to him in his cell or at the place of execution. He might be provided an alcoholic beverage or drug to help him brace up for the ordeal. The prisoner was escorted by several men who provided support in case he faltered, and he was followed closely or led by his religious adviser if he had one. The condemned was placed on the trapdoor where his wrists and arms, knees and ankles were pinioned and the noose was adjusted. At some point during the proceedings he was given an opportunity to speak to the spectators, and once his speech was finished the final preparations were concluded, including a black hood pulled over his head or a blindfold tied over his eyes. It was then but a moment before the trap was sprung. A physician was required to be in attendance, and he would pronounce the moment of death; then the body was deposited into a coffin. People of the West were familiar with death by gunshot but hanging continued to be a mystery and preoccupied the interest of the public, so at times articles were published describing the sensations experienced. Of course there was no opportunity to ask the subject of a legal hanging as the law required that they be "hanged until dead," but failed suicides by hanging and scientific study provide insight into the sensations. As early as April 16, 1869, the *Walla Walla Statesman* (Washington) published an article entitled "How it feels to be hanged."

> "We are told that hanging, if successful — that is, if it breaks the person's neck — is the most sudden death he can die. It ruptures the spine in the immediate neighborhood of the *medulla oblongata*, and thus breaks up communication of the nerve force, or vital power, to the organs that carry on the human machinery. If the man's neck is not broken the first action of the cord is to close the trachea, or windpipe, and thus stop the supply of air. It also compresses the large veins in the neck which return blood to the heart — the jugulars — but does not entirely compress the large arteries that carry blood to the brain, for these lie deep. The immediate physiological effect is congestion of the brain — a congestion not dissimilar in its commencement from the congestion of drunkenness, which is generally regarded as agreeable, and the consequences of this congestion — a consequence that perhaps follows in three minutes after the pressure of the cord is felt — is the total abolition of conscious sensation. The man may struggle and writhe in a way

terrible to see, but these struggles are like those of convulsions generally — painful only to the beholder. Therefore, if a man is hanged successfully, he feels only the one sickening sensation of the plunge before he gets to the end of the rope; three seconds of horror. If he is hanged successfully, by strangulation, he feels the same three seconds, and in addition, between the pressure of the cord and the deep congestion of the brain, three minutes of swimming, drowsy, uncertain uneasiness — at worst, three minutes and three seconds; and this is all we give of misery to murderers. Compare with this the pain that man suffers before he dies from an ordinary illness — the drawn out wretchedness of his three weeks of fever, the days of agony with rheumatism, and the bent-forward, restless nights before this rheumatism finally brings his damaged heart to a standstill; the months of slow death entailed by a cancerous stomach; in fine, compare the history of any disease with the short shrift of hanging, and then reflect that our humanity now obliterates the murderer's three minutes and three seconds by the use of chloroform. Really it is a fine age, and if a man is tired of this world and wants to get out on easy terms, the thing for him to do is to cut his neighbor's throat and be hanged under chloroform."

One of the main criticisms of hanging as a means of execution was that the condemned's neck was, all too often, "unbroken and he would perish by the long and painful process of strangulation." John Burns, however, spoke from personal experience in refuting that perception. He recalled,

"Some time during the [Civil] war ruffians, who desired to be thought [bush] whackers, came upon me at my house, intending to compel me to give up some money I was supposed to have. I had none, and told them so, but they did not believe me and their next move was to cut a cord out of a bedstead, tie one end around my neck, throw the other over a joist overhead, and pull me up till my feet were clear of the floor. This they did four times, questioning me between whiles. I lost consciousness every time as soon as my feet left the floor but felt no pain at any time, and after the second hoist I meant to sham continued insensibility when they let me drop again, since to lower me they just let go the rope and I fell to the floor, but this was beyond my power. My first consciousness was that I had raised my body to a sitting position, which put shamming out of the question. I experienced no pain when the rope tightened, nor when I was suspended, nor after I was released, except the soreness caused on my skin by the chafing of the rope. I weighed about two hundred pounds, which insured that the rope was fully tightened each time."

Dr. D. S. Lamb, an ex-surgeon of the United States Army, studied the subject of hanging and in 1894 reported in the *St. Louis Globe-Democrat*:

"DEATH BY HANGING–

"The Three Different Stages Through Which the Victim Passes

"I have made the subject of death by hanging a long study. From my observations during my experience in the army I feel justified in saying that death by hanging is the most exaggerated of all modes. It may be immediate and without symptoms but the subject must pass through three stages before death.

"In the first stage the victim passes into a partial stupor lasting from thirty seconds to two minutes, but this is generally governed by the length of the drop, the weight of the body, and the tightness of the constriction. There is absolutely no pain in this stage; the feeling is rather one of pleasure. The subjective symptoms described are intense heat in the head, brilliant flashes of light in the eyes, deafening sounds in the ears and a heavy numb feeling in the lungs. In the second stage the subject passes into unconsciousness and convulsions usually occur. In the third stage all is quiet except the beating of the heart. Just before death the agitation is renewed, but in a different way from that in the second state. The feet are raised, the tongue has a peculiar spasm, the chest heaves, the eyes protrude from the orbits and oscillate from side to side, and the pupils dilate. The pulse can, in most cases, be felt ten minutes after the drop.

"I once knew a man who was desirous of ascertaining if there was any suffering by hanging and in order to find out he placed a rope around his neck and stepped off a bench, intending to step back again, but he became immediately unconscious and would have died in a few minutes had it not been for the timely arrival of a friend. He said he experienced all the feelings that I mentioned in the first stage."

This three-stage process depended upon the rope being properly knotted and adjusted. The knot was carefully positioned on the left shoulder just behind the jaw so that it would press upon the carotid artery, cutting off blood to the brain which resulted in unconsciousness in a few seconds. This positioning of the knot forced the head to snap backward and dislocate the vertebrae. Ideally, during a legal hanging, the spine would be dislocated between the first and second or the second and third cervical vertebrae and the spinal cord would be severed, or at least severely compressed, cutting off all sensation to the torso and extremities.

Before one execution by hanging the trapdoor gallows was described as "ready and in fact every detail for the execution has been carefully arranged. The gallows is of the regulation pattern, very strong built, and has a drop of six feet. The rope is of best quality hemp, and 1½ inches in size," but there was no regulation design for gallows. Each sheriff, when required to do so, hired a local carpenter to design and build a gallows for his county, and the builder might rely on designs of other gallows, the military's design, or common sense. The trapdoor and release mechanism were of particular concern and the drop, the distance a man would fall, had to be calculated correctly. The distance a particular man should drop was determined by a mathematical formula based upon his weight where a one hundred ninety-six-pound man required a six-foot drop and for each deduction of seven pounds in weight two inches were added. Scaffolds of the trapdoor design, paid for with county funds, were usually disassembled and stored for reuse. Another type of gallows used a heavy weight as a "counter-poise" so that, when the weight was dropped, the condemned man was jerked up with such suddenness it dislocated the man's vertebrae.

Hemp was used almost exclusively for a hangman's rope because the strands were longer and stronger than flax, the other commonly available material at that time. The hemp material was beaten until soft and then twisted into strands, and three strands were twisted around a central strand called "the heart" to form a rope. A very thick rope was ordered from the manufacturer so that, even after soaking and stretching, it was still thick enough to prevent it from cutting into the neck of the condemned. Upon arrival the rope was soaked in water and stretched to remove elasticity, and then the rope was tested for the condemned's weight, usually by dropping a comparable weight through the trapdoor the required distance or by jerking up the equivalent weight of the condemned man. The loops of a hangman's noose were not a set number but seven loops were most often used, though on occasion a hangman might use as few as five or as many as thirteen loops. The point where rope grated on rope was lubricated with grease, soap, or wax to make the strands slide more easily and cinch tightly.

Most hangings were successful, according to newspaper accounts, and even when the prisoner strangled to death the condemned was reported to be unconscious within seconds after the jerk or drop. Early executions were intentionally as public as possible as this was believed to deter other would-be murderers, but in the mid–1870s the phenomenon of privacy during executions swept throughout the West, and territories and states required that gallows be constructed within a wall or enclosure of high board fencing, or have a special building erected or selected for the purpose. Laws were often very specific in excluding and including citizens of the jurisdiction as witnesses, and the number of invitations was greatly limited. However, there was no national guideline requiring executions to be private, and a public hanging occurred in the "civilized east" as late as August 14, 1936, when Rainey Bethea was publicly hanged at Owensboro, Kentucky.

When execution was by firing squad rifles were used most often, though a few executions in the Indian Territory were by pistol. When three or more firearms were used a portion of the arms might be loaded with powder only so that each shooter could later rationalize that his weapon did not fire the fatal bullet. This accommodation was intended to steady the shooter's aim. Firing squad members ranged from one to nine men.

When execution was by electrocution the person's head and leg were shaved to prevent resistance to the electric current. The person was then strapped to a chair with belts across his chest, groin, legs, and arms. A metal skullcap-shaped electrode was placed over the scalp and forehead atop a moistened sponge, and this sponge must not be too wet or it could short-circuit the electric current nor too dry as it would have a very high resistance to the current; and another electrode was attached to the leg over a moistened sponge to complete the circuit. After the prisoner has the opportunity to speak his final words he is usually blindfolded. The execution team then vacates the execution chamber and the warden signals the executioner, who applies the electricity from a rheostat, allowing him to increase or decrease the voltage. The jolt can be between 600 and 2500 volts and can last for twenty to sixty seconds. After the current surges, it is turned off but may be turned on a second time before the body is examined. The doctor must wait a few seconds for the body to cool before he can check for vital signs, and if there is any sign of life additional jolts of electricity are applied until the prisoner is pronounced dead. The prisoner's hands often grip the chair and there may be movement of the limbs so violent it can result in dislocations or fractures, the tissues swell, defecation and urination may occur, and steam or smoke may rise from the body which smells like burning flesh. At the postmortem examination the internal organs may be hot enough to blister the doctor if touched, so the autopsy is delayed while the internal organs cool. There may be third-degree burns with blackening of the flesh where the electrodes met the skin of the scalp and leg, and the brain will appear cooked in most cases. During early times the moistening agent was a water and salt or a water and acid solution but then a conductive jelly called Electro-Creme was developed.

When execution was by lethal injection the condemned was escorted into a sterile room where he lay down on a gurney and his chest, waist and legs were strapped while his arms were strapped to extensions. A medical technician then inserted an intravenous cannula (IV), or fourteen gauge catheter, into the vein of each arm while the executioners were hidden from view, the second catheter a back-up in case the first failed. Once the condemned was prepared, the window coverings were drawn or raised and the witnesses were allowed to see the condemned, and he was asked if he had any last words. Upon the condemned concluding his statement or declining to speak, the warden or his representative ordered the execution to proceed. Before the lethal injection protocol proceeds the tubes are flushed with ten milliliters of a heparin solution to prevent clotting, and then a one thousand-milliliter bag of saline solution is attached and the tubes are flushed, and are flushed again between each drug. During the earliest days a two-drug combination was used but this was quickly changed to a three-drug combination, and these drugs are administered through the tubes leading to the arms of the condemned man.

Sodium thiopental, or Pentathol, is a strong, short-acting barbiturate which causes rapid unconsciousness when injected into the blood stream. In a lethal injection protocol, two to three grams in eighty cubic centimeters of an aqueous solution, or about ten times the anesthetic dose, are injected. In time this dosage could cause death in most individuals in a brief time period.

Pancuronium bromide, or Pavulon, which is sometimes reported as the similar drug vercuronium bromide, is a very strong muscle relaxant that paralyzes the diaphragm. In a lethal injection protocol fifty milligrams of this drug are administered. This dosage could cause death by asphyxiation in most individuals in a brief time period.

Potassium chloride is used during heart surgery to stop the heart, and in a lethal injection protocol one hundred milliequivalents performs the same function.

While the injection process can take up to five minutes, the condemned is typically unconscious in one to two minutes and dies in four to eight minutes. In late developments two states, Ohio and Washington, have adopted a single drug protocol by administering the sedative drug in a dosage up to three times the fatal amount. This new protocol has been challenged in the federal courts and affirmed. The drug sodium thiopental became scarce in early 2010 as the single company that produced it discontinued production, but in several executions Pentobarbital was substituted. This new drug was challenged in the federal courts and affirmed for use.

Executions State by State

Before NEBRASKA became a state on March 1, 1867, there were two men hanged in separate executions. After statehood the county sheriff maintained responsibility for conducting fourteen executions of fifteen men, the last George W. Morgan, hanged on October 8, 1897. In 1903 the responsibility for executions was moved to the prison where Gottlieb Neigenfind became the first man hanged in the prison on March 13, 1903. The scaffold, the same which had been used in Douglas County, was moved to the prison and erected in the west corner of the unoccupied cell house at the west end of the yard. This gallows was twenty feet tall, painted black, and crossing it from east to west was a heavy beam with a hole at the center where the rope was tied. The trapdoor was at the center, measured four by four feet and was held in place by a wooden trigger. The platform was reached by a wide stairway of a dozen steps located on the north side of the structure and beneath the platform, directly beneath the trapdoor, the large stones of the floor were removed and the dirt was removed to ensure there would be clearance for the prisoner's feet after he dropped. By 1908 the new cell block had been completed with death row cells directly across from the guard station, and by October 1910 the death chamber had been moved into the thirty-by-fifty-foot frame warehouse at the northwest corner of the prison. The wooden lever trapdoor release had been replaced by four electric buttons, including three dummies, so no one knew who sprang the trap. By the time Albert Prince was hanged on March 21, 1913, the gallows had been moved to "the little red death house" in the southwest corner of the prison yard. Between February 14, 1868, and March 21, 1913, when Albert Prince became the last man hanged in Nebraska, twenty-three men were hanged during twenty-two executions. After Prince was hanged the state adopted the electric chair as the sole means of execution and Cole Alson became the first man to die by this method on December 20, 1920. Nebraska's code, Chapter 29, §2504, read, "The mode of inflicting the punishment of death in all cases shall be by causing to pass through the body of the convicted person a current of electricity of sufficient intensity to cause death." This law would create some difficulty when it came time to execute Joseph Thomas MacAvoy on December 30, 1943, because the chair had not been used for some time, and needed parts for repair, but an execution was not a priority during wartime, so the execution was delayed until March 23, 1945, after the chair had been put in good working order. The death chamber was in the hospital, and the condemned man was moved to a hospital room hours before he was to be electrocuted. After Timothy Iron Bear was executed on December 1, 1948, the death chamber was moved to a basement room beneath the warden's offices. Only two men were executed in this room, the last Charles Starkweather on June 25, 1959. Thirty-five years would pass before another man would be executed in Nebraska, and when Harold L. Otey faced the executioner on September 2, 1994, the electric chair had been moved back to the hospital wing. On February 8, 2008, the Nebraska Supreme Court found the electric chair "cruel and unusual" punishment, and in November the state legislature banned its use, but twelve men remain on death row in Nebraska.

Before KANSAS became a state on January 29, 1861, there was one murderer, John Coon, Jr., executed by firing squad. After Kansas became a state and until 1888 twenty men were executed, four shot and six hanged under military authority and ten men hanged by civilian authority. Civilian authority was the county sheriff, who had responsibility for conducting executions between December 29, 1865, when John Hendley was hanged and November 21, 1888, when Jake and Joe Tobler died on the gallows. After the Toblers were hanged, no other person was executed in Kansas before the death penalty was abolished in 1907. Between September 5, 1930, when the federal government executed Carl Panzram, and June 22, 1965, when the state executed James Latham and George York, forty-five men were executed during twenty-six executions: fifteen hanged by the state; three hanged by the federal government; and thirty men hanged by the military, most at the Disciplinary Barracks at Fort Leavenworth including fourteen German prisoners of war. After World War II ended military executions were conducted at the state prison until February 14, 1957 when the hangings were moved back to Fort Leavenworth. The death penalty had been restored in Kansas in time to hang Ernest Hoefgen on March 10, 1944, as Kansas retained hanging as its sole method of execution. On June 22, 1965 York and Latham became the last men to die on a Kansas gallows. In Kansas there is not a designated death row, but nine men sentenced to death were housed in the Administrative Segregation section of the prison on December 31, 2010.

Before OKLAHOMA became a state the Oklahoma Territory was formed in 1890 by dividing the Indian Territory approximately in two with the dividing line running north and south, and the territory was formed from leased district lands, the Cherokee outlet, and "No Man's Land" in the western part of what would later become the state of Oklahoma, where nearly twenty tribes had lived. On November 16, 1907, the Indian Territory, then occupied only by the five civilized tribes, and the western portion comprising the Oklahoma Territory were combined to become the state of Oklahoma. Before 1907 there were two men executed in the territory in separate executions: one shot and one hanged; and between 1840 and 1899 thirty one men were hanged and thirty-six men were executed by firing squad in the Indian Territory. However, the U.S. Congress passed the Curtis Bill in July 1898, which took jurisdiction for criminal matters from the tribal councils and placed it in the federal courts, and between 1899 and 1907 nine men and one woman were executed under federal authority in the Indian Territory during seven executions.

The first federal court dealing with crimes in the Indian Territory was set up at Van Buren, Arkansas, where, on June 24, 1870, Amos McCurtain became the only man hanged there for a crime in the territory. A federal court was then established at Fort Smith, Arkansas, where Tu-ni-ah and Young Wolfe were the first from the Indian Territory to be hanged on October 8, 1873, and Richard Smith was the last from the Indian Territory to be hanged on January 25, 1889. Hanging was considered by most tribes to be the most disgraceful way to die, but the Cherokee tribe did not adhere to that view and built a permanent gallows at their National Prison in Tahlequah. The Chickasaw tribe had no prison but they built a substantial jail facility at Tishomingo. After statehood the county sheriff was responsible for conducting executions until March 31, 1911, when Frank Henson became the last man hanged by a county, and during that period seven men were hanged in separate executions.

The state legislature then adopted the electric chair as the exclusive method for executing murderers, moved executions to the prison, and on December 10, 1915, Henry Bookman became the first person to die by that method, and in all eighty-three men would die by electrocution with the last being executed on August 10, 1966. In preparation for the first execution by electric chair, Warden R. W. Dick had prison electrician W. M. Treadwell design and build the chair in a chamber in the basement beneath the main prison building. He used heavy oak, and he attached to the chair eight heavy black leather straps two inches wide to bind the chest, waist, wrists, arms, and ankles of the condemned man. A leather mask was used to cover the man's eyes and forehead, and Treadwell installed a means to attach the rear of the mask to the chair back to restrain the head of the condemned. A copper helmet and copper leg band were designed and lined with sponge, and the sponges were moistened to complete the connections, and to these electrodes were attached heavy gauge copper wires. The wires were attached to a rheostat, or "control panel," which allowed the executioner to adjust the level of current from 600 to 2500 volts and had a switch to turn the current on and off. The dynamo, which hummed loudly as it generated electric current, was located in an adjacent room, and it was turned on before the prisoner was brought into the chamber. One or several days before the execution the condemned was taken from his regular cell and moved to a special cell in the basement, near the death chamber. The witnesses were usually ushered into the viewing area just before the prisoner appeared, and they were separated from the death chamber by a metal grating. Even though the state had a law requiring the exclusive use of the electric chair, this did not apply to the federal government, and on June 19, 1936, Arthur Gooch was hanged in Oklahoma by federal authorities, and then two soldiers were hanged by the military at Fort Sill, one on September 26, 1944, and the second on August 14, 1945.

The nationwide moratorium on the death penalty ended executions in Oklahoma for twenty-four years but when they resumed, with the execution of Charles Troy Coleman on September 10, 1990, his death was by lethal injection, and in all ninety-four men would die by that method before John David Duty was executed on December 16, 2010. Oklahoma was the first jurisdiction in the world to adopt lethal injection as their primary method of execution, though Texas was first in the United States to use the method in 1982, but Oklahoma retained electrocution as an alternative if lethal injection was found unconstitutional and the firing squad as an alternative if both methods were found unconstitutional. In 1977 Oklahoma's chief medical examiner A. Jay Chapman proposed the use of drugs to end the lives of condemned prisoners. Dr. Stanley Deutsch, chair of the Anesthesiology Department at the Oklahoma University School of Medicine outlined the protocol, and the bill passed into law the same year. On December 31, 2010, seventy-seven individuals were housed in special sections of the prison, awaiting adjudication of appeals on their death sentences or a commutation of sentence. The commutation process in Oklahoma is typical of such administrative processes nationwide; in Oklahoma the governor can grant clemency only if a majority of the five members of the state Board of Pardons and Parole votes to recommend clemency following a hearing, and members may choose to vote, abstain, or recuse themselves. The governor, however, can grant a temporary reprieve while asking the board members to reconsider a vote against clemency.

NEBRASKA

The first Europeans to see the land that would become Nebraska were the Pedro de Villasur party in 1720, and they found the land inhabited by the Arapaho, Cheyenne, Omaha, Oto, and Sioux Indian tribes. The region was claimed by France but in 1763 those claims west of the Mississippi River were ceded to Spain. In 1800 France reacquired possession and in 1803 sold the region to the United States as part of the Louisiana Purchase. Nebraska became a territory on May 30, 1854 with passage of the Kansas-Nebraska Act. Nebraska remained a relative wilderness until 1860 when the government began granting free land to homesteaders. Nebraska became the 37th state on March 1, 1867.

Tator, Cyrus H.
August 28, 1863

In early June 1863 Horace Wilson, a boy gathering driftwood in the Missouri River bottoms, found a body floating in a stream not far from Sulphur Springs, and men working nearby recovered the body. An inquest was held and the remains were identified as Isaac H. Neff. It was determined he had been cruelly murdered two days before being submerged in the stream, weighted down with logging chains wrapped about the arms, neck and legs. Neff had recently arrived in Omaha from Denver, bringing three unloaded wagons to look for freight to return to Denver, and he was in the company of his freighting partner Cyrus H. Tator. A party of men was sent to examine the area around Sulphur Springs. They found two of Neff's wagons abandoned there, and it appeared they had been standing several weeks. The third wagon was missing, and the party determined that a few days earlier Tator had driven that loaded wagon west toward Denver. Sheriff Thomas L. Sutton was soon on the trail of Tator and captured him in Colfax County, arrested him for the murder of Neff, and took his prisoner to Omaha where he was lodged in the county jail. The Omaha district court was then in session, with Judge W. P. Kellogg presiding, so rather than delay to the next term of the court a special grand jury was convened, and Tator was indicted on June 17. Tator's trial commenced two days later. The evidence showed the motive for the murder was robbery, as Tator wanted to gain possession of their joint property, and after killing Neff he sold two teams to Heber P. Kimball, who was the strongest witness against him. He also tried to sell the wagons but, failing, left them standing where they were found. After several days of testimony and brief deliberations the defendant was convicted of first degree murder and sentenced to hang on Friday, August 28, 1863. The case was appealed to the territorial supreme court, exceptions taken and overruled and a writ of error denied, and the matter was handled with such efficiency that there was no delay in the proceedings.

The gallows was built at Sulphur Springs, right on the spot where it was determined the murder took place, and it was a plain framed apparatus of four erect beams with a platform and trapdoor in the center. On the day of the execution a crowd of over two thousand men, women and children gathered at an early hour and, anticipating the large turnout and the need to preserve order, Sheriff Sutton requested and received from General McKean a guard of forty soldiers from Company C, 7th Iowa Cavalry. During the morning the Rev. T. B. Lemon administered the Holy Communion to the prisoner in his cell and remained with him until 11:00 A.M., when Sheriff Sutton brought the prisoner out of his cell. Sutton was assisted by City

Marshal Thomas Riley. They placed the prisoner in a buggy, drove him to Sulphur Springs, and escorted him onto the scaffold. Tator took his place at the railing and addressed the large crowd, reading a carefully prepared statement that took thirty minutes to complete. He called on God to witness that "I am an innocent man, I did not murder Neff, and I am ignorant of the author of the deed." The Reverend Lemon then offered a prayer while the prisoner was positioned on the trapdoor and the noose was cinched tight by the sheriff. Next the sheriff and city marshal bound his wrists and ankles and pulled the black cap over his face. The trap was sprung at 1:00 P.M. and Tator dropped to his death, breaking his neck in the fall. The attending physician pronounced him dead after several minutes but the body was not cut down for twenty-two minutes. The remains were lowered into the coffin provided and taken away to await a requisition by his friends.

Sources: *The Omaha Daily Nebraskian* (NE): August 29, 1863. *The Omaha Weekly Nebraskian* (NE): September 4, 1863; *The Weekly Hawk-eye* (Burlington, IA): September 2, 1863; Sorenson, Alfred. *History of Omaha from the Pioneer Days to the Present Time.* Omaha: Gibson, Miller & Richardson, Printer, 1889.

Diercks, Casper F.
August 16, 1866

On August 15, 1866, William Henry Hamilton, an eleven-year-old boy, was herding cattle for his father on their farm in Otoe County, five miles from Nebraska City. That evening the boy failed to return home so a search was made, and the dead body of the boy was found with his feet buried in the mud of the nearby creek, his body in a stooping position. The boy had been shot three times: in the right eye; under the right arm; and in the right ear — and the cattle were missing. The body was pulled from the mud and carried to the Hamilton farmhouse where a coroner's jury was convened, and the jurors determined that the person responsible was a man known as "Cash," who had driven Hamilton's cattle to Nebraska City and sold them. A reward of $200 was posted. The search for Cash began, and it was quickly learned that he had crossed the river on the ferry into Iowa. Two hundred armed and angry men started in pursuit, and early the following day they captured Casper Frederick Diercks, alias Cash, at Plum Hollow, Iowa. The prisoner was taken back to Nebraska City and would have been lynched if it had not been decided to give him a trial in a "People's Court." Two other men thought to be involved were Sebastian Deitch and R. P. Ford, and they had been jailed in the interim. At 10:30 A.M. two thousand men, women, and children assembled in the public square and elected D. J. McCann president of the court and J. Dan Lauer as secretary. A jury composed of old, influential citizens was then empaneled to try the prisoners while another committee was appointed to guard the jail to prevent escape, suicide, or a lynching. Twenty special policemen were appointed to keep order and attorneys were appointed for the defense and prosecution. The three prisoners were brought forth and the jury heard the testimony of seven witnesses, including Deitch and Ford, which sealed the fate of their partner in crime. The jury then retired to deliberate and they quickly found Diercks guilty of "willful murder," but recommended that Deitch and Ford be held for the regular session of the district court. A proposition to hang Diercks immediately was voted down and it was decided to give him until 6:00 P.M. to put his life in order. Deitch and Ford were later tried, convicted of being accomplices to cattle stealing, and sentenced to long prison terms.

While the condemned man waited his execution he was allowed to consult with the Methodist reverend H. F. Davis and, during his last hours on earth, bequeathed all his worldly possessions. When his time came the condemned man stepped from his cell and was escorted onto the platform, where a prayer was offered by the Reverend Davis as the prisoner was positioned on the trapdoor. The prisoner took the noose in his hand and said, "Holding as I do this rope, which is to send me into eternity, I declare that I am guilty of the larceny, but of murder, I am not." He was then questioned and denied knowing who killed the boy, then said, "May God have mercy on my soul!" As he was speaking to the crowd he had been prepared by having his wrists and ankles pinioned and the noose adjusted about his neck. When he finished his plea for God's mercy the trap was sprung and he dropped to his death. He struggled for a few minutes but then hung lifeless and as soon as he was pronounced dead he was cut down, lowered into a cheap pine coffin, and given to the Reverend Davis for burial.

Source: *Andreas' History of the State of Nebraska — Otoe Co. — Part 5.*

Baker, Otway R.
February 14, 1868

Will R. King owned and operated a grocery store in Omaha, Douglas County, Nebraska. He had a fire at his new store location which prevented him from moving in, but he did not suspect any of his employees of being involved in the arson. The fire had been set by Otway R. Baker, King's porter, who did not want King to move into the store too early for his robbery plan to work. By November King was situated at his new location when, on the afternoon of November 20, there was another large fire in the vicinity of King's new store. Baker had set that fire as a diversion to keep King's bookkeeper, Woolsey D. Higgins, from depositing $1500 in currency he had received that day. The fire spread and caused far more damage than Baker intended but it served its purpose, as Higgins missed his opportunity to deposit the money. After the store closed, Higgins, who always carried the keys, locked the money in the store safe. Both Baker and Higgins slept at the store, and Baker retired at 8:30 P.M. He fell asleep and did not know when Higgins retired, but at midnight Baker arose and got an axe from the store's stock. He then stealthily removed the keys from Higgins' person but, he later said, he thought that Higgins was only shamming sleep and would report him so he struck a hard blow to Higgins' head with the sharp edge of the axe. Higgins let out a long breath and Baker thought he was about to call out, so he struck him again. Higgins' head was laid open, his brain exposed through two gaping wounds, and he was dead in moments. Baker then opened the safe and took out the money. He put his plunder in a can, took it to Eleventh Street between Harney and Howard Streets, and buried it under the west side sidewalk. Baker returned to the store, went into the basement, piled boards up to the floor beneath their sleeping rooms, and soaked rags in coal oil. He set the pyre ablaze, believing that the floor would collapse and conceal the details of the murder and robbery. Baker then went to the back door and as soon as the room was filled with smoke he shot himself in the arm, threw the pistol into the flames, and at 1:00 A.M. ran out yelling, "Fire! Murder! Thieves!" The fire department arrived but was unable to get control of the fire and the store was gutted. However, several men had rushed into the burning building and recovered Higgins' body, saw that the safe was opened and empty, and observed that there were matches spilled all over Baker's bed. This latter development was a mere coincidence which pointed the finger of blame at Baker, while in fact the matches had been knocked over by a stream of water from the fire truck. Baker claimed that he was awakened by the crackling of the flames and chased an intruder into the basement, where he was shot, but when his wound was treated it was apparent that it was self-inflicted so his story was disbelieved. Baker was arrested and lodged in jail, charged with murder, robbery, and arson. At the inquest over Higgins' remains the coroner's jury recommended that Baker be held without bail and charged as the sole author of the deed, and he was charged accordingly. Baker was indicted on April 23, 1867, and on the following day he was arraigned in Judge George B. Lake's courtroom. Baker's trial commenced on May 1 after great difficulty in empaneling a jury, and once they heard the testimony they could not agree so the case was carried over to the October term. The second trial was just as contentious but the jurors finally reached a verdict of "guilty as charged in the indictment" and Baker was sentenced to hang. The case was appealed to the state supreme court, but on January 28, 1868, Baker gave his attorney, Colonel Savage, a full signed confession of guilt and told where the money was hidden so the appeal was withdrawn. Baker was then brought before Judge Lake and resentenced to hang on February 14, 1868.

Days before the execution, the gallows was erected in a ravine a half mile from the capital and, on the morning of February 14, it was guarded by volunteers from the fire department under command of Fire Chief William L. May. During his final days Baker had been visited by Father Egan, who helped him brace up and resign himself to his fate, and Father Egan was with him that final morning. At an early hour the sheriff and deputies, Baker's defense attorney, and several invited guests appeared at the cell of the condemned man. The death warrant was read and then Baker was escorted from the jail into the street. The procession boarded two buggies, surrounded by a vast crowd which had gathered to catch the first glimpse of the prisoner. The two buggies, followed by a third buggy carrying the press, moved at a solemn pace to the site of the gallows, with the crowd following. Once at the gallows the parties dismounted and Baker climbed the stairs onto the platform. Only the sheriff, Father Egan and Colonel Savage accompanied the prisoner, and he immediately took his place on the trapdoor. He had either declined to speak or was not asked, but without delay the sheriff pinioned his wrists and ankles, adjusted the noose about his neck, and pulled on the black hood. In but a moment the trap was sprung and Baker dropped seven feet, breaking his neck in the fall. The body hung for sixteen minutes before the attending physicians made an examination and pronounced him dead. The body was then cut down, placed in the coffin provided by the county, and given to Father Egan, who saw to the burial at the Catholic Convent that afternoon.

Sources: *Andreas' History of the State of Nebraska — Douglas Co. — Omaha — Section 4*; Sorenson, Alfred. *History of Omaha from the Pioneer Days to the Present Time.* Omaha: Gibson, Miller & Richardson, printers, 1889.

Richards, Samuel D.
April 26, 1879

In the summer of 1878 Samuel D. Richards was arrested, charged with petty larceny of a watch, and lodged in the Buffalo County, Nebraska, jail. He was tried and convicted of petit larceny and sentenced to a brief jail term. While behind bars he met a prisoner named Harrelson, who was serving a much longer jail term for theft of lumber from a bridge. Harrelson and Richards became friendly and Richards agreed that, upon his release, he would go to the Harrelson farm and look after his family — a wife, two young daughters and a baby boy — and work the farm. Harrelson then escaped, fled from the area, and was not heard of again. Richards, seeing the vulnerability of Mrs. Harrelson, went to the farm intent on getting possession of the property. Soon after Richards arrived on the farm, the entire Harrelson family disappeared. When questioned Richards explained that Mary L. Harrelson had left with her children to join her husband, but only after she had sold the farm to him. Richards said that Mrs. Harrelson would not tell him where her husband had settled, and the explanation seemed plausible so no investigation was undertaken. Richards, fearing a growing suspicion of foul play, fled and next appeared at the home of Peter Anderson, a well-to-do Swede who lived alone on the southeast quarter section number 6 in the Sherman Township, one mile east of Keene and southwest of the county seat at Minden in Kearney County. Soon trouble erupted between the two men but Richards continued his employment on the Anderson farm. On December 8, 1878, Anderson, feeling ill, appeared at the home of neighbor Godfrey Boostrom seeking help. The symptoms were a swollen tongue and other evidence of poisoning so after Anderson was given an antidote he was encouraged to stay the night. However, Anderson insisted that he had to return to his farm. In the morning Boostrom sent his nine-year-old boy, Swan, to check on the welfare of Anderson but the boy could find no sign of the ailing man. When the boy returned home Boostrom hitched up a team and wagon and went to the Anderson farm, where they saw Richards hitching Anderson's grey horse and black mule to a wagon. The boy was sent to ask Richards about Anderson, and was told the farmer would soon return from a neighbor's house, and Richards invited the Boostroms to wait inside the house. Upon entering they found the place in shambles, as if ransacked, and the stove was red hot as if someone was about to prepare a meal. After quickly checking the cellar, and finding nothing, they went outside in time to see Richards riding southwest on Anderson's horse leaving behind the mule and wagon. They did not pursue Richards but instead gathered neighbors for a thorough search of the Anderson property. They quickly found a newly dug grave in the cellar beneath a pile of coal, and they dug out the dead body of Anderson, his head crushed in with a hammer. Boostrom contacted the authorities and a search began for Richards. The fugitive's description was widely circulated, and a two hundred-dollar reward, the highest amount allowed by law, was offered for his arrest. The fugitive was first traced to Red Cloud and then to Hastings, and from there the trail led through Chicago, Illinois, to Falls City, Ohio, thirty miles south of Cleveland, where Richards was arrested and taken to Steubenville to await extradition. Finally the fugitive was on his way to Nebraska in the custody of Sheriffs T. L. Martin of Buffalo County and D. Anderson of Kearney County. As soon as Richards reached Chicago on December 26 he confessed:

> "... I went west about two years ago, and have spent most of the time since then in Nebraska, although I have been further west; soon after arriving in Nebraska I fell in with another man and we traveled together under assumed names; we did very little

work while in Nebraska. I had some money when I went west, and got more; I did not work for it, but got it in different ways. After traveling with my partner for a while we had a difficulty and he disappeared near Sand Hill. The circumstances that led to his disappearance was a cartridge from a revolver I carried. I shot the man; I did not bury him. There was no serious trouble between us. I then roamed about the state until October when I ran across Mrs. Mary L. Harrelson near Kearney, in Buffalo County, whose husband had broken jail and run away. The last of October or the first of November, I gave out that she had gone to meet her husband, and had sold me all of her property. Her dead body, and the bodies of her three children, were found under a hay-stack. I put them there after I killed them, and being afraid suspicion would rest on me after they were found, I ran away and went to Kearney County where I got work on a farm belonging to Peter Anderson, who was quite well off. He and I had a fight, and he got killed between my fists and a hammer. It was only about a little trouble that arose between us; it was not about money. I did not get any money from any of the people I killed. The pretended confessions which say I did are false. The Anderson affair occurred in the early part this month [December] and I left soon after. I started from Kearney County two weeks ago Monday and stopped Tuesday until Friday in Hastings, Nebraska, then came here on the Chicago, Burlington and Quiney Railroad, arriving at 6 o'clock Saturday evening, and got shaved at the Clifton House. I had side whiskers when I got here and had them cut off, and left at 9:45 the same evening for Wheeling, West Virginia where I staid over Sunday and then went up to Mount Pleasant, where I was arrested by two citizens who knew me. I had expected lynching when I got back to Kearney, but the officers say I will get a fair trial. However, it is immaterial to me how the matter ends. I have committed the crimes, and will take my punishment like a man, let it come in whatever way it may."

During the time that Richards was a fugitive suspicion was raised about the sudden disappearance of the Harrelson family. A search was organized and their dead bodies were discovered buried in a hay stack. Mrs. Harrelson and her daughters, ten-year-old Daisy and four-year-old Mabel, had their skulls crushed with a flat iron, and Jessie, the two-year-old baby, had been flung against a wall inside the house and his brains had been bashed out.

Richards was lodged in the jail at Minden and indicted in early January 1879 for the murder of Anderson, and his trial commenced within days. He was easily convicted on his own confession and the evidence at the scene of the crime, and on January 16 the jury returned a verdict of guilty as charged in the indictment. Richards was sentenced by Judge Gaslin to hang on April 26, 1879 and he was taken to Lincoln and lodged in the prison, then returned to Minden on April 25. By the time Richards was returned to Minden the scaffold had been erected on the southeast corner of the courtyard near the Minden jail, and a tall pine-board fence was raised to enclose a sixteen-foot-square area around the gallows. On the final morning the crowd began to assemble at an early hour and demanded to see the murderer, so Sheriff Kieran put him in a wagon and drove him around the public square in the hope this would settle them. The crowd continued to grow until it swelled to twenty-five hundred strong by noon, when they suddenly surged forward and, in violation of Nebraska law, tore down the fence so they could see the condemned man expiate his crime on the gallows. Soon after the fence was down the sheriff went to Richards' cell and read the death warrant, and then the procession formed. The party exited the jail and made their way through the crowd onto the stairs, and Richards climbed onto the platform with a firm step. He was asked if he had anything to say and he spoke for five minutes, saying he was not guilty of the crime under which he was convicted. When he finished speaking his religious adviser recited several prayers and then asked everyone to join the condemned man in singing the hymn "There Is a Fountain Filled with Blood," and two versions were sung. Richards then had his wrists and ankles pinioned, the noose adjusted, and the black cap drawn over his head, and he talked the entire time. At 1:17 P.M. the sheriff kicked the lever, the trap was sprung, and Richards dropped six feet, breaking his neck in the fall. There was only a slight twitching of his legs before hanging motionless, and after ten minutes the attending physicians determined that Richards' heart had ceased to beat and pronounced him dead. The body hung a sufficient time to ensure he could not revive before he was cut down and deposited in the coffin provided by the county. There was no designated cemetery in Minden at the time, as families each had their own family cemetery on their properties, so the remains were taken to a nearby draw and buried. The local doctors had requested the opportunity to perform an autopsy but that request had been denied and a guard was placed over the grave to protect it from grave robbers. The following night the guard was removed, the body was exhumed, and the doctors held their autopsy in secret. The body was then returned to the grave and reinterred. Later, after the body had become completely skeletonized, the bones were dug up and scattered about the streets of Kearney, and the *Kearney County Gazette* of November 1, 1882, claimed to have Richards' skull on display in its window.

Sources: Bang, Roy T. *Heroes Without Medals—A Pioneer History of Kearney County Nebraska*. Warp Publishing Company: Minden, NE, 1952, 104; *Decatur Daily Republican* (IL): December 27, 1878; *Dubuque Herald* (IA): December 22, 1878; April 27, 1879; *Kearney County Gazette* (NE): November 1, 1882; *The Richmond Gazette* (OH): May 1, 1879.

Casler, Orlando
May 20, 1879

On July 11, 1878, C. C. Cowden and his small son were fishing on the Blue River near Seward, Seward County, Nebraska. Cowden's son told his father, "Pa, there is a man on the other side of the river." The story was, at first, discounted as the father could see nothing from his vantage point, but at the insistence of his son he moved from behind a tree and confirmed his son's observation, a man floating in the river, so they hurried back into town and sounded the alarm. Coroner J. H. Woodward, accompanied by several hundred Seward citizens, hastened to the scene where a Mr. Mahaffey swam across the river and attached a stout fishing line to the remains, and the body was towed across the river. A coroner's jury was impaneled and the inquiry begun, but no foul play was suspected until Dr. Woodward noted an ugly bruise above the right eye, inflicted by a blunt instrument with such force that the skull was exposed but not fractured. The body was immediately stripped and examined and a bullet wound was found in the right breast. The bullet had entered from the front about an inch and a half from the breastbone, passed through the lung and came out an inch to the left of the backbone. The bullet had severed an artery and a vein and shattered the end of one rib, but had missed the heart. It was a fatal wound but not one which would have produced instant death, so the deceased may have been deposited in the river while yet alive.

The pockets of the deceased were searched and in them was found an unsigned postcard to the man's wife — Elizabeth "Lizzie" Munroe of Arkansas City, Colley County, Kansas. There was also a letter from the wife of the deceased identifying him as "George," and upon his right arm was a tattoo "G. L. M." From the evidence it was determined that the deceased was George L. Munroe, and it was deduced from the postcard that he had been murdered for his team and wagon, valued at $300, and for $155 in money. There was no clue to the murderer so the officers began a search for Munroe's outfit. They circulated inquiries which were soon rewarded with intelligence that the team and wagon were in the possession of Orlando Casler, a farmer residing at Beaver Crossing. The circumstances of his possession of Munroe's outfit were such that an examination had already been held at Beaver Crossing but there was no evidence of foul play at that time. Deputy sheriff Osborn went to the Casler farm on July 13 and arrested Casler without resistance. The deputy took his prisoner to Seward where the coroner's inquiry was continuing. A number of men also came from Beaver Crossing and testified that George L. Munroe had come to that place shopping for land to move his family from Kansas, and had mentioned that he wanted to sell his outfit but had not seemed motivated. On July 6 he was seen conversing with Orlando Casler and that evening he accompanied Casler to his farm two miles northeast of town. Munroe spent the night, and the following day, Sunday at 11:00 A.M., the two men started for Seward in Munroe's outfit. On Monday Casler returned to Beaver Crossing with Munroe's wagon, team, and property but without Munroe, and it was this development that had first aroused suspicion as Casler had no means with which to buy the outfit. In Seward Casler testified before the coroner's jury that he and Munroe had arrived at Seward at 8:00 P.M. and encamped in the bottoms near the slaughterhouse of Hennegin & Ashton, and then went into town to buy items for their dinner. When they returned they found that four men from Peru, Nebraska, had camped nearby and, after a brief conversation with them, Casler suggested that he and Munroe move upriver to avoid being pestered by mosquitoes. Munroe agreed and it was the last time the men of Peru saw the murdered man. In the morning Casler asked the Peru residents to help him catch his horses, but when they drove them toward Munroe's wagon Casler turned the horses away, and they were captured some time later at another location.

Casler immediately took charge of the team and, alone, hitched them to the wagon. When asked by the Peru men about Munroe, Casler said his partner had become ill, went into Seward for medicine, and had his breakfast at the boarding house of E. C. Moore. Casler drove the outfit into Seward where he bought a number of items, and several people noticed that he was soaked from head to foot, but he said he had become drenched chasing his horses through wet grass. On his way home he stopped at the farm of Morris Underhill and there a rifle and satchel were seen in the wagon, but these items disappeared until the grass was burned off the prairie and they were discovered, and Casler insisted that Munroe had taken these items when he left for Kansas. Casler also testified that he had traded an eighty-acre homestead and $100 for the outfit and property and said he had gotten the money from the Seward County Bank. The entire story of Casler was quickly disproved, and he was arrested pending the finding of the coroner's jury. The coroner's jury then retired to the place where Munroe and Casler had camped and found a clear trail where a body had been dragged to the edge of Lincoln Creek. It was supposed that the body sank at first but, when it began to decompose, the gasses brought it to the surface and it floated down to the Blue River where it was found. As the circumstantial evidence mounted a search was made of Casler's farmhouse and there, in his mattress, were found the personal papers of Munroe and several deeds, and several items of Munroe's property. As Casler sat in his cell his clothes were collected and it was discovered that several stains had been carefully washed from his shirt, but there were several blood stains still visible on his pants. By July 15 the coroner's jury completed their inquiry and concluded, "George L. Munroe came to his death by a deliberate shot from a revolver in the hands of Orlando Casler, the same being with the intent to kill." Casler was charged with the murder of Munroe and held over for action by the grand jury.

In November Casler was indicted and held for trial. Casler's attorneys, through clever legal manipulation and pettifogging, had much of the evidence excluded, and then advised their client to plead guilty to second degree murder to avoid the death penalty. Casler, confident that he could get a much shorter sentence than life in prison, refused and his trial commenced on January 28, 1879. Casler also insisted on taking the stand and proved to be an excellent witness in his defense. The trial concluded at noon on February 3 and then the arguments continued until the following day at 5:00 P.M., when the jury retired to deliberate. The jurors were out only one hour before returning a verdict of "guilty of murder in the first degree." On February 6 the prisoner was brought into court where Judge Post declared "that he be remanded to the County jail of Seward County, there to remain until Tuesday, the 20th day of May, 1879 when between the hours of 10 A.M. and 2 P.M. he (is) to be hanged by the neck until dead."

Casler maintained hope for a commutation of sentence from Governor Albinus Nance, and his attorneys worked feverishly to that end, but they had dismissed as futile any chance for a successful appeal to the supreme court. As the fatal day neared the attorneys took Casler's wife and children before the governor to plead for clemency, and then the family returned to Seward to spend as much time as possible with the condemned man. Next came Casler's sister, Mrs. Thomas S. Tinsdale, who also pled for her brother's life before she returned to Seward. The attorneys continued their efforts until Sunday evening, May 18, when the governor announced that he would telegraph his decision to the Seward authorities on Monday afternoon. The attorneys returned to Seward to wait, and on Monday evening they learned that the governor declined to intervene.

On May 10 Casler wrote his "dying statement" giving a brief history of his life and professing his innocence. Two days later he published a revised version in which he suggested that tests of his revolver could prove his innocence. On Saturday, May 17, Casler's children bade him farewell for the last time, while still hoping for some respite which would save their father's life. The scaffold and enclosure were under construction; Sheriff Sullivan was concerned that the citizens would tear down the twenty-five-foot fence, and wrote to Governor Nance asking for help. The governor sent an aide who pointed out how disgraceful it would be if the citizens circumvented the law by tearing down the enclosure, and equally disgraceful if Seward County needed troops to enforce the law which required privacy in executions. The sheriff finally agreed and enlisted the support of leading citizens to help ensure compliance. On Monday afternoon, still concerned over talk that the enclosure would be breached, Sullivan deputized and armed thirty-five men to guard the perimeter. Casler had asked that he be buried in a new suit and his sister promised him one, but she reneged. He also asked to be buried at Beaver Crossing and this was granted, so a coffin was purchased by the family for that purpose and placed inside the enclosure. On Monday morning Sheriff Sullivan was busy trying to recall invitations, as he had sent out far too many. As the Sheriff cancelled invitations of local dignitaries Casler was visited by a barber who gave him his last shave; and later when told that the governor had refused to intervene the condemned man remarked, "Well, it is all right. A man has only one time to die, and I am as nearly ready now as I ever will be." That afternoon Sheriff Sullivan proposed to Casler that he might write out his confession and seal it in an envelope, to be opened only after his death. The prisoner turned his back on the sheriff, but later commented that he would prefer to speak to the crowd from the gallows, and added that he would "give them Hell," meaning those who had testified against him. The Reverend Hapgood, Casler's Baptist minister, had been attending to Casler's religious needs but expressed disappointment "that Casler had not confessed to a crime of which there seemed so little doubt of his guilt." The condemned man had displayed "exquisite nerve" throughout the waiting period and had not weakened as his time drew near. That final evening a terrible storm arrived and the newspaper reporters observed, "This is just such a night as that on which Casler killed George L. Munroe." Casler retired at 10:00 P.M. his final night and slept soundly until, at 5:00 A.M., he sprang from his bed and asked for water to wash before breakfast. Soon afterward his wife and sister arrived to visit with the condemned man, but they would remain in the jail when he was marched to the gallows. While they were visiting thousands of spectators arrived from all parts of the region and soon more than three thousand people had gathered outside the enclosure, which measured fifty by thirty feet, with one wall the southeast side of the jail and the other three walls were made of boards. At 10:30 A.M. Casler was brought out under a heavy guard for a breath of fresh air, and he was allowed to mount a wagon and address the crowd. He said, "I am looking my last upon Earth, and I am about to die an innocent man. As God gave me life and breath, I declare that I am innocent of the murder of George L. Munroe, for the murder of whom I am about to die." He was then returned to his cell where he continued visiting his wife and sister. As the hour neared for the execution twenty armed deputies were deployed around the enclosure fence. However, at 11:15 A.M. the crowd suddenly surged forward and tore down the eastern portion of the wooden fence, and as the deputies struggled to save that portion of the fence the southern portion was torn down also. In less than three minutes the entire enclosure had been destroyed and the crowd stood upon the boards, so the deputies erected a makeshift railing to protect the gallows. The crowd, intent on seeing the execution but not preventing it, approached the railing in an orderly fashion and quietly awaited the arrival of Casler. At 1:15 P.M. the crowd was rewarded when the condemned man, wrists tied behind his back, appeared and walked to the twelve-by-twelve foot gallows' platform with an escort of half a dozen lawmen, county clerk Graham, and the Reverend Jencks. They walked to the west side where the stairs were located, ascended quickly, and the prisoner took his place behind the four-by-four foot trapdoor. He was prompted to center himself on the trap and he did so without further encouragement. Graham then read the lengthy death warrant while Casler stared into the eyes of each reporter, located directly in front of him beneath the gallows, and then glanced at the rope dangling just above his head. The rope had been purchased and prepared for a previous execution but that man had his sentence commuted, so Sheriff Sullivan had soaped it anew for the current event. When Graham concluded, Casler was invited to speak to the crowd, and he repeated his claim of innocence. His pulse was measured at seventy, and as the Reverend Jencks read scripture and prayed for his soul, Casler was prepared with his knees and ankles tied. Next, at Casler's request, everyone joined in singing the hymn "What a Friend We Have in Jesus," and then Casler spoke briefly, saying nothing new. Sheriff Sullivan carefully positioned the noose about Casler's neck and pulled the black hood over his head, but tying it in back dislodged the noose and there was a delay while it was repositioned. At that moment it occurred to Casler that he still wore his boots and he asked if he should pull them off.

Sullivan said, "No! It is all right."

Casler then said, "But I don't want to die with

my boots on. Drop me in my stocking feet." When the sheriff made no reply Casler again asked that his boots be removed. Instead Sheriff Sullivan took several steps backward, kicked the block from beneath the trigger, and with a tap of his foot, at 1:30 P.M., he sprang the trap. Casler dropped a little more than five feet, which was not sufficient to break his neck, and his body convulsed for several minutes as he strangled to death. At eight minutes respiration ceased and a minute later, at 1:39, Casler's heart ceased to beat and he was pronounced dead. He hung a while longer, to ensure he could not be revived. The body was then cut down, placed in its coffin, and delivered to Casler's brother for interment at Beaver Crossing the following day.

Sources: *The Daily Nebraska State Journal* (Lincoln): May 16–17, 1879; May 20–21, 1879.

Smith, Milton W.
July 24, 1885

Fifty-eight-year-old Milton W. Smith had been married to the same woman for many years but he had led a wandering and dissolute life, often disappearing for lengthy periods only to return and seek reconciliation. His wife always took him in and their relations would be congenial for months, and they had six children as a result of these "visits," but Smith would inevitably wander off again. Mrs. Smith was an industrious woman, not inclined toward taking any sort of charity, and she supported the family by taking in washing and performing other matronly duties for local families. One day in June Smith returned home drunk and beat his wife, then drove her and the children outdoors where they were forced to spend the night. He was arrested and released on a bond but his subsequent actions led to his surrender by his bondsman. In court he promised to leave the area and upon being released he wandered north to Lone Pine but he returned in early October for his court appearance, as agreed. In the meantime Mrs. Smith had filed for divorce alleging drunkenness, cruelty and neglect and had a "peace warrant" issued. Smith threatened to kill his wife when he learned of her action to end their marriage. On Thanksgiving day, November 27, 1884, at 6:00 P.M. Mrs. Smith saw her husband hanging about her home and, alarmed, went to the county judge and obtained assurances that he would handle the matter, so she returned home. Just at dark Mrs. Smith was seated at the table with their youngest child on her lap when Smith stealthily opened the door, took deadly aim, and without hesitation or warning snapped the firing pin, but it failed to fire. Mrs. Smith tried to rise but the second round fired, the bullet striking her in her side. Mrs. Smith collapsed but screamed out in pain, and this alarm brought a large crowd to the scene. A search was begun immediately for Smith and, when found in the cornfield near the house, he presented his pistol and threatened to shoot the first man who approached him. Two men ignored his threat, leaped on him and wrestled him to the ground. He was taken to jail while the crowd called out to hang him, but he made it safely to his cell. There it was found he had two pocket knives and had used one to gash his throat in two places on each side of his wind pipe. He lay on the floor of the jail as if a corpse and this further angered the crowd, as they thought the attempted suicide a sham, so a doctor was called and it was first pronounced that he would die of his wounds. There was still strong talk of lynching but the citizens were restrained as they awaited word on Mrs. Smith's condition. They were determined, however, to ensure that Milton Smith paid for his crime as they believed Mrs. Smith would rest easier if she knew her husband could not come back and kill any of the children, and it was rumored that he had tried twice to shoot his youngest child but the firing pin only snapped. Mrs. Smith lingered in great pain before succumbing to her wounds at 10:30 P.M. Friday, and she was buried in the Osceola cemetery the day following her death. At his examination the prisoner was held to answer to the Polk County grand jury and remained behind bars to be tried at the March term of court. He was destitute so M. A. Miller was appointed to represent him, and they began to establish a defense by claiming that Smith's wife had badgered and belittled him for years, and this was the reason he so often left home and stayed away for long periods. He claimed that he had spent Thanksgiving day with his wife, and she had spent the holiday morning insulting and humiliating him so thoroughly that he had become miserable. He said that in an insane moment he shot her. At his trial, which lasted four days, the prosecution presented evidence that his defense was a ruse to avoid the death penalty, or perhaps even gain an acquittal, and the jury rejected his claims and found him guilty of first degree murder. Judge Norval then sentenced him to hang on July 24, 1885, and when sentenced his only remark was that he was being convicted on false evidence and perjured testimony.

On the Tuesday before his hanging, Smith's appetite failed him and he was not able to eat for several days, nor sleep soundly. On Wednesday evening the lumber was delivered to the open area south of the jail and work began on the enclosure, which would keep the crowd from viewing the execution. The gallows, a trapdoor model, was built within and the enclosure was surrounded by a wire fence to hold back the large number of spectators expected. By Thursday evening the structures were in place and the gallows was tested. Smith had hoped for a commutation and had submitted two petitions and letters to Governor James W. Dawes, claiming age as justification for a commutation, but the governor had also received petitions supporting the execution. On his final evening he was told that his application for commutation or respite had been refused. Smith had weakened during his time in jail but braced up until the sounds of preparation caused him to begin breaking down. When he learned his last hope to avoid the hanging had failed he called for spiritual consolation, so Deacon Ben Campbell responded and prayed with the condemned man until late Thursday evening. He slept a portion of the night, from sheer exhaustion, but awoke at an early hour and was restless and uneasy. He refused to have a priest in attendance and talked to everyone but his guards and the sheriff, but Campbell returned to the cell at 8:00 A.M. and remained with Smith to the end. At 10:00 A.M. deputy Beitzer appeared in the enclosure and announced that Smith would appear in about twenty minutes. Sheriff Hamilton then went outside the enclosure and secured a box for the prisoner to stand upon when addressing the witnesses, and placed it on the platform. This served as a signal to the mass of two thousand men, women and children who refused to be denied admission, so they rushed forward trampling the wire fence. They then tore down the enclosure, all in less than five minutes, and just as quickly became orderly while they awaited the arrival of Smith. There was nothing that Sheriff Hamilton could do at that time, as the hour of execution was at hand, so he went to the prisoner's cell and told him his time had come. The sheriff had been there earlier to read the death warrant, with Ben Campbell supporting the prisoner, so now he took Smith out of his cell and bound his wrists and arms. The procession formed and the prisoner was immediately marched onto the platform where he was asked if he had anything to say, and when he said "Yes!" he was helped onto the box. He looked down at the throngs of people and said, "Fellow Citizens, I am about to be executed for a crime of which you have heard reiterated both in print and by hearsay and of which I am innocent, and that is deliberate premeditated murder. May the Lord help you all to form a correct judgment. My enemies I forgive and pray and bless all my friends, is all I ask." He was then helped down from the box and positioned on the center of the trapdoor. The prisoner's ankles were tied, the black hood drawn over his head, and the noose was adjusted. The prisoner then said, "I commend my spirit to the Lord on high and my body to the hands of wicked men," and when Smith ended his final speech at 10:30 A.M. Sheriff Hamilton sprang the trap. Smith fell seven feet, breaking his neck, and he hung motionless. It was thought he had died instantly but was not pronounced dead for five minutes, then the body was allowed to hang for seven minutes more, to ensure he could not be revived, before being cut down. The remains of Milton W. Smith were lowered into the coffin provided by the county and immediately conveyed to Potter's Field for burial.

Sources: *Osceola Record* (NE): July 23, 1885; July 30, 1885; *Weekly Nebraska State Journal* (Lincoln): December 5, 1884; July 31, 1885.

Reynolds, James
May 21, 1886

James Reynolds was born in Howard County, Missouri, on December 6, 1862. Reynolds' father was ill so, as the oldest, he had to go to work to support his family of four sisters, two brothers, and both parents rather than attend school. In 1885 Reynolds was working for Mr. J. S. Long when James Pinkston decided to move to Nebraska and offered Reynolds a position, at the urging of his son John who was about the same age as Reynolds. Reynolds had $65 when they started in mid–July and the Pinkstons, James and son John, each had the same amount besides owning the outfit. Along the trail the men spent their money on necessities as if from one family and, upon arriving in Cheyenne County, Nebraska, they took up adjoining homesteads. Then the three men began building a house on the elder Pinkston's property. They planned to build a house on each property, a requirement to "prove up" on their homestead claims, then return to Missouri for the winter and return in the spring to work and live on their claims. On September 16, 1885, the three men sat down in their tent to take account of the money they had spent on the trip to Nebraska and were soon quarreling. According to Reynolds the elder Pinkston suddenly jumped to his feet, declared that everything belonged to him, and that he would settle matters to suit himself. Reynolds claimed that he suggested they drop the matter until everyone was in good humor, and they could then settle the accounting. James Pinkston insisted that they settle the matter "now or not at all." Pinkston argued that Reynolds should not be concerned about a few dollars, and Reynolds claimed he replied it was not the matter of a few dollars but the thought of the elder Pinkston "trying to beat me out of it" after being friends for several months. Reynolds then claimed the contested amount was $15 and said the elder Pinkston yelled, "Don't you tell me that I am trying to beat you out of $15." According to Reynolds, Pinkston then advanced toward him so he said, "Go back and sit down and let's talk this thing over in a quiet way. Let's not get mad." Pinkston insisted, "We will settle this thing now, as we have commenced it." Reynolds said he replied, "We cannot settle this the way you want unless we knock it out. It seems to me you want a fight." Pinkston then shook his fist in Reynolds' face and said, "I would just as soon fight as not," and the fist was slapped away with a warning for Pinkston to sit down. It was then, according to Reynolds, that Pinkston hit him and a fist fight commenced, during which John Pinkston tried to get his father to calm down. As the fight continued they came near where the camp ax lay on the ground and the elder Pinkston grabbed it but as he raised it Reynolds grabbed the ax handle with his right hand and overpowered the older man. He struck him on the head and as the old man collapsed, John Pinkston struck Reynolds with a club and Reynolds said, "You want some of it too, do you?" Reynolds parried the club with the ax, pushed the younger Pinkston back with his left hand, and then struck him on the head with the ax. Reynolds insisted that he did not think the blows were fatal, but after he gathered his composure he found that both men were dead. He claimed that his first thought was to go to town and tell the whole thing, but first he went through their pockets and took all their money. It was dark so that instead of starting for town he hitched up the team to the wagon, placed the bodies on the hind part of the running gear, and sat in front of them on the reach, holding them on with one hand and driving with the other. He took the bodies to the sand draw where he buried them. He returned to the tent and changed his bloody clothes, throwing them into the tent, and then set the straw tick afire to burn up the evidence. According to Reynolds, after burning the tent he mounted one horse and started for the house of Mr. Num, intending to tell him the story, but then manufactured another story in the hope it would exonerate him but he was immediately suspected of foul play and arrested. A search of the camp soon showed the truth of the murders, and the bodies were easily discovered where they had been buried. Reynolds next tried an insanity dodge but was not good at it, so at his examination he was held over for the grand jury. He was tried at the spring term of the court and found guilty of premeditated murder, and was sentenced to hang on May 21, 1886.

It seemed that everyone expected a respite or commutation so when the day grew close, and no action had been taken, a scaffold had to be hurriedly built on the west side of the jail. It was twelve feet square with the platform seven feet above the ground, and the trapdoor was in the center. Sheriff Eubanks had delayed the execution until 3:00 P.M. in case there was last minute word from Governor James W. Dawes, but finally the procession formed and Reynolds marched to the gallows escorted by deputy Moore and the Rev. Leslie Stevens. Once upon the platform the prisoner stepped onto the trapdoor and stood firm while the sheriff tied his wrists and arms, knees and ankles. He was then asked if he had anything to say to the witnesses and he declined, but turned to the Reverend Stevens and said, "Make a good prayer for me, and when you get through I want to go." The short prayer was finished at 3:20 P.M., and with the pronouncement of "Amen!" the trap was sprung, as the reverend began reciting the Methodist Episcopal burial service. The knot had been exceptionally large and this caused the noose to slip behind Reynolds' neck, but he strangled to death with only a few convulsions. At 3:40 P.M. Reynolds was pronounced dead by the attending physicians and the body was cut down. The remains were lowered into the coffin provided by the county and turned over to the Reverend Stevens for burial.

Sources: *Nebraska Weekly State Journal* (Lincoln): May 28, 1886.

Marion, William J.
March 25, 1887

John Cameron, a nineteen-year-old Iowan, boarded with twenty-three-year-old William Jackson Marion and his wife Lydia at Grasshopper Flats, Clay County, Kansas. In late April 1872 Cameron and Marion started for the Wild Cat district which was one and a half miles from Wolf Creek, or sixteen miles from Beatrice in Gage County, Nebraska. Cameron was driving a fine team of bay mares and an almost new wagon, and he had already agreed to sell the outfit to Marion for $315, and Marion had given a deposit of $30 to seal the deal. The men planned to visit Lydia's parents, John and Rachel Warren, before starting out for Steele City to get work on the St. Joseph & Denver Railroad. On May 3 the two men started west but on May 6 Marion returned to Wolf Creek with the wagon and team, and also had Cameron's light brown trunk containing all his clothes except what he had been wearing, all of Cameron's papers, ink and paper, and both pairs of Cameron's boots. John Warren saw his son-in-law wearing a nearly new pair of Cameron's boots when they met at Snow's blacksmith shop in Beatrice in mid–May, but Marion said he had swapped his old boots for them. The suspicion of foul play was growing, so near the end of May Marion went to Rulo and remained for a month and then left for Kansas. Over the next decade his whereabouts remained a mystery. On Thursday morning, March 20, 1873, the remains of a man about five feet eleven inches tall were found buried in the mud along the banks of Indian Creek, a tributary of the Blue River near Blue Springs on the Otoe and Missouri Indian Reservation. The man had been shot in the head three times with a small caliber pistol, and the condition suggested he might have been there nearly a year as there was only a little flesh on the skeleton and some light brown hair attached to the skull, but the clothing was entirely intact. The remains were collected, placed in a pine box, and taken to Beatrice where they were stored in the rear of Wallace Buchanan's store. On Saturday morning Coroner Job Buchanan convened a jury for an inquest and took testimony from John Warren and Lydia Marion. Both witnesses identified the clothing of the deceased as resembling that of Cameron when last seen: a brown vest, a blue shirt, and brown pants with small stripes. Warren said that when questioned Marion had told him that he had completed the deal for the team and wagon and headed back to Wild Cat while Cameron returned to Kansas, and Marion explained that he had Cameron's property because, without the wagon, the young man had no way to take it along. Warren also testified that when they left Marion had a small caliber navy revolver with him. Based upon all the evidence the jury found, "...the said John Cameron came to his death on or about the 4th day of May, 1872, by means of a bullet or bullets shot from a revolver in the hands of Jackson Marion, and the same was done by the said Jackson Marion feloniously." A warrant was issued for the arrest of Marion and his description was circulated widely: five feet ten inches tall, dark brown hair worn short, whiskers and moustache lighter than his hair, light complexion, stoop-shouldered, size seven boots. On December 12, 1882, Sheriff Nathaniel Herron went to southern Kansas and returned to Beatrice with Marion on December 30. The prisoner had been arrested in Kansas on a charge of grand larceny and, though he used a false name, he was recognized as the Nebraska fugitive. He had been hiding in the Indian Territory all those years but made the mistake of returning to Kansas. He was charged with murdering Cameron and on April 20, 1883, he was indicted, immediately tried, and his trial concluded on May 3. Marion was tried upon a carefully constructed chain of circumstantial evidence which left no doubt as to his guilt; the defendant was convicted of first degree murder, and on May 24 he was sentenced to hang on June 26. At his first trial the judge pronounced the sentence, rather than the jury as prescribed by law, and this proved to be error sufficient for the state supreme court to grant a new trial. Marion's second trial commenced in February 1885, and on March 3 the jury found him "guilty as charged in the indictment."

On April 17, 1885, following motions by the defense, Marion was sentenced to hang. Once again appeals delayed the proceedings but this time the state supreme court affirmed the lower court and the date for Marion's execution was set at March 11, 1887, fifteen years after anyone had seen John Cameron alive. An application was sent to Governor John M. Thayer praying for a commutation of sentence to life in prison, and the governor granted a two-week respite to consider the matter, but after careful consideration the governor refused to intervene and the new date for execution was set at March 25, 1887. There were no further delays in the proceedings.

The scaffold was erected east of the jail building within a forty-foot-square area surrounded by an eighteen-foot fence. The platform was only six feet above ground level but an excavation three feet deep had been dug beneath the four-foot-square trapdoor. On Thursday all was in readiness for testing and the condemned man asked Sheriff E. Fay Davis if he could inspect the apparatus. The sheriff granted his request and when they entered the stockade a bag of sand was about to drop to test the half-inch Manila rope, so the prisoner asked to see the trap sprung to see how it would work. The sheriff sprang the trapdoor using the bar which extended into the jail, so no one would know who sprang the trap at the fatal moment, and Marion said, "It works nice, don't it?" On his final night Marion ate a hearty supper at 7:00 P.M. and then had a long consultation with the Rev. G. H. Albright, his spiritual adviser. The condemned man retired at 8:30 P.M. but could not sleep so he dictated an address to the citizens of Gage County. He finally fell asleep at 11:00 P.M. and, though he awoke briefly once, he slept soundly until 6:00 A.M. Outside the crowd began to grow at an early hour, and Company C of the militia, with bayonets fixed, formed a cordon to protect the enclosure fence. By the time set for the execution there were more than five hundred spectators surrounding the stockade. Once the prisoner was awake the barber shaved him and then Marion brushed his new grey coat, vest and dark pants, made his toilet, and dressed. At 7:00 A.M. his breakfast arrived and his appetite did not fail him. After eating a hearty morning meal he was closeted with his spiritual adviser until 10:00 A.M. when visitors were admitted for a brief period. Soon Sheriff Davis appeared with several other lawmen as witnesses and he read the death warrant to the prisoner. Marion realized that his time was near at hand and said, "I never shirked when duty called, and I am ready to go." He then turned to the reverend and said, "I confess before the Almighty that I am a sinner. Further than that I will not deny my guilt, neither will I confess it." At 11:05 A.M. Marion, unshackled, stepped out of his cell and the procession formed. They marched at a solemn pace into the stockade and Marion mounted the platform with a firm step, unassisted, and then the Reverend Albright offered a brief prayer for the salvation of Marion's soul. Marion was next given an opportunity to speak to the one hundred fifty witnesses but there was a delay of several minutes as he seemed in deep thought, during which a death-like silence prevailed. Finally William Wymore, Marion's uncle, was allowed to mount the scaffold and encourage his nephew to speak to the crowd. Marion said,

> Well gentlemen, I suppose you are all waiting to hear what I have to say. You are waiting patiently to hear me make some confessions. You have been waiting sometime, some years, some months, some weeks, thinking to get a full confession of guilt out of me. No man has anything to show where I have confessed that I have committed any crime. I confess that I am a sinner, the same as any other law-abiding citizen or church member. I've made no confession to nobody and I've got no confession to make. All I have said is to go to the dockets for four years and see wherein there have been men indicted, convicted, and sentenced and not hung, or convicted and not sentenced. Then I want you to compare my case. May God help everybody; friends and foes, nearest and dearest; the enemy and the prejudiced as much as the brother, the sister, the mother. All I have to say is God help everybody, that including everything. That is all I have to say.

He concluded at 11:15 A.M. and was positioned on the center of the trapdoor where his wrists and arms, knees and ankles were pinioned, the noose was adjusted, and the black cap was pulled over his head. The trap was sprung at 11:20 A.M., and Marion dropped six feet, breaking his neck. Dr. D. E. Waldron and the newspaper reporters were allowed to approach the area under the trapdoor and, after only a few twitches, the body hung motionless and he was pronounced dead in fifteen minutes. At 11:45 A.M. the remains were lowered into a coffin, carried outside the stockade, and put on display where more than one thousand men, women and children filed past. The Reverend

Albright then took possession of the body, as no one had applied to bury the deceased. Marion was buried in the Potter's Field section of the Beatrice cemetery at 4:00 P.M., following a brief sermon by the reverend.

William Wymore, Marion's uncle, for years made every effort to prove that William Jackson Marion was innocent of the murder of John Cameron. In August 1891 Wymore swore to the editor of the *Beatrice Express* that he had found John Cameron alive in LaCrosse, Kansas. Wymore reported that when asked about his disappearance for two decades Cameron explained that he had fled to Mexico to avoid a shotgun wedding when a girl tried to claim he was the father of her child. According to Wymore, Cameron was not aware that he had been reported dead nor that anyone had been convicted and executed for his murder, as he had been mining in Mexico, Colorado and Alaska. Wymore had his relative, Dud Marion, write out the statement for Cameron, who was literate and could have written it himself, and Wymore made no effort to have the statement taken by a notary public nor from a disinterested third party. Cameron, according to Wymore, "was afraid of his own shadow," refused to return to Beatrice, and soon afterward conveniently disappeared never to be heard of again. On December 12, 1986, Nebraska's Governor Robert Kerrey granted Marion a posthumous pardon to become effective on March 25, 1987—the 100th anniversary of his execution. The governor wrote, "Upon consideration of the application and the evidence submitted in support thereof, the [Pardon] Board did find that the said William Jackson Marion is a fit subject for clemency."

Sources: *Beatrice Express* (NE): March 27, 1873; August 3, 1891. *Beatrice Republican* (NE): April 2, 1887. *Daily Pharos* (Logansport, IN): March 26, 1887. *Beatrice Daily Sun* (NE): October 15, 1929. *Evening Gazette* (Cedar Rapids, IA): March 25, 1887. *Marion v. Nebraska, 16 Neb. 349* (1884); *Marion v. Nebraska, 20 Neb. 233* (1886). *The Daily Northwestern* (Oshkosh, WI): March 25, 1887. *The Galveston Daily News* (TX): March 26, 1887.

Hoffman, David W.
July 22, 1887

At 9:10 P.M. on Tuesday, January 11, 1887, the southbound Missouri Pacific Express train left Omaha, Nebraska, on the Burlington & Missouri road carrying sixteen thousand dollars in the safe and eighteen silver bars, each worth one thousand dollars. At 11:30 P.M., when the train was one mile north of Dunbar traveling at forty miles per hour, and only a few feet from a forty-foot embankment, it was derailed. The engine was thrown from the tracks and the drop-lever was driven entirely through the body of engineer James B. DeWitt of Wyandotte, Kansas. DeWitt was killed instantly, and Fireman Frank Denter was slightly injured. The baggage car was thrown from the tracks and lay two hundred feet distant, at the bottom of an embankment in a frozen creek, where express messenger Frank Chenowith was so severely injured that it was thought he would die. Chenowith survived but was permanently crippled. All of the passenger cars were derailed and fell on their sides but had not been tossed about so that none of the fifty-five passengers were seriously injured, though they were badly shaken. Just as the train reached the point where it derailed two men were seen running from the tracks into a ravine, presumably to avoid being killed in the impending disaster. Men were soon on the scene to help the injured and investigate the derailment, and they found a claw bar and wrench. These tools had been used to remove spikes and fishplates from two rails, and the rails had been moved only a few inches inward so that the engineer could not see the danger ahead. At daybreak the following morning two sets of boot tracks were found in the snow, first going southward to the baggage car where it appeared that the two men had not been able to loot the car because of a break in the creek's ice. From there the boot tracks led up the creek bank into a cornfield and directly to the farm of John Hoffman, lying three hundred yards north of the wreck. The appearance of foot tracks were documented and later were matched exactly to those of David Hoffman and James Bell. A coroner's jury was summoned and the first witnesses questioned were the Hoffmans—John and his wife, and John's brother David. Testimony revealed that John had gone to his well just before 11:30 P.M. and saw two men on the tracks, one he recognized as his brother David. Mrs. Hoffman testified that soon after the wreck David Hoffman and James Bell walked up to the Hoffman farmhouse, and Mrs. Hoffman suggested they hurry after John to lend aid to the injured. The two men went to the wreck and offered to help but then immediately returned to the farmhouse without rendering any aid. David Hoffman and James Bell gave conflicting testimony, especially about their route to the farmhouse, and as soon as they left the witness stand they were arrested by Sheriff McCallum.

On Thursday night Missouri Pacific rail detectives George Fairchild and Frank K. Tutt checked into Dunbar's Grand Pacific Hotel, and just before midnight the prisoners were separately brought to their room for questioning. Each man quickly confessed and blamed the other, but otherwise the stories they told were consistent. Each said they had been friendly for over a week, since Bell had come to town from Unadilla fourteen miles north of Dunbar. Both men had worked on railroads, Bell as a reater and Hoffman as a brakeman, but they were now unemployed, short of cash, and interested in leaving Nebraska to search for opportunities elsewhere. On the morning of January 11 an Unadilla farmer named Rogers, who held a chattel mortgage on Bell's team, came to Dunbar to prevent him from selling the team. During the early evening of January 11, Bell and Hoffman were in Moffat's Saloon, drinking heavily as they had for the past week, and had a row which resulted in their arrest. They posted security for their appearance in court and were released. They returned to the saloon but by 10:00 P.M. had become so boisterous that Sheriff McCallum ordered the saloon closed. The two men started for the Hoffman farm, following the railroad tracks, but when a half mile from town they broke into a section house and stole a wrench and claw bar. They went another half mile and removed the spikes and fishplates. As they worked on the rails Bell had second thoughts and suggested that they go home without tampering further but Hoffman replied, "It don't make a damn bit of difference how many get killed. We want the money." They had no idea what treasure might be aboard the train but were certain it would carry enough money for their purpose. The headlight of a locomotive suddenly appeared in the distance so, as soon as the rails were loosened and moved a few inches, the two men ran to a ravine to await the wreck. After the prisoners confessed they were taken to the jail at Beatrice to avoid a lynching. The sheriff had heard talk of vigilante action and had encouraged a rumor that the men would be taken out by train, but instead they were spirited away from Dunbar by sleigh, and ten minutes after they departed the jail was assaulted by a mob. Once the vigilantes determined that the prisoners were not in a cell they dispersed. The prisoners had their preliminary examination in Beatrice on January 21 and were held over for action by the grand jury, and Hoffman was tried for the murder of DeWitt. One of the most trying moments occurred when James Bell, who had turned state's evidence, took the stand and related all the details of the crime. Hoffman was found guilty of first degree murder after only a half hour of jury deliberations, and on Monday, April 11, 1887, Judge Chapman sentenced the prisoner to hang at Beatrice on Friday, July 22. The trial of Bell was to commence the following day, but he pled guilty to being an accomplice and received a sentence of ten years in prison. Neither appeal nor application for clemency would delay the fatal date.

Hoffman had been attended by the Revs. R. Pierson and J. B. Stuart during his final days and had frequent visits by many family members. On Sunday one of the clergymen suggested he write a letter "giving the cause of his downfall." The letter was published verbatim, to show his lack of education, but added nothing to the record. On his final night the condemned man retired at 1:30 A.M. and asked that his brother Timothy be allowed to spend the night with him, but later relented saying he would sleep better alone. He arose at 6:30 A.M. and ordered his usual breakfast, supplemented with bananas and oranges. At 8:00 A.M., Company B of the Nebraska National Guard was deployed around the courthouse, and forty minutes later the death warrant was read to the prisoner in his cell. After 10:00 the sheriff went to the cell door and told Hoffman his time had come, and the procession formed. The prisoner was escorted from the jail by the Reverends Pierson and Stuart with deputies in front and in back, and he reached the stairs to the scaffold at 10:20 A.M. Once on the platform he declined to make a speech and took his place on the trapdoor. While a prayer was offered for his soul, his wrists and arms, knees and ankles were bound, the noose was adjusted, and the black hood pulled over his head. At 10:24 the trap was sprung and Hoffman's body dropped straight downward and rebounded, then the muscles of the body contracted, the knees were drawn up, and the flesh quivered. His hands clenched and unclenched for a few moments then hung motionless. In eight and one-half minutes he was pronounced dead, and it was later determined that his neck had been broken in the fall. The body was cut down, deposited in the coffin provided, and turned over to an undertaker for delivery to Unadilla on Saturday afternoon, July 23 for burial.

Sources: *The Beatrice Republican* (NE): January 22, 1887; April 23, 1887; July 30, 1887.

Haunstine, Albert
May 17, 1891

Albert Haunstine, Hiram Roten and William Ashley, Roten's uncle, were neighbors in Roten Valley, Nebraska. The men had been friendly toward one another until there was a theft of school property. On November 9, 1888, Roten and Ashley, officers of the school board, were asked to investigate the theft of lumber and a clock. At the school house the two men found a clear set of wagon tracks and followed them to the farm house of Albert Haunstine. The two men were confronted by Haunstine who demanded to know why they were there and, when told of their purpose, he went into his house and returned with the stolen clock, and then confessed his crime. As the two men returned to their wagon with the clock, Haunstine reached inside his front door, brought out his rifle, and shot both men in the back. He then rifled their pockets and took forty dollars, their watches, and their firearms — a rifle and a revolver. Haunstine and his wife fled to Arnold, switched teams, and then continued on to Madison. Meanwhile the family and friends of Roten and Ashley became concerned by their continued absence and formed search parties. After several days they found the bodies in front of Haunstine's house. A description of Haunstine was circulated and a reward posted. Haunstine had sent his wife by train to Columbus and he followed later, but as he disembarked from the train he was arrested by deputies who had tracked him. Haunstine was lodged in the Custer County jail, and at his examination he was held to answer to the grand jury. He was indicted in early March 1889, and his trial at Broken Bow followed immediately. The defendant was convicted of first degree murder and sentenced to hang on September 6. However, his defense team of C. L. Gutterson, A. R. Humphry and N. V. Harlen filed appeals which delayed the execution until 1891. After the conviction was upheld by the state supreme court the date for Haunstine's execution was set for April 17. Next a question was raised regarding the prisoner's sanity, and the execution could not proceed until the matter was resolved. At the last moment Governor John M. Thayer granted a thirty-day respite so the matter could be resolved, and when the crowd of spectators learned of the delay they rose up and several times tried to lynch Haunstine, but finally they were calmed and dispersed. The prisoner was found sane and then rescheduled to hang on May 17, 1891.

The scaffold had been constructed in 1884 by John S. Lamb for the Grand Island execution of George Hart, but his death sentence had been commuted to life in prison, and this scaffold was borrowed by Custer County. The authorities, hoping to limit the number of spectators, would not release the time of execution so crowds began to gather at an early hour outside the sixteen-foot enclosure built on the south side of the courthouse. However, as preparations indicated that the moment was at hand the crowd surged forward, tore down the fence, and fifteen hundred men, women, and children gathered around the gallows. Haunstine was brought out of the jail after noon, made his way through the crowd, and took his place on the platform. He was positioned on the trapdoor and Sheriff Jim Jones asked if he had anything to say. The condemned man begged for forgiveness, and then told the crowd, "I am very sorry for the trouble I have given the public, and ask forgiveness for what I have done. Remember that little things grow into big ones and don't wait till you come to what I have before you seek salvation. The committing of little sins led me on to the commission of the crime which has brought me where I now stand." Haustine, a Catholic, was then blessed by Father Haley of Broken Bow and Father Wolf of Grand Island, who had attended him in his cell for weeks. As the priests spoke the prisoner's wrists and arms, knees and ankles were pinioned and the noose was adjusted. When the priests concluded the black cap was pulled over the prisoner's head and the trap was sprung at 1:02 P.M. Haunstine dropped through but the rope unraveled and he fell to the ground. The stunned prisoner was picked up and escorted onto the platform a second time as a new noose was being prepared, and at 1:05 P.M. Haunstine dropped six feet, breaking his neck in the second fall. Death was pronounced in eleven and a half minutes, and the body was cut down eighteen minutes after the drop. The remains were placed in a coffin and given to his brother for burial.

Sources: *Lincoln Evening News* (NE): May 21, 1891.

Furst, Christian
Shepherd, Charles
June 5, 1891

Just after sundown on December 10, 1889, Carl J. Pulsifer, a grain dealer at Crowell, Dodge County, Nebraska, locked his office and left for his home a half mile from town where his wife and eight children awaited his arrival. A half hour later the report of three pistol shots aroused the inhabitants of the town and a party of men started along the thoroughfare toward the sound of the gunfire. The leading men in the party, rushing forward, stumbled over the dead body of Pulsifer. He had been shot through the heart and his pockets were turned out, and it was later determined he had been robbed of twenty dollars. The first clue to the perpetrators occurred when two men — Charles Shepherd and Christian Furst — excitedly rushed into the farm house of farmer Schumacker four miles west of Crowell where they bought a loaf of bread and hurried on their way. Tracks at the scene revealed that two men had committed the murder and had headed west, and the time it would take to reach Schumacker's farm coincided with their arrival there after the shots were heard. A posse was formed, and they tracked the two men from Schumacker's farm to four miles north of Crowell, but there they lost the trail. A reward of nineteen hundred dollars was posted for the arrest and conviction of the murderers: one thousand dollars by Pulsifer's brother, five hundred dollars by Governor John M. Thayer, and four hundred dollars by Sheriff Mallon. At 3:00 A.M. on the morning of December 12 two young men rode into Scribner on a pair of spent horses they had stolen from Grove's farm. They tried to steal a fresh team but were discovered and had to flee on foot. An alarm was raised and a large party of men pursued them into the brush along the Elkhorn River, where they were captured without resistance. They were returned to Scribner and separated, one being held in jail and the other at the Clifton House under a close guard. The two men were well known in Scribner as Shepherd worked at Spangler's blacksmith shop and Furst worked in Joseph Shepherd's livery. A telegram was sent to Sheriff Mallon in Fremont, who hurried to Scribner to take custody of the two prisoners. Word of their capture had spread; the sheriff arrived just in time to deputize a small force of responsible citizens to prevent a lynching, and they kept a large crowd of angry farmers at bay. The two prisoners were taken safely to Fremont and lodged in the county jail. Another Scribner resident, thought to have knowledge of the crime, was also arrested, and the three were joined by a fourth man from Crowell. As soon as twenty-three-year-old Shepherd and twenty-two-year-old Furst were behind bars, each tried to be first to inform on his partner. Each prisoner confessed all the details of the robbery and murder, but pointed their finger at the other as the one who fired the fatal bullet. At their preliminary hearing on December 20 the two men thought to know something of the crime were questioned, exonerated, and released; but Furst and Shepherd again recited their confessions and pled guilty. The prisoners waived an examination and were held for the next session of the district court, which convened in January. The two defendants were easily found guilty of the first degree murder of Pulsifer, their confessions being the most damning evidence against them. They were sentenced to hang but the admission of the confessions was grounds for an appeal, which delayed the proceedings. On February 17, 1891, fourteen months after the murder, the state supreme court affirmed the lower court's judgment and sentence and also dismissed the issue of insanity as a defense in the case, and the date for the executions was set for June 5, 1891. On May 20 Shepherd's parents arrived in Fremont to plead with Governor John M. Thayer for a respite or a commutation of sentence for their son, but applications for both condemned men were already being considered. Two weeks before the hanging the scaffold was being erected within an enclosure in the jail yard, and when the governor finally announced, on June 3, that he would not intervene on behalf of the prisoners he also sent word to the sheriff to prepare for the affair. The governor was concerned that the crowd would tear down the enclosure, as had recently occurred at the hanging of Albert Haunstine in Broken Bow. He authorized the sheriff to mobilize the local militia and deploy them around the enclosure fence, bayonets fixed, facing the crowd, and remain on post until both men were pronounced dead.

On the morning of June 5 there was a slight drizzle falling but it did not dampen the spirits of the curious citizens who assembled in large numbers near the jail. However, unlike the affair at Broken Bow, the crowds were calm and orderly. At mid-morning the sheriff went to the cell of Furst and Shepherd where he read the death warrants and the reports on the appeals and applications. The prisoners had risen early that morning and prepared for their deaths by making their toilet, eating a light breakfast, and donning their burial suits. They were asked about their condition and Furst, speaking for both of them, said, "If everybody felt as happy as we do, this would be a nice world." Both men said they had embraced religion, were confident of salvation, and had resigned themselves to their fates. They stepped out of their cell and the procession formed, with eight sheriffs and ex-sheriffs escorting them to the scaffold. The condemned men walked with a firm step into the enclosure and onto the platform. They were asked if they had anything to say to the few witnesses gathered below the scaffold and Furst declined, but Shepherd confessed the crime and tried to exonerate Furst. They were then positioned on the trapdoors where their ankles and knees, wrists and arms were bound. The nooses were brought forward and positioned, and the black caps were pulled over their heads. In a moment the trap was sprung and the two murderers dropped to their deaths, breaking their necks in the fall. Beneath the platform Drs. Deveries, McDonald, Brown, and Inches waited and, deploying two to each man, one listened to the heartbeat while the other monitored the pulse. Furst hung lifeless and was pronounced dead in fourteen minutes but Shepherd displayed slight convulsions for several minutes and was not pronounced dead until nineteen minutes had lapsed. The bodies were then cut down and released to their respective family members: Furst's remains going to his brothers and sisters and Shepherd's remains going to his father.

Sources: *The Lincoln Evening News* (NE): February 18, 1891; May 20, 1891; June 3, 1891; June 5, 1891.

Neil, Ed
October 9, 1891

Ed Neil, sometimes spelled Neal, but often using the aliases Livingston and Katen, was a notorious cattle and horse thief. Neil had been convicted of stealing cattle in Iowa and served a term in the state penitentiary. Upon his release he went to Kansas, watched for a promising opportunity, stole cattle and horses and again was captured, convicted and sentenced to a term in prison. Of course, these rustling jobs were only the ones where he was caught, and certainly there were many others. As soon as Neil acquired the money from the sale of the stolen livestock he began spending freely, flaunting his newfound wealth until it raised suspicion, and this had led to his arrest, but his two convictions were the direct result of the testimony of the owners. Upon his release from his second prison term Neil went to Omaha, Nebraska, and in early 1889 he saw an excellent opportunity to rustle on the farm of Allen and Dorothy Jones, an aged couple living near that city. They owned a fine herd of cattle and an excellent string of horses so in February he went to the farm, found Allen at work, and shot him dead. He then went into the house and, finding Dorothy in the kitchen, shot her dead without hesitating a moment. He buried the bodies in the manure pile and the following day drove the cattle and horses to market. Neighbors missed the couple in two days and one man went to check on their welfare, but when he found them absent and the livestock gone, the neighbors formed a search party and quickly found the bodies. They suspected Neil, and a posse trailed him to Omaha where he had boarded the train for Kansas City. A week after the murders Neil was arrested in Kansas City for stealing cattle there, a crime committed almost as soon as he arrived, and he was again discovered because he was flaunting his newfound wealth. After his arrest the authorities saw that his description matched that of the Nebraska murderer, which had been circulated widely. They notified Omaha lawmen, and Neil was returned to Omaha where he confessed to the murders. He was tried at the spring term of court, convicted, and sentenced to hang. The evidence was entirely circumstantial but carefully linked so that there was no reasonable doubt as to his guilt. The case was appealed to the state supreme court, and after two years of "legal manipulations and pettifogging" the justices affirmed the lower court on June 29, 1891; the date for Neil's execution was set for October 9. No further appeals nor applications for executive clemency would delay the proceedings.

On Wednesday, October 7, 1891, a drayman drove up Harney Street, turned north on Eighteenth Street and dropped a load of lumber on the southwest corner of the courthouse grounds. Shortly two men with post hole augers appeared and bored ten holes to a depth of two feet, then raised ten four- by four-inch timbers sixteen feet in length. These timbers were the supports for the enclosure, and soon carpenters were busy enclosing an area forty feet square with eighteen-foot boards. The gallows, which had been stored in the basement of the jail, was brought out and assembled in the southeast corner of the enclosure using heavy carriage bolts. The invited guests would stand about the gallows but tables and chairs were provided for member of the press, located six feet from the place the body would appear beneath the platform. On Thursday morning the rope was attached and the entire apparatus was inspected and tested by dropping a bag of sand weighing two hundred pounds. On Thursday Neil was visited by Jo Clark, a fallen woman who was suspected to be his sister, and he gave her a written confession to present to Governor John M. Thayer but she found the governor away from the capitol and returned to Omaha. On his final night Neil retired at 9:30 P.M. and within ten minutes was sound asleep. Just after midnight he turned over on his bunk and quietly said, "You can't do it!" It seemed he was still asleep when he spoke but he awoke at 3:00 A.M. and, after asking the time twice during the next hour, he said, "I wish it was morning." Father Riggs arrived at an early hour and they engaged in religious exercises before his morning meal. He then ate a hearty breakfast and spent most of the morning alone, except for the constant presence of his death watch. At 11:30 A.M. Sheriff Boyd, accompanied by deputy Tierney and jailer Horrigan, went to Neil's cell on the second floor and prepared him for his walk to the gallows. The first sound heard by the prisoner was the turning of the key in the third of four iron gates, and when the lawmen entered his cell he weakened and fell to his knees. He was given whiskey to help him brace up and then he was able to stand for the reading of the death warrant. The procession formed with the sheriff in front, followed by the prisoner with Tierney and Horrigan on each side, and followed by Fathers Riggs and McCartney; last came the death watch guards. Neil walked with a firm step, his hands clasped in front and his head bowed, but he was not shackled. The procession proceeded along the iron balcony and down the stairs, through the corridors into the jailer's office and into the kitchen of the jailer's residence to the door in the west wall of the south wing. The procession exited into the gallows' enclosure where Neil raised his head for only a moment to gaze at the witnesses. With head bowed again he walked slowly to the stairs and ascended to the platform of the scaffold, where he stepped cautiously onto the trapdoor. Sheriff Boyd asked Neil if he had anything to say and he stepped forward to the rail and said, "I went to the Jones farm that night alone, and killed those old people, and I hope I shall be forgiven, particularly by the Jones family, and all people in Omaha whom I may have offended. I hope I shall be forgiven as I expect to be above." He then stepped back onto the trapdoor where his wrists and arms were bound and his ankles shackled. The black cap was drawn over his head and the noose was adjusted at 12:07 P.M., and in a moment the lever was drawn backwards, the trap was sprung and Neil dropped six feet. The surgeons in attendance stepped forward to monitor vital signs and found that Neil's neck had not been broken in the fall, though there were no signs of struggling, and it took forty-five minutes before the attending physicians pronounced him dead. The body was then cut down and given to Fathers Riggs and McCartney for burial in the Holy Sepulcher Cemetery the following day.

Sources: *Lincoln Evening News* (NE): June 30, 1891; October 8–9, 1891. *The Waterloo Courier* (IA): October 14, 1891.

Dixon, Clinton E.
June 24, 1892

Twenty-three-year-old Clinton E. Dixon was a private in the Sixth U.S. Cavalry stationed at Fort Niobrara, Douglas County, Nebraska, and his immediate superior was Corporal Thomas Carter. In late 1891 Carter was ordered by his captain to drive a number of unsavory characters from the grounds of the fort. Carter efficiently did his duty with all but one black courtesan, Lillie Lewis, who had recently been intimate with Private Dixon. Carter, to complete his task, took a flat board and paddled Lewis, then physically ejected her from the fort with a warning not to return. Dixon, who was intoxicated at the time, took offense at the treatment of his paramour, got his carbine, and shot Carter dead. Dixon was arrested and, since the murder was between soldiers on a military post, he was held for trial in the U.S. Circuit Court at Omaha. Dixon's trial commenced in January 1892, he was convicted of first degree murder, and on January 20 he was sentenced to hang on April 2. An application was sent to President Benjamin Harrison praying for a pardon, so the date of execution was postponed to April 23 while the matter was under consideration. The president denied the pardon on April 6 saying, "The element of malice aforethought is clearly proven; also the purpose to kill." Next came an application to the president for a commutation of sentence to life in prison, and the president again granted a respite to expire on May 23, but the matter was not concluded by June 4 so on that day the respite was extended to June 24, 1892. This time the president decided that there was no justification to interfere further and ordered U.S. Marshal Brad D. Slaughter to proceed with the hanging.

The marshal had a stockade built just outside the Douglas County jail at Omaha. Inside the enclosure the gallows was erected and three electric buttons were provided to spring the trapdoor, two being dummies so no one would know which man sprang the trap. Marshal Slaughter announced that the execution would take place during the early afternoon hours but this was a ploy "to mislead morbid and curious people." Five hours before the stated time Marshal Slaughter went to Dixon's cell and read the death warrant. The small procession then formed and the condemned man walked into the enclosure and onto the platform escorted by his religious adviser, Father Riggs. When asked if he had anything to say to the small party of witnesses he declined. The condemned man then prayed with his priest as his wrists and arms were bound, his knees and ankles were pinioned with straps, the noose was cinched in place, and the black hood pulled over his head. Marshal Slaughter gave the signal and the three buttons were depressed, one springing the trap, and Dixon fell breaking his neck. The body hung motionless while the attending physicians monitored his vital signs, and when his heartbeat ceased the doctors pronounced him dead. Dixon's remains were lowered into his coffin, given to Father Riggs, and buried that evening.

Shortly before the hanging Lillie Lewis had been convicted in police court of a minor offense and lodged in the Douglas County jail to "board-out" a $350 fine. On the Sunday night following the execution Lewis became irrational saying she believed an angry mob was coming to lynch her. She demanded to be put in the most secure cell in the jail, and she was accommodated. Somehow she became aware that she had been moved into the cell that Dixon had occupied until the previous Friday morning, and she began to howl, froth at the mouth, and she finally collapsed into unconsciousness. She could not be revived for four hours but when she was finally aroused she was completely demented. Lewis was then committed to the state asylum for the insane.

Sources: *Alton Daily Telegraph* (IL): April 6, 1892. *Davenport Daily Leader* (IA): June 6, 1892. *Evening Times* (Monroe, WI): June 25, 1892. *Logansport Daily Pharos* (IN): April 29, 1892. *The Daily Huronite* (Huron, SD): June 25, 1892. *The Lincoln Evening News* (NE): January 20, 1892. *The Salt Lake Tribune* (UT): June 27, 1892.

Hill, Harry
March 1, 1895

On Wednesday evening, November 1, 1893, the Akeson family was just sitting down to supper in their farmhouse near Manley, Cass County, Nebraska, when two masked men rushed in and, at gunpoint, ordered Matthew Akeson to throw up his hands. Akeson had, just that day, received a large sum of money so when Akeson did not comply the robber armed with a revolver fired one shot, the bullet striking Akeson in the head, killing him instantly. The robber then emptied his revolver at Akeson's son and two hired hands, wounding them slightly. The second robber, who was armed only with a club, attacked Mrs. Akeson and beat her so brutally it was thought she would die but, after some time, she recovered. During the attack the robber's masks slipped and both men were recognized as Harry Hill and Joe Benwell, ex-farmhands who had been hired by Akeson's son at Weeping Waters and put to work husking corn. They had been discharged when the work was done and had returned to Weeping Waters, where they planned the robbery. Their descriptions and names were circulated and printed in the local newspapers, and two days later Joe Conway, a Lincoln bartender, recognized the two men as they entered a saloon at Twentieth and O Streets. Conway notified Police Chief Cooper and Detective Malone, and when they arrested the two fugitives Benwell gave his real name but Hill claimed he was George Rogers, until papers in his pocket showed his name as Harry Hill, formerly a hack driver in Omaha. The men then admitted they had worked on the Akeson farm but denied the assault and shooting. The day after their arrest Benwell weakened and made a full confession, naming Hill as the one who fired the fatal shot and he admitted beating Mrs. Akeson. The two men were examined and held for action by the grand jury, indicted, and tried at the spring term of the court. Both men were found guilty but Benwell had not committed murder and had cooperated, so he was sentenced to life in prison while Hill was sentenced to hang. Hill's defense of insanity was dismissed by the jury so deliberations were brief. The appeals commenced but on November 9 the state supreme court denied the appeal and set the date for execution at March 1, 1895. The proceedings would not be delayed further by applications for executive clemency nor by appeals.

A fence of sixteen-foot boards enclosed an area twenty-six feet square behind the jail. The entire enclosure was roofed to ensure no one could see inside from rooftops or windows. The scaffold, twelve feet square, was erected in the center of the enclosure, and the three-foot-square trapdoor, located in the center of the platform, allowed for an eight-foot drop. The entire apparatus was tested by Sheriff Eikenbary at 5:00 P.M. on the day before the hanging. Hill had remained composed during the long wait for the fatal day and was attended by Father Carney of Plattsmouth, Father Nugent of Louisville, and Father Cook of Hamburg, Iowa. On his final night he talked freely of his feelings, insisting that, "My sins have been forgiven, and whatever my fate might be in this world I am sure of salvation in the beyond. It makes little difference to me now what they say about me. It can do me no good or no harm. I shall be beyond its reach. What this world thinks of me doesn't concern me now, but I want only to say that I will walk up that scaffold tomorrow without a single pang, and that if I have ever injured any one I am sorry for it. I leave this life without a hard feeling toward any one and I am only anxious for the end to come." Everyone acquainted with Hill seemed certain that his profession of religion was genuine, and he slept soundly that last night and arose at 6:00 A.M. He ate a hearty breakfast before the priests arrived and they remained with him to the end. At 9:00 A.M. the death warrant was read to Hill in his cell and then the procession formed. Hill walked to the scaffold with a firm step, unassisted, and took his place on the trapdoor where he declined to speak to the one hundred witnesses in the enclosure. The last sacrament was administered by the three priests and then Hill shook hands with officers and friends. The straps were applied to his wrists and arms, ankles and knees, and the noose was adjusted. The hood was immediately pulled over his head, and at 9:06 A.M. Sheriff Eikenbary pulled the lever which sprang the trap. Hill plunged seven and one-half feet, breaking his neck. The attending physicians then began monitoring his vital signs, and in sixteen minutes his pulse stopped and he was pronounced dead. The priests took charge of Hill's remains and saw to his burial.

Sources: *The Evening News* (Lincoln, NE): February 16, 1894; February 25, 1894; November 9, 1894; March 2, 1894; March 1, 1895. *The Nebraska State Journal* (Lincoln): November 9, 1894.

Hoover, Claude H.

August 7, 1896

Claude H. Hoover worked for his brother-in-law and Councilman of the First Ward Samuel DuBois and lived in the DuBois house at 3197 South Thirteenth Street, Omaha, Nebraska. On December 13, 1895, Hoover and DuBois argued over Hoover's treatment of his sixteen-year-old half-sister because of her relationship with another girl, whom Hoover claimed was not fit company for his sister. Immediately after the argument DuBois fired Hoover, and Hoover threatened to kill DuBois the next time they met. Hoover immediately went to a store and bought a revolver and ammunition. Four hours after his termination Hoover, in an intoxicated condition, was in a small shoe store at 418 South Thirteenth Street discussing the difficulty he had with DuBois and said, "I wish he was here now. I would give a quarter if he was." Within a minute DuBois appeared at the door, entered, and walked to within two feet of Hoover. Hoover jumped to his feet and, without hesitation, pulled his new revolver as he yelled out, "I've got you now where I want you, you ___ ___." He fired two shots at DuBois, the bullets striking him in the left side just above his heart. DuBois was a large man, Hoover small, so DuBois grabbed Hoover and as they struggled Hoover said, "I told you I would kill you." DuBois took away the pistol and dragged Hoover into a nearby drug store. He turned over custody to several men as he exclaimed, "He has shot me. Oh! My poor wife and children." DuBois then walked to the rear of the store and sat down to await the arrival of physicians. On examination he was found to be fatally shot and was removed to the Presbyterian hospital, where he lingered until the following day and then died, and was buried on December 17. Hoover had been arrested right after the shooting and lodged in the county jail. After DuBois died a coroner's jury was convened and they charged Hoover with his murder, and at his examination the prisoner was held for action by the grand jury, which was then in session. Hoover was indicted and his trial commenced two weeks after the killing. His defense was that he was either insane or intoxicated, but his attorneys were not able to substantiate either claim and he was found guilty of first degree murder. On December 30, 1895 Hoover was sentenced to hang on April 17, 1896. The case was appealed to the state supreme court and on February 5, 1896, the justices granted a stay of execution while they considered the case. On July 31 the supreme court denied the appeal and set the date for execution at August 7, 1896. The sheriff then ordered a close death watch on his prisoner, to be certain he would not commit suicide and cheat the hangman. On August 1 Hoover's attorneys began a brief campaign to have Governor Silas A. Holcomb grant a reprieve to allow their client time to prepare for death, citing the absence of his spiritual adviser the Rev. J. M. Wilson, and requested a delay until his arrival. The governor was not in his office but, upon receiving the request, he denied the application on August 3. During Hoover's time in jail he had remained composed and maintained a hearty appetite. He became agitated for a brief time when told of the governor's action but quickly regained his composure. His sister was his only visitor, and he had shown great contrition for his rash act and expressed sorrow for the bereavement he had caused his sister and her children.

By August 5 a tight board fence eighteen feet high enclosed an area forty feet square in the southwest corner of the jail yard. In the southwest corner of the enclosure the parts of the scaffold were assembled using heavy timbers secured by carriage bolts, and the trapdoor at the center of the platform allowed a seven-foot drop. The electric release consisted of four buttons, three dummies, so that no one would know who actually sprang the trapdoor. The apparatus was tested on the morning of August 6 and worked perfectly. Cards of admission were distributed to very few but included several sheriffs and any doctor who asked to attend. The Revs. C. W. Savidge and J. M. Wilson, who had quickly returned from the East, had been attending to the prisoner's religious needs and promised to be with him at the fatal moment. On the final evening Hoover's supper of pork chops and watermelon was served at 6:00 P.M., and an hour later the Reverend Wilson arrived and was admitted at once. The two men prayed and sang hymns for an hour before they were joined by the Reverend Savidge, and the three then joined in until 1:45 A.M. After the clergymen left Hoover talked with his guards until 2:30 A.M., and then slept until 5 o'clock. He had a few words with his guard and then slept again until 6:45 A.M., when he arose for breakfast. He dressed in a black suit, with white shirt and black tie, and put a white rose in his buttonhole. He then ate heartily as he talked with his guards. His attorneys appeared at 8:30 A.M. and said there was no more they could do, so the prisoner assured them he had resigned himself to his fate. Next came the reverends, and they prayed and sang fervently, particularly four hymns that Hoover favored but especially "I Was Once Far Away from the Savior." Hoover made it a point to shake hands with his guards as they went off duty. The crowd began to gather at an early hour, and by 9:00 A.M. there were several hundred men and boys, and a few women, at the corners of Eighteenth and Harney Streets. An hour later the crowd had doubled but all were orderly. Chief Sigwart had twelve men stationed around the courthouse square, and no persons were allowed to gather there. Several more policemen were deployed on the courthouse lawn, and a reserve force of twenty men stood by. Sheriff McDonald had limited the witnesses to several county sheriffs, a few physicians, and the press. At 10:45 A.M. the sheriff tested the apparatus once more and it again worked perfectly. The reverends had asked to have until 11:00 and this had been granted, so the sheriff and deputies did not arrive at the cell door until 11:23. One of Hoover's daytime death watch guards put his arm gently around Hoover's shoulders and escorted him from the cell. The sheriff then read the death warrant and the procession formed, with a deputy in the lead, then came the sheriff followed by Hoover with two deputies on each side, next came the reverends, Dr. E. W. Lee and County Physician Mercer, and finally the press. They progressed at a solemn pace and the men already in the enclosure quietly parted to let them pass. Hoover ascended the stairs with the sheriff, three deputies, the two reverends, and Hoover's attorney Mr. Powers. The attorney spoke first, making a long speech detailing all he had done to save the life of his client, and then he read the statement written by Hoover:

> Omaha, Aug. 6, 1896 — On the day I took the life of my friend and brother-in-law Samuel DuBois, I was drunk. Most of the events of that afternoon are a blank to me and what I remember appears like a dream. I know no more about it. It was not my conscious and intentional act. I say this believing I have but one day more to live. My death must be laid at the door of intemperance. I was crazed by drink, and I killed my friend. I made my sister a widow and took from his children, whom I love, their natural protector. I hope God has forgiven me.

The statement was followed by Hoover's statement that he was forgiven and his salvation was firmly fixed, and ended with "God bless you all. I am ready." The Reverend Wilson then offered a fervent prayer followed by the benediction of the Presbyterian church, which brought the religious services to a close. The sheriff stepped forward and adjusted the black hood over Hoover's head while the deputies pinioned his wrists and ankles. The noose was adjusted, and at 11:37 A.M. the sheriff and three deputies each stepped back to one of the four electric buttons. On the sheriff's signal, each man pushed a button, and the trap was sprung. Hoover dropped with a thud and swung around three times, then slowly the rope unwound and the body hung motionless. The doctors approached and monitored Hoover's vital signs, and at 11:50 A.M. pronounced him dead. The body hung another seven minutes and was then cut down and placed on an undertaker's stand. Hoover's mother had requested that the body not be taken to the morgue or to an undertaker's parlor, as she did not want her son's remains to be displayed to the public, so Undertaker Michael O. Maul took charge on her behalf. Maul removed the black suit, the body was wrapped in a black shroud, and Hoover's remains were delivered to the home of Hoover's mother and sister at 3197 South Thirteenth Street. On Sunday funeral services were conducted at 2:30 P.M. by the Reverend Wilson at the Castellar Presbyterian Church, and burial followed immediately afterward; and a memorial service was planned for 8:00 P.M. in the People's Church, with a sermon written by Hoover and delivered by the Rev. Charles W. Savidge.

Sources: *The Lincoln Evening News* (NE): December 17, 1895; December 30, 1895; February 5, 1896; February 11, 1896; February 20, 1896; March 18, 1896; April 18, 1896; April 22, 1896; June 3, 1896; July 14, 1896; July 29–31, 1896; August 1, 1896; August 3, 1896; August 6–7, 1896.

Morgan, George W.
October 8, 1897

Martin Boeker, a coal hauler, boarded at Widow Gaskill's home at 1418 Howard Street in Omaha, Douglas County, Nebraska. On November 3, 1895, at 5:00 P.M. eleven-year-old Ida Gaskill was sent to call Boeker to dinner but when Ida did not return a search was made. At 1:00 A.M. the dead body of Ida Gaskill was discovered hidden in an old chest in a vacant house at 1807 Half-Howard Street, just behind 426 South Eighteenth Street. The young girl had been choked to death, either during or after a brutal sexual assault. There were finger marks on Ida's larynx and also below her left ear and under her chin. Her face was swollen and discolored, her eyes and tongue were protruding, and there was bruising upon her head and lower limbs. Boeker was immediately suspected and arrested but he quickly proved he was not involved. Ida's ten-year-old brother, Willie, then reported that he had seen George Morgan in the vacant building at 4:00 P.M. on the day Ida disappeared. Morgan had asked Willie to send Ida to him so that he could send her on an errand, and Willie told Ida of the request and did not see his sister after that. The lawmen hurried to the home of George W. Morgan, a collar-maker who lived with Ed Sanford in a house near the vacant house, and found Morgan asleep in his bed still wearing his bloody clothes. Morgan and Sanford were arrested but Sanford proved an alibi and was released. Morgan was charged with the rape and murder of Ida Gaskill; it was then determined that Morgan had previously served a term in prison for burglary and four years earlier had been acquitted of sexually assaulting a girl named Noyes, but he had spent a year in jail. Mrs. T. F. Agnew, who lived across from the vacant house, reported that she had seen

Morgan in the vacant house earlier on the day Ida disappeared and said he had tried to lure two young girls into the house, but they ran off. Morgan said that on the afternoon that Ida went missing he, Ed Sanford, Bill Thompson and Alex Murray were in his room playing cards and drinking. He said he went for a walk and met Ida Gaskill, who told him she had called for Boeker to come to dinner but he had not answered. According to Morgan he then went to Boeker's office but he was not in. Morgan said he returned to his room and remained there until 8:00 P.M. He could not explain the blood on his clothes but later claimed it was blood from a butchered steer. He pled not guilty but was held over for action by the grand jury. The entire community was incited to lynch Morgan so after his arraignment Morgan was taken by train to Lincoln by deputies Boehme and Rasmussen and lodged in the penitentiary. On November 17 deputy Drexel took the prisoner from the prison and returned him to the county jail in Omaha where Morgan was indicted, tried and convicted of first degree murder. The case of circumstantial evidence was a strong one, and each element had been linked so carefully that the jury had no difficulty in finding him guilty after brief deliberations. Morgan was sentenced to hang but appeals delayed the execution for nearly two years. On August 5, 1896, Morgan was delivered to the prison to await the fatal day, and on June 3, 1897, the state supreme court denied the final appeal. Next came delays as efforts commenced to convince Governor Silas A. Holcomb to intervene. On September 30 the Reverend Father Peters, Chief Gallagher, John A. Creighton and others went to see the governor but he declined to intercede on Morgan's behalf.

On October 1 the sheriff visited the governor and learned that there was no chance for a reprieve or commutation of sentence, so he immediately began preparations for the hanging. When told of his impending doom Morgan resigned himself to his fate, continued his constant reading of religious matter and passed the time in comparative peace, sleeping well and maintaining a good appetite. On the Saturday before his execution a Mass was held, and he received confirmation at the hands of the bishop. Morgan was returned to the Omaha jail and had seemed to weaken as October 8 neared, but on his final night he had regained some of his lost spirit and said that Father Peters had spiritually prepared him to meet his fate. He ate a hearty supper, including a dessert of several fresh fruits. Father Peters came at 7:00 P.M. and stayed an hour. At 9:00 P.M. the barber arrived to shave the prisoner, and Morgan said, "Give me a good shave, Jack, for it may be a long time before you get a chance to shave me again." As Morgan was being shaved fifty people gathered outside and only departed when police officers ordered them to disperse. Sheriff McDonald tested the gallows twice and determined that it worked efficiently. On the final morning he appeared at Morgan's cell at 11:00 A.M. and read the death warrant. The procession was then formed and marched at a solemn pace from the jail onto the scaffold, arriving fifteen minutes later. The condemned man took his place on the trapdoor, and when asked if he had anything to say, he made a long rambling speech but declined to confess. Next his wrists and ankles were pinioned while Father Peters offered a fervent prayer and commended the soul of Morgan to the care of his Maker, and then came the black cap and the noose. Three men — Sheriff McDonald, deputy John Lewis, and deputy George Stryker — each stepped to a button, and on a signal from the sheriff the buttons were pressed, the electric release was activated, and the trap was sprung at 11:34 A.M. Two of the buttons were dummies so none knew who actually activated the trapdoor release. Morgan dropped straight down but did not break his neck, and strangled to death in ten minutes. Attending physicians monitored Morgan's vital signs and pronounced him dead at 11:44 A.M. The body was immediately cut down and given to Father Peters, who announced that it would receive proper interment.

Sources: *Nebraska State Journal* (Lincoln): September 29, 1897. *The Evening News* (Lincoln, NE): June 3, 1897.

Neigenfind, Gottlieb
March 13, 1903

On April 21, 1901, Gottlieb Neigenfind married Anna Peters, the widowed daughter of Albert Breyer — a prosperous farmer living six miles east of Pierce, Nebraska. Mrs. Peters had four children when they married, and tumultuous marital relations commenced immediately because Neigenfind was addicted to drink and had an ugly temper. The couple soon separated and on September 26, 1901, Mrs. Neigenfind was granted a divorce. The couple had one child, a boy born after Gottlieb moved out, but the wife was given custody of the boy and his father had never seen him. Anna moved back to the Breyer farm to live with her father and mother while Neigenfind remained in Pierce. Neigenfind blamed his in-laws for his marital difficulties and talked wildly of revenge on them and his wife, but soon left Pierce without incident and went to Kansas. After a year, on Thursday morning, September 11, 1902, Neigenfind returned to Pierce and went directly to the Breyer farm to speak with his ex-father-in-law, and the result of that heated discussion was that Anna's ex-husband was ordered off the property. Neigenfind left but returned a few hours later and demanded that his wife return to live with him, but she refused and was counseled by her parents to have nothing more to do with her ex-husband. Neigenfind then demanded to see his son but his wife said the boy was no longer his son and he could not see him. Neigenfind returned to Pierce where he bought a five-shot revolver and ammunition. He returned to the Breyer farm at dusk and found Mr. Breyer in the yard. An argument followed and Neigenfind, without provocation or hesitation, shot Breyer. Mrs. Breyer was keeping an eye on the two while they argued, and she immediately ran into the yard yelling for Neigenfind not to shoot her husband again. He then fired several shots at Mrs. Breyer, who fled for her life as two bullets struck her but none were fatal. Neigenfind then stood over the prostate figure of Albert Breyer and shot him three more times, reloading to finish the work, and killing the old man where he lay helpless. Neigenfind's ex-wife ran into the yard when she heard the shots but, fearing for her life, she fled to the other side of the barn. Neigenfind intercepted her there and shot her dead, then raised her skirts and shot her again to mutilate her genitalia. The murderer next started to run down the road but encountered the younger sister of his ex-wife. He attacked her, tearing at her clothing, but he did not shoot her nor try to sexually assault her. Anna's sister then sounded the alarm, and posses were organized, but they could not find the fugitive. It was later learned that Neigenfind had only walked three miles from the Breyer farmhouse and spent the night with an old acquaintance, who had heard nothing of the affair. The next morning the friend rode with Neigenfind to within two miles of Winside in Wayne County where Neigenfind hitched a ride with County Commissioner Cullen, made his way to the Rehmus farm, and there secured a job. During the next week the hue and cry went on and finally Cullen became suspicious, but he did not know where Neigenfind had gone. Liveryman Dave Leary secured a few clues which led him to drive toward the Rehmus farm, but four miles south of Winside he encountered Rehmus and Neigenfind driving cattle along the road. Leary hurried around the herd to the Cullen place, and when the herd arrived the county commissioner identified the fugitive. Leary, with Perry Borum, armed themselves with shotguns and went ahead of the herd to lay an ambush. When Neigenfind came abreast of them they ordered him to put up his hands and surrender, but he drew his revolver and grabbed Rehmus as a shield. Neither Leary nor Borum could fire at Neigenfind for fear of hitting Rehmus, but the murderer fired freely at them emptying his revolver. Neither man was hit. Rehmus finally managed to tear himself free, and shotgun fire was returned, bringing down Neigenfind with a dozen nonfatal wounds. The murderer was loaded in a wagon and taken to Winside, and as soon as he could be moved he was taken to the penitentiary to avoid a lynching. Near the end of October the prisoner was taken back to Pierce and tried for murder. The case was a strong one, with eyewitnesses and incriminating physical evidence, so on November 7 defendant Neigenfind was convicted of first degree murder, and a few days later he was sentenced to hang on March 13, 1903. Neither appeal nor application for executive clemency would delay the proceedings, the first conducted in the prison under the new law.

For three weeks prior to the execution Neigenfind had been living in isolation in a small cell in the hospital ward, located in the center of the prison yard. He was under a close death watch but he had remained cheerful and showed little sign of nervousness or concern. On his final night he went to bed at 9:00 P.M. and slept so soundly that even the hoarse whistle of the prison, which sounded at 5:30 A.M., failed to awaken him. He finally awoke on his own at 6:30 and talked with death watch guards John Burke and John Hudson, who took his breakfast order of beefsteak, eggs, broiled mackerel and cocoa. He dressed in his new, black burial suit and then busied himself looking over his letters and books until, at 9:45 A.M. the death warrant was read to him. He thought this was the signal to start and asked, "Are you ready for me?" but was told the warden was not yet ready, so he sat down again. At 11:00 Ensign Swanson and Lieutenant Long of the Salvation Army arrived with a bouquet of roses. He thanked the ensign, and she replied, "God bless you, good bye," and then asked, "We will meet in heaven, won't we?" and he replied, "Yes, yes!" The prisoner was then sequestered with the Rev. George Allenbach of the German Lutheran Church and the two men prayed together. He confided that the previous night he had asked a guard if he understood what it meant to be born again and was told it meant reborn of spirit, not flesh. He pondered that for a moment and then said, "Well, I'll tell you John. You go to the phone Saturday morning and I'll call you up and tell you all about the other world." The delay continued so he ate a hearty dinner at noon. The apparatus, the same used in Douglas County and moved to the prison, had its final test and then Neigenfind was notified that they were ready for him. He exited his cell and was accompanied by deputy warden Jones on one side; on the other was night cell house keeper James McNeill with the Reverend Allenbach following. They walked one hundred yards to the cell house door and went directly to the scaffold where the prisoner ascended unaided. Waiting on the platform were Dr. Burkner and guards W. B. Baird, James Stewart, and M. F. Greene, who were in charge of the execution. As soon as the condemned man was on the platform the Reverend Allenbach offered a prayer in German and ended by commending Neigenfind's soul to God. The prisoner was then asked if he had anything to say but he only shook his head, so he was directed onto the trapdoor. The Reverend Allenbach shook hands with the prisoner, blessed him, and retired from the scaffold. Neigenfind's wrists were bound behind and straps were applied to his ankles and legs just above his knees. The black cap was pulled over his head and the drawstring tied at his neck. Next came the noose, a heavy piece of ⅞-inch Manila, and the knot was placed behind the left ear. At 12:32 P.M. two men on the platform and three below pressed electric buttons, all dummies but one, so no one knew who had sprung the trap. Below thick boards were brought and placed over the depression in the floor so that Drs. Willmeth and Houtz could approach the hanging figure and monitor his vital signs. At 1:05 P.M. the doctors pronounced Neigenfind dead, and fifteen minutes later the body was cut down. The remains of Neigenfind were placed in a coffin and prepared for shipment to Pierce for burial, the cost paid for by the German Lutheran congregation of Lincoln. However, before Neigenfind could be buried his body was put on display and viewed by thousands of curious citizens, and this later was the cause of great outrage among many Nebraskans.

Sources: *The Lincoln Evening News* (NE): March 13, 1903.

Rhea, William
July 10, 1903

William Rhea, whose real name was William Klein, was only eighteen years old in 1901 but he was already a well established member of a band of twenty outlaws who rendezvoused at the farm of Mrs. M. D. Williams near Sydney, Dodge County, Nebraska. In late December 1900 Rhea and Edward Gardner planned the robbery of Herman Zahn's saloon in Snyder. They arrived in town on the afternoon of January 2, 1901, with William Darrell, alias William Burton, and began drinking in another saloon before going to Zahn's place of business at 7:30 P.M. At 9:00 P.M. the three men had an altercation with several men outside the saloon, and someone warned Zahn that the three troublemakers were armed. Soon Rhea entered the saloon, with Gardner close behind, Darrell remaining outside. As the two passed through the door into the saloon they donned masks and pulled their pistols. Inside were a dozen men playing cards, and another dozen men had entered just in front of them. Zahn was seated at a table as the men ordered everyone to raise their hands, and everyone complied, including Zahn, who had a chair in his hands as he approached the robbers. Zahn cried out, "Don't shoot!" However Rhea, without further warning or hesitation, shot Zahn in the stomach, the bullet entering on the left side just below the navel. Zahn collapsed to the floor in excruciating pain. Darrell was watching the streets but at one point entered and threw up his hands as well. Gardner told Darrell to lower his hands and held the twenty-four patrons at bay by waving his pistol about and firing warning shots into the ceiling. Rhea went around the counter and broke open the cash box and cash drawer, finding $75, then returned to the body of Zahn, pistol-whipped and kicked the saloon keeper and took his watch and $8. Rhea and Gardner than terrorized the patrons for a brief period before taking their leave, one robber leaving by the front door and two by the rear. The town, at the sound of gunfire, had mobilized and the robbers and townspeople exchanged shots as the three robbers ran to the railroad tracks. A few men followed, to see where they went rather than to engage them, but their track was soon lost. Zahn was carried to his home. The doctor was summoned, and he probed for the bullet but could not find it; Zahn died in ninety minutes. Sheriff Kreader of Fremont and detective Charles Franklin of Lincoln were telephoned, and they arrived the next day, Franklin bringing two bloodhounds. At noon on the following day they started out with a posse of twenty men. Later that day Gardner was captured by Billy Kerkow and taken to Crowell, seven miles from Snyder. The posse had found that the three men had separated, with Darrell heading north to West Point and Rhea and Gardner heading east toward the Elkhorn River. The posse had traced Gardner and Rhea to a frame house a half mile from Crowell and, in searching, found evidence that a straw stack was inhabited. They searched and found Gardner, who was then armed only with a razor, and he had to surrender without a fight. Rhea, who was still armed with his pistol, put up resistance so the posse set the straw stack afire. Rhea was burned out and managed to escape during a running gun battle. In Crowell Gardner was mistakenly identified by Emil Zahn, Herman's brother, as the one who had shot the saloon keeper, but Emil may have been distracted by the distinctive feature of Gardner missing two fingers on his left hand. When the sheriff arrived at Crowell with Gardner they learned that Darrell had also been captured that morning in West Point, unarmed and without resistance, and when arrested Darrell had Zahn's watch in his pocket. Gardner and Darrell were lodged in jail at Fremont to prevent a lynching. On January 5 Sheriff Phillips of Cuming County, after a brisk gun battle, captured Rhea in the timber along the Elkhorn River. Rhea had been wounded once while fleeing from Snyder and three more times during two subsequent gun battles but none of his wounds were life-threatening.

At his examination Rhea was held over for action by the grand jury, and he was indicted. His trial commenced in the district court in early February, and on February 16 the case went to the jury. Rhea was convicted of first degree murder, but the jury was out for twenty-four hours because one juror fought against the death penalty. The juror was finally convinced, and Rhea was sentenced to hang. There began a series of appeals, applications and motions for injunctions which delayed the execution for two years. Governor Ezra P. Savage, when the question came to him, set precedent by granting a reprieve of one year so the matter could be dealt with by his successor in the governor's office. Governor John H. Mickey, when the matter was presented, denied Rhea's application for executive clemency. After all efforts failed Rhea was finally sentenced to hang on July 10, 1903.

Gardner was the second man to be tried and the case went to the jury on February 25. Gardner was found guilty of the murder of Zahn but not of firing the fatal shot, so on the following day he was sentenced to life in prison. The trial of Darrell commenced in early March, and Darrell was only charged with aiding and abetting Rhea and Gardner, but on March 8 he was acquitted of all criminal charges and released.

The scaffold was in the west cell house, which had not yet been equipped with iron cells. This was the second time the scaffold was put to use in the prison, with Neigenfind being the first under the new law which moved executions into the prison. The hanging apparatus had six buttons to activate the release, including five dummies, so no one would know who sprang the trap. The prisoners were required to move the scaffold from storage and assemble it with heavy carriage bolts; this agitated them greatly, and they protested. The prisoner who was put to work washing the platform was as pale as if he were the condemned man. As a result Warden Albert D. Beemer assigned as few guards as possible to the execution, and the rest remained on duty to keep the prisoners under control. Rhea, who had been confined in an isolation cell in the hospital ward, spent his final night serenely sleeping and apparently unconcerned. He arose at 7:30 A.M. and had his breakfast, eating heartily of ham and eggs. At 10:30 he was visited by Prison Chaplain Ralph K. Williams who remained with him for forty-five minutes. At 11:30 Warden Beemer and prison clerk E. B. Fairfield appeared at Rhea's cell to read the death warrant, which took eighteen minutes. The warden had been advised that Rhea's attorneys were making a last-minute appeal to the state supreme court asking for a respite, so he agreed to postpone the execution until 2:00 P.M. or earlier if all remedies were exhausted, and he advised Rhea of the reason for the delay. Mrs. Beemer then visited the prisoner, read to him from a small book, and upon leaving the hospital building, was in tears. Next his dinner was served, an elaborate menu completed by a huge piece of pie. At 1:00 P.M. Warden Beemer learned that the application to Governor John H. Mickey and the court injunctions had been denied, and he began final preparations. He sent deputy warden Delahunty and death watch guard Stewart to escort Rhea to the execution chamber. When they opened the door to his cell he came out and stated he would say nothing on the scaffold. The procession proceeded across the yard to the south door of the west cell house. He walked twenty feet to the stairs, took off his black felt hat, and ascended onto the platform with each deputy supporting one arm. On the platform he took his place on the trapdoor and gazed about, inspecting the scaffold, the rope, and then the witnesses. It took but two minutes to apply the straps to his ankles and knees, wrists and arms, and then the noose was adjusted and the black cap was pulled over his head. At the signal six buttons were depressed and the trap was sprung, and Rhea shot downward. There were convulsive movements of the lower limbs as the feet were raised slightly every ten seconds for a minute and a half. Boards were brought forward and placed across the depression in the floor so that the attending physicians could monitor Rhea's vital signs, and they stepped up after five minutes. At nine minutes the pulse was at ninety and the dozen doctors present thought his neck had not been broken, so when he was pronounced dead at thirteen minutes Rhea was allowed to hang another eight minutes. The body of Rhea was then cut down and lowered into a wicker basket by undertaker Walton G. Roberts, and upon close examination the doctors confirmed that the dead man's neck had been broken in the drop. The remains were taken to Roberts' funeral parlor and prepared for burial the following day. The cost of the interment was paid for by Rhea's well-to-do uncle who lived in Mt. Vernon, Indiana.

Sources: *The Lincoln Evening News* (NE): January 5–6, 1901; February 19, 1901; February 27, 1901; March 9, 1901; June 17–19, 1903; July 2–13, 1903. *Nebraska State Journal* (Lincoln): February 16, 1901; February 27, 1901; March 7, 1901.

Clarke, Harrison
December 13, 1907

At 10:00 on the evening of March 7, 1906, three black men, Harrison Clarke, Calvin Wain and Clarence "Pink" Gathright, started from Wain's house intent upon a crime spree. Each carried a pistol, and Wain's wife had sewn masks to hide their identities. They went directly to the saloon of Henry King at 32nd and Q Streets where the occupants, including one woman, were robbed and the cash drawer was rifled. They next went to the saloon of Julius Grimm at 13th and U Streets where they held eight occupants at bay while they cleaned out the till. The robbers arrived at the terminus of the Albright-Benson streetcar line at 12:30 A.M. just as the last car was pulling up for its return to Omaha. They waited for another car to start the return trip before attacking that last car. Ed Flury, the conductor, saw the three men running toward him but had no idea of the danger until one called out, "Throw up your hands," and he then saw that they were masked with pistols drawn. In response Flury pulled his revolver and immediately was the target of a fusillade of gunfire, with as many as two dozen shots fired in his direction. Flury was wounded before he could return fire but it seemed just a minor wound to his wrist so, after the robbers fled, he continued with his regular duties. Motorman Patterson drove the car on the return trip, unaware of Flury's wound. Finally the seriousness of Flury's wound became apparent, and Patterson rushed the wounded man to Drs. McCrann and Carson, who sent him to St. Joseph's Hospital. On March 15 after lingering for an entire week, mostly in an unconscious state, Flury died of his wound. Clarke had entrusted a portion of his share of the plunder to a woman but she became concerned when she saw how outraged the population had become over the shooting, and she informed on the three robbers. Early on March 9 Clarke and Wain were behind bars but they were steadfast in their silence. However, later that day Gathright was also captured, and as soon as he realized his precarious situation he confessed every detail of the robberies. As a result three revolvers and some of the plunder were recovered.

Gathright's confession was published in the same newspaper edition as the announcement of Flury's death, and this raised concern of a lynching. That night a large mob of angry men appeared at the jail and would have hanged the three prisoners but for the clever work of Sheriff McDonald in hiding them in the courthouse. Six days after Flury died, on March 21, Clarke also confessed the details of the crime spree and admitted he was the leader of the men, but he could not say who fired the fatal shot as he claimed all were firing at the same time. An information was immediately filed against Clarke charging him with first-degree murder. On April 9 Clarke and Wain were arraigned and pled not guilty but Gathright, who had turned state's evidence, was not brought into court. Clarke's trial commenced on April 10 with the empaneling of a jury, and the following day he was found guilty of the first-degree murder of Flury. The evidence against him was strong, and the testimony of Gathright and his own confession ensured his conviction. Calvin Wain's trial commenced on May 31, and he was also convicted of first-degree murder, but the evidence seemed to indicate that he had not fired the fatal bullet so he was only sentenced to life in prison. A week later Clarence Gathright pled guilty to second-degree murder and was sentenced to twenty years in prison, and the three men were lodged in cells at the prison, Clarke to await the fatal day. On June 26 motions for a new trial were denied, and Clarke was resentenced to hang on November 26, 1906. Appeals to the state supreme court were filed on October 11 so an order suspending sentence was issued. The case was heard on June 4, 1907, but the death sentence was affirmed on July 18, and the new date for the execution was set at August 30, 1907. On July 31 the first death warrant was issued but on August 15 the case was appealed to the supreme court for a rehearing. Five days later Governor George L. Sheldon received the first petition pleading for clemency, and the order postponing the execution was issued two days later. On September 16, 1907, Gathright, Wain and Clarke filed affidavits stating Clarke had no part in the murder of Flury, but Flury's employer countered with a petition pleading for the governor to deny clemency, and the governor refused to act while the case was being considered by the supreme court. On November 9 the rehearing was denied by the supreme court, and Clarke's date of execution was rescheduled for December 13, 1907; the second death warrant was issued on November 11. There was another hearing based upon Clarke's claim that he had not been given a fair trial, which began on December 3 and was continued on December 10, but it was resolved in the negative so finally, with all efforts concluded without judicial relief for the condemned man, the execution could proceed on schedule. Clarke had conducted the major effort for his own relief, and on the final day he had prepared an affidavit declaring himself insane. However, the supreme court had already declared in the Frank Barker case that "applications for insanity hearings which manifest only a delaying tactic" would have no effect.

During his days in prison Clarke had favored cigars and at times smoked them incessantly, and he had been allowed his guitar which he sometimes played, at other times merely strummed almost absentmindedly, and often sang along. On Thursday night Father Moran visited and tried to get the prisoner to repent but failed to get any response. On his final night Clarke started writing letters before he retired under the watchful eye of death watch guard C. C. Tanney, and the prisoner slept quietly, rising only briefly to smoke a cigar. He arose at 6:00 A.M. and finished writing his letters. The traditional breakfast for condemned men, ham and eggs, had been served the previous morning so while he worked on his letters he ordered his final breakfast and, when it arrived, he ate with great relish. Clarke then told the attendant, "It looks like 12 o'clock to me now, sure enough," indicating he expected no further delays in the proceedings. At 7:15 A.M. Clarke was taken to the prison chapel where he told deputy warden James Delahunty, "You're very kind, deputy, to let me stay in the cell house last night. I fully expected to go to the death cell." From the chapel he was taken directly to the little isolated building in the center of the prison yard where the condemned men waited for the procession to form. Here he was stripped of his jail garb and given his burial clothes — a black suit, white shirt and black necktie — and placed in the south cell. His first visitor in his new surroundings was Father Moran, who remained for twenty minutes. After the priest left, Clarke's wife arrived; they talked through the bars, and he gave her his letters to post. She shed a few tears but was generally composed. Soon after she left Benton Bell and Fred L. Smith, friends of

Clarke, arrived but he refused to see them, saying "Go away from here. I don't want to see you. You are trying to hang me." They left but returned and were again told to leave. Next came the Rev. John L. Marshall with two parishioners, but Clarke refused to see them, saying to the deputy, "I do not want to see anybody, deputy, until I pass off," and no further visitors were admitted to the prison. At 11:00 A.M. a letter was received from Clarke's mother, which he read as his noon meal was served. Judge Cornish had telephoned and asked that the execution be postponed pending a matter then before him, and asked that the warden send any witnesses who could testify to Clarke's sanity. Between 12:15 and 2:00 P.M. a party of doctors examined Clarke, and afterward Dr. J. M. Birkner pronounced the prisoner perfectly sane, so at 2:15 Warden Albert D. Beemer received a phone call from Judge Cornish saying that he would not interfere further. Preparations then proceeded beginning with the reading of the death warrant by prison clerk E. B. Fairfield at 2:20 P.M. At 2:30 the procession was formed with a guard on each arm of the prisoner and deputy warden Delahunty leading the way. They marched the short distance into the broom factory and to the east end where the black gallows had been erected. Clarke climbed onto the platform where the Reverend Marshall offered a special blessing. The prisoner was positioned on the trapdoor where his wrists and ankles and legs were strapped, but as the black cap was produced Clarke said, "I would like something, some rocks or a big bag of sand on my feet." The guards tried to calm him but he turned toward the warden and twice shrieked that he wanted something heavy on his feet so that he might drop quickly, and the warden replied, "You have got your shoes on." Clarke then turned to the crowd of witnesses and said, "Good-bye, everybody. You are hanging an innocent man who did not commit murder. Tell mother to pray for me." The noose was adjusted and the black cap pulled over his head and the electric buttons, all but one being dummies, were pressed and the trap was sprung at 2:39 P.M. Four doctors rushed forward and began monitoring vital signs, and at the end of twelve minutes they pronounced Clarke dead. The body was then cut down and placed in a casket, loaded into a hearse, and taken to the undertaking rooms of Castle, Roper & Matthews. Warden Beemer had given permission to the undertakers to display the remains only to those authorized to view them, but word was received that the parlor was about to open its doors to the public so the governor's office telephoned and pointed out that to do so would violate state law. The same day word was received from Clarke's mother, Mrs. Mary J. Clarke of Troy, Missouri, to send the remains there for burial, and this was done with the greatest expediency.

Sources: *The Lincoln Evening News* (NE): March 14, 1906; March 19, 1906; March 23, 1906; April 12–14, 1906; June 1, 1906; June 8, 1906; December 12–14, 1907.

Barker, Frank
January 17, 1908

On Sunday, January 31, 1904, thirty-year-old Daniel Barker and his wife Alice, in company with Dan's twenty-five-year-old brother Frank and his sweetheart Lizzie Renkle, attended evening church services in Innavale, Nebraska. On the way back to Daniel's farm Miss Renkle scolded Frank for his lack of ambition and said, "I will never marry you until you can provide me with as good a home as your brother gives his wife." When the couples reached the farmhouse Daniel and Alice disembarked and went into the house, leaving Frank to drive Ms. Renkle home. The Barkers, not knowing when or if Frank would return, locked the doors and retired for the night. At 1:00 A.M. Dan and Alice were awakened by loud knocking on their front door, and Dan got up to let his brother enter. As soon as Dan opened the door Frank, who stood with pistol in hand, shot Dan in the heart. Dan collapsed onto the sitting room carpet and bled to death in seconds. Frank then went to the bedroom searching for Alice and found her cringing beneath the bed. Frank, to avoid a struggle, shot her once in the back and once in the head killing her instantly, and then dragged the body from its hiding place. Neither bullet had exited and Alice lay in such a position that she did not bleed on the bedroom floor, so Frank carefully lifted her remains and took them out to the buggy. He then collected the body of his brother, put it in the buggy, grabbed the ax, and started for the Republican River one mile away. He stopped the buggy along the river bank and chopped a hole through the ice but then Frank became concerned that the weakened ice, with the weight of himself and a body, might crack and deposit him in the frigid waters.

With the bodies still in the buggy he drove back to the farm and went into the cowshed. He dug a hole four feet deep and deposited the bodies in the grave and after he covered them with dirt he shoveled a large pile of manure on top of the grave. Frank next put up the horse and cleaned the buggy before he went into the house and rolled up the blood-soaked sitting-room carpet, then took the carpet to the cowshed and hid it. Frank returned to the house and scrubbed the blood stains on the floor before he retired. The following day he rifled through the house looking for all the money and valuables his brother had cached, and on Wednesday he went into Innavale and deposited $100 with merchant Charles Hunter, perhaps to show his fiancée that he had suddenly become quite prosperous. It was well known that Frank had little or no money of his own but that Daniel had at least $200 hidden in the Barker farmhouse. Daniel and Alice Barker were very active in the community so when they had not been seen for several days friends began to wonder about their absence. The deputy sheriff at Innavale was encouraged to question Frank and was told that Dan and Alice had gone to Red Cloud where they boarded the train for Denver, but a telephone call to Red Cloud quickly disproved this story. On February 4 Frank left the farm at an early hour to conduct some business at Red Cloud, and his neighbors took that opportunity to institute a systematic search of the Barker farm. The search party first followed buggy tracks to and from the Republican River where they found the place where a buggy had stopped near a hole recently chopped through the ice. It was then suspected that the dead bodies of Dan and Alice Barker had been pushed through the ice into the river, and a call to the deputy at Red Cloud led to the arrest of Frank Barker on suspicion of murder. The search for evidence was continued the following day, and the blood-soaked carpet was discovered in the cowshed. When it was noted that a large pile of manure, for no apparent reason, had been moved from one location to another within the shed the search party became suspicious. The manure was dug away, and beneath it the party found freshly dug dirt; when this was removed the bodies of the Barkers were discovered. Now the investigation took on a new purpose, and during a search of the farmhouse the party found a belt buckle and a knife burned in the stove. They carefully documented the dark stain on the floor of the sitting room, and it was clear that it had recently been cleaned quite vigorously. All the evidence pointed to Daniel's twenty-five-year-old brother Frank as their murderer. The bodies were taken to Innavale, and a coroner's jury found that Frank Barker was responsible for the death of his brother and his brother's wife. At the spring session of the grand jury Frank Barker was indicted and immediately afterward tried for murder in the first degree. The evidence was overwhelming, and Frank even admitted the killings, but insisted "I committed the crime while under the influence of an uncontrollable murder lust." The defense tried to show insanity, arguing that Frank Barker suffered from a dual personality and that the crime was committed while under the influence of his alter ego. This defense failed, and Barker was found guilty of murder in the first degree and sentenced to hang on September 2, 1904. Appeals were filed and this stayed the execution, but the supreme court finally reviewed the case and on April 5, 1905, the justices affirmed the judgment and sentence of the lower court and set the date of execution at June 16, 1905. Just as the supreme court was about to consider the issue of Barker's sanity Governor John H. Mickey, citing the precedent set by Governor Ezra P. Savage in the William Rhea case, on the day before the execution granted a reprieve of two years so that the next governor could deal with the matter. Alice's sister, Mrs. Anna McCord, had written asking for financial assistance so that she and her children could attend the execution, arguing that "the blood of my murdered sister cries out to me," and the postponement for two years came as a heavy blow.

The insanity proceedings began in the district court on June 7, 1907, and on July 14, after twenty hours of deliberations, one juror disagreed on Barker's sanity so the matter was tried again. The second jury, on September 29, found Barker sane, and the court set the date for his execution at January 18, 1908. The defense then asked for a new trial but that motion was denied, and on January 8 and 13 matters before the state supreme court were denied. On January 15, 1908, application was made to Governor George L. Sheldon for executive clemency — a respite or a commutation of sentence — but on January 17 the governor refused to intervene.

The entire time that Barker was in prison he continued to promote the "insanity dodge" and feigned a dual personality. Some days he would mope about his cell while on other days he displayed a cheerful and exuberant personality. Sometimes his food went untouched for days, and then at other times he would eat heartily and with such relish it amazed his guards. He was the first condemned prisoner kept on the first floor of the new cell house, directly across from the guard station, and this gave him a constant audience for his antics. His attorney was tenacious in trying to get Barker a new trial, a commutation or removal to the asylum on a finding of insanity, and his efforts continued to the last minute. To accommodate Barker's attorney the warden had postponed the execution from noon to 2:30 P.M. Even though work was still under way to obtain some relief for Barker he finally gave up hope that final evening and resigned himself to his fate, but still he wrote a letter to Governor Sheldon asking him to come to the prison for an interview.

During his final afternoon Barker received a touching letter from his sister and spent the evening hours writing a response. During the night he was restless except for an hour or two of fitful slumber between two and four o'clock. At 6:30 A.M. deputy warden James Delahunty came to the cell and was given the letter Barker had written to his sister, and was asked to post it. Barker said, "It's pretty tough," but would say little else. The prisoner had no appetite and did not order breakfast so the regular fare was provided, though he ate little. The standard routine was to move the prisoner to the hospital isolation ward on the morning of the execution and then return him to the death row cell on the first floor just before the march to the gallows, but Barker was moved to the second floor hospital ward and kept there. Death watch guard C. C. Tanney had kept a close watch over his ward throughout the night, until relieved at 7:00 A.M. by James McNeill, who would watch over Barker until the last moment, and preparations for the execution moved forward at a steady pace. The governor arrived mid-morning and had a long interview with Barker but at the close the executive told the condemned man he had heard nothing to justify his interference with the execution. At 11:00 the prisoner was allowed to bathe and shave, and he then dressed in his burial clothes — a black suit provided by the warden. As the hanging had been postponed he was fed dinner and he ate sparingly. At 1:15 the prison clerk, E. G. Heilman, appeared at Barker's cell and read the death warrant, and soon afterward Dr. E. A. Carr appeared at the prison gate stating he had been sent by Barker's defense attorney to determine the prisoner's sanity. The two were sequestered for a time, and when the doctor appeared he announced that Barker was perfectly sane. During his last hour Barker was visited by his religious counselors, the Rev. John L. Marshall and Chaplain Johnson, and the prisoner insisted that he had been a Christian for two years and was assured of salvation. At 2:50 P.M. the guards appeared at the door to the hospital cell and Barker was taken out. He took his place between guards McNeill and McCorkel, each taking an arm, and they escorted their ward down stairs, across the yard, and into the broom factory where the gallows had been erected at the far end. When he reached the foot of the stairs he paused and glanced at the apparatus for a brief moment, then climbed onto the platform. At 2:55 P.M. his wrists and arms, knees and ankles were pinioned, but he was not asked if he wanted to address the witnesses as he had previously said he had nothing further to say. He kept his eyes downcast, except for a brief moment when he gazed down at the crowd beneath him, and after his hat was removed he closed his eyes and did not open them again. The noose was adjusted, the black cap was pulled over his head, and at 2:56 P.M. the trap was sprung. Barker's head was jerked to one side, and the body began hitching and swaying, accompanied by the gurgling and spitting sounds of strangulation. At 3:07 P.M. he was pronounced dead, and the body was lowered into a basket and removed to the undertaking rooms of Castle, Roper & Matthews. At first there seemed an opportunity to have the body surrendered to the medical college for dissection, and W. H. England, the juror who had disagreed on Barker's sanity, wanted to confirm a diseased brain by conducting an autopsy and offered to pay the expense. However, it was proposed that relatives would soon come forward to claim the remains so the body was ordered to be held for a week. Two days later, however, the officials at the prison agreed to pay for Barker's funeral, citing that "he had been a model prisoner and worked industriously for several years." They noted that the state owned a plot of ground in the Wyuka Cemetery and that Barker was entitled to a decent burial, even though his relatives could not bear the expense. Barker was buried on January 22.

Sources: *The Lincoln Evening News* (NE): February 5, 1904;

August 24, 1904; February 11, 1905; March 6, 1905; March 13, 1905; May 6, 1905; May 17, 1905; June 5, 1905; June 12, 1905; June 15–16, 1905; June 27, 1905; January 13, 1908; January 15–18, 1908; January 20, 1908.

Shumway, R. Mead
March 5, 1909

On August 31, 1907, thirty-one-year-old Missourian R. Mead Shumway, who refused to use his first name of Robert, went to the Gage County, Nebraska, farm of Jacob Martin, near Adams, and asked for work. He was hired as a farmhand and put to work in the fields. On September 3, according to Martin, he attended a primary election and upon his return he found blood stains on the first floor of his farmhouse. He followed the trail of blood to the upstairs bedroom and there found his wife Sarah wrapped in bedclothes and pushed under the bed. He pulled the dead body out and found that her head had been crushed and her throat had been cut from ear to ear, and it was later determined she had been raped before being murdered. Martin sounded the alarm and a search was made for Shumway, but the farmhand was gone and also missing was a horse and buggy, a pistol, and $200. The trail went south, and posses were soon following. They tracked the fugitive to Seneca, Kansas, where he was arrested on September 5. When Shumway was being brought back to Nebraska by train he managed to escape as he stepped onto a platform by darting into the crowd of curious onlookers, and the two officers in charge could not shoot for fear of wounding or killing a bystander. Soon a large crowd was in foot pursuit but the escapee eluded capture in a cornfield and then walked to Superior, Missouri, where he boarded a train for Oregon, Missouri, where he was again captured on September 26. He had taken a job on a farm but could not hide his identity as he had worked in that area before and was well known. Shumway persistently denied his guilt, saying that on the day of the murder he was working in the field and when he returned to the house he found the blood and, as the husband had, tracked it to the bedroom. He said that after he found the body he was afraid he would be suspected of murder so he fled. Shumway was held to answer to the grand jury, indicted, and tried at the fall term of the district court. The defendant was found guilty of the first degree murder of Sarah Martin and sentenced to hang on January 29, 1908. The evidence was entirely circumstantial but was presented in such a convincing manner that there was no reasonable doubt to his guilt, but juror Peters argued against the death penalty before finally acquiescing. Soon after the conviction and sentence of death the juror who had fought so hard against the death penalty, but finally weakened, became despondent and committed suicide. The appeals process began in earnest, and on January 24, 1909, the *Sunday State Journal* announced that the rehearing had been denied and that "Mead Shumway Must Hang." The grounds for the appeal were that the defense had been deprived of peremptory challenges during jury selection, and the court divided three to three with one justice abstaining as he had a previous interest in the case. The new date for Shumway's execution was set at February 19, 1909, but the prisoner applied for a one hundred-day reprieve from Governor Ashton C. Shallenberger, citing petitions from two communities in Illinois where Shumway's family lived. While the governor considered the application the state supreme court granted a stay of execution only thirty-five minutes before the trapdoor was to be sprung. The following day the governor refused to interfere, emphasizing that the condemned man had five hearings and each time had been denied relief. However, the supreme court's stay had been issued by telephone while Shumway's attorneys argued that he was feebleminded or insane, and the justices had granted sufficient time to explore the prisoner's condition. Shumway had been prepared for his death and had been baptized on February 16, and he had heard the death warrant read minutes before the phone call came. The examination into the mental state of Shumway found him sane, and the date for his execution was finally set for March 5, 1909. The Rev. I. F. Roach arrived at the penitentiary at 11:30 A.M. on March 4 and was with the prisoner continuously until his execution. Shumway gave the Reverend Roach a number of small possessions and letters to be given to relatives and friends, including an epistle to his sweetheart. Shumway, though disappointed by the results of his appeals and applications, had resigned himself to his fate and remained composed. On the fatal day after 2:00 P.M. the death warrant was again read to him in his cell and the procession formed at 2:30 P.M., with guards McCorkle and Sheff Sanderson of Clay County on each arm and the Rev. I. F. Roach leading the way. The prisoner was marched to the scaffold, and once on the trapdoor he looked down at the one hundred witnesses and proclaimed his innocence. He was prepared by having his wrists and arms, knees and ankles pinioned with straps; the noose was positioned, and the black cap was pulled over his head. His final words were, "I am an innocent victim. May God forgive everyone who has said anything against me." The trap was sprung at 3:33 P.M. but the drop did not break Shumway's neck, and he squirmed, breathing hard, until he choked to death because the knot had slipped from behind the left ear and had lacerated the flesh under his chin. Shumway had confessed to the Reverend Roach that he had committed many petty crimes throughout his life but was innocent of the murder of Mrs. Martin, and he asked that the reverend tell his story to young men in a sermon, to serve as an example to them. He then asked that the reverend ensure that his body did not go to the medical college for dissection but be buried by his family. On the day following the execution Fred Shumway of Adams arrived in Lincoln and took charge of R. Mead Shumway's remains and shipped them to Waverly, Illinois, for burial.

After the horrible murder of his wife Jacob Martin's health began to steadily deteriorate. On Thursday, September 29, 1910, after a few days of illness, Jacob died at Tecumseh, Nebraska. Later there were rumors that he had made a deathbed confession that he was the murderer of his wife, but the couple had lived together happily for many years, were prosperous and content with their lives. There was no report of any marital discord nor any reason to suspect he could have murdered his wife. Those who claimed that there was a deathbed confession failed to consider the overwhelming evidence upon which Shumway was convicted and the fact that Mrs. Martin was "ravished" by the killer. A deathbed statement, as a matter of policy, would have been recorded by a notary public but no such affidavit exists.

Sources: *The Sunday State Journal* (Lincoln, NE): January 24, 1909; February 17, 1909; February 19–20, 1909; March 6–7, 1909; October 3, 1910.

Taylor, Bert M.
October 28, 1910

At 8:00 P.M. on the evening of April 28, 1908, Bert Taylor went to the house in Minden where his wife had died a short time previously. His sisters-in-law, seventeen-year-old Pearl and thirteen-year-old Ida, were living there while attending school, and they let him enter. Taylor played cards with a man named Peterson but at 9:30 the two men left and went to a saloon where Taylor drank heavily, and he was seen by the night watchman at 11:30 P.M. making his way back to the house. When he arrived he pounded on the door, and when Ida asked who was knocking he replied, "a crazy Negro." Taylor forced entry and dragged Pearl into the sleeping room where he sexually assaulted his seventeen-year-old sister-in-law. During the assault Taylor beat Pearl unconscious so Ida had not heard a suspicious sound. Soon Taylor came out of the sleeping room and went to the kitchen, but as he returned toward the sleeping room Ida heard Pearl groaning, so Taylor beat Ida into unconsciousness, laid both bodies on the bed, poured kerosene about the room and the bed clothes, and set them afire. Taylor fled, confident the flames would hide his crime, but Ida recovered her senses and dragged her sister from the room onto the porch before summoning help, and neighbors came quickly and put out the flames. Pearl was taken to a neighbor's house, and doctors were summoned but they pronounced her case practically hopeless. Pearl lingered for eight days before dying on May 7. Immediately after the crime posses were organized, and a search was started with an ever widening circle, but Taylor was nowhere to be found. The citizens were outraged and, if Taylor had been found then, he would have been lynched. When Pearl died he was charged with her murder. His description was circulated and a reward of two thousand dollars was posted, but it was nine months before he was found as he had first fled to Kansas and later went to Enid, Oklahoma. From Enid he wrote a letter to Kearney County Sheriff Wyatt claiming his innocence and insisting there was another man responsible, one who was his double in appearance, and said he was on the trail of the murderer. Taylor drifted toward California, and in January 1909 he told fellow workers at a railway grading camp that he was wanted for murder in Nebraska, so Taylor was arrested and returned to Nebraska. Even though nearly two years had passed feeling still ran high so he was not jailed at Minden. When his trial commenced he was finally returned to Minden, and in May 1909 he appeared in Judge

Dungan's courtroom. Ida had identified him as the murderer of her sister immediately after the crime and did so again at trial. Taylor claimed insanity and also presented the story of his "double" who had committed the crime, but the jury did not believe his defenses and on June 2 convicted him of first-degree murder. He was sentenced to hang on September 17, 1909, and was taken to the penitentiary and registered as prisoner 5285. Appeals followed. On May 20, 1910, the state supreme court upheld the lower court's judgment and sentence, and the date for Taylor's execution was then set for October 28, 1910.

The condemned man had weakened so he was taken to the special cell in the hospital to spend his final weeks under close guard. He was returned to his cell on October 27, and on his final night he slept until midnight, then became restless, and in the morning his appetite failed him. The execution had been set for 2:30 P.M., and Warden T. W. Smith delayed until he received the final word that neither the supreme court nor Governor Ashton C. Shallenberger would intervene. The governor stated, "I do not care to hear the other side. I have fully made up my mind to deny the application before me. I note from a letter written by the defendant Taylor, attached to the bill of exceptions in this case, that the crime for which he was convicted was committed two and one half years ago. It seems to me that ample time has been given his counsel to inquire into his mental condition. If there is any criticism that may be urged against our system of jurisprudence it is the delay occasioned by the procedure of our courts in bringing to justice those who are guilty of such heinous crimes as is disclosed by the record in this case." The gallows had been erected in the thirty- by fifty-foot frame storehouse at the northwest corner of the prison. The scaffold, painted black, was at the south end, and the witnesses were grouped on the north end of the building. The march to the gallows was a solemn affair with the Rev. John L. Marshall and prison chaplain James T. Huff accompanying the prisoner, though there were no services on the platform. The procession had formed with one guard on each side of the prisoner, three guards in front and three guards behind to ensure that he did not falter or resist. Taylor entered the storehouse by the north door and climbed the stairs with a firm step where he took his place on the trapdoor. His wrists and ankles were pinioned by official executioner George Stryker before he was given the opportunity to speak to the witnesses, and he said, "I am innocent. I was convicted on circumstantial evidence. I am going to a better place." He then once again blamed his "double," before he said, "Good bye, everybody, good bye." After he completed this brief statement the black hood was pulled over his head and the noose was adjusted, and at 2:37 P.M. the trap was sprung. There was one release button on each side of the gallows and one man was posted at each button, so no one knew which button activated the trapdoor release. Taylor dropped seven feet, breaking his neck in the fall, and prison physician Dr. H. B. Lowry, with three doctors assisting, monitored his vital signs and pronounced him dead in twelve and one-half minutes. He was buried in the prison cemetery plot the next morning.

Sources: *Lincoln Evening News* (NE): February 12, 1910; October 11, 1910; October 24, 1910; October 26, 1910; October 28, 1910. *Nebraska State Journal* (Lincoln, NE): October 8, 1910; October 29, 1910.

Johnson, Thomas
May 19, 1911

On Wednesday evening, October 13, 1909, Frank Williams, a porter on the rail line between Denver and Salt Lake City, went for supper, and upon his return to the rail yards at 9:45 P.M. he heard a man moaning. He started to move closer to the sound but, thinking of the danger which might await him, started to walk away just as he encountered switchman James C. Mitchell. The two men, now emboldened by their number, went to investigate and found the body of Henry R. Frankland of Chicago, husband and father of two, who was lying in a pool of blood beneath the Tenth Street viaduct in the rail yards. There was a three and one-half inch cut on the left side of his neck which had severed the jugular vein; another cut on the left side started on the cheek and extended back behind the neck and was two inches deep; and a third cut was located high on the left side of Frankland's neck, in the hair, and was about three inches long though it was not deep. Frankland's pockets were turned out and his valuable, distinctive watch and chain were missing. The men called for a stretcher to take Frankland into the station where a doctor would have light to treat the wounds, but Frankland bled to death before he could be moved. During the day Frankland had been seen in the company of Williams, a bridge carpenter named James Tull, and another black man named Thomas Johnson. They had been at Woolstein's Saloon but left at closing at 8:00 P.M. Johnson and Frankland were next seen together in the rail yards after 8:30 P.M., and Frankland was found in his dying condition minutes later. It did not take long to clear Williams, Mitchell, and Tull of any part in the killing, and the search for Johnson intensified. On Friday morning detectives W.T. Deveresee and H.A. Cunningham arrested Johnson in Union Station and found he had shipped two grips to Chicago, so they sent for them to be returned. On his person they found only $15.75 which he claimed was pension money, but they also found a pocket knife with a bloody blade. Coroner Heafey scheduled an inquest for Friday morning, and testimony proved that Johnson was seen with the murdered man moments before he was killed. Two hours later he was seen in the Humboldt Hotel scouring stains from his clothes and carrying the watch and chain which, by its description, was positively identified as belonging to Frankland. When Johnson was searched the police found that his left shirt cuff and coat sleeve were stained with blood. Frankland's watch, which Johnson had pawned the day following the murder, was recovered, and Bernice Willhoit, with whom Johnson spent the night after the murder, identified it as the watch in the possession of Johnson that evening. Johnson insisted that he had bought the watch from another black man that evening and had been in the terminal when the murder was committed, but the coroner's jury did not believe him and found that Frankland had been "murdered by the hand of Thomas Johnson," and the prisoner was charged with murder. On October 17 Johnson was arraigned in Judge Crawford's court, heard the reading of the information, waived his preliminary hearing, pled not guilty, and was held over for action by the grand jury. That evening the body of Frankland was shipped to Chicago for burial. Johnson's trial commenced in early February, and although the evidence was circumstantial it was carefully linked to show that Johnson was unquestionably the murderer of Frankland. The jury spent just a half hour in deliberations before returning a guilty verdict as charged in the indictment. On February 10, 1910, Johnson was sentenced to hang on June 6, and he was immediately delivered to the prison. Johnson's attorneys then filed the usual appeals, and this delayed the proceedings for a year, but finally the state supreme court affirmed the judgment and sentence of the lower court and set the date for Johnson's execution at May 19, 1911. His attorneys next filed an application with Governor Chester H. Aldrich praying for executive clemency, but the application was denied.

Johnson resigned himself to his fate, and during his time in the penitentiary he was a "good convict." He had once secured a section of gas pipe and a knife but never made any attempt to escape, and he surrendered the contraband items to the warden voluntarily. He professed to be a member of the Baptist Church, spent his last weeks engaged in prayer, and said "I am a better man than I have been since the time I was a boy at my mother's knee." He spent most of his final evening talking with guard J. J. Andrus and said, "I have no malice towards anyone. I haven't the slightest hard feeling. I forgive everyone." He finally retired, awoke at 4:00 A.M. but quickly fell asleep again, and slept soundly until he awoke at 7:00 A.M. He dressed in his burial clothes and then ate a hearty breakfast. He spent the morning singing hymns and writing letters and ate a hearty dinner at 11:30 A.M. At 12:47 P.M. Chief Clerk T. J. Ward said to Johnson, "I have something here I've got to read to you Thomas," and Johnson replied, "I know it; that's all right." Ward then read the death warrant. Next Doctor E. J. Seward, assisted by Drs. Borgium, Olson and Spradling, were admitted to examine Johnson. At 1:15 P.M. Ollie Jackson, the black evangelist, was admitted and they talked at length through the bars of his cell in the hospital. The newsmen arrived next, and he said he did not want to turn them away and said, "My time is so near that it seems useless to make a statement." However, he told the reporters he was a Christian, assured of his salvation, and was prepared to die. He was asked if he had any friends he wanted to invite to the execution and he replied, "I would not want to see another man killed, and I don't want to have my friends do something which will be unpleasant to them." At 1:21 P.M. executioner G. B. Stryker made his final examination and test of the gallows and, after being satisfied with its efficiency, he admitted the one hundred fifty witnesses who had gathered in the prison's assembly room. At 2:08 P.M. the procession formed, and Johnson was escorted by guards James McNeill and John Kopeley on either side in case he needed support, with the warden following. They entered the warehouse where the gallows had been erected, and as he reached the stairs, he turned to Ollie Jackson, smiled, and bid him farewell. Once on the platform he looked back, smiled again, and said to Jackson, "Goodbye, meet me in heaven." Stryker then directed him onto the trapdoor and, as he muttered incoherent prayers, he was prepared by having his wrists and arms, knees and ankles pinioned and the noose adjusted. The black hood was pulled over his face at 2:13 P.M., and in a moment the four electric buttons were pushed by four men, all but one being a dummy switch, and the trap was sprung. Johnson dropped, and Dr. Seward later said he was certain that Johnson's neck was broken, but the body suffered two violent convulsions. Johnson was pronounced dead at 2:27 P.M. but hung four minutes longer before being cut down. The body was placed in the coffin provided and given to Jackson, who would see to his burial and services at graveside. Johnson had family in Georgia but did not want them to know the details of his death.

Sources: *Nebraska State Journal* (Lincoln): October 14–17, 1909; February 10, 1910; May 26, 1910. *The Evening Standard* (Ogden, UT): May 20, 1911. *The Lincoln Daily Star* (NE): May 19, 1911. *The Lincoln Evening News* (NE): May 25, 1910; May 19, 1911.

Prince, Albert
March 21, 1913

In early 1912 there was a great deal of unrest among the convicts at Nebraska's state prison, and there had been attempts to escape. One of the prisoners who had tried to escape was Albert Prince, who arrived on December 6, 1909, to serve twelve and one-half years for assault with intent to kill. His efforts were thwarted by deputy warden Edward D. Davis, and Prince swore he would have revenge. On Sunday, February 11, Davis was in the prison chapel overseeing services, and as noon approached the congregation of convicts and visitors arose to sing the last hymn. Prince was among the worshipers and had taken great pains to be seated at the end of a pew. Suddenly Prince rushed at Davis and, using a small corn knife, stabbed the deputy warden six times. Davis was rushed to the hospital and then to the living quarters over the offices where surgery was performed. The doctors said that not one of the wounds would have been fatal by itself but in combination they were mortal, as four wounds penetrated the abdomen, and Davis bled to death within hours. Prince was subdued, taken directly to the solitary confinement cells, and locked in. He was indicted for the murder of Davis, tried in May and convicted, and on May 21 he was sentenced to hang on August 30. The appeals process began immediately which stayed the execution, but after the state supreme court affirmed the judgment and sentence Prince was scheduled for execution on March 21, 1913. He then filed a second appeal but it was quickly denied. The last hope for Prince seemed to be his application for executive clemency requesting a respite or commutation, which was presented to the Board of Pardons and promptly rejected on March 10. Then the opponents of the death penalty, on general terms and those on behalf of Prince in particular, began circulating petitions among clergymen, legislators, and women's clubs and planned to present them to Governor John H. Moorehead on the morning of the execution. Their reasoning was that, since there was legislation pending which would abolish the death penalty in Nebraska, it was proper to commute Prince's death sentence to life imprisonment. The petitions were delivered but the governor declined to intervene. The issue of insanity was then raised and disposed of on March 13 when Dr. J. S. Butler pronounced the prisoner sane.

Prince, on his final evening, requested that he be allowed complete solitude until the fatal noon hour arrived, and this was granted so he retired to his solitary hospital cell. The warden restricted access only to those Prince approved, which included his brother, three ministers, and a few faithful friends, and he told them, "When the drop goes down, I am going up. I'm going to heaven." He asked for a small meal at 10:00 P.M. but then refused to eat anything after midnight Friday, a custom begun weeks previously when he began fasting on Fridays, and he slept little during the night. At 9:00 A.M. the death warrant was read by Warden Fenton, with prison chaplain the Rev. P. C. Johnson in attendance, and Prince stated he would not speak on the scaffold and requested that he not be asked for last words nor asked any questions. The reverend then administered the last sacrament, and afterwards Prince said he did not want any clergy to accompany him on his death march. At 11:00 A.M., the earliest time noted in the death warrant, Prince began dressing in his burial suit, and then the Rev. J. H. May arrived and prayed with the prisoner for an hour. At noon all the prisoners were marched into the dining room, and after eating they were locked in their cells. At 12:20 the witnesses arrived, including the coroner, five sheriffs, newspapermen, and several officials. Prison physician Dr. Williams offered Prince an opiate at 1:05 P.M. but he refused, and then he was examined by Drs. Williams, Rowe, Seward, Taylor and Spier and found to be in perfect health. At 1:30 P.M. the prisoner's wrists were bound, and then he was escorted from his cell into the "little red death house" in the southwest corner of the prison yard. He climbed the stairs and immediately took his place on the trapdoor, showing no emotion of any kind. His ankles and knees were quickly strapped, the noose was adjusted, and the black cap was pulled over his head. At 1:35 P.M. executioner George Stryker gave the signal to four men whose fingers were poised over four electric switches, three of which were dummies, and the trapdoor was sprung. Prince dropped through, breaking his neck in the fall, and four doctors observed while Dr. Rowe applied the stethoscope and monitored the prisoner's heartbeat until he pronounced Prince dead at 1:51 P.M. Prince had bequeathed his brain to Dr. M. G. Welch, and after it was collected the Reverend May took charge of the remains and arranged for the burial the following day, following a brief ceremony.

Sources: *Lincoln News* (NE): March 13, 1913; March 21, 1913. *Sheboygan Press* (WI): March 21, 1913. *Alaska Citizen* (Fairbanks): March 4, 1912. *Fort Wayne News* (IN): March 20, 1912. *Janesville Gazette* (WI): March 10, 1913; March 21, 1913. *New York Times* (NY): March 15, 1912.

Cole, Alson B.
Grammar, Allen V.
December 20, 1920

Allen Vincent Grammar of Palmer, Nebraska, married the daughter of Lulu Vogt, sometimes Voght, of nearby Elba. In January 1917 eighteen-year-old Alson B. Cole began working for nineteen-year-old Grammar doing odd jobs on his farm and driving him around the state buying cattle. When Cole's car was in Brandies Garage for repairs, and he was not able to pick it up due to a lien against it, he and Grammar arranged a ruse to get the car, and Cole immediately sold it and bought an Oakland roadster. He forged a check in Grammar's name for the difference in price of $300, with his employer's permission. Then, at the direction of Grammar, Cole went to Denver and then to his brother's ranch in Wyoming to wait for the bad check matter to settle down. Cole returned to Central City, Nebraska, on July 1 where he met Grammar and his wife and they returned to Palmer.

On July 4 everyone gathered at the Vogt home for Independence Day festivities but Grammar took Cole aside, told him to stay away from the house, and brought him food. Grammar demanded that Cole kill his mother-in-law "because she tried to poison me," but his real motive was probably to gain possession of her property and money, and he threatened Cole with a term of at least fifteen years in prison on the forged check if he refused. Grammar told Cole that after the killing he would have to leave town and then, after Cole wrote that he was settled, Grammar would send him $500 to make his escape into Canada. Grammar left his automobile with Cole and returned to the Vogt house, and just before midnight the Grammars entered Samuel Vogt's automobile and started for Palmer.

Cole, after waiting a reasonable time, went to the Vogt home, awoke Lulu Vogt who was alone, and told her there had been a terrible car wreck and she needed to go with him. Mrs. Vogt dressed quickly and they started off in Grammar's car but soon Cole stopped, saying that he thought one of their tires was going flat, and then he strangled Mrs. Vogt to death and left her body along the side of the road. Cole drove into Central City, and the following day he saw Grammar and asked for money but Grammar, after telling Cole he had better leave town immediately, said he had no money to give him at that time. Cole left and later that day the body of Mrs. Vogt was found and the investigation into her murder began.

Cole had gone to Janesville, Wisconsin, and taken a job on a farm. Then he wrote to Grammar for money but, instead of getting the money promised, he was arrested two days later and taken to Omaha. Cole first concocted an obviously false story, but eventually he confessed to the crime and implicated Grammar. Later he would claim that he only confessed because he was deprived of food and water, tortured and beaten. Grammar was lodged in jail and after a brief time he also confessed, then recanted his confession and protested his innocence to the end including a lengthy written statement released after his death.

The two men were indicted for murder, and their trial began in St. Paul, Nebraska, in mid–March, but on March 22 Cole changed his plea to guilty, and would later claim on appeal that he was promised a life sentence for cooperating. Grammar was convicted and both men were sentenced to die in the electric chair, the first such executions in Nebraska since the law changed to end hangings. Appeals followed, and over the next three years Grammar was reprieved ten times and Cole was reprieved eleven times before, on July 8, they received their final reprieve to August 6. Grammar's attorney filed a petition for a writ of habeas corpus in the U.S. Circuit Court of Appeals, so the current reprieve was extended for both men to November 11 when Grammar's petition was denied. The execution date for both men was then set for December 20, 1920.

Grammar's wife would not give up the fight, and she stood by her husband and refused to believe he was guilty, which alienated her from her entire family. During his years on death row Grammar was attended by the Rev. Thomas Maxwell, and he and Mrs. Grammar were with him when, at 2:00 A.M., he consented to have a newspaper delegation visit him in his hospital room across from the death chamber. He said, "Well Gentlemen, it has been a long fight but it looks like the end is here. I appreciate whatever has been said in the newspaper published with the best of intention, no matter if inaccuracies did occur. I have only the highest praise for my attorneys Mr. (Sterling F.) Mutz and Mr. Campbell. I know Mr. Mutz did all in his power for me. I have prepared a statement which is in the hands of my attorney and he will make it public after it is over. I have withheld this statement until after my death because I felt it best to do so." He shook hands with everyone present and they retired. Meanwhile Cole was busy talking with his attorney, John M. Priest, and with his two religious advisers, L. A. Gregory and G. E. McFadden. Both condemned men had offered to go first, so after the newsmen retired it was decided that the order would be decided by the attorneys guessing the date of a coin in the warden's pocket, the closest to go last, and J. M. Priest won. At 2:39 Warden W. T. Fenton read the death warrant to Grammar first, and a few minutes later did the same for Cole. While the six witnesses joined the newsmen in the viewing area Grammar was taken into Cole's room and they shook hands, and in a few minutes, as Grammar started for the death chamber, he stopped into Cole's room for a final goodbye. At 3:16 A.M. Grammar entered the death chamber escorted by the Reverend Thomas and Warden Fenton, and Boston executioner E. B. Currier, assisted by a team of five men, strapped the prisoner to the heavy chair. Grammar spoke his final words, "Good bye, warden," and then declined to speak to the witnesses. Sponges were moistened and one was placed under the helmet and one under the electrode attached to his leg to complete the circuit. On the signal of the warden the first jolt of 2000 volts was administered, then reduced to 300 volts, and then turned up to 2000 volts again before being turned off at 3:21 A.M. As soon as the body cooled at 3:24 A.M. Grammar was examined and pronounced dead by Dr. I. D. Munger. The body was removed, and in six minutes Cole was escorted into the death chamber by religious advisers Gregory and McFadden and the warden, and he shook hands with everyone present. He asked, "Is Dobry here?" referring to Charles Dobry, the district attorney who prosecuted the case, but Dobry had left the chamber only minutes earlier. Cole then declined to speak further and was prepared as Grammar had been. The electricity was applied in the same manner beginning at 3:35, and he was pronounced dead at 3:39 A.M. Grammar's body was turned over to his wife and father to be taken to Palmer for burial, but no one had claimed Cole's body so it was turned over to a local undertaker to be prepared for burial.

Sources: *Arizona Silver Belt* (Globe): July 21, 1917. *Beatrice Daily Sun* (NE): March 22, 1918; December 21–22, 1920. *Greeley Tribune* (CO): July 8, 1920. *Muskogee Times-Democrat* (OK): April 15, 1920.

King, James B.
June 9, 1922

Twenty-eight-year-old James B. King, a black convict at the Nebraska penitentiary serving an indeterminate sentence for burglary, was a troublesome prisoner, and during the first part of 1921 he committed a number of petty violations of the prison's rules. Guard Robert L. Taylor, who worked in the cell block where King lived, reported him on several occasions, and King spent from three days to a week in a solitary cell as punishment for each violation. As a result King threatened to stab Taylor. King's grudge against Taylor grew until on May 11, 1921, King accused Taylor of taking his comb and not returning it, and a heated argument followed. As Taylor moved on King yelled after him, "Well, you will hear from me." The prisoners went to their supper meal and at 5:00 P.M. were returning to their cells, King at the front of the line, when he stepped out and took a position at the rear. Taylor was at his post at the foot of one of the stairways leading to the cells on the second and third floors, and it was his duty to see that the prisoners marched in an orderly and quiet fashion going to the dining hall and returning to their cells. The line had passed Taylor's post when King, the last man, suddenly pulled out his jail-made eight-inch knife fashioned from a file and, without warning or hesitation, plunged it into Taylor's throat. Taylor turned and started to run up the stairs but King followed and stabbed him twice in the back and once in the left arm. Before Taylor could reach the second floor landing he collapsed and rolled down to the first floor. Convict Joe Elmore was standing ten feet away from Taylor's prostrate body, and as soon as the attack ended he called for help. King stood over Taylor for several seconds, and then said, "I got nothing to lose," as he turned and walked to his cell. Several attendants carried Taylor to the prison hospital but the guard's wounds were terrible, and he had already lost so much blood that he died within a half hour. After King was in his cell, convict H. T. Ritchie asked, "What's the trouble?" and King replied, "I just killed one of them ___ that sent me to the hole (solitary cell) the other day, and I am going to get the other one as soon as he gets to this cell." The guards soon arrived with the prison physician, and guard Marion Jones found the knife hidden in a broom. King denied knowing how the knife got there or how it had been smeared with blood. The guards took King to the warden's office, and he was questioned but the deputy warden, thinking the questioning heavy-handed, took King to the library where he confessed. He would not sign the confession, however, until May 13 when he was taken to court for his arraignment, and he pled not guilty. King was tried in the Lancaster County Court the following month, convicted of first-degree murder, and sentenced to die in the electric chair. An appeal followed which stayed the execution, but the state supreme court affirmed the judgment and sentence of the lower court, and King's date with the executioner was set for June 9, 1922. Neither the Board of Pardons nor the governor would intervene.

On his final morning, after 9:00 A.M. the prisoner was brought to a room in the hospital. Newsmen were admitted, and King told them he had slept well and ate a hearty breakfast, and when asked about fear of the electric chair he replied, "I have no fear." The death warrant was read to King, and then the newsmen retired to the viewing area where they joined the other witnesses. At 9:57 the march to the death chamber began to the death cell in the northwest corner of the second floor of the cell block, adjacent to the hospital. At 10:00 King entered and stood while a prayer was offered by the Rev. Thomas B. Maxwell, and then he declined to speak to the witnesses. He took his seat in the heavy chair and was strapped in by a team of five assistants. Executioner E. B. Currier of Boston, Massachusetts, checked everything, and when Warden W. T. Fenton gave the signal, at 10:06, he applied a jolt of 2,000 volts of current for two minutes. Currier turned the current off to let the body cool, and then the attending physician checked for a heartbeat, after which Currier applied a second jolt of 2,000 volts at 10:10; at 10:11 A.M. the prisoner was pronounced dead. After the body cooled King's remains were removed and sent to the college of medicine at the University of Nebraska, according to his last wish.

Sources: *Sioux City Journal* (IA): June 10, 1922.

Simmons, Walter R.
August 11, 1925

On May 14, 1922, Frank Pahl, a garage owner in Spencer, Nebraska, disappeared after closing his garage. The following day Pahl's body was found buried in a shallow grave under a bridge outside Spencer, his pockets turned out and $180 missing. There were no clues until two days later when a farmer reported that the night of the murder a man had slept in his barn, and when he was discovered the next morning he fled on foot, leaving behind his automobile. When the farmer found the car with the interior splattered with blood he called the authorities. The investigation revealed that the car belonged to twenty-four-year-old Walter Ray

Simmons, a well-known bootlegger about Spencer, and the search for him began. Simmons was soon captured in Norfolk, Nebraska, and lodged in the jail at Spencer, but when there was talk and then actions suggesting that a lynching was imminent he was whisked away to another jail. Simmons was returned to Spencer and tried for murder, and Pahl's wife testified that the money found in Simmons' pockets when he was arrested was her husband's money, but Simmons claimed that Pahl had been murdered and robbed by other bootleggers when he showed his money while buying liquor, though he was present. Simmons could not explain why he had Pahl's money, why his car was splattered with Pahl's blood, and why he had fled when first discovered. He was convicted of first-degree murder and sentenced to die in the electric chair, but his attorneys' appeals were among the most aggressive in Nebraska history, and by August 1925 he had received twenty-three reprieves. The state Board of Pardons denied his petition for a commutation. The last effort to save their client's life was a petition to the U.S. District Court praying for a writ of habeas corpus, but this was denied and his date with the executioner remained August 11.

Simmons, a former cowboy, baseball player and deputy sheriff, conspired with three other convicts to escape from the penitentiary, overpowered two guards, and broke out one of the cell bars before being overpowered by other guards. After the escape attempt was foiled the condemned prisoner was kept under a constant "death watch" guard. Simmons spent his last hours writing his final statement, which he delivered to his attorney: "There is but a few moments left; there is a hereafter and that if I were leaving the world with a lie on my tongue I wouldn't have the chance I have if I tell the truth, and realizing that as I do , and believing that to be true, the only thing that I can say is that I am innocent. I am dying without any prejudice against anyone — all is forgiven by me and I ask forgiveness in place of it as much as possible." He also wrote a letter to his sister and bequeathed $500 for the education of Walter Ray, Jr. At 6:30 A.M. the witnesses were in position in the viewing area, and Simmons was taken to the room in the hospital across from the death chamber, where Warden W. T. Fenton read the death warrant. His head and left leg were already shaved and his pant leg split when he appeared in the chamber after 7:00 A.M. and was strapped to the heavy chair. There is no record of final words before the mask was tied in place, and sponges were moistened and placed beneath the helmet and leg electrode, which completed the circuit. At 7:05 the current was turned on and 2,000 volts coursed through Simmons' body, reduced, and then turned up to 2,000 volts again. The current was turned off after five minutes, and when the body cooled Simmons was pronounced dead by the attending physician. The body was then removed from the chair and sent to a local funeral home to be prepared for burial. Simmons' wife and four children, his father and invalid mother lived in Baltino, Montana, but there is no record that they requisitioned the remains.

Sources: *Kokomo Tribune* (IN): August 11, 1925. *Lebanon News* (PA): August 11, 1925. *Wisconsin Rapids Tribune* (WI): August 11, 1925.

Bartlett, Henry E.
April 29, 1927

On the evening of October 18, 1924, Charles W. F. Searling picked up thirty-three-year-old Henry E. Bartlett, an ex-convict, at Kearney, Nebraska, and drove him to Minden. Bartlett had seen a pistol in a hardware store he wanted, and they planned to burglarize the store for the gun and other valuable items. After they were inside, however, the local police arrived led by Chief of Police Asa L. Ransom and, while Bartlett hid, they captured Searling and put him in the city jail. After the store was cleared of lawmen Bartlett came out of hiding, found his gun and ammunition, went to the jail (which was not staffed as the police force was so small) and shot the lock off the cell door. Bartlett and Searling then fled from Minden in Searling's car while a posse was being formed, after the gunshots were heard. Searling, later, described the events that followed:

> We drove out of town and were stopped on the D. L. D. Highway about four miles north and two miles east. A man (Ransom) approached the car and threw a flashlight and gun within a few inches of my face and said, "you are the birds we want." The officer had his head stuck in through the car door, his body resting against the car when, in about twenty seconds, the shooting started. I slid down in my seat and started the car, and drove away as fast as I could. We zigzagged towards the west and stopped at one farm to get water and a

man came out and talked to us. We drove on into Hastings and separated at Hastings, and at the place we got water. I looked to see if Bartlett had been shot in the hip, at his request. I could not see anything wrong.

Bartlett made his way to Kearney where he went to see Dr. J. J. Camerson and had the bullet wound treated, claiming it resulted from an accidental discharge. The doctor had not heard of the shooting at Minden so he did not report it for several days. The investigation continued, but it was not until April 1925 that Sheriff W. C. Condit captured Searling at Hastings, said he wanted to check the motor number on his car, and put him in a state police vehicle. They rushed him out of town, and along the way Condit obtained a confession, implicating Bartlett as his partner in the burglary and the murderer of Ransom. Searling was lodged in the Hall County jail at Grand Island and said they could find Bartlett at work in the monument factory at Kearney. When they arrived a man operating a crane was asked if he was Bartlett, but he pointed to two men further down the railroad tracks, and one officer approached them and learned that the man operating the crane was Bartlett. Sheriff Condit had been suspicious of the man, and he and a deputy remained with the crane operator and then arrested Bartlett. They took him to his home and asked to search but his wife required a search warrant, so one was obtained. In the house the officers found two pistols, onc of thc caliber that killed Ransom. Bartlett was then lodged in jail with Searling. On April 23 the two prisoners were taken to Minden where a large, angry mob had formed outside the jail, but they made it safely to their cells, and Sheriff Renus Kargo placed a heavy guard over them. Their trial began in Minden in October, and Searling, who had turned state's evidence, took the stand on October 26 and related all the details of the killing. Bartlett was convicted of first-degree murder and on October 29 was sentenced to die in the electric chair on March 5, 1926. The case was appealed, which stayed the execution for a year, but finally the date for Bartlett's execution was set for April 29, 1927. Searling's trial was to follow but, as he had agreed, he pled guilty to second-degree murder and on November 12 was sentenced to a term of twelve years in prison. Searling's sentence was commuted, and on December 24, 1930 he was released. Bartlett's attorneys did not file an appeal for executive clemency but their client tried the "insanity dodge," and on April 22, a week before the execution, they filed a petition asking for a sanity hearing, but it was denied by Judge W. A. Dilworth.

On Thursday his mother and sister came to the prison but he refused to see them, and several clergymen also tried to see the condemned man but he declined all efforts at religious consolation. Early on the morning of his execution Bartlett was removed from his cell, placed in a wheelchair, and rolled to a room in the hospital across from the death chamber. He had spent his last days feigning insanity and paralysis and continued the ruse to his last moments of life. After the witnesses were in place, after 6:00 A.M. the prisoner was carried to the electric chair, placed in the seat, and strapped in. There is no record of a statement, or even if he was asked, but his continued ruse of insanity would have prevented him from speaking to the witnesses in any case. A mask was tied over his face, and two sponges were moistened and placed beneath the helmet and the electrode attached to his left leg. The executioner then turned on the current at 2,000 volts, turned it off and then on again. After the body cooled the doctor pronounced Bartlett dead at 6:33 A.M., and then the body was removed and sent to a local funeral home to be prepared for burial as arranged by his mother.

Sources: *Ada Evening News* (OK): April 29, 1927. *Beatrice Sun* (NE): October 22, 1924; April 24, 1925; October 30, 1925; April 22, 1927; December 24, 1930. *Sioux City Journal* (IA): November 11, 1925.

Carter, Frank
June 24, 1927

Forty-six-year-old ex-convict Frank Carter, aliases Louis Clark and Pat Murphy, believed he was suffering in the advanced stages of paresis, a disease which ends in paralysis and insanity. He was a tramp of small stature who, in February 1926, was in Omaha, Nebraska, when he decided to go on a shooting spree using the silenced .22-caliber automatic pistol he had purchased in Chicago two years earlier. On February 14 he saw dairyman William L. McDevitt on an Omaha street and shot him in the head once, killing him instantly, but he did not rob him. Two days later he murdered aged doctor Austin D. Searles by shooting him once in the head in his office and later claimed that he shot Searles because he would not give him money and failed to cure his disease. He complained of Searles and his other victims, "They failed to show proper respect for my small pistol." After killing Searles he shot at silhouettes through lighted windows during hours of darkness, including the windows of several doctors. On the evening of February 19 he shot at Council Bluffs, Iowa, railroad detective Ross Johnston six times from ambush, hitting him four times, but he recovered; a man he shot in the face during daytime hours also recovered. Omaha newspapers recommended a blackout during the hours of darkness to avoid being shot by the "Phantom Sniper," and businesses came to a standstill after Carter fired indiscriminately through the window of Thompson's drug store in downtown Omaha. The description of a suspicious man seen near several of the shootings was circulated. On February 22 railroad foreman C. C. Bruce, while operating a handcar, saw Carter crawling from a haystack near the tracks outside Bartlett, Iowa, and hurried into town to notify Constable Dave Morgan. The constable formed a small posse and arrested Carter without resistance, and the prisoner was quickly returned to Omaha. Carter readily confessed to the killings and to at least fifty other crimes, but insisted he never killed anyone before McDevitt, and said, "I shot because I didn't want to get caught. I just got the inclination to shoot." When he mentioned paresis he was examined by Dr. F. S. Lovely, the disease was confirmed, and the doctor predicted that Carter would soon go insane and would die shortly afterward. Carter told his guard, "I'm going to try to get away if I can and I'll kill any number of men who get in my way when I start." On February 23 he was charged with two counts of murder and arraigned, he pled not guilty, and his three-week-long trial began in Judge Goss' Omaha courtroom on Monday, March 1. His attorneys pleaded insanity but prosecution experts testified that the disease had not resulted in legal insanity at the time of the shootings, and he was convicted of two counts of first-degree murder and sentenced to die in the electric chair. His court-appointed attorneys then filed an appeal which stayed the execution for over a year, but finally the state supreme court justices affirmed the judgment and sentence of the lower court, and Carter was scheduled to die on June 24, 1927.

On his final day Carter arose at 4:00 A.M., and after breakfast he asked for the reporters. The newsmen were admitted, and Carter, obviously pleased with the turnout, said, "I've never had so many reporters before." He then confessed to forty-three murders; most of them were obviously fictional. He professed a religious fanaticism and said he once killed a man who "doubted Heaven and Hell," and said he had committed so many murders, "I forgot the names of my victims and the details of the crimes." He said he believed in a supreme being but denied the existence of an omnipotent power. After the newsmen departed for the viewing area Carter was moved to a room in the hospital across from the death chamber, and just after 6:00 A.M. he walked to the chair at a brisk pace and took his seat. He then gave directions to the guards to tighten this strap or that, and when the blindfold was produced he asked executioner W. S. Gilbert of New Jersey to leave his eyes uncovered, as he was "anxious to watch the reporters send out the story." He then turned to the reporters and said, "Well boys, I guess you're going to get a big kick out of this. Ain't very often a condemned man gives you such a swell story as I am giving you, is it?" He then told the Rev. Thomas Maxwell, as he prayed, "Chaplain, I think you had better commend my soul to the Lord under the name of Pat Murphy instead of Carter, because He will know me better under that name." As Carter talked two sponges were moistened and placed beneath the helmet attached to his head and under the electrode which was attached to his leg. When the attendants stepped away Carter yelled out "Turn on the juice," just as Gilbert flipped the switch and 2,000 volts of electricity coursed through his body. The electricity was turned off at 6:14 A.M., and Carter was pronounced dead.

Sources: *Ada News* (OK): February 22, 1926. *Independent* (Helena, MT): February 23–24, 1926. *Indiana Gazette* (PA): February 23, 1926. *New York Times* (NY): February 20, 1926; February 25–26, 1926; March 21, 1926. *Oelwein Register* (IA): June 24, 1927. *Sheboygan Press* (WI): February 23, 1926; June 24, 1927. *Syracuse Herald* (NY): July 5, 1925.

Sharp, Frank E.
October 19, 1928

Fifty-year-old Frank and forty-eight-year-old Harriette Sharp had been married for two years, and their relationship was seriously troubled. Each had children by prior marriages, and Frank's son Cletus lived in Bethany, Nebraska. On the evening of March 16, 1926, the couple had a heated quarrel before Frank and his wife started for a dance in Havelock. At 9:30 P.M. Sharp's parked car was seen by visitor's to Minte Schmidt's farm two miles northeast of Havelock, and they saw a second car which drove off soon afterward. At 7:00 A.M. they checked on the car still parked at the roadside and found Harriette's body lying on the rear seat of the blood-splattered automobile, her head horribly crushed. They called the authorities, and deputy sheriff Ira Vorhies, who was already searching for Mrs. Sharp, searched the car and found a bloody hammer and a bloody hammerhead believed to be the murder weapons. Soon afterward the handle from the hammerhead was found a mile away. Earlier that morning Sharp had stumbled into the farm of George Carey near Bethany and said he had stopped his car between University Place and Bethany to repair a flat tire. He said a large car pulled up and one of two men got out, tied his wrists with wire and tied on a blindfold before ordering him back into his car. He said his wife fainted as one of the robbers got in and drove about fifty yards, then ordered him out of the car and drove off abducting his wife. The authorities had been called and they launched an area-wide search for Sharp's car, until notified the next morning it had been found. Sharp was arrested later that day after deputy Vorhies asked him to explain the bloodstains on his clothing, and Sharp replied, "Well, it's not from her." He was lodged in the University Place jail but the following day, when there was strong talk of lynching, the prisoner was moved and hidden. The investigating officers took Sharp's clothing for evidence and sent it to the Bureau of Bacteriology for examination. Investigating officers took his shoes and matched them to foot prints by a creek near the scene of the murder, where the murderer had washed his hands, and when told of the similarity in the prints Sharp said, "I wasn't up there; I can't account for it." Once the hammer handle was found it was examined by a fingerprint expert, and a clear palm print was lifted, which matched Sharp's right palm. The car's tires were also checked, and all were found to be in perfect condition, with neither a puncture nor a repair. Officers were looking for Cletus Sharp, believing he had gone to the scene, driven his father to a point near the Carey farm, tied his wrists and blindfolded him, and then left him there, but it was never proven he was an accessory. Sharp was tried and convicted of the first-degree murder of his wife and sentenced to die in the electric chair. The case was appealed, and the state supreme court overturned the judgment of the lower court on technical errors and granted him a new trial. He was once again convicted and sentenced to die, but this time the justices affirmed the lower court's judgment and sentence. Sharp's date with the executioner was set for October 19, 1928, and everything was handled so expeditiously, even two petitions to the state Board of Pardons, that only two and one-half years had passed when, on the day before his execution, Sharp was visited by Governor Adam McMullen in his cell. The governor, in response to a letter sent by Sharp, said he would not intervene, and later efforts by Sharp's family to have the governor reconsider granting clemency also failed.

On his final day Sharp arose at 4:00 A.M., and after breakfast was served he was moved into a room in the hospital near the death chamber. The witnesses were in place by 6:00 A.M., and soon afterward Sharp was escorted into the chamber and took his seat in the electric chair. He was strapped in and then was asked if he had any last words, and he replied, "I am innocent of this crime but I am ready to go." He was then blindfolded, and two sponges were moistened; one was placed under the helmet while the other was placed under the electrode attached to his left leg to complete the circuit. Executioner W. S. Gilbert of New Jersey, upon the signal from Warden W. T. Fenton, applied 2,000 volts of current. After a minute it was turned off, and then in a moment a second jolt was applied. When the current stopped the body was allowed to cool briefly before the doctor stepped forward and at 6:29 A.M. pronounced Sharp dead. The body was then removed from the chair and sent to a local funeral parlor to be prepared for burial, as arranged by his aged mother, seventy-five-year-old A. G. Sharp.

Sources: *Beatrice Sun* (NE): March 18, 1926. *Indiana Evening Gazette* (PA): March 18, 1926; October 19, 1928. *Oelwein Register* (IA): March 17, 1926. *Ogden Standard-Examiner* (UT): October 18, 1928. *Sioux City Journal* (IA): October 19, 1928.

Sherman, Henry
May 31, 1929

Nineteen-year-old Henry Sherman, a farmhand on the Ponchon farm at Rushville, Nebraska, was infatuated with thirteen-year-old Ellen "Nellie"

Ponchon, and he showed her much unwanted attention. On the evening of May 17, 1928, Sherman, who had been drinking, was chastised for his drinking and for his attention to the child. He was warned to cease his actions or be fired, and he planned revenge for the next morning. As the family sat around the breakfast table at a very early hour, preparing for the day's work on a farm, Sherman excused himself and returned with his shotgun. He first shot Nellie's father, Roger, in the wrist, arm and back, and he staggered into the hallway where he collapsed and bled to death. He next turned the gun on Nellie's grand-mother, Eugenia Ponchon, and shot her in the jaw, killing her instantly, and she fell next to the table. He quickly turned on Nellie's mother, Hattie, and shot her in the head, also killing her instantly, and her body was found slumped in a corner of the room. The entire room was splattered with blood as Sherman grabbed a six-month-old baby from its crib and beat its head on a chair and the table, but he did not kill the infant. He took Nellie upstairs, where four other children were asleep, and he raped her. When he threatened the other children and threatened to kill Nellie, she pleaded for her life so she could care for her brothers and sisters, and to save them she convinced Sherman to take her to a neighbor's house. Sherman told her to get dressed so they could go to Rushville. Instead they drove in the Ponchon automobile to Clifford Davis' farm where Sherman confessed his crime and prepared to surrender. The authorities were called, and Sheridan County Sheriff Robert M. Bruce arrested Sherman and lodged him in the Rushville jail. Sherman confessed the crime and motive, saying he killed the Ponchon family to get the girl and her parent's money and farm, and claimed he had "spells" and was having a spell when he killed the Ponchons. The day following the murders the prisoner was arraigned and held over for trial. Sherman's trial for killing Hattie Ponchon began on June 25, and Burwell attorney F. M. White presented a defense of insanity and mental inferiority. However, the prosecution showed that Sherman was aware of what he was doing when he committed the murders, and when the district attorney began to describe the murder scene Sherman cried out, "Man, don't go into that!" The defendant was convicted of first-degree murder and sentenced to die in the electric chair, but his attorney filed an appeal, which stayed the execution for months. The state supreme court affirmed the judgment and sentence of the lower court, and Sherman's date with the executioner was set for May 31, 1929. Efforts to gain a commutation of sentence from the Parole Board or clemency from Governor Weaver failed.

During his time on death row Sherman was attended by prison chaplain the Rev. Thomas Maxwell. On his last night Sherman retired at 11:30 P.M. but arose several times during the night before dressing at 3:30 A.M. After breakfast was finished at 4:00 A.M. the Reverend Maxwell arrived and was with the prisoner when, at 6:10 A.M., Warden W. T. Fenton and overnight guard B. A. Diltz moved the prisoner to a room in the hospital across from the death chamber. The death warrant was read by Warden Fenton in the presence of ten reporters, and Sherman told them, "I'm as good as could be expected. I haven't a thing to say here, but I'd like to say something in the other room." After the reporters joined five doctors and a number of lawmen in the witness area Sherman was escorted into the chamber. As he stood in front of the chair he said, "I want you gentlemen to know that I am sorry for the awful crime and that I have gone though lots of suffering. I have confessed my sins and believe that I have been forgiven by God. The only reason I asked for mercy was on account of my father and sisters and brother. I know I am guilty and deserve this, and I am ready to go." He then took his seat, was strapped in, and the black mask was tied over his face by New Jersey executioner W. S. Gilbert. Two sponges were then moistened with an acid solution, and one was placed beneath the helmet strapped to his head, the other beneath the electrode attached to his left leg to complete the circuit. At the signal from the warden the executioner flipped the switch and 2,300 volts of electricity coursed through Sherman's body for nineteen seconds. Sherman lurched into the straps, his body tensed, and wisps of smoke arose. After the body cooled Dr. B. A. Finkle and the four other doctors gathered around and searched for a heartbeat, but suddenly Sherman gasped and started to breathe so they stepped back while a second jolt of electricity was applied. After the body cooled again Dr. B. A. Finkle searched for vital signs and announced, "It is 6:35 o'clock and Henry Sherman is dead." After the witnesses were escorted from the chamber the body was removed and sent to a local funeral home to be prepared for burial at Rushville, where his father and two sisters lived.

Sources: *Beatrice Sun* (NE): June 27–28, 1928; May 31, 1929. *Reno Gazette* (NV): May 19, 1928. *Waterloo Courier* (IA): May 31, 1929.

MacAvoy, Joseph T.
March 23, 1945

Sixteen-year-old Anna Milroy, a high school junior, took a summer job on a farm near Sutton, Nebraska, in 1943. After work on Saturday, August 7, she met her sisters and a neighbor girl in Sutton, and they stopped at a filling station for gasoline. Anna, who said she was tired and wanted to go home, went to the restroom but never returned. After searching the filling station the girls believed that Anna had gone home but on Sunday, when they discovered Anna had not returned home, a search began. However, it was not until noon on Monday, when Ray Carlson, a farmer cutting weeds along the highway eighteen miles south of Sutton, found the nude, battered body of Anna with a chisel driven into her head, and he called the authorities. Late Monday afternoon a blood-splattered automobile was seen parked in Sutton, and this led the police to twenty-four-year-old Private Joseph Thomas MacAvoy, a soldier at Harvard Army Airfield, who was out on bond after attacking a woman in Hastings. Private MacAvoy, who had recently been demoted from sergeant, was arrested by State Sheriff Lloyd Mengel, and by 5:30 A.M. Tuesday the prisoner had signed a detailed confession. MacAvoy said he had just bought his car when he saw Anna in the gas station and took her for a ride on a lonely road, but would not say if she went willingly or was abducted. He said she refused his advances so he struck her with his fist, then took the crank from his car and bashed in her skull and dumped the body in a clump of weeds and returned to the airfield. He said he washed the crank and put it in another soldier's car, and on Sunday evening returned to the scene to confirm the body was still there. MacAvoy denied raping Anna, but the evidence showed otherwise. He was arraigned and pled "not guilty by reason of insanity," and he was held over for trial. MacAvoy was tried at the December 1943 term of the district court, and the defendant testified, "I hit her with the crank, but I didn't use the chisel. Somebody else did that." On December 11 he was convicted of first-degree murder and sentenced to die in the electric chair on December 30, but that date had to be abandoned because the warden could not get parts to repair the electric chair, as an execution was not considered a priority during time of war. MacAvoy's attorney saved the day when he filed an appeal which stayed the execution for more than a year before the state supreme court affirmed the judgment and sentence of the lower court. MacAvoy's date with the executioner was then set for March 23, 1945. Efforts for a commutation of sentence from the Board of Pardons failed, and the governor refused to intervene. During the delay the parts were obtained and the chair was repaired.

During MacAvoy's months on death row he was attended by Father Frank Sherman of Lincoln, and he became resigned to his fate in those last days. The priest was with him on his final morning when Warden Neil Olson appeared at his cell door after 5:00 A.M., and the prisoner was escorted to a room in the hospital, just fifty-five steps from the electric chair. Once the witnesses were in place the death warrant was read by the warden, and then MacAvoy was brought into the chamber. He took his seat and was strapped in, then asked if he had any last words, and he said only, "Goodbye Chaplain, goodbye Warden." The black mask was tied over his face, and two sponges were moistened with an acid solution; one was placed under the helmet placed on his head, and the other was placed under the electrode attached to his left leg to complete the circuit. Warden Olson gave the signal, and at 5:58 A.M. the first shock of 2,300 volts was applied for twenty seconds and then turned off, but there was still a heartbeat so a second shock was applied at 6:00 A.M. At 6:01 prison physician Dr. B. A. Finkle pronounced that MacAvoy was dead. After the witnesses were escorted from the chamber the body was removed and sent to a local funeral home to be prepared for burial.

Sources: *Billings Gazette* (MT): August 10, 1943. *Council Bluffs Nonpareil* (IA): March 23, 1945. *Racine Journal-Times* (WI): August 10, 1943. *Sheboygan Press* (WI): December 11, 1943.

Iron Bear, Timothy
December 1, 1948

Twenty-three-year-old Timothy Iron Bear, a South Dakota Indian, had already served two prison terms, one for car theft and one for forgery, when he was paroled from the Nebraska penitentiary on July 20, 1947. He immediately found work on the Stollar ranch thirty miles south of Rushville, Nebraska, and he moved into the bunkhouse. After only a few days Iron Bear became dissatisfied with the wages agreed upon, and on July 24 he went to the main house and argued with sixty-year-old John W. Stollar and his fifty-eight-year-old wife Grace. When the dispute escalated Iron Bear left, but quickly returned with an axe and chopped the couple to death, John first and Grace a few seconds afterward. He then threw down the murder weapon, took the keys to the Stollar automobile, and fled north. The bodies were found on Saturday night, July 26, and in searching the bunkhouse Iron Bear's parole papers were found hidden among his blankets. A description of Iron Bear and the Stollar automobile was broadcast, and on Monday, July 28 he was arrested by Indian police fifty-five miles north of Pine Ridge, South Dakota, still driving the Stollar automobile. On Tuesday morning Iron Bear was turned over to Sheridan County Sheriff F. L. Green and lodged in the Rushville jail. The Indian refused to talk of the murders with lawmen, but at his preliminary hearing that afternoon he confessed and pled guilty to two counts of murder and one count of car theft. Judge Clarence Benshoter bound him over without bail, and within days Iron Bear was sentenced to die in the electric chair for the murder of Grace Stollar. He was delivered to the state prison at Lincoln while his case was being appealed. More than a year passed before all efforts for relief or clemency were exhausted, and then Iron Bear's date with the executioner was set for December 1, 1948.

During his months on death row Iron Bear was attended by the Rev. Father Joseph Sinkula, and the priest spent all day November 30 with the condemned man. After midnight Warden James M. Jones and six guards, with the priest, moved the prisoner from his death row cell to a room in the hospital where the death warrant was read. Iron Bear was dressed in white, and the condemned man was especially proud of his new white slippers; looking down to admire them he said, "At least I won't die with my boots on." Once all the witnesses were in place Iron Bear was escorted across the hall into the death chamber, and he took his seat in the heavy chair. Warden Jones asked, "Do you have anything to say, Tim?" but he declined to speak. He was strapped in, and the black mask was tied over his face. Then two sponges were moistened with an acid solution; one was placed under the helmet placed on the crown of his head, and the other was placed under the electrode attached to his left leg to complete the circuit. Twice during the time he was being prepared Father Sinkula bent over and whispered words of encouragement. Warden Jones gave the signal at 1:00 A.M. The first shock of 2,300 volts was applied for twenty seconds, then turned off, and this was followed by a second shock at 1:02 A.M. At 1:05 A.M. the prison physician used his stethoscope to listen for a heartbeat and pronounced Iron Bear dead. After the witnesses were escorted from the chamber the body was removed and sent to a local funeral home to be prepared for shipment to Allen, South Dakota, as arranged by the Rev. Jim Blue Bird of the Native American Church.

Sources: *Beatrice Sun* (NE): July 29, 1947. *Racine Journal-Times* (WI): July 29, 1947. *Sheboygan Press* (WI): December 1, 1948.

Sundahl, Ronald D.
April 30, 1952

Sixteen-year-old Bonnie Lou Merrill, a high school senior, took a part-time summer job as a car hop in Columbus, Nebraska, twenty miles from her home in Silver Creek. On Sunday morning, August 27, 1950, Betty Lou completed her shift at 1:30 A.M. and went on a date with Clifford Burgess, to avoid being pestered by Herman Fried. Burgess arrived in a car driven by nineteen-year-old Ronald D. Sundahl, married and father of two, and they drove to a roadside restaurant for soft drinks and danced to jukebox music. By 2:30 A.M. Bonnie Lou said she was tired and wanted to go home. Burgess was dropped off several blocks from Bonnie Lou's boardinghouse. She always wanted to be dropped off a block away, and Burgess saw the brake lights when the car stopped again. However, Sundahl had convinced Bonnie Lou to accompany him to Babcock Lake, or perhaps he abducted her, as it was only his word on how the two ended there. Once at the remote location Sundahl demanded sex from Betty Lou, and when she said "No!" he strangled her until she went limp, then dragged her from the car and beat her with a hatchet until she was dead. He buried the body in a shallow grave among tall weeds and drove back to Columbus, where he stopped at the same drive-in where Betty Lou worked, before returning home. Betty Lou had been calling her mother daily so when her mother hadn't heard from her daughter all week she reported her missing on Friday, September 1, and the search for the missing girl began. Officers first searched her room and found everything in order and her savings of $80 in a purse, and then they questioned employees at the drive-in restaurant, which led them to Burgess. Once he told of the events of Sunday morning the officers brought in Fried and Sundahl for questioning, and neither man gave them any useful information but Sundahl turned over a bottle of liquid makeup. He said he had asked Bonnie Lou to dance while she was making up her face, and she still had the bottle in her hand, so he put it in his pocket and forgot about it. The next day Betty Lou's body was discovered, her head bashed in, her neck broken, and skin was found under her fingernails showing she had scratched her attacker. Her purse lay nearby with her money, lipstick, and the key to her room. On September 2 Columbus' Police Chief E. J. Nickolite had the three suspects — Burgess, Sundahl, and Fried — brought in for further questioning but the Chief quickly focused on Sundahl. The Chief had Sundahl strip to the waist and wash vigorously, and as the liquid make-up washed away, deep scratches appeared on his arms. Sundahl then confessed to the murder. He said, "Something snapped when I put my arm around her and squeezed." In December 1951 he was tried and convicted of first-degree murder, and on January 6, 1952, Judge R. D. Floury sentenced him to die in the electric chair on April 22. There was no appeal but there were four applications for a commutation of sentence. The State Board of Pardons denied the last petition on April 19, and the date of execution was set for April 30.

During his final days he read his Bible, comic books, and western novels, and also listened to the radio. The death chamber had been moved to a "garishly lighted basement room under the offices of Warden Herbert Hann of the State Penitentiary." Warden Hann read the death warrant to the prisoner in his death row cell before midnight, while the witnesses were being brought into the witness area. Once all the witnesses were in place Sundahl was escorted into the death chamber, and he took his seat in the heavy chair. Warden Hann asked, "Do you have anything to say, Ron?" and the prisoner murmured, "No." He was strapped in, the black mask was tied over his face, and then two sponges were moistened with an acid solution; one was placed under the helmet placed on the crown of his shaved head, and the other was placed under the electrode attached to his shaved left leg to complete the circuit. Warden Hann gave the signal at 12:04 A.M., a shock of 2,250 volts was applied, and at 12:07 A.M. the prison physician used his stethoscope to listen for a heartbeat and pronounced Sundahl dead. After the witnesses were escorted from the chamber the body was removed and sent to a local funeral home to be prepared for burial.

Sources: *Racine Journal-Times* (WI): January 6, 1951. *Republic* (Mitchell, SD): April 30, 1952. *Statesville Record* (NC): May 1, 1952. *Wisconsin State Journal* (Madison): September 3, 1950.

Starkweather, Charles
June 25, 1959

Eighteen-year-old Charles Starkweather met thirteen-year-old Caril Ann Fugate in 1956, and an unlikely romance blossomed, much against the wishes of her parents. After Fugate crashed Starkweather's car, and his father was liable for the cost, he was forced to leave home. He had a job as a garbage collector and began to use his route to plan bank robberies, but his efforts to form a gang failed. On November 30, 1957, Starkweather went to a Lincoln, Nebraska, filling station to purchase a stuffed dog for his girlfriend, but he was refused credit by the twenty-one-year-old attendant, Robert Colvert. Starkweather left but soon returned with a twelve-gauge shotgun, which he left in his car; after two false starts, he entered the station with the shotgun, took Colvert hostage, stole $100 from the cash register, and drove Colvert to a remote location outside Lincoln. Colvert was ordered out of the car but then he began struggling with Starkweather and the shotgun discharged, wounding Colvert, and he collapsed. Starkweather then killed his helpless victim with a single shotgun blast to his head. On January 21, 1958, Starkweather went to the Fugate home but found that Caril was not there and instead became embroiled in a heated argument with Marion and Velda Fugate about his unseemly relationship with their young daughter. Starkweather returned to his automobile and took out his shotgun, shot Marion and Velda to death, and then strangled and stabbed their two-year-old baby girl, Betty Jean, to death. When Caril returned home they buried the bodies in separate places in the backyard and remained in the house until January 27, warning everyone away with a note saying everyone had the flu. When Caril's grandmother became suspicious she called the police but when they arrived they found that the couple had recently departed, and while searching they found the bodies. Starkweather's arsenal now included the twelve-gauge shotgun, a .22-caliber rifle, a .32-caliber revolver, and a large knife. Starkweather and Fugate drove to Bennett, Nebraska, to the farmhouse of family friend seventy-year-old August Meyer, and Starkweather shot him in the head, killing him instantly. After ransacking the house for money they tried to drive away, but their car became hopelessly mired in mud and they had to abandon it. Seventeen-year-old Robert Jensen and sixteen-year-old Carol King stopped to give them a ride, and they were taken hostage. Starkweather forced them to drive to an abandoned storm shelter in Bennet, and he shot them to death and stole their automobile. They next drove to the exclusive area of Lincoln and selected the home of C. Lauer Ward, where they took Clara Ward and her maid, fifty-one-year-old Lillian Fencl, hostage. He used his knife to stab both women to death, inflicting many wounds on each body. When C. Lauer returned home Starkweather shot him to death as soon as he entered his home. The couple then loaded the valuables they had collected from the house into Lauer's 1956 Packard automobile and fled into Wyoming. They knew that the large, expensive car they were driving would draw attention so they watched for their opportunity to switch vehicles. They spotted a Buick parked along the highway fifteen miles east of Douglas, parked behind the Buick, and woke thirty-seven-year-old salesman Merle Collison before Starkweather shot him to death with his .22-caliber rifle. The car had a push pedal emergency brake, unfamiliar to Starkweather, so when he tried to drive off the car stalled. Twenty-nine-year-old Joe Sprinkle of Casper, Wyoming, stopped to help, Starkweather brandished his .22-caliber rifle, and an argument and struggle for the rifle followed. Just then deputy sheriff Bill Romer pulled up to investigate the three cars parked along the highway and Fugate ran to him yelling, "It's Starkweather! He's going to kill me!" Starkweather jumped into the Packard and a high-speed chase followed. He ran the first roadblock, but when a bullet shattered his windshield and a glass shard cut him he surrendered. Starkweather and Fugate were lodged in the Douglas, Wyoming, jail and Starkweather confessed, but claimed that Fugate had nothing to do with the murders, then changed his story several times, and Fugate insisted she was being held hostage. Starkweather said, "I always wanted to be a criminal but not this big a one. I wasn't mad at anyone, I just wanted to be somebody." The couple signed extradition papers on January 31, 1958, and were returned to Lincoln and lodged in jail to await their arraignment and trial. Their trials began in Judge Harry A. Spencer's Lancaster County district courtroom in May. Starkweather was convicted of ten counts of murder and sentenced to die in the electric chair, and Fugate was convicted of being an accessory to the murders and sentenced to serve a life term with the possibility of parole; she was released after serving seventeen years. Starkweather was delivered to the prison and lodged in a death row cell while his case was appealed. It took nearly a year to dispose of the judicial remedies. The Board of Pardons refused to grant a commutation of sentence, and Governor Ralph Brooks declined to intervene. A flurry of final appeals was filed on his last day, and the last of these was denied at 8:30 P.M. on June 24, 1959, just three and one-half hours before the scheduled execution.

Before midnight thirty-five witnesses were moved into the viewing area of the death chamber, which was now located in a "garishly lighted basement room" under the warden's offices. Once the witnesses were in place deputy warden John Greenholtz read the death warrant to the prisoner in his cell and then escorted the prisoner to the death chamber, where he took his seat in the heavy chair. Greenholtz asked Starkweather, "Is there anything you would like to say?" but the prisoner only shook his head. He was then strapped to the chair and the black mask was tied over his face. Two sponges were moistened with an acid solution, and one was placed under the helmet placed on the crown of his shaved head, the other placed under the electrode attached to his shaved left leg to complete the circuit. Greenholtz gave the signal exactly at midnight, and five jolts of 2,200 volts of electricity were applied. At 12:05 A.M. prison physician Dr. B. A. Finkle used his stethoscope to listen for a heartbeat and pronounced Starkweather dead. After the witnesses were escorted from the chamber the body was removed and sent to a local funeral home to be prepared for burial in Lincoln's Wyoka Cemetery.

Sources: *Montana Standard* (Butte): January 31, 1958; June 25, 1959.

Otey, Harold L.
September 2, 1994

In June 1977 twenty-six-year-old Harold Lamont "Walkin' Willie" Otey worked as a horse walker at the Ak-Sar-Ben racetrack outside Omaha, Nebraska. Twenty-six-year-old photography student Jane McManus rented a house with her sister across the street from the racetrack, and she caught the attention of Otey. On the evening of June 11 Otey broke into McManus' house and found Jane in an upstairs bedroom, raped her, then strangled her with her belt and stabbed her fifteen times before he crushed her skull with a hammer. He fled leaving his bloodstained hunting knife in the kitchen. McManus' brother stopped by to check on his sister and discovered the body, and frantically called for the police. The investigation continued for six months but there seemed no clues until Otey attacked a girl with a knife in Douglas County, with rape the most likely motive, and his proximity to the McManus killing in time and place was determined. Otey was nowhere to be found, as he often moved from racetrack to racetrack around the country, but in January 1978 Otey was found working at the Florida Downs racetrack near Tampa. Otey was arrested, and over a two-day period he spoke with officers for eight hours and gave a detailed confession which was tape recorded, and he confessed to committing over ten rapes, but no murders, over the past six years. Otey was extradited to Douglas County, arraigned, and after he recanted his confession he pled not guilty and was held over for trial. The trial began in April, and on April 13, 1978 the jurors found Otey guilty of "first degree murder in the commission of a sexual assault." On June 20 Otey was sentenced to die in the electric chair but over the next sixteen years he delayed his execution time and time again, and in the process he lost three appeals in the state court and three federal appeals. In 1991 he filed a state court action appealing his clemency hearing, and he filed a federal civil rights action on the same basis. His only success was his state challenge to the clemency hearing when Judge Bernard McGinn granted a brief stay of execution. After his execution date was set for September 2, 1994, a new flurry of appeals were filed in the state and federal courts, but his final hope for a stay of execution ended when the U.S. Supreme Court justices declined to hear his case, for the eighth time. The Board of Pardons denied his application for a commutation of sentence, and Governor Ben Nelson refused to interfere.

This would be the first execution in Nebraska in thirty-five years, and the electric chair had been moved back to the death chamber in the second-floor hospital wing of the cell block. As the day approached the witnesses were sent invitations, and the executioner was hired and paid $300 for his services. The chair was tested using a fifty-five gallon drum of water, and it worked perfectly. For days the ten men chosen for the execution team practiced the procedures and checked and rechecked every bit of the equipment, and one member of the team similar in size to Otey stood in during practice. On Thursday Otey was moved into hospital room No. 7 where a constant death watch was maintained, and later that day more than twenty newsmen were given a tour of the hospital and death chamber. Otey refused his final meal. At 11:00 P.M. all the visitors were escorted from the prison, and then Otey's head and left leg were shaved. Director of Correctional Services Harold Clarke and Warden Frank Hopkins then brought in the official witnesses, and they heard Otey's last statement: "It'll be good to have an end to it." Warden Hopkins read the death warrant, and then the official witnesses, including four invited by Otey, left to join the newsmen in the witness area. At 11:30 P.M. a call was made to the Board of Pardons, and the line was kept open until midnight. Just before midnight the prisoner, shackled but not sedated, was escorted to the electric chair by Captain of the Guards Dallen Johnsen and his team. The curtains between the chamber and the witness room had been closed while Otey was strapped to the chair, under the observation of two independent government officials. The curtains were then drawn back so that the witnesses could identify the man about to be executed, and then the curtains were drawn closed again. The face mask was tied over Otey's face and two sponges were moistened with an acid solution; one was placed beneath the helmet electrode attached to the crown of his head, and the other was placed beneath the electrode attached to his left leg to complete the circuit. At that moment there was a brief delay as the final call was made to the Board of Pardons but there was no respite forthcoming, so the execution team retired from the chamber and then the curtains were drawn open. At 12:23 A.M. the warden gave the signal to the executioner, in a small room behind a one-way mirrored window, who applied four jolts of 2,450 volts of electricity. Otey's body surged against the straps with each jolt. The electricity was turned off at 12:25, and after the body cooled a deputy sheriff, acting as coroner, checked for vital signs and pronounced Otey dead at 12:33 A.M. The warden then relayed that information to the newsmen and to the members of the Board of Pardons. A mortician was then admitted, and he removed the body from the chair and delivered it to the morgue of the Lincoln General Hospital for an autopsy.

Sources: *Cedar Rapids Gazette* (IA): September 2, 1994. *Columbus Telegram* (NE): June 14, 1977; August 3, 1977. *Omaha World* (NE): March 23, 1994; August 28, 1994; September 2, 1994.

Joubert, John J.
July 17, 1996

At about 8:00 P.M. on August 22, 1982, eleven-year-old Richard Stetson left home to jog in the city of Portland, Maine, but when he had not returned by dark his parents called the police. The next day a motorist found Stetson's partially nude body on the side of the I-295 highway. Stetson had been molested, bitten, strangled and stabbed. A suspect was lodged in jail, and it took eighteen months before he was proven innocent and released, but this misdirection delayed the investigation and the case went cold. Meanwhile nineteen-year-old John Joseph Joubert enlisted in the U.S. Air Force to get out of Maine, and he was stationed at Offutt Air Force Base in Omaha, Nebraska. Several times during the third week of September 1983 the brother of thirteen-year-old Danny Joe Eberle noticed a white man following him in a tan automobile while he pedaled his route delivering the *Omaha World- Herald* newspaper in Bellevue, a suburb of Omaha. Danny Joe also had a newspaper route and on the evening of Sunday, September 18, 1983, he disappeared while delivering newspapers. When he did not complete his route, and customers called, a search was made and his bicycle was found at his fourth of seventy houses. There appeared to be no sign of a struggle but a search began. Eberle had been abducted by John Joseph Joubert, who drew his knife and covered the boy's mouth to keep him from screaming, took him to his automobile and drove him to a remote location along a gravel road. Three days later Eberle's body was discovered beside a roadway outside Papillion, Nebraska, four miles from where he had been abducted, and he had been stripped to his underwear, his ankles and wrist bound with an unusual rope, his mouth taped; his abductor had stabbed him nine times. The Federal Bureau of Investigations (FBI) was called in to investigate the kidnapping, a federal crime. The investigation included rounding up of known pedophiles, and this included a young man who had molested two young boys a week after the Eberle murder. However, the prisoner did not fit the profile established by the FBI. He was released due to a lack of evidence, and the case went cold. On December 2, 1983, twelve-year-old Christopher Walden was abducted while walking to his elementary school in Papillion, Nebraska, about three miles from where Eberle's body had been found, and witnesses said they saw a suspicious white man in a tan car in the vicinity. Walden's body was found two days later five miles from Papillon, but Walden had not been bound, the body was better concealed, and he was killed immediately after being abducted. At 8:15 A.M. on January 11, 1984, Barbara Weaver, a Papillion pre-school teacher, called the police to say that she had seen a young man driving in the area, and when the driver saw her writing down his license plate he stopped and threatened her before fleeing. The car was not tan, but it was traced and found to be rented by John Joubert, an enlisted radar technician from Offutt Air Force Base. The officers learned that Joubert's automobile, then in a shop for repairs, was a tan Chevrolet Nova sedan. A search warrant was issued for Joubert's barrack's room, and rope consistent with that used to bind Danny Joe Eberle was found. The FBI determined that this unusual rope had been made for the United States military in South Korea. Joubert, an assistant scoutmaster, was arrested that afternoon and questioned about the rope, and he admitted getting it from the scoutmaster. Robert K. Ressler, the FBI's head profiler at the time, while presenting the case of the two Nebraska boys to a training class at the FBI academy, was approached by a police officer from Portland, Maine, when he noted similarities to the Stetson case. They determined that Joubert lived in Portland, Maine, when the Stetson boy was murdered, and comparisons of bite marks proved that Joubert was the murderer. When confronted with the mounting evidence Joubert confessed to killing the two Nebraska boys, and on January 12, 1984, he was charged with their murders. At his arraignment Joubert pled not guilty, but on July 3 he changed his plea to guilty. He had been evaluated by psychiatrists several times and found to have been legally sane at the time of the killings, though medically he was found to be very seriously disturbed. A panel of three judges determined the degree of his crimes to be first-degree murder, and they sentenced him to die in the electric chair on both counts. His attorney filed every motion, appeal, petition and application he could to save his client's life, or at least delay his execution, and nearly succeeded when, in 1995, he filed a writ of habeas corpus in the United States federal courts arguing that the aggravating factor of "exceptional depravity" was unconstitutionally vague, and the court agreed. The state appealed to the United States District Court for the District of Nebraska which overturned the appeal, saying that he had shown sadistic behavior by torturing Eberle and Walden. After a dozen years on death row Joubert's date with the executioner was set for July 17, 1996. At his hearing before the Board of Pardons Joubert said he had psychosexual fantasies for many years and asked the board to spare his life so he could be studied, but they denied his application, and then his appeal to the governor was also denied.

A month before his execution Joubert told a reporter for the *Omaha World-Herald*, "It was the power and the domination and seeing the fear. That was more exciting then actually causing the harm." As the day approached the witnesses were sent invitations, the executioner was hired, and the chair was tested. For several days the ten men chosen for the execution team practiced the procedures, and checked and rechecked every bit of the equipment, and one member of the team similar in size to Joubert stood in during the practice sessions. On Thursday Joubert was moved into hospital room No. 7 where a constant death watch was maintained, and later that day more than twenty newsmen were given a tour of the hospital and death chamber. At 11:00 P.M. his visitors were escorted from the prison, and then Joubert's head and left leg were shaved. The director of correctional services and the warden then brought in the official witnesses, and they heard Joubert's last statement: "I do not know if my death will change anything or if it will bring anyone any peace." The warden then read the death warrant, and the official witnesses, including Joubert's girlfriend, left to join the newsmen in the witness area. At 11:30 P.M. a call was made to the Board of Pardons, and the line was kept open until midnight. Just before midnight the prisoner, shackled but not sedated, was escorted to the electric chair by the captain of the execution team and his team members. The curtains between the chamber and the witness room had been closed while Joubert was being strapped to the chair under the supervision of two independent government officials. The curtains were then drawn back so that the witnesses could identify the man about to be executed, and then the curtains were drawn closed again. The face mask was tied over Joubert's face, and two sponges were moistened with an acid solution; one was placed beneath the helmet electrode attached to the crown of his head, and the other was placed beneath the electrode attached to his left leg to complete the circuit. At that moment there was a brief delay as the final call was made to the Board of Pardons but there was no respite forthcoming, so the execution team retired from the chamber as the curtains were drawn open. Joubert turned to look at his girlfriend and mouthed the words "I love you," and kissed, and she returned the gesture. At 12:13 A.M. the warden gave the signal to the executioner, in a small room behind a one-way mirrored window, who applied four jolts of 2,450 volts of electricity and Joubert's body surged against the straps with each jolt. The electricity was turned off at 12:15, and after the body cooled a deputy sheriff, acting as coroner, checked for vital signs and pronounced Joubert dead at 12:22 A.M. The warden then relayed that information to the newsmen and to the members of the Board of Pardons. A mortician was then admitted, and he removed the body from the chair and delivered it to the morgue of the Lincoln General Hospital for an autopsy, where it was found that during his execution Joubert incurred a four-inch brain blister on the top of his head and blistering on both sides of his head above his ears.

Sources: *Journal-Tribune* (Marysville, OH): July 17, 1996. Ressler, Robert K. and Tom Shachtman. *Whoever Fights Monsters: My Twenty Years Hunting Serial Killers for the FBI.* New York: St. Martin's Press, NY, 1992. *Sitka Sentinel* (AK): July 17, 1996. *Cedar Rapids Gazette* (IA): September 23, 1983; December 14, 1983.

Williams, Robert E.
December 2, 1997

Forty-year-old Robert E. Williams, a black railroad laborer, had been having marital difficulties when he kidnapped, beat and threatened his wife with a knife. He was arrested, lodged in the Lincoln, Nebraska, jail, arraigned and held over for trial with bail being set at $2,000, but he paid 10 percent to a bondsman, and on August 9, 1977, he was released. Early on the morning of August 11 Williams went to the northeast Lincoln duplex apartment of twenty-five-year-old Patricia McGarry, a white woman with whom he was acquainted, and they were soon involved in a loud, heated argument. McGarry's four-year-old son ran to his upstairs bedroom and hid as twenty-five-year-old Catherine M. Brooks, the white woman who lived in the other half of the duplex, heard the commotion through the walls and, leaving her five-year-old daughter in their apartment, went to McGarry's aid. As soon as Brooks arrived Williams shot McGarry in the face, killing her, and then he beat and raped Brooks before shooting her to death.

Williams may have thought it better to hide out for a while so he broke into a nearby house, captured the twenty-five-year-old white woman who lived there, and held her hostage from 9:45 A.M. until 4:00 P.M. During the six-hour ordeal Williams forced the woman to engage in sexual acts six times. After he fled she called the police, but in the meantime Brooks' parents had become concerned about their missing daughter, and the police found their five-year-old granddaughter alone, then obtained a key to the McGarry residence and at 5:00 P.M. discovered two dead bodies.

Williams had been on the prowl for an automobile, and he carjacked a Minnesota man driving a 1967 red, two-door Chevrolet Impala and forced him to drive from Fridley to St. Paul, Minnesota. In Cheyenne County the Impala, then being driven by Williams while his captive was bound in the front passenger seat, was pursued by a deputy sheriff but Williams lost the officer during a high-speed chase. In St. Paul Williams pulled his captive from the car and then searched for another automobile, and he found twenty-year-old Catherine Billings, a railroad worker, returning to her blue 1969 Dodge Polara. Williams shot her twice, inflicting serious but not fatal wounds, then raped her before driving to a remote field where he pushed her out of the car. Williams drove to Sioux Falls, Iowa, and on August 12 began looking for another automobile.

He waited near the home of Virginia Rowe. When Rowe returned from her beauty parlor appointment he captured her at gunpoint, took her to the upstairs bedroom, raped and then shot her to death, and her husband found her body later that day. Williams stole Mrs. Rowe's automobile and drove back to St. Paul, where he abandoned that car. The search for Williams was intense, covering at least the three-state area in which his crimes were being committed, and on August 19 he was captured in Lincoln, Nebraska. Williams was arraigned on two counts of first-degree murder in Nebraska and one count in Iowa, as well as numerous counts of sexual assault and auto theft, and he underwent two psychiatric examinations in preparation for his preliminary hearing set for October 14 on one sexual assault charge. In 1978 Williams was tried for two murders in Nebraska, found guilty of two counts of first-degree murder, and sentenced to die in the electric chair. He was then taken to Sioux City, Iowa, and tried for the murder of Virginia Rowe, convicted of first degree murder, and sentenced to serve a term of life in prison. Williams was returned to Nebraska and lodged in a death row cell while his case was appealed. The matter dragged on for nineteen years, and during that time one of Nebraska's death sentences was overturned by the state supreme court justices, but the other death sentence was affirmed. After every avenue of judicial relief was exhausted Williams faced the Board of Pardons, but they refused to grant clemency, and Governor Ben Nelson declined to intervene.

As the day for the execution approached invitations were sent to the five media and ten official witnesses, the executioner was hired, and the chair was tested, and it worked perfectly. For days the men chosen for the execution team practiced the procedures with one member from the team, similar in size to Williams, standing in during practice, and they checked and rechecked every piece of equipment. Early Tuesday morning Williams was moved into hospital room No. 7, where a constant death watch was maintained, and at 8:00 A.M. all the visitors were escorted from the prison. Williams' head and left leg were then shaved before the director of correctional services and the warden brought the official witnesses into the room, and they heard Williams' last statement, "I'm on my way. I just appreciate living long enough to be blessed by so many people that God has led into my life, and my last statement would be that I hope that this incident will inspire other people to find another way." The warden read the death warrant and then the official witnesses left to join the news men in the witness area. At 9:30 A.M. a call was made to the Board of Pardons, and the line was kept open until 10:00 A.M. when the prisoner, shackled but not sedated, was escorted to the electric chair by the execution team. The curtains between the chamber and the witness room had been closed while Williams was strapped to the chair, and then the curtains were drawn back so that the witnesses could identify the man about to be executed. Williams took this opportunity to tell Virginia Rowe's husband, "I am sorry, Mr. Rowe. I love you brother," and waved one hand. Rowe waved back and then the curtains were drawn closed again. The face mask was tied over Williams' face, and two sponges were moistened with a mild acid solution, one placed beneath the helmet electrode attached to the crown of his head while the other was placed beneath the electrode attached to his left leg to complete the circuit. At that moment there was a brief delay as the final call was made to the Board of Pardons but there was no respite forthcoming, so the execution team retired from the chamber and the curtains were drawn open. At 10:16 A.M. the warden gave the signal to the executioner, secreted in a small room behind a one-way mirrored window, who applied four jolts of 2,400 volts of electricity, and Williams' body surged against the straps with each jolt. On the first and third jolts smoke appeared on the right side of Williams' head and his left knee. The electricity was turned off at 10:17, and after the body cooled a deputy sheriff, acting as coroner, checked for vital signs and pronounced Williams dead at 10:23 A.M. The warden then relayed that information to the newsmen and to the members of the Board of Pardons. A mortician was admitted, and he removed the body from the chair and delivered it to the morgue of the Lincoln General Hospital for an autopsy.

SOURCES: *Columbus Telegram* (NE): August 15, 1977, September 7, 1977. *Muscatine Journal* (IA): August 12, 1977. *Newport News* (RI): August 15, 1977. *Salina Journal* (KS): September 3, 1977.

KANSAS

The land that would become Kansas was explored by Francisco Vasquez de Coronado in 1541, and he found the land inhabited by the Osage, Pawnee and Kansa Indian tribes. France later claimed the land, ceded it to Spain in 1762, regained possession in 1800, and in 1803 sold the region to the United States as part of the Louisiana Purchase. On May 30, 1854, the Kansas-Nebraska Act established the Kansas Territory. Kansas was west of the Mississippi River in the central part of the country, so situated that it played a pivotal role in settling the West, as it served as a staging area for wagon trains traveling west. The Kansas Territory became the 34th state on January 29, 1861.

Coon, John, Jr.
January 18, 1853

On Saturday, November 11, 1852, fifteen-year-old John Coon, Jr., was locked in the Wyandotte jail and charged with murder. On the previous evening Coon and Martin Big-arms had a drunken brawl with Curtis Punch, and the two men beat Punch mercilessly, but it was Coon who struck the fatal blow with a fireplace poker. After completing their investigation the Indian sheriffs released Martin Big-arms but held Coon, and six days later on Friday, November 17 the court convened to empanel a jury. Coon's trial commenced two days later with testimony and arguments concluded in one day, and at dusk, following brief deliberations, the jury returned a verdict of "guilty of first degree murder." The prosecuting attorney then argued that the evidence, at most, could only support a verdict of manslaughter but Coon was sentenced to die by firing squad on January 18, 1853. The application for clemency sent to President Millard Fillmore was denied, and nothing further would delay the proceedings.

On January 15, 1853, the council met to arrange for the execution of Coon, and they settled the matter at 11:00 P.M. At 1:00 P.M. on January 18 the condemned man was brought from the jail and boarded a wagon, where he took a seat upon his coffin. The wagon was escorted by a party of six armed Wyandotte Indians and a small number of witnesses. The six executioners — James Barnet, Thomas Pipe, Isaac Zane, H. C. Long, Louis Lumpey, and Joseph White — marched along in a solemn procession led by Matthew R. Walker and Philip Brown. They proceeded for two hours until they reached the place chosen for the execution, and then the condemned Indian was taken out of the wagon and stood up with a clear field of fire behind. The six executioners took up their positions in a line facing the place where Coon stood. The prisoner's wrists and ankles were secured, a handkerchief was tied over his eyes, and a target was pinned to his chest over his heart. At exactly 3:30 P.M. Walker gave the signal, six rifles fired simultaneously, and the condemned man dropped to the ground — dead. His body was lifted into the coffin; it was nailed shut, and Coon was buried on the spot.

Sources: *The Republican Compiler* (Gettysburg, PA): February 28, 1853. *The Journal of William Walker.*

Raymond, Joseph
November 24, 1861

On November 22, 1861, twenty-three-year-old private Joseph Raymond, a Mexican whose real name may have been Jose Ramon, of Company C, 7th Kansas Cavalry, was in Leavenworth, Kansas, with friends when they broke into a store and stole merchandise and money. The following day, when quite drunk, Raymond and two other soldiers went to "the Garden City House," demanded entrance, and when refused fired their pistols into the house. Raymond, who was missing a right finger, then bloodied both hands breaking out windows, and once they were inside they took all the liquor they could find. They threatened the owner, Mrs. Geiger's, daughters at gunpoint and tried to get them upstairs to the bedrooms, but Mrs. Geiger plied them with wine and "saved her daughters' virtue" while her barkeeper went for help. When the soldiers left Raymond stole silver coin and a silver watch, then went to another house and abused the female occupants in a similar manner. The three men were arrested, and Colonel Charles R. Jennison called a court of inquiry. Raymond was positively identified and charged with stealing, and through the Colonel's diligence he was able to determine the other two soldiers were not guilty of that capital offense during time of war. Raymond was tried at a drumhead court martial, found guilty, and sentenced to be shot on Sunday, November 24, 1861. During the early morning hours of his final day Raymond was attended by regimental chaplain the Reverend Ayres, who accompanied him to a quadrangle formed by the soldiers. The companies had formed on three sides while a firing squad of twelve men was within, and at 9:00 A.M. Raymond took his place, making the fourth side. He was allowed to kneel while the Reverend Ayres delivered an "impressive prayer." His wrists were bound but when the blindfold was produced he declined, and this was granted. Colonel Jennison then read the order of execution and said that he regretted the need for the execution, "but if such a crime went unpunished no man's life was safe, the honor of no woman secure, (and) all property was in danger." The prisoner then confessed and stood unflinching as the order to fire was given, and each of a dozen bullets struck his body killing him instantly. The Army physician examined the body and pronounced Raymond dead before it was placed in a coffin, carried a short distance from the parade ground, and that afternoon he was buried in the grave dug the previous day.

Sources: *Adjutant General's Report—1885*: List of U.S. Soldiers Executed by United States Military Authorities during the Late War. Alotta, Robert I. *Civil War Justice: Union Army Executions Under Lincoln.* Shippensburg, PA: White Mane Publishing Co. Inc., 1989. *Conservative* (Leavenworth, KS): November 25, 1861. Johnson, Edward C., Gail R. Johnson, and Melissa Johnson Williams. *All Were Not Heroes: A Study of U.S. Soldiers Executed by U.S. Military Authorities During the Late War.* Chicago, IL: E. C. Johnson, 1997.

Driscoll, Alexander
March 18, 1862

Twenty-seven-year-old private Alexander Driscoll had been a member of Company H of the 7th

Kansas Regiment for six months when he was confined in the guardhouse and charged with robbery and stabbing a member of Company H. He managed to escape and fled south but was captured, returned to the guardhouse, and charged with desertion. He was tried before a drumhead court martial on March 8, found guilty, and sentenced to be shot at sunset on Tuesday, March 18, 1862. In the evening Driscoll was taken to a field near Humboldt, Kansas, marched under guard to an open area where soldiers had formed on two sides of a quadrangle, the firing squad of five men were on the third side of the formation and Driscoll was placed at the other end near his coffin. The General Order was read to him, and he was allowed to kneel and pray; when he arose a blindfold was tied over his eyes. The officer of the day stepped back, gave the signal, five rifles erupted as one, and five bullets struck Driscoll in the chest killing him instantly. The Army physician made his examination and pronounced Driscoll dead; the body was lifted into a coffin and buried in the grave prepared a short distance from the place he died.

Sources: *Adjutant General's Report—1885*: List of U.S. Soldiers Executed by United States Military Authorities during the Late War. Alotta, Robert I. *Civil War Justice: Union Army Executions Under Lincoln*. Shippensburg, PA: White Mane Publishing Co. Inc., 1989. Johnson, Edward C., Gail R. Johnson, and Melissa Johnson Williams. *All Were Not Heroes: A Study of U.S. Soldiers Executed by U.S. Military Authorities During the Late War*. Chicago, IL: E. C. Johnson, 1997. *The Daily Conservative* (Leavenworth, KS): March 27, 1862.

Bell, John
July 11, 1862

In mid–June 1862 two soldiers, one of the 2nd Ohio Cavalry and the other of the Tenth Kansas Cavalry, went to the home of Juba Davis on Mill Creek and raped his young daughter while his wife was restrained and forced to watch as the men took turns. Davis was warned by neighbors that there were cries for help coming from his house, and with a large party of men, Davis hurried three miles to his home and captured the soldiers, took them to town, and turned them over to the military authorities. The two men were taken to Fort Scott where General Doubleday decided to send them to Fort Leavenworth for court martial. However, the following day deputy sheriff Peter Puck appeared with a civil writ, the soldiers were surrendered to him, and he took them to Marmaton for trial. During the night the jail was surrounded, the prisoners were taken out and hanged. It was then decided that the Army should handle its own criminal matters to conclusion.

Twenty-four-year-old John Bell was a private in Company I, 2nd Kansas Cavalry, which was headquartered near Iola, Kansas, in July 1862. On the evening of July 4 Bell and several other soldiers started toward Humboldt, Kansas, where there was to be a dance. When they reached the home of Mrs. Elizabeth Haywood they stopped and asked for directions, but she said there was no such event, so they turned about and started back to their camp. After riding a mile the soldiers missed Private Bell and another soldier, and he reappeared in Iola after midnight. Bell and the other soldier, almost too drunk to ride, had returned to the Haywood home and demanded water, which was provided. They rode off but soon returned and demanded food, and this was also provided but only the other soldier ate. Bell insisted that the other soldier needed to sleep so they took him upstairs and returned to the first floor. Bell attacked Mrs. Haywood, threw her to the floor, threatened to shoot her, and raped her. Just then an officer and three soldiers arrived but Bell convinced them to continue on to camp, but meanwhile Mrs. Haywood went into the bedroom of her son and sent him for help from a neighbor. Bell returned and raped Mrs. Haywood twice more, and then Mrs. Haywood's son returned with two Abrams boys, and soon their father followed. Mrs. Haywood asked him to note Bell's appearance for later identification and asked him to follow, but he had no horse. Bell then got his friend and they returned to Iola, arriving after midnight.

On July 5 the rape was reported and on July 7 the men of Company I were lined up and Bell was positively identified. Between July 5 and July 7 Bell had confessed the rape to Private Thomas Leach, and he provided a deposition. On July 8 Bell was tried by twelve officers at a drumhead court martial, a legal proceeding happening on the spot on a battlefield or along a line of march. He was found guilty of rape under the articles of war and was sentenced to hang. The judgment and sentence was reviewed by Colonel W. F. Cloud and approved, and General Order 55 was issued on July 9.

It was planned to hang the prisoner at sunset so the gallows was erected during the day but a large crowd of men, women and children began to gather, partly because of the intense outrage at the crime and partly because it was quite an event for an entertainment-starved public. Colonel Cloud postponed the execution until the following day but a number of citizens loitered near the camp waiting to give the signal that the hanging was about to happen. The evening of July 10 the company commanders were ordered to have their companies ready for parade at sunrise, and before dawn the men were marched in formation near the gallows. As soon as Bell appeared a small contingent of stalwart citizens raised up from the grass to watch, but the crowd was quite small so the process continued.

The prisoner climbed the stairs with a firm step and took his place on the trapdoor where his wrists and arms, knees and ankles were bound and the noose was adjusted. There is no record of a statement but as soon as the blindfold was tied over his eyes the trap was sprung and Bell dropped to his death. An Army physician monitored vital signs until Bell's heart ceased to beat, and then he was pronounced dead and cut down. The body was deposited into a coffin, carried a short distance from the parade ground and buried in the grave which had been prepared two days earlier. The companies were dismissed and the gallows was torn down.

Sources: *Adjutant General's Report—1885*: List of U.S. Soldiers Executed by United States Military Authorities during the Late War. Alotta, Robert I. *Civil War Justice: Union Army Executions Under Lincoln.* Shippensburg, PA: White Mane Publishing Co. Inc., 1989. *Dubuque Herald* (IA): June 22, 1862. *General Order No. 55, Headquarters 2d Kansas Cavalry*: July 9, 1862. Johnson, Edward C., Gail R. Johnson, and Melissa Johnson Williams. *All Were Not Heroes: A Study of U.S. Soldiers Executed by U.S. Military Authorities During the Late War.* Chicago, IL: E. C. Johnson, 1997. *Manhattan Express* (KS): July 22, 1862.

Hoy, Jeremiah
July 28, 1862

William Clarke Quantrill was a teacher at Lawrence, Kansas, but in 1859, as the abolitionists and secessionists exchanged words and deeds, he was charged with various minor crimes and fled. He was sympathetic to the pro-slavery faction, and when hostilities commenced between the Union and Confederate forces at the beginning of America's Civil War, Quantrill joined the Confederate fight, first as an irregular. He became adept at guerrilla tactics, formed his own force of men, and became a scourge along the Missouri and Kansas border. He attacked any business concern supporting the North and murdered any individuals sympathetic to the Union. He was declared an outlaw in 1862 after his men participated in the capture of Independence, Missouri. Soon afterward Quantrill was commissioned a captain in the Confederate army but still led his own forces, consisting of three hundred regulars and as many as seven hundred fifty men who were loosely allied. Among his regular troops was a man named Jeremiah Hoy, alias Solomon Perry Hoy, who was a civilian from Johnson County, Kansas. On July 22, 1862, Hoy was tried before a military commission convened at Fort Leavenworth. The commission, appointed on May 23, 1862, consisted of Captain D. S. Vittum, Lt. F. C. Kiser, Lt. L. B. Reed and Lt. Asa W. Farr acting as recorder. Samuel W. Carpenter, the principal witness against Hoy and a "detective" for Colonel Robert B. Mitchell, was sent on a scout specifically to locate and document the movements of Quantrill's guerrilla band. He testified that "in the latter part of March or early April, when seventy-five rods distant I saw Quantrill leading a force of forty-two men toward the Blue Ridge Crossing bridge five miles below Kansas City, so I dismounted, tied my horse in the brush and crept as close as I dared, about 35 rods distant." Carpenter said he took out his notebook and began recording the descriptions of the men riding with the guerrilla leader, including Jeremiah Hoy, whom he recognized from previous encounters with the man. A local farmer named Allison with his son and a Union soldier in uniform crossed the bridge, Allison riding a bay mare and the boy bareback on a mule. When they reached the opposite side they were confronted by Quantrill's band. At gunpoint the farmer, his son, and the soldier were ordered to dismount, and then a brief conversation followed. Carpenter testified that he thought he might be discovered and started to make his way from the scene when he heard a pistol shot and turned back to see Quantrill holding a smoking gun and the soldier lying dead on the ground. While Carpenter watched, Quantrill shot the elder Allison and ordered his men to take the saddle from Allison's horse and move it to the mule for the boy. Carpenter said that Quantrill next told the Allison boy, "Go back to Kansas City and tell the sons of b__s you saw

Quantrill's band kill your father." Quantrill then turned to his men and said, "Boys, bring the d__d dead carcasses on the bridge and we'll roast them." The men had already set the bridge afire so the younger Allison had to hurry across as the body of his father and the soldier were thrown into the flames.

Carpenter hurried to Kansas City and led Colonel Mitchell's force after the Quantrill band as they fled, then numbering only twenty-six, and on March 22 Hoy and four other men were captured by Colonel Mitchell following a skirmish near Little Santa Fe, Missouri. They were first taken to Shawneetown and then to Fort Leavenworth, Kansas, where four prisoners were examined and released by Lt. H. B. Sturgis, but Hoy was held for trial and charged with several offenses including murder. Hoy pled not guilty to all charges and, in his defense, confessed that he was present at the killing of Allison and the soldier but insisted that he was not a willing member of Quantrill's band but had been conscripted against his will. At the close of the testimony the commission members conferred, found Hoy guilty of "killing a man named Allison of Missouri and of a U.S. soldier of Maj. Charles Banzhaf's First Missouri Cavalry command on March 20, 1862, at the bridge crossing in Jackson County, Missouri; also of burning that bridge; and of treasonable acts in levying war against the United States." They sentenced Hoy to be "publicly shot to death according to military usage at such time and place as the General commanding the Department of Kansas shall direct." The proceedings were reviewed by Major F. A. Calkins, approved and forwarded to Major General James G. Blunt who, on July 26, fixed the date of execution at July 28, 1862.

The execution took place in the field just south of the barracks at Fort Leavenworth. Colonel John T. Burris was present with Captain John Conover acting as officer of the day and commanding a dozen troops from the Fort Leavenworth garrison, who were assigned as the firing squad. A detachment went to the guardhouse and pinioned Hoy's arms. The condemned man was then escorted onto the field by the firing squad, directly to the spot where he was about to die. A large number of troops had been assembled under arms to witness the execution, and they were standing nearby in formation. Hoy was wearing a new black suit, his burial clothes, and proudly wore the felt hat provided by the Army. He was directed to kneel, and as he complied the hat was taken from him. A clergyman read a divine prayer, which "took ten minutes but seemed an eternity to the witnesses." Meanwhile the firing squad took their places twenty yards distant. After the prayer concluded Hoy was helped to his feet, and the officer of the day read the death sentence. The prisoner was then directed by the attending guard to kneel again and Hoy's composure began to fail him as he "swayed like a leaf in the wind." Just as the guard stepped away the officer of the day gave the order to fire, and "twelve volumes of fire erupted from the rifles." One ball went through Hoy's head, and two more penetrated his body; he fell forward onto his face and lay motionless. Drs. Quindor and Sinks went immediately to examine the body and pronounced Hoy dead. The remains were then placed in a coffin while the firing squad and troops left the field, marching to a lively tune played by the band. The coffin was loaded into a wagon, driven to the military burial grounds, and interred without ceremony.

Sources: *Court-Martial case file KK-151. Daily Milwaukee News* (WI): August 6, 1862. *Leavenworth Daily Conservative* (KS): July 29, 1862. *The Daily Gazette* (Janesville, WI): August 7, 1862. *The State Journal* (Lawrence, KS): August 6, 1862.

Horne, Carl
February 13, 1863

John Philip Friend, sometimes spelled Freund, lived with his wife Catharine and their five-year-old son James on a farm one mile from Easton, Kansas. Carl Horne, a thirty-five-year-old ex-soldier, had boarded with the Friend family since June. On September 5, 1861, the dead body of John Friend was found buried in a haystack on his farm, his head and chest crushed. It was later determined he had been dead seven days. A search was immediately made for Catharine and James but they were nowhere to be found, and Horne was missing also. During the investigation which followed it was learned that Horne and Catharine Friend, using the alias Catharine Grossman, had been married at Leavenworth on September 2 and, with James, had started two days later for St. Louis, Missouri, on their honeymoon. On the day after the body was found Deputy U.S. Marshal Shott started after the couple and overtook them at

Elwood. The following day, September 7, they were in jail at Leavenworth charged with the murder of Catharine's husband. Horne's trial commenced in Judge William McDowell's courtroom on November 25, 1861, and lasted three days, and the jurors deliberated only two hours before returning a verdict of guilty of first-degree murder. Catharine Friend was tried two days later, found guilty of murder in the second degree, and sentenced to ten years in prison. On December 7 Horne was brought into court for sentencing. The defense presented a motion for a new trial, which was quickly denied, and the prisoner was sentenced to hang on January 24, 1862. The defense attorneys next took an appeal to the Kansas supreme court, and this acted as a stay of execution. The justices heard the case in early February 1862 and sent the case back for a new trial. On December 10, 1862, Horne's second trial commenced in Judge Samuel D. Lecompte's Leavenworth courtroom. Once again the trial took three days, and on the 13th Horne was found guilty after brief jury deliberations. Horne was brought to court for sentencing on December 30, and after overruling the motion for a new trial, the judge sentenced Horne to hang on February 13, 1863. Nothing would further delay his date with the hangman.

Horne resigned himself to his fate, and two days before he was to die he was discovered by a reporter in a cheerful mood, willing to discuss his current predicament. A gallows of "Hickory, neatly put up, and painted a dark drab color" had been erected on the north side of the Leavenworth jail within an fenced enclosure and had been thoroughly tested. On the fatal day, as early as 10:00 A.M., a crowd began to gather, and some climbed the fence, but soon a militia force arrived armed with bayoneted rifles, cleared the fence, and kept the crowd at bay. The sheriff had sent out a limited number of invitations, and only those invited were admitted to witness the execution. The witnesses marched into the enclosure after noon. At 12:30 P.M. the procession appeared, and Horne climbed the stairs onto the platform. A deputy sheriff read the death warrant, and this was followed by a brief statement, in German, by the condemned man. Horne then made a speech in English during which the condemned man professed his innocence and stated he regretted ever knowing Philip Friend. He was then positioned on the trapdoor, his arms and legs were pinioned, the black cap was pulled over his head, and the noose was adjusted. One minute after 1:00 P.M. the sheriff gave the signal, and the trap was sprung. Horne's body dropped, breaking his neck in the fall, and fourteen minutes later he was pronounced dead. After hanging a while longer the body was cut down, placed in the cheap wooden coffin provided by the county, and buried without ceremony.

Sources: *Atchison Daily Champion* (KS): February 20, 1879. *Leavenworth Daily Conservative* (KS): December 8, 1861; December 11–14, 1862; December 28, 1862; December 31, 1862; February 12–14, 1863. *Leavenworth Daily Times* (KS): September 7–8, 1861. November 26–28, 1861; December 3, 1861; December 6–8, 1861.

Shirley, John
May 6, 1863

On the evening of April 22, 1863, John Shirley, John McBride and Charles Radcliff were at the bar in the Cincinnati House in Leavenworth, Kansas. They systematically fed drinks to William Keyes, a recently discharged soldier with his mustering out pay filling his pockets. When Keyes was sufficiently drunk the three men convinced him to accompany them to an area behind the hospital on the military reservation where they clubbed him into unconsciousness, robbed him of $1,100, and threw his body in a ravine. The entire affair occurred during the early morning hours of April 23, and the robbers were so brazen that they were seen by many witnesses. Later in the day all three men were arrested but they had cached all but $77 of the stolen money. The men were lodged in the civilian jail at Leavenworth but the following day they were moved to the guardhouse, as the town was then under martial law. A military commission was convened the following day, April 24, headed by Captain R. H. Hunt. The evidence proved that Shirley and McBride were principals in the robbery while Radcliff was determined to be an accessory. Radcliff was sentenced to a long term of imprisonment at hard labor while Shirley and McBride were sentenced to hang. The findings were reviewed and approved by Major General James G. Blunt but McBride was later reprieved and sentenced to a prison term, leaving only Shirley to hang.

The hanging of John Shirley on May 6, 1863, was a public affair, and people from all over the region flocked to Leavenworth to see the hanging. By noon there were more than three thousand men, women, and children surrounding the gallows. The scaffold had been erected on the open ground south of the guardhouse, and at 1:15 P.M. the entire command, consisting of five companies of Infantry, were assembled in full uniform under arms. The company band then formed in front of the guardhouse and played a solemn tune as the carriage, which was to carry the prisoner to the scaffold, arrived. Captain J. T. Gordon placed Shirley aboard, and the carriage, with the Reverend Dr. Davis already aboard, started for the gallows. Shirley showed no sign of weakening as they arrived, and he climbed the stairs with a firm step, taking his place upon the trapdoor. Captain Graham read the death warrant, and then Shirley was allowed to kiss his two small brothers. The condemned man turned his attention to the crowd and stated, "I have but one word to say and that is this: I hope my friends will lead a different life from what I have. I've led a very indifferent life; and furthermore, I hope you will not meet the same doom which I have come to — the gallows...." The preparation of Shirley was managed with great efficiency, and his arms and legs were pinioned, the black cap pulled on and the noose quickly adjusted so that the trap could be sprung at exactly 1:30 P.M. In fifteen minutes the attending physicians pronounced him dead and the body was cut down. The remains of John Shirley were placed in a wagon pulled by a six-mule team, which was followed by marching troops as the band "played a lively air." Shirley was buried that evening.

Sources: *Leavenworth Evening Bulletin* (KS): April 22–24, 1863; April 29, 1863; May 4, 1863; May 6 1863; May 8, 1863. *Leavenworth Daily Conservative* (KS): February 11, 1863; April 23, 1863; May 3, 1863; May 6–7, 1863.

Summers, John W.
May 13, 1863

Twenty-two-year-old John W. Summers, sometimes spelled Sommers but nick-named "Fort Sumpter" by his fellow soldiers, was a native of Indiana who enlisted in Company E of the Kansas 2d Volunteer Cavalry and arrived at Iola, Kansas, near Fort Riley about May 1, 1862. He was paid at the end of September, and, with pockets filled, he was sent on a foraging mission to find anything the company could eat. He would later claim that he was captured by a rebel guerrilla band on October 1 and kept prisoner for twenty-four hours. He was then given the opportunity to swear "to support the Confederate States of America and not to take up arms against them or aid and abet their enemies," or he could choose to be shot, and he chose to swear allegiance. Summers was free for the next four months, and in early January 1863 he enlisted in Company C of the 3rd Wisconsin Cavalry under Captain E. R. Stevens, but again he deserted. On March 20, 1863, Summers was captured at Neosho Falls and taken to Fort Scott, Kansas, where a commission had convened on March 11, 1863, to try a number of pending cases dealing with civilians. On March 26, drawing from the complement of commissioned officers, Summers' general court-martial commenced on a charge of desertion. First Summers complained that he should not be tried while shackled as this was against military procedure and was prejudicial, but this was overruled as there was fear he might try to escape, and next he succeeded in having Captain Stevens excluded as judge because it was he who had brought the charges against him. The case for the prosecution consisted of the testimony of 2nd Lt. Agustus J. Lovellette and Privates Bryon Alden and Alison Eggleston. Summers presented his own defense and concluded on March 27 with the reading, by the judge advocate, of his carefully prepared written statement:

> "I am arraigned before you under very grave charges, and the evidence adduced in the prosecution must appear very conclusive in the eyes of the court (viz.) my desertion from the service of the United States. Gentlemen: ... I belonged to Capt. Gardner's Comp. E, 2d Regt., Kas. Vols., the company to which I belonged was encamped between Keithsville and Cafeville, Mo. on or about the 1st day of October, '62. I obtained leave of absence from my company commander to leave camp for the purpose of purchasing a few necessities in the shape of chickens, butter, etc. I had not proceeded but a short distance from camp before I was surprised and surrounded by an armed party of mounted guerrillas who made a prisoner of me, and gave me a choice of either taking an oath of allegiance to the Southern Confederacy, or to be shot; as a necessity I took the oath and went with them to Carthage; after arriving there I was released. I then proceeded to Fort Scott, Kas. From here I went to Lawrence, Kas. where I was arrested by the Provost Marshall of that place 'on suspicion of being a Confed. spy,' he at the same time took from me my papers and forwarded me to Fort Leavenworth as a prisoner where I was detained 13 days in the guard house. When I was released and set at liberty, through the influence of Lieut. Hunt of the 2d Kas. Vols., he at the same time procuring the situation of teamster from me from the 2d Master to

drive a team between Forts Scott & Leavenworth. I was under the conviction after the arrival of the train in Fort Scott that it would then proceed in the direction of Springfield, Mo. and that I would have a chance of joining my Comp. On my way down from Leavenworth to Fort Scott I met with an accident on the road by having one of the wagon wheels run over my foot which incapacitated me from any further use in the 2d employ until my foot would get better, so I went to a private boarding house in the vicinity of Fort Scott and remained there until my means were exhausted; as a means of necessity I joined the 3d Wis. Cavy where I remained about two months at the expiration of which I was ordered on a foraging expedition which I accompanied. After having helped to load the wagons I told some of the men of the party that I was going to an adjacent house for my washing, it being late when I went I concluded to stay there all night. Next morning I got on my horse and went to Fort Scott after which I went back to the house where I got my washing done, some of the 3d Wis. Cavy had been there in my absence in search of me and threatened that when they saw me they would shoot me whether I surrendered or not; after my hearing this report I was afraid to go back to the 3d Wis. fearing that they might put their threats into execution. I at the same time being under supposition that I really did not belong to that Reg, as I was never mustered into it, and as a ground work for that supposition was the paymaster not paying me in consequence. I was also under the conclusion that I came under the President's Proclamation of Pardon to all deserters joining these Regs. up to a stated time...."

The commission, after considering all the evidence, found Summers guilty of twice deserting from the service of the United States Army and sentenced him to death by firing squad. The proceedings were reviewed, approved, and forwarded to Major General James G. Blunt who, on May 8, fixed the date of execution for Wednesday, May 13, 1863. The aide to General Blunt wrote:

"In reviewing this case the General commanding has felt it his imperative duty to approve the findings and sentence of the court which inflicts the severest punishment known to military law for the crime of desertion, trusting that this example may be a warning to others and prove satisfactory to the interests of the service. The crime of desertion has long been treated with great leniency and the impunity with which it is committed is calculated to destroy the discipline and efficiency of the Army; (after passing sentence of death the court very justly states that the prisoner has been twice tried by the same court for desertion from different regiments), hence the necessity of inflicting the severest penalty of the law."

It would appear from the statements of General Blunt's aide that Summers had been tried in absentia for his first desertion, and that previously the crime of desertion had not been punished as a capital offense. After word of General Blunt's action was received Summers was allowed continuous religious conversation and was attended by the Rev. T. T. Insley, who was pastor of the local M. E. Church, assisted by the Reverends Leard and Harden. On Monday, May 11, the prisoner was baptized by immersion and afterward expressed penitence, professing his conversion and insisting, "I would not exchange my hope for Heaven for a pardon." On the fatal day the prisoner was removed from the guardhouse before 11:00 A.M. A detachment of soldiers of the 12th Regiment Kansas Volunteers under direction of Sergeant Pleasant of Company E, with the reverends and the entire command of infantry and cavalry soldiers, marched to the solemn music of the band as the procession made its way to a place on the prairie a half mile from town. Summers took his place on one side of a hollow square: on two sides of the hollow square were the officers and men delegated to act as witnesses; the third side consisted of the firing squad of seven men under command of Captain James H. McKay of Company F; and directly opposite the firing squad was the prisoner, the guard detail, the reverends, and Post Adjutant Lt. Marshall M. Ehle. Seven rifles had been loaded by Captain McKay so that none of the soldiers knew which rifle contained a blank load. The prisoner never showed any sign of fear and was allowed to kneel and pray. He then stood as Lt. Ehle read the record of the court-martial and the death sentence. One guard was then detailed to tie on a blindfold but Summers requested that he be allowed to see, and this was granted. He then looked to the firing squad and called out, "Take good aim and do your work well." Summers was positioned a few feet in front of his coffin, where he again knelt. His wrists had not been bound, and as he awaited that awful moment he raised his hand toward heaven in prayer. In that instant, at 12:15 P.M., Captain McKay gave the order to fire. Six leaden balls penetrated the body of the young deserter, and he lurched forward onto his face; for a moment blood spurted out the holes in his back where the bullets had exited. The post physician attended Summers and pronounced him dead in seconds. The body was then lifted into its coffin, and

Summers was buried that evening after a brief graveside service by the Reverend Insley.

Sources: *Daily Conservative* (Leavenworth, KS): May 17, 1863. *The Whig* (Beaver Dam, WI): June 2, 1863. RG 153: Records of the Judge Advocate General's Office, Entry 15: Court-Martial Case Files (Army), 1809–1894; 7E3:14/5/02; Box # 1514; File # NN-105.

Frizzell, Claudius C.
May 27, 1863

Vernon County, Missouri, organized a militia company in March 1863, and Augustus Baker, a local farmer, was elected Captain. Claudius C. Frizzell, sometimes spelled Claudeus C. Frizell, had anticipated being elected to the position and was greatly disappointed when the captaincy went to Baker. On March 6 Frizzell and a man named Upton went to Baker's house and, pretending congeniality, gained entrance. Baker and his wife were in the parlor with their visitors when Frizzell suddenly pulled his pistol and, without warning or hesitation, shot and killed Augustus Baker. The two murderers then ransacked the house for valuables and fled, leaving Mrs. Baker unharmed and anxious to testify against them. Troops were dispatched, and they tracked the men to a house in Cedar County, Missouri. They captured Frizzell but Upton jumped out a window and fled, never to be heard of again. Frizzell was lodged in the Fort Scott guardhouse on May 13, and the following day he was tried before a military commission, Captain H. F. Rouse presiding and Lt. Marshall M. Ehle serving as Judge Advocate. The prisoner was found guilty of murder and robbery. Eight days later, on May 21, Major General James G. Blunt reviewed and confirmed the findings, and Frizzell was sentenced to hang on May 27. On the fatal day Frizzell marched resolutely to the gallows, which had been erected near the government corral. He read his Bible as he walked, mounted the stairs with a firm step, and took his place on the trapdoor. After the reading of the death warrant the prisoner was quickly prepared, with his arms and legs pinioned, the black cap pulled on, and the noose adjusted. In but a moment the trap was sprung and Frizzell dropped to his death. After hanging a sufficient time to ensure he would not revive he was lowered into his coffin and buried later that day.

Sources: *Leavenworth Daily Conservative* (KS): May 7, 1863; May 22, 1863. *Leavenworth Evening Bulletin* (KS): May 20–22, 1863. *The Whig* (Beaver Dam, WI): June 2, 1863.

Griffith, William
October 30, 1863

In 1854 began a struggle to determine whether Kansas should enter the Union as a free or a slave state. Free-state and pro-slavery factions became rivals, bad feelings resulted, and men were attacked but rarely killed. The Trading Post had become a center for a pro-slavery group, and in 1858 Charles Hamilton was a leader among the pro-slavery faction. He was a native of Georgia who had come to the border area in 1855 with the express purpose of making Kansas a slave state but Hamilton and his friends were driven out. He soon sent back word to constituents "to come out of the territory at once, as we are coming up there to kill snakes, and will treat all we find there as snakes."

On May 19, 1858, thirty men under Hamilton's leadership crossed into Kansas and rendezvoused at the Trading Post. They started on the road toward Missouri, capturing eleven unarmed "free-staters" along the way. Most of the prisoners knew Hamilton and believed he meant them no harm. However, Hamilton herded them into a ravine and ordered them to form a single file line facing east, while Hamilton's men formed another line on the east side of the ravine. Hamilton then gave the order to fire, firing the first shot himself as a signal. Hamilton next ordered his men to finish the job with pistols. Five free-staters died, four were seriously wounded, and two men went unscathed; the six only survived by feigning death. Hamilton's forces then fled into Missouri. The massacre became known as Marais des Cygnes from a poem later published by John Greenleaf Whitter.

In September 1863 William Griffith, a married man with five children, the youngest a newborn, was arrested by troops from Fort Leavenworth and charged with murder. The prisoner was turned over to Sheriff E. B. Metz and held in a house at Mound City, as there was no jail, and security was provided by a detachment of Linn County militia. Griffith's trial commenced in Judge Solon O. Thatcher's courtroom on October 3, 1863. Griffith was identified by one of the massacre survivors — William Hairgrove — but the defendant insisted he had only helped capture the eleven men and had not taken part in the shooting. The trial lasted two days, and the jury, during three hours of deliberations, chose to disbelieve Griffith's self-serving testimony and convicted him of murder. The defendant was then sentenced to hang on October 30, 1863.

A gallows was erected in a wood west of town on the opposite bank of Little Sugar Creek. The gallows was of the "twitch-up" design, where a heavy counter-poise weight dropped, jerking the condemned man upward and dislocating his vertebrae; this was the first reported use of this gallows design in the west. Acting Sheriff C. S. Wheaton was in charge; he mobilized a force of two hundred militiamen to provide crowd management, and he ignored the law requiring that executions be conducted privately. As the moment approached the crowd swelled to thousands coming from several counties to witness the spectacle, and the crowd included a large number of women.

A little after noon Griffith was conveyed to the wood where he stepped onto the wooden platform a few inches above the ground. His wrists, knees and ankles were bound and the noose was adjusted. The black cap was pulled over his face at 1:07 P.M., and in but a moment William Hairgrove, one of the survivors of the massacre, cut the restraining rope with a hatchet; the four hundred pound weight dropped, jerking Griffith upward. The body rebounded and hung motionless while the attending physicians monitored his vital signs, and in twenty-five minutes they pronounced him dead. His remains were cut down, placed in a coffin, and given to his family for burial.

Sources: *Daily Journal of Commerce* (Kansas City, MO): October 8, 1863; November 3, 1863.

Lockman, Charles
November 12, 1864

In November 1864 elements of Companies D and F of the 2nd Colorado Cavalry were on their way to Fort Leavenworth, Kansas, under command of Lieutenant William Wise. On the morning of Thursday, November 12, when seven miles southwest of Lawrence, Kansas, privates Charles Lockman and John Gross (sometimes Grace or Groce) argued. Lockman fell back but suddenly rode up to Gross with his pistol drawn and shot him in the heart, killing him instantly. Lockman was arrested and tried by a drumhead court-martial, found guilty of murder, and sentenced to hang that afternoon. At 1:00 P.M. Lockman was hanged by a sergeant and three privates from his own company. There is no record of a statement, but Lockman's wrists and ankles would have been bound, the noose adjusted, and a blindfold would have been tied over his eyes. In a moment Lt. Wise gave the signal and Lockman was hanged a sufficient time to ensure death. The body was then cut down and buried on the spot. The body of Gross was sent to Fort Leavenworth for burial.

Sources: *Adjutant General's Report—1885*: List of U.S. Soldiers Executed by United States Military Authorities during the Late War. Alotta, Robert I. *Civil War Justice: Union Army Executions under Lincoln.* Shippensburg, PA: White Mane Publishing Co. Inc., 1989. Johnson, Edward C., Gail R. Johnson, and Melissa Johnson Williams. *All Were Not Heroes: A Study of U.S. Soldiers Executed by U.S. Military Authorities During the Late War.* Chicago, IL: E. C. Johnson, 1997. *Leavenworth Daily Conservative* (KS): November 13, 1864; November 15, 1864.

Hendley, John
December 29, 1865

John T. Jones owned a farm in Franklin County, Kansas, and in June 1865 he hired Texan John Hendley as a farmhand. Nearby was the farm of the Sutton family. Mrs. Sutton was an accomplished seamstress, and Hendley hired Mrs. Sutton to sew a hunting shirt. He provided the material, but when he received the shirt there was a quarter-yard remnant of ribbon material missing, and this angered the ill-tempered Texan. On June 28 Hendley went to the Sutton farm, demanded the remnant, and used profane and abusive language against Mrs. Sutton and her sister. Mrs. Sutton's husband John intervened and ordered Hendley to leave his house, but Hendley refused saying he would leave when he was ready, and became ready as soon as John Sutton produced a gun. Once Hendley was outside he acted as if he would not leave so Sutton fired a single round inflicting a minor wound to his arm. In response Hendley drew his revolver, rushed the house, and upon entering immediately shot Sutton in the breast inflicting a mortal wound. Sutton lingered for a day before dying from his wound while Hendley fled toward Bloomington.

The fugitive was captured on June 30 and charged with the murder of Sutton, and the prisoner was taken to Ottawa, where he had his examination before justice of the peace Dow. He was held for action by the grand jury and remanded to the custody of Sheriff Robbins, who took his prisoner to Leavenworth and lodged him in the Douglas County jail. The district court convened at Lawrence in November, and Hendley was tried in Judge D. M. Valentine's courtroom. The trial lasted several days, and on November 11 the case went to the jury, which deliberated for only one hour before returning a verdict of guilty of first-degree murder. Two weeks later Hendley was brought into court, and Judge Valentine sentenced him to hang on December 29, 1865. Neither appeal nor application for executive clemency would delay the proceedings.

During his final days the condemned man displayed "a stoicism better becoming a savage than a man reared in Christian society." He slept soundly his final night and arose the following morning in a cheerful mood. He ate a hearty breakfast, his appetite never failing him while behind bars. He dressed for his burial, and after 11:00 A.M. the death warrant was read to him in his cell; then he was escorted to the gallows. He mounted with a firm step and took his place on the trapdoor. There is no record of a statement to the crowd. His limbs were bound, the noose adjusted, and a black bag pulled over his face. The trap was sprung, and before noon Hendley was pronounced dead by the attending physician. After hanging a sufficient time the rope was cut, his body was lowered into the awaiting coffin, and he was buried later that evening.

Sources: *Daily Tribune* (Lawrence, KS): July 2, 1865; November 12, 1865; December 30, 1865. *Weekly Tribune* (Lawrence, KS): November 30, 1865. *Madison County Courier* (Edwardsville, IL): January 11, 1866.

Wa-tee-cha, Ernest
January 19, 1866

On January 31, 1865, Ernest Wa-tee-cha, a Quapaw Indian soldier assigned to Company A of the Sixteenth Kansas Cavalry, was on furlough in Ohio City, Kansas, shopping at the local mercantile. Wa-tee-cha, a graduate of the Osage Mission School, saw local farmer William Hastings receive a large sum of money and on impulse decided to rob him. Wa-tee-cha watched Hastings until his victim started for his farm in Ottumwa and followed him onto the prairie. After traveling several miles from town Wa-tee-cha rode up to Hastings and asked him about purchasing his horses, then fell back and shot the unsuspecting farmer in the back. The wound was a mortal one but it did not kill Hastings immediately, and the farmer put up a stiff resistance which drove off Wa-tee-cha empty-handed. Hastings turned around and drove his team and wagon a considerable distance toward town to the nearest house, where he was taken in and cared for. Hastings never lost consciousness and told the residents the details of the shooting, and described the man who had attacked him. A posse was soon organized and put on the trail of Wa-tee-cha. They quickly overtook and captured the soldier and brought him to the bedside of Hastings, who identified him as the man who had shot him. Hastings, in contemplation of his impending death, then dictated an ante-mortem statement before dying the day following the attack. In late November Wa-tee-cha was tried in Judge D. M. Valentine's courtroom at Lawrence, Kansas. The trial lasted two days and concluded on November 23 when the jury, after deliberating only one hour, returned a verdict of guilty of first-degree murder. Within a week Judge Valentine sentenced Wa-tee-cha to hang on January 19, 1866. Nothing would intervene to delay the execution.

During his final days Wa-tee-cha was attended by Father Hermann, who had been his teacher at the Osage Mission School, and the priest remained with him during that final morning. At a few minutes before noon Sheriff Ogden appeared at the cell door and the procession formed, led by the sheriff with the priest on the Indian's arm guiding him. Wa-tee-cha ascended the stairs to the gallows' platform with a firm step and took his place on the trapdoor. Father Hermann then read the Catholic service for the dying while the condemned man held a crucifix firmly in both hands, staring down at it as he listened. Father Hermann and the prisoner then knelt for prayer, and upon their rising, Sheriff Ogden read the sentence of the court, then offered Wa-tee-cha the opportunity to speak. The condemned man said he wanted his body given to the Catholic Church for burial, then to the spectators he said that he was sorry for his past life; was guilty of the crime for which he was convicted; but now he was truly repentant and felt that God had forgiven him. He said he hoped his fate would be a warning to others to avoid bad company and to live a Christian life. He then bade farewell to Father Hermann and the sheriff as his limbs were pinioned, the noose adjusted, and the black cap pulled over his head. At five minutes past noon the trap was sprung, and Wa-tee-cha dropped straight through, breaking his neck in the fall, but there were two convulsive movements before the body hung motionless. His vital signs were monitored by the attending physician; in fifteen minutes his heart ceased to beat and he was pronounced dead. Five minutes later the body was cut down, lowered into the coffin provided, and given to Father Hermann for burial at the Mission School cemetery.

Sources: *Kansas Patriot* (Burlington): February 10, 1866. *The Weekly Tribune* (Lawrence, KS): November 30, 1865; January 25, 1866.

Lewis, Benjamin
August 10, 1866

In March 1866 the horribly burnt and decomposed remains of an Indian known as "Blacksmith" were found a short distance southeast of Miami, Kansas. Evidence pointed to a Peoria Indian named Benjamin Lewis, and he was arrested on suspicion of being the murderer. It was presumed that Lewis had first murdered Blacksmith before burning the body, but the condition of the corpse prevented determination of the cause of death. Before his arrest twenty-seven-year-old Lewis, in a drunken state, paraded about town bragging, "Me kill white man — soldier — got heap money — got revolver — me big Indian — kill more white men." His ranting had been dismissed as an alcohol-induced fantasy until Blacksmith's remains were found, but then it was decided to investigate. In jail Lewis was questioned and he proudly told where the remains of the soldier were buried, and the authorities found the decomposed remains not far from the designated spot, six miles north of Paola, Kansas. Lewis was charged with murdering the soldier and given a preliminary examination before a Miami justice of the peace. During the hearing, and from evidence found with the second set of remains, the authorities determined that the murdered soldier was Ben M. Jones of Company F of the Fourteenth Kansas Cavalry, missing since late 1865. Lewis, they learned, had deserted from Company F of the Fourteenth Kansas Cavalry at Fort Scott on December 19, 1864, and it was thought that he may have murdered Jones when he was recognized as a deserter. The prisoner was held for trial, which commenced in the district court at Paola on July 2, 1866. Judge D. M. Valentine, after careful consideration, admitted the defendant's confession into evidence, and the following day the case went to the jury. After brief deliberations they returned a verdict of guilty of first-degree murder. On July 5 Judge Valentine sentenced Lewis to hang on August 10, 1866, and nothing would delay his date with the hangman.

The day and night before his execution Lewis spent with his wife, laughing and talking as if they did not have a care in the world. At 7:00 A.M. on his final day, while the prisoners were eating breakfast and the jailer was away, Lewis managed to escape and hid in the brush near town. A large posse searched and within an hour the prisoner was back in his cell, ironed and manacled. During the forenoon the prisoner was visited by a delegation of Indian chiefs, led by Chief "Major" Battista Peoria, but he said he was not affected by his impending doom. At noon the condemned man ate a hearty dinner and then waited quietly in his cell. A reverend appeared in a half hour and Lewis was told that his time had nearly expired and if he had anything to say or request, now was the time. Lewis requested a final farewell with his wife, and it was granted. He then stood and the sheriff removed the manacles and tied his wrists.

The gallows had been erected west of town among the timber, there being no suitable yard at the jail. The prisoner was loaded in a wagon and driven by Sheriff Reaney, accompanied by a deputy, to the gallows. A large crowd accompanied the wagon to the scaffold, and there they joined the crowd of men, women and children who had assembled on the site. Lewis dismounted, made his way through the crowd accompanied by the lawmen and the reverend, climbed the steps with a firm step, and took a seat in the chair provided. First a prayer was offered by the attending clergy, and then the sheriff addressed the prisoner "in relation to the solemn and painful duty devolving upon him." The sheriff then read the death warrant and, when finished, he asked Lewis if he had anything to say to the spectators. The condemned man stood, stepped forward, and gazed at the crowd, and the large number of spectators seemed to please him. He said, "My friends, I speak to you. My friends, I leave this world now. My friends, I hope we all meet together. My friends, I speak no more." Lewis then stepped back and took his seat but the sheriff prompted him to stand and move to the center of the trapdoor. The deputy tied his ankles while the sheriff adjusted the noose and pulled on the black cap. The sheriff then stepped back and waited as the reverend announced, "May God have mercy on your soul," and at that moment, 2:00 P.M., the trap was sprung. Lewis' body shot straight down, breaking his neck in the fall, but there were several convulsions before the body hung motionless. The attending physicians monitored his vital signs and pronounced him dead in eight minutes, but the body was allowed to hang until 2:15 before it was cut down and lowered into the coffin provided by the county. The remains were immediately driven to the "Indian burying grounds" near town and interred after a brief graveside ceremony.

Sources: *Leavenworth Daily Conservative* (KS): July 15, 1866; August 18, 1866. *The New York Times* (NY): August 26, 1866.

Bates, Martin W.
February 20, 1867

Martin Bates, a newly married nineteen-year-old man with twin baby boys, was suspected of stealing horses, and in late September 1866 he was arrested by deputy sheriff John Polley. There was no jail in Osage County at that time so Polley took the prisoner into his home. Bates wore leg shackles but was very cooperative as he awaited trial. Polley and his wife were not concerned when they went to visit a neighbor on October 3 and left Bates in the custody of John's crippled father, Abel Polley, who also served as justice of the peace. Abel was busy reading the Bible as Bates slipped into the loft and got a loaded double-barreled shotgun as he prepared to make his escape. He later claimed that he only tried to scare the old man but Abel Polley was determined to thwart the escape of his prisoner, and they grappled for the gun. The fight was so violent that the stock of the shotgun was broken off but the struggle finally ended with a fatal shot to the body of Abel Polley. The elder Polley lived for several days before succumbing to the fearful body wound. After shooting the old man Bates removed his shackles with an ax and fled into Johnson County. A reward was offered, and his description was circulated, so within a week he was recognized and captured. This time Bates was taken to Lawrence where they had a substantial jail structure. An extra term of the district court was convened in December 1866, and Bates was tried before Judge John Watson of Emporia. Bates was convicted of first degree murder and sentenced to be hanged on February 20, 1867, "within a proper enclosure in the courtyard of the jail."

Sheriff William Cozine was responsible for conducting the hanging of Bates. There was no such enclosure at that time, and lumber was difficult to obtain and therefore very expensive, so the sheriff had a gallows constructed inside the courtroom, which had a high ceiling. The room being quite small only six witnesses were admitted, including four county officials and two clergymen, one Methodist and one Catholic. Bates was bareheaded and barefooted as he was led from his jail cell onto the scaffold. He knelt between the two clergymen facing the trapdoor, and they prayed for ten minutes. The Catholic Priest held a crucifix in front of Bates' face the entire time and told him to keep his eye on it. When the prayer was done Bates arose and stepped forward onto the trapdoor. His arms and legs were pinioned and the black cap was pulled over his head. As soon as the noose was in place the trap was sprung and Bates dropped to his death, breaking his neck in the fall. He was cut down after hanging a sufficient time to ensure he could not be revived, carried out through a blinding blizzard, and buried "over behind the hill."

There followed a terrible outrage by Judge Watson, as the hanging had not been carried out according to his sentence, and he insisted that the hall of the courtroom had been desecrated. He was indignant and told everyone concerned, but the work was done and nothing he said would change it.

Sources: *Emporia News* (KS): January 5, 1867; February 20, 1867. *Kansas Weekly Tribune* (Lawrence): October 11, 1866. *Kansas Daily Tribune* (Lawrence): February 23, 1867. *Topeka Weekly Leader* (KS): January 3, 1867.

Holderman, Scott
November 15, 1867

John Carver was a stranger passing through Linn County, Kansas, but he was forced to lay over at the home of Jack "uncle Jackie" Williams, Scott Holderman's father-in-law, when he had an attack of ague — a malady characterized by alternating shaking chills and fever, aches in the bones and joints, and debilitating weakness. Carver had recuperated by September 25, 1865, and continued on his way. Scott Holderman, Elias Foster, and a man named Ward saw Carver's condition and his possessions, and they were determined to rob him. Holderman and Foster had met and become friends during the Civil War when they were serving in Company D, Sixth Kansas Cavalry in Arkansas, and they began a life of crime after being mustered out. Foster was the "thinker" of the two, Holderman more of a follower, and Foster decided the three men would trail Carver from the Williams' farm, which was three miles from Trading Post, to some desolate location and murder him for his money, valuables, and traveling outfit. Carver had only traveled three miles when he was overtaken by the three young men and brutally murdered. The boys did not take care in hiding the body, and it was discovered seven weeks later.

At the inquest it was determined Carver's death had come by violence, by persons unknown to the jurors, but the exact cause of death could not be determined due to the advanced state of decomposition. The investigation was conducted by Sheriff David Goss, and he soon suspected Holderman, Foster, and the man named Ward.

Foster was found first, in Bates County, Missouri, but he was well mounted and managed to outdistance all of the posse but one man, and the two exchanged shots at various times during the pursuit. Foster finally decided he would stop the man by shooting his horse, and waited until the pursuer fired and missed. Foster then turned and prepared to fire but unknown to Foster his pursuer had a repeating rifle and now, with a stationary target, the posse man unhorsed Foster. Now afoot it was not long before Foster was captured near Butler. He was taken to Mound City and lodged in a house under close guard, there being no jail. Foster, as soon as he was arrested, confessed all the details of the murder of Carver and informed on Holderman and Ward, and warrants were issued for their arrest. Two months later Foster was moved to the jail at Lawrence but on May 5, 1867, lawmen were transporting Foster to Garnett, and were in the area of Sugar Creek at 9:00 P.M. when a mob of fifty men took the prisoner from the officers. The two lawmen, under threat of being shot, were ordered to drive toward Mound City but Sheriff Goss, after driving a short distance, returned to search for his prisoner, and after daybreak he found Foster hanging from a limb.

Ward was the next man arrested in Lawrence, but Foster's confession did not implicate him as a principal in the killing. Ward was tried, convicted of second-degree murder, and sentenced to serve a ten-year prison term. The search for Scott Holderman continued and, as often happens, chance played a part in his capture. The brother of Sheriff David Goss, William Goss, lost his way in heavy rain during a trip into Missouri on July 2, 1867. He stopped at an isolated cabin for directions, and the woman who answered the door was Scott Holderman's wife. Goss recognized her immediately, got his directions and left, and as soon as he returned to Kansas he notified his brother. There was a small country store in the vicinity of the cabin, and the proprietor agreed to let the sheriff know when Holderman was at home. Sheriff Goss returned to his home and awaited word, and finally in mid–July 1867 he heard that Holderman had returned. A small posse was organized; they surrounded the cabin before calling for Holderman to come out, and he came out shooting. The fugitive was shot in the bowels and had no choice but to surrender, or die of his wound. He was treated, and as soon as he was able to travel he was taken to Mound City and held in a house under heavy guard. He had his examination on August 3, was held over for trial, and remanded to the custody of the sheriff who took him to Lawrence and lodged him in jail. In mid–September Holderman's trial commenced in Judge D. P. Lowe's courtroom in Lawrence and lasted nearly a week. The evidence, though entirely circumstantial, was strong, and the confession of Foster played a major role. The defendant was convicted of murder in the first degree, the jury deliberating only one hour, and on September 25 Judge Lowe sentenced Holderman to hang on November 15, 1867. The defense attorneys did not file a motion for a new trial, nor was there an appeal nor an application for clemency. Holderman was held in the Douglas County jail at Lawrence, and on the fatal day he was taken from his cell to the gallows, built within an enclosure in the jail yard. Outside there was a large crowd but they were kept back from the high fence. As Holderman stood on the platform he looked down at the thirty-five invited witnesses while his wrists, knees and ankles were bound, and the noose was adjusted. The black cap was pulled over his head at 11:25 A.M.; in but a moment the trap was sprung, and Holderman broke his neck in the fall. After he was pronounced dead by the attending physician his body was cut down, deposited in a coffin, and given to his wife for burial.

Sources: *The* (weekly) *Border Sentinel* (Mound City, KS): May 10, 1867; September 20–27, 1867; November 22, 1867. *The Kansas Daily Tribune* (Lawrence): November 18, 1867.

Baughn, Melvin E.
September 18, 1868

Melvin E. Baughn was born in Virginia in 1836 and was orphaned at the age of fourteen. He made his own way the best he could and claimed to have worked as a bartender, hostler, and pony express rider during his youth. When the pony express company went bankrupt, he claimed, he was paid only pennies on the dollars owed him and, to recover from his near penniless state, he became a guerrilla raider, a Jayhawker, in Missouri. He was captured, convicted and served two years and three months of a ten-year sentence before being pardoned, and he claimed this close association with hardened criminals put him on the path of lawlessness.

Once free he joined a gang, and they stole horses near St. Joseph but the owners, hearing of the efforts of the thieves to take the herd into Kansas, obtained a warrant and pursued them. Upon reaching Seneca, Nemaha County, Kansas, the posse learned that the party of four horse thieves — Melvin E. Baughn, Zack Mooney, and men named Strange and Jackson — were less than an hour ahead of them. They obtained a Kansas warrant and continued on their trail. Jackson and Strange were captured less than a mile east of Seneca and taken to Doniphan County, examined and released when it was proven that their string of horses did not include the stolen stock. Three deputies from Doniphan County, Missouri, then continued on the trail of Baughn and Mooney and, carrying arrest warrants for the two fugitive horse thieves, arrived in Seneca on November 19, 1866. Sheriff William Boulton organized a posse and sent scouts out in all directions to search for clues; one party of scouts learned the whereabouts of Baughn and Mooney, and the posse pursued them for fifteen miles. The advance party of three men — Charles Ingram, Henry Hillix, and Jesse Dennis — went out on the road to Capioma and soon overtook Baughn and Mooney. As the deputies rode up to the men their intentions were known, and the two wanted men opened fire on the three lawmen. In the exchange of gunfire Dennis was shot in the back and died within minutes, Hillix was seriously wounded but survived, and Ingram was uninjured. Bullets also fractured Baughn's right arm and Mooney's right leg but they still managed to escape. Ingram could not pursue the horse thieves alone so he returned to Seneca with the injured Hillix and the body of Dennis.

On January 6, 1867, Baughn was arrested at Leavenworth, Kansas, but one month later he made his escape and then, with several others, robbed the store of a Mr. Craig in Wathena to get a stake of $800. He remained free for fifteen months, and during that time he went to St. Louis where he spent his share of the plunder. In May 1868, now penniless once again, Baughn went to Sedalia, Missouri, where he had a valise in storage under the alias Joe King. After confirming the valise was still there he left without paying the fee, and this raised suspicion. The clerk left the window ajar and waited, and after dark Baughn appeared. When he tried to enter through the window the clerk shot him, the bullet taking off a finger and glancing off his skull, but he still managed to escape. Baughn was arrested two days later and lodged in the jail at Warrensburg, Missouri, and on June 25, 1868, Nemaha County Sheriff A. Kyger arrived to identify the prisoner. Baughn insisted his name was Bigger but the prisoner perfectly matched Baughn's description, which had been widely circulated, and he was extradited to Seneca. There he was positively identified as Baughn and charged with the murder of Dennis.

The prisoner had been afraid he would be lynched but the sheriff assured him he would protect his prisoner from a lynch mob at the cost of his own life, and he had at least one opportunity to keep his promise. Mooney eluded capture for some time but was later lynched for stealing horses, rather than for the murder of Dennis. A special term of the district court convened during the first week of August and Baughn was taken into Judge R. S. Graham's courtroom for trial. Following the presentation of evidence the jury deliberated briefly before returning a verdict of guilty of first degree murder, and on August 7 Baughn was sentenced to hang on September 18, 1868. Neither appeal nor application for clemency delayed the fatal day.

During the time Baughn awaited the day of his execution he was visited frequently by the Revs.

W. C. Stewart and Gray, and they helped him resign himself to his fate. On the final evening the two clergymen visited and prayed with the prisoner until he retired at midnight. On his final morning Baughn arose at an early hour and ate a light breakfast, as his appetite failed him for the first time. He then dressed in his burial suit — black alpaca, pleated bosom shirt, and slippers. He had requested that his body be taken to Doniphan County for burial, and a friend had arrived to handle the matter.

The gallows had been built on the south side of the Nemaha County jail within the jail yard and close to the jail door within a tall canvas stretched over a wooden framework. Outside a rope barricade had been installed and this was guarded by fifteen armed men determined to keep the one hundred spectators from rushing in, as only those with invitations were permitted to witness the execution. At 3:00 P.M. the witnesses were admitted, including several prominent citizens, officers of the court, two physicians, the Reverends Stewart and Gray, and newspaper reporters.

At 3:10 P.M. the condemned man was marched out of the jail by the sheriff, and when he appeared he said, "It's rather rough." He then handed two hand-written communications to the Reverend Stewart and was escorted onto the platform. The Reverend Stewart followed, and after Baughn was seated the reverend offered a prayer; then the prisoner shook hands with everyone on the platform. The condemned man was positioned on the trapdoor and his limbs were pinioned, the noose was adjusted, and the black cap was placed on his head but not pulled down. He was then given the opportunity to speak to the witnesses, and he said, "I believe it is customary for persons in my position to have something to say. With me it is different. I have nothing. I have been arraigned, tried, convicted, and I am here to suffer the penalty of the law. That is all." The death warrant was then read and the cap was pulled over his head. The sheriff announced, "Melvin Baughn, you have just five minutes to live," and this warning was repeated at two and one-half minutes and at one minute. At 3:18 P.M. the rope restraining the trapdoor was cut and the trap was sprung. Baughn dropped but his neck was not broken in the fall and he strangled to death, though his struggles were slight. The attending physicians monitored his vital signs and found that in seven minutes his pulse ceased and in two more minutes his heart stopped beating. After the attending physicians pronounced him dead Baughn's remains continued to hang for eighteen minutes before being cut down. His wrists were untied before the body was lowered into a coffin, taken into the jail, and propped up for display. Many curious citizens filed through to view the remains of Melvin Baughn, and the following day the body was released to his friend to be taken to Missouri for burial.

Sources: Gray, P. L. *Gray's Doniphan County History: A Record of the Happenings of Half a Hundred Years*. Bendena, KS: The Roycroft Press, 1905. *Leavenworth Times and Conservative* (KS): September 24, 1868.

Dickson, William
August 9, 1870

In March 1870 William Dickson was arrested for the murder of Jacob Burnett, a Jewish peddler from Leavenworth, Kansas. Dickson was found with Burnett's watch in his possession after Burnett's body was found on the road to Delaware City. The murder was a particularly atrocious one, as Burnett had been shot five times and stripped of all his money and valuables. Dickson had been released from prison on March 7, destitute after serving a three-year sentence, and three days later killed Burnett. The evidence was circumstantial but strong enough to hold Dickson for trial at his March 19 examination before Judge Rees. The community was outraged, and there was talk of a lynching, but cooler heads prevailed and it ended with talk. The trial commenced on June 13 and lasted four days. After the case went to the jury they were out only fifteen minutes, just long enough for one vote, before returning a verdict of guilty of first degree murder. On June 19 Dickson was sentenced to hang on August 9, 1870. Neither appeal nor application for executive clemency delayed the proceedings.

The county had an old gallows, which had been stored since 1863, and this was taken out and refurbished. It was erected in the northwest corner of the jail yard, a rather small area making the privacy requirement difficult to comply with. There were vantage points all about the city and thousands took up positions where they could watch the execution, including many "boys and girls of tender age." Sheriff McFarland had invited a large number of witnesses but still hundreds of the uninvited clamored for admission. At 11:45 A.M. the condemned man was taken from his cell and marched out of the jail and onto the scaffold. He was positioned on the trapdoor, and his wrists and arms, knees and ankles were pinioned, the noose was adjusted, and the black cap was pulled over his head. A few minutes after noon the trap was sprung and Dickson dropped, breaking his neck. Attending physicians monitored his vital signs and after pronouncing him dead the remains were cut down and deposited in the coffin provided by the county. The coffin was put in a wagon and driven to the cemetery where Dickson was buried, without ceremony, in an obscure grave.

Sources: *Leavenworth Daily Commercial* (KS): March 11, 1870; March 13, 1870; March 19, 1870; June 14–17, 1870; August 5, 1870, August 9–10, 1870. *Leavenworth Times and Conservative* (KS): March 11, 1870; March 13, 1870; March 19, 1870; June 14–17, 1870; August 9–10, 1870.

Mosier, Lee
November 15, 1887

On October 27, 1886, Hugh B. Lawler was driving Lee Mosier, a mentally challenged twenty-year-old, and a youth named Robert Arner into Kansas from Anthony, Indian Territory. Mosier was sitting in the bed of the wagon, and Arner was on the seat next to Lawler. After traveling thirty miles, as dusk was approaching and the men were preparing to stop for the night, Mosier suddenly raised a double-barreled shotgun, put the muzzle near the back of Lawler's head, and fired one barrel of heavy shot. The blast took off the entire top of Lawler's head, killing him instantly, and then Mosier turned the gun on Arner but the boy talked him out of firing the second barrel upon his promise of secrecy. Mosier kept the wagon and team but allowed Arner to leave, and the boy hurried home to sound the alarm. A posse was organized, and Mosier was captured in Harper County the following day. The prisoner was taken to Sedgwick and lodged in the county jail. At his examination he was held over for the term of federal court scheduled to convene in Wichita in September 1887. As his defense he claimed that he had been hired by Mrs. Lawler to kill her husband, but there was no corroborative proof, and she was never charged in the murder. The trial of Mosier commenced in the federal court in early September and concluded on September 15. Mosier pled guilty, but testimony was taken for the record, and the case went to the jury, which in minutes returned a verdict of guilty of first-degree murder. Even though Kansas had abolished the death penalty fifteen years earlier, the federal death penalty still applied, and Mosier was sentenced to hang on November 15, 1887. Neither appeal nor application for clemency from the president delayed the execution.

The gallows was built on the west side of the Sedgwick County jail within a thirty-foot-square enclosure consisting of a high board fence. On the fateful day Mosier was provided brandy to help him brace up for the ordeal, and he consumed a pint. He walked from the sheriff's office into the enclosure after 9:00 A.M. and took his place on the trapdoor, facing the fifty-four witnesses the sheriff had invited. Outside a large crowd had gathered and, though they were not rowdy, several of the bolder men had loosened boards to peek through. His wrists and arms, knees and ankles were strapped, the noose was adjusted with the knot behind his left ear, and the black cap was pulled over his head at 9:32 A.M. In a moment the trap was sprung and Mosier dropped, breaking his neck. Attending physicians beneath the scaffold monitored his vital signs and pronounced him dead at 9:53 A.M. After hanging a bit longer Mosier's remains were cut down, placed in the wooden coffin provided by the government, taken to the Sedgwick cemetery, and buried in Potter's Field that evening.

Sources: *Atchison Daily Globe* (KS): November 15, 1887. *Daily Beacon* (Wichita, KS): September 6, 1887; September 15–16, 1887; November 15, 1887. *Times* (Kansas City, MO): November 16, 1887. *Morning Eagle* (Wichita, KS): September 16–17, 1887, November 16, 1887. *Xenia Daily Gazette* (OH): November 16, 1887.

Tobler, Jake
Tobler, Joe
November 21, 1888

During the early days of August 1885 Frank Cass and A.P. Goodykountz, two prominent merchants from Vinita, Indian Territory, started on their way through Texas toward home. They were near the Sac & Fox Agency in the Indian Territory when they set up camp on August 16. Jake and Joe Tobler, black brothers aged twenty-three and twenty-one respectively, arrived at the same place at a late hour and camped nearby.

During the night the Toblers arose and crept up on the two sleeping merchants, and each man shot one of the sleeping figures, killing each instantly. The Toblers took their team of horses and wagon, then stripped the bodies of four dollars, a gold watch and a ring before they drove to their uncle's home. The bodies were found and identified by a brother of one murder victim, and then a half-breed came forward and said he had been nearby, heard the shots, and saw the two murderers ride off. A posse of seven men was soon on the trail of the murderers, and on August 19 the Toblers were arrested for murder; both prisoners immediately confessed to the posse men. They were taken to Wichita and lodged in jail to await action by the grand jury. Both prisoners were indicted, and Jake's trial commenced on September 5. There was considerable argument from the defense to exclude his confession but it was admitted and, along with the testimony of the half-breed and his possession of the stolen property when arrested, his fate was sealed. The jury only deliberated for fifteen minutes before returning a verdict of guilty as charged in the indictment—first-degree murder. The following day the trial of Joe Tobler commenced and concluded, with the same result except that the jury only took seven minutes to reach a conclusion. Appeals and applications for executive clemency delayed the executions for several years but finally the Toblers were sentenced to hang on November 21, 1888, the same day Thomas Thurber was sentenced to hang. Both men were first held in the old jail but soon they were moved to the new jail where they shared cells with Thurber and a man named Frazier. Both condemned men were model prisoners, never giving jailer Ed Darnell any trouble.

On the night before the execution the scaffold was tested at 10:00 P.M. and worked perfectly. The execution was scheduled between 9:00 A.M. and noon. Even before the earlier hour parties with the necessary credentials were touching the electric bell at the jail entrance, and by 9:00 A.M. most of the witnesses were present. The crowd of eighty-four consisted of deputy marshals, doctors in the interest of science, newspaper representatives, and the Reverend Gates of the First M. E. Church assisted by Mr. and Mrs. Cole and Mr. Harper, a ministerial student. The witnesses moved around the jail in a quiet manner talking in a low tone as there was concern that the condemned man would break down. There was interest in how the prisoners had spent the night, and the jailer answered that they had been rather nervous; scarcely sleeping an hour after 3:30 A.M., they played cards, ate peanuts, and drank spirits. Shortly after 9:00 A.M. Mr. and Mrs. Cole and Mr. Harper gained admittance to the prisoners' cell where they sang hymns and offered prayers. The prisoners put on a sober face and at the close they seemed concerned, but they were joking each other about their bravery, each wanting to bet that the other would make a "fool" of himself. They lighted cigars and walked nervously about the cell and called for stimulants, which were given, and were asked if they wanted to see the other prisoners. They said yes and in charge of Sheriff Hays and Deputy Metcalf went into another department to say good-bye. As they passed by the cells they were met with ready hands and asked, "How are you, Joe and Jake; do you think you can stand it?" and the answer was usually "Yes, oh yes! We ain't scared." They returned to their cells where the time went slowly by, and at times an awkward silence prevailed.

Charles Howard of Topeka was in charge of the execution, and he was assisted by Joe McClellan, sheriff of Kingman County; W. A. Jarrett of Caldwell; Jack Stillwell of the Indian Territory; Deputies H. Metcalf and Henry Dillard of Topeka. The death trap had been built in the main corridor of the jail by Mr. Wagoner of Wichita, and the gallows was designed after an improved plan, resting upon the gallery running around the corridor twelve feet above the jail floor. The trapdoor separated in the center by means of a toggle joint which could be sprung easily by a lever, positioned a few feet to the rear, and the ropes ran through two iron rings imbedded in the ceiling. At 10:18 A.M. deputy Howard beckoned for the jailer to open the door leading to the cell of the doomed men, and he was accompanied by Jarrett and McClellan. The prisoners stepped into the hall where they were informed by Howard that the hour of execution was at hand; it was his duty to read the death warrant and see that they be executed according to law. As the officer read the warrant Jake drooped his head and fanned himself with his hat. Joe turned his face upward toward the heavy iron rings. When deputy Howard read, "And you shall be hanged by the neck until dead," his voice faltered and the deputies seemed more touched at that moment than at any other time. After Howard concluded they were given another stimulant, their wrists were bound, and they started for the scaffold with Mr. and Mrs. Cole and Mr. Harper leading the way up the stairway. The brothers were followed by Dillard and Metcalf, and behind them were Stillwell and McClellan. At the scaffold the prisoners and deputies stepped upon the platform. Their arms and knees were pinioned, and as Stillwell was strapping Joe's knees he indicated he wanted his shoes removed. In a moment they were off. This caused Jake to think of making similar preparations so Metcalf relieved him of his boots. The brothers were then positioned over the center of the trapdoor and the deputies pinioned their ankles. Mrs. Cole then delivered a prayer on behalf of their souls, "so near eternity," and she prayed in a most fervent manner. Jake seemed unconcerned over the situation and looked as stolid, impudent and daring as ever but Joe's eyes became moist, his lips trembled, and he began to show evidence of weakening and seemed to fear a breakdown, so he looked back at Stillwell, who advanced and was told to "stop that woman." The deputy whispered to Mr. Cole who conveyed the desires of the prisoner to his wife and a minute later she announced "Amen!" Howard said, "Now, boys, if you have anything to say you can do so now," but the answer from Jake, in a gruff and positive manner, was "No!" This was followed by Joe who, in a more subdued tone, replied, "No." The deputies drew the black hoods from their pockets and as they were being pulled on Joe, in a low tone, said "Good-bye." The nooses were next and the deputies quickly had them in place. The prisoners again simultaneously said, "Good-bye," and worked their hands as though they wanted some one to clasp them, so the deputies shook them by the hands and stepped back. Stillwell went to the lever, and McClellan had his hand on the key and stood poised until they were beckoned by Howard to go ahead. The locking key was removed, the lever pulled, and the trap was sprung at 10:25 A.M. The drop was four and one-half feet. Jake never moved a muscle, being dead from a broken neck a moment after the drop, while Joe at the end of fifty seconds drew his shoulders slightly forward and during the second minute drew up his legs twice. At the end of the sixth minute County Physician Rentz pronounced both men dead, but they were allowed to hang fifteen minutes. A few of the spectators left before they were cut down and placed in their coffins. At the undertaker's parlor they were viewed by hundreds of people and then the bodies were turned over to the Wichita Medical Society.

Sources: *Atchison Daily Globe* (Kansas): November 22, 1888. *Daily Beacon* (Wichita, KS): September 3–7, 1888; September 17, 1888; November 21, 1888. *Morning Eagle* (Wichita, KS): September 5–7, 1888; September 16, 1888; September 21–22, 1888; November 21, 1888.

Panzram, Carl
September 5, 1930

Carl Panzram was born in 1891 on a desolate farm in northern Minnesota. In 1898 his father abandoned the family and he became "incorrigible," and as a result he was sent to the Minnesota State Training School in 1903, a reform institution for juveniles where he experienced sexual abuse and beatings. After two years Lizzie Panzram took her son home, and he was relegated to working the fields, but soon he hopped a freight train and began wandering across the Midwest.

Over the next two decades Panzram would commit burglaries, robberies, sexual assaults, and murders in a dozen states and serve several terms in prisons. He would manage to escape from a half dozen jails and use many aliases to avoid capture for his previous offenses. In October 1923 Panzram arrived at the Dannemora Prison just ten miles from the Canadian border. He made his first attempt at escape within a few months by climbing one of the prison walls but fell thirty feet onto a concrete step and broke both legs and ankles, and his spine was also badly injured. He received no medical attention for his injuries and was carried into a cell and dropped on the floor. In July 1928, after serving five hard years, Panzram, now somewhat crippled and more angry than ever, was discharged from Dannemora. Within two weeks he committed a dozen burglaries and killed at least one man during a robbery, was arrested, and at his booking gave his real name for the first time in years.

During his first few days in the Washington, D.C., jail he made several remarks about killing children, so inquiries were made in other states, and word came back that he was a hunted man. Panzram was determined to escape so he chipped away at the concrete surrounding the metal bars in his cell window, but one of the other prisoners informed on him. Panzram was removed from his cell, brought to an isolated area, and handcuffed around a thick wooden pole, and a rope was tied to the handcuffs. He was hoisted up until only his toes touched the ground, and he was left this way for a day and a half. During the night Panzram admitted to the murders of several young boys. Panzram confessed to the murder of fourteen-year-old Alexander Luszzock, a Philadelphia newsboy murdered the previous August, and also that of twelve-year-old Henry McMahon of New Salem, Connecticut. Each day that went by Panzram told more but rookie guard Henry Lesser took pity on the prisoner, treated him kindly, and got Panzram to agree to write his life story. In this extraordinary twenty-thousand word confession Panzram gave details of twenty-two murders, all of which were later confirmed. He supplied dates, times and the places where the crimes occurred as well as his arrest history spanning several continents.

His trial for the burglary and housebreaking opened on November 12, 1928, with Panzram acting as his own attorney. Panzram took the stand in his defense but not only admitted the burglary but told the court that he had remained in the house for several hours hoping the owners would return so he could kill them. He was found guilty on all counts, and Judge Walter McCoy sentenced him to serve fifteen years on the first count and ten years on the second count, to run consecutively at the federal prison in Leavenworth, Kansas.

Panzram, facing a term of twenty-five years, arrived at the prison on February 1, 1929, and was taken to see Warden T. B. White. As the warden read the rules of the institution Panzram stood quietly and when the warden finished the prisoner said, "I'll kill the first man that bothers me." Panzram was assigned to the laundry room where he could work all day alone, sorting and washing inmate clothes. His supervisor was Robert Warnke, a small, balding man who was notorious for writing up prisoners for minor infractions and enjoyed using his supervisory position to wield power. Panzram had trouble with Warnke, which caused him to be sent to a solitary cell several times. On June 20, 1929, Panzram was working in the laundry at his usual detail. Leaning against the door was a four-foot long iron bar used as a support for the wooden transport crates. Without a word he picked up the heavy bar and approached Warnke, who was preparing paperwork. Panzram raised the bar high over his broad shoulders and brought it down squarely on the man's head, and Warnke's skull broke instantly. He screamed, "Here's another one for you, you son of a bitch!" and continued to smash the bar onto the man's head, sending blood, brains, and skull bone all over the room. There were other inmates in the laundry that day so Panzram decided that he should kill the others as well. He chased them around the room, shouting, cursing, swinging the huge iron bar, smashing bones, desks, lights, breaking up the furniture into pieces and sending the terrified inmates crawling up the walls to get away from the raging madman. A general alarm sounded in the prison and dozens of guards armed with submachine guns and high-powered rifles came running to the laundry. The guards looked through the bars into the room where Panzram stood holding the twenty-pound steel bar like a baseball bat, his clothes shredded and covered from head to toe with fresh blood, and he told them, "I just killed Warnke." The guards opened the door and Panzram walked quietly to his cell and sat down on his bunk.

Panzram's trial for Warnke's murder commenced in Judge Hopkins' courtroom on April 14, 1930, at 9:30 A.M., and Panzram remained defiant and uncooperative. When asked if he had an attorney he replied, "No, and I don't want one!" When asked for a plea he stood and sneered at the court, "I plead not guilty! Now you go ahead and prove me guilty, understand?" The prosecutor called a parade of witnesses including Warden White, five Leavenworth guards, and ten prisoners who testified they saw Panzram smash the skull of his helpless victim with an iron bar while Warnke lay unconscious on the floor. The jury took just forty-five minutes to arrive at a verdict and found the defendant guilty of murder with no recommendation for mercy. Judge Hopkins remanded him back to Leavenworth until "the fifth day of September, nineteen thirty, when between the hours of six to nine o'clock in the morning you shall be taken to some suitable place within the confines of the penitentiary and hanged by the neck until dead." Panzram told the judge, "I certainly want to thank you, judge, just let me get my fingers around your neck for sixty seconds and you'll never sit on another bench as judge!" U.S. marshals then dragged him out of the courtroom.

On the morning of April 15, 1930, a meeting was arranged between Panzram and Dr. Karl

Menninger, a Harvard graduate and one of the pioneers of modern psychology. Panzram was brought into the room at 8:30 A.M. where the doctor said good morning and Panzram replied, "I want to be hanged and I don't want any interference by you or your filthy kind. I just know the more about the world and the essential evil nature of man and don't play the hypocrite. I am proud of having killed off a few and regret that I didn't kill more! I am saying I am responsible and I am guilty and the sooner they hang me the better it will be and gladder I will be. So don't you go trying to interfere with it!" Panzram was then returned to his cell. For Panzram the death sentence seemed a relief, and he resisted all attempts to have a stay of execution granted. On May 30 Panzram wrote to President Herbert Hoover, emphasizing that he was "perfectly satisfied with my trial and the sentence. I do not want another trial. I absolutely refuse to accept either a pardon or a commutation should either or the other be offered to me."

On his final night he was restless and paced his cell until daybreak. In the morning the death warrant was read to him, his wrists and arms were bound, and at 5:55 A.M. he was escorted to the gallows. A handful of newspapermen and a dozen guards acted as witnesses. As soon as he appeared in the prison yard he began cursing his mother for bringing him into this world and cursed "the whole damned human race!" He was escorted by two deputy U.S. marshals as he walked briskly to the wooden scaffold and climbed the thirteen stairs onto the platform. The deputies attempted to place a black hood over his head but before they could complete their task Panzram spit in the executioner's face and said, "Hurry up you bastard, I could kill ten men while you're fooling around!" After the hood was secured the deputies stepped back, and at exactly 6:03 A.M. the trap was sprung. Panzram dropped five and a half feet, and his body jerked repeatedly and swung from side to side. Dr. Justin K. Fuller monitored his vital signs and pronounced him dead at 6:18 A.M. The *Sunday Star* later reported, "A hangman's noose at Leavenworth, Kansas, this morning snuffed out the life of Carl Panzram, a man who swore he hated all humanity with a consuming passion.... [H]e was the most criminally minded man in America." After the body was removed from the gallows an autopsy was performed at the prison hospital, and later that same day he was carted over to the prison cemetery in a wheelbarrow, buried on row No. 6, grave No. 24, and the only identification on his tombstone was number "31614."

Sources: *Chicago Evening American* (IL): April 16. 1930. *Washington Post* (D.C.): October 28, 1928.

Applegate, Glen
Suhay, Robert J.
August 12, 1938

In early 1937 Glen Applegate and Robert J. Suhay were paroled from the Great Meadows prison in Comstock, New York. They went to New York City and in March stole a car and drove to Ketonah, New York, where, with another man, they robbed the Northern Westchester bank of $18,300 and fled west.

Federal Bureau of Investigation (F.B.I.) agents investigating the robbery, the second at that bank in two weeks, knew the men who had committed the crime and learned that a package had been sent to Suhay at general delivery in Topeka, Kansas. Three agents set a trap to capture the bank robbers when they came to pick up the package, and one of the agents was Wimberly W. Baker. Twenty-seven-year-old Baker was new to the force, and this was his first big case. The three agents spent three days staked out in key positions in the post office waiting for the clerk to give the signal, and finally, just before noon on April 16, Applegate appeared at the general delivery window. It was Baker's turn in the key position so he walked up to Applegate and told him to raise his hands, but Suhay had stayed back to keep watch, and he came up behind Baker and shot him in the back with one bullet from his automatic pistol. When Baker was spun about Suhay shot him in the chest, and in the excitement that followed he shot Baker twice in the legs as they started to flee. When Baker collapsed to the floor the other two agents took up the chase. In the gun battle that followed more than twenty shots were exchanged, and Suhay was wounded in the left wrist while bystander O. D. Davis, who was writing at one of the lobby tables, was shot in the foot.

The two fugitives escaped and drove to Sabetha, Kansas, where they wrecked their car and then telephoned Dr. Sam Hibbard from a farmhouse a few miles north of town. Hibbard went to the farmhouse and was confronted by two armed desperadoes, who forced the physician to drive them into Sabetha in his own automobile and go to his office, where he bandaged Suhay's arm wound. Applegate and Suhay then forced Dr. Hibbard to drive them several miles north of Sabetha, ejected him from the car, and continued their flight northward toward Lincoln, Nebraska. Frank Stone, Jr., assistant director of the Kansas Highway Patrol said, "The strongest guard on the highways we've ever had was organized for the pursuit," and later that evening the two fugitives were captured without resistance at Plattsmouth, Nebraska, by Sheriff Homer Sylvester. Suhay gave his true name but Applegate claimed to be Alfred Power when arrested. Their black coupe, bearing New York license plates, was found wrecked in a ditch near the farmhouse where they had captured the doctor, and a wrecker was dispatched to impound the automobile. Dwight Brantley, in charge of the Kansas City division of the F.B.I., said Dr. Hibbard led officers to $6,954.15 after the fugitives gave the doctor the key to their hotel room and said there was a lot of money, and he could have it; and when arrested the two men had $11,000 concealed in their clothing, constituting nearly all the loot taken from the New York bank.

Meanwhile agent Baker had been rushed to the hospital where Dr. C. E. Joss removed the bullets but reported that Baker's bowels had been perforated; his condition was pronounced critical. His recovery was said to be doubtful, but agents stood by to donate blood. Two days later, on April 18, Baker died of his wounds, and the following day the two prisoners, though they admitted to the shooting, pled not guilty to a murder charge. United States Attorney S. S. Alexander said there would be a prompt indictment for murder before the federal grand jury in June, and he said the death penalty would be demanded.

On June 3 the two defendants pled not guilty before Judge Richard J. Hopkins, and their trial began the following day. Suhay had confessed to the shooting, and his written statement was introduced at trial. F.B.I. ballistics experts testified it was his gun which fired the fatal bullets. Applegate's written confession was also introduced but his statement, that he had bought an automatic pistol "for the express of shooting it out with any officer who attempted to arrest him," had been redacted when he objected. The defense did not produce a single witness but claimed that the two fugitives thought they were being held up and shot the agent in self-defense, and they relied upon evidence of who fired the first shot as their entire case. The case went to the jury on June 25, and they deliberated only three hours and twenty-five minutes before returning a verdict of guilty of first-degree murder, but they withheld a recommendation for mercy. Judge Hopkins ordered the two convicted murderers to return on June 29, when they were sentenced to hang at the federal penitentiary at Leavenworth, but they appealed their conviction, which stayed the execution for a year. Their appeals from the death sentence were confirmed by the United States Circuit Court and the United States Supreme Court and finally, after all legal efforts were exhausted on June 10, 1938, Applegate and Suhay were resentenced to hang between 3:00 and 8:00 A.M. on August 12, 1938. Applegate, when he heard the sentence, told a prison guard, "That's a good break; that's good luck. It could have been Friday the 13th." All that remained was the application to President Franklin D. Roosevelt praying for executive clemency, but this was denied.

Both men shunned religious counseling during their stay in prison. On their final night the two condemned men ate a plain prison dinner and then sprawled on their cots to read detective story magazines until the lights were turned out. They were aroused before 3:00 A.M. but the twenty-seven witnesses, including Baker's father and younger brother, had already been admitted to the moonlit prison yard near the double gallows for some time. The warden appeared at their cells, and the two men were escorted into the yard where they climbed the thirteen steps onto the platform. Forty-five-year-old Applegate continued to show indifference but twenty-six-year-old Suhay gritted his teeth and would not speak, for fear he might weaken. Once they were upon the trapdoor the prison chaplain tried to speak with them but Applegate said, "You'll have to go a Hell of a long way to visit with me." Their limbs were strapped and the nooses adjusted when Applegate turned to Suhay and said, "Let's shake and go together," but he was ignored. Suhay declined to speak to the witnesses but Applegate said to the persistent chaplain, "You can't do me any good; all of my friends are in Hell." Deputy U.S. Marshal Ray Buschausen appeared with the death warrant, and Applegate said, "The scaffold can't be too high nor the time too quick for me." The death warrant was read and immediately afterward the black caps were pulled over their heads and the trap was sprung. Both men dropped, breaking their necks, and after the prison physician pronounced them dead they were cut down and lowered into their coffins. The remains were later taken to a crematorium and the ashes shipped to relatives.

Sources: *Daily Capital News* (Jefferson City, MO): June 24, 1937; June 26, 1937. *Lincoln State Journal* (NE): June 25, 1937. *The Abilene Reporter-News* (KS): August 11, 1938. *The Dallas Morning News* (TX): April 17–19, 1937; June 11, 1938. *The Hutchinson News* (KS): December 30, 1937; May 31, 1938. *The Lowell Sun* (MA): August 12, 1938. *Waterloo Daily Courier* (IA): August 12, 1938.

Brandon, Levi
July 26, 1943

In 1942 twenty-three-year-old Private First Class Levi Brandon was attached to the service detachment of the command and general staff school at Fort Leavenworth, Kansas. On New Year's morning 1943 Brandon, emboldened by an assault to commit rape in Kansas City for which he had not been arrested, raped and murdered a seventeen-year-old waitress in Leavenworth, Kansas. He was soon arrested and charged with both offenses. At his general court-martial on February 8 he was found guilty, the case was reviewed and approved by higher authority, and on June 26 the sentence of death was confirmed by presidential order. The date for Brandon's execution was set for one month hence, and he was held in the disciplinary barracks at Fort Leavenworth, known as "the Castle." After 2:30 A.M. on his final morning the commandant appeared at his cell and read the order for execution. The prisoner was then taken out and escorted into the prison yard where he mounted the gallows with a firm step and took his place on the trapdoor. He declined to speak to the two dozen witnesses, including a chaplain who prayed for him as he was prepared by having his wrists and arms, knees and ankles strapped, the noose adjusted, and the black cap pulled over his head. In but a moment the trap was sprung and he fell, breaking his neck. An Army doctor was in attendance to pronounce him dead, and, after he had hung a sufficient time to ensure he could not be revived, he was cut down and deposited in his coffin. His remains were turned over to his family in Kansas City, Kansas, for burial.

Sources: *Globe Gazette* (Mason City, IA): July 26, 1943. *Oakland Tribune* (CA): July 26, 1943. *The Brainerd Daily Dispatch* (MN): July 26, 1943.

Hoefgen, Ernest
March 10, 1944

On September 18, 1943, thirty-one-year-old Ernest Hoefgen stopped to pick up a hitchhiker near Peabody, Kansas. After driving a short distance Hoefgen felt that his passenger, eighteen-year-old Kansas State University student Bruce Smoll, had become suspicious of his intentions so he quickly drove into a cornfield and shot Smoll to death before robbing him. In December Hoefgen was arrested with his wife Pauline, but she was absolved of any part in the slaying when her husband, on December 26, confessed to the killing. He was held over for the grand jury, indicted, and tried at the spring term of the court. Hoefgen was found guilty of first-degree murder and sentenced to hang on March 10, 1944, and neither appeal nor application for executive clemency would delay the proceedings.

After Hoefgen was arrested his wife, whom he said he loved dearly, abandoned him, and three days before he was hanged he was served with divorce papers. The prisoner was consoled and received religious counseling from Chaplain T. F. Rudisill, and he had resigned himself to his fate so on his final day he was able to eat two hearty meals of fried chicken and finished with a supper of steak and fried onions. Just before 1:00 A.M. Warden Robert Hudspeth appeared at the door to death cell No. 2, one of four death cells, and said, "This is the time," and Hoefgen replied, "Okay." Hudspeth then read the death warrant before the prisoner was marched across a narrow prison street into the old brick warehouse where Chaplain Rudisill, who accompanied him, retired at the foot of the thirteen stairs of the newly constructed gallows. The prisoner told the warden, "I'm sorry I couldn't give my life for my country and that I have to go out this way. I love my wife," and then he climbed the stairs and took his place on the trapdoor. His wrists and arms, knees and ankles were strapped, the noose was adjusted, and a blindfold was tied over his eyes. The trap was sprung by an anonymous out-of-state executioner at 1:01 A.M., and fifteen minutes later he was pronounced dead. The warden said the body would be held for two days, pending a requisition for it, but then would be buried in the Mount Muncie cemetery where the prison had a small plot.

Sources: *Jefferson City Post-Tribune* (MO): March 10, 1944. *The Abilene Reporter-News* (KS): December 27, 1943. *The Troy Record* (NY): March 11, 1944.

Brady, Fred L.
Knox, Clark B.
April 15, 1944

On January 9, 1943, forty-five-year-old Fred L. Brady tried to rob Joe Williams at gun point but, after shooting and killing Williams, Brady fled without taking the $1,700 Williams had in his pockets. Brady was quickly captured at Winfield, Kansas, and when taken before Judge Stewart S. Bloss he pled guilty. Then on January 13, to his surprise, he was sentenced to hang on March 20. Appeals stayed the execution, and the matter continued under review until all avenues of relief were exhausted in March 1944. Then his date of execution was set for April 15, and he was lodged in one of the four death row cells at the state prison in Lansing. In early February 1944 Governor Andrew Schoeppel rejected a final effort to save Brady's life and ordered the execution to proceed.

On August 2, 1943, Kansas City Police Officer Edward F. Nugent was on his way home when he was stopped by a woman on Seventh Street and Washington Boulevard, and she reported that while she was waiting for a bus a man ordered her into a dark alley. The man said he would shoot her if she cried out, and she got as far as the alley entrance when she suddenly turned and ran into the street, right in front of Nugent's car. After relating the details the woman got into Nugent's car and they drove around the area until she saw the man walking on Seventh Street. The man was detained and searched by the officer, but Nugent failed to find a nickel-plated .38-caliber revolver with a two-inch barrel. Nugent flagged a car and asked for help, and one man volunteered, so they got into Nugent's car with the volunteer behind the officer and the suspect seated behind the woman. Nugent started for the police station but suddenly the suspect drew the revolver, put the barrel an inch from Nugents' head, and fired once, killing him instantly. The volunteer then wrestled the weapon from the suspect's grip, but the out-of-control car ran over a curb and during the confusion the suspect escaped through an open window. Forty minutes later Clark B. Knox was arrested two blocks from the murder scene. Paraffin tests proved he had recently fired a gun, he was identified as the shooter, and he was jailed on a charge of murder. Knox was tried and found guilty of first-degree murder and sentenced to hang at the prison in Lansing. Appeals followed but were quickly adjudicated, and on February 15, 1944, Governor Andrew Schoeppel decided the execution should proceed. The final effort to save Knox's life was a claim of insanity, so on March 31 the governor empanelled a committee of doctors to consider the matter but they found him sane.

Both convicted murderers were scheduled to die on April 15, and it was decided that Brady would go first, shortly after midnight, while Knox would follow at sundown. Brady was attended by Father P. Delahunty, prison chaplain, during his final days, and the priest was with him that last night. At 1:00 A.M. Warden Robert M. Hudspeth appeared at the door to Brady's death row cell and read the death warrant to the prisoner. He was then taken out and escorted across the narrow prison street to the old brick warehouse where the gallows had been erected a month earlier for the execution of Ernest Hoefgen. The prisoner climbed the thirteen stairs and took his place on the trapdoor but, being a hardened career criminal with four previous prison sentences, he refused to speak to the witnesses. His wrists and arms, knees and ankles were bound, the noose was adjusted, and a blindfold was tied over his eyes. At 1:17 A.M. the trap was sprung by an out-of-state executioner, and Brady was pronounced dead in fifteen minutes. The body was then cut down and placed in the coffin provided by the state. There was no requisition for the remains so he was buried in the prison plot of the Mount Muncie cemetery.

The gallows was then prepared for the execution of Knox who had, as a last request, asked for "soda pop and a candy bar"; these were provided, and then he asked for gum. When Warden Hudspeth appeared at his cell door at 7:00 P.M. he was vigorously chewing his gum and would continue until standing on the trapdoor. The death warrant was read to him, and then he was escorted across the narrow prison street into the old brick warehouse where the same procedures were conducted as for Brady eighteen hours earlier. Knox declined to speak to the witnesses so the trap was sprung at 7:30 P.M., and he was pronounced dead fifteen minutes later. The body was cut down, placed in the coffin provided, and the remains were turned over to the sister of the deceased for burial.

Sources: *Joplin Globe* (MO): March 31, 1944. *Lincoln Sunday Journal and Star* (NE): April 16, 1944. *Rapids Daily Tribune* (WI): April 15, 1944. *San Antonio Express* (TX):

January 14, 1943. *The Abilene Reporter-News* (KS): April 16, 1944. *The Brainerd Daily Dispatch* (MN): April 14, 1944. *The Hutchinson News-Herald* (KS): January 22, 1943; May 9, 1943; February 15, 1944.

Richie, Alfred B.
April 21, 1945

In late June 1944 Corporal Peter De Fusco, assigned to Camp Phillips in Kansas, was making plans for a furlough to his hometown of Uniontown, Pennsylvania. He withdrew $1,100 he had saved and was planning to leave on June 28. On the evening of June 27 he was seen walking with his friend, twenty-six-year-old Sergeant Alfred B. Richie, about five hundred yards from their barracks, and that was the last time De Fusco was seen alive. De Fusco's dead body was discovered concealed beneath a hedge near the infantry area of the camp, covered with grass; his head had been crushed, and his pockets were empty. While the investigation was under way De Fusco's remains were shipped to Uniontown with Sgt. Richie as his honor guard. At Uniontown Richie declined to attend his friend's funeral. On Sunday, July 2, the sergeant was arrested in a Pittsburgh hotel room on a charge of murder, and he had $1,065 in his pockets. He was returned to Camp Phillips and lodged in the guardhouse, and his three day trial began on August 17. On August 19, before a general court-martial of nine Army officers, Richie was found guilty of murdering De Fusco for the purpose of robbery, and he was sentenced to hang. Eight months passed while the record of the court-martial was reviewed by the general staff and then considered by the U.S. Supreme Court before sending it to the president for review, and after President F. D. Roosevelt died on April 12 President Harry S Truman affirmed the judgment and sentence and set the date for Richie's execution at April 21, 1945.

There is no record of details for the execution of Richie. The Army censored the facts of the case during the time it was being investigated and may have censored the details of the execution. Nationwide newspapers were overflowing with articles about the progress of the war in Europe, as great deeds were being accomplished and the Nazi regime was on the verge of collapse. The war in Europe would end in weeks but the newspapers also had many articles about the war in the Pacific theater and about the many men in both theaters who had died heroic deaths and were awarded medals. In local papers were articles about soldiers returning home and about their reunions with their families and their plans for the future. Still it seems unlikely that, without some aggressive censorship by the military, there would not be at least some mention of the execution in the newspapers of Kansas, in newspapers from Uniontown, Pennsylvania — De Fusco's hometown, or in North Carolina's newspapers — Richie's home state.

Sources: *Nevada State Journal* (Reno): July 9, 1944. *The Daily Courier* (Connellsville, PA): July 7, 1944. *The Daily News* (Huntingdon, PA): July 5, 1944. *The Mexia Herald* (TX): August 25, 1944. *The Monessen Daily Independent* (PA): August 18, 1944. U.S. Army Court Martial Case #264081.

Beyer, Walter
Demme, Hans
Scholz, Willi
Schomer, Hans
Seidel, Berthold
July 10, 1945

In early January 1944 forty-year-old Corporal Johannes Kunze of the Afrika Korps was a prisoner of war (POW) at the internment camp in Tonkowa, Oklahoma. He offered to trade information on German defenses for a transfer to a California POW camp and permission to remain in California after the war. The Americans agreed and interviewed Kunze but they were using a German POW as a clerk and gave him the notes to transcribe. The clerk made two copies and smuggled one to thirty-two-year-old First Sergeant Walter Beyer, the ranking noncommissioned officer in the camp.

On November 4, 1943, after the Americans retired for the night Beyer called a meeting of POWs, put Kunze on trial, and read the transcribed notes aloud. The mass of men found Kunze guilty and immediately beat him to death. The commotion raised an alarm, and in thirty minutes the guards quelled the disturbance and began examining the men for evidence they had participated in the murder.

Five men were singled out as ringleaders and most guilty in the beating: Beyer; twenty-three-year-old Hans Demme; thirty-year-old Berthold Seidel; twenty-two-year-old Willi Scholz; and twenty-seven-year-old Hans Schomer, all veterans of the Afrika Korps and described as "fanatical Nazis." Their general court-martial was held on

January 25, 1944, at Camp Graber, Oklahoma; they were found guilty and sentenced to hang. They were taken to the disciplinary barracks at Fort Leavenworth to await the review and approval by general staff, and this took some time, but finally in April 1945 the trial record and sentences were approved. The German government was notified and an exchange was proposed, but before any action could be taken the Nazi regime collapsed. The order for execution was then given to President Harry S Truman, who signed the death warrants and set the date for July 10, 1945, making these five POWs the first foreign prisoners executed on American soil.

When told of their fate Beyer said, "Someday they will see that this is wrong." But Seidel complained, "Damn bastards! Isn't it enough that they have destroyed Germany?" When the day arrived the men requested to die in their German uniforms, and this was granted, but their last meal consisted only of the regular issued rations. Beyer insisted it was his right to go first so just after midnight he was conducted to the gallows where Colonel William S. Eley, commandant of the disciplinary barracks, read the execution order, which was translated into German. Beyer's wrists and arms, knees and ankles were strapped and the noose was adjusted before he was asked if he had anything to say. There is no record of any of the prisoners making a statement to the military witnesses, so the black hood was pulled over his head and the trap was sprung. An Army doctor was in attendance to monitor vital signs, and he pronounced Beyer dead. One by one the remaining four soldiers marched to the gallows, were prepared in the same manner, and hanged. As each body was cut down the remains were deposited into a coffin, and after all five men were dead they were carried to the cemetery on the nearby hillside and buried.

Sources: *Fort Worth Historical Society*: "German POW Execution," www.ftlvnhistsoc.org/German_POW_execution.htm. *The Independent Record* (Helena, MT): July 10, 1945.

Gauss, Erich
Straub, Rudolph
July 14, 1945

Twenty-three-year-old Horst Gunther, a soldier in the Afrika Korps, was captured in Tunisia on May 9, 1943. He was transported to the Camp Aiken prisoner-of-war camp in South Carolina, but soon his fellow prisoners from the Afrika Korps began to suspect him of collaborating with the enemy — the U.S. military. He was tried in a "kangaroo court" in absentia, convicted of treason, and sentenced to die. Thirty-two-year-old Sergeant Erich Gauss and thirty-nine-year-old Private Rudolph Straub were chosen to carry out the sentence. On April 6, 1944, the two executioners managed to lure Gunther out of his tent into a compromising situation and, using a ligature, garroted him to death. The two men then hanged the body from a telephone pole to make it appear a suicide. There were five witnesses to the murder, the murder was discovered by guards, and the guilty parties were quickly identified. Gauss and Straub were tried before a general court-martial and sentenced to hang, then shipped to the disciplinary barracks at Fort Leavenworth, Kansas, while the case was under review. The general in command upheld the judgment and sentence of the tribunal, and the order for execution was then given to President Harry S Truman, who signed the death warrants and set the date for the hanging at July 14, 1945. When the day arrived the men requested to die in their German uniforms, and this was granted. The gallows could accommodate only one man, and Gauss went first. Once the prisoner was on the trapdoor Colonel William S. Eley, commandant of the disciplinary barracks, read the execution order, which was translated into German. Gauss' wrists and arms, knees and ankles were strapped and the noose was adjusted before he was asked if he had anything to say. There is no record of Gauss making a statement to the military witnesses, so the black hood was pulled over his head and the trap was sprung. An Army doctor was in attendance to monitor vital signs, and as soon as he pronounced Gauss dead the body was cut down, deposited into a coffin, and set aside to await the remains of Straub. Soon Straub appeared at the gallows and, when asked, said, "What I did was done as a German soldier under orders. If I had not done so, I would have been punished when I returned to Germany." He was then prepared in the same manner and hanged. After Straub's body was cut down it was deposited into a coffin, and both coffins were carried to the prison cemetery on the nearby hillside and buried.

Sources: *Fort Worth Historical Society*: "German POW Execution," www.ftlvnhistsoc.org/German_POW _execution.htm.

Reichl, Edward J.
August 22, 1945

Thirty-seven-year-old Private Edward J. Reichl harbored a grudge against thirty-five-year-old Private Adam Bucholz because Bucholz had failed to stop his truck to give Reichl a ride when he was three miles from the Coast Guard camp at Gualala, Mendocino County, California. On November 17, 1943, Reichl confronted Bucholz at the camp, and during an argument Reichl pulled out a pistol and shot Bucholz to death. Reichl was arrested immediately and lodged in the guardhouse at Hamilton Field. He was tried at a general court-martial, found guilty of first-degree murder, and on February 15, 1944, was sentenced to hang. Reichl's defense was that he was too drunk to premeditate a murder, as required under the 92nd Article of War, and he claimed to have been a chronic alcoholic for the past decade, but strong testimony showed that he had been sober at the time of the shooting. Reichl was delivered to the disciplinary barracks at Fort Leavenworth, Kansas, while his case was under review. The court-martial record and sentence was twice reviewed by President Harry Truman and each time he refused to intervene. The last denial of a plea for clemency came on August 10, 1945, ten days before Reichl's date with the hangman.

Reichl spent his last night writing letters to his wife in Santa Rosa, California, and his sister in Chicago, Illinois. The place chosen for the hanging by Raymond Orr, Quartermaster was a warehouse elevator shaft in Building 465 because he wanted a place that was indoors to ensure privacy. The elevator was raised to the third floor and a platform was built on the first floor, with a three-foot-square trapdoor providing a seven-foot drop. A ⅞ inch rope of hemp was used and tied across a beam installed on the second floor. Reichl's hanging was a test of the new apparatus as seven German prisoners of war, convicted of murder, were to be hanged in sequence in three days. Before midnight a guard detachment conducted Reichl, wearing an army uniform without insignia, from his cell in the disciplinary barracks to the gallows in Building 465 where he took his place on the trapdoor. Colonel William S. Eley, Commandant, then read the death warrant and record of appeal. When Reichl interrupted with a cough Eley asked, "Are you all right?" and the prisoner replied, "I'm fine, sir." His wrists and arms, knees and ankles were bound. Then Colonel Eley asked if he had anything to say, and he replied, "Yes, I have. I'm not guilty of premeditated murder. It was a drunken shooting," then he turned to the fifteen army officials and the newspaper reporters and said, "Good-bye Chicago. I love every street and alley in Chicago." The noose was adjusted and the black hood was pulled over his head at 12:08 A.M., and the trap was sprung immediately. Reichl dropped, breaking his neck in the fall. An Army doctor monitored his vital signs until his heart ceased to beat at 12:24 A.M. and then he was pronounced dead. Arrangements for his burial had been made by his family in Chicago, as his wife had not been heard of for several months, and Reichl's sister Rose Michalski had filed a missing person's report for the wife.

Sources: *Alton Evening Telegraph* (IL): August 22, 1945. *Daily Journal Gazette* (Matoon, IL): August 22, 1945. *The Piqua Daily Call* (OH): August 22, 1945.

Fischer, Helmut C.
Franke, Fritz
Kuelsen, Guenther
Ludwig, Heinrich
Reyak, Bernhard
Stengel, Otto
Wizuy, Rolf
August 25, 1945

World War II raged on and the battle with German U-boats stretched from the North Atlantic to the Caribbean. On May 9, 1942, German U-boat 352 was sunk by depth charges when southwest of Cape Hatteras. The U.S. Coast Guard Cutter *Icarus* was on the scene and plucked thirty-three sailors from the sea, but fifteen men died with their boat. On July 31, 1943, German U-boat 199 was sunk by depth charges dropped from three aircraft, one American and two Brazilian, and twelve sailors were taken prisoner while forty-nine perished. On August 7, 1943, German U-boat 615 was sunk by depth charges in the Caribbean Sea southeast of Curacao, and forty-three sailors were rescued while four died. It was the policy of the United States to imprison their prisoners of war (P.O.W.s) far from the east coast. Papago Park near Phoenix, Arizona, became the major internment camp for U-boat crews and in 1944 was home to more than four thousand men.

Werner Drechsler (sometimes Drexler) was also a U-boat sailor rescued when U-118 was sunk off the Azores in 1943 but he was first taken to Fort Hunt, a special naval internment and processing center. He became an American agent and collected information on U-boat prisoners processed through Fort Hunt but bound for Papago Park. After Drechsler was compromised he was transferred to the Army's 9th Service Command which had jurisdiction over all P.O.W.s in the West. His record was flagged to keep him away from U-boat crews, so he was housed at Fort Leonard Wood in Missouri.

However, on March 12, 1944, Drechsler was mistakenly transferred to Papago Park, and as soon as he arrived he was recognized by members of his crew. A large committee was formed, a "kangaroo court" convened, Drechsler was tried in absentia, convicted and sentenced to die. Only six and one-half hours after he arrived he was attacked by at least seven men and brutally beaten until he was helpless, then he was dragged into the shower room and hanged from a rafter. His body was discovered the following morning by guards. During the investigation one man was immediately identified from wounds to his hands suffered while beating Drechsler, and soon six others joined him. The seven included: twenty-four-year-old Helmut Carl Fischer; twenty-three-year-old Fritz Franke; twenty-two-year-old Guenther Kuelsen; twenty-one-year-old Heinrich Ludwig; twenty-year-old Bernhard Reyak; nineteen-year-old Otto Stengel; and eighteen-year-old Rolf Wizuy, all from the three U-boats first mentioned. While these seven men were formally charged with Drechsler's murder, nearly every prisoner in the camp was involved. The seven murderers all signed statements admitting their guilt as they felt it was their honor and duty to murder an American agent. At their general court-martial on March 15, 1944, they were found guilty and sentenced to hang at Fort Leavenworth. However, before the executions progressed Adolf Hitler sentenced seven American P.O.W.s to hang and then proposed a trade, but before any action could be taken the Nazi regime collapsed. As soon as the seven Americans were out of danger preparations for the execution of the seven German murderers proceeded. They had been transferred to the disciplinary barracks at Fort Leavenworth and the trial and sentence had been reviewed and approved, so on June 3 President Harry S Truman issued an executive order setting the date for execution at August 25, 1945. The place chosen for the hangings by Raymond Orr, Quartermaster, was the warehouse elevator shaft in Building 465 (see Reichl, Edward J.). Twenty-four hours before their execution the death warrants were read to the men in their cells, and then the seven men received the last rites from the Roman Catholic chaplain. They spent their final day writing letters to family and friends in Germany, writing out their wills, and receiving religious counseling. Just after midnight the first of the seven men was taken from his cell and escorted to Building 465 where he took his place on the trapdoor. His wrists and arms, knees and ankles were bound and he was asked if he had anything to say, but there is no record of a statement by any man. The noose was then adjusted, the black hood was pulled over his head, and the trap was sprung immediately. The process was repeated six times more, and as each man was pronounced dead his body was cut down and deposited into a coffin stored in the warehouse basement, while guards returned to bring the next prisoner. By 3:00 A.M. all seven men had been hanged, and shortly after dawn the seven caskets were conveyed to the cemetery on the nearby hillside and buried.

Sources: *Brainerd Daily Dispatch* (MN): July 19, 1945. *Fort Worth Historical Society*: "German POW Execution," www.ftlvnhistsoc.org/ German_POW_execution.htm. *San Antonio Express* (TX): August 26, 1945. *The Fresno Bee* (CA): August 25, 1945.

Gumtow, George F.
Tate, Cecil
July 29, 1947

Late Monday night, May 12, 1947, two circus roustabouts, who had been hitchhiking and were without funds, decided to break into a home in Calista, Kansas, and rob the occupants: sixty-year-old grain elevator operator William W. McClellan, his thirty-six-year-old son, Arnold, and his thirty-four-year-old son, Raymond. They broke in, captured the men, and took from them $4.50, missing $6 in Raymond's pocket, but then Arnold tried to run and was shot down. The two men, certain they were guilty of a murder, were about to kill William McClellan to eliminate the witness but before they could pull the trigger he pleaded that they spare his son Raymond. Thirty-four-year-old Raymond was paralytic and defective in speech, and the two murderers felt he could do them no harm so, after they shot William to death, they left Raymond unmolested and fled to Kingman, Kansas, nine miles away. Raymond managed to drag himself out of his house and crawl to the home of his nearest neighbor, then managed to let the residents know he needed help. The neighbors went to the McClellan home, found the two dead men, called the authorities, and within seven hours the two murderers were arrested at a Kingman hotel. Twenty-one-year-old George F. Gumtow and twenty-two-year-old Cecil Tate, as soon as they were behind bars, gave a detailed account of the murders and signed their confessions so by Wednesday County Attorney John McKenna had filed first-degree murder charges. The prisoners waived their preliminary hearing before Justice of the Peace W. H. White, but he appointed Charles H. Stewart to represent the two prisoners. On June 2 the two defendants were brought into the district courtroom of Judge Clark Wallace and they pled guilty, possibly expecting to get a life sentence in consideration of their cooperation, but the judge sentenced them to hang at the state prison at Lansing on July 29. Appeals did not delay the proceedings, and on July 22, one week before the executions, Governor Frank Carlson considered their pleas for clemency. Their attorney argued that the murders were not premeditated but the County Attorney countered that the robbery was premeditated and under Kansas law that made it first-degree murder. The governor said "...where the governor is asked to interfere with the judgment of the court some solid basis should appear to justify such action; but a most painstaking consideration of the present cases fails to show any extenuating circumstances which would justify any clemency at my hands, so the law will have to take its course. The applications are denied." A last-minute appeal for clemency for Tate arrived from Texas Governor Beauford Jester, probably at the urging of his family in Jacksonville, Texas, but it was denied by Governor Carlson.

The two men maintained their composure during their final days, bracing up with the help of several Catholic priests, and when midnight neared Warden Robert H. Hudspeth appeared at the doors to their death row cells and read the death warrants. The two men were taken out and escorted across the narrow prison street into the old brick warehouse. At one end was the double trapdoor gallows lighted with three powerful lamps. At the foot of the stairs the prisoners, warden and three priests conferred, and the condemned men were asked which one wanted to be hung first, but both said they wanted to be hung together so they climbed the thirteen steps and took their places on the trapdoors. Once in place the warden asked if they had anything to say to the twenty witnesses, and Gumtow, who appeared on the verge of collapse, said, "I have nothing to say that I know of." Tate then took his turn and said, "Warden, I want to shake your hand," and after they shook hands their wrists and arms, knees and ankles were bound, the nooses were adjusted, and the blindfolds were tied over their eyes. At 12:01 A.M. the warden raised and dropped his hand as a signal, and the trap was sprung by an out-of-state executioner brought in for the purpose. In fifteen minutes both men were pronounced dead by the attending physicians, and the bodies were cut down and deposited into their coffins. The remains of Tate were sent to his family in Jacksonville, Texas, and Gumtow's remains were shipped to his family in Battle Creek, Michigan.

Sources: *Joplin Globe* (MO): July 29, 1947. *The Anniston Star* (AL): July 29, 1947. *The Emporia Gazette* (KS): May 15, 1947; July 22, 1947. *Union-Bulletin* (Walla Walla, WA): June 3, 1947.

Miller, George
May 6, 1950

On February 3, 1947, forty-eight-year-old Mike Churchill, chief of the Osawatomie, Kansas, police department, with officer Harvey Earp and Mrs. Miller, went to the home of fifty-nine-year-old George Miller, a black section hand charged with beating his wife the previous night during an argument over money. With arrest warrant in hand Churchill approached the house, but Miller was hiding in a rear shed. When the lawman came within range Miller stuck the barrel of his shotgun through a hole in the shed's door and shot down Churchill with a single shotgun blast, and the lawman bled to death in minutes. Miller fled, and once word of the killing spread a large mob formed and began searching for the fugitive. A three-year-old child found Miller hiding in a garage loft two hours after the killing, and within minutes the mob surrounded the structure and demanded Miller's surrender. When Miller refused the mob began firing shotguns, rifles and pistols into the structure and finally captured Miller, and were about to lynch him when officers intervened and lodged him in the jail at Lawrence in neighboring Douglas County. On the day following the killing first-degree murder charges were filed against the prisoner, and later, when it was safe, he was brought back to Paola for trial. He was indicted, tried at the spring term of the court, convicted of first-degree murder, and sentenced to hang. However, the appeals process stayed the execution, and the matter dragged on for three years. Finally all avenues for judicial relief were exhausted, the application to Governor Frank L. Hagaman, praying for a commutation of sentence, was denied, and the date for Miller's execution was then set for May 6, 1950.

Miller showed no nervousness as the time for his death approached, and on his final day he made no special request for a last meal, so Warden Robert H. Hudspeth provided him with several cards for the prison store and he cashed them in for candy bars. After midnight the warden appeared at the cell door and read the death warrant, and then Miller, dressed in prison denims with wrists bound, was escorted by three guards across the narrow prison street and into the old brick warehouse. He walked to the stairs of the gallows, brightly lit by three large lamps, and when asked if he had anything to say to the twenty-seven witnesses he replied, "Yes, I'm ready to go. I've been ready." He hurried up the stairs and took his place on the trapdoor where his arms, knees and ankles were pinioned, the noose was adjusted, and the black cap was pulled over his head. Miller had been so anxious that there was a brief delay as the executioner awaited the hour of 1:00 A.M., and then the trap was sprung. Miller dropped, breaking his neck in the fall, and the prison physician monitored his vital signs until he pronounced him dead in thirteen minutes. The body was then cut down and deposited in the coffin provided. Miller had first asked to be buried at Osawatomie but after he was visited by his sister, his step-daughter, and a granddaughter he requested burial at the Mount Muncie cemetery at Leavenworth. The coffin was taken to Leavenworth and buried according to his final wishes.

Sources: *Atchison Daily Globe* (KS): May 5, 1950. *Record-Eagle* (Traverse City, MI): February 4, 1947. *The Anniston Star* (AL): May 7, 1950. *The Charleston Daily Mail* (SC): May 6, 1950.

McBride, Preston F.
April 6, 1951

On Wednesday, February 15, 1950, twenty-four-year-old Preston F. McBride engaged a taxi cab in Hutchinson, Kansas, driven by sixty-two-year-old John Watkins. After they were under way McBride pulled a .22-caliber pistol and forced Watkins to drive to a lonely road outside of Derby, Kansas, and then, while Watkins was still behind the steering wheel, he shot him to death. The body was discovered the next day and McBride, being his last passenger, was arrested. He readily admitted to killing Watkins, and as soon as he began talking Federal Bureau of Investigation and Treasury Department agents were called in because McBride said drugs were being flown from Mexico into San Antonio but were bound for Kansas, and he named the man responsible. He said he was being paid handsomely to deliver the drugs in Kansas and that one of his narcotic dealers offered him $1,500 to "rub out" Watkins, and said he was given the .22-caliber pistol and ammunition.

McBride was indicted in mid–April and his defense was insanity, but on April 22 a Reno County jury convicted him of first-degree murder, and Judge F. B. Hettinger sentenced him to hang at the Kansas State Prison on July 1, 1950. His attorneys filed appeals and on May 25 the Kansas state supreme court granted a stay while they considered the trial record. The supreme court affirmed the lower court's judgment and sentence and on February 6, after the time expired to file an appeal with the U.S. Supreme Court, the justices set the date for execution at April 6, 1951. An application pleading for a commutation of sentence was sent to Governor Edward F. Arn, but it was denied.

During his final days McBride was baptized into the Catholic church by prison chaplain Father Patrick H. Delahunty and Father Jerome Twomey of Horton, Kansas. On Thursday McBride visited with his parents and requested that they bury him at the Mount Carmel cemetery in Wichita, and the parting was very emotional. Once his parents left his priests were called and they remained with him, praying, until Warden Charles A. Edmondson arrived to read the death warrant just before 1:00 A.M. The prisoner was then taken out of his cell and escorted into the death chamber in the old brick warehouse by the warden and chaplain Delahunty. He walked up the thirteen steps and took his place on the trapdoor where he was asked if he had anything to say to the twenty-five witnesses, and he said, "God bless everybody, and may God have mercy on my soul." He then turned to the priest and said, "Father pray for me. Everybody pray for me, and I'll pray for you." While this exchange was going on the attendants applied straps to his arms, knees and ankles and adjusted the noose. McBride then kissed a crucifix offered by the priest and the black cap was pulled over his head. The rope was held at a right angle by a prison official while the trap was being sprung at 1:01 A.M. McBride dropped straight down, breaking his neck, and in thirteen minutes prison Dr. Peter Combs pronounced him dead. The body was then cut down, deposited in the coffin provided by his father George, and given to his parents for burial according to his last request.

Sources: *San Antonio Express* (TX): February 17, 1950. *The Atchison Daily Globe* (KS): May 25, 1950. *The Emporia Daily Gazette* (KS): February 7, 1951; April 6, 1951.

Lammers, James
January 5, 1952

On December 13, 1950, the trailer of the Lammers family in the Fred Worman trailer park at Troy, Kansas, was discovered on fire at 12:30 A.M. The entire trailer was consumed and the bodies of twenty-three-year-old Genevieve Lammers, an eight-month-old boy, and two girls aged two and three were burned beyond recognition but twenty-eight-year-old James Lammers, the husband and father, was supposed to have left the previous day to look for work. The family had moved into the trailer home only eight weeks earlier when James found work as a bulldozer operator at Troy, but he was laid off two weeks before the fire. There were only two trailers in the park at the time, and it was the resident in the other trailer, Mrs. Frank Gorcham, who first discovered the flames but she could do nothing to extinguish the blaze. At first it appeared that the point of origin was an oil heater that had exploded, and it appeared that Mrs. Lammers had tried to get out as her body was found near the door, but the children's bodies were found in their beds as if they died in their sleep. The investigation continued, the source of the fire was proven to be arson, and James Lammers was arrested. He soon confessed that he had strangled his wife to death before setting the trailer ablaze to hide the crime, leaving his three children to perish in the flames; and on December 28 County Attorney Robert Guier filed first-degree murder charges against Lammers. The defendant was indicted and tried at the spring term of the court, found guilty of first-degree murder, and sentenced to hang. The appeals process delayed the execution for nearly a year, but finally in late 1951 all avenues of judicial relief were exhausted, and Lammers was scheduled to hang on January 5, 1952. The last appeal to Governor Edward F. Arn, praying for executive clemency, was rejected.

Lammers spent his final year in a death row cell at the Kansas State Prison at Lansing. He was attended by prison Chaplain Patrick Delahunty and had resigned himself to his fate when the warden appeared after midnight to read the death warrant. A few minutes before 1:00 A.M. his wrists were bound and he was escorted from his cell by two guards, crossed a snow-covered baseball diamond into the old brick warehouse, and climbed thirteen stairs onto the gallows. He took his place on the trapdoor and was quickly prepared by having his arms, knees and ankles strapped and the noose adjusted. Just before the black cap was pulled over his head he said, "I have been treated very well." The black cap was then pulled on at 1:01 A.M. and the trap was sprung immediately. Lammers dropped, breaking his neck, and prison Dr. A. R. Starrett pronounced him dead in nine minutes. Chaplain Delahunty then performed the last rites of the Roman Catholic church before the body was cut down and placed in the coffin provided. His parents, Mr. and Mrs. Fred Lammers of Fordyce, Nebraska, were notified by telegram when the execution was completed but they had not yet requisitioned the body so it was buried in a prison plot.

Sources: *Atchison Daily Globe* (KS): December 13, 1950; January 6, 1952. *The Emporia Daily Gazette* (KS): December 28, 1950.

Germany, Nathaniel
May 21, 1954

On October 23, 1947, just before midnight eighteen-year-old David W. Gray, a Kansas City junior college student, and his seventeen-year-old college girlfriend Mary Lou Johnson were parked along the roadside of "lover's lane" when Nathaniel Germany, a twenty-three-year-old black truck driver, pulled up behind them. He went to the window of the car and, at gunpoint, took them out and tried to intimidate Gray, intending to rape his girlfriend. He had tried the same ploy on August 31 and on October 5 and had raped two white women after threatening to kill their escorts. However Gray would not weaken, refused to get out of his car, and bargained for the release of Johnson. When Germany agreed Gray told Johnson to leave immediately and go directly to the nearest house. After Johnson had walked a short distance away Gray exited his automobile and Germany demanded the car keys and his wallet, and when Johnson heard them arguing she turned to see Gray throw the keys in Germany's face, then heard a single gun shot. She rushed to her boyfriend and, it being a brightly moonlit night, clearly saw Germany run into the woods before she realized Gray was dead. She went for help and reported the murder to the authorities.

The police soon received an anonymous tip, and detectives Joseph Shick and Frank Steach arrested Germany at his home. The prisoner first said, "I just thought I would have a little fun," but later gave a full confession which was transcribed and signed. On November 1 the prisoner appeared before Judge Jack Dear and tried to enter a plea of guilty to one count of murder and two counts of rape, but it was rejected and he was remanded to the custody of Sheriff John Theroff. Germany was indicted, tried, and found guilty of first-degree murder, but the issue of insanity was raised, and in February 1948 Germany was sent to the asylum for observation. He remained there for thirty-three months before a panel of doctors pronounced him sane. He returned to court in late October 1952 and was sentenced to hang on December 3, but then the appeals process commenced which further stayed the execution. Germany's court-appointed attorneys launched a vigorous effort to save the life of their client and delayed his execution for another eighteen months. Finally all avenues of judicial relief were exhausted and only an application to Governor Edward F. Arn for a commutation of sentence remained, but this was rejected and the date for Germany's execution was set for May 21, 1954.

During his final days Germany was attended by the Rev. T. E. Freeman, and through his influence the condemned man resigned himself to his fate. He spoke to newsmen on his final night and told them, "We all sin and we all have to die. Everyone was born to die. I believe in Jesus Christ and I know he will save me. You fellows better get right with God." After midnight the warden appeared at the cell door and read the death warrant, and then the prisoner was taken out and escorted across the narrow prison street into the old brick warehouse. He walked to the gallows and climbed thirteen stairs to take his place on the trapdoor. His wrists and arms, knees and ankles were strapped, the noose was adjusted, and the black cap was pulled over his head. There was a delay as he began to pray, "I'm in your hands, oh Lord. Please forgive me. Please save me. Keep me. Oh my God, give me strength." When he concluded at 1:01 A.M. the trap was sprung and the prisoner dropped, breaking his neck in the fall. The attending physician monitored his vital signs, and when his heart ceased to beat he was pronounced dead, cut down, and deposited in his coffin. He was buried the following day.

Sources: *Atchison Daily Globe* (KS): January 9, 1953. *Emporia Daily Gazette* (KS): October 31, 1947; November 1, 1947. *The Brownsville Herald* (TX): May 21, 1954. *The Great Bend Daily Tribune* (KS): May 21, 1954. *The News* (Fredericksburg, MD): November 1, 1947.

Martin, Merle W.
July 16, 1954

Early on the morning of June 23, 1952, thirty-one-year-old Deputy Sheriff Willard Carver and Patrolman Floyd Gaunt were investigating a suspicious automobile bearing a Missouri license tag stalled in a ditch three miles west of Zarah in Johnson County, Kansas. It proved to be a stolen vehicle so the officers set up a stake-out to see if the car thieves returned. The two men soon appeared in a pick-up truck they had stolen from a nearby farm, intending to pull their stolen car from the ditch. Carver and Gaunt ordered the two men to surrender but both men drew weapons and exchanged shots with the lawmen. Carver managed to fire three rounds before he was shot down by .45-caliber bullets, the same caliber carried by Martin, and then the two men ran from the scene.

The following day Charles Wilford Isgrigg was discovered hiding in a cornfield and captured, and his partner was identified as forty-two-year-old Merle William Martin, known in Illinois, Missouri and Kansas as the "pillowcase burglar" as he always took away his loot in a pillow case. Martin avoided capture for some time, and on August 11 he was placed on the Federal Bureau of Investigation "ten most wanted" list. After Martin lost his partner, his ex-brother-in-law, he picked up his girlfriend, and they were traveling together until Martin was captured at St. Louis, Missouri, on August 30, 1952. He was returned to the Johnson County jail and at his examination was held over for the grand jury, but he continued to deny firing the fatal bullets. Martin and Isgrigg were indicted for murder in November; on the 29th Martin was convicted of first-degree murder and sentenced to hang at the Kansas State Prison at Lansing. The evidence against Martin was conclusive but it was just as clear that Isgrigg did not fire the fatal bullets, so when he was brought into court three days later he pled guilty and was sentenced to serve a life term. Martin was soon delivered to the prison and lodged in a death row cell while his attorneys launched an aggressive campaign of appeals. However by the end of May 1954, after two years of judicial reviews, Martin's final chance for a respite or new trial was denied, and he was scheduled to die on July 16, 1954. A week before the execution his final plea for a respite was rejected by the U.S. Supreme Court, and an application was submitted to Governor Edward F. Arn praying for a commutation of sentence, but this was denied. The issue of insanity was raised by the attorneys, and at their request prison Dr. Peter Combs examined the prisoner on July 15 and pronounced him sane.

Martin had no religious affiliation when he arrived at the prison but in his final days he was baptized into the Catholic faith by prison chaplain Father Patrick H. Delahunty and Father Jerome Twomey of Horton, Kansas. The two priests were with him his final evening praying, and through their influence he finally confessed in writing: "Now that I am about to die I wish to set the record straight before I go to meet my maker. *Isgrigg did no shooting.* On June 23, 1952 I fired the shots that killed Officer Carver near Zarah, Kansas. We, Isgrigg and I, were taken by surprise by Officer Carver and Officer Gaunt. The only words spoken by either of the officers was "hold it," then they both started shooting. I could see no one but I thought several people were shooting at us and I emptied my revolver and escaped. It was not my intention to shoot anyone and I am very sorry that it happened. The loved ones of Officer Carver have my sincere sympathy. Merle William Martin." Martin's statement was in response to an earlier sworn statement by Isgrigg in which he claimed he had fired the bullets which killed Carver, in an attempt to save Martin through perjury.

After midnight Warden Charles A. Edmondson appeared at the cell door and read the death warrant, and then the prisoner was taken out and escorted by the warden and Father Delahunty into the death chamber in the old brick warehouse where twenty-five witnesses awaited his arrival. At the foot of the thirteen stairs he was asked if he had anything to say to the witnesses, which included Carver's brother Earl, and he said, "I would like to thank all of my friends who helped and all those who tried to help and have prayed for me. If there are any Catholics among you I would appreciate it if they would pray for me." He then walked up the stairs and took his place on the trapdoor where his wrists and arms, knees and ankles were strapped, the noose was adjusted, and the black cap was pulled over his head. The trap was sprung at 1:03 A.M. and Martin dropped to his death, breaking his neck in the fall. Dr. Peter Combs was in attendance and monitored Martin's vital signs until he pronounced him dead thirteen minutes later. The body was then cut down and deposited in the coffin provided by the state, and he was buried in the prison plot in the Mount Muncie cemetery.

Sources: *Atchison Daily Globe* (KS): July 15–16, 1954. *Daily News* (Greensburg, IN): August 11, 1952. *Hope Star* (AK): July 17, 1954. *Post-Tribune* (Jefferson City, MO): June 24, 1952.

O'Brien, Bernard J.
July 31, 1954

On May 7, 1952, thirty-year-old Warrant Officer Bernard O'Brien, assigned to the U.S. Navy Medical Training Center, murdered his wife Dorothy with a trench shovel at their home near Degerndorf, Bavaria, Germany. He carried her body to their car and later drove it at a high rate of speed into a tree between Bad Aibling and the Munich-Salzburg autobahn. He reported it as an accident and said his wife had been killed in the crash but after a two-day investigation and an autopsy, which showed Dorothy was dead before the crash, he was arrested and charged with her murder. In mid–June he faced a general court-martial at Munich, took the stand in his defense, and admitted he struck his wife twice with the shovel but insisted it was because "she nagged me until I didn't know what I was doing. I only wanted to make her suffer, not kill her." U.S. Army criminal investigator Raymond McNine testified that O'Brien struck his wife on the head while she was asleep, then gave each of his two children a glass of milk and told them their mother was ill and he was going to rush her to the hospital. McNine said that O'Brien confessed that he had dressed his wife, carried her to the car, and driven around with the body in the car for two hours before he got up the nerve to crash it into the tree. Captain Helen E. King, an Army nurse, then testified that O'Brien told her he was divorced and had promised to marry her.

On June 19, 1952, O'Brien was found guilty of first-degree murder and sentenced to hang. He was delivered to the disciplinary barracks at Fort Leavenworth, Kansas, while the verdict and sentence were reviewed and approved by the general staff. The appeals process then commenced. By May 1954 all avenues of judicial relief were exhausted, and the matter was referred to President Dwight D. Eisenhower. The President rejected the plea for clemency, issued an executive order for the execution to proceed, and set the date for July 31, 1954.

During his time in prison O'Brien was attended by Chaplain Major Milton E. Berg, who administered the last rites of the Lutheran Church on Friday afternoon. The prisoner had fully resigned himself to his fate when Commandant James W. Davis appeared at his cell door and read the death warrant. The prisoner, dressed in drab Army khakis without insignia, was handcuffed, taken out, and driven seven miles to the state prison at Lansing. He entered the prison yard just before midnight and walked directly to the scaffold where he was asked if he had anything to say, and he replied, "Not a thing at all." With complete composure he climbed the thirteen stairs and took his place on the trapdoor. While Chaplain Berg prayed for his soul his knees and ankles were bound, the noose was adjusted, and the black cap was pulled over his head. The trap was sprung at 12:01 A.M. and the prisoner dropped, breaking his neck in the fall. Two Army doctors were in attendance, and they immediately opened O'Brien's shirt, and, using stethoscopes, monitored his heartbeat until they pronounced him dead at 12:13 A.M. Then the body was cut down and deposited in the coffin provided by the Army. O'Brien, as a last request and with the approval of his mother, had bequeathed his remains to the University of Kansas Medical Center at Kansas City for medical research, and the body was delivered later that day.

Sources: *Dallas Morning News* (TX): July 30, 1954. *Las Vegas Optic* (NM): July 31, 1954. *Lubbock Journal* (TX): June 19, 1952. *Morning Avalanche* (Lubbock, TX): June 20, 1952. *Pharos-Tribune* (Logansport, IN): July 31, 1954. *The Mexia Daily News* (TX): June 19, 1952.

Beverly, Chastine
Riggins, James
Suttles, Louis M.
March 1, 1955

On September 19, 1951, fifty-two-year-old Harry Langley, a cab driver, was beaten to death with rocks and robbed of his money and cab near Waynesville, Missouri. He was found and rushed to the hospital but he died the following day. It was not long before three black soldiers were arrested and charged with his murder: twenty-two-year-old Chastine Beverly of Balty, Virginia; twenty-four-year-old James Riggins of Tallahassee, Florida; and twenty-four-year-old Louis M. Suttles of Chattanooga, Tennessee.

On October 5 a general court-martial was convened at Fort Leonard Wood, Missouri, consisting of six officers and three enlisted men, and the first ten of fifty-five witnesses were called. After six days of testimony all three defendants were found guilty of murder on October 10, 1951, and sentenced to hang at the Kansas State Prison at Lansing, and they were delivered to the U.S. disciplinary barracks at Fort Leavenworth. The appeals process then began in earnest, the executions were stayed, and it took four years to dispose of the legal avenues for relief. Then military authorities and President Dwight D. Eisenhower upheld the death sentences fixed by the court-martial, and the date of the hangings was finally set for just after midnight on March 1, 1955.

Twenty military witnesses gathered in the state prison yard at Lansing and when midnight neared Commandant Colonel James W. Davis went to the cells in the disciplinary barracks and read the death warrants to the prisoners, all dressed in Army uniforms stripped of insignia, and then Beverly was taken out and driven eight miles to the state prison. He went directly into the prison yard and onto the scaffold, taking his place on the trapdoor.

Colonel Davis asked if he had anything to say to the witnesses and he replied, "Nothing at all, sir." His wrists and arms, knees and ankles were strapped, the noose was adjusted, and the black cap was pulled over his head while an Army chaplain prayed with him. At 12:02 A.M. the trap was sprung and Beverly dropped, breaking his neck. After the attending physician pronounced him dead he was cut down and deposited in his coffin. Meanwhile Colonel Davis had started for the disciplinary barracks and soon returned with Riggins. The same process was gone through and Riggins also declined to make a statement. The trap was sprung at 12:43 A.M., and after the prisoner was pronounced dead he was deposited in his coffin while Colonel Davis went for Suttles. The third condemned man arrived in the prison yard at 1:14 A.M. and declined to make a statement, so he was quickly prepared and dropped within a few minutes of his arrival, and after his remains were deposited in the coffin provided the three bodies were transported back to Fort Leavenworth and buried later that morning.

Sources: *Daily Capital News* (Jefferson City, MO): October 12, 1951. *Joplin Globe* (MO): October 5, 1951. *The Ada Evening News* (OK): October 9, 1953. *The Salina Journal* (KS): February 28, 1955. *Tribune* (Chillicothe, MO): March 1, 1955.

Edwards, Thomas J.
Moore, Winfred D.
February 14, 1957

On March 1, 1953, Thomas J. Edwards of Ardmore, Oklahoma, a nineteen-year-old black soldier, beat to death Maria Stowasser at Kitzingen, Germany. Edwards was tried by general court-martial and found guilty of murder, and on April 1, 1953, he was sentenced to hang. On June 30, 1953, Winfred D. Moore of Virginia Beach, Virginia, a nineteen-year-old black soldier, engaged a cab to drive him from Fort Bragg to Fayetteville, North Carolina, but before the cab was off the post he shot to death and robbed taxicab driver Charles Pettit. Moore was arrested and in August he was found guilty of murder at his general court-martial, and on August 19 he was sentenced to hang. Both men were delivered to the disciplinary barracks at Fort Leavenworth, Kansas, to await the outcome of their appeals. With them was John T. Lee, also sentenced to die for the shooting death of Sergeant Stanley R. Wade at Neb Ulm, Germany, on June 22, 1953, but he would cheat the hangman. The appeals process took nearly four years to conclude but finally all avenues of judicial relief were exhausted. Edwards dispatched two letters to President Dwight D. Eisenhower asking for a reprieve but on his final day he received a telegram from the White House notifying him his plea had been rejected.

During the time the cases were under review the State of Kansas notified Colonel James W. Davis that they would no longer execute Army prisoners at the state prison, so a temporary platform was built in Fort Leavenworth's station power plant with the traditional thirteen stairs. As the time for their execution approached both men became resigned to their fate and displayed an unexpected calmness. Edwards was chosen to go first, as the gallows would only accommodate one man at a time. Before midnight Commandant Colonel James W. Davis appeared at the cells of the men and read the orders of execution, and then Edwards, dressed in a regulation olive drab uniform without insignia, was led out. He was taken to the execution chamber with a guard on each arm, mounted the scaffold and took his place on the trapdoor. In all thirty military men were present, several attending to the prisoner and the remainder as witnesses. Edwards' wrists and arms, knees and ankles were bound and the noose was adjusted. Edwards was then asked if he had anything to say but he declined, so the black cap was pulled over his head at 12:01 A.M. and the trap was immediately sprung by a master sergeant. Edwards dropped, breaking his neck in the fall, and in fifteen minutes he was pronounced dead by the Army physician in attendance. While the body was being cut down and deposited into a coffin Colonel Davis returned to Moore's cell, and they returned just before 12:30 A.M. The procedure was completed when the prisoner declined to speak and the trap was sprung at 12:32 A.M. Moore's body twitched for several minutes but he was pronounced dead in fourteen minutes, and it was determined that his neck was broken in the fall. Moore was deposited into his coffin and his remains were released to family members for burial. There was no requisition for the remains of Edwards so he was buried in the fort cemetery.

Sources: *Lebanon Daily News* (PA): February 14, 1957. *The Albuquerque Tribune* (NM): February 14, 1957. *The Daily Times-News* (Burlington, NC): February 14, 1957. *The*

Mexia Daily Journal (TX): February 14, 1957. *The Salina Journal* (KS): December 18, 1953.

Ransom, Ernest L.
April 3, 1957

In early June 1953 twenty-one-year-old Ernest L. Ransom, a private assigned to the 933rd Anti-aircraft Artillery Automatic Weapons Battalion in Korea, shot a Korean guard to death while the Korean was on duty, and then he raped a fourteen-year-old Korean girl. He was arrested and faced a general court-martial convened at Inchon. He was found guilty of murder and rape; on June 5, 1953, he was sentenced to hang at Fort Leavenworth, Kansas, and within days of his crime he was transported to the disciplinary barracks at Fort Leavenworth. The case was reviewed by the general staff and they approved the verdict and sentence. The appeals process then commenced and the case dragged on for four years, but finally in February 1957 the U.S. Supreme Court denied the appeal, and the matter was forwarded to President Dwight D. Eisenhower for review. The president issued an executive order for the execution to proceed and set the date for April 3, 1957.

Ransom would be the third man hanged on the new gallows built in Fort Leavenworth's station power plant. As the time for his execution neared Ransom became resigned to his fate and displayed great composure. On Tuesday, before midnight, Commandant Colonel James W. Davis appeared at the cell door, and Ransom, dressed in a regulation olive drab uniform without insignia, was led out. He was taken to the execution chamber with a guard on each arm, where he mounted the scaffold and took his place on the trapdoor. Colonel Davis then read the order of execution and concluded, "May the Lord have mercy on your soul." In all twenty-five military men were present, several attending to the prisoner and the remainder as witnesses, but the prisoner declined to speak to them. Ransom's wrists and arms, knees and ankles were bound, the noose was adjusted, the black cap was pulled over his head at 12:01 A.M., and the trap was immediately sprung. Ransom dropped, breaking his neck in the fall, and in fifteen minutes he was pronounced dead by the Army physician in attendance. The body was cut down, placed in the coffin provided, and prepared to be shipped to Garysburg, North Carolina, where his parents, Mr. and Mrs. Lester Ransom, would see to the burial.

Sources: *The Daily Times-News* (Burlington, NC): April 2, 1957. *The News-Palladium* (Benton Harbor, MI): April 3, 1957.

Thomas, Abraham
July 23, 1958

On Tuesday, February 23, 1954, twenty-eight-year-old Sergeant Lafayette Bennett and thirty-two-year-old Corporal Edward Peters, black soldiers, arranged a rendezvous with German girlfriends Walburga Wenderoth and Anna Weigel at a small cottage at Gersthofen near Augsburg, Germany. Twenty-six-year-old Abraham Thomas, a black private first class, was interested in one of the girls and was insanely jealous when he learned of the tryst. He took his Army-issue carbine and an ax and followed the two couples, and after they were preoccupied he burst into the cottage and shot all four dead. He then used the ax to bludgeon, hack and mutilate the bodies. The bodies were found almost immediately, and within two hours Thomas was arrested and lodged in the guardhouse.

Thomas was formally charged with premeditated murder on February 28, and his general court-martial was scheduled to be held at Augsburg on April 5. Thomas pled guilty to the charges and specifications, and on April 15, 1954, he was sentenced to hang at Fort Leavenworth, Kansas, but he remained in Germany while the verdict and sentence were reviewed by the general staff and approved; then the long appeals process commenced. Thomas arrived at Fort Leavenworth in June 1954 to await the outcome of the appeal, and four years passed before the U.S. Supreme Court affirmed the finding of the court-martial. The matter was then referred to President Dwight D. Eisenhower, and he affirmed the verdict and sentence, issued an executive order to proceed with the execution, and set the date for July 23, 1958.

Thomas would be the fourth soldier hanged on the platform built in Fort Leavenworth's station power plant. As the time for his execution neared Thomas found comfort in religious counseling and became resigned to his fate. On Tuesday before midnight Commandant Colonel James W. Davis appeared at Thomas' cell door and the prisoner, dressed in a regulation olive drab uniform without insignia, was led out. He was taken to the execution chamber with a guard on each arm, where he mounted the scaffold and took his place on the trapdoor. Colonel Davis then read the order of execution and concluded, "May the Lord have mercy on your soul." In all thirty military men were present, several attending to the prisoner and the remainder as witnesses, but the prisoner declined to speak to them and only turned to Colonel Davis and thanked him for his treatment while a prisoner. His wrists and arms, knees and ankles were bound, the noose was adjusted, the black cap was pulled over his head at 12:04 A.M., and the trap was sprung immediately. Thomas dropped, breaking his neck in the fall, and in seventeen minutes he was pronounced dead by the Army physician in attendance. The body was cut down, placed in the coffin provided, and prepared to be shipped to Montezuma, Georgia, for burial.

Sources: *Appleton Post-Crescent* (WI): July 24, 1958. *Charleston Daily Mail* (SC): March 28, 1954. *The Columbus Daily Telegram* (NE): July 23, 1958. *The Corpus Christie Caller Times* (TX): February 28, 1954. *The Logansport Press* (IN): April 7, 1954.

Day, John E., Jr.
September 23, 1959

On December 23, 1950, twenty-two-year-old John E. Day, Jr., a black private serving in Korea, made sexual advances toward the wife of Korean civilian Lee Hak Chum, sometimes given as Lee Mak Chun, in Seoul. Chum came to her defense but Day pulled a pistol and shot Chum to death. Day was immediately arrested, and in January 1951 he faced a general court-martial. Day was found guilty of murder and on October 1, 1951, he was sentenced to hang at Fort Leavenworth, the first American to receive a death sentence during the Korean conflict. He was transported to the disciplinary barracks at Fort Leavenworth while the case was under review. The verdict and sentence were approved by the general staff and then the appeals process commenced. The case was considered numerous times but finally the U.S. Supreme Court, after eight years, approved the verdict and sentence, and the matter was forwarded to President Dwight D. Eisenhower. The president carefully considered the matter before issuing an executive order to proceed with the execution and set the date for execution at September 23, 1959.

Just before midnight Commandant Colonel Weldon W. Cox appeared at the cell door and escorted Day into the power plant building and onto the gallows platform. The prisoner took his place on the trapdoor where Colonel Cox read the warrant for execution of sentence. When the reading concluded Day declined to speak to the witnesses, and, while the chaplain prayed for his soul, Colonel Cox retired and turned preparations over to three sergeants. While the chaplain continued praying the three sergeants bound the prisoner's limbs with straps, adjusted the noose, and pulled the black cap over his head. At 12:02 A.M. the trap was sprung and Day dropped, breaking his neck in the fall. An Army physician was in attendance and he pronounced Day dead in fifteen minutes, and then the remains were lowered into the coffin provided. He was buried in the military portion of the cemetery later that day.

Sources: *Daily Herald* (Utah County, UT): September 23, 1959. *Dallas Morning News* (TX): September 25, 1959.

Bennett, John A.
April 13, 1961

In 1954 nineteen-year-old Army private John A. Bennett, a black soldier, was assigned as an ammunition handler and truck driver with the 11th Anti-aircraft Battalion stationed in Austria. On December 21 Bennett saw an eleven-year-old girl walking to her home in Siezenheim and abducted her. He brutally raped the girl and then choked her to death so she could not identify him, but he was identified as the murderer and arrested. On February 8, 1955, a general court-martial convicted Bennett of rape and murder. He was sentenced to hang at Fort Leavenworth, Kansas, and he arrived at the U.S. disciplinary barracks on April 29, 1955. The sentence was reviewed and more than two years later, on July 2, 1957, the sentence was approved by President Dwight D. Eisenhower. The case was appealed aggressively, and in March 1960 Federal Judge Walter A. Huxman stayed the execution just before Bennett was to hang. The judge said he would consider the claim that "racial hostility" surrounded the court-martial and that he (Bennett) should have been tried by Austrian authorities and not by the military tribunal. Huxman finally rejected the appeal, and then Bennett's attorneys tried every means and legal manipulation to save the life of their client, but to no avail. On February 27, 1961, the Secretary of the Army ordered the execution to proceed and set the time and date for 12:01 A.M. on April 13. The prisoner's final plea was a telegram sent to President John F. Kennedy, but relief was denied and he made his preparations for death.

Just before midnight Commandant Colonel Weldon W. Cox appeared at the cell door and escorted Bennett into the prison yard and onto the new yellow and gray gallows platform. He took his place on the trapdoor, and Colonel Cox read the warrant for the execution of sentence. When the reading concluded Bennett turned his head to the colonel and said, "I wish to take this opportunity to thank you and each member of the staff for all you have done in my behalf," and then asked the chaplain to pray for him. Colonel Cox concluded "May God have mercy on your soul," before retiring and turning the preparations over to three sergeants. While the chaplain prayed the sergeants bound Bennett's limbs with straps, adjusted the noose, and pulled the black cap over his head. At 12:05 A.M. the trap was sprung and the prisoner dropped to his death, breaking his neck in the fall. An Army doctor was in attendance, and he pronounced Bennett dead in seventeen minutes, and then the remains were lowered into the coffin provided. He was buried in the military portion of the cemetery later that day.

Sources: *Dallas Morning News* (TX): March 11, 1960. *Post-Tribune* (Jefferson City, MO): April 13, 1961.

Andrews, Lowell L.
November 30, 1962

Eighteen-year-old Lowell Lee Andrews spent Thanksgiving evening, November 27, 1958, with his family—fifty-year-old father William L., forty-one-year-old mother Opal, and twenty-year-old sister Jennie Marie, who was a senior at Oklahoma Baptist University. Andrews, a sophomore at the University of Kansas, had returned home to the Wyandotte County family farm for the holiday but kept secret that he had just failed a course. He had been an honor student throughout his time in high school and reportedly had the highest I.Q. score of any student on record, so he was having difficulty dealing with his recent failure. Lowell's father was a Trans World Airline mechanic but he was idle because his union had gone on strike the previous week, and this added to the tension in the home.

On Friday evening at 6:00 P.M. the family sat down to a quiet supper, and afterward they all gathered in the living room to watch television. After an hour Lowell retired to his bedroom but returned shortly with his twenty-one shot .22-caliber rifle and a .22-caliber Luger pistol and, using the rifle, he shot his father, mother and sister. His father staggered into the kitchen and collapsed and Lowell thought he might still be alive so he emptied the clip from his pistol into the prostrate body, shooting him seventeen times in all. He had shot his mother four times, and she was found lying on her back near a wall in the living room while his sister was shot three times and found facedown near the wall opposite her mother; the women had apparently died instantly. Lowell then went through the house pulling out drawers and throwing about the contents, opened a window and removed a screen to make the killings look like a burglary gone wrong. Lowell drove back to his college in Lawrence, and along the way he stopped to throw the guns in the Kansas River, then made a point to talk with a fellow student to build his alibi. Afterward he went to the Granada Theater to watch a movie and at midnight returned to the family farm near Wolcott, west of Kansas City, and "discovered the bodies." He called the sheriff's office saying, "There's been a shooting at my house," and when deputy sheriff Albert Gilhaus arrived he found Andrews sitting on the porch calmly petting his dog. He told the detective that his family had been slain by burglars, and the family's Baptist Rev. V. C. Dameron was called to attend to the boy.

In three hours Andrews weakened and confessed to the reverend, who said of him, "He was particularly sensitive to suffering. I bet he never had a fight in his life, and yet he calmly told me every detail of the shootings." The confession was written out and he signed it, and then explained, "It wasn't a case that they wouldn't give me what I wanted, it was a case they couldn't.... I would like to have a sports car; and I would have liked to have a million dollars." He said his motive was that he wanted to inherit the two hundred fifty-acre farm and the family's $1,800 savings account, but later said, "I'm not sorry and I'm not glad. I just don't know why I did it." His attitude caused sheriff's Lt. Ralph Athey to observe, "He was the most unconcerned murderer I ever met." Andrews denied that anything was bothering him and insisted he had not had any type of disagreement with his family before the shooting, and on Saturday the prisoner was arraigned on a charge of first-degree murder. The question of insanity was raised, and a three-doctor panel examined the prisoner and found him legally sane at the time of the murders, though there was some question of schizophrenia.

Andrews was then indicted, tried and convicted of first-degree murder at the spring session of the court, and he was sentenced to hang. However, the trial judge only instructed the jury on a verdict for first-degree murder, and this was the basis for numerous appeals, which delayed the execution for several years as the state supreme court and then the U.S. Supreme Court considered the case. Andrews was scheduled to hang on September 11, 1962, but Justice Byron White of the U.S. Supreme Court then granted a stay on August 29, 1962. The justices considered the matter for the second time and denied the appeal, and the date for Andrews' execution at the state prison in Lansing was scheduled for November 30, 1962. His attorney, James R. Ahrens, refused to give up and filed a writ of habeas corpus with the U.S. District Court in Topeka, but this was denied on the evening before the execution, and efforts to have Governor John Anderson grant executive clemency failed. Ahrens insisted his client was insane and said he would try one last appeal to Judge Delmas C. Hill of the Circuit Court of Appeals in Wichita, but to no avail.

During his final days the prisoner was visited by his maternal aunt and uncle, and they agreed to see to his burial. He was attended by his family pastor, the Rev. V. C. Dameron, and the reverend helped him prepare for his death. Just before the appointed hour Warden Sherman H. Crouse appeared at the cell door and read the death warrant. The prisoner was then taken out and escorted to the gallows by the Reverend Dameron. The entire enclosure was lit by a single unshaded light bulb, and the harsh light gave it an eerie appearance as Andrews took his place on the trapdoor. He was asked if he had anything to say and he replied, "No, I don't believe so." This, however, was not positive enough for the warden so he asked again if there was a last request, and Andrews said emphatically, "No!" The prisoner's wrists and arms, ankles and knees were strapped, the noose was adjusted, and the black cap was pulled over his head. In but a moment the trap was sprung and Andrews dropped to his death, breaking his neck in the fall. He was allowed to hang a sufficient time to ensure he was dead before the body was cut down and placed in the coffin provided by his mother's sister, Mrs. Major P. Herrington of Decatur, Illinois. Mrs. Herrington arranged for his burial next to his family in the Mount Salem Cemetery in Jacksonville, Missouri, but would not disclose any of the details of the services to the newspapers.

Sources: *Cumberland Evening Times* (MD): November 30, 1962. *Denton Record-Chronicle* (TX): November 30, 1958. *The Constitution-Tribune* (Chillicothe, MO): November 30, 1962. *The Daily Telegram* (Columbus, Nebraska): November 29, 1958. *The Bee* (Danville, VA): November 29, 1962. *The Cedar Rapids Gazette* (IA): November 30, 1962. *The Hutchinson News* (KS): August 29, 1962. *Western Kansas Press* (Great Bend): November 30, 1962.

Hickock, Richard E.
Smith, Perry E.
April 14, 1965

During the early part of 1959 twenty-eight-year-old Richard Eugene Hickock and thirty-one-year-old Perry Edward Smith were cell mates serving terms in the Kansas State Penitentiary for burglary and bad checks. Another convict, who had worked for Herbert Clutter in 1948, spoke of the great wealth he was certain was in the Clutter home and told of a hidden safe which contained that wealth. Hickock and Smith decided that after they were released they would rob the Clutter home near Garden City in Finney County, Kansas. Smith was paroled in July and he returned to his home in Las Vegas, Nebraska. Hickock was paroled a month later and went to his parents' home in Edgerton, Kansas. After a brief delay Hickock contacted Smith and told him to join him in Kansas City to prepare for the planned crime, and the two men rendezvoused in November.

On the evening of November 15 the two ex-convicts drove to a point near the Clutter farm and just after midnight, armed with a shotgun and knife, they broke into the house through the unlocked door to Clutter's office. They found forty-eight-year-old Herbert Clutter in pajamas and asleep in the downstairs bedroom near the office, shook him awake and questioned him, but he insisted he had no safe nor any money in the house. He was taken upstairs where the two burglars captured forty-five-year-old Bonnie Clutter, sixteen-year-old daughter Nancy, both in pajamas, and the fifteen-year-old son Kenyon dressed in blue jeans and T-shirt, and locked them in the bathroom. Hickock kept guard over the family while Smith searched the house but he could find no safe so he stole their portable radio and put it in their car. The two robbers then took Herbert to the basement, threw him onto a mattress cover, tied him hand and foot, and gagged him. Soon he was joined by Kenyon, who was tied to a sewer pipe and gagged. They then returned upstairs and took Mrs. Clutter and her daughter to their respective bedrooms and tied them to their beds. Once everyone was securely tied both men returned to the basement and cut Herbert Clutter's throat, then shot Kenyon in the head with the shotgun, and afterward returned to Kenyon's dead father and shot him in the head as well. The two robbers returned upstairs and shot Nancy first and then Bonnie Clutter, point blank in the head. All of the Clutters died instantly from the initial wounds inflicted.

The two murderers were certain they left no witnesses before they fled to Las Vegas, Nebraska. Eight hours later two of Nancy's girlfriends arrived from Holcomb to ride to Sunday school with their friend and, getting no answer but finding the door open, entered and went to Nancy's room. When they found her murdered they ran out, screaming, and the person who had driven them to the farm called the sheriff's office. Coroner Dr. Robert Fenton examined the remains and determined that the women were not molested and, though the phone lines had been cut, it seemed nothing was missing from the house and nothing appeared disturbed so the authorities were baffled as to a motive. The Kansas Bureau of Investigation collected two footprints, one in the dust of the basement and another bloody footprint on the mattress cover beneath Herbert Clutter, but they could find no other clues for seven weeks.

Just before Christmas the ex-employee of Clutter, still in prison but now conscience-stricken upon learning of the murder of the Clutter family, contacted the authorities and told them that one of the men they were seeking was Hickock, now a parole violator. After New Year's Day the authorities arrested Hickock in Las Vegas, Nebraska, and on Sunday night, January 3, he provided a full confession and named Smith as his accomplice. The authorities went to the Hickock family home in Edgerton, Kansas, and found the shotgun and knife and also a pair of boots which matched the footprints in the dust in the Clutter basement. It was not long before they arrested Smith, and officers found a pair of boots with a track that matched the bloody footprint on the mattress cover on which Herbert Clutter was killed. Hickock's confession revealed that the holdup had netted them a radio, a pair of binoculars, and less than $50 in cash.

The trial of Hickock and Smith began at Garden City, Kansas, in late March 1960; they were found guilty of first-degree murder, and when the jury sentenced them to die by hanging the pair displayed no emotion. The defense did not challenge the state's case but made strong pleas for life imprisonment rather than the death penalty. Logan Green, who assisted County Attorney Duane West in the prosecution, told the jurors it was up to them to see that the laws of the state were enforced. Green acknowledged the pleas by defense attorneys Harrison Smith and A. N. Fleming but said, "I wish these two men (the defense attorneys) had been present Nov. 15 to make a plea for mercy for Nancy Clutter. I dare say there would have been six bodies found instead of four." The prisoners were taken to the penitentiary and lodged on death row to await the day of their execution, but the attorneys began the appeals process, which delayed the hangings for five and one-half years.

Finally all efforts had been exhausted, including the application to have the governor commute their sentences to life imprisonment, and the executions were scheduled for just after midnight on April 14, 1965. The gallows could only accommodate one man so just before midnight the prison's warden went to Hickock's cell and read the death warrant, and then he was escorted to the gallows. He took his place on the trapdoor and was asked if he had anything to say, and he replied, "I don't have any hard feelings. You are sending me to a better place." His wrists and arms, knees and ankles were strapped, the noose was adjusted, and the black cap was pulled over his head. In a moment the trap was sprung, and he broke his neck in the fall. He was pronounced dead by the prison physician at 12:41 A.M., and then the body was cut down and deposited in its coffin. Meanwhile the warden returned to Smith's cell and read the death warrant. The warden escorted Smith to the gallows and he chewed gum as he walked, winked at the witnesses, and smiled faintly. However, once on the trapdoor Smith complained, "I think it's a Hell of a thing that a life has to be taken in this manner.

I think capital punishment is legally and morally wrong." He was then quickly prepared and the trap was sprung. Smith was pronounced dead at 1:19 A.M. and the body was then cut down and deposited in the coffin provided, and the remains of both men were released to their families for burial.

Sources: *Dallas Morning News* (TX): March 30, 1960. *Garden City Telegram* (KS): January 4, 1960. *Press Telegram* (Long Beach, CA): April 14, 1965. *The Daily News* (Huntingdon, PA): January 4, 1960. *The Salina Journal* (KS): November 16, 1959; January 4, 1960.

Latham, James D.
York, George R.
June 22, 1965

On May 25, 1961, nineteen-year-old James Douglas Latham and eighteen-year-old George Ronald York escaped from the Army stockade at Fort Hood, Texas. They were bitter racists who resented having to take orders from black officers, but Latham had been jailed for stealing $40 from a fellow soldier and York was jailed for twice going absent without leave. They fled to Baton Rouge, Louisiana, and on May 27 used a wrench to brutally beat forty-three-year-old Edward J. Guidroz, a fish peddler, left him for dead, and stole his money and pickup truck. Guidroz recovered but Latham and York were sure they had committed a murder and later said that, having killed once, they decided they might as well continue to murder and rob.

They next went to Florida, and two days later, on May 29, they met twenty-five-year-old Patricia Ann Hewitt and forty-three-year-old Althea Ottavio of Valdosta, Georgia, who were vacationing in Jacksonville, Florida. The women were on their way to the dog races, and the two men befriended the women, then strangled them to death before they stole their money and automobile, found a .38-caliber revolver in the glove box, and etched three notches on the grips. On June 7 they were in Tennessee when they encountered seventy-one-year-old John Wittaker, a porter for the Louisville & Nashville Railroad, shot him dead near his home in Tullahoma and stole $40, and notched their gun handle once more. York later said they chose Wittaker "because he was black," and Latham added, "We don't feel bad about killing a nigger."

They continued on their murder spree into Illinois, and on June 8 they shot to death fifty-eight-year-old Albert E. Reed near Litchfield as he was driving to work and stole what little money he had in his pockets and his bright red automobile. Later that same day they bludgeoned to death sixty-nine-year-old service station owner Martin Drenovac near the Chain-of-Rocks bridge over the Mississippi River. On June 9 they arrived in Kansas, and when near Wallace they pulled to the side of the road and feigned engine trouble. Sixty-two-year-old Otto Ziegler, a Union Pacific Railroad employee, stopped to help them, and they saw that he was well dressed and were certain he would have money. They shot him with both a .38-caliber and a .22-caliber pistol, killing him instantly, and they robbed him of $51.

Robbery was the purpose of every killing up to that point but on June 10 the two murderers were in Craig, Colorado, and stopped at a dairy bar where they met eighteen-year-old Rachel Moyer, a motel maid. They invited her to join them at a local carnival and afterward took her to an isolated location near the river where they raped, robbed and shot her to death.

The two murderers continued fleeing westward and later the following day, June 11, they were captured at a police roadblock near Grantsville, Utah. Both prisoners talked freely of the killings and said, "We thought we were doing them (the victims) a favor by putting them out of their miseries in this rat race. Everyone believes in the idea of one man stomping another for his own gain. That's the problem." After authorities carefully weighed all the evidence in each killing it was decided the Kansas case was the strongest, and the prisoners were returned to Sharon, Kansas, for trial in the slaying of Ziegler. However, there was so great an outrage at Sharon that the trial was moved to Russell County, Kansas, on a change of venue. Both men were arraigned, given a preliminary hearing, and indicted, and their trial began on October 24, 1861.

Defense attorneys concentrated their final arguments on pleas against the death penalty, and neither York nor Latham took the stand in their defense. Marvin Thompson, one of the four court-appointed defense attorneys, argued that the state failed to prove premeditation, a requirement in first-degree murder convictions, and contended, "It's our position that it's not a first degree murder case. It's not even a very good second degree murder case." The defense attorneys also argued that there was serious doubt of the youths' mental condition, citing their Army record, which listed mental disturbances. After a thirteen-day trial the jury deliberated for six hours and forty-five minutes before rejecting the argument that the defendants were insane and found them guilty. On November 7 the two defendants were sentenced to hang on January 30, 1962, at 12:01 A.M. CST at the Kansas State Prison in Lansing. As the sentence was pronounced the two condemned men stood with heads bowed as Judge Benedict P. Cruise told the condemned youths to use the brief time remaining in their lives to turn to God.

An aggressive appeals campaign stayed the executions but when the first round of appeals concluded the date for execution was rescheduled for June 20, and the *Dallas Morning News* announced that the condemned killers had been granted a thirty-day stay of execution by the U.S. Circuit Court of Appeals at Denver, Colorado. The two condemned men had just ordered their last meal and flipped a coin to determine which should be hanged first when informed of the respite. Roy Cook, attorney for the killers, argued that their constitutional rights had been violated because they were denied court-appointed counsel at their preliminary hearing, but the three appeals justices upheld the murder convictions. Under the unanimous decision the two prisoners were granted ninety days for filing a further appeal with the U.S. Supreme Court. The appeals process then dragged on for another two years but finally, after the fifth appeal to the U.S. Supreme Court was denied, all avenues for judicial relief were exhausted. The date for their execution was set for June 22, 1965, four years after they were arrested, and Governor William H. Avery refused to intervene.

Two days before their date of execution the two prisoners were interviewed and they continued to express their anti-social feelings, calling life a rat race, and Latham, who had "I hate the World" tattooed on his arm, said, "You can't blame us and you can't blame our parents. It's the whole damn world's fault." York said, "I always wanted to know what it's like on the other side and now I'll get to see. We'll be able to sit over there and laugh at the rest of you guys trying to figure out what's going to happen. Y'see we'll already know." The two prisoners spent their final day fully resigned to their fate and had repented and found religion. They asked that prison chaplain the Rev. Edgar Meissner read the twenty-third Psalm, and both men donated their eyes to the University of Kansas Medical Center. Warden Sherman Crouse said that both men remained cheerful throughout that final day and fully enjoyed their elaborate final meal. The prisoners said, "We killed together, so we expected to die together," but the gallows could only accommodate one man at a time, and Latham won the coin toss so he went first.

Just before midnight the warden appeared at the cell door and read the death warrant to Latham, then the prisoner was escorted to the gallows where he took his place on the trapdoor. When asked if he had anything to say he responded, "There is nothing to say but that I am going home to heaven, and I hope to meet you people up there. I know it wouldn't do much good to say I'm sorry. God has forgiven me and I hope you people can see fit to do the same." Latham's wrists and arms, knees and ankles were strapped, the noose was adjusted, and the black cap was pulled over his head while the Reverend Meissner read the twenty-third Psalm, and when he finished the trap was sprung. Latham dropped, breaking his neck, and in sixteen minutes he was pronounced dead, cut down, and deposited in his coffin. The warden then retired to the cell of York and read his death warrant and he was escorted onto the scaffold. When asked if he had anything to say he replied, "I'm not mad at anybody." He was prepared while the Reverend Meissner performed his duty and then the trap was sprung. York was pronounced dead nineteen minutes after the fall; the body was then cut down and deposited in his coffin. After their eyes were donated the remains were released to their families for burial.

Sources: *Dallas Morning News* (TX): November 8, 1961; December 4, 1961; July 13, 1963; June 20, 1963. *Independent* (Long Beach, CA): June 22, 1965. *News Journal* (Mansfield, OH): June 22, 1965. *The Salina Journal* (KS): June 15, 1961; October 30, 1961. *The Salt Lake Tribune* (UT): November 8, 1961. *Tucson Daily Citizen* (AZ): November 6, 1961. *Waterloo Sunday Courier* (IA): June 20, 1965.

Oklahoma

In 1541 Francisco Vazquez de Coronado became the first European to see the land that would become Oklahoma, but it was the French who explored the eastern region. France claimed the area but ceded it to Spain in 1763; then in 1800 France reacquired the region. Three years later France sold Oklahoma to the United States as part of the Louisiana Purchase, excepting the panhandle, which was acquired from Mexico in 1845. The area was inhabited by the Osage and Quapaw Indians but by 1818 they had ceded all claims to their land, and a number of treaties signed by various tribes over the next twenty-five years turned over most of the remaining land, which was then occupied by a number of Indian tribes relocated by the U.S. Government under their policy of "relocation and concentration." The Indian Territory was established when, in 1830, the United States Congress passed a bill that required all eastern Indian tribes to cede their land to the government and move west to a designated region. The Eastern Cherokee tribe, under the leadership of Chief John Ross, fought against this "removal and concentration" policy by every means at their disposal. However, the tribe was split between the majority who wanted to remain on their ancestral lands and a large minority who favored the removal and the compensation to be paid. The Removal Party, led by John and Major Ridge and Elias Boudinot, wrote the Treaty of New Echota in 1835, and it was signed by many of the party members. In response the majority of the tribe, citing their Indian constitutional prohibition to selling Cherokee lands without approval of the National Council, branded the treaty signers as traitors. However, the signing of the treaty by such a large number of tribal members undermined the efforts of John Ross, and on August 1, 1838, the removal began, with the last group of the eastern Cherokees arriving in the Indian Territory about April 1, 1839. Cherokee Indians had been moving west to the region that would become the Indian Territory since 1794, but in 1828 the U.S. Government made a treaty with the western Cherokees and they were removed in 1832. By the time the eastern Cherokees arrived the western Cherokees, called "the Old Settlers," were well established. However, the Old Settlers were greatly outnumbered and, though everyone favored unification of the Cherokee Nation, the Old Settlers resisted the imposition of the far more sophisticated government of the eastern tribe. The Old Settlers felt that these "newcomers to their lands" should assimilate into the western tribe's culture and adopt their government, while the Ross party believed in the majority rule. To add to the confusion a third faction, the Treaty Party or signers of the Treaty of New Echota, were at odds with everyone and were declared outlaws, and some were marked for death. In June 1839 one hundred fifty members of the Ross party, in defiance of their leader, chose to execute the leaders of the Treaty party and managed to murder John and Major Ridge and Elias Boudinot before outrage ended their campaign. However, the conflicts and the politically motivated killings continued well into the 1840s. The Oklahoma Territory was carved out of the Indian Territory on May 2, 1890, and on November 16, 1907, the Oklahoma Territory and Indian Territory were recombined to become the State of Oklahoma, America's 46th state.

Smith, Archilla
January 1, 1841

Archilla Smith was a prominent member of the eastern Cherokee tribe but he was at odds with the majority when, in 1835, he favored removal to the Indian Territory and signed the Treaty of New Echota, often called the "false treaty." He was branded a traitor so in 1837 he was among the first of his tribe to move west. When the remainder of his tribe arrived Smith was already well established in the region, and, branded an outlaw and a part of the despised "treaty party," he formed a gang of murderers and horse thieves from among his family and friends.

In the late fall of 1839 just before dusk Smith was visiting a small village of Creeks who had been allowed to stop on Cherokee lands, and all the men had been drinking. Suddenly John MacIntosh, whose Indian name was Ah-kungh-yah-shee, appeared on horseback, riding hard among the men and bragging "What a man I am!" MacIntosh was also drunk and he charged at the men several times, bumping against the man holding the reins for Smith's horse which freed the animal from his grip, and once crashing into the hut of Paul which knocked off several boards. Smith had finally had enough, and the next time MacIntosh passed he grabbed his reins and the two men began to argue, then MacIntosh struck at Smith with a fist or with the whip in his hand, and Smith responded by pulling his knife and slashing at MacIntosh several times, missing. On the next thrust, however, Smith buried the knife blade into MacIntosh, and the wounded Indian rode off a short distance before he fell from his horse. None of the Indians present saw Smith stab MacIntosh nor did they see him fall from his horse as it had grown dark, but when Smith returned to the group he still had the knife in his hand. Smith left and in the morning light MacIntosh's body was discovered, carried into Paul's house, prepared for burial, and buried that evening.

A warrant was issued for the arrest of Smith for the murder of MacIntosh but it was not until early December 1840 that officers surrounded Smith and took him prisoner. Jails had not yet been built in the Nations so Smith was kept under close guard in various residences, and he was moved every few days to prevent a rescue. On December 15 he was delivered to the court and the proceedings began, with Looney Price acting as judge and Isaac Bushyhead prosecuting. After the preliminaries of seating a jury were completed many Indians testified about the events of that night, and after six days the jury retired. They deliberated for three days, and on the ninth day the jury reconvened to clarify certain testimony, then found Smith guilty of murdering MacIntosh. On Saturday, December 26, 1840, Judge Price sentenced Smith to hang at Tahlequah, the capital of the Cherokee Nation, on January 1, 1841. Looney, also the chief justice, reviewed the law and the facts and found nothing to recommend a change in the sentence, and many friends and family of the condemned man signed a petition which was delivered to the principal chief but he declined to intervene.

On his final night Smith drew up his will, and when that was done about midnight he lay back on his bed and watched for an opportunity to escape, but one of the guards noticed his movements and came closer thus preventing the attempt. Earlier, Stand Watie had tried to bribe a guard to let Smith escape, but the offer was refused. At 10:30 A.M. a wagon carrying a coffin pulled up to the hut, and Smith came out and boarded. His wrists were bound behind as he rode, seated in a chair, the three-quarters of a mile to the place of execution but the gallows had not arrived so the sheriff chose a tree for the purpose. A grave had been dug, but the family had decided to requisition the remains and see to the burial. A large crowd had gathered and moved to the tree, and just before noon the wagon was drawn beneath a stout limb.

The Reverends Young Wolf and Worcester were in attendance. The latter offered a prayer in English, and this was followed by Young Wolf offering a prayer in the Cherokee tongue. Smith then stood in the wagon and spoke to the crowd, and he condemned the authorities at Tahlequah, said he was preordained to die in this manner and did not fear death, apologized when he began to cry, and concluded "I have no more to say." Many in the crowd came forward to shake Smith's hand but the Sheriff, seeing it was nearing noon, ordered that no more come forward. Smith was told to climb upon the chair and then onto the plank stretched across the wagon bed, and he cooperated. The noose and black hood were adjusted and then the wagon was driven out. Smith dropped but his feet reached the ground, so several spectators quickly grabbed the rope and pulled him up until he swung free. He was examined, and it was found his neck had been broken in the drop and he had died instantly, without a struggle. Smith hung for an hour to ensure he could not be revived, and then the body was cut down and given to the relatives for burial.

Sources: Dale, Edward E. and Gaston Litton. *Cherokee Cavaliers.* Norman, OK: University of Oklahoma Press, 1939. Payne, John H. *Indian Justice; A Cherokee Murder Trial at Tahlequah in 1840.* Norman: University of Oklahoma Press, 2002.

West, Jacob
October 11, 1843

On August 8, 1843, following the biennial elections, Jacob West led a party of six men, including sons George and John West, in an attack on three election judges counting ballots in the Saline District. During the melee that followed George West stabbed Isaac Bushyhead, who had been the prosecutor of Smith, killing him, and all the men beat

David Vann, treasurer, and Elijah Hicks, associate Judge of the Cherokee Supreme Court, but Vann and Hicks survived and recovered. A large crowd finally surged forward and captured Jacob and John West, but George and the other three men escaped.

Jacob was tried and convicted of murder as he had led the party, even though he did not inflict the fatal wound. Jacob was sentenced to hang at Tahlequah on October 11, 1843. John West was tried and convicted as an accessory to murder and sentenced to receive one hundred lashes at a public flogging. On October 11, 1943, Jacob West was escorted onto the gallows and he took his place on the trapdoor. There is no record of a speech nor of the preparations, but these are relatively standard for this occasion. After he was pronounced dead his remains would be turned over to friends for burial. Four days later, on October 15, John West was publicly flogged, and he survived the ordeal.

Sources: Dale, Edward E. and Gaston Litton. *Cherokee Cavaliers*. Norman, OK: University of Oklahoma Press, 1939. *New Orleans Picayune* (LA): November 2, 1843. *Van Buren Intelligencer* (AR): November 11, 1843.

Radcliffe, Dick
February 21, 1844

Dick Radcliffe, a wealthy half-breed Cherokee, became intoxicated and during a heated argument with his wife he murdered her. He was arrested and taken to Tahlequah for trial, convicted of murder, and sentenced to hang. On appeal the principal chief refused to grant a commutation or pardon. On February 21, 1844, he was taken to the gallows, where he took his place on the trapdoor, his arms and wrists, knees and ankles were bound, the noose was adjusted, and a blindfold was tied over his eyes. There is no record of a statement. In but a moment the trap was sprung and Radcliffe dropped, breaking his neck in the fall. After all signs of life ceased the body was cut down and prepared for burial.

Sources: *Edgefield Advertiser* (SC): February 21, 1844.

Ootacauhur
February 9, 1845

In December 1844 Ootacauhur, a Cherokee Indian, murdered his wife near Tahlequah, the capitol of the Cherokee Indian Nation in the Indian Territory. He was tried, convicted, and sentenced to hang on February 9, 1845. On the morning of his last day he was escorted onto the gallows, where he took his place on the trapdoor and was asked if he had anything to say, but there is no record of a speech. He had his wrists and arms, knees and ankles bound, the black hood pulled over his eyes and the noose adjusted, and in a moment the trap was sprung. The condemned man fell to his death, and the body was then cut down and turned over to friends for burial by his tribe.

Sources: *New Orleans Picayune* (LA): February 26, 1845.

Unnamed
Unnamed
Unnamed
September 27, 1845

Three unnamed Cherokee Indians murdered a man named Bigelow and were arrested, tried at Tahlequah and sentenced to hang. On September 27, 1945, they were taken to the gallows, and they took their places side by side on the trapdoor. There is no record of a statement by any of the condemned men, but after they were in position their wrists and arms, knees and ankles were pinioned, the nooses were adjusted, and their eyes were blindfolded. In a moment the trap was sprung and all three men dropped to their deaths. After they had hanged a sufficient time to ensure they could not be revived they were cut down and deposited in their coffins.

Sources: *New Orleans Picayune* (LA): October 9, 1845.

Faught, Wheeler
April 23, 1846

In early 1846 it was decided that John "Stand" Daugherty, murderer of James Starr and a member of the Ross party, should be killed for revenge. Wheeler Faught, a member of the Treaty Party of the Eastern Cherokee tribe, was assigned to decoy Daugherty into a compromising situation where he could be murdered. Wheeler did his duty and Daugherty was killed and scalped. All of the participants escaped except Faught who was captured, tried, and sentenced to hang at Tahlequah on April 23, 1846. On the fatal day he mounted the scaffold and took his place on the trapdoor, and when asked if he had anything to say he confessed his crime. He then named fellow tribesmen Tom Ellis, Jim William, Washington Starr, John Ryder, James Taylor, and a white man named Madison Gerring as his co-conspirators. His wrists and arms, knees and ankles were bound, the black hood was pulled over his head, the noose was adjusted, and the trap was sprung immediately. Faught broke his neck in the fall, and as soon as his heart ceased to beat he was pronounced dead, cut down, and turned over to friends for burial.

Sources: Dale, Edward E. and Gaston Litton. *Cherokee Cavaliers*. Norman, OK: University of Oklahoma Press, 1939. *New Orleans Picayune* (LA): April 22, 1846.

Smoker Glass
November 6, 1846

Smoker Glass, a Cherokee Indian, murdered Wild Cat Campbell, another Cherokee, and was quickly captured, tried, convicted, and sentenced to hang at Tahlequah on November 6, 1846. On his final day he was brought forth, and he took his place on the trapdoor where his wrists and arms, knees and ankles were bound and he was asked if he had anything to say, but there is no record of a statement. He was then blindfolded, the noose was adjusted, and in a moment the trap was sprung. After he had hung a sufficient time to ensure he could not be revived the body was cut down and prepared for burial.

Sources: *New Orleans Picayune* (LA): November 25, 1846.

Takatokah
July 2, 1847

During June 1847 Takatokah murdered a woman at Beatrice's Prairie. He was arrested and taken to Tahlequah for trial, convicted and sentenced to hang on July 2. When the day arrived he was taken to the gallows where his wrists and arms, knees and ankles were bound and he was asked if he had any last words, but there is no record of a statement. In a moment the trap was sprung and Takatokah dropped to his death, and after hanging a sufficient time to ensure he could not be revived he was cut down and prepared for burial.

Sources: *Van Buren Intelligencer* (AR): July 30, 1847.

Scales, Henry
October 21, 1876

Seymour Thornton, a black man, and his wife Nan lived at Fort Gibson in the Indian Territory in 1876. During the early part of the year Henry Scales, a black man and former city marshal at Fort Gibson in the Indian Territory, coaxed Nan away from Thornton and they lived together as man and wife. This led to several heated verbal confrontations but no aggressive action was taken by either man until, on the morning of July 25, 1876, Nan told Scales that her husband had threatened his life.

Scales strapped on his pistol belt and started downtown, where he met Thornton coming in the other direction on horseback. Scales drew his pistol and snapped it twice, but it either misfired or snapped on empty chambers. Thornton then called out that he was unarmed and Scales demanded to know if he had threatened his life. Thornton denied it but offered to take back anything he might had said. Before Thornton could say anything further Scales drew a bead on his target and shot him with the next, single shot. Thornton's father then happened onto the scene and, seeing his son in his final death throes, fired at Scales, who fled afoot into Fort Gibson with Thornton's father in close pursuit. Scales ran into the store of Mr. Percival, who was then city marshal, and surrendered while begging to be protected. Thornton's father had acquired a shotgun and as he came into the store he aimed at Scales, but a patron wrenched the weapon from his hands before he could fire.

Five men were then deputized to take the prisoner to the Greenleaf courthouse, Illinois District, and Scales was turned over to Sheriff Lovely Rogers. His trial was set for August 26 but postponed to September, and when Judge Richard Fields became sick the trial was postponed to October. By October 12 the jury of eleven Indians and one white man had heard three days of testimony, they found Scales guilty of murder, and he was sentenced to be hung on October 21.

During his final days Scales was attended by the Rev. Jack Bown, and he had braced up so that he "met his sad fate with sorrow but fortitude." Three hundred people gathered about the scaffold to hear Scales speak, and he gave good advice and seemed almost cheerful as his wrists and arms, knees and ankles were bound. The black cap and noose were adjusted by Sheriff Rogers and then the trap was sprung. Scales dropped, breaking his neck, he was pronounced dead by an attending physician, and he was buried by the Reverend Bown that evening.

Sources: *Cherokee Advocate* (Tahlequah, I.T.): July 29, 1876; October 18, 1876; November 11, 1876. *Indian Journal* (Muskogee, I.T.): October 19, 1876; October 21, 1876.

Look-Back
October 31, 1876

Look-back, a Cherokee Indian, was tried at the Cooweescowee District court during the latter part of October 1876 for his second offense of horse stealing. He had survived the one hundred lashes he received on his first conviction so this time he was sentenced to be hanged on Tuesday, October 31, 1876, at the courthouse. He met his fate with the typical stoicism of the Indian, and his body was turned over to members of his family for burial by the tribe.

Sources: *Indian Journal* (Muskogee): November 9, 1876.

Dirt Seller
October 15, 1877

In June several full-blooded Cherokee Indians were involved in a card game in the Saline District of the Cherokee Indian Nation, and everyone was drinking liquor. Wilson and Jones began to argue and then began to fight. Dirt Seller, one of the other players, stabbed Jones in the back of the head causing a mortal wound. Wilson then picked up a stick and beat Jones, breaking his arms and pummeling his body. Jones lingered for a day before dying. There were a number of witnesses present and immediately after the attack they arrested Wilson, though Dirt Seller was able to flee. A pocket knife was found at the scene and thought to be the murder weapon but after examining the wound it was found caused by a large butcher's knife.

Wilson was lodged in jail; soon afterward Dirt Seller was captured and he joined Wilson behind bars. They were tried in late August, found guilty, and sentenced to hang at Tahlequah on Monday, October 15, 1877. They arrived at the Tahlequah jail on September 5 along with their signed order of execution. The Cherokee Supreme Court reviewed the court records and commuted the sentence of Wilson to life in prison but affirmed the sentence for Dirt Seller, who had struck the fatal blow.

Dirt Seller had been shackled but on Thursday, October 11, he managed to remove the shackles and made a desperate attempt to escape. As he fled he slammed one of the jail doors behind him but guard Rice Foreman shot through the bars of the door striking him in the hip. The condemned murderer continued to flee so Foreman shot again. Dirt Seller was returned to his cell and on examination it was found none of his wounds were serious.

On the fatal morning, just before the procession formed, the prisoner's friend Samuel Downing visited but said he would not accompany him to the gallows, and Dirt Seller asked, "What, are you afraid to see me hung?" Downing replied "No!" as the prisoner was taken from the cell. Dirt Seller was unable to walk to the platform due to the hip wound so two men supported him as he made his way onto the scaffold where he was seated. He called for his children, the oldest being only seven, and they all came onto the platform and bade their father good-bye before returning to the crowd of spectators. The Rev. J. D. Hillman next asked if the prisoner had anything to say, and Dirt Seller replied, "Yes, I am ready to die!" but then asked the reverend to pray for him and said he wanted to speak afterward. Once the reverend announced "Amen" Dirt Seller began,

> "I have only a short time to live. The law will be satisfied but I cannot confess that I am guilty. I do not deny that I cut the man, but the knife produced in Court was not the one used. I do not believe I cut the man hard enough to kill him. The knife I used was short and narrow bladed. A man named Jones scuffled with me. I don't believe it. But the man, who took him off the ground, killed him. At the time I cut the deceased I had two knives, one a large one in a scabbard and in the scuffle afterwards the large one dropped out. I picked it up and had it in my hand. I asked a prosecuting witness whether he believed that cut in the head was the cause of death of the deceased. He said no, it was not the cut but the beating he believed killed him. The murdered man threw up from the effects of whiskey and afterwards vomited a great deal of blood. This is all I have to say."

A shroud was pulled over Dirt Seller's body and then he was allowed to kneel and pray, and after a half minute he said, "I am ready" and was helped to his feet. His wrists and ankles were bound, the black hood was pulled over his head, and the noose was adjusted. In a moment the trap was sprung and

Dirt Seller broke his neck in the drop. The attending physician monitored his heart beat and in ten minutes pronounced him dead. The body was then lowered into the coffin provided, and the remains were turned over to his family for burial by the tribe.

Sources: *Cherokee Advocate* (Tahlequah, I.T.): September 5, 1877; October 17, 1877.

Satanoke
June 20, 1879

In February 1879 Satanoke and Anatecher murdered Foxtail by shooting him to death. All three were members of the Creek Indian tribe. Both murderers were apprehended and tried for murder, but after they were both convicted and sentenced to be shot on June 20 the chief, in reviewing the evidence, was convinced that Satanoke fired the fatal shot and pardoned Anatecher. On the morning of June 20 Satanoke arrived at the courthouse at 10:00 A.M. in the company of Captain Childers. Services were then conducted by the Rev. James McHenry, and then Judge Coweto Mico gave a speech emphasizing the effect and result of murder and told all to take warning from the execution. Satanoke was then given the opportunity to address the crowd of two hundred fifty, and afterward he passed among them saying good-bye to as many as he could. His wife and infant child were brought forward and he bade them a final farewell, and after his family retired he inspected his coffin and pronounced it a good job.

At 11:55 A.M. Satanoke was told his time had come so he took his seat in the chair provided, where he removed his boots and arranged his clothing. When he was ready he asked what guns would be used and he was shown two shotguns, but he asked that Spencer rifles be used, and this was granted. Satanoke sat erect, was blindfolded, and a piece of red ribbon was pinned to his chest over his heart. At exactly noon the command was given to fire and both rifles reported as one, and two bullets struck their target, killing Satanoke instantly. The body was then laid out on the ground, and his family took possession to arrange for burial.

Sources: *Indian Journal* (Muskogee): June 26, 1879.

Wheat, John
December 3, 1879

In 1879 John Wheat shot and killed Creek Indian Charles Torrey. At his trial he claimed that Torrey had fired at him three times before he returned fire with a single shot, which killed Torrey, so it had been a killing in self-defense. The jury did not believe the defense and convicted Wheat of murder and sentenced him to hang in the Chickasaw National Prison in Tishomingo on December 3, 1879. On the morning of the execution a huge crowd gathered around the outer prison walls, but there were few witnesses inside. Wheat walked onto the scaffold at noon and took his place on the trapdoor. While his wrists and arms, knees and ankles were being bound he spoke to the witnesses, telling them he wished to meet everyone he knew in heaven, that he had tried to serve the Lord while he was in jail, and he hoped he had received forgiveness for his sins. He was then asked about the murder but he persisted in his claim of self-defense. When it was clear there was no more to be said the black hood was pulled over his head and the noose was adjusted. At 12:23 P.M. the trap was sprung, and Drs. R. O. Trout, L. M. Carvons, and W. A. Reese monitored vital signs for twenty minutes before they pronounced Wheat dead. The body was then cut down, deposited into the coffin provided, and turned over to his family for burial.

Sources: *Cherokee Advocate* (Tahlequah, I.T.): December 3, 1879.

Hawley
September 7, 1880

Hawley, a Creek Indian with a jealous streak, shot to death another Creek Indian he thought was being too attentive with his wife. He was tried and convicted of murder and sentenced to be shot at Eufaula on Tuesday, September 7, 1880. When the day arrived he appeared at the place of the execution where one hundred Creek Indians had gathered. He took his place on the ground in a kneeling position on a quilt, and one friend grabbed each wrist and hand and spread them widely. The executioner, a relative of the murdered Indian, took his place a few yards away and fired a single shot from his rifle, which struck the target pinned over Hawley's heart. The condemned man fell forward, was laid out on the quilt, and he bled to death in minutes. The body was then prepared for burial.

Sources: *Indian Journal* (Muskogee): September 16, 1880. *New Orleans Picayune* (LA): September 8, 1880.

Dixon, Chester
September 10, 1880

Seventeen-year-old Chester Dixon, a full-blooded Choctaw Indian, lived with his mother and step-father five miles from Atoka. Their nearest neighbors were Choctaw Indians Washington and his wife Martha. In September 1879 Washington returned home from Atoka and found his wife dead, her head severed from her body and the torso and limbs chopped and hacked with an axe, and the murder weapon lay beside the victim. Washington called for help, and others reported they had seen Dixon leaving the house at about the time the murder would have occurred, and he was drenched in blood.

Dixon was arrested but denied the killing. He was tried and convicted, sentenced to be shot at noon on September 10, 1880, and was then released on his promise to appear, as was the custom. Choctaw law had no provision for an appeal so when Dixon was overcome by an uncontrollable fit after his conviction, and it was revealed he was subject to such fits and not responsible for his actions, he could not seek relief on that account. On September 9, 1880, Dixon and his step-father went to Atoka and ordered his coffin, then made the arrangements for his burial. Friday morning one hundred persons gathered about the courthouse to watch the execution but at 11:30 A.M. Dixon had not appeared. A reporter for the *Indian Journal* asked if he might break his parole and was told, "If he is alive he will be here within ten minutes, just as sure as the sun shines," which was followed immediately by the exclamation, "Here he comes."

Dixon rode up on his pony, dismounted, and sat on a tree stump with his head bowed as if in meditation. An aged Indian then approached him and told him, in the Choctaw tongue, to meet his fate as becomes a Choctaw brave and remember that nothing but his life could atone for the life he had taken, and to meet his fate feeling that his people had done justice in condemning him. Dixon then raised his head and gave the old Indian a hearty handshake, and he next walked about and shook hands with several others until, at 11:45 A.M., Sheriff William Nelson brought Dixon a change of clothes and he dressed in his burial suit.

As soon as Dixon was ready the sheriff directed him to the spot where the shooting would take place and Dixon stood facing his coffin. His step-father took his right hand and a cousin took his left hand while the aged Indian made a mark of charcoal over his heart, and the sheriff tied on a blindfold and directed Dixon to kneel. Once Dixon was on his knees Abner Woods, Dixon's cousin and the man he had chosen to shoot him, appeared and walked to within five paces. Woods took careful aim with his Winchester rifle, fired a single shot which struck the boy's heart, and Dixon collapsed forward and died without a struggle. Dixon's mother came forward and took charge of the remains, which were buried soon afterward with only a few friends present.

Sources: *Indian Journal* (Muskogee, I.T.): September 18, 1880. *Kane Weekly Blade* (PA): October 21, 1880.

Arneta
September 29, 1881

On April 15, 1881, Arneta, a Cherokee Indian, was drunk and became determined to get a supply of several gallons of whiskey he knew John Dry, a half-breed living at Long Prairie in the Going Snake District, had brought into the district to sell to the Indians. Arneta went to the home of Dry and shot him in the head three times, stabbed him ten times, then decapitated the body to be certain he was dead. He left the body where it fell and went to the home of a neighbor and, with a promise of ample whiskey, he convinced the neighbor to help him hide the body. They collected the remains and hid them in a remote location, laying out Dry with folded arms and then covering him with leaves. The two men went into the village and shared their whiskey with other men, became drunk and began talking about the crime, and soon they were arrested and jailed. A party searched for and found Dry's remains, and Arneta was charged with his murder. Arneta was tried in May and on May 25 he was convicted and sentenced to hang on August 10. Many thought that Arneta's sentence should have been commuted so the Chief took it under advisement, but finally he decided that the execution should proceed and the date was set for September 23.

The gallows was erected in the yard at the National Prison at Tahlequah, Indian Territory. Before being taken to the scaffold Arneta provided a detailed confession and listened to the reading of the death warrant. After 1:30 P.M. he was escorted from his cell onto the platform where he climbed the stairs with a firm step and gazed down at the large crowd. Deputy sheriff Thorne, while binding his ankles, asked if he had anything to say and Arneta spoke for several minutes commending the laws of the Territory and saying he deserved death, but made no allusion to religion or eternity. When he concluded his wrists were tied behind, the black hood was pulled over his head, and the noose adjusted. At 1:50 the trap was sprung and Arneta dropped five and one-half feet, breaking his neck. The doctor in attendance monitored his vital signs and pronounced him dead almost immediately. The body was then cut down, deposited into its coffin, and released to friends and family for burial.

Sources: *Cherokee Advocate* (Tahlequah, I.T.): April 27, 1881; May 25, 1881. *Galveston Daily News* (TX): September 30, 1881. *Indian Journal* (Muskogee, I.T.): September 29, 1881. *Syracuse Morning Standard* (NY): May 4, 1881. *Waukesha Freeman* (WI): May 12, 1881.

Haney
Lilley
April 3, 1882

Ockchunhaijo was an old hermit and miser, nearly seventy years old, who hoarded his money and lived in a crude hut in a remote location. Still, the old Indian and his habits were well known and he was respected among members of his tribe. Twenty-year-old Haney tried to rob the old man and broke into his hut, but was detected and driven away, arrested and charged with larceny. While he awaited trial Haney began to plan the murder of the old man, and thereby remove the only witness to his crime of attempted larceny. He enlisted the aid of twenty-four-year-old Lilley and a young teenager named Jones, and on the evening of February 12, 1882, the three men went to Ockchunhaijo's hut and demanded entry, but the old man recognized their voices and refused. They tried to break in but the old man threw himself against the door and frustrated their efforts, so Haney and Lilley fired bullets through the door, riddling the old man's body with six bullets and killing him in minutes. After the shooting the three men fled without gaining entry. Haney was immediately suspected and this led to his arrest and that of Lilley and Jones. They were tried, convicted, and sentenced to death, but Jones was a mere boy so the principal chief pardoned him, while clemency for Haney and Lilley was sternly denied and they were told to prepare for death.

Before their executions both men adopted the Methodist religion and were baptized. They told their friends they were at peace with God and would be admitted into His kingdom. On April 3 at 5:30 P.M. the two men were escorted to a gentle elevation a short distance west of Ockmulgee where they were allowed to say goodbye to one hundred friends and witnesses in attendance. Guards then stood them a few feet apart on the spot where they were to die, bound their wrists behind, and tied on blindfolds. At the order "Fire!" two rifles reported and each man was struck in the heart by a single bullet, they both fell forward, and in six minutes both men were pronounced dead. The remains were then given to relatives for burial.

Sources: *Galveston Daily News* (TX): April 4, 1882. *Indiana Democrat* (PA): April 27, 1882. *Salt Lake Daily Tribune* (UT): April 9, 1882.

Pettit, Willis
May 5, 1882

On Wednesday, February 22, 1882, at 7:30 P.M. Willis Pettit, a black man, went to the Johnson home where Margaret Bird, a black woman, and her daughter Julia had gone to visit Grace Johnson, who was ill. Pettit demanded that Julia return to him, as she had been living with him as his mistress but had left him at the prompting of her mother. Julia refused and her mother strongly supported her decision. Pettit backed toward the front door, over which hung a musket, and he half-closed the door as he continued to talk to Bird. Suddenly he grabbed the musket and shot Bird, with the ball striking her just below her left eye and lodging in her brain. Bird died instantly as Pettit threw down the musket and fled. A posse was organized by Sheriff Sanders, and they searched all night but could not find the murderer, but at 8:00 A.M. Pettit was marched into town in chains. He had spent the night hiding at the house of another of his concubines a mile from the murder and had asked a black man to put him in chains to prevent a lynching and take him to town. The prisoner was lodged in jail at Tahlequah, and his defense was that he had not intended to kill Bird but had fired at Julia. He was tried, convicted of murder, and sentenced to hang on May 5.

On the day of his execution Pettit was marched onto the platform, smiling and laughing as his wrists and arms, knees and ankles were bound. There are no details of his speech other than his persistent claim that he had meant to shoot Julia. The black hood was pulled over his head, the noose was adjusted, and the trap sprung. Pettit must have broken his neck in the drop, as there is no mention of a struggle, and he was buried that evening.

Sources: *Cherokee Advocate* (Tahlequah I.T.): February 24, 1882. *Chester Times* (PA): May 6, 1882. *Galveston Daily News* (TX): March 3, 1882.

Lucas, Ruben
May 31, 1882

Thompson McKinney, a half-breed Choctaw, had a trading post in the little village of Oaklahoma in the Choctaw Nation. On December 15, 1881, McKinney began a tour of villages and towns along the Arkansas border, and by December 20, while on the return trip by way of Oak Lodge, he stopped at the home of deputy sheriff Lewis Lucas. Ruben Lucas was spending the holidays with his cousin and when, after visiting a few hours, McKinney said he would go visit an elderly Choctaw he knew and return to the Lucas home for supper, Ruben asked to go along. The two men started out on fresh ponies, well armed.

In a few hours Ruben returned to his cousin's home and said McKinney had decided to stay with his friend and continue home from there. His speech was rambling and disjointed, his clothes torn and blood-stained, and he seemed apprehensive. Lewis accused Ruben of murdering McKinney but he denied the charge, and a heated argument resulted. While the two men were arguing McKinney's riderless pony appeared, lathered and with the saddle splashed with blood. A party was organized and a search was made of the entire surrounding countryside, but no trace could be found of McKinney. Ten days passed before his body was discovered in a remote ravine, carefully hidden, and it had been hacked and bashed horribly.

While the search continued Ruben was kept under such a close watch he was a virtual prisoner. He had maintained an indifferent attitude until told of the body, then said, "I killed him. I am ready to die." He appeared in Judge Rufus Fulsom's San Bois circuit court on May 1, and when asked to enter a plea Ruben yelled out, "Guilty!" then demanded that he be executed immediately. The judge refused the request, gave a brief speech about the atrocity of the crime, the high standing of the victim, and the sorrow of his friends, then told the prisoner to make his peace with God and gave him thirty days to prepare. Lucas was taken back to his prison cell, complaining that he did not need a day to prepare. During his final weeks he was sullen and withdrawn, and the warden reported that the prisoner said he had calculated carefully on the crime and punishment before he murdered McKinney.

Lucas, on his final morning, said he was glad that doomsday had finally arrived. Everything was in readiness at 12:20 P.M., and the prisoner was brought forth from his cell to the place of execution, three hundred yards distant in the courthouse yard. After the prisoner passed among the two hundred witnesses, including friends and relatives of McKinney and himself, he said his last goodbyes and took a seat on his coffin. A target was then pinned to his chest and a blindfold tied on. The executioner took his position a dozen feet from the prisoner; at exactly 1:00 P.M. the command "Fire!" was given and a single bullet pierced the target, and his heart, and Lucas died in seconds. The body was then laid out on the ground and the coffin lid removed, and the body was deposited. The remains were released to his family and buried that evening.

Sources: *Galveston News* (TX): June 1, 1882.

Luckey, Daniel
June 9, 1882

In December 1881 Daniel Luckey, a black man, was among a crowd of people in Gibson, Cherokee Nation, who mistook a youth named Cobb for a man against whom they all had a grudge. Cobb was shot by everyone in the crowd, his body riddled with bullets, and he died instantly. Everyone managed to flee except Luckey, who was captured and lodged in jail. He was tried, convicted of murder on circumstantial evidence, and sentenced to hang at the National Prison in Tahlequah, Indian Territory, on June 9, 1882. On the fateful day Luckey, shouting, singing and praying, was escorted onto the scaffold just before noon. He took his place on the trapdoor and was asked if he had anything to say to the one hundred witnesses, and he stated that he was innocent, that he died for others, and that he was going home to heaven. His wrists and arms were bound, his knees and ankles strapped, and then the death warrant was read to him. When the reading concluded the black hood was pulled over his head and the noose was adjusted. The trap was sprung immediately, and the doctor in attendance monitored his vital signs until his heart ceased to beat and then pronounced him dead. After hanging twenty minutes the body was cut down, deposited in the coffin provided, and buried.

Sources: *Galveston Daily News* (TX): June 10, 1882.

Running Bird
August 9, 1883

On August 20, 1882, Running Water, alias Orton, was taunting Running Bird until Running Bird, in a fit of intense passion and anger, murdered his antagonist. There was a long-standing feud between the two men, and there had been a number of incidents of taunting by Running Water, but Running Bird, who came from a reputable Indian family, had always refused to react violently until the day of the murder. The crime occurred in the Delaware District of the Cherokee Nation so Running Bird was tried there, convicted of murder, and sentenced to hang. There was some delay as Chief Bushyhead considered the matter but finally he declined to intervene and the date for the execution was set for August 9, 1883. The gallows was erected in the yard of the National Prison at Tahlequah, and Running Bird was escorted onto the platform before noon. There is no record of a speech but his wrists and arms were bound, his knees and ankles tied, a black hood pulled over his head, and the noose adjusted, and the trap would have been sprung at about noon. He hung until the doctor in attendance pronounced him dead, and then he was cut down, deposited in his coffin, and given to his family for burial.

Sources: *Newark Daily Advocate* (OH): August 10, 1883. *New Orleans Picayune* (LA): August 10, 1883.

James, Levi
December 14, 1883

On July 4, 1883, Levi James, a full-blooded Choctaw Indian, attended a celebration at Haskett City, three miles from his home. He was accompanied by James Fulsom, also a full-blooded Choctaw Indian. Both men came from respectable families, James being the son of Circuit Judge Davis James and Fulsom the son of the Rev. Willis Fulsom. James overindulged in liquor and "became stupidly drunk," so Fulsom and another friend took him home to be sure he arrived safely. When they arrived James insisted that Fulsom spend the night but he refused, and James then became quarrelsome. Fulsom and the other man started to leave, and James said if Fulsom left he would kill him. The two men continued at a leisurely gait when suddenly James, who was still mounted, started his horse at a run and when in pistol range fired a single shot which struck Fulsom in the back, killing him in minutes.

James fled into the Chickasaw Nation and hid for four months, but finally in early November he was recognized, arrested, and returned for trial. He was convicted in late November and sentenced to be shot to death in the courthouse yard at Sculleyville, eight miles from Oak Lodge, on December 14, 1883. When the moment arrived James took his position and the death warrant was read, then his wife and five children were allowed to bid him farewell and embrace him for the last time before being led away. James knelt upon a blanket and the black hood was pulled over his head. The sheriff then held his right hand and wrist while a deputy took hold of the left hand and wrist as the executioner came forward to within five paces. The executioner held a Colt revolver and took careful aim until the sheriff said "Fire!" and then he sent a single bullet through James' heart, killing him in two minutes. The body was lowered onto the blanket, laid out, and lifted into the coffin, and the remains were delivered to his wife for burial

Sources: *New York Times* (NY): December 15, 1883.

Barehead, Sarbee
August 4, 1885

In early August 1883 sixteen-year-old Sarbee Barehead, a full-blooded Creek Indian, murdered Okilissar, a fellow tribesman. There were reports that he had killed an entire family and later a preacher, but there was no confirmation in the record. He was convicted of murder and sentenced to be shot, but he fled. On July 30, 1885, an officer of the Creek Light Horse Guard learned the whereabouts of Barehead, and with a detachment of six men they swooped down on him. There was a running gunfight on horseback for three miles but Barehead reached an unoccupied house and hurried inside, where he found a second loaded revolver on a shelf. He reloaded his pistol and engaged the Light Horse posse in a gun battle, standing in the open doorway with a pistol in each hand. While returning fire he recognized one of the men in the posse, and after being shot in the leg he proposed to surrender to this man, and the offer was accepted. Barehead was taken before a judge who granted him five days to make his preparations, and he was shackled to prevent an escape. He was allowed to choose his executioners, and he selected Lewis Asberry and John Doctor, both excellent shots and one his cousin.

On the day of his execution, August 4, Barehead was taken to a wooded hill near Eufaula in the Indian Territory where one hundred fifty people awaited his arrival. He was seated on his coffin in front of an oak tree as the two executioners took their positions ten feet in front of him, Navy Colt revolvers in hand. His breast was bared and a piece of white plaster was pasted over his heart. A blindfold was then tied over his eyes but he pushed it up and asked that he be allowed to see, but Captain Philip Raiford, who was in charge, refused, and Barehead allowed the blindfold to be pulled down again. Raiford announced "Ready!" and the two executioners knelt and took aim, and at the command "Fire!" both pistols reported simultaneously. Both bullets struck the plaster target and pierced Barehead's heart, and his head slumped forward as he groaned twice. He died in seconds, was laid out on the ground, lifted into his coffin, and buried that afternoon.

Sources: *Evening Gazette* (Cedar Rapids, IA): August 6, 1885. *The New Era* (Humeston, IA): September 3, 1885.

Dyer, Saffron
August 21, 1885

Morgan Pah-ta-cher, a full-blooded Chickasaw Indian, was elected constable of Pontotoc County in the Chickasaw Indian Nation in late August 1884. One of his first duties was to arrest Saffron Dyer, also a full-blooded Chickasaw Indian, for larceny. The constable, with a deputy, went to Dyer's house near Stonewall and, anticipating trouble, they approached with Winchester rifles at the ready. The front door was opened a crack, and as soon as Pah-ta-cher stepped onto the porch Dyer fired from behind the door, the bullet striking Pah-ta-cher in the chest; as the constable fell dead his rifle discharged. Dyer then stepped out and fired twice at the fleeing deputy, the bullets striking him in the arm and side, but neither wound was fatal.

Dyer managed to avoid capture until Christmas day when he was lodged in the Tishomingo jail. His case came up for trial in Judge B. W. Carter's courtroom at the July session, and he was convicted of first-degree murder. He had claimed self-defense, testifying that there had been rumors that Pah-ta-cher said he would not take Dyer alive, but he was unable to produce a single witness to corroborate his claim. On July 30 Judge Carter sentenced Dyer to hang at the National Prison in Tishomingo on August 21, 1885. After carefully reviewing the facts of the case the principal chief refused to intervene.

When the fatal day arrived the death warrant was read to the condemned man in his cell, and then Dyer was escorted onto the gallows in the prison yard, where a hundred witnesses had gathered. He took his place on the trapdoor where his wrists and arms, knees and ankles were bound. He was asked if he had anything to say but there is no statement on record. The black hood was pulled over his head and the noose adjusted, and a moment later the trap was sprung. A doctor was in attendance and monitored his vital signs until his heart ceased to beat, and then he pronounced Dyer dead. The body was cut down, and he was buried in the Nation's cemetery in a neat walnut coffin.

Sources: *Indian Journal* (Muskogee, I.T.): August 21, 1884; December 26, 1884; July 30, 1885; August 27, 1885

Weston
November 2, 1885

Weston, a full-blooded Choctaw Indian, murdered his wife in late 1884. He was tried, convicted, and sentenced to die by firing squad. He reported to the place of his execution on the day designated and took his place on the quilt that had been prepared, kneeling and facing his executioner. A large audience watched as a target was carefully pinned over his chest and he was blindfolded. Two men then each took hold of a wrist and hand and spread his arms wide. A squad of executioners, a departure from the single executioner which was the custom, took careful aim from only a few yards away and each fired a single shot. Weston died instantly as it was reported that his body was riddled with bullets. Once he was dead his body was laid out on the quilt, his coffin was brought forward, he was deposited in it, and the cover was secured.

Sources: *Savannah Morning News* (GA): November 3, 1885.

Burris, Anderson
November 14, 1885

Anderson Burris, a twenty-two-year-old full-blooded Choctaw Indian, murdered his wife in late July 1885 and was arrested. He was tried in August and sentenced to be shot to death on November 13. The case was reviewed and the sentence affirmed by the council, and the principal chief refused to grant clemency or a reprieve. On Wednesday, November 11, 1885, Burris was taken to Atoka by Deputy Roberts and was turned over to Sheriff Hoke. The prisoner attended a prayer service conducted by Baptist Rev. J. S. Morrow and after the congregation left the condemned man spoke with the reverend through an interpreter. He said he was resigned to his fate, he was at peace with his God, and he was prepared to die.

On Thursday Burris, with a small posse, started for the place of execution and spent the night at the home of Deputy Carnes, where he was given his burial suit of checkered trousers and a white shirt, and he took from his old clothes a Jews harp and asked that it be given to his brother. At supper he said grace in the Choctaw tongue and after the meal spent the hours until bedtime smoking his pipe. He rested peacefully throughout the night, and at 9:00 A.M. the party traveled three miles to the place of execution at the court grounds of the Pushmataha district.

Burris was served lunch at noon, along with the twenty men in his company, and then the doctor in attendance, a white man dressed in buckskins with long flowing hair, offered Burris a stimulant but it was refused. The death warrant was then read to him but he requested a delay until his friends arrived, but when none appeared by 1:30 P.M. the death warrant was read again. Burris talked with one of the officers and expressed his willingness to die, then turned toward the spectators and prayed in the Choctaw tongue. He took off his shirt, exposing a black charcoal mark over his heart, and he knelt. The sheriff took his right hand and deputy Carnes the left, and they extended his arms. Another deputy stepped off ten paces, turned, and took careful aim with his Winchester rifle, and in but a moment he fired and the bullet struck Burris in the heart, killing him instantly. After the doctor pronounced him dead he was buried on the spot by the officers.

Sources: *Galveston News* (TX): November 15, 1885; September 25, 1894. *Logansport Daily Pharos* (IN): September 24, 1894. *Savannah Morning News* (GA): November 14, 1885.

Newton, Samuel
March 5, 1886

In October 1884 Samuel Newton went riding with his wife in search of game, and when they got to a lonely spot he fell back, drew his pistol, and shot her to death. He hid her body in the woods but she was found several days later. Her remains had been badly mutilated and partially eaten by wild hogs, the head being entirely severed from the body and lying some distance from the torso. It was at first thought the animals had killed Newton's wife but his queer actions led to a careful inspection of the remains, which focused suspicion on Newton, and he was arrested. He was tried at the spring term of the court, convicted, and sentenced to die at the Masholatubbee courthouse in the Choctaw Nation. He received a respite on June 6, just before he was to be shot, and his execution would be delayed for another nine months as various appeals followed, so it was not until early 1886 that all avenues for relief were exhausted and the date of execution was set for March 5, 1886.

Newton was led from his cell at 10:00 A.M. and seated on a blanket. When given the opportunity he confessed that he had murdered his wife but said, "I was urged by some unforeseen power." He was blindfolded and a white paper target was pinned over his heart. Two attendants, one on each side, held his wrists and hands firmly while the executioner, with rifle in hand, knelt in front and at point-blank range fired a single round through his heart, killing him instantly.

Sources: *Daily Republican* (Oscatur, IL): June 6, 1885. *Indian Journal* (Muskogee, I.T.): March 6, 1886. *New York Times* (NY): March 7, 1886. *Savannah Morning News* (GA): March 7, 1886

Atowah
Saunds
June 3, 1887

On about May 15, 1887, Atowah, Saunds and a friend, all Seminole Indians, were drinking together, and as the night progressed they began to quarrel and then fight, ending with the death of their friend. They were arrested, tried, and convicted of murder, in part on their own confessions. They were sentenced to die on June 3 and were released into the community. On the morning of June 3 both men reported to the place of execution on Little River where they mingled with family and friends of each condemned man and the murder victim, two hundred in all. Religious services were conducted and when the hour neared each man made an address, warning against the use of liquor. The death warrants were then read and the men were conducted to blankets spread on the ground a short distance apart, the ends of which were staked down. They knelt, blindfolds were tied over their eyes, and then officers took hold of each man's wrists and hands and spread them to fully expose their chests. The executioners then advanced and, taking careful aim, simultaneously fired a single round into each man's heart. The men fell forward with a lurch, were carefully turned over and laid out on the blankets. The first man died in six minutes and the second in eight minutes. The bodies were then given to friends and family for burial.

Sources: *Lebanon Daily News* (PA): June 6, 1887. *New York Times* (NY): June 7, 1887.

Spade Sunshine
September 9, 1887

Long John Watt, a full-blooded Cherokee Indian, had a horse stolen in April 1886, and he suspected Spade Sunshine, also a full-blooded Cherokee Indian, both living in the Sequoyah district. Horse stealing, for a first offense, could result in a public flogging of one hundred lashes and on a second conviction the prisoner could be put to death, but Watt never pursued the prosecution of Sunshine. On Christmas Day 1886 Sunshine found Watt in a crowd of people, walked up to him, and without a word spoken pulled his revolver and fired a single shot, the bullet striking Watt just below the lower left rib and passing through causing almost instant death. Friends ran to Watt and with his last breath he said, "Spade Sunshine shot me. I thought he was my friend."

Sunshine was arrested and taken to the prison at Tahlequah, tried in Judge J. P. Drew's courtroom, and convicted of murdering Watt. On March 2 he was sentenced to hang on May 27, but he received three respites delaying the hanging to September 9. Before the first respite, on May 27, Sunshine was only moments from being executed, standing on the trapdoor with his coffin beneath the scaffold, when the respite arrived. When September 9 arrived Sunshine was escorted from his prison cell to the scaffold, and there he told the crowd the details of the crime, but insisted he did not get justice at his trial and told the spectators, as he had testified at his trial, that Long John had threatened his life, "and it was him or me." He then took his place on the trapdoor where his wrists and arms, knees and ankles were bound, the noose was adjusted, and he was blindfolded. The trap was sprung at 11:48 A.M., and Sunshine dropped, breaking his neck in the fall. After hanging a sufficient time to ensure he could not be revived his body was cut down and deposited in its coffin.

Sources: *Galveston News* (TX): September 10, 1887. *Indian Journal* (Muskogee, I.T.): March 2, 1887. *San Antonio Light* (TX): September 10, 1887. *Huronite* (Dakota Territory): September 9, 1887.

Wright, John
August 11, 1888

On July 19, 1887, John Wright murdered Timothy Jefferson. He was captured, tried and convicted, and sentenced to die by shooting. The condemned man was set free to handle his affairs while his case was being reviewed, and it took a year before the sentence was affirmed and the date for Wright's execution was set for August 11, 1888. On the designated day Wright reported to the White Silver Springs courthouse yard. When directed he took his place kneeling on a blanket spread on the ground in front of the courthouse, with his back to a large tree. A target was pinned over his heart, he was blindfolded, and his wrists and hands were held by his brothers. The sheriff then approached to point-blank range and shot him through the heart with a single shot from his pistol, and he bled to death in five minutes. His brothers then took the body and saw to the burial.

Sources: *Galveston Daily News* (TX): August 12, 1888. *New York Times* (NY): August 13, 1888. *Reno Evening Gazette* (NV): August 14, 1888.

Puslee, Lyman
December 14, 1888

In 1888 Lyman Puslee, a full-blooded Choctaw Indian, murdered his brother. He was tried and convicted and sentenced to die by shooting at Ushkaomma. His case was appealed but on December 8 the supreme court affirmed the judgment and sentence. On the day designated, December 14, several hundred Choctaw Indians witnessed the execution as he sat on his coffin, erect and calm while his wrists and ankles were being bound. A target was pinned over his heart, but he declined to have a blindfold, and when the executioner gave the command to fire the condemned man did not flinch. Three bullets from Winchester rifles pierced the target and he died instantly. His body was laid out and then lifted into the coffin, which was stored nearby and brought forward.

Sources: *Logansport Journal* (IN): December 15, 1888. *New York Times* (NY): December 9, 1988. *Savannah Morning News* (GA): December 15, 1888.

Dunawa, Fred
Dunawa, George
April 17, 1891

In April 1890 a white family named Chambers moved to the Going Snake district and took up residence on the Wash Lee farm. The Chambers had two pretty, young daughters and Fred Dunawa became infatuated with one of them, wooed and won her, and they were married. On September 24, 1890 Fred Dunawa heard that a disreputable piece of gossip was being spread about his wife by Wash Lee's wife. This resulted in a minor confrontation, and then the men of each family took up the fight. On the evening of September 27 the two Dunawa boys and Wash Lee happened to meet near the Chambers' house, and an argument escalated into a fight. Lee was armed only with a small knife and a rock while the Dunawa boys were armed with pistols. The Dunawa boys riddled Lee's body with bullets but he lived in excruciating pain for two days before dying. Fred and George Dunawa were immediately arrested and lodged in jail, and when Lee died they were charged with his murder. The Dunawa boys were tried at the February term of the court, convicted, and both were sentenced to hang at the National Prison in Tahlequah on April 17, and nothing would delay the proceedings.

At 12:50 P.M. the two brothers, dressed in blue and wearing buttonhole bouquets, were brought from their cells and escorted onto the gallows. They took their places on the trapdoor, and the Reverend Wilson of the Tahlequah Baptist Church prayed for their souls. When asked if they had anything to say Fred responded, "I acknowledge my crime, I did it willfully. I have been a great sinner all my life until a few days ago. I confessed my sins to God and believe He has forgiven me." He then spoke a few words of advice in the Cherokee language before he asked for a drink of water. Both boys drank and then George declined to speak. Their mother had been on the scaffold, and Fred called out his last good-bye as she was being helped from the platform. His wife, who had been with him in the jail, had remained there as she could not bear to see his execution. During the talking and praying the men's wrists and arms, knees and ankles had been bound, and then the nooses were adjusted and the black hoods pulled over their heads at 1:10 P.M. In but a moment the trap was sprung, and both condemned murderers broke their necks in the fall and died without a struggle. The bodies hung for twenty minutes before the attending physicians pronounced them dead and they were cut down. The bodies were deposited into coffins and given to their family for burial.

Sources: *Galveston Daily News* (TX): April 17–18, 1891. *Kansas City Times* (KS): April 18, 1891

Parnochie
June 19, 1891

Parnochie, alias Lish Brown, a Seminole Indian living at Wewoka, on May 12, 1891, attacked Sam-o-gee, a Seminole band chief, with a hoe. He hacked his victim to death and mangled the body beyond recognition. He was immediately arrested and tried, convicted, and sentenced to be shot at Sasawka on June 19. On the morning of the execution a large crowd of Indians had gathered on the execution grounds. The Light Horse brought the prisoner at the appointed time and placed him in a seated position. A bright piece of cloth was then pinned over his heart, and two executioners took their positions six feet from the prisoner, so that the barrels of their Winchester rifles were only inches from his chest. At 11:00 A.M. the signal was given and both rifles reported simultaneously, both bullets struck Parnochie in the heart, and he died in seconds. Parnochie fell forward, and his body was carefully laid out and then lifted into the coffin, which was stored nearby and brought forward. The body was given to his family for burial.

Sources: *Arkansas Gazette* (Little Rock): June 23, 1891. *Muskogee Phoenix* (I.T.): June 11, 1891; June 18, 1891.

Urnest
July 7, 1891

Urnest and another full-blooded Seminole Indian had an argument about June 7, and Urnest knocked him senseless with a hoe, then used the hoe to kill the helpless Indian by chopping his body in two. He was quickly arrested and lodged in jail, tried according to Seminole law, and sentenced to be shot. At 9:00 A.M. on his execution day he was taken to the Council Grounds at Waheka and told he had two hours to live. He walked freely among his friends and family and those of his victim. When the time neared the captain of the Light Horse came forward and told Urnest to sit upon a flat rock nearby and prepare for death. Urnest took his seat, faced the crowd, and crossed his arms across his chest. The captain blindfolded him with a handkerchief, then beckoned to two of his Light Horse to advance and instructed, "When I give the word, fire at the top button of his coat." He stepped back and said "Fire!" and the two rifles reported simultaneously. The condemned man drew up his arms and twitched nervously so two officers ran forward, took him by the arms and laid him on his back on the grass, where he bled to death in two minutes. Everyone in the crowd then filed past to look at the dead man, and after all had passed by the coffin was brought from a wagon and the body was deposited. The lid was screwed on, the coffin was loaded into the wagon, driven to the grave that had been prepared yesterday, and buried with the greatest respect.

Sources: *Muskogee Phoenix* (I.T.): July 9, 1891. *Newark Daily Advocate* (OH): July 9, 1891.

Frog, John
Wolf, Jackson
July 28, 1891

On July 3, 1891, the Seminole Indians at Wewoka, Indian Territory, were preparing for the celebration of the forthcoming Independence Day holiday. Three of the Indians involved in the preparations were John Frog, Jackson Wolf, and Harg, and Frog and Wolf began quarreling with Harg. The argument resulted in a struggle and Frog bested Harg, but then all three men retrieved their rifles and in the shooting that followed Harg was killed.

The Indians did not recognize self-defense as justification so Frog and Wolf were arrested and charged with Harg's murder. The law required that Harg's death be avenged so that the families would not feud, which could result in the deaths of many tribal members for generations to come. The trial of Frog and Wolf commenced within days and "it was marked with great deliberations," and it was Wednesday before it closed. All the testimony relative to the killing was taken, and then came those interested who had a right to influence the council. First came relatives of the dead man who told how the widow and children were without support; how Harg had been a good man to them and how the tribe had lost a valuable member. Then came the friends of the accused who argued that no good would come from taking two men from the tribe. They, too, had wives and children who would suffer and the tribe would have to care for them. The hearing adjourned after the council announced that their decision would be pronounced on July 22, and the prisoners were remanded to the custody of the Light Horse Brigade.

On the day that the decision was to be rendered the council gathered in the stockade surrounding the courthouse and met behind closed doors. They began to discuss the matter and, though they resolved all issues in minutes, they remained sequestered so that the decision would not seem hasty. In seven hours the council emerged and the old chief announced,

> "Let all be silent that they may hear the decree of the council. Blood has flowed from the body of Harg. The widow and children cry for food and there is none to give them. Death came through John Frog and Jackson Wolf, and it is our thought there was no cause for the shedding of blood. Now this is our decree: When the sun shall kiss the death rock on the sixth morning, then shall John Frog and Jackson Wolf pay the debt by giving their lives into the family of Harg, that they may wipe out the stain, for our fathers have said it, that blood must be wiped out by blood. And to the widow and children of the murdered man shall be given the substance of John Frog and Jackson Wolf sufficient to keep them from want for one year. It is so decreed."

The two condemned man were kept under a heavy guard by the Light Horse Brigade, and the captain was held responsible for delivering them to the place of their death on July 28, 1891.

On the final morning the two prisoners were aroused at daybreak as drums began to beat in the village, and they were brought their last meal. After breakfast they were escorted into the stockade, a fifteen-foot-high enclosure built of heavy logs. A dozen feet from the eastern side was a large rock semicircular in shape, known as the "death rock" because all executions since 1866 had taken place there. The huge rock, which had been buried deep except for two feet above ground, was so situated within the enclosure that the sun would not strike it until 11:00 A.M. Already gathered in the enclosure were the families of the murdered man and the families of John Frog and Jackson Wolf, as well as the entire company of fifty men consisting of the council, a few invited guests, and the Light Horse Brigade.

The prisoners' bonds were removed and they were allowed to mingle among those in the enclosure, and they moved about chatting in what seemed more a holiday atmosphere than their last moments of life. The rock was avoided by everyone until the hour neared and the two men began to wend their way among the people, saying their final farewells, and drawing ever nearer the rock. The family of Harg then withdrew from the rest of the witnesses and cast lots among themselves as to who would avenge the death of Harg. Once this was decided the two condemned men walked to the rock singing their death songs, first in a low tone but increasingly louder until those outside could hear them and know the hour was near. The two condemned men walked side-by-side and then sat upon the rock nearly shoulder-to-shoulder. They folded their arms below their hearts and, without the slightest sign of fear, looked toward the family of Harg.

Six men armed with rifles stepped out and took their places ten yards in front of Frog and Wolf. The captain of the Light Horse Brigade then stepped forward and blindfolded the two condemned men, stepped away, and ordered "Fire!" All six rifles reported and the two condemned men lurched forward and lay on the ground, perfectly still. On examination it was determined that the condemned men had died instantly. The bodies were collected and it was announced, "The decree of the council has wiped out all blood feud between the families," and the whole tribe united in the ceremonies attendant upon the burial, as if they had died in battle.

Sources: *Fort Wayne Gazette* (IN): August 6, 1891. *The Arizona Republican* (Phoenix): August 8, 1891. *The Indiana Progress* (PA): August 12, 1891. *Weekly Wisconsin* (Milwaukee): December 13, 1891.

Waner, John
April 15, 1892

In July 1891 fifty-year-old John Waner, Ball Christie and John Muskrat conspired to murder George Daugherty in the Flint District. Though Waner did not fire the fatal bullets, he assisted the other two men in the murder. He was captured and tried in January, convicted, and sentenced to hang at the National Prison at Tahlequah on April 15, 1892. Nothing would arise to delay his execution. Waner was nervous during his last several days but he was composed when his final day arrived.

Before noon the prison gates were flung open and three thousand people rushed in and gathered at the foot of the gallows. As soon as the crowd settled, at noon, the prisoner was handcuffed and brought out by Sheriff Wash Mayes and several deputy marshals. He was dressed in a black suit with cravat and white gloves, and once upon the scaffold the handcuffs were removed and he sat in the chair provided. When asked if he wanted to speak he walked to the railing and reviewed his past criminal experiences, confessed that he was guilty of the crime but said that it was done in the heat of passion, then warned against the use of whiskey and bad associations. He said, "...I say again, I am guilty, but others were also implicated. I am not satisfied to pay the death penalty alone. Had three been punished I should have no regrets. Ball Christie, John Muskrat and I killed George Daugherty," and he then commented on the murder of George Hewing, but said it would all be published in the *Advocate*. He insisted that if he had been a member of a "protective organization," as the other two men were, he would not have been convicted.

After he concluded he took his seat and a hymn was sung. He then knelt for prayer with the Reverend Hawkins, and upon arising he took his place on the trapdoor. His wrists and arms, knees and ankles were bound by Sheriff Mayes, the black hood was pulled over his head, the noose adjusted, and at 12:55 P.M. the trap was sprung. Waner broke his neck in the fall and in thirteen minutes the doctor in attendance pronounced him dead, and seven minutes later the body was cut down and deposited into a coffin.

Sources: *Indian Journal* (Muskogee, I.T.): April 20, 1892. *Muskogee Phoenix* (I.T.): April 21, 1892.

Bearpaw, Thompson
December 30, 1892

In mid–1891 Raspberry Manus, a Cherokee, was a witness against Thompson Bearpaw's brother at Fort Smith, Arkansas, on a charge of selling whisky in the Indian Territory. Bearpaw's brother was sentenced to serve a term at the Detroit House of Corrections, but in early August 1892 Bearpaw received a letter from the warden saying his brother was very ill and would probably die.

On August 22, 1892, a social affair was given at the home of Cucumber at Tahlequah; as the night progressed dancing was called for, and Thompson Bearpaw, a capable violinist, was recruited as the musician. After playing two sets Bearpaw gave the instrument to Cucumber and joined the other dancers. Everything seemed to go well for a while but suddenly during a whirl Bearpaw pulled out a .44 Colt revolver and aimed it at Raspberry Manus saying, "This is the way me and my brother used to do when we went to dances," and immediately fired. The first bullet struck Manus in his arm, and he tried to shield himself behind a woman. A second shot was fired right by the woman's neck and this bullet struck Manus in the breast. Manus collapsed as everyone ran for the doors, and then Bearpaw leisurely took aim at his helpless victim and shot him a third time, killing him instantly. Bearpaw fled into the woods and evaded capture until October when a sheriff's posse surrounded him and took him prisoner without resistance while he was seated on a log with his fully loaded Winchester rifle on his lap. Bearpaw was lodged in jail, and his trial in November was long and tedious, but he was convicted of first-degree murder. When Judge Gunter sentenced him to hang at the National Prison at Tahlequah on February 28, 1893, he fainted.

During his time in prison Bearpaw was cheerful, but as the day for his hanging neared he became concerned because of the heavy overcast that persisted. He believed in the old Cherokee legend that if a condemned Indian was executed on a cloudy day his spirit would not reach the happy hunting ground. Bearpaw's wife and daughter visited his last night, and a guard overheard him ask her to bring poison so he could cheat the hangman, so the watch was doubled.

Bearpaw slept until 8:00 A.M. and refused breakfast, then spent the morning with the Rev. Lacy Hawkins. At 12:30 P.M. the death warrant was read and interpreted, and two deputies escorted Bearpaw to the gallows. He mounted the scaffold with a firm step, and when asked if he wanted to speak he said, as interpreted, "I am sorry for what I have done. I acted in the heat of passion and hope those who are listening will take warning and never indulge in fire-water." A hymn was sung and a prayer offered by the Reverend Hawkins. While this was going on High Sheriff D. W. Mayes had his deputies bind Bearpaw's wrists and arms, knees and ankles, pull the black hood over his head, and adjust the noose, and when the reverend announced "Amen!" the sheriff sprang the trap. Dr. R. L. Fite waited beneath the scaffold and monitored vital signs for eleven minutes before pronouncing the prisoner dead. The body was then cut down, deposited into a coffin, and given to his family for burial.

Sources: *Arkansas Gazette* (Little Rock): December 31, 1892. *Daily Review* (Decatur, IL): January 1, 1893. *Muskogee Phoenix* (I.T.): November 24, 1892; January 5, 1893.

Loring, Elias
March 10, 1893

Elias Loring, a full-blooded Chickasaw Indian, had been raised during a part of his youth by Susan "Granny" Cravatt, and after he became a man he moved to a home not more than a mile from hers. Loring was rumored to be a "bad Indian" and once had been charged in the brutal beating death of Philip Colbert, but on the night before the trial began the only witness, Philip's brother Icom, was mysteriously murdered, and Loring was set free. Loring had a wife but he took a mistress into his home, and his wife dared not complain, and he was not faithful to his wife or mistress.

On January 30, 1893, Agnes Bellei, a Chickasaw Indian who lived near the home of eighty-year-old Cravatt thirty miles from Pushmataha, was visiting her neighbor. After 9:00 P.M. the two women were inside when Granny suddenly arose and went to the door, opened it, and invited someone to step in and sit. Bellei thought it strange as she had heard no sound, but then came the sound of heavy footsteps on the porch walking toward the threshold. In a moment a hulking figure, concealed in heavy wrappings and with a slouch hat pulled down, stood in the doorway, and as soon as he was close he fired his pistol once, the bullet striking the old woman in the temple. Granny collapsed to the floor, dead instantly, and in the flash of the gunfire Bellei saw that the figure was twenty-six-year-old Elias Loring. Loring hurried away, passing Granny's granddaughter Amy, and he was recognized again. Loring hurried home and when a peddler called he told him that he had been very sick with pneumonia as the result of a curse placed by Cravatt. Granny, he insisted, was a witch, and Loring said he was certain that the only way to lift the curse, and save his life, was to kill her.

Philip Johnson, the sheriff of Jackson County, was called to the scene and started a search for Loring, and in thirty-six hours he had his prisoner lodged in jail. Loring claimed that he had been bedridden and could not have fired the fatal shot, but in early February he was indicted by the grand jury, and on February 14 he entered a plea of not guilty. His trial followed immediately but the peddler, to whom he had confessed, was not available to testify. However, Bellei testified that she saw Loring shoot Granny, and then the defense produced a clergyman who said he sat with Loring until 8:00 P.M. that night and the defendant was not able to get out of bed. There were, however, a number of facts which corroborated the testimony of Bellei, and Loring had enough time to do the deed after the clergyman left, so he was found guilty of murder, and circuit Judge Hampton of the third district, on the following day, sentenced Loring to be shot to death on March 10, 1893. He was remanded to the custody of the sheriff while the case was appealed, but Justice Everett refused to hear the matter as it was based entirely on baseless technicalities and not on new facts or evidence.

Loring was kept in jail until the day arrived. Before noon he was taken out to the enclosure where a large crowd had gathered, and he mingled among them and bid farewell to all his friends and family. Just before noon he was told to take his place on the flat rock which had served as the place of execution for thirty years. He sat and faced the crowd, folded his arms below his chest, and looked at Sheriff Johnson as he took careful aim. The sheriff fired a single shot which struck Loring in the center of his chest and he fell forward. He was then laid out on a quilt spread on the ground where he bled to death in minutes. The body was then lifted into a coffin and given to the tribe for burial.

Sources: *Daily Citizen* (Iowa City, IA): March 12, 1893. *Galveston News* (TX): March 11, 1893. *Pittsburgh Press* (PA): April 1, 1893. *Savannah Morning News* (GA): March 11, 1893.

Bird, James
June 30, 1893

In January 1892 James Bird, a black Choctaw, became angry at his mother-in-law and attacked her with a knife, hacking her to death so brutally that she was partly dismembered. When tried he pled guilty to manslaughter and was sentenced to be publicly flogged, and one hundred lashes were administered. His wife then refused to live with him but allowed him to visit her occasionally, but this arrangement wore on Bird until late one night in mid–April 1893 he went to his wife's home, called to her, and when she came out he shot her in the head, killing her instantly. He avoided capture until mid–May when he surrendered to a deputy marshal, and he was lodged in the U.S. jail, then delivered to the sheriff of Sculleyville County and moved to the jail at San Bois in Gaines County. In late June he was tried at the Choctaw court in Wilburton, convicted of murder, and on June 20 he was sentenced to be shot on June 30, 1893.

When the hour of 11:00 A.M. neared Bird took his seat upon a plank in front of a large tree, where he was blindfolded and a white paper target was pinned over his chest. Ed Loomis and Robert Anderson then each grabbed a wrist and held his arms out, baring his chest to executioner Sheriff John Perry of Gaines County. The sheriff took his position five paces from the condemned man, took careful aim with his Winchester rifle, and fired a single bullet through his heart. Bird did not die and cried out, and tried to raise up but he was held down by his attendants. He was then gagged with a handkerchief to stifle his screams, and he bled to death in three minutes. As soon as Bird was dead his body was deposited into the coffin provided and carried to the grave, which had been dug previously, and buried.

Sources: *Galveston News* (TX): July 1, 1893. *Muskogee Phoenix* (I.T.): June 22, 1893.

Mayes, Sam
October 6, 1893

On July 3, 1893, Sam Mayes, grandson of Chief Joel B. Mayes, and Jim Christie, son of the notorious outlaw Ned Christie, were drinking and playing cards at Mike Pritchett's at Barren Fork. During the game Mayes was the loser, and he had also bet and lost several sentimental trinkets, and this angered him. It was quite dark when they left together and Christie was heard to say, "I'll be a witness against you, here or at Fort Smith." The next morning Christie's dead body was found about where they were last seen together. Christie had been shot in the back of his head, his throat was cut from ear to ear, he had been stabbed several times and the body had been mutilated, and his head was crushed with a rock. The body had been dragged a short distance through mud and around the body were boot tracks, all of which matched Mayes' boots. Mayes claimed that he and Christie were attacked by a third man and he had fled, only to turn around and see the man attack Christie who lay helpless on the ground.

When the area was searched there were no tracks except Mayes' and Christie's boot tracks, and a .44-caliber and .38-caliber bullet casing were found and collected. Mayes could not explain why he had not gone to Christie's aid, called for help, or made any attempt to report the attack. Mayes was arrested and lodged in jail, and at his first trial in late July the jury, deadlocked, could not decide on his guilt. A new jury was seated for his second trial in August. On August 23 the jurors found him guilty of premeditated murder and he was sentenced to hang at Tahlequah on October 6.

On his final day Mayes was brought from his cell at 12:30 P.M. and he took his place on the gallows, where he was asked if he had anything to say to the small number of witnesses in the yard. With Henry Dick as his interpreter he said,

> Friends, I have made a full confession and no doubt you will see it in a few days, but my time has come and I wish to make you a short talk. The crime for which I am about to suffer the penalty, I confess to have committed, though it was not premeditated murder. I got justice and am satisfied. Boys, I will give you some good advice. Don't carry pistols, get drunk and be tough, I am a specimen of that kind of a boy, and you see what it has led me to. No matter how much you try to hide your crimes the law will always find you out. Parents, see that your children do not grow up to be drunkards. Correct them in their evil ways and see that they grow up to be righteous men. Boys, do not let my last words pass by unheeded, take warning from me and obey your parents. This is all I have to say, Farewell!

While he spoke the straps were applied to his wrists and arms, knees and ankles, and as soon as he concluded a prayer was offered by the Rev. N. Bilting. The noose was then adjusted, the black hood was pulled over his head, and the trap was sprung immediately. Drs. Fite and Murray waited below the gallows and monitored vital signs until they pronounced Mayes dead in twelve minutes. The body was then cut down, deposited in a coffin, and turned over to relatives for burial.

Sources: *Cherokee Advocate* (Tahlequah, I.T.): July 8, 1893; October 7, 1893. *Muskogee Phoenix* (I.T.): October 12, 1893.

Ponaska, Tom
October 9, 1893

In late 1892 Tom Ponaska, a Creek Indian, learned that light horseman Simon Tully had made application for a writ to arrest him for horse-stealing, but a family feud aggravated the circumstances. Ponaska lay in wait and shot down Tully, then escaped. He made a nuisance of himself throughout the Creek Nation until a reward of $500 was issued for his capture, and he was cornered in early September 1893, arrested, and lodged in jail. He was quickly tried for murder, convicted, and sentenced to be shot to death in front of the courthouse at Wellington on Friday, October 9.

On Friday afternoon he was brought out of his cell when all was in readiness and he took a seat upon his coffin, folded his arms, crossed his legs, and stared at light horsemen Johnson and Edwards, his executioners, who were three yards distant. The two men took careful aim with their Winchester rifles at the white paper target pinned over Ponaska's heart and, at the signal of the high sheriff, they fired simultaneously. One bullet struck just above the target and the other pierced the center of the target, and Ponaska slumped over and bled to death in minutes. His body was lifted into the coffin, the lid was secured, and he was buried later that day.

Sources: *Belleville Telescope* (KS): October 13, 1893. *Janesville Gazette* (WI): October 10, 1893.

Dick, Joseph
February 16, 1894

In early August 1893 twenty-five-year-old Joseph Dick, a Creek Indian, had some difficulty with Thomas Gray, a member of his tribe. He snuck up behind Gray in a remote part of an abandoned orchard near Eufaula and shot him in the back three times, killing him instantly. He left the body of Gray, a member of his tribe, to decompose and be devoured by animals, expecting the remains would never be discovered. Gray's unexplained absence started a search but it was three weeks before two boys, exploring the old orchard, stumbled upon the skeletal remains. They notified the authorities and the bones were collected and buried. Dick was immediately suspected, arrested, tried, convicted and sentenced to be shot on September 4. Chief Perryman then granted a respite to February 16, 1894, to consider the matter, but the council could find no reason to interfere and ordered the execution to proceed. However, in the meantime Dick agreed to return to custody, as the Creek Indians had no jail, if he was allowed to go to the many Christmas celebrations and dances throughout the area. He was released, and the next morning he reported for breakfast. On another occasion Dick was released to get a load of firewood, and returned in three hours with the wagon loaded. After that he was allowed his freedom on the promise he would return for meals, and he never disappointed his captors. A week before his execution Dick was baptized into the Baptist church.

On the appointed day Dick confessed his crime to his attorney, Bunnie McIntosh, and it was McIntosh who told him his time was up. The two men marched out of the courthouse shortly before 3:00 P.M. Dick was asked if he had anything to say but he declined, and then the Rev. William McCombs prayed for his soul. McIntosh then made a brief speech before Dick was blindfolded and sat upon a box in front of a large tree. He leaned back against the tree trunk while McIntosh pinned a target over his heart. Robert Hawkins and John Hawkins then took their positions five yards in front of the condemned man, aimed their rifles, and at the command of Captain Barney Green they each fired into the target, the bullets entering Dick's heart less than an inch apart and exiting his back into the tree trunk. Dick gasped and groaned, fell back, and was then carefully lifted to the ground, where he lingered for six minutes before he died. His remains were then given to his family for burial by the tribe.

Sources: *Arkansas Gazette* (Little Rock): February 25, 1894. *Indian Journal* (Eufaula): February 22, 1894. *The Galveston News* (TX): February 17, 1894.

Tulmoskey
March 1894

The romantic tale of a full-blooded Seminole Indian stealing a horse to ride one hundred miles to be by the side of his dying lover is just too good to be true, but it is included here because of the insistence by many that it is true. According to the reminiscence of April 4, 1907, in late February or early March 1894, Tulmoskey learned that his sweetheart was dying but he had no horse, so he immediately stole one to ride to her bedside. The law in the Indian Territory, generally, was that for the first offense of horse-stealing the thief was punished by one hundred lashes inflicted at the public flogging post, but for a second offense he was sentenced to die. It might be presumed that one horse, being ridden hard, could not have carried its rider the entire distance and would have to be replaced at regular intervals along the route, and a string of fresh horses would be needed to ride one hundred miles, so Tulmoskey may have stolen as many as a dozen horses.

When Tulmoskey returned home he was arrested, taken to Wewoka, tried and sentenced to be shot to death in three weeks. The condemned man was released to handle his affairs and, on the designated day, he appeared at Wewoka for his execution. As the hour neared he dressed in his best clothes and then was taken into the council courtyard where he mingled with his friends, relatives, and curious residents. Just before 11:00 A.M. he was told by the Light Horse, the Seminole Indian police, that he should take his position, and he sat upon the execution rock with his back to the huge white oak tree behind, where he was blindfolded and a white paper heart-shaped target was pinned to his chest. A Light Horse officer, a crack shot, took his position fifteen paces in front of Tulmoskey and upon the hour fired a single bullet from his Winchester rifle, striking the center of the target. After it was confirmed that Tulmoskey was dead his body was lifted and carried into the nearby forest where he was buried in an unmarked grave.

The main problem with this wonderful tale is that there is no record of the event in any of four Indian newspapers between March 1 and March 29, 1894, nor in any other newspaper in the United States. The reminiscence reports that this was the last execution of a Seminole Indian; on October 9, 1896, John Bloss, or Pulmusky (note the similarity in the name), was the last full-blooded Seminole Indian executed; and the tale mentions the Curtis Act, which at the time of Bloss' execution was being discussed, written and revised five times before it was passed on June 28, 1898.

Sources: *Guymon Herald* (OK): May 16, 1909. *Oklahoman* (Oklahoma City): April 14, 1907; May 16, 1909. *New State Tribune* (Muskogee, OK): April 4, 1907.

Allen, Jim
September 24, 1894

In 1889 twenty-year-old Jim Allen, a full-blooded Choctaw Indian, was arrested in Jackson County, Oklahoma, on a charge of larceny, and the principal witness against Allen was another Choctaw Indian named Dixon Hunter. To avoid a prison sentence Allen lay in wait for Hunter and decapitated him with an axe. Sarah Battlesi, a Choctaw squaw, saw the murder but Allen threatened her with the same fate if she reported the crime. Battlesi, after four years, told authorities the details of Hunter's murder. Allen was arrested, brought to trial in August 1894, convicted of murder in the first degree, and sentenced to be shot on September 24, 1894. Neither appeal nor application for clemency sent to Governor William C. Renfrow delayed the proceedings. The prisoner was kept in the Pushmataha jail, a flimsy affair from which he could have easily escaped, but the condemned man believed escape would brand him a coward — a fate worse than death.

On the day of his execution a large crowd, including thirty Choctaw Indians, assembled at the Pushmataha courthouse grounds at an early hour. The early arrivals were rewarded when the prisoner made his appearance at 8:25 A.M. for Christian services followed by Indian ceremonies. After returning to his cell Allen's spiritual adviser explained that he could not expect forgiveness if he did not confess his sins, and the prisoner replied, "I am guilty. I killed Dixon Hunter."

At 1:00 P.M. Deputy Robert Jackson placed a lemon crate five paces from the courthouse door and then brought Allen from the jail. When Allen asked if his "tricke" had come — meaning his coffin and burial clothes — he was assured they had arrived. He then knelt to pray and upon rising rolled open the bosom of his shirt revealing a quarter-sized white mark painted over his heart. He took his seat on the crate facing the courthouse door while Deputy Jackson retired into the courthouse and, staring at his watch and with his .44-caliber Winchester at hand, he waited.

Seconds before the designated time of 2:00 P.M. a distant dog barked, and Allen, thinking it an omen, was distracted, so deputy Jackson seized upon that opportunity to shoot the condemned man once in the heart. Allen froze for several seconds before lurching backward onto the ground and uttering several loud groans. Blood spurted four feet into the air from the half-inch hole in his breast so two Indian companions stuffed cotton and rags into the wound to stem the gusher, and Allen bled to death in eight minutes. The remains were buried that evening.

Sources: *Logansport Daily Pharos* (IN): September 24, 1894. *The Galveston Daily News* (TX): September 25, 1894.

Pratt, Caleb
November 2, 1894

Caleb Pratt, a black Choctaw, had a disagreement with another Choctaw Indian and killed him. He was captured, tried and convicted of murder in August 1894 and, though he admitted the killing, he insisted it was an accident. Judge Hamilton then sentenced him to die by shooting on September 24 at the Pushmataha courthouse, with Jim Allen. The case was appealed, which stayed the execution, but on September 25 the decision went against Pratt and he was sentenced to be shot on November 2, and the responsibility once again fell upon Deputy Bob Jackson. After noon on the day of execution Deputy Jackson placed a wooden crate a short distance from the courthouse door and then brought Pratt from the jail. Pratt prayed and then opened his shirt, revealing a white mark painted over his heart. He took his seat on the crate facing the courthouse door while Deputy Jackson retired into the courthouse and, staring at his watch and with his .44-caliber Winchester in hand, he waited. Seconds before the designated time of 2:00 P.M. Deputy Jackson took careful aim and fired, and

Pratt lurched forward onto the ground and bled to death in minutes. The remains were buried that evening.

Sources: *Advocate* (Newark, NJ): November 4, 1894. *Logansport Daily Pharos* (IN): September 24, 1894. *Galveston Daily News* (TX): September 25, 1894.

Lewis, Silan
November 5, 1894

When the Choctaw tribe was removed from their homeland to the Indian Territory two opposing political parties developed. The National Party, known as the Eagles, was progressive and wanted to have all the tribal lands divided into tracts granted to individual members of the tribe, and the Eagles were friendly toward the settlement of whites on Choctaw lands. The opposing party was known as the Standpatters or Buzzards, and they wanted to maintain the status quo of tribal ownership of their lands, and they did not want whites settling on tribal lands. Over time members of the two parties became bitter enemies until, in 1892, there was a hotly contested election for tribal chief with Wetson Jones representing the Buzzards and Jacob Jackson representing the Eagles.

On September 10, 1892, the Buzzards held a campfire meeting near Wilburton, and fifty-two-year-old Silan Lewis, one of the leaders, said, "The best way to end the friendship between the Eagles and the whites is to kill the Eagles, then forbid whites to settle on Nation land." The next morning six of the leaders of the Eagle party were found shot to death within forty miles of the encampment, and among them was Joe Hoklatubbe of the Hartshorne district, as well as Elias Colbert, Frank Frascier, Robertson, Nelson, and one other, but they did not find Green McCurtain and Abner Persie. Frascier's wife and her mother recognized four of the murderers, including Silan Lewis and Simon Wade. When Chief Green McCurtain, commander of the Light Horse, went to Tuskahoma to investigate, Silan Lewis admitted to being in the party which attacked the cabin of Hoklatubbe, killing him.

Lewis was arrested and he was soon joined by Simon Wade and twenty-four others, all charged in the murders of the Eagle leadership. Lewis and Wade were tried for Hoklatubbe's murder in Judge Holston's Mosholtubbe district courtroom and sentenced to be shot to death on September 8, 1893. They were kept in jail, and when the day arrived they were taken out to the court grounds ten miles from Wilburton, and they alternately sang their death songs and prayed. Their graves had been dug on a little hill four hundreds yards distant, but visible to the crowd gathered for the executions. They were stripped to the waist and seated upon their coffins but then Robert Benton, captain of the Light Horsemen, rode up and announced that the two men had been granted new trials by Judge Holston.

The prisoners were returned to their cells, all twenty-seven defendants were retried, and they were all found guilty and sentenced to die. This time, however, Lewis was to die alone, first, on November 5, 1894, and this time he was released on his promise to appear for his execution. His case was reviewed by the supreme court of the Choctaw Nation and affirmed on October 6. On the day of the execution he was to appear at noon at the isolated location selected, but at 11:30 A.M. a young boy galloped in and yelled that a force of one hundred heavily armed Buzzards was coming to rescue Lewis. All those present, over one hundred armed men, took up defensive positions until, at 11:55 A.M., Lewis rode up alone, dismounted, and said it had been a joke on the spectators and execution party.

He then began his farewells to all present and distributed his earthly belongings, and finally he said, "Time up. I choose my friend Lyman Persley (*sic*) as my executioner." Lewis had been friends with Sheriff Pursely since childhood, and the sheriff was one of the best shots in the Nation. Lewis then prayed and followed that with a short talk. He concluded his statement by pulling off his coat, vest and boots and he opened his shirt so that Sheriff Pursely could paint a cross over his heart. The condemned man took his position, knelt, and a red handkerchief was tied over his eyes, to prevent flinching, and then two men each took one wrist and held Lewis firmly. Pursely took his position five paces back and took careful aim with his Winchester rifle, but he hesitated for just a moment so Lewis shouted, "Shoot, Lyman!" and took a deep breath. This was just enough to move the target and caused the bullet to miss Lewis' heart by a fraction of an inch, causing a wound an inch above the right nipple and passing entirely through Lewis' body. Lewis threw his head back and sank to the ground, blood spurting from the wound, and he lay there moaning and writhing in pain. It was decided not to fire a second shot, as there was still concern that a force of Buzzards might be nearby awaiting some signal to attack for revenge. The two men holding a wrist continued to hold Lewis while a third man rushed forward to hold his legs. Pursely then took a rag and covered his friend's mouth and nose and in three minutes the condemned man had been suffocated to death.

A man among the spectators took a photograph, and this would create quite a controversy among the U.S. senators who were considering a bill to remove jurisdiction for criminal cases from the Indian tribal councils. As a result of this bungled execution Lewis was the last man executed by the Choctaw Nation, and within three years jurisdiction over criminal matters passed into federal hands.

Sources: *Elgin Echo* (IA): November 8, 1894. *Galveston News* (TX): February 16, 1895. *Kokomo Tribune* (IN): November 25, 1926. *Minnetonka News* (MN): November 9, 1894. *Savannah Morning News* (GA): November 6, 1894. *Stillwell Democrat-Journal* (OK): March 19, 1970.

Milligan, John
March 13, 1895

Twenty-one-year-old John Milligan, a black man, lived with the Clark family, Gabe and Hannah and their six-year-old grandchild Lucy, in a hut in Deep Fork township northeast of Oklahoma City, Oklahoma County. Milligan had lived with the couple for over five years and was treated as an adopted son, but Milligan refused to work so the old man had to support the family. On the evening of November 3, 1893, Milligan attacked the elderly black couple with an axe and first struck a blow at the head of the old man, but it was a glancing blow and a terrible struggle ensued. Hannah awoke and rushed to her husband's aid but they were overpowered by the younger man, and he crushed their skulls, and then he cut their throats from ear to ear. He next turned his attention to Lucy and, though she pleaded, "Oh John, don't hurt me, don't kill me," he hit her on the head with the ax, cut her throat, and left her lying on the bed. He was certain that all three were dead when he ransacked the cabin and stole $200, with which he planned to return to Tennessee. When found, Mrs. Clark was dead, her husband was in a dying condition and lasted only a few weeks, and it was believed that Lucy would also die of her wounds. However, Lucy was young and strong, finally rallied, and lived to testify against Milligan. As soon as the crime was discovered Milligan's description was widely circulated, published in a special edition of the *Globe-Democrat*, and a reward was posted. The murderer had fled to St. Louis where he was recognized and arrested on November 6, but he gave the name William F. Odin. The description of Milligan tallied so closely, however, that he was subjected to close questioning, and he finally admitted he was Milligan. He then claimed that the couple had first attacked him and he had killed them in self-defense, and insisted that Lucy had been injured in the struggle. Questioning continued and he eventually weakened, confessing every detail, but then justified the murders by stating it was only his intention to rob the Clarks and when discovered in the act of searching the cabin he felt the only way he could avoid arrest was to commit murder. Milligan was returned to Oklahoma City, lodged in the county jail, and indicted, and his trial commenced in Judge Henry W. Scott's courtroom in early February 1894. He was convicted of first-degree murder; within a few days he was brought into court and the date of his execution was set for April 6, 1894. Appeals and applications for executive clemency delayed the proceedings until November when the territorial supreme court affirmed the lower court, and the date for Milligan's execution was scheduled for January 11, 1895. Then began the efforts of those opposed to the death penalty on general terms, led by Dr. J. R. Furlong. On November 29 Milligan escaped from the jail by crawling through a ventilator, only to be recaptured in two days by Charlie Fightmaster. He was returned to his cell and heavily shackled. Milligan then worked the "insanity dodge," and his bizarre behavior apparently worked well enough for the guards to become complacent. On January 1, 1895, Milligan again escaped, this time by jumping through a glass door, but he was bareheaded, barefooted, and in his shirt sleeves as he made his way in two inches of snow. He was easily tracked to a haymow a few miles from Choctaw City and recaptured by Harry and Jim DeFord.

After he was returned to his cell, he was rewarded with a continuing delay as Governor William C. Renfrow affirmed the respite granted by the acting governor so he could consider the matter. On the day before the execution Dr. Furlong and A. C. Scott went to the governor and discussed the imminent execution of Milligan, but the governor decided that the enormity of the deed and the heartlessness displayed by the murderer would not permit his intervention. The sheriff was informed to proceed, and he then sent out invitations to the jury of twelve citizens, several officers, the county physician and attorney, other appropriate officials, and five friends of the condemned man. The fairgrounds would no longer work for the gallows site, so during Milligan's last week a tall fence was erected around the jail yard, and the gallows was constructed within the enclosure. Milligan was weighed and found to be one hundred eighty-seven pounds, so the gallows was tested with a two-hundred-pound sack of sand, and the apparatus worked perfectly. On the morning of the execution a canvas was stretched over the gallows to prevent any view from neighboring buildings. On the day before the execution Milligan's spiritual advisers spent the entire day with him trying to distract him from his impending doom, but he was weakening and it was thought he would have to be carried onto the scaffold, and the death watch — James W. DeFord, Tom Owens, and jailer Garver — were on the alert for any attempt to cheat the hangman.

On Wednesday, March 13, 1895, Milligan arose early and paced restlessly until Deputy Jim DeFord asked what he would like for breakfast, and Milligan replied, "Jimmie, this is the last breakfast I will get to eat, and I will leave it all to you." DeFord went to the Saddle Rock Restaurant and ordered the best breakfast they could prepare. At 9:00 A.M. Sheriff Harry DeFord appeared at the cell door and read the death warrant. Milligan was attended by Friar C. C. Calf and the Reverends Harper and Ross who prayed and sang hymns with the condemned man, and Milligan said, "In two hours I will be sitting on the throne with God." He took great pains in dressing and said of his appearance, "I look so nice, I wish my sister could see me now." Dr. Furlong was in the cell with the prisoner and told him, "John, poor boy, I strove hard to save your life. I first strove hard to have the Governor commute your sentence to life imprisonment; and after I failed in that, I then tried hard to have the legislature abolish the death penalty in the territory. I did this because I was and am thoroughly convinced that the infliction of the death penalty is wrong...."

The prisoner's arms were bound behind him, and at 11:55 A.M. the procession formed, with Sheriff DeFord leading with the prisoner, deputy sheriffs in front and rear, and the procession was followed by the clergymen. The prisoner was escorted onto the scaffold and positioned on the trapdoor where his knees and ankles were bound, and next came the noose and black cap. The coroner's jury of twelve men and the others invited by the sheriff, and five friends invited by the condemned man, waited patiently beneath the gallows while Sheriff DeFord and several deputies entered the small booth where the release was located. At 12:03 P.M. a sharp blow from a hatchet severed the cord, the trap was sprung, and Milligan dropped to his death. Dr. Feigenbaum waited beneath and monitored vital signs until he pronounced him dead. The body was then cut down and lowered into a coffin in preparation for burial later that day.

Sources: *Iowa State Reporter* (Waterloo): March 21, 1895. *Logansport Pharos* (IN): February 14, 1894. *San Antonio Daily Light* (TX): April 6, 1894. *Journal* (Logansport, IN): December 2, 1894. *Oklahoman* (Oklahoma City): March 13–14, 1895. *Fort Wayne News* (IN): January 2, 1895. *Nebraska State Journal* (Lincoln): November 7–8, 1893.

Bark, Walter
March 22, 1895

On Sunday evening, August 16, 1891, Walter Bark and Johnson Reese, full-blooded Cherokee Indians, stopped at the house of a tenant on Widow Reese's place for dinner, and they began drinking whiskey. Bark had earlier given Reese a $5 gold piece to buy whiskey but he did not buy the liquor, and when Bark asked for the return of the gold piece Reese refused to return the money. They began to argue so Reese left. When he had passed the fence Bark and two others came out, and Bark and Reese again argued, with the fence between them. Suddenly, without warning or hesitation, Bark drew his six-shot revolver and shot Reese once through the breast, and Reese collapsed. Bark then climbed over the fence and shot him two more times as he lay helpless on the ground. Bark next turned his pistol toward the witnesses and emptied his revolver at them as they ran for cover, missing his targets. Bark fled into Texas where he lived with a white woman, and no one knew where he was during that time. In late 1894 Bark went to Fort Smith to collect his share of the per capita money which was about to be paid. He went on a spree and was arrested for disturbing the peace, and Sheriff John Brown of the Illinois district, who was in town, recognized Bark and knew there was a $250 reward posted for his arrest. When Bark was released from the local jail Brown made his arrest and delivered his prisoner at Tahlequah. Bark was tried for the murder of Reese and sentenced to hang on February 22, 1895, but he was given a respite to March 22 so the principal chief could review the case, but the chief declined to intervene.

Thirty-year-old Bark was lodged in the prison to await his execution. On his final day Bark was taken out of his cell at 12:30 P.M., and High Sheriff Resche and City Marshal Wyle escorted him to the gallows behind the jail building. On the platform he was asked if he had anything to say, and he talked for a half hour to the large crowd of Cherokees, insisting he was innocent of murder and concluding, "I make this statement in the presence of men realizing full well that in a few minutes more I will be in the presence of God." He was then positioned on the trapdoor where his wrists and arms, knees and ankles were strapped and the noose was adjusted. Bark, at that moment, began to collapse and an attendant helped him stand. In a moment the trap was sprung and Bark broke his neck in the fall. A doctor waited beneath the gallows and monitored vital signs until he pronounced Bark dead fourteen minutes after he dropped. The body was then cut down and deposited in the coffin provided by the Nation, and he was buried later that day.

Sources: *Cherokee Advocate* (Tahlequah, I.T.): August 18, 1891. *Statesman* (Boise ID): March 23, 1895. *Indian Journal* (Eufaula, I.T.): March 29, 1895. *Savannah Morning News* (GA): March 23, 1895.

Davis, Frog
September 13, 1895

On Monday, June 3, 1895, Sheriff James T. Musgrove and Deputy Griffin of the Cooweesoowee district, went to the home of Tom Davis, Frog Davis' uncle, located on Bird Creek, which was a tributary of the Verdigris River east of Catoosa. Musgrove was going to serve an arrest warrant on Frog Davis for selling stolen horses and cattle to the Osage Indians. Musgrove dismounted and started for the main house, but Davis was hiding in a log stable, and he took aim at the sheriff through a crack in the wall. Davis fired once, the bullet striking the sheriff in the abdomen. Griffin took cover behind a tree, and Davis fled into the woods and made his way toward Tulsa. Musgrove was carried into the house where he bled to death in an hour. Davis' description was circulated and a reward was posted, and a posse of U.S. marshals and Indian police took up his trail. On June 19 Davis was at the home of Henry Wilson on Pigeon Creek, nine miles north of Okmulgee in the Creek Nation. The Wilsons got Davis drunk and then disarmed and chained him, and they took their prisoner to Tahlequah, the capital of the Cherokee Nation. Davis was lodged in a cell at the National prison, quickly tried, convicted of murder, and sentenced to hang on September 13, 1895.

On his final day the death warrant was read to the prisoner in his cell, and at 11:13 A.M. Davis was brought from his cell by prison officials, and he joined High Sheriff Roach and the Reverends Lamar, Deter and Bitting on the gallows. He was immediately asked if he had anything to say and he stepped to the front of the scaffold and said,

> I killed James Musgrove and would have killed Griffin had he not hidden himself behind a tree; I could not see him. I shot Musgrove because he came after me. I came back from Stillwater [Minnesota] penitentiary with the intention of being a man, but they would not let me — Shave Alberty prosecuted me for carrying a pistol. I told them I had just come back from over the road. Gentlemen, there never was a braver man on this stand than Frog Davis. My uncle told me to die like a man. I am prepared to go; I have read the Bible and said my prayers for three years. I would have been a good boy always had the people given me an opportunity — they forced me to do wrong. My intention, when I first started out and killed James Musgrove was to show you what a man is; Bill Cook and Cherokee Bill would not have been a circumstance. My friends sent me a telegram, saying that 100 men were after me. I would have fought, killed and died like a man if my friends had been true men; those whom I took to be my friends. I tell you, gentlemen, no one knows the trouble I have gone through with; I have suffered ten thousand deaths in my time. I have been run over enough to make any man bad. Gentlemen, if they had allowed my witnesses, I would have come clear. Gentlemen, I tell you my folks were the bravest men that ever lived. Well, I have no more to say. I hope I shall meet you all in Heaven. I am prepared to meet my God. I would like to have John Taylor and Harrison Foreman to see that I am buried on Bird Creek. I thank you all for your kind attention. Good bye.

The Reverend Lamar then told the witnesses that Davis had deceived him, claiming his innocence until just before he was brought from his cell. The reverend then warned the boys to "take an example of the unfortunate man who is about to meet his death on account of leading a wicked life." Davis then stepped forward again and said he had lied to the reverend because he was advised to protest his innocence, "as long as there was any show of hope," and continued, "Gentlemen, tell my folks, please, that I died like a man. I confess before God and men that I killed James Musgrove." He was guided to the center of the trapdoor and the Reverend Deter spoke a few words while the prisoner's wrists and arms, knees and ankles were being bound. Before the noose could be adjusted he yelled, "Tell them all I died like a man — I am the bravest man that ever stood on this gallows. Good-bye." Just then he saw someone in the crowd he recognized and called out good-bye to him as the noose was cinched and the black hood was then pulled on, and then he called out through the cloth "Good-bye!" one last time. The trap was sprung at 11:35 A.M. and Davis did not break his neck in the fall, so it was ten and one-half minutes before Drs. Fite and Murray pronounced him dead from strangulation. His body was then cut down and given to his friends for burial on Bird Creek, in accordance with his last wish.

Sources: *Arkansas Gazette* (Little Rock): September 14, 1895. *Muskogee Phoenix* (I.T.): June 19, 1895; September 19, 1895. *Sandusky Register* (OH): June 5, 1895.

Timmy Jack
May 1, 1896

In the spring of 1896 Timmy Jack, a Creek Indian, rode to a "stomp dance" at a friend's house. One of Timmy Jack's best friends, Jimmie Brown, was also in attendance but during the festivities the two men began to argue, then wrestle, and finally the situation deteriorated into a fight. No one tried to stop them, as they were evenly matched and neither man seemed able to hurt the other, but suddenly Timmy Jack drew his knife and drove it into the heart of Jimmie Brown, and he bled to death in minutes. Timmy Jack was restrained and held for the authorities, arrested, and lodged in the Creek Nation jail at Okmulgee. He was tried before Judge Freeland Marshall in late April, and on April 24 he was sentenced to die on May 1, 1896. He was set free on his promise to appear at the Council House for his execution. The case was reviewed by Chief Isparcher but he refused to interfere.

Early on the morning of his execution Timmy Jack mounted his pony and rode into Okmulgee. He went to the store and bought his burial clothes — a black suit, white shirt and white tie, and then went to the blacksmith shop to inspect his coffin, and after he approved, it was delivered to the courtyard of the Council House. The fence had been torn down around the courtyard and a large crowd of spectators, including friends and family, gathered. When the condemned man arrived he moved among the crowd bidding them farewell until told his time had come. He walked to the northeast corner and sat upon a box in front of a large tree. His wrists were handcuffed and his ankles shackled, a blindfold was tied on and a white paper target was pinned over his heart. Timmy Jack had chosen Captain Berryhill, of the light horsemen and his relative, to shoot him and had asked that it be done with his Winchester rifle. Berryhill stepped off fifteen feet, turned and knelt, then took careful aim. He fired a single bullet and missed the target, but Timmy Jack fell forward, writhing in agony, until he bled to death in ten minutes. Once he was dead the handcuffs, shackles and blindfold were removed and he was given to his family for burial.

Sources: *Hearne Democrat* (TX): May 14, 1926. *Iola Register* (KS): April 24, 1896. *Muskogee Phoenix* (I.T.): May 14, 1896.

Homes, Charles
May 8, 1896

Thirty-five-year-old Charles Homes, a Choctaw Indian, had trouble with his son-in-law Wilson Katiatubbi, who lived with his wife at Springtown. Early on the morning of November 2, 1895, Homes went to the home of the Katiatubbi and, with ax in hand, crept into the bedroom while his daughter and son-in-law were still asleep. He struck a single blow to his son-in-law's head, laying it open and killing him instantly. He then grabbed his daughter and, after threatening her, took her along as he fled. At her first opportunity she escaped and reported the murder, and Homes was soon arrested and lodged in jail. He was tried in the Boggy Creek court in early March 1896, and on March 16 he was convicted and sentenced to be shot on March 27. Homes was released while the case was under review, and it was decided to grant a respite to May 8. The judgment and sentence were affirmed and the principal chief refused to interfere, so that there was no delay in the proceedings.

Homes reported to the Pushmataha courthouse on the day of his execution and was inside until, at 1:53 P.M., he was led out wearing a black robe covering him to his ankles. Religious services were conducted while the condemned man took his seat on a box five paces in front of the courthouse door. Deputy Robert Jackson then tied on a blindfold and pinned a two-inch white paper target over Homes' heart, then the deputy retired into the courthouse. Two deputies took hold of Homes' wrists to support him after he was shot, but there was a brief delay as Deputy Jackson counted down to the hour of 2:00. In the shadows of the doorway Jackson held his Winchester rifle at the ready, and when the hour arrived he raised it to his shoulder, took careful aim and shot Homes once, missing the target by two inches. Homes was lowered onto the ground where he writhed in agony for ten minutes before he finally bled to death. His wife had been present at the execution so the body was given to her for burial.

Sources: *Cedar Rapids Evening Gazette* (IA): March 16, 1896. *Fort Wayne Post* (IN): May 5, 1896. *Muskogee Phoenix* (I.T.): May 14, 1896.

Talton, Robert
July 31, 1896

On November 16, 1892, Robert Talton, alias Bill Taylor, had some difficulty with Jesse W. Elliott, of Vinita, at Catoosa. Talton suddenly grabbed hold of Elliott and cut his throat from ear to ear, so deeply that he was able to twist his head from his shoulders. Talton fled, and Elliott's friends posted a $500 reward for his capture, and Sheriff John F. Blair added another $100 to the reward. Talton was arrested by Officer Charlie Smith of Purcell and lodged in jail at Tahlequah. He was tried in December 1892, convicted of murder, and sentenced to hang on February 28, 1893. On December 26 the Cherokee Supreme Court convened to review the judgment and sentence, and they granted a new trial. Talton was once again convicted and sentenced to hang, but the case was reviewed for several years until on May 19, 1896, the supreme court justices affirmed the judgment and sentence of the lower court, and Talton's date with the hangman was set for July 31. The case was appealed to Chief Mayes, and on July 30, the day before the execution, he refused to interfere.

Before noon the gates to the National Prison were opened and a crowd of curious spectators rushed in and surrounded the gallows. At noon Talton appeared, handcuffed and escorted by deputy marshals. He took his seat on the gallows and was asked if he had anything to say, but there is no record of a speech nor of religious ceremonies. When the formalities were concluded Talton took his place on the trapdoor where his wrists and arms, knees and ankles were strapped, the noose was adjusted, and the black hood was pulled over his eyes. In a moment the trap was sprung, and the doctor in attendance, posted beneath the trapdoor, monitored his vital signs until his heart ceased to beat and then pronounced Talton dead. After hanging a while longer the body was cut down, deposited in the rough wooden coffin provided, and was buried that evening.

Sources: *Galveston News* (TX): November 30, 1892. *Muskogee Phoenix* (I.T.): January 5, 1893.

Swimmer, James
Williams, Henry
September 18, 1896

For some time there had been ill feelings between James Swimmer and Eli Baldridge, both full-blooded Cherokee Indians. On Saturday, September 14, 1895, both men had been in Braggs all day, and after noon they happened to meet at Louis Dolson's restaurant where they had a brief exchange of words, but it was not a heated exchange. Swimmer suddenly pulled a revolver and, without hesitation, shot Baldridge twice in the chest killing him instantly. Swimmer was immediately subdued and disarmed, arrested, and taken to Tahlequah where he was lodged in jail. He was tried at the spring session of the court, convicted, and sentenced to hang on August 20. During his time in jail he found religion and was baptized.

Eighteen-year-old Henry Williams, a black man, had an argument with another black youth, Crockett Mackey, at Fort Gibson during the early part of 1896. Without provocation or excuse he murdered Mackey and was arrested, tried at the spring session of the court at Tahlequah, and convicted of murder. Williams was sentenced to hang on August 20, with Swimmer.

Chief Mayes reviewed the cases and on the day of the execution he granted a thirty-day respite to September 18, but he could find no further reason to interfere. Before noon the gates of the National Prison were opened and the crowd of spectators rushed in and surrounded the gallows. The two men, handcuffed and escorted by deputy marshals, were brought out and seated on the gallows, which could accommodate up to three men, and the handcuffs were removed. When asked if they had anything to say each man took his turn at the railing, Williams first, who said he had found religion and been saved, and then he confessed his crime. Swimmer came next and insisted he was not afraid to die, and then he made a long speech. The two men returned to their chairs and a hymn was sung, followed by a prayer offered by the Reverend Hawkins. When the Reverend announced "Amen!" the two men took their places on the trapdoors where their wrists and arms, knees and ankles were bound, the nooses were adjusted, and the black hoods were pulled over their heads. In a moment the trap was sprung and both men broke their necks in the fall. After the physicians in attendance pronounced the two men dead their bodies were cut down, deposited into the rough wooden coffins provided, and they were buried later that day.

Sources: *Fort Wayne News* (IN): September 19, 1896. *Iola Register* (KS): September 20, 1895. *Muskogee Phoenix* (I.T.): September 18, 1895; September 19, 1896.

Bloss, John
October 9, 1896

In April 1896 John Bloss, a full-blooded Seminole also known by his Indian name Pulmusky, killed Joe Factor. He was arrested along with Parnosey, who was thought to be his partner in the crime, and they were tried at Wewoka. Bloss was convicted of murder and sentenced to die by shooting and then he was given his freedom, but Parnosey was acquitted when it was shown that Bloss alone was responsible for Factor's death. Bloss reported to his place of execution in Wewoka on Friday, October 9, 1896. The Light Horse brought the prisoner to the spot of his execution at the appointed time and placed him in a seated position. A bright piece of cloth was then pinned over his heart, and two executioners took their positions six feet from the prisoner, so that the barrels of their Winchester rifles were only inches from his chest. At 11:00 A.M. the signal was given and both rifles reported simultaneously, both bullets struck Bloss in the heart, and he died in seconds. Bloss fell forward and his body was carefully laid out and then lifted into the coffin, which was stored nearby and brought forward.

Sources: *Fort Wayne News* (IN): October 12, 1896. *Middleton Daily Argus* (NY): October 12, 1896. *Muskogee Phoenix* (I.T.): October 15, 1896.

Hadworth, Charles
Welsh, Henry
October 11, 1896

Charles Hadworth and Henry Welsh, half-breed Seminoles, brutally murdered a Seminole squaw on June 10, 1895, and were arrested and taken to Wewoka for trial. They were convicted, sentenced to die by shooting, and then were set free. On Sunday, October 11, 1896, only two days after John Bloss was executed, the two condemned men reported at Wewoka. When the time came the Light Horse brought the prisoners to the spot of their execution in the courtyard at the appointed time and seated them on their coffins and tied on blindfolds. Paper targets were pinned over each man's heart, and four executioners, two for each condemned man, took their positions twenty feet from the prisoners. At 11:00 A.M. the signal was given and all four Winchester rifles reported simultaneously, two bullets striking each man in the heart, and each man fell back onto his coffin and bled to death in seconds. The two men were then laid out, the lids of the coffins were removed, they were deposited, and buried that evening.

Sources: *Iola Register* (KS): October 16, 1896. *Kansas City Star* (MO): October 12, 1896. *Muskogee Phoenix* (I.T.): October 12, 1896.

Choka Ebin
June 14, 1897

On May 23, 1897, Choka Ebin, a full-blooded Creek Indian, murdered Laura Anthony and was arrested and taken to the capitol of Coeta. Ebin was tried, convicted, and sentenced to die by shooting at Perry on June 4, but on the day of his execution he was sick and could not ride to his execution, so the governor granted him a ten-day respite. On Monday, June 14, Choka Ebin appeared at Perry and surrendered. When the moment arrived he was placed on his knees and his executioners, his father Riley Ebin and brother Palko Ebin, took up their positions a dozen feet away armed with Winchester rifles. At the signal the executioners fired at the target pinned over Choka Ebin's chest, struck dead-center, and he died in seconds. The body was then lifted into a coffin and his father and brother took him home for burial.

Sources: *Chicago Tribune* (IL): June 16, 1897. *Galveston News* (TX): June 13, 1897. *Waterloo Daily Courier* (IA): June 17, 1897.

Chickasaw Tom
June 11, 1897

Chickasaw Tom was a half-witted Creek Indian who reveled in childish pranks, including silly petty thefts. However, he never stole anything of great value except for the two times he had made off with someone's horse, and so he was tolerated. However, it seems likely he was punished for his first two horse-thefts as the penalties were progressive, with fifty lashes for a first offense and one hundred lashes for a second offense inflicted at a public gathering, and death was inflicted for a third offense. One day in early 1897 Chickasaw Tom's very fine pony was missed and he was determined to find it. He scoured the countryside for several days and then found another fine pony grazing, and decided to take it only to help him find his animal. He made a bridle of bark, mounted, and continued his search for several days more before he found his pony. He set free the pony he was riding, moved his makeshift bridle to his pony, and returned to Okmulgee. However, he was arrested for horse-stealing and, when tried and found guilty in Judge Freeland Marshall's courtroom, he was sentenced to die on June 11. A large party of influential men then tried to convince Judge Marshall to reduce the sentence but he refused; they returned on the day before the execution but again he declined to interfere.

On the morning of June 11 Chickasaw Tom mounted his pony and rode into Okmulgee where he went to the store and bought his burial clothes. He then reported to the courthouse, where his coffin had been loaded into a wagon, and as the hour neared he boarded the wagon and was driven to the Old Indian Graveyard northeast of Okmulgee, escorted by a detail of Light Horsemen. At the graveyard his coffin was unloaded and placed near his grave, which was just then being dug. He moved among the crowd of friends and family saying his final farewells until he was told to take his place on a large rock near his grave. He was blindfolded, his wrists were handcuffed, his ankles were shackled, and a white paper target was pinned over his heart. Captain Mose Asberry then paced off fifteen feet, knelt, and took careful aim with his Winchester rifle. He fired a single bullet, which pierced Tom's heart, killing him instantly. The body was laid out, cleaned and dressed, deposited in the coffin, and buried immediately.

Sources: *Hearne Democrat* (TX): May 14, 1926.

Watka, John
November 19, 1897

John Watka, a half–Creek and half–Choctaw Indian, lived with Lucy Gooddy in a hut at Brush Hill for a year. When she left him her sister Addie moved in, but in 1895 she also left him. Watka blamed Jonas Deer, a fellow Creek Indian, and when Deer decided to marry Louise Grayson he did not do so in the Indian way, having learned from Watka's experience. On May 20, 1897, Watka and Deer, with an Indian crew, were working on a Brush Hill road together and Deer taunted Watka for not taking action against him after accusing him of causing his women to leave him. Watka rushed at Deer and the two men fell to the ground and struggled, but Deer was larger and was about to pummel Watka when others pulled Deer off. The men stepped between them, expecting Watka to rush at Deer, but instead he ran to his pony and galloped off to his nearby hut. In a few minutes he came riding back at a gallop, and the men warned Deer he was returning with his Winchester rifle. Deer refused to look up from his work digging a ditch with an ax. Watka rode up and fired a single round without even raising the rifle, the bullet striking Deer in the left side, piercing his heart and killing him instantly. He immediately fled north into the Cherokee Nation and eluded capture for three months.

A reward of $150 was offered by Chief Isparcher and this was matched by Chucmarthle, Deer's father. John West, U.S. Marshal at Muskogee, sent Creek Indian Ben Wadsworth after Watka, and he joined a band of Creeks at Fort Gibson. Wadsworth immediately befriended Watka and after several days got him drunk and they rode away together. When they reached a cabin Wadsworth convinced him to stop and sleep, and when he awoke he was a prisoner. He was tied to his horse and, with Wadsworth riding behind, they went to Muskogee.

He was charged with Deer's murder, and on September 26 he was taken to the courthouse nine miles west of Eufaula for trial in Judge Cub McIntosh's courtroom. He was found guilty of first-degree murder and sentenced to be shot to death on October 30, then placed under "nominal restraint" at the hut of Joe and Emarthe Tiger, Light Horsemen, on Lynch Mountain. He worked in the cornfield and could have escaped at any time, but he made no attempt to flee, and when a *Sunday World* reporter visited he reenacted the crime and then posed in an execution scene. As the date approached the judgment and sentence were under review, and he was given a reprieve to November 9; when the decision of the lower court was affirmed the date of execution was set for November 19, but on October 31 newspapers across the country published detailed stories of his execution the previous day. Early on the morning of the November 19 execution the Light Horsemen escorted their prisoner to Eufaula, with pistols in their belts and rifles in hand, because while he would not try to escape his family and friends were free to rescue him without any stigma of cowardice attaching.

When the party arrived Watka was free to mingle with the men who had come to watch the event, until Light Horseman Captain Barney Green announced the time was near. Watka then walked to the quilt spread on the ground and knelt. He opened his shirt bearing the white mark over his heart, and then his wrists were tied behind. After the blindfold was tied over his eyes two executioners took their places five paces in front and took careful aim with their Winchester rifles. At the command of Green they fired simultaneously, killing Watka instantly. He fell forward as Green and his deputies came forward, untied his wrists and laid out the body. The quilt was then lifted and the body was carried directly to the grave which had been prepared nearby.

Sources: *Iola Register* (KS): November 1, 1897. *Sunday World* (Tulsa, OK): November 7, 1897. *Waterloo Courier* (IA): November 17, 1897.

Brooks, K. B.
Perkins, Charles
July 1, 1898

In July 1898 the U.S. Congress passed the Curtis Bill taking jurisdiction for criminal matters from the tribal courts in the Indian Territory. The first cases to be tried in the federal court at Muskogee, Indian Territory, were those of Charles Perkins and K. B. Brooks.

On October 28, 1897, a Mr. Combs hired thirty-three-year-old black man K. B. Brooks to do some work for him while he went to Coffeyville, Kansas, on business. Combs left at home his three daughters: Lulu age sixteen, Cora age eleven, and Ida age five years. After dark the children retired, but after a brief period Brooks entered their bedroom and, when Lulu asked Cora to light the lamp, he fell on Lulu's bed and attempted to attack her, but she began to struggle and scream. Brooks then struck her on the head with a club, knocking her unconscious. When her sister screamed Cora grabbed Ida and they fled into the darkness and hid. Brooks then went to look for the two younger girls to prevent them from going to the neighbors for help, but he could not find them, so he returned to the house and found that Lulu had regained consciousness and fled. He pursued her and found her ten feet from the house, still dazed. He struck her so hard with the club he broke it into three pieces, but he knocked her unconscious and nearly killed her. Brooks then raped the unconscious victim and fled.

Meanwhile Cora took her sister to the Hicks home a mile and a half distant and told what happened, and a party went to the Combs house and found Lulu in the house in bed and in a terrible state. A physician was summoned and he treated the injured girl, and she told the details to the authorities. The entire community was notified and were ready to lynch Brooks if found. Deputy Ledbetter was then put on Brooks' trail, and he followed him for a week. Immediately after the assault Brooks went to the house of Moore Gibson three miles distant, borrowed a blanket, and slept in the barn. In the morning he went into the house for breakfast when Gibson saw blood on his hands, inquired, and was told Brooks had slapped Lulu Combs. Brooks then started for the Osage District.

Deputy Ledbetter captured him on November 4 and took him before Commissioner Jackson for a preliminary examination, and he was held over for trial in the U.S. Court. On April 28 he was convicted of rape in Judge John R. Thomas' courtroom and sentenced to hang on July 1, 1898, and nothing would occur to delay the proceedings.

On December 2, 1897, a fifty-five-year-old black man, Charles Perkins, alias Henry Whitfield, went to the home of Nancy Adkins, a black woman who lived with her mother, and found several people already there, one being George Miller. Perkins, who was infatuated with Nancy, entered the conversation but soon began to verbally abuse his hostess over some trivial difficulty that occurred previously, and Miller objected to his tone and words. Perkins left, went across the street, but soon returned to the gate and began calling to Nancy to come out. John Williams arrived and told Nancy that Perkins was calling to her, but she refused to go out, so Perkins went across the street and lay in wait for Miller. Miller left at 11:00 P.M., and Perkins suddenly appeared and said, "Now I said I would kill you and I am going to do it." Perkins reached for his pocket pistol as Miller began to struggle with him, but he pulled the evolver and shot Miller twice in the body, killing him instantly. Perkins fled to Atoka where he was captured by Marshal Laflore, returned to Muskogee, held over for trial in the U.S. Court, and on April 2 was tried in Judge John R. Thomas' courtroom. Perkins was convicted of murder, and on April 27 he was sentenced to hang on July 1, and nothing would arise to delay the proceedings.

On their last night both condemned men ate a hearty supper but they remained restless until Marshal Bennet offered consolation and comfort. They retired at 11:00 P.M. and seemed to sleep soundly but awoke early. They had not lost their appetite when breakfast was served after 6:00 A.M. and seemed in good spirits. They had little to say, except when Brooks persisted in denying his guilt. Hundreds of curious citizens had gathered outside the stockade at an early hour but only ten invitations, a blue card signed on one side by Marshal Bennett and with the name of the witness on the other side, had been issued, and these men joined the officials in the stockade. The coffins were propped against the back of the gallows underneath, in readiness for the moment they would be needed. After breakfast the two men dressed in their burial suits and seemed to be weakening when, at 8:00, a party of colored men and women came to pray with them and Brooks broke down and cried.

After the congregation left Father Charles, assisted by a minister, spent time with the prisoners, and at 9:00 Marshal Bennett appeared and read the death warrants at the cell doors. Brooks handed a photograph to the Marshal and asked that it be sent to his family in Paris, Texas, and then they were taken from their cells and handcuffed. Father Charles, two black ministers, Marshal Bennett, jailer Lubbes, Turnkey Wilkerson and Judge Barker went ahead, and when the two men arrived at the scaffold at 9:17 A.M., each escorted by two guards, they took their places on the trapdoor. The handcuffs were removed and their wrists and arms, knees and ankles were strapped, and then everyone prayed and sang hymns. The marshal asked if they had anything to say and Perkins declined, but Brooks spoke for five minutes, declaring his innocence, and said, "I am a stranger in a strange land and the object of oppression on account of my color. I am being persecuted because I am without money and friends, except for God, in whom I trust that he will see me home to Him." Brooks then thanked the lawmen for their kind treatment and said, "Good-bye, everybody."

The black caps were pulled over their heads and the nooses adjusted by Lubbes and Wilkerson, and at 9:32 A.M. Judge Barker sprang the trap. Local Drs. Fite, Blakemore, and Thompson, assisted by Drs. Chad Thompson and Beattie of Anna, Illinois, monitored their vital signs and pronounced Perkins dead in three minutes, and Brooks was pronounced dead seven minutes later. The bodies were then taken down and deposited in their coffins, and the examination showed both men had broken their necks in the drop. The remains were driven to the Baptist church for services and both men were buried in the local cemetery later that day.

Sources: *Duluth News Tribune* (MN): July 2, 1898. *Hutchinson News* (KS): July 4, 1898. *Muskogee Phoenix* (I.T.): April 28, 1898; May 5, 1898; June 30, 1898; July 7, 1898.

Goings, William
July 13, 1899

In the spring of 1897 William Goings, whose Indian name was Walla Tonka, and fellow Choctaw Indian Wallace Crosby murdered William's uncle,

Sampson Goings, an Indian deputy. This was reportedly the seventh murder by Goings so both Indians were tried by the Choctaw tribal council, found guilty, and sentenced to be shot in late July 1897. The Indians were released from custody on the understanding that when the time came for their execution they would appear at the designated place, which was the custom and had never been violated. Goings was a famous Indian ball player and his team had a game — a cross between tennis and football, but with the rough and tumble tactics of the latter — in Kansas City on August 1 so the game was postponed a few days and the execution was postponed until November 4.

When the date arrived Goings appeared at Alikchi, Indian Territory, and made ready to face the firing squad, and hundreds of whites and Choctaw Indians gathered nearby to witness the spectacle. However, on Wednesday, November 3, a courier arrived from Tuslahomo, the Indian capital, with a stay of execution pending a new trial granted by the supreme court of the Choctaw Nation. When the courier arrived Goings observed, without emotion, "Maybe me play more ball now." He was retried at the December term of the Choctaw court, again convicted and sentenced to die by firing squad, and then a series of writs of habeas corpus followed as the U.S. federal courts tried to establish their jurisdiction over the Indian Territory, but the date was finally set for early 1899.

Goings, in the meantime, had joined Buffalo Bill's Wild West Show, which featured Indian ball games for audiences in the north and east, and the show was in Michigan when the word arrived that the time was near. However, Goings went missing and was chased through Arkansas and Louisiana, but he kept hidden in the mountains until the day set for his execution had passed, and he then returned to the Indian Territory.

However, since he had already been sentenced all that was required was to set the new date of execution, and it was scheduled for July 13, 1899. An application was made to Federal Judge John R. Thomas pleading for a writ of habeas corpus, and it was granted and telegraphed from Tulsa. A deputy arrived at Alikchi at dawn Thursday and presented the writ to District Attorney Clay and Sheriff Thomas Watson, and it required them to deliver Goings to Muskogee on July 22, but the sheriff refused to receive it and asserted that only Choctaw Judge Abner James could stop the execution. A runner was dispatched but Judge James was ill and returned a verbal order to continue with the execution, unless there could be shown some law which allowed the federal court to intervene. The sheriff and district attorney could find none and proceeded with preparations for the execution to occur at 2:00 P.M.

On the fatal day a few minutes before 2:00 P.M. four Choctaw Indians appeared and prepared the site in front of the courthouse by delivering Goings' coffin, spreading a quilt nearby, and positioning a bench four paces away from the quilt. In a moment thirty-year-old Goings appeared with the sheriff and deputy, with twenty Light Horsemen marching on either side. As he passed through the spectators he bid them farewell, then knelt on the quilt and was blindfolded. The sheriff bared his bosom, painted a white mark over his heart, and then stepped back four paces and rested his Winchester rifle on the bench. He fired one shot but the bullet missed its mark. Goings fell backwards and moaned piteously for an hour before he bled to death. Water was poured down his throat several times, hoping to strangle or drown him and put him out of his misery but this failed to complete the task.

While the execution was being conducted the Light Horsemen, armed with Winchester rifles, had faced the crowd and kept two deputy U.S. Marshals from interfering. The U.S. Congress, between the time Goings was first sentenced to die and the time of his execution, had abolished the jurisdiction of the Indian tribunals, and as Goings lay dying District Attorney Clay observed, "We are making history" by defying the federal court. On July 15 U.S. Marshal Bert Brown and a posse left Antlers for Alikchi with arrest warrants for twenty-seven persons charging them with contempt for refusing the writ sent by Judge Thomas. The posse returned to Antlers on July 18 with District Attorneys A. H. Clay and Simon Tyler, the latter also clerk of the court. Sheriff Watson could not be found, and the other twenty-four warrants were not served at the time.

Sources: *Hawarden Independent* (IA): July 20, 1899. *Logansport Daily Reporter* (IN): July 14, 1899. *New York Times* (NY): November 7, 1897; July 14, 1899. *The Galveston Daily News* (TX): July 15, 1899. *Weekly Wisconsin* (Milwaukee): July 22, 1899.

Cully, George
July 21, 1899

On September 27, 1897, Dick Carr sold a load of cotton to Mr. Turner and received payment. Twenty-eight-year-old George Cully, sometimes Curly, who was living with his aunt west of Muskogee, saw Carr receive the money and was determined to rob him. He waited while Carr made a number of small purchases from various merchants, and that evening the farmer left for his home in Choska. Cully followed as far as Drew's ferry on the Arkansas River, shot Carr to death, took a little more than $50 from his pockets, and stole the items he had purchased at Muskogee. He then threw the body off the wagon and drove to his aunt's home. Cully was captured a short time after the killing and was identified as the man who had shot a merchant at Miami during a robbery a few days earlier, but he was charged with Carr's murder. He was tried at the October term in Judge John R. Thomas' courtroom at Muskogee, found guilty, lodged in the U.S. jail on October 28, 1897, and on December 24 was sentenced to hang on February 25, 1898. The case was appealed, after a year under consideration the judgment and sentence were affirmed, and on May 6, 1899, Judge Thomas set the date for execution at July 21.

A week before the execution a *Muskogee Phoenix* reporter was at the U.S. jail and, with jailer Lubbes, happened to stop by Cully's cell. They found him angry and he showered them with epithets. Jailer Lubbes said that Cully was restless and at times showed signs of weakening, but he had never before acted as he did that day. Several days before his execution Cully relented and asked to be baptized, and the Reverend Solomon performed the service. After being baptized he wrote out a confession for the reverend but it was sealed by the church. His death watch was assigned on the evening of July 20, and jail officials decided it would be better to hang Cully early so they set the time for 8:00 A.M. After breakfast the death warrant was read to Cully in his cell, and then he walked to the gallows with a firm step, where he spoke only a few words. This was followed by the singing of a hymn and a prayer by the Reverend Solomon. After the religious services concluded Cully's wrists and arms, knees and ankles were strapped, the black hood was pulled over his head, the noose was adjusted, and without a moment's delay the trap was sprung. Cully dropped, breaking his neck, and a vein in his neck was also severed, and death was instantaneous. After only a few minutes the attending physician pronounced Cully dead and the body was cut down, deposited into the coffin provided by the Reverend Solomon and delivered to him for burial that afternoon.

Sources: *Muskogee Phoenix* (I.T.): May 11, 1899; July 13, 1899; July 20, 1899; July 27, 1899.

Brown, Cyrus
Craig, Matthew
August 25, 1899

In late 1896 Cyrus Brown, a tramp, became ill, and Daniel Cuthbert, a sixty-year-old white man who lived on a houseboat on the Arkansas River near Webbers Falls, nursed him back to health. As soon as Brown recovered he shot Cuthbert in the back, weighted the body with stones and threw it in the river. Brown sailed the houseboat to Fort Smith and continued to live on the boat until the body washed ashore. Following an investigation Brown was arrested at Fort Smith and returned to Muskogee for trial. The defendant was found guilty of first-degree murder, and on July 23 he was sentenced to hang on December 18, 1897. The case was appealed to the U.S. Supreme Court, which remanded the case back to the appellate court for the Indian Territory, where the judgment and sentence were affirmed. The date for Brown's execution was then set at August 25, 1899.

On March 14, 1899, Deputy U.S. Marshal Joseph P. Heinrichs, with a posse man, arrested Matthew Craig for selling whiskey in the Indian Territory. There was no jail at Tahlequah so the marshal took his prisoner to his home for the night and they slept in the same bed, so he could keep a close watch on his prisoner. The posse man bedded down outside while Heinrichs' wife and two daughters slept in another bedroom. At 3:00 A.M. Mrs. Heinrichs and the girls were awakened by a gunshot and they rushed into the other bedroom where they found the marshal dead. Craig had fled through a window, and he was pursued, quickly recaptured, and lodged in jail charged with murder. The posse man was also arrested and charged as an accessory for passing the gun to Craig. The trial of Craig began on Friday, May 5, 1899, and his defense was that he had been placing his pistol under the bed when it discharged accidentally, killing the marshal. The jury rejected the defense as preposterous and found Craig guilty of murder in the first degree, and the defendant was convicted and sentenced to hang. The date of execution was set at August 25, 1899.

The gallows was erected in the U.S. jail yard at Muskogee. Both men had resigned themselves to their fate, though neither professed religion, and they slept soundly their last night. They arose that final morning and ate a hearty breakfast before they were escorted from their cells onto the scaffold. They took their places on the trapdoors and refused to make a statement to the thirty witnesses gathered beneath the gallows, including the Heinrichs family. They knelt but while the Reverend Butler prayed for their souls Brown arose, lighted a cigarette, and uttered an oath. Once Craig arose the two condemned men had their wrists and arms, knees and ankles strapped, the black caps were pulled over their heads, and the nooses were adjusted. In a moment the traps were sprung and both men broke their necks in the fall. Attending physicians monitored their vital signs, and when their hearts ceased to beat they were pronounced dead and lowered into the coffins provided. The bodies were buried at government expense that afternoon.

Sources: *Fort Gibson Post* (I.T.): August 31, 1899. *Iola Daily Register* (KS): August 25, 1899. *Logansport Journal* (IN): August 26, 1899. *Muskogee Phoenix* (I.T.): May 11, 1899.

Barrett, Charles
Wright, Dora
July 17, 1903

Twenty-two-year-old Charles Barrett was convicted in late December 1902 of murdering on December 3, for the purpose of robbery, section hand John Hennessey at Calvin twenty miles south of McAlester. Hennessey was a miserly man, known to have hoarded a great deal of money, so Barrett lay in ambush and shot him to death, and it seemed apparent that the work was done by one man. Barrett was arrested, tried, convicted, and on June 3, 1903, Judge Clayton sentenced Barrett to hang on July 17, 1903. In his last moments, after making a number of false confessions, the condemned man insisted that he had been helped in the murder by Isaacs "the barber" and Tom Stennet, and they shared $1,052.

In late 1902 and early 1903 Dora Wright, living at Wilburton, had been abusing and beating seven-year-old Annie Williams for months. On February 2, 1903, a whipping and a sharp blow to the head killed the little girl, and then Wright mutilated the body and burned her with a hot poker trying to make it look as if she had been sexually assaulted. The evidence of previous injuries were explained as punishment because the girl had been intimate with several white men, whom she could not name. An examination, however, showed that the specific injuries that led to her death, and meant to show the sexual assault, were inflicted after the girl was dead. Wright was charged with her murder, tried before the end of the month, and convicted, and on June 3 Judge Clayton sentenced Wright to hang on July 17. Her case was appealed but the lower court was quickly affirmed. When President Theodore Roosevelt was asked to intervene he replied, "if that woman was mean enough to do a thing like that, she ought to have the nerve to meet her punishment."

On their last night both condemned prisoners slept soundly, with Wright arising at 4:45 A.M. and Barrett arising fifteen minutes later. They both refused breakfast and then spent the next forty-five minutes with their spiritual advisers: The Reverend Cameron for Barrett and the Reverend Roebuck for Wright. When asked at 6:45 both prisoners said they were ready, and five minutes later jailer J. C. Wilkinson pinioned their wrists and arms. Wright was dressed in a stiffly starched white dress, and Barrett was dressed in a plain suit when he told the *Phoenix* reporter, "I have nothing to fear, and although my sins are great, I know I am forgiven." They were then escorted from their cells as they bid the other prisoners farewell, and at 6:58 they mounted the scaffold, Barrett in the lead. They had previously declined to speak to the one hundred witnesses, and the death warrants had been read to them previously so, while the black hoods were pulled over their heads and the nooses adjusted by U.S. Marshal Frank Genung, another attendant strapped their ankles and knees. At 7:00 A.M. Genung gave the signal and the traps were sprung by Deputy Marshal Henry Donothan. In twelve minutes Barrett was pronounced dead and in less than a minute the same was pronounced for Wright. The bodies were immediately cut down and taken from the jail yard. No one had requisitioned the remains so both bodies were buried at government expense later that afternoon.

Sources: *Columbus Enquirer* (KS): July 18, 1903. *Emporia Gazette* (KS): July 17, 1903. *Hutchinson News* (KS): July 17, 1903. *Muskogee Phoenix* (I.T.): July 18, 1903.

Binyon, Rufus
September 22, 1905

In 1900 Rufus Binyon lived with his wife, both black, and Mary Hawthorne, a orphaned black girl of eight years, at Ran, I.T. On May 18 Mrs. Binyon went to the neighbor's home for sorghum, and during her absence her husband became enraged at the young girl over some trivial matter and, as he often did, he began to whip and beat her. He killed the girl and, to cover the crime, he started a large fire in the fireplace and threw in the body. Rufus went into the fields and began hoeing corn. When his wife returned she found the girl's body in the fire and sounded the alarm, yelling that the child had fallen into the fire and burned. Neighbors rushed to the house and found the child's body still in the fire, so horribly burned that the flesh peeled off when they tried to remove the remains from the flames. Still, numerous wounds were apparent on the head and body inconsistent with falling into the fireplace, and the next day Doctor Bernard examined the remains and concluded that a head wound three inches long had penetrated and crushed the skull, and this was a fatal wound. Witnesses also found that Mary's "private parts," her genitals, were swollen, lacerated and torn, suggesting a sexual assault though no charge would be filed.

The doctor, who had seen Rufus Binyon at noon on the day of Mary's death, said Binyon had mentioned that he had violently whipped the child earlier that day. A neighbor then said, "He told me that he whipped this child twice the day he killed it, and the last time he whipped it he said he put it in the bed. It was sick some way or another, and he put it in the bed, and he went to the field. He was hoeing corn, and when he and his wife come back to dinner he claimed they found the child dead in the bed. And then he said to his wife that they was 'into it and they had to get out of it some way.'" Binyon confided that it was then they decided to burn the body so he sent his wife away, and when she began yelling her alarm Rufus was seen walking from the house. He confessed all the details of the killing and burning to several others as well.

Binyon was charged with the murder of Mary Hawthorne and indicted on December 20, 1900. The matter dragged on for a year but finally on January 15, 1902, he was tried, found guilty of murder, and sentenced to hang. His defense was insanity but he insisted that he "had a complete forgetfulness of the entire matter," but the jury refused to accept the defense believing he was shamming insanity. The case was appealed, but on September 23, 1903, the judgment and sentence of the lower court was affirmed. The case was then appealed to the U.S. Supreme Court, again affirmed, and the date for Binyon's execution was set at September 22, 1905. The petition for a commutation of sentence sent to the Board of Pardons was denied, and the application for executive clemency sent to President Theodore Roosevelt was also denied.

Binyon seemed to realize he would not be saved from the hangman, and he seemed in a listless stupor his final days. He was attended by Bishop Arnett of Ohio, and this helped him brace up for the ordeal. The gallows was erected within an enclosure in the jailhouse yard in Ardmore. The prisoner awoke his final morning and was served breakfast, then prepared for his death and waited in his cell until the death warrant was read to him. He was escorted onto the scaffold where he sang "I'm Going Home to Die No More," then said "Good-bye everybody, be good people." Bishop Arnett read the Lord's Prayer and prayed for the soul of Binyon, and when the Bishop said "Amen," Binyon announced, "I am ready." His wrists and arms, knees and ankles were strapped and a black hood was pulled down below his waist. The noose was then adjusted and at exactly 2:00 P.M. the trap was sprung. Binyon dropped, breaking his neck in the fall and in fifteen minutes the doctor in attendance pronounced him dead. His body was then cut down, placed in the coffin provided, and delivered to his wife for burial.

Sources: *Binyon v. United States*: 1903 IT 15; 76 S. W. 265. *Daily Northwestern* (Oshkosh, WI): September 22, 1905. *Tishomingo News* (I.T.): September 27, 1905.

Williams, Grant
November 3, 1905

In mid–1904 Grant Williams, a Negro construction laborer, was working on the Ardmore division of the Rock Island rail line. In August he received his wages from paymaster James Dolan but protested that the pay was not enough for the work he had done. He was not given more money and did nothing until October 19 when he took his pistol, went to the paymaster's railcar, shot Dolan to death, and wounded a contractor who was in conversation with Dolan. As Williams left the car he saw a man lurking nearby and shot him to death as well, but this man was a tramp who was never identified. Williams fled to Russellville, Arkansas, and it was nearly a year before he was recognized, arrested, and returned for trial. He was easily convicted on the evidence and sentenced to hang on November 3, and he was lodged in the new federal jail at South McAlester. Williams was suffering from advanced consumption (tuberculosis) and a brain tumor, but in September he managed to pry loose a water pipe in his cell and made a desperate attempt to escape. He failed to gain his freedom, and as the date for his execution neared he began to deteriorate rapidly, and it was thought he might cheat the hangman.

On his final morning the death warrant was read to Williams in his cell after 9:30 A.M. Williams was too weak to walk to the gallows erected at the rear of the cell block, out of view of the other prisoners, so he was strapped to a board and carried by four men onto the scaffold. He was in no condition to speak, so he was not asked, and the board was propped in position on the steel trapdoor while the black hood was pulled over his head and the noose adjusted. At 10:00 A.M. the trap was sprung, and Williams broke his neck in the fall. In ten minutes the doctor in attendance pronounced him dead. The body was cut down, deposited in the coffin provided by the U.S. Government, and buried before sundown.

Sources: *Muskogee Democrat* (I.T.): November 3, 1905. *Muskogee Phoenix* (I.T.): November 2, 1905. *Muskogee Pioneer* (I.T.): November 11, 1905.

Cotton, Robert
September 4, 1906

During the early part of 1905 Robert Cotton and his wife Cynthia, a black couple, living at Vian in the Indian Territory, were having marital difficulties. On August 6 Robert, an escapee from the Tennessee penitentiary, took a large butcher knife and stabbed his wife seventeen times about her upper torso and mid-section, which nearly cut her body in two. He was captured and lodged in the jail at Vinita where he confessed to the crime. He was tried in the U.S. Circuit court at Sallisaw, convicted of first-degree murder on May 26, 1906, and on June 1 he was sentenced by Judge Parker to hang at Vinita on September 4. Nothing would interfere with the proceedings.

Cotton had braced up for his death with the help of ministers from the A.M.E. Church at Vinita. At noon on September 4 he walked onto the gallows with a firm step and took his place on the trapdoor. He made a brief speech, confessing once more to the murder of his wife, while his wrists and arms, knees and ankles were strapped. While a minister prayed for his soul the black hood was pulled over his head and the noose was adjusted, and at 12:10 P.M. the trap was sprung. Cotton dropped, breaking his neck in the fall, and in two minutes the attending physician pronounced him dead. The body was then cut down and turned over to the minister from the A.M.E. Church for services and burial that evening.

Sources: *Checotah Times* (I.T.): September 7, 1906. *Emporia Gazette* (KS): September 4, 1906. *Evening News* (Ada, OK): June 1, 1906. *Galveston Daily News* (TX): May 27, 1906. *Weekly Sentinel* (Fort Wayne, IN): September 5, 1906.

Ford, Frank
June 12, 1908

A black couple, twenty-four-year-old Frank Ford and his wife Jane, lived with their newborn infant on a farm near Manitou in Comanche County, Oklahoma. Early on the evening of June 16, 1907, Jane retired with her baby "enfolded in her arms." Her husband had been away during the day but later he would never discuss his whereabouts or give any reason for his actions. The couple had been experiencing marital discord for some time, due mostly to Frank's brutal treatment of his wife. Frank returned home at a late hour and stealthily entered the house. He drew his revolver as he rushed to the bedside and, without hesitation or warning, shot his wife twice. The wounds were fatal and Jane died in seconds, and Frank immediately fled, leaving his baby unattended. Neighbors, alerted by the baby's crying, discovered the ghastly scene and notified authorities, and a posse was formed and they were soon on the trail of the murderer.

By nightfall Frank Ford was found a few miles

from his home, arrested and lodged in a jail cell at Lawton, to prevent a lynching in Manitou. During the time Ford was jailed he refused to talk of the crime. As Ford sat in a Lawton jail cell the County of Tillman was formed from a portion of Comanche County, and the place where the crime occurred was located in the new county. This caused some delay in bringing the murderer to justice but finally, on January 23, 1908, the jail at the new county seat of Frederick was completed, and Judge J. T. Johnson transferred the case to the jurisdiction of Tillman County. On Wednesday, April 22, a jury was empanelled at the district court at Frederick, and the trial commenced during the morning hours. Ford put up little defense to substantiate his plea of not guilty so the case went to the jury that afternoon. Deliberations only lasted thirty minutes before the jurors returned a verdict of guilty of murder in the first degree. Ford was sentenced to hang on June 12, 1908; there was no delay due to an appeal, and on June 11 the *Lawton Constitution-Democrat* announced that Governor Charles N. Haskell would not interfere. An application had been submitted asking for a ten-day respite to apply for a commutation of sentence, and Governor Charles N. Haskell consulted with Judge Johnson, who recommended no interference. The governor then notified Tillman County Sheriff Frank Carter to proceed, and the sheriff posted a death watch over the prisoner to prevent suicide.

The gallows had been erected within an enclosure, which permitted those interested in seeing the prisoner to catch a glimpse before he dropped through the trapdoor. The "special hemp rope" and straps had been borrowed from Vernon, Texas, where it had been tested by hanging wife-poisoner George W. Morrison some time earlier. It was decided to conduct the execution at an early hour so a crowd of nearly fifteen hundred men, women and children had gathered outside the enclosure by 6:00 A.M. Inside the jail Ford had risen early and ate a hearty breakfast before dressing in his burial clothes, consisting of a gray suit, white collar, and black tie. At 6:40 A.M. Sheriff Carter, Sheriff Rufe LeFors of Lawton, four Tillman County deputies, and Ford's religious adviser, the Rev. J. W. Owens of Lawton, joined the condemned man in his cell. Sheriff Carter read the death warrant and then Ford was escorted out of the jail and onto the platform where the party joined six county sheriffs invited to witness the affair. Beneath the scaffold waited the twelve-man coroner's jury and two physicians. Ford was asked if he had anything to say to the witnesses, and he said, "Young men and boys, your parents will never advise you wrong. Obey them. My disobedience has brought me to this scaffold. I am ready to die but if I had my life to live over again it would be different." When he concluded everyone joined in the singing of a hymn and then the Reverend Owens read the fourteenth chapter of John before offering a prayer for the soul of the condemned man. The prisoner requested that the hanging be delayed while he smoked a cigarette, and this was granted. In only a few minutes Ford announced he was ready and the straps were applied to his wrists and arms, knees and ankles, the noose was placed around his neck but not yet adjusted when Ford asked if he could have a mirror, as he wanted to see himself. A mirror was brought forth and his image, prepared for death, caused the condemned man to smile. Next the black hood was pulled over his head, the noose was carefully positioned, and Sheriff Carter asked, "Are you ready, Frank?" Ford replied, "All ready!" The lever was pulled, the trap was sprung at 7:00 A.M., and Ford's body dropped seven feet. His neck was broken in the fall, and the body hung motionless as the two attending physicians monitored his vital signs, one taking his pulse while the other listened to his heartbeat. In forty-three minutes he was pronounced dead by the county physician, and the body was cut down. Ford's remains were lowered into the coffin provided by the county and buried at county expense that afternoon.

Sources: *Lawton Constitution-Democrat* (OK): January 23, 1908; April 23, 1980; June 11–12, 1908.

Hopkins, John
August 28, 1908

On Sunday evening, January 5, 1908, thirty-five-year-old John Hopkins, an Indian farmer and widower with three children, drove his buggy to the home of his brother, Ezra Hopkins, located four miles northwest of Seneca in the east part of Ottawa County, Oklahoma. A beautiful nineteen-year-old school teacher named Lena Craig boarded with Ezra, and John had been aggressively pursuing the girl, demanding that she marry him. She had agreed to accompany him to church and boarded the buggy but, unknown to

Ms. Craig, John had become more determined than ever to marry her. Hopkins had said earlier that day, "I shall propose to her once more and if she does not accept, no other man shall have a chance to win her." He had armed himself with a revolver, and during the afternoon of January 5 he went to Joplin and consumed a steady supply of liquor to give him the courage to act if rejected again. Once Ms. Craig was aboard the buggy they started toward town but John, being anxious, made his demand before they had driven seventy-five yards, and was just as quickly rebuffed. Without further discussion or hesitation he pulled his revolver and shot Ms. Craig four times: once in her left arm, once in her left side, once in her abdomen, and once in her face between her nose and left eye. The young girl was not yet dead so John pulled out his pocketknife, opened the larger blade and cut her throat, then cut his own throat so deeply he severed the windpipe but not a vein or artery. Neighbors heard Ms. Craig calling for help as soon as the revolver was seen and they hurried to her aid. Hopkins fled but was not immediately pursued as Ms. Craig was still alive, and rushing the wounded girl to medical care seemed the greater priority. However, several of her wounds were mortal and she died on Monday at 1:00 A.M. On Tuesday at 3:00 P.M. Lena Craig was buried at Racine, her family's home, six miles east of Seneca.

Shortly after the murder Hopkins was trailed to the home of another brother and cornered, but even in his terrible condition he put up a struggle and was finally subdued when a deputy knocked him unconscious with the butt of his Winchester rifle. He was taken to Seneca, lodged in jail, and given medical treatment, and as soon as he was able to talk he confessed. There was strong talk of lynching so by January 10 the sheriff had moved his prisoner to the county jail at Miami. Hopkins was indicted by the Ottawa County grand jury, and his trial commenced in Judge Brown's Miami district courtroom on March 13. He was easily convicted of first-degree murder upon his own confession, the statements of eyewitnesses, and the physical evidence. On May 16 Judge Brown sentenced Hopkins to hang on June 26 but Governor Charles N. Haskell granted a sixty-day respite to consider the matter. On the day before the execution the governor decided not to interfere with the proceedings, leaving August 28 as the date set for the execution.

A scaffold and walkway were built early that final week, and Hopkins asked for the opportunity to help build it, but this request was denied. Many clergymen had made overtures to counsel him on his spiritual welfare but the condemned man rejected all offers. On the prisoner's final night a reporter from the *Miami Record-Herald* visited the prisoner but the condemned man would say nothing and continued "pacing in his narrow cell like a caged animal." His hands worked convulsively as he paced and he was extremely nervous and pale. His brother Robert was admitted at suppertime but the two men talked little. The prisoner spent a restless night and in the morning arose and prepared for his execution. He had not had a good appetite for many days but he ate a hearty breakfast that final morning, and then he was handcuffed to prevent suicide when shaved by a barber.

When the escort arrived at the cell door at 11:30 A.M. Hopkins went to his old coat, pulled a knife from the pocket, and handed it to deputy sheriff John Lucky saying, "Here John. I just wanted to show you I could beat you to it if I wanted to." Hopkins was then removed from his cell, his wrists and arms were bound, and the procession formed in the jail corridor. Hopkins walked into the enclosed walkway at a solemn pace, first appearing at 11:46 A.M., climbed the stairs unassisted and took his place upon the trapdoor. When asked if he had anything to say to the small crowd of witnesses he replied loudly, "Gentlemen, I am going, but I am going an innocent man. If the dead were alive they would tell you I am innocent," then he turned to Deputy Lucky and added, "Cut your dog loose." The black hood was pulled over his head while his legs were being bound, the noose was adjusted, and at 11:51 A.M. the string was pulled by deputy Lucky, which sprang the trap. Hopkins dropped straight down, breaking his neck in the fall, and he hung motionless until the attending physician pronounced him dead in eight minutes. The body hung another seven minutes before being lowered into a basket and taken to Fribley's undertaking parlor to be prepared for burial. Hopkins' body was shipped to his relatives in Seneca, Missouri, on the Shawnee reservation, and he was buried next to his wife who had died five years earlier.

A week after the hanging Deputy Lucky complained that he was haunted by the memory of the hanging. He said,

I have not slept a minute since I pulled the string

> which meant death to Hopkins, who had become a friend of mine during the time he was in jail. The last thing he said to me, before we left the jail to go to the scaffold, was "John, you have treated me better than I was ever treated while a free man and I love you for it." When these remarks were made, I felt that they were the true thoughts of a human and not the expression of flattery. I was tempted to protest against performing my duty, but the second thought, which led me on, is the one which has made my life miserable. I would not hang another man if offered a million dollars. I would rather have my conscience easy than to possess all the money in the state of Oklahoma and my duty in the future does not embrace hanging my friends.

Sources: *Miami Record-Herald* (OK): August 28, 1908. *Nashua Reporter* (IA): September 10, 1908. *The Chillicothe Constitution* (MO): January 7, 1908; January 11, 1908. *The Evening News* (Ada, OK): May 18, 1908. *The Galveston Daily Times* (TX): August 29, 1980. *The Lawton Constitution-Democrat* (OK): September 10, 1908. *The Logansport Daily Reporter* (IN): January 7, 1908. *The Ottawa County Beacon* (OK): August 29, 1908.

Johnson, Will
December 11, 1908

On the evening of January 23, 1908, Will Johnson, a black man, murdered Mrs. Mary Cuppy, a white woman aged seventy-three, who lived two miles from Shawnee in Pottawatomie County, Oklahoma. The victim was beaten to death but there was no evidence of an attempt to rape the woman, nor was anything taken from her purse. The reason for the murder was never revealed even when Johnson pled guilty at his first trial, and it was thought he intended robbery but was frightened off by the sound of approaching people.

Immediately after the details of the murder became known and Johnson was behind bars, the community became incensed and there was strong talk of lynching but Sheriff E. A. Pierce spirited his prisoner away and lodged him in the Oklahoma County jail. Johnson was brought back to the county seat of Tecumseh in Pottawatomie County for trial, and, after his guilty plea, he was sentenced to hang on May 18, 1908. However, due to error in receiving the plea and the manner of sentencing, a new trial was granted. Johnson was tried and convicted again, and this time he was sentenced to hang on July 17, 1908. This date of execution was stayed by an appeal to the state supreme court, which affirmed the lower court's judgment and sentence in October, and the date for execution was next fixed at November 13, 1908. Three days before Johnson was to hang an appeal was filed in the federal court and a reprieve was granted by Governor Charles N. Haskell to end on December 11, which allowed the courts sufficient time to consider the matter. The *Ada News* reported that Johnson's coffin had been nailed together, the grave was dug, and the rope was being soaped when the telegram arrived postponing the execution. In all, the murderer had two trials, a half dozen appeals, and three reprieves before the fatal day finally arrived.

On the morning of December 11 an optimistic Johnson arose at an early hour, still anticipating another delay or perhaps even his release from custody, and he ate a hearty breakfast before dressing in the new suit provided by the county. As 11:00 A.M. neared Sheriff Pierce appeared at the cell door and read the death warrant, and then the procession formed. The march to the scaffold took only a few moments, and once upon the platform the condemned man took his place on the trapdoor and was asked if he had anything to say, and he replied only, "Send my body to my old mother in Texas." His wrists were bound and his arms strapped to his body, his knees and ankles were strapped together, the noose was brought forward and positioned, and the black hood was pulled over his head. At 11:07 A.M. the trap was sprung by Sheriff Pierce, and in eight minutes Dr. Byrum of Shawnee pronounced Johnson dead. The body hung a while longer before being lowered into the undertaker's basket and conveyed to a funeral parlor, where the remains were prepared for shipment to Texas.

Sources: *The Evening News* (Ada, OK): November 14, 1908; November 29, 1908; December 12, 1908. *The Lawton Constitution-Democrat* (OK): May 18, 1908.

Armstrong, Henry T.
November 19, 1909

Henry T. Armstrong, a breed Indian of the Otoe tribe, coveted the fine team and wagon of Isaac Fell and was determined to have it for his own. Early on December 17, 1908, Armstrong went to the farm of Isaac Fell, a plot leased from the Otoe tribe, and asked for the farmer. He learned from Fell's wife, Ada, that her husband had gone to Red Rock. Armstrong then enlisted the help of Fell's former employee Albert Mitchell, a feeble-minded youngster who was easily manipulated, and the two men hurried toward Red Rock to intercept Fell.

On the evening of December 17 Fell stayed at the home of Andy Ward while Armstrong and Mitchell spent the night nearby at the farm of a man named Breckenridge. Armstrong and Mitchell, armed with a Winchester rifle and a .44-caliber revolver, arose early and set up an ambush along the road. They captured Fell alive and unharmed, and then bound their prisoner. Armstrong wanted the new harness that Fell had recently acquired but it was not with the team, so Armstrong wrote an order for the harness. Armstrong forced Fell to sign the order and, leaving Mitchell with the revolver to guard their prisoner, he presented the order to Fell's wife. She honored the order, recognizing her husband's signature, and had no reason to suspect foul play. As soon as Armstrong returned he threw Fell into the wagon bed and the two kidnappers drove east.

On the morning of December 19, when the party was at the eastern edge of the Otoe reservation, Armstrong pulled out the .44-caliber revolver and murdered the helpless farmer with one shot to his head. He covered the body with straw and drove eight miles to a point near Morrison in Noble County where he knew of an abandoned well. He threw Fell's body into the well and then burned the blood-soaked straw. Armstrong disguised himself by cutting his long hair and removing two gaudy rings from his ears. The two men continued to the home of Mitchell's father near Morrison, and Armstrong remained there for three days. The disappearance of Fell was the talk of the neighborhood and, fearing detection, Armstrong left Mitchell at his father's home and continued north with the team and wagon and made his way to the home of "Captain" Joseph Whipple, a man of Indian extraction. Fell's body was quickly discovered, and just before Christmas Albert Mitchell was arrested on suspicion of being involved in the murder. Under close questioning the youngster quickly broke down and confessed every detail of the kidnapping and killing, naming Armstrong as the one who fired the fatal shot, but the arrest of the young man quickly led to his mental deterioration and he became hopelessly deranged. Mitchell was tried in mid-February, acquitted on a defense of insanity, and committed to the state insane asylum.

As soon as Mitchell informed on his companion the search for Armstrong began in earnest and his name and description were widely circulated. Within a few weeks after being named as the murderer several Sac and Fox Indians living in the vicinity of McLoud informed on Armstrong, and he was arrested at Whipple's home in mid–January. Armstrong was lodged in the jail at Perry; in February he was indicted for murder and was tried in mid-February 1909. Armstrong was convicted of first-degree murder and sentenced to hang on March 29. The case was appealed to the state supreme court, and this resulted in a stay of execution until the justices affirmed the lower court's judgment and sentence in October.

On October 18 the prisoner was taken into the district court for re-sentencing, and Judge William Bowles asked if he had anything to say before pronouncing sentence. Armstrong replied, "Yes I have something to say. What I did I was forced into doing at the point of a Winchester" (trying to shift blame to Mitchell). "I never killed Fell nor any other man. You can and may hang me, but if you do, then justice will complete another travesty. The blood of an innocent man will be on the hands of those who condemn me to die. Never has it been said that my people were afraid to die; I am not afraid to die. When the trap is sprung my spirit will be the sooner released from its imprisoning clay, free to soar and join my father's in that land of abundance which we are taught to believe is open after death to those who have not sinned against their fellow beings." Judge Bowles then sentenced Armstrong to hang on November 19, 1909.

All that remained to save Armstrong's life was an application to Governor Charles N. Haskell requesting executive clemency — a commutation of sentence to life in prison or a respite to continue the fight to spare the life of the convicted murderer. The governor, two days before the execution, notified Sheriff A. C. Nicewander that he would not intervene. On Wednesday before the execution workmen began assembling the scaffold. It was within a twenty foot high enclosure erected at the corner of the Perry jailhouse yard so that the prisoner could enter without being seen by spectators outside. The workmen completed construction on Thursday and the apparatus was tested.

During his time in jail Armstrong displayed typical Indian stoicism and seemed almost unaware of his impending death. He declared that no Indian ever feared death and he would not betray the good name of his tribe. He believed in spirits and admonished those who were about to execute him that his spirit would return and walk the streets of Perry nightly to remind those who did the deed that his blood was on their hands. On November 19 Chief Pipestem, whose Indian name was Shu-mon-eca-the, went to Perry and told the authorities, "I came here in response to the wishes of my people who have become incensed because Armstrong had said his spirit would walk the streets of Perry after the hanging. I want to tell him that the Otoe Indians do not believe him and are not afraid of him. They do not like him and he does not like them, but they are not made superstitious by his threats." Armstrong had no friends among the whites nor among the Indians, and his only visitor during his entire time of incarceration was Father Willebrod.

On the morning of his final day Armstrong arose at an early hour and prepared for his death by dressing in a new black suit and satin shirt. After breakfast he retired and immediately fell into a deep sleep. As soon as the witnesses were admitted to the enclosure at 9:15 A.M. Sheriff Nicewander went to Armstrong's cell accompanied by newspaper men, a number of county sheriffs, and Father Willebrod. The final death watch guard, Joe Kerns, had to shake the prisoner awake, and as he arose he hung a crucifix about his neck. Father Willebrod read the last confessional, and then Armstrong was escorted into the jail corridor, where the procession formed. In the lead was the Noble County sheriff followed by the prisoner with Father Willebrod on one arm and layman Thomas Phillips on the other arm, and then came the visiting sheriffs, the jury which had convicted him, the coroner's jury which would sign the death certificate, several bailiffs and officials, and last, Mrs. Ada Fell, the wife of the murdered man.

The prisoner climbed the stairs with a firm step, and once in place on the trapdoor he was given a cigar. The sheriff next read the lengthy order of execution and when asked, "Have you anything to say why the death sentence should not be imposed?" Armstrong replied, "It is the will of the Lord." He then kissed the crucifix as the priest read the last exhortation while his wrists and arms, knees and ankles were pinioned and the noose of three-quarter-inch hemp rope was positioned about his neck. As the black hood was produced the expression on the condemned man's face changed, according to the reporter from Ada's *Evening News*, into "a full realization of his awful doom. It was an indescribable expression eliciting the sympathy of the hardest heart. It was the parting look of a hopeless, utterly ruined, outcast, friendless human." The black hood was pulled over his head at 10:30 A.M. and Sheriff Nicewander sprang the trap, and the body dropped eight feet. Drs. Bruce Watson and D. D. Brengle waited beneath the scaffold where one monitored Armstrong's pulse while the other listened for his heartbeat and, after twenty minutes, the doctors conferred and pronounced him dead. The body was then lowered into an undertaker's basket, the noose was removed, and the remains were taken to the local funeral parlor to be prepared for burial. The remains were given to Father Willebrod for burial, and after the body was taken away Mrs. Fell said, "Justice has at last been done, and I am happy. Did I hate to see the man's neck broken? Why not ask if I have lost the love that I bear my little children? Had the sheriff not officiated, I would have sprung the trap myself, had I been permitted."

Sources: *The Evening News* (Ada, OK): October 19, 1909; November 18, 1909; November 20, 1909.

Hunter, Alf
April 8, 1910

Alf Hunter, a black man whose real name was James Kingsbury, and his wife Pearl lived in Oklahoma City and had been having marital difficulties during the first half of 1908. They argued constantly and sometimes the arguments became quite heated. In mid–May Pearl left her husband for the third time in as many months and rented a room at the boarding house at 507 East First Street. During the forenoon hours of Tuesday, May 19, Alf went to the boarding house, sat with Pearl in the parlor and after a long and pleasant conversation they reconciled. However, within hours they were again arguing and Pearl, fearing for her safety, fled.

Alf spent the afternoon and early evening hours tracking down his wife, and by 8:00 P.M. he was convinced that Pearl was hiding in the home of Charles and Susie Pride, a black couple residing at 325 East First Street. He appeared at the front door of the Pride home and demanded admittance but when he was denied entry by Susie Pride he became enraged and began to kick at the door. Mrs. Pride went out the back door, came around the house from the rear, scolded Hunter, and told him that if he broke the door he would have to pay for it. Hunter then yelled, "Damn you! I'll shoot you and pay for nothing!" Hunter then pulled one of the two semi-automatic pistols he carried and fired six shots at Susie Pride, two bullets striking her in her neck and another in her side, killing her instantly. When the shooting started Hunter's wife fled out the back door of the Pride house and hid from authorities and her husband for days.

As soon as the killing was done Hunter fled east and south toward the Canadian River bottoms, but the shots had been heard by Chief of Police Post and he phoned the police station. Officers Burnett, Davis, Connors, and Colt, joined by Deputies Ballard and Casey, took an automobile and went to the scene of the shooting, learned the direction Hunter had fled, and were in close pursuit. With the officers traveling in an automobile and Hunter afoot they overtook him at the "dumps" near the river bottoms, but Hunter kept up a withering fusillade from his two semi-automatic pistols and finally made his escape through the woods that skirt the river.

Meanwhile, the body of Susie Pride was taken to the undertaking parlor of J. H. Marshall, an autopsy was performed, and the remains were held for an inquest by Justice William H. Zwick on May 21, 1908. The coroner's jury found that Susie Pride had been murdered by Alf Hunter and a warrant was issued for his arrest. Sheriff George W. Garrison then did everything he could to find and arrest Hunter.

Hunter hid for a while among friends in Oklahoma City, who kept him informed of the movements of lawmen, but finally he managed to get out of Oklahoma City and fled to Watonga. In Watonga Hunter had a number of friends who would hide him from the authorities, so he sent a man to guide his wife to his hiding place. Sheriff Garrison learned of this development and convinced Pearl and her guide to take him along. On June 5 Garrison enlisted the services of Deputy M. R. "Fate" Sanders of Arcadia and deputized former night police chief Todd Warden, and the three lawmen boarded the train for Watonga in the company of Hunter's wife and her guide. Hunter had a man in Watonga watching and learned of his wife's betrayal, snuck into Watonga, confronted his wife at East Second Street, and shot her.

After Pearl was shot the party of lawmen started for the hills in pursuit of Hunter, with Blaine County's Sheriff George McArthur and Deputies Billy Phillips and Jim Rouse close behind. At 7:00 P.M. McArthur's party rendezvoused with Garrison's party, and when they reached the hiding place three miles east of Hitchcock they came upon Hunter and six friends in a field, and an attempt was made to arrest Hunter. However, upon seeing the lawmen approaching Hunter's party began firing at the officers, firing seventeen shots, and the gunfire was returned. One of Hunter's friends was wounded slightly and Deputy Sanders was seriously wounded, but he recovered within a year. Hunter then ran to a haystack and climbed on top, where he lay in wait for the lawmen. As soon as Sheriff Garrison was in range Hunter fired, killing the sheriff, so the lawmen then returned to town to gather a larger, better armed posse while Hunter and his friends fled, each in a different direction. In Watonga McArthur gathered a posse of fifty heavily armed men and they started on the trail of Hunter.

Meanwhile word of the murder of Garrison had spread far and wide and in Oklahoma City more than one hundred men armed with revolvers, Winchester rifles, and shotguns gathered at the train station demanding to join the posse. Men from all over Oklahoma took up arms and soon there were more than two hundred fifty men interested in locating Hunter and his six companions, and many were determined to see them lynched as soon as they were captured. A reward of $3,200 was offered for the capture of Hunter, and it was thought that if the gang was not located and wiped out it could result in a statewide race riot. The fugitive group dispersed but the description of Hunter was circulated widely.

Still, it was not until late September 1909 that Hunter was arrested by Jefferson County Sheriff Philpot at Pine Bluff, Arkansas. At first it was not certain they had the right man, since nearly sixteen months had passed, so he was brought to Kingfisher where Henry Daugherty, Susie Pride's brother, identified him as Alf Hunter. Hunter was returned to Watonga where he was lodged in jail, and at his examination he was held over to answer to the grand jury and was indicted. Hunter was tried at the fall session of the district court, convicted of the murder of Garrison, and sentenced to hang. His defense team immediately began an aggressive appeals process, which delayed the execution for more than a year, but finally on March 4, 1910, the state supreme court affirmed the lower court's judgment and sentence, and Hunter's date for execution was set at April 8.

The condemned man was taken to the penitentiary at McAlester to be held until the date of his execution, and his attorneys then began a campaign to obtain a commutation of sentence. As the fatal date approached the prisoner was returned to the jail at Watonga where, by April 7, the scaffold had been erected twenty feet from the jail within a twenty-foot board fence enclosing a thirty-foot-square area. Even as Sheriff McArthur awaited word from Governor Charles N. Haskell, jailer Perry Southwick tested the rope and, finding it too long, made a second test. The time for the execution had been set for 7:00 A.M. but the sheriff was persuaded to delay until 10:30 as many people were coming in on the 10:00 train. The entire Garrison family had come to witness the execution, and the murdered man's sons, Harvey D. and Brick Garrison, were permitted to assist on the scaffold. Hunter's brother Jack and his aged father, Joe, had arrived from Little Rock, Arkansas, and Joe Hunter purchased a black suit for his son's burial. During Hunter's final afternoon Father P. P. Schaffer of Union City heard Hunter's confession and then baptized him into the Catholic religion. At 7:10 P.M. Governor Haskell formally denied the request to intervene and told Sheriff McArthur to proceed with the execution. When the condemned man was told of the governor's action he said, "This thing of being hanged does not bother me. But I want to go on record as being the opposite of being a bad man. I became bad in Arkansas because I and my people were double-crossed by the white men. We got no justice, no law. As soon as I found out these conditions I started to carry a gun. I never saw Sheriff Garrison until the day I killed him. No one is more sorry than I that I killed him. When he ran for sheriff I worked for him among the Negroes and was his friend. But then it's all right."

Hunter had slept well his final night and arose early to eat a hearty breakfast of ham and eggs. He dressed in his new burial suit and then sat with his religious adviser until the sheriff arrived before 10:30, his wrists and arms were bound, and the procession was formed. Father Schaffer led the way with crucifix held high, then came Sheriff McArthur, and next was the prisoner with Watonga's Deputy Sheriff W. B. Skeene on one arm and Hydro's Deputy O. C. Allen on the other arm. It was a short walk from his cell into the enclosure, and as soon as he exited the jail building he was met by his father for a last tearful good-bye. The condemned man marched onto the scaffold with a firm step and gazed down at the seventy-five witnesses assembled beneath. Waiting on the scaffold were Sheriff M. C. Binion of Oklahoma County, Sheriff T. L. Garrison from Texas, and Harvey and Brick Garrison. When he was asked if he had anything to say he said,

> I am bound here like a sheep for the slaughter. I can't get away and I know I am going to be killed. The cause of my being here is the fact that no justice is afforded to the Negro race. I could obtain none in Arkansas and I could get none here, so I was forced to become a fugitive and carry a gun. I am sorry for the death of Sheriff Garrison. I know he was a good and brave man. I killed him in a fair fight, however, and if I had been white I would not have hung for the deed. I am not a criminal nor a habitual lawbreaker but am a victim of circumstances. In conclusion I would say that although I am not a brave man, justice is the only thing that I ever begged for, and right in this courthouse men stood up and swore falsely against me and against Ellis, who is at present in jail because he was supposed to have been my accomplice. They swore by the God that gave them life and I pray that he will forgive them as I do now. Well, friends, I bid you good-bye. I die in a great faith and pray for you all, that you may meet me in the land of rest. Amen! Amen!

Sheriff McArthur then read a telegram from Mrs. Garrison in San Antonio, Texas, addressed to the Rev. G. McManis, which said, "Read this to Alf Hunter before his execution. By your act on June 15, 1908 (*sic*), you took from me all that was dear, my husband, and left me to a cold, cruel world, alone and without support in my old age. I send you this message of peace, and God be with you and forgive you as I have." Hunter wept as he acknowledged the letter. The sheriff then read the death warrant, and afterward Deputy Skeene directed Hunter to take his place on the trapdoor. His knees and ankles were pinioned by O. C.

Allen, and Harvey Garrison stepped from the rear to position the noose. Skeene then pulled the black hood over Hunter's head and, stepping back, gave the signal to the sheriff who sprang the trap. Dr. W. R. Kelley monitored vital signs and pronounced Hunter dead in six minutes. Kelley said, "The man's neck was broken and the spinal column separated. It was one of the quickest hangings in the history of the state. He never knew anything after he felt the trap give beneath his feet." Hunter's body was then taken down, placed in an undertaker's basket, and laid on the steps of the courthouse so that the throngs of curious citizens could file past and view the remains. Alf's brother Joe stood at the head of the corpse and took a collection to pay for transportation to Little Rock and for the funeral, and he collected $75. The money was given to Hunter's father, who then placed the remains of his son in an express wagon which drove to the local undertaking parlor. The body was prepared and shipped Friday evening.

Sources: *Lawton Constitution-Democrat* (OK): June 11, 1908. *New Castle News* (PA): June 6, 1908. *Oklahoman* (Oklahoma City): May 21, 1908. *Evening News* (Ada, OK): March 4, 1908; August 7, 1908; April 8–9, 1910. *Ogden Standard* (UT): June 6, 1908. *Oklahoma City Times* (OK): May 21, 1908; September 28, 1909. *Oklahoman* (Oklahoma City): October 3, 1909.

Black, John
April 15, 1910

On Thursday afternoon, October 14, 1909, John Black, a black man, took up a position on the road two miles south of Holdenville in Hughes County, Oklahoma, and, armed with a revolver, sat on a stump to wait for men to pass so he could rob them. During the early morning hours he robbed Ed Nicholson, ordering him to turn out his pockets. Meanwhile J. P. Stephens took $35 from the household funds and started for town at 10:00 A.M., driving his team and wagon. When Stephens came upon Black the highwayman stopped him at gunpoint and robbed him of the $35. Black would later claim his gun fired accidentally, but the next that was seen of Stephens was when his team returned to his farm and his body was found on the front seat face downward, one hand still clutching the lines and with the brake set. He was still alive and was immediately moved into the house, but he died in minutes without speaking a word.

A number of people had seen Black so a description of the suspected murderer was circulated, and Calvin's city marshal Carter was notified to be on the lookout for the fugitive. With D. S. Hood, Carter searched a freight train that had come into his city, and they found a man hiding in a refrigerator car near the engine. He matched the description of Black so they took him to jail and conducted a thorough search. They found a $20 gold certificate and a $10 and $5 bill, the exact denominations Stephens had on him when murdered and robbed. The officers also found a .45-caliber Colt revolver with one expended shell. The prisoner then confessed to being Black and confessed to robbing Nicholson, but he denied shooting Stephens, saying a partner had killed the farmer. He said that after he robbed Nicholson his partner said "You give me the gun and I'll stay here until I get some of these fellows." Black claimed he went across the field and had not gone far when he heard the fatal shot fired, his partner caught up with him and told him what he had done and gave him the money and gun before running away. Black said he went to the Rock Island tracks and buried his distinctive clothing — a blue jumper and overalls — then walked to Bilby and boarded the train to Calvin where he was arrested.

Several men had already been jailed but Nicholson had cleared them, but when Black was returned to Holdenville he was positively identified as the lone highwayman. Sheriff King then went to the place where Black said he discarded his clothes, found them, and recovered them for evidence. On Friday morning, October 15, Black was arraigned and pled not guilty, but later on appeal he would say his plea was more out of fear of mob violence and the potential of a lynching than a denial of guilt. That evening there was strong talk of lynching so Sheriff King and deputy Bailey took their prisoner in a buggy and drove into the country east of town. A lynching party tried to overtake them but they could not find the prisoner. On Saturday at noon the sheriff arrived in Wetumka, boarded the train for Muskogee, and deposited his prisoner in jail there.

Black was not returned to Holdenville until November when the defendant was tried in Judge Caruthers' courtroom during the fall term, and he presented no defense. Black had not realized that he had been seen by a large number of men, all of whom testified that he was acting alone on the road, but it was his confession that sealed his fate.

The jury retired at midnight with instructions that if they reached a verdict they could seal it and deliver it on Friday, November 12, 1909. After forty-five minutes deliberating the jurors retired under guard of two bailiffs. However, a crowd of over two hundred men became restless and the sheriff was afraid of another attempt to lynch the prisoner so the judge called the jury back to court to determine if they had reached a verdict, and they reported they had found the defendant guilty of murder in the first degree and recommended the death penalty. On Friday morning Black stood before Judge Caruthers for sentencing, and Black asked that he be allowed time to send for his people. The judge stated that the sentence had to be set for not less than thirty nor more then sixty days. The judge then, after a lengthy speech, said, "I now sentence you to be hanged by the sheriff of Hughes County, Oklahoma, in the manner provided by law, on the 17th day of December, A.D. 1909 by the neck until dead. May God have mercy on your soul."

The appeal process delayed the proceedings for four months but the judgment and sentence of the lower court was finally affirmed, and the date for Black's execution was set for April 15, 1910. An application praying for executive clemency was then submitted by Black's priest but after carefully considering the matter Governor Charles N. Haskell, on the morning of the execution, telephoned Father Paul J. Gillen saying that he saw nothing in the application that justified his interference. The application for commutation included a statement by Black, and according to the *Ada Evening News* of April 16 Black had claimed that he "pleaded not guilty at trial, later, however, confessing to the crime, and saying that he would have entered a plea of guilty had he not feared mob violence. Black said the verdict was rendered at nighttime, at demand of a mob, and that any other verdict would most probably have resulted in a lynching. The evidence presented at the trial, Black insisted, was only circumstantial. He said the murder of Stevens (*sic*) was accidental, as only robbery was intended." The application suggested that if he had cooperated and pled guilty the court would have only sentenced him to life in prison. The priest had asked for an early return so that, if refused, he could prepare the condemned man for the gallows, and immediately after hearing of the denial the priest hurried to Black's cell.

Black had received spiritual support continuously from Father Gillen during his time behind bars. On the fatal day Black walked from the jail into a cold drizzling rain, one officer on each arm to ensure he did not falter. He mounted the scaffold with a firm step and, when asked, talked to the crowd of one thousand witnesses for nine minutes, relating the details of the murder for which he was about to die. He forgave everyone and begged for forgiveness from them. He then took his place on the trapdoor where his wrists and arms, knees and ankles were bound with straps, the noose was adjusted, and the black hood was pulled over his head. At 1:27 P.M. all was in readiness, and Sheriff King sprang the trap. The attending physicians, waiting beneath the gallows, monitored his vital signs and pronounced him dead in eight minutes. The body was then cut down, lowered into the waiting coffin, and buried that evening.

Sources: *Holdenville Times* (OK): October 22, 1909; November 12, 1909. *The Evening News* (Ada, OK): April 16, 1910.

Henson, Frank
March 31, 1911

On Sunday evening, October 9, 1910, miners working outside Dawson in Tulsa County, Oklahoma, were engaged in a dice game in a "joint," a house where they regularly gambled, when a dispute arose over the point being made and the distribution of the winnings. This disagreement quickly escalated, and a messenger was sent to bring Dawson's deputy sheriff, Charles Stamper, to prevent the altercation from turning deadly. When the deputy entered he was deeply resented by the black miners, and several pulled their pistols and started shooting at the deputy. Stamper returned fire, wounding three miners, two fatally, but he was shot in the head at close range. The deputy did not die immediately but lingered for several hours before succumbing to the fatal wound. The armed combatants included Frank Henson, one of the black miners, who fled the scene with other miners who had scattered to avoid being shot. Those involved in the gunfight then spilled over into the community, and innocent citizens had to scramble for cover, as the shooting became wild and unrestrained. Henson was identified as the man who had shot Deputy Stamper, and the following day he was arrested, with four others, and lodged in the Tulsa County jail. Henson was indicted in the fall and tried, and on November 23, 1910, he was convicted of murdering Deputy Stamper. The case was appealed. On January 5 the Ada *Evening News* announced that the lower court's judgment and sentence had been affirmed, and Henson was sentenced to hang on January 27, 1911. However, there were further delays as Governor Lee Cruce took office on January 9 and granted a respite to consider the matter. The governor found no justification to intervene so Judge Poe set the date for Henson's execution at March 31, 1911, and nothing further would delay the proceedings.

To ensure privacy the scaffold was erected within a fenced enclosure near the old Tulsa County jail at the corner of Detroit Avenue and East Second Street. On the fatal day Henson was escorted onto the platform by his religious adviser the Reverend Netherland. When prompted Henson looked down at the twenty witnesses and made a speech lasting five minutes, during which he admitted his guilt and his willingness to expiate his crime on the gallows. He stepped back onto the trapdoor and, as he was being prepared, the Reverend Netherland read a funeral prayer. Henson's knees and ankles, wrists and arms were pinioned, the noose was adjusted and cinched tightly, and the black hood was pulled over his head, and when the Reverend announced "Amen!" the trap was sprung by Tulsa County Sheriff William M. McCullough. Henson dropped straight through, breaking his neck in the fall, and the attending physicians came forward and monitored vital signs until Henson's heart ceased to beat, then pronounced him dead. The body hung a while longer and was then cut down, deposited in the coffin provided, and buried that evening following services by the Reverend Netherland.

On June 30, 1911, the Ada *Evening News* announced that the "Hanging Site is Bare." The newspaper reported, "Whether it is another incident of the work of the divine, pointing a warning or merely a freak of nature, the fact remains that the spot in the jail yard at the side of the county court house over which Frank Henson, a black man, was hanged this spring for killing Charles Stamper, deputy sheriff, is devoid of any particle of vegetation, while all around it high weeds are growing profusely ... attaches of the sheriff's office and other departments of the county government have almost become superstitious about the circumstance."

Sources: *Advocate* (Victoria, TX): October 11, 1910. *Northwestern* (Oshkosh, WI): March 31, 1911. *Ada Evening News* (OK): January 6, 1911; June 30, 1911. *Oklahoman* (Oklahoma City): April 1, 1911

Bookman, Henry
December 10, 1915

Richard C. Hardin, a white man, lived next to George Booth, a black man, and the families were on friendly terms. On the Booth farm, near Fame in McIntosh County, lived Booth's sixty-year-old wife Lizzie and their twenty-eight-year-old farmhand Henry Bookman. During the afternoon of April 2, 1915, Hardin went to the Booth home to buy a used buggy wheel, as the wheel on his buggy had broken, but George was not home so Hardin waited on the porch with Lizzie. Bookman was working in the field but suddenly appeared on the porch and told Lizzie that he was feeling ill, then asked for water with soda. Bookman, who had always been friendly with Hardin, had not said a word to him before Lizzie went into her kitchen to fix the medicinal drink, but when she heard a shot fired she rushed out to see Bookman fire a second load of buckshot at Hardin. The first shot had nearly torn off Hardin's right hand and the second shot nearly severed his left arm at the shoulder. When Lizzie had left the men, only seconds earlier, Hardin had been standing in the doorway but when she returned Bookman was standing in the doorway and the double-barreled shotgun which hung over the door was in his hands. He started beating Hardin over the head with the gun barrel, and Hardin raised his right arm to ward off the blows and cried out for help and for Bookman to stop the attack. Lizzie also yelled for Bookman to stop but the farmhand ignored the pleas of both. Lizzie then ran into the farmyard yelling for help, and in a few moments Hardin followed, but he only managed to stumble fifteen feet before he collapsed, and then Bookman beat him to death with the butt of the shotgun.

Bookman was about to leave when George returned and he and his wife convinced the murderer to stay and surrender. Bookman was arrested by Sheriff McCune and taken to the jail at Eufaula, but was quickly moved to McAlester and lodged in a prison cell for safekeeping. Two weeks earlier

Crockett Williams had been arrested, the jail had been overrun, and Williams had been lynched. Sheriff McCune suspected it could occur again, and his suspicions were confirmed when a large mob overran the jail at 2:00 A.M. and were allowed to search the cells before they dispersed. Meanwhile, in McAlester, Judge R. W. Higgins issued an order for a special session of the district court to begin on April 28, but then moved the date to May 21. A jury was seated by May 23; Bookman's trial lasted six days, and on May 29 he was convicted of first-degree murder, rejecting his plea of self-defense. Judge Higgins then sentenced him to die in the electric chair on August 6, the first such sentence in Oklahoma. The date was stayed to October 6, but extended to October 11 when the court of criminal appeals affirmed the judgment and sentence of the district court, and the date of execution was then set for Friday, December 10. Nothing would arise to delay the proceedings further.

On Monday, December 6, Bookman was removed from his regular cell and moved to the special death cell across from the execution chamber. During his time on death row Bookman was attended by prison chaplain the Rev. A. B. Johnson, and on this final day the reverend was assisted by three long-term convicts as they prayed and sang hymns throughout Thursday afternoon. Late Thursday Warden R. W. Dick received a petition from Bookman's attorney asking for a stay of execution on the grounds that his client was insane, and Bookman claimed he remembered nothing of the killing and told the officials, "I don't know why they goin' to kill me. Guess it's cause they got me in here. Nah, I ain't guilty; I never done nothin' to be killed for." After a careful examination the officials pronounced the prisoner sane, he immediately ceased the bizarre behavior he had displayed for weeks, and the execution proceeded on schedule.

When the sun had set the prisoner begged Warden Dick, "Oh, Mr. Warden, let me see de sun one mo' time," but the request was denied. Later in the evening the reporters were admitted and the condemned man told them, "Why be afraid to die? A man has ter die sometime," and when asked if he was "all right with the Lord?" he replied "Yeh, Yeh! Me and de Lord am all right. I'se prayed and prayed and am ready." He then sang his favorite hymn before concluding, "I'm going to meet my Jesus over there." After a stimulant was administered the death warrant was read to Bookman by Warden Dick and then, just before 1:00 A.M., the heavy cell door was swung open. The Reverend Johnson and a guard each took an arm and escorted Bookman the short distance to the oak chair, with the prisoner mumbling a prayer as he walked. The prisoner took his seat and his chest, waist, arms and ankles were secured with heavy leather straps, and then the copper helmet and leg band, lined with moistened sponge, were strapped in place. A black leather mask was placed over his eyes and forehead and attached to the chair. The electricity, set at 1,500 volts, coursed through Bookman's body for ten seconds at 1:01 A.M., and the body jerked taut and shot upwards, straining against the straps. His fists clenched, there was a grunt, saliva spewed from his mouth, and then he relaxed as the current was turned off. Dr. C. C. Shaw checked for vital signs and ordered another surge, and 2,300 volts of electricity were applied for seventeen seconds; Bookman was pronounced dead at 1:03 A.M. One minute later the body was removed and sent to a local funeral home to be prepared for burial in the prison cemetery, as he had lost touch with all the members of his large family after he left home.

Sources: *Ada Evening News* (OK): December 10, 1915. *Eufaula Democrat* (OK): April 9, 1915.

Towery, Cecil

November 6, 1916

On the afternoon of August 4, 1916, black brothers Will Towery and twenty-two-year-old Cecil, walked with their seventeen-year-old cousin, Clarence Scott, to a house along the Grayson Highway in McIntosh County, Oklahoma, where they could buy Choctaw beer. After they had drunk a quantity of beer Charles Vaughn, an oilman from Morris, drove up and went inside. He did not drink any beer and soon was ready to continue on to Morris, and the Towery brothers and Scott asked to ride along. Vaughn agreed and they went into Morris where they spent an hour while Vaughn conducted his business, and Vaughn bought a quart of whiskey which he placed under the seat in the tonneau where the Towerys were riding. Vaughn drove the Towerys and Scott back to the house along the highway, but when they arrived Vaughn noticed that both Towery boys were much drunker than before, checked for his bottle of whiskey and found it missing. He accused the Towery brothers of stealing his whiskey and they denied it, so he said he was going to report them to the authorities, and the Towerys and Scott agreed to go along. Cecil got into the passenger seat and Will and Scott climbed into the tonneau seat.

When they were a half mile from town one of the Towerys convinced Vaughn that he had to stop, and as soon as they pulled over an argument started, followed by a violent struggle between the Towerys and Vaughn, and Scott fled. The youngster quickly returned to the automobile and learned that Will had grabbed Vaughn and pushed him backward over the tonneau, and Cecil then pulled out a straight razor and inflicted two deep neck wounds, each severing a major vein or artery, and Vaughn had bled to death in seconds. Scott then ran to town for help while Will convinced Cecil they had to flee, but after they had gone only a short distance crossing a field Cecil returned to the automobile, afraid that if he was captured he would be lynched. Cecil was found at the side of the road, surrendered and was lodged in the jail at Okmulgee. Vaughn's body was taken from the tonneau and returned to Morris.

Later that night it became clear that a large mob was forming to lynch Cecil Towery, so at 11:30 P.M. the officers decided to take him to the jail at Muskogee. As they drove from the city they were confronted by a large mob of angry men, so they turned off and made it to the jail at Sapulpa. Again a mob began to form so on August 7 the prisoner was moved to the Eufaula jail. The following day Cecil's brother Will surrendered to avoid being hanged, and he joined Cecil in jail, and then both men confessed the details of the murder. Late on August 8 a large mob of men started for Eufaula, and sixteen automobiles arrived at the jail at 2:00 A.M. the next morning, fully loaded with angry lynchers who were allowed to search the jail. Once the mob was certain the Towery brothers were not present they returned home, and then the officers brought the prisoners from a nearby cornfield and started for McAlester where the Towerys were lodged in a prison cell.

Within the week the brothers were arraigned, and Cecil pled guilty, recanting his earlier confession while claiming that he alone had murdered Vaughn, while Will pled not guilty, and his trial was set for August 28. On the day following the start of the trial the case went to the jury at 6:00 P.M., and after dinner the jurors took one ballot and found Will Towery guilty of first-degree murder, and recommended a sentence of death. Judge Clay then sentenced Cecil to die in the electric chair on November 6, 1916, and afterward he sentenced Will to die with his brother. Defense attorneys W. H. Twine and J. D. Epps filed appeals, and the judgment and sentence for Cecil was quickly affirmed, while for Will it was reversed, and he was granted a new trial. Their efforts to receive clemency failed when Governor Williams refused to intervene, and the date remained unchanged.

During Cecil's weeks on death row he was attended by prison chaplain the Rev. A. B. Johnson and by Pastor A. L. Russell, and a week before his death he embraced religion and was baptized, and then he read his Bible continuously thereafter. He was moved from his regular cell to the cell across from the death chamber several days before the execution, and as midnight neared the newspaper reporters were admitted. Towery told them, "I am ready to go. I am guilty and it is all right for the law to take my life. Choctaw beer was the cause of my crime." The reporters hurried to the witness area, and then the prisoner was escorted from his cell by his two clergymen, and took his seat in the heavy oak chair. His waist and chest, wrists and arms, and ankles were strapped to the chair, and after the sponges were moistened the copper bands were attached to his head and leg. A black mask was tied over his eyes and forehead and it was secured to the chair back. At 12:52 A.M. 1,500 volts from the electric control panel were turned on for five seconds, and then Dr. C. C. Shaw pronounced the prisoner dead, but to be certain he could not be revived another surge of 1,900 volts was applied for four seconds. After the body went limp, and it was again confirmed he was dead, the remains were removed and prepared for burial.

Sources: *Checotah Times* (OK): August 11, 1916. *Haskell News* (OK): November 6, 1916. *Muldrow Sun* (OK): November 6, 1916. *Muskogee Times-Democrat* (OK): August 5, 1916; August 8, 1916; August 30, 1916.

Taylor, Chester
Williams, Willie
Young, Charles
April 13, 1917

In 1916 a black couple, forty-three-year-old Chester Taylor and his wife Millie, lived in a tent near Oilton in Creek County, Oklahoma. On August 24 Millie told her husband that she was going to a dance, but he forbade her to attend. When the opportunity presented itself Millie snuck out and went to the dance. When she returned home she quietly entered their darkened tent, believing her husband was asleep. However, her husband was lying in wait with an axe and split open her skull killing her instantly. Taylor was arrested and lodged in the jail at Sapulpa, tried in Judge E. B. Hughes' courtroom in February 1917, and convicted of first-degree murder on February 23. Judge Hughes then sentenced Taylor to die in the electric chair on April 13, 1917, and he responded, "God bless you Judge." There was no transcript of the trial submitted for review and no attempt to obtain clemency or a respite.

On Sunday, December 26, 1915, at 2:30 A.M. Muskogee police officer Sam Neal saw a suspicious black man carrying a large, heavy gunny sack. When he confronted thirty-two-year-old Willie Williams, alias Charlie Green, the suspect dropped the sack, pulled a .38-caliber Colt revolver, and shot Neal in the right arm. Neal was right-handed and could not draw his weapon so he struggled with Williams for the pistol, but Williams overpowered the officer and shot Neal through the head at point-blank range, causing a mortal wound. Neal collapsed in a pool of blood in the middle of the street while Williams fled. Officers arrived from headquarters in minutes and found Neal unconscious, but the officer regained consciousness on the way to the hospital, identified his murderer and gave the details of the shooting. Neal died at 6:00 A.M. An investigation revealed that Williams had just burglarized the Bohart hardware store and was carrying away his loot when discovered by Neal, and his description was broadcast widely. Within a few hours of the shooting Williams, with Homer Matthews, boarded the Midland Valley train at Porum and was recognized, so Deputy Sheriff Dick Shumate, City Marshal Oscar Poole and the train's conductor approached the men to make an arrest. Williams pulled his revolver but a cartridge hung in the cylinder and he was taken into custody without firing a shot, and Williams and Matthews were rushed to the jail at Tulsa to prevent a lynching.

In late February the two men were taken to Muskogee for their preliminary hearing before Judge deGraffenried; they pled not guilty, and their trials were separated. Williams' trial began on February 23 and he tried to lay the murder on Matthews, but Matthews proved that he was not with Williams when the murder occurred. There was some thought of pleading insanity, as there seemed no other defense and no exculpatory evidence was presented, so Williams changed his plea to guilty, and on March 10 he was sentenced to die in the electric chair. His attorney filed an appeal which stayed the execution but the court of criminal appeals affirmed the judgment and sentence of the district court and set the date for execution at April 13, 1917.

On December 2, 1916, twenty-six-year-old Charles Young, a black man, was on a spree in a black settlement in Tillman County, Oklahoma, when he encountered George Good, a white man who had come to pick up his laundry. Young murdered Good but later insisted the killing was accidental. He was tried at the early spring term of the court, convicted of first-degree murder, and sentenced to die in the electric chair on April 13, 1917. There was no transcript of his trial submitted for review and clemency was denied.

Several days before the executions the men were removed from their regular cells and taken to special cells near the death chamber, and during these last days the three men were attended by prison chaplain the Rev. A. B. Johnson, who was assisted by two other ministers. The clergymen were at the door to their cells, praying and singing hymns, as each man was brought out and escorted to the electric chair. The order of execution was not recorded, nor were any last words of the condemned men, but between 5:00 A.M. and 5:30 all three men were electrocuted. There were fifty witnesses in the viewing area when the first man appeared and he took his seat in the heavy oak chair. His waist and chest, wrists and arms, and ankles were strapped to the chair, and after the sponges were moistened the copper bands were attached to his head and leg. A black mask was then tied over his eyes and forehead, and it was secured to the chair. The first jolt of electricity, ranging from 1,500 to 2,300 volts, was applied from the electric control panel, and then the current was turned off and on again for a brief period before the doctor pronounced the prisoner dead. After the body was removed the second man was brought in and the same procedures followed, and then the third man, and afterward the bodies of all three condemned men were removed from the prison and prepared for burial.

Sources: *Fort Gibson Gazette* (OK): December 30, 1915. *Muldrow Sun* (OK): April 27, 1917. *Muskogee Times-Democrat* (OK): February 23–24, 1916; April 13, 1917. *Sequoyah County Democrat* (OK): February 23, 1917.

Prather, John H.
May 3, 1918

At 1:00 A.M. on the morning of March 9, 1911, eighteen-year-old John Henry Prather and four other young black boys accosted plumber W. H. Archie on Third Street as he was returning to his home in Oklahoma City. They knocked him to the ground, beat him and stole $70, and then Prather, who had a pistol, fired a single shot which killed Archie. The five murderers were quickly captured and lodged in jail, and Prather confessed to firing the fatal shot. He told the authorities, "I have been wanting to kill a white man for a long time."

All five prisoners were held over at their arraignment, and all but Prather pled not guilty to murder, while Prather pled guilty hoping to get a reduced sentence for cooperating. By April 7 James Holmes, Elijah Turner, Charles Posey, and Bud Johnson were convicted of murder, and on April 29 Judge W. R. Taylor sentenced all five men to hang on June 21. The cases were being appealed while applications were pending with Governor Cruce, and the governor granted reprieves for all five men, Prather first to July 7 and then to July 28. Prather's application was still pending as Sheriff Jack Spain stood in Prather's cell, preparing to escort him to the gallows alone, but just then the commutation to a life sentence arrived and Prather was taken to the prison that evening. The sentence of Holmes was soon afterward commuted to life imprisonment while the appeals for Turner, Posey and Johnson continued for more than a year. Their judgments and sentences were affirmed on September 4, and then on September 28 Governor Cruce commuted their sentences to life imprisonment.

In early 1917 Prather's cell-mate was Charlie Ross, and when he told Ross that he was going to kill a prison guard and escape he was severely criticized. Prather then murdered Ross, and in July he was tried in the Pittsburg County district court and convicted of first-degree murder. Judge R. W. Higgins sentenced Prather to die in the electric chair, but his case was appealed which stayed the execution. The judgment and sentence of the court was affirmed, and the date of his execution was set for May 3, 1918. On May 1 he received word that his petition for a rehearing in the court of criminal appeals had been denied, and he was moved to a cell near the electric chair. Governor Williams had considered the case and declined to intervene.

The time for Prather's execution was set between midnight and dawn but there is no detailed record of the execution, nor even a mention of a policy of censorship. He may have received a stimulant shortly before the heavy iron doors were swung open, and then Prather would have been escorted to the heavy oak chair where the prisoner took his seat and his chest and waist, wrists and arms, and ankles were secured with heavy leather straps. The copper helmet and leg band, lined with moistened sponge, were secured in place next and a black leather mask was placed over his eyes and forehead and attached to the chair back. The electricity, set between 600 and 2,300 volts at the "electrical control panel," coursed through Prather's body for at least several seconds while the witnesses looked on, and after the doctors confirmed that there were no vital signs a second jolt of electricity was administered as required by the regulations. The prison physician pronounced Prather dead before the body was removed and sent to a local funeral parlor to be prepared for burial.

Sources: *Ada Evening News* (OK): October 1, 1912. *Checotah Times* (OK): May 5, 1911; September 28, 1917. *Emporia Gazette* (KS): July 28, 1911. *Muskogee Times-Democrat* (OK): June 21, 1911; May 1, 1918. *Star Gazette* (Sallisaw, OK): August 4, 1911.

Brown, James
November 8, 1918

On Friday morning, May 18, 1917, two large black men, at gunpoint, held up the entire crew of the Iron Mountain freight train near Vian, Oklahoma. Shortly after the robbery was reported the Vian deputy sheriff encountered two likely suspects, and following a shoot-out, during which no one was injured, they escaped. Later two black men resembling the fugitives were captured at Vian, but they proved to be the wrong men and were released.

On the following evening, May 19, two black men robbed Glenn Jacobs and his father-in-law on Brushy Mountain road northeast of Muskogee while the two men were on their way to the Arkansas River on a fishing trip. One of the robbers shot Jacobs through the heart, and the Coca-Cola salesman bled to death in seconds. His father-in-law was not injured and he provided a good description of the robbers, which matched the robbers of the freight train crew.

On Sunday, May 27, at 11:30 P.M. Fort Gibson's deputy sheriff, Henry Rees, with town marshal Milo Willey, deputized citizens Monte Mountcastle and Louis Sleeper, surrounded "a little Negro hut on the outskirts of town" and captured thirty-two-year-old James Brown, alias Jerry Moore, without resistance. The prisoner was taken to Muskogee overnight. In the morning he confessed and named Sam Shaw, alias Sam Crittenden, as his accomplice and the man who shot Jacobs. The following day, Tuesday, Shaw was arrested by Haskell's city marshal Jones and he also confessed, but claimed it was Brown who shot Jacobs. Jacobs' father-in-law had at first corroborated Brown's story, but when he was able to see the two men standing side-by-side he identified Brown as the murderer.

On Friday, June 1, the two prisoners were arraigned before Judge Vernon and they pled not guilty, their hearing was set for Monday morning, and they were held over for separate trials. Brown then tried the "insanity dodge" but after a brief period of bizarre behavior he abandoned the obvious ruse. Jury selection for Brown's trial began in Judge R. P. deGraffenried's courtroom on July 2, and presentation of the evidence was completed the following evening. The jurors then deliberated less than twenty minutes before returning a verdict of guilty of first-degree murder and recommending the death penalty. Shaw's trial began on Thursday, July 5, and on Sunday, July 8, he was also convicted of first-degree murder, without recommendation for the death penalty. Brown was then brought into court and Judge deGraffenried sentenced Shaw to a term of life in prison while Jacobs was sentenced to die in the electric chair. Both men were delivered to the prison while Jacobs' attorney, Kelly Brown (no relation), filed an appeal. The court of criminal appeals affirmed the judgment and death sentence in mid–1917, and the date for Brown's execution was set for September 28. Governor Williams then intervened and granted a reprieve to October 26, 1917, but after a year of further delays the date of execution was finally set for November 8, 1918, and the governor declined to interfere further.

The execution of James Brown was set between midnight and dawn, but there is no detailed record of the execution, nor even a mention of a policy of censorship. The condemned man would be moved from his regular cell to a cell near the death chamber days or hours before the date set. Typically, a stimulant would be administered before the death warrant was read to the prisoner in his cell, with his clergyman present if he had accepted religious counsel. The heavy cell door would then be swung open, and he would be escorted the short distance to the oak chair where he would take his seat and his chest, waist, arms and ankles would be secured with heavy leather straps. The copper helmet and leg band, lined with moistened sponge, would be strapped in place and a black leather mask would be placed over his eyes and forehead and attached to the chair back. The electricity, set between 600 and 2,300 volts, would course through his body for several seconds, and after being checked by the physician another surge of electricity would be applied. After the prisoner was pronounced dead his body would be removed and sent to a local funeral home to be prepared for burial, and in Brown's case his burial was probably in the prison cemetery.

Sources: *Checotah Times* (OK): September 28, 1917. *Haskell News* (OK): May 30, 1917. *Muskogee Times-Democrat* (OK): May 26, 1917; May 28, 1917; June 1, 1917; July 2–3, 1917; November 8, 1918.

Braught, T. R.
May 23, 1919

On Monday evening, November 13, 1916, Drumright police officer Sam Cook took a sawed-off double-barreled shotgun and went looking for Creek County deputy sheriffs T. R. Braught and M. H. van Sickle. Cook had been a police officer until several months earlier when he was removed on charges brought by the two deputies, but Cook had been reinstated over the deputies' objections. Cook found the two deputies standing on Main Street, and as he stepped into the middle of the street he fired both barrels at the deputies without giving warning or hesitating, but neither deputy was struck by the heavy buckshot. Cook took cover behind a telephone pole to reload while Braught returned fire with his pistol, but he was not able to shoot his attacker. The two deputies realized that they were at a disadvantage against a man with a shotgun so they ran into a hardware store where Braught obtained a Winchester rifle and ammunition and then, returning to the street, opened fire. The first bullet struck Cook over his heart killing him instantly. The two deputies then drove to Sapulpa and surrendered to the sheriff, and at their preliminary hearing the killing was found to be self-defense and they were released.

On July 1, 1917, thirty-nine-year-old Braught, Otis Robbins, who was a cousin of Sam Cook, and Elgie Kessenger were drinking together at "the Hump," a once notorious roadhouse four miles from Oilton. During the early morning hours Braught threatened Robbins' life several times, but took no action and everything seemed friendly when they left at 5:00 A.M. Braught and Robbins went to Braught's automobile and drove to the Oklahoma Garage in Oilton where Robbins was shot to death. Braught, who was no longer a deputy sheriff, surrendered and was lodged in the Sapulpa jail. He claimed that over the past months Robbins had threatened his life many times, making the statements to Braught's wife and to a justice of the peace in Drumright, and he said that Robbins had twice armed himself and gone looking for Braught "to pay a debt." The prisoner claimed that when they parked the automobile Robbins took Braught's pistol from the glove box and said, "You killed my cousin, Sam Cook. I'm going to shoot you with your own gun and see how you like it." Braught said they struggled for the gun and it went off, accidentally killing Robbins. While Braught was in jail his wife was murdered in a Drumright hotel by Back Davis, a friend of Robbins and Cook, so one of Braught's key defense witnesses was not available when he was tried in the Creek County district court at Sapulpa during the early fall session. He was convicted of first-degree murder and sentenced to die in the electric chair on November 23, 1917. Appeals followed and it was not until early 1919 that the court of criminal appeals affirmed the judgment and sentence of the Creek County district court, and the date of electrocution was set for May 23. Governor J. B. A. Robertson was repeatedly petitioned for clemency, but he declined to interfere and said, "If the death penalty is to be retained in Oklahoma it must, in justice, apply in Braught's case."

As the date approached Braught was removed from his regular cell and lodged in a special cell near the death chamber. He was attended by the prison chaplain and his assistants, and the last services were conducted in the passageway outside his cell at 4:00 P.M.; then he was returned to his cell. His brothers and sisters were allowed to step up to the bars, and they bid him farewell and exchanged kisses, but he began to cry when the sister who had worked so hard to obtain a commutation stepped forward, and he said, "It is not that I must die within a few hours that hurts, but it is the thought that I have brought this disgrace and humiliation upon you."

After his family left he was offered a stimulant, but he refused. The death warrant was read just after midnight, and then the heavy cell door was swung open and Braught was escorted into the death chamber. He professed religion and insisted that the killing of Robbins was accidental, and then he knelt and prayed. Upon arising he took his seat in the heavy oak chair and his chest and waist, wrists and arms, and ankles were secured with heavy leather straps. He watched as the straps were being applied, smiling all the time while the clergyman and his assistants sang the hymn "I Am Going Home" over the sound of the dynamo humming in the next room. The copper helmet and leg band, lined with moistened sponge, were secured in place, and then the black leather mask was placed over his eyes and forehead and attached to the chair back. At 12:36 A.M. the first surge of electricity, set at 1,500 volts, coursed through Braught for five seconds, and the body jerked taut against the creaking straps. After three attending physicians checked for vital signs, and pronounced him dead, another surge of electricity was applied as required by the regulations. One minute later the body was removed and shortly afterward was released to relatives, who had the remains sent to a local funeral home to be prepared for shipment to Afton, Ohio, for burial on Saturday afternoon.

Sources: *Ada Evening News* (OK): May 23, 1919. *Haskell News* (OK): November 126, 1916. *Muskogee Times-Democrat* (OK): May 23, 1919.

Betterton, Monroe
July 9, 1920

Monroe Betterton and his first wife, living in Barry County, Missouri, were having marital difficulties, and one day they quarreled and he beat her insensible. She was rushed to the hospital but soon died. There is no record of him serving time, but by 1908 Betterton claimed to be remarried, and he and his second wife were having similar difficulties. They were in Neosho, Missouri, and decided to go to Monett, where Betterton had relatives. As they walked down the railroad tracks they began to quarrel, and when they were just two miles from town Betterton pulled out his knife and stabbed his wife in the heart, killing her instantly. He left the body beside the tracks, and a crew from a freight train found her. Betterton's description was sent to Monett and vicinity. He was arrested at Monett, lodged in the Mt. Vernon jail, tried for murder in Judge F. C. Johnston's courtroom, convicted of first-degree murder and sentenced to serve a ninety-nine year term in prison.

In 1918 forty-eight-year-old Betterton obtained a parole and he returned to Monett, where he met and courted forty-four-year-old Mrs. Lockwood, and they were soon married, but marital discord arose immediately, they quarreled constantly, and were soon divorced. However, when Betterton's son married Mrs. Lockwood-Betterton's daughter the couple reconciled and they were remarried at Mt. Vernon during the first week of July 1919. The Bettertons returned to their home in Vinita, Oklahoma, where the same difficulties that led to their divorce quickly reappeared. On July 9, 1919, the couple quarreled, and when Mrs. Betterton turned away from her husband he pulled out a pistol and shot her in the back. She soon died of the wound, and Betterton was arrested and lodged in the jail at Vinita.

He was tried in Judge Brewster's Craig County courtroom during the second week of November, and on November 13 the jurors returned a verdict of guilty of first-degree murder and recommended the death penalty. When the prisoner appeared before Judge Brewster for sentencing he was described as "the man with the glassy eye, the drawn cheek — with every mark of a murderer — and the man without a friend," and then Betterton was sentenced to die in the electric chair on January 23, 1920. On November 25 a notice of appeal was filed, which stayed the execution, and the court of criminal appeals considered the case for months before affirming the judgment and sentence of the lower court. Betterton's date for execution was then set at July 9, 1920, exactly one year after the murder was committed. The condemned man was then examined by staff from the state hospital and pronounced sane, to avoid any last minute delays by requests for a sanity hearing. Governor Robertson, when petitioned for clemency, declined to intervene.

Several days before his date in the electric chair the prisoner was removed from his regular cell to the special cell near the death chamber beneath the main building. At noon on his final day he issued a statement once again proclaiming his innocence, and insisted that his soul had been saved. One reporter was allowed to visit him in his cell ten minutes before midnight and the prisoner told him, "I am not guilty of the crime with which I am charged. I am ready to die. I am ready to meet my God. I do not fear death, but I do not want to die for a crime which I did not commit." After the death warrant was read by Warden Fred C. Switzer the reporter joined one hundred witnesses and they were ushered into the viewing area.

At 12:10 A.M. the heavy cell door was swung open, and the prisoner was escorted into the death chamber. Warden Switzer asked him, "Have you anything to say before you die?" and Betterton replied, "No sir." Betterton took his seat in the oak chair where his chest and waist, wrists and arms, and ankles were secured with heavy leather straps, and he looked straight ahead the entire time of preparation. The copper helmet and leg band, lined with moistened sponge, were strapped in place and a black leather mask was placed over his eyes and forehead and attached to the chair back. Chaplain J. E. Rogers then read a passage of scripture which was followed by a prayer, after which Betterton said, "Thank God!" As everyone stepped away Betterton, anticipating the current, called out, "Good-bye and bless you all." The electricity, set at between 600 and 2,300 volts, coursed through Betterton's body for several seconds at 12:12 A.M., and his body jerked taut and strained against the straps. The doctor in attendance quickly checked for vital signs and pronounced him dead, but then a second jolt of electricity was applied as required by regulation to ensure death. One minute later the body was removed and sent to a local funeral home to be prepared for burial

Sources: *Ada Evening News* (OK): July 9, 1920. *Muldrow Sun* (OK): July 2, 1920. *Muskogee Times-Democrat* (OK): November 25, 1919; July 9, 1920. *Neosho Times* (MO): July 17, 1919.

Blakely, Robert W.
Ledbetter, John
February 25, 1921

Thirty-eight-year-old Robert W. Blakely, a Brushy Mountain farmer, had been having criminal intimate relations with his step-daughter, eighteen-year-old Effie May Alford, for some time when, on August 1, 1920, she told him to stop. She threatened to report him for rape and he countered by threatening to kill her if she went to the authorities. When she filed a complaint Blakely fled, and deputies were searching for him.

Early on Wednesday morning, August 14, the fugitive returned home to his wife, step-daughter and six children and convinced them to go to Arkansas and start life anew. The next morning Mrs. Blakely went into Muskogee and tried to sell the crops in the field. During the early afternoon hours, while Mrs. Blakely was still in town, Effie May went to the spring and talked with a man who had stopped for water. Blakely saw them, and he became jealous thinking he might be her new lover. As soon as his step-daughter returned he accused her, they argued, he drew his .45-caliber automatic pistol, and as Effie May begged for her life he shot her to death. He fled and was trying to make his way into Arkansas, but at the river he was captured by Jess Herd and Chester White. He still had the .45-caliber pistol and two clips of cartridges, but Herd "got the drop on him" and he had no choice but to surrender or be shot. Blakely's wife was jailed as his accomplice, but she was later cleared and released.

After Blakely was arrested he confessed that he had shot his step-daughter when she said she wanted to go to a neighbor's house for thread, but he believed she was going to summon the authorities, and he said that at that moment he "decided to end it all. I killed her and am ready to die." In late November Blakely was tried in Muskogee and convicted of first-degree murder, and on December 2 he was sentenced by Judge B. B. Wheeler to die in the electric chair on February 25, 1921. There were no delays from appeals nor from petitions for clemency.

On Sunday, August 15, 1920, Robert Moreland, a recent acquaintance of twenty-five-year-old divorcee Pearl Darrow, spent the day with her, and at 6:30 P.M. they started walking to a spiritualist meeting. On the way they met thirty-one-year-old John Ledbetter, who had been dating Darrow for a year, and he tried to convince his sweetheart to return to her home at 1303 Galveston Street in Muskogee. Darrow refused and the three continued walking along a narrow path near M Street, but at one point they had to walk single file with Moreland in front, Darrow next, and Ledbetter in the rear. As they neared the corner of M and Fredonia Streets Ledbetter suddenly pulled out a Colt .45 revolver and shot over Darrow's shoulder, the bullet striking Moreland in the back and killing him instantly. Ledbetter then put the barrel of his pistol to Darrow's head and said, "Your time has come too, damn you!" Mrs. Darrow cried out, "John, don't shoot — listen, think what little May will say," referring to her eight-year-old daughter, whom Ledbetter had grown to love. They walked only a few yards before they met Mrs. William Byrd, and Ledbetter left Darrow with her and fled. He was not seen again until 7:00 A.M. when he was arrested by Police Captain England in a house near the stockyards in North Muskogee.

Later that day Ledbetter had his preliminary hearing before Judge Fred Zick and the primary witness against him was Darrow. Ledbetter claimed self-defense and said that he saw Moreland "fooling with something in his pocket, and I thought he had a gun," but Moreland was unarmed. Based upon this evidence and the testimony of Darrow, Ledbetter was held over for trial. He was tried in late November, and he was convicted of first-degree murder. On December 2 Ledbetter appeared in court for sentencing and was asked by Judge B. B. Wheeler if he had any reason why sentence should not be passed, and he said he did not have a fair trial and that Mrs. Darrow had lied in her testimony. The judge said, "The court is of a different opinion," and then sentenced him to die in the electric chair on February 25, 1921, the same date as Blakely. It was thought that an appeal would delay the execution for months, but the matter was handled so expeditiously that the date remained unchanged, and the governor refused to intervene.

On February 19, after Blakely had resigned himself to his fate and no longer feared he was going mad, he told the warden, "I know I've been a fool and a mean man. I'm sorry I killed Effie May. But that does no good. It is not the ordinary sorrow now that will help me, it's only the goodness of God, and that is what I am relying on...." The prisoners were moved into cells in the basement of the main building near the electric chair days before their execution. On the afternoon of his final day Blakely told the warden, "I can go to heaven just as well from one place as another, but I don't want to be left to rot in the penitentiary graveyard. I don't want my children to have to come to the penitentiary to see my grave. If you grant this wish I am willing to meet my fate with a smile and pay the penalty for my crime."

While Blakely sat, reading his Bible and praying, a priest was admitted to Ledbetter's cell and for the first time he heard the Lord's Prayer. That evening, as midnight approached, the men were offered a stimulant but there is no record of one being administered, and then the death warrants were read to both men. Ledbetter was taken out first and he was escorted to the chamber where he confessed his crime to seventy-five witnesses. He took his seat in the oak chair and the Lord's Prayer was recited while his chest and waist, wrists and arms, and ankles were secured with heavy leather straps. Next came the copper helmet and leg band, lined with moistened sponge, and these were secured in place. A black leather mask was then placed over his eyes and forehead and attached to the chair back. Minutes after midnight electricity, set between 600 and 2,300 volts, coursed through Ledbetter and his body stiffened and strained against the straps, and then a second jolt of electricity, as required by regulation, was administered. Dr. J. W. Echols checked for vital signs, and six minutes after the first surge of electricity began he pronounced Ledbetter dead. As Ledbetter's body was being removed prison officials returned to the death row cells and brought in Blakely. As soon as he appeared he announced, "We reap what we sow," and then he confessed the crime before saying, "I want to leave a message to the young people of Muskogee. I would ask them to be converted. I hope to meet you all in heaven. I am going home to glory." He then took his seat and the same procedures were followed as for Ledbetter, and twelve minutes after Blakely walked into the chamber Dr. Echols pronounced him dead. The bodies were removed from the death chamber and sent to a local funeral home to be prepared for burial.

Sources: *Ada Evening News* (OK): September 16, 1920. *Muskogee Times-Democrat* (OK): August 16, 1920; August 18, 1920; November 4, 1920; December 2, 1920; February 19, 1921; February 24, 1921. *Wichita Times* (KS): February 25, 1921.

Thomas, Eli
July 15, 1921

On Saturday, August 7, 1920, a group of people, all black, were having a picnic at the grounds outside Calhoun, Oklahoma, just south of Sallisaw in Leflore County. Twenty-year-old Selma Mayfield, a local farmer, was riding by on his horse when twenty-year-old Eli Thomas, one of the picnickers, stepped into the road and asked Mayfield where he was going. Mayfield replied, in a joking manner, "I'm going to Hell if I don't start praying more." Thomas replied, "I'm going to send you to Hell right now," as he pulled his .45-caliber six-shooter and fired at Mayfield. Upon seeing the pistol Mayfield started to slide off the opposite side of his horse, but the first bullet struck him in the leg. Thomas fired a second shot immediately and this bullet ricocheted off the horse's neck and struck Mayfield in the abdomen. The wounded boy managed to stumble several yards before he collapsed, and Thomas stood over him and took careful aim for the coup de grace, but several man ran forward and disarmed and captured Thomas. They sent for Sheriff Carter and he soon arrived, arrested Thomas, and took him to the Leflore County jail; Mayfield was rushed to the hospital.

Early Monday morning, after Mayfield died, the white farmers in the area began to form a large, angry mob, and they stormed the jail intent on lynching Thomas, but the sheriff heard of their plans and had taken his prisoner to the Sequoyah County jail. Thomas was returned to Leflore County for trial, and on September 4 he was found guilty of first-degree murder and sentenced to die in the electric chair. Two weeks later the transcript of the trial and all the evidence was presented to Governor Robertson for review, and he declined to interfere. Then the case was taken to the court of criminal appeals, and it took months before they affirmed the judgment and death sentence and set the date for the execution at July 15, 1921.

As the day for the execution approached Thomas was moved from his regular cell to a death row cell in the basement of the main prison building, near the electric chair. After noon on his last day his head and leg were shaved and he was offered a stimulant, but there is no record he accepted. The death warrant was read to Thomas by the warden just before midnight, and then the heavy cell door was swung open. The prisoner was escorted into the death chamber and he made a brief speech to the witnesses, who were standing behind the grating between the chamber and the witness area. Thomas took his seat in the oak chair where his chest and waist, wrists and arms, and ankles were secured with heavy leather straps, and then the copper helmet and leg band, lined with moistened sponge, were secured in place. A black leather mask was placed over his eyes and forehead and attached to the chair back. The electricity, set between 600 volts and 2,300 volts, coursed through Thomas' body for several seconds, and the body stiffened and strained against the straps. When the current was turned off the body relaxed and the attending physician checked for vital signs, and he pronounced Thomas dead a few minutes after midnight. Then another surge of 2,300 volts of electricity was applied, as required by regulation to ensure death. The body was then removed and sent to a local funeral home to be prepared for burial.

Sources: *Ada Evening News* (OK): July 15, 1921. *Muskogee Times-Democrat* (OK): August 9, 1920; September 18, 1920.

Sabo, Steve
March 17, 1922

On the morning of September 18, 1921, while eighteen-year-old Sophie Sabo was asleep in her parents' home in Coalgate, Coal County, Oklahoma, her forty-nine-year-old uncle Steve Sabo snuck into her bedroom, beat and raped her. He then stabbed her seven times and thinking she was dead he fled, but Sophie managed to walk to the home of neighbor Joe Nicholas before she collapsed. She then named her uncle as the man who had stabbed her before she lapsed into unconsciousness, and she died soon afterward without regaining consciousness.

It was during the autopsy at Coalgate that the coroner discovered Sophie had been raped, and the citizens of Coalgate were even more infuriated by this development. Immediately after the attack posses were formed and highly motivated men combed the area for several days before Sabo was found hiding at the bottom of an abandoned coal mine. He resisted arrest when discovered but he was quickly overpowered, arrested, and lodged in the jail at Atoka in the adjoining county, to prevent a lynching. When a large, angry mob followed the prisoner to Atoka he was smuggled out of the jail and taken to a railway crossing where the train was flagged down and Sabo was taken to the penitentiary at McAlester. While being taken to the prison Sabo confessed to Sheriff R. W. Freeman that he had stabbed his niece, but he said nothing of the rape. Sabo was returned to Coalgate and tried at the winter 1921 term of the Coal County district court. On December 13 he offered to plead guilty in exchange for a life term but this was rejected by the prosecution, and the case went to the jury on December 14 after the defense closed without calling a single witness. The defendant was found guilty of murder in the first degree and sentenced to die in the electric chair on March 17, 1922, but he was kept in the Coalgate jail while efforts were being made to file an appeal or a petition praying for a commutation of sentence. When all efforts failed he was delivered to the prison on February 16, 1922, and nothing would arise to delay the proceedings.

Several days before his execution Sabo was taken from his regular cell and moved to a special death row cell in the basement of the main prison building, near the death chamber. Mid-day Thursday a barber was brought to the cell and he shaved Sabo's head and left leg, and his burial clothes were delivered. During his time at the penitentiary Sabo remained sullen and silent, refusing to talk to anyone on any subject. Before midnight Thursday the witnesses were ushered into the viewing area, and they took their places behind the grating that separated them from the electric chair. Shortly after midnight Sabo appeared and when he entered the chamber he was asked if he had anything to say. He claimed he was innocent, and concluded, "Sometime you'll find out who killed Sophie."

He then took his seat in the heavy oak chair where his chest and waist, wrists and arms, and ankles were secured with two-inch-wide black leather straps. A copper helmet was placed on his head and a copper band was attached to his leg, each lined with moistened sponge. A leather mask was next tied over Sabo's eyes and forehead, and this was attached to the chair back to restrain his head. While the preparations were being made not a word was spoken, the only sound the humming of the dynamo in the next room. Wires from the helmet and leg band led to a rheostat, or "control panel," which allowed the executioner to adjust the level of current from 1,500 to 2,300 volts, and this had a switch to turn the current on and off. At 12:13 the executioner applied a jolt of 1,500 volts for several seconds, and then the attending physician checked for vital signs and at 12:14 A.M. pronounced Sabo dead. The executioner, as required by regulation, then reapplied the electric current set at 2,300 volts for several seconds more, to ensure death. As soon as the body cooled it was removed and sent to a local funeral parlor to be prepared for burial. No one from the Sabo family had claimed the remains so on Saturday Sabo's body was buried in the prison cemetery.

Sources: *Ada Evening News* (OK): March 17, 1922. *Logansport Pharos-Tribune* (IN): March 17, 1922. *Muskogee Times-Democrat* (OK): March 17, 1922. *San Antonio Evening News* (TX): March 16, 1922.

Watkins, Sam
May 5, 1922

On February 9, 1922, thirty-nine-year-old Sam Watkins, a farmer at Caney, Oklahoma, went to the nearby Jones farm to see Jones' fourteen-year-old daughter. Mr. Jones was away but Cora Jones, the girl's mother, threatened Watkins, telling him that if he did not stop having sexual relations with her young daughter she would tell her husband. Watkins, knowing that Mr. Jones might kill him, or at least he would be exposed to criminal prosecution and a long term in prison, picked up an iron pipe and beat her to death in front of her children. He dragged her body to the hog pen and threw it in, expecting them to consume the remains. The body was found and saved from the hogs on Thursday afternoon, and Watkins was immediately arrested.

As soon as the prisoner was in the county jail he confessed to the killing and his motive, and the circumstances so outraged the citizens that he was quietly removed to a jail in an adjacent county to prevent a lynching. On Friday night two hundred fifty masked, mounted, and heavily armed men surrounded the jail and angrily demanded the prisoner, so Sheriff Phillips allowed a committee to enter and search the jail, and when they found the cells empty the mob dispersed.

On February 13 Watkins appeared in Judge J. H. Linebaugh's Atoka courtroom, confessed and pled guilty to murdering Cora Jones, and then asked the judge for seventy-five days to put his affairs in order. The judge took the testimony of five witnesses, to create a record for review, before sentencing Watkins to die in the electric chair on May 5, and on February 14 the condemned man arrived at the prison to await his date with the executioner. The prisoner was lodged in the regular cells while his case was reviewed, but nothing would arise to delay the proceedings.

During his short time at the prison he was attended by Chaplain J.E. Rogers, and he found peace and resignation. Watkins was visited by his wife of fourteen years on Monday, May 1, and she convinced him that if he persisted in his request to be buried at Caney his remains would almost certainly be dug up, mutilated and burned. He told her, "They can kill my body and they may burn it, but they cannot kill my soul," but then he agreed to be buried in the prison cemetery. Immediately after the visit his wife departed for Oklahoma City to continue her campaign to obtain a commutation, or at least a reprieve.

Early on May 3, two days before his execution, the prisoner was moved to a death cell in the basement of the main prison building, near the electric chair, and that afternoon the barber was brought in to shave his head and leg. As he was being moved he bragged to his guards, "If I had a half day start, I would have gotten a gun, caught a freight train and gone to the hills of Arkansas, where they never would have caught me." During his last day, Thursday, Watkins confessed twice to the murder of Cora Jones but then contradicted himself, saying, "I am innocent and happy and ready to go. I am going to meet my mother, little brother, and baby sister in heaven tonight." He was offered a stimulant but there is no record he accepted. Before midnight prison officials appeared at his cell door and read the death warrant before the heavy cell door was swung open. The Reverend Rogers, who had been with him constantly for several days, and a guard each took an arm and escorted Watkins the short distance into the death chamber. He stood before the grating separating the witnesses from the death chamber and made one of the longest speeches ever by a condemned man, during which he thanked the prison officials for their kindness, said that he was dying without hatred in his heart, and concluded, "I wish that old judge at Atoka would get right with God."

The prisoner then took his seat in the heavy oak chair where his chest and waist, wrists and arms, and ankles were secured with heavy black leather straps. The copper helmet and leg band, lined with moistened sponge, were secured in place, and a black leather mask was placed over his eyes and forehead and attached to the chair back. At 12:14 A.M. the first jolt of electricity, set at between 600 and 2,300 volts, coursed through Watkins' body for several seconds, and his body stiffened and strained against the straps. After the current was turned off the attending physician checked for vital signs and pronounced Watkins dead at 12:17. Another surge of electricity, set at 2,300 volts, was applied for several seconds more as required by regulation to ensure death. The body was then removed and sent to a local funeral home to be prepared for burial in the prison cemetery.

Sources: *Ada Evening News* (OK): February 16, 1922; May 5, 1922. *Courier and Reporter* (Waterloo, IA): February 11, 1922. *Victoria Advocate* (TX): May 5, 1922.

Harvey, Aaron
Pope, John
January 13, 1924

In late March 1923 Lydia B. Pope left her forty-five-year-old husband John "Jack" Sr., and her nineteen-year-old son John "Jack" Jr., took along their infant son and moved in with her parents — Mr. and Mrs. Tom H. Hansell. After a month of soul-searching Lydia realized that her turbulent and abusive relationship with her husband would never improve, so on April 25 she filed for divorce and he was served. Her husband was determined to collect on her $2,000 life insurance policy before the divorce proceeded so during the early morning hours of April 26 the elder Pope had his son drive him and twenty-one-year-old Aaron "Red" Harvey to the Hansell house near Haworth in McCurtain County, Oklahoma. Harvey went to the front door, which was barred, while Pope went to a side window. They took careful aim into the house where five people were sleeping, and they shot them, killing instantly all but a four-year-old boy. However, to be certain they were all dead, they broke down the door and checked each body, and shot again each person who showed any sign of life. In all they fired eleven shots from a shotgun and automatic pistol, killing Lydia Pope, their infant son Hubert Pope, Mr. and Mrs. Hansell, and their four-year-old son Aubrey Hansell.

The men fled but within hours they were tracked down by a posse of determined men when near the Red River, in the region between Oklahoma and Texas, and they were captured without resistance. As soon as they were in custody the Popes confessed and implicated Harvey, though he denied guilt, but there was a certainty that the prisoners would be lynched if returned to Haworth so they were lodged in the jail at Paris, Texas. Several days after the killings the prisoners were returned to Haworth for their hearing, and all three defendants confessed and pled guilty to their part in the five murders. On May 10 Judge G. T. Arnutt sentenced the elder Pope and Harvey to die in the electric chair on July 13, and the younger Pope was sentenced to serve a life term in prison. The sentencing was done at a very early hour, and the prisoners were immediately taken to the state prison to prevent a lynching by the outraged Haworth citizens. Governor J. C. Walton was against the death penalty so over the next several months he granted two reprieves, the first to October 13 and the second to January 13, 1924, but when Governor Trapp took office he refused to interfere, and the date for the double execution remained January 13, 1924. Nothing would arise to further delay the proceedings.

During their months awaiting execution both men were attended by the prison chaplain, and each man resigned himself to his fate. Two weeks before their execution Pope confessed again, and on his last evening he wrote out his confession once more asserting he had promised to pay Harvey $500 from the insurance money for killing his wife. On Saturday morning, January 12, the two men were moved from regular prison cells to death cells in the basement of the main prison building, near the death chamber. During the day Harvey asked several times for drugs, but was denied, and there was some concern he might break down completely but he rallied. Pope's son was allowed a visit and the condemned man told him, "Son, forgive me for the great wrong I did you in getting you into trouble. Take an example in the remembrance of what sin has done for your father and live an upright life." After they parted Pope said he was relieved that his son had been converted.

The two condemned men posed for photos during the early afternoon hours, and then the barber was brought in to shave their heads and legs. At 9:00 the two men were permitted to shake hands and they forgave each other. As midnight approached fifty-two witnesses, including six doctors led by prison physician J. W. Echols, were ushered into the viewing area and took their places behind the grating that separated them from the electric chair. The death warrant was read to both prisoners by Warden Harry Townsend, and at the stroke of midnight the cell doors were swung open and both men were escorted into the chamber. There is no record of a statement by either man.

Pope was first to take his seat in the heavy oak chair where his chest and waist, wrists and arms, and ankles were secured with heavy black leather straps, and then the copper helmet and leg band, lined with moistened sponge, were secured in place. A black leather mask was placed over his eyes and forehead and attached to the chair back. The electricity, set between 600 and 2,300 volts, coursed through Pope's body for several seconds, and the body stiffened and strained against the straps. When the current was turned off and the body relaxed, the attending physicians checked for vital signs, and at 12:14 A.M. they pronounced him dead. A second surge of electricity was then applied, as required by regulation to ensure death, and Pope's body was removed.

The same procedures were then followed for Harvey and at 12:25 he was pronounced dead. The bodies were delivered to a local mortuary to be prepared for burial, and hundreds of people gathered around the undertaker's chapel and demanded to view the remains, but none were admitted. The following morning the bodies were returned to the prison cemetery and buried, following a simple ceremony by the prison chaplain, and no one was allowed to attend but a few prison officials and guards and a detail of prisoners, who had dug the graves and would fill them in.

Sources: *Ada Evening News* (OK): May 10, 1923; January 13–14, 1924. *Joplin Globe* (MO): January 13, 1924. *Oklahoman* (Oklahoma City): January 13, 1924.

Birkes, Richard
September 5, 1924

On August 2, 1923, twenty-three-year-old Richard Birkes was released from the Oklahoma Penitentiary at McAlester. One week later, on August 9, 1923, Birkes, with Allison Ivey and Raymond Thomas, went to Vinita and hired a car to drive them to Ketchum in Craig County, Oklahoma. When they were halfway between the two towns the men drew pistols, captured the driver, and threw him out. They continued on to Ketchum and at 11:00 A.M. parked in front of the First State Bank of Ketchum. Thomas stayed in the driver's seat with the engine running while Birkes and Ivey went into the bank, and Birkes ordered, "Raise your hands, this is a hold-up." Cashier Frank Pitts would not raise his hands, and Birkes immediately began shooting at him. Once Pitts collapsed with a fatal wound the two robbers scooped up all the money they could find and ran outside to the waiting automobile.

They fled southward and were pursued by a hastily formed posse of police officers and citizens, but they eluded capture. On the evening of the robbery Thomas tried to join a posse several miles from Ketchum, but he was recognized and arrested. He was taken to Ketchum, and when he was threatened by a large, angry lynch mob he confessed to save his life, claiming he was the driver and Birkes did the shooting, and then he was lodged in the Craig County jail. He gave a good description of Birkes and Ivey, and the following day the two fugitives were surrounded by a heavily armed posse as they hid in tall grass outside a cemetery one mile north of Vinita. They were captured without a fight and lodged in the Craig County jail, and at their hearing they were held over for trial.

The trial of Birkes and Ivey began on Monday, November 5, and at 6:30 P.M. on November 7, after five hours in deliberations, the jurors found the two defendants guilty of murdering Pitts and determined that Birkes fired the fatal shot. Ivey was sentenced to serve a life term in prison while Birkes was sentenced to die in the electric chair. On November 8 the trial of Raymond Thomas began, and he was convicted of being an accomplice to Pitts' murder and sentenced to serve a life term in the penitentiary. An appeal was filed for Birkes which stayed the execution for months, but finally the court of criminal appeals affirmed the judgment and sentence of the lower court. On September 2 Birkes' aged mother and his wife pled with Governor M. E. Trapp for Birkes' life, and he told them, "The law of an eye for a eye and a tooth for a tooth is a good law where both have an equal chance and in a case of murder with robbery as a motive it certainly can be applied." They presented the governor with a confession from Ivey and Thomas which said that Birkes did not fire the fatal shot, but on September 4 the governor said, "This confession has no bearing upon the sentence imposed upon Birkes, as each of the three men who entered the bank for the purpose of robbing it was a potential murderer equally guilty of causing the death of the cashier. I feel that the death sentence is warranted in certain instances, including the case now under consideration," and concluded, "I can find no reason why the verdict of the court should not be carried out."

Several days before his execution Birkes was moved from his regular cell to a special cell in the basement of the main prison building, near the death chamber. On Wednesday the barber was called, and he shaved Birkes' head and leg. Before midnight Thursday seventy-eight witnesses were ushered into the viewing area while Warden W. S. Keys was reading the death warrant. At the stroke of midnight the cell door was swung open and the prisoner was escorted into the death chamber where he was asked if he had any last words, and he told the witnesses, "I am not guilty of this crime but I am not afraid to die." Birkes then took his seat in the heavy oak chair where his chest and waist, wrists and arms, and ankles were secured with heavy leather straps. The copper helmet and leg band, lined with moistened sponge, were secured in place, and a black leather mask was placed over his eyes and forehead and attached to the chair back. Once Birkes was ready everyone stepped back, and he waved at the spectators as he called out, "Turn it on boys." Just at that moment the electricity, set at 2,300 volts and slowly decreased to 600 volts, was switched on. It coursed through Birkes' body for several seconds, and his body stiffened and strained against the straps. When the current was turned off the doctor in attendance checked for vital signs and at 12:05 A.M. pronounced the prisoner dead. Then another brief surge of 2,300 volts of electricity was applied for several seconds, as required by regulation to ensure death. The body was then removed and sent to a local funeral home to be prepared for burial, as arranged by his mother.

Sources: *Ada Evening News* (OK): August 9–10, 1923, September 4, 1924. *Chillicothe Constitution* (MO): September 3, 1924. *Muskogee County Democrat* (OK):.November 8, 1923. *Perry Journal* (OK): September 6, 1924.

Scott, Leroy
May 29, 1925

Frank Daniels, a former prison guard, was working as a taxi driver in McAlester in Pittsburg County, Oklahoma, on Wednesday, July 23, 1924, when, at 10:30 P.M., twenty-year-old Leroy Scott, a Creek freedman, engaged him to drive to Crowder, eleven miles north. When they reached Crowder Scott asked the driver to take him to the home of relatives living on Gaines Creek near the river crossing between Pittsburg and McIntosh Counties. When they reached the bridge crossing of Gaines Creek on the Jefferson Highway, thirty-five miles north of McAlester, Scott said the house was some distance off the road and he would walk. Scott paid his fare and dismounted, then told Daniels that he had a flat tire. When Daniels got out to check Scott struck him on the head three times with an automobile crank, crushing his skull and killing him. Scott rifled his pockets finding $20, threw the body in the creek, and then drove Daniels' automobile into Muskogee where he abandoned it.

Daniels' body was found on Sunday, July 27, and Scott was immediately arrested at Muskogee, as he was the last person seen with Daniels, and he confessed and even reenacted the crime for the officers. Scott was returned to McAlester on Monday, July 28, and immediately appeared before Justice of the Peace Thompson for his arraignment. He pled guilty and waived his preliminary hearing. He was then lodged in the prison as there was strong talk of lynching the prisoner. Scott quickly changed his plea to not guilty, and he was tried in the last week of August in Judge Enloe Vernon's courtroom. On August 30 he was found guilty of first-degree murder after only fifteen minutes of deliberations, and when the verdict was announced made a "sneering laugh." On September 6 Scott was sentenced to die in the electric chair on November 14 and returned to his prison cell.

Scott's court-appointed attorneys filed a notice of appeal which stayed the execution, but with his confession and initial plea of guilty in the record there was little they could argue in his behalf so, on March 7, 1925, the court of criminal appeals affirmed the judgment and sentence of the district court. The date for Scott's execution was then set for Friday, May 29, 1925, and nothing further would arise to delay the proceedings, as Scott refused to petition the governor for clemency.

Several days before his execution Scott was moved from his regular cell to a special cell in the basement of the main prison building, near the death chamber. On Wednesday the barber was summoned, and he shaved the prisoner's head and leg. On Thursday evening Scott was offered a stimulant, but there is no record he accepted, and as midnight approached the witnesses were ushered into the viewing area, separated from the death chamber by a metal grating. The warden read the death warrant to Scott in his cell, and at the stroke of midnight the cell door swung open and Scott was escorted into the chamber. There is no record that he was asked for a statement, or if one was made. At 12:15 A.M. the condemned man took his seat in the oak chair where his chest and waist, wrists and arms, and ankles were secured with heavy leather straps, and the copper helmet and leg band, lined with moistened sponge, were secured in place. A black leather mask was placed over his eyes and forehead and attached to the chair back. The electricity, which could be regulated between 600 and 2,300 volts, coursed through Scott's body for several seconds beginning at a low intensity but increased gradually to the maximum, and Scott's body stiffened and strained against the straps. When the current was turned off the attending physician checked for vital signs, and at 12:20 A.M. he pronounced Scott dead. Another brief jolt of electricity, set at 2,300 volts, was then applied as required by regulation to ensure death. The body was then removed and sent to a local funeral home to be prepared for burial.

Sources: *Ada Weekly News* (OK): July 31, 1924; March 8, 1925. *Independent* (Helena, MT): May 29, 1925. *Joplin Globe* (MO): September 7, 1924, May 29, 1925. *Morning Avalanche* (Lubbock, TX): August 31, 1924. *Oakland Tribune* (CA): May 29, 1925. *Sioux City Journal* (IA): May 30, 1925.

Washington, Johnnie
December 4, 1925

On November 9, 1924, El Dorado's city marshal and night watchman, Otto Holler, was on patrol when he discovered a black man in the process of breaking into a local business. When he tried to arrest twenty-seven-year-old Johnnie Washington, sometimes Johnny, the burglar fled but suddenly turned and opened fire on the officer, wounding him fatally. Washington was soon captured, and he was tried in the Jackson County district court. He was convicted of first degree murder, and Judge A. S. Wells sentenced him to die in the electric chair on June 19, 1925. June 19 was celebrated among the blacks as emancipation day, which confused the matter, and Warden W. S. Keys, thinking that an appeal was pending, failed to execute Washington; when the warden discovered his mistake in August he sought legal clarification. Washington's attorney then filed an appeal based upon the fact that his client "was officially dead," but this argument was rejected and on November 2 the date of execution was set for November 19. As Washington sat in his cell, head shaved and dressed in his burial clothes, Governor W.J. Holloway intervened and granted a two-week reprieve to December 4 while a request for a writ of habeas corpus was being considered, and he reviewed the case once more. The appeal was denied on December 2. The governor refused to interfere further, so preparations for the execution moved forward quickly.

As soon as word was received that there would be no further delays in the proceedings Washington was removed from his regular prison cell and moved to a special cell in the basement of the main prison building near the death chamber. The barber was brought in and Washington, for the second time in two weeks, had his head and leg shaved. He was asked if he had any last requests but he refused any considerations and would not make a statement. Before midnight the witnesses were ushered into the viewing area, which was separated from the death chamber by an iron grating. Warden Keys read the death warrant to the prisoner in his cell, and at the stroke of midnight the cell door was swung open and the prisoner was escorted into the death chamber.

He took his seat in the oak chair where his chest and waist, wrists and arms, and ankles were secured with heavy leather straps, and the copper helmet and leg band, lined with moistened sponge, were secured in place. A black leather mask was placed over his eyes and forehead and attached to the chair back. The electricity, which could be set between 600 and 2,300 volts, began at a low intensity and was steadily increased for several seconds, and as it coursed through the prisoner's body he stiffened and strained against the straps. The current was then shut off, and the attending physician checked for vital signs; at 12:05 A.M. Washington was pronounced dead. Another surge of 2,300 volts of electricity was then briefly applied, as required by regulations to ensure death, and one minute later the body was removed and immediately sent to a local funeral home to be prepared for burial.

Sources: *Ada Evening News* (OK): November 18, 1925; December 3–4, 1925.

Bruster, Theodore
O'Neil, Willie
Wigger, Walter
June 29, 1928

On Thursday, January 13, 1927, twenty-year-old Theodore Bruster, Leroy Baker and George

Moss, all black, tried to rob aged storekeeper William Heenan. They fired a shot at Heenan when he resisted and then fled empty-handed. The following afternoon Bruster armed himself with a rifle and returned to the Heenan store on the outskirts of Muskogee and without hesitation shot Heenan in the left eye, then when the old man lay writhing on the floor he took an axe and struck him in the back of the head. Bruster then cleaned out the cash register before he fled. When Heenan's body was discovered he was rushed to the hospital and, though he was expected to die, he was still alive on Sunday morning. The three men had been arrested on Saturday and they each confessed to their part in the Thursday attempted robbery, and Bruster confessed to the Friday affair. Baker and Moss were arraigned on Sunday morning and pled guilty, and were immediately sentenced to serve ten years in prison. No action was taken against Bruster until Heenan died, and then he was charged with murder. He was tried in the district court at Muskogee, convicted, and sentenced to die in the electric chair, but an appeal stayed the execution. The court of criminal appeals affirmed the judgment and sentence of the lower court, and Bruster was finally sentenced to die on June 22, 1928. On February 9 he was examined by the heads of three institutions and found sane, so that a late request for a sanity hearing would not delay the proceedings.

On the night of February 27, 1925, twenty-two-year-old Willie O'Neil, a black man, and another unmasked black man entered the store of Moody Jackson near the fairgrounds on the east side of Oklahoma City, Oklahoma. O'Neil was armed with a pistol and he shot Jackson before cleaning out the cash register, but the storekeeper survived to testify. The two men fled, and within minutes they entered the streetcar of motorman Mark H. Hipsher and robbed the fare box. As they fled Hipsher armed himself with a pistol and pursued the robbers, but before he was more than a few yards from his streetcar O'Neil shot him through the breast, killing him, and he collapsed with his unfired pistol in his hand. Police were tracking down leads, including a small coupe which had been seen near both robberies, and soon they had Willie O'Neil in jail. O'Neil was identified by Jackson as the robber with the gun, and he was convicted of first-degree murder in the Oklahoma County district court and sentenced to die in the electric chair. His attorney filed an appeal, and the court of criminal appeals considered the case for months, finally affirming the judgment and sentence of the lower court on December 29, 1927, and the justices set the date of execution for March 9, 1928. On February 9 O'Neil had been found sane, preventing a delay from a late request for a sanity hearing, but he was later reprieved to June 22.

Thirty-year-old Walter Wigger, an ex-convict, had been courting nineteen-year-old divorcee Ruth Harris and they had been engaged, but she broke off their relationship and turned her attention to a Galena, Kansas, miner. On the night of October 23, 1926, Wigger waited in the yard of Harris' Picher, Oklahoma, boarding house, and when she returned home he confronted her. When she insisted that their relationship was ended Wigger pulled out his pocketknife with the razor-sharp long blade extended and slashed her throat so deeply that she was nearly decapitated by the single gash. Harris was rushed to the Picher hospital where she died in thirty minutes. Wigger was quickly captured, and he still had the bloody knife in his pocket. He claimed then, and throughout his trial, that he could not remember anything that happened that night.

He was arraigned on October 25, and two days later he told Judge W. M. Thomas that he waived his preliminary examination. On November 2 Harris' body was shipped to Fayetteville, Arkansas, for burial. Wigger was tried in the Ottawa County court in Miami in late November, convicted of first-degree murder, and sentenced to die in the electric chair. His attorney filed an appeal, and the court of criminal appeals considered the case for months before affirming the judgment and sentence of the lower court. Wigger was examined by the heads of three institutions and declared sane on February 9, preventing any delay from late requests for a sanity hearing. Wigger's execution date was then set for June 22, 1928.

Five men had been scheduled to die sequentially on June 22 but Governor Henry S. Johnston granted them a seven-day reprieve to June 29, and later the sentences of two men would be commuted to life in prison, but Bruster, O'Neil and Wigger still faced the executioner. On Wednesday morning, June 27 the three condemned men were moved from their regular cells to the special cells in the basement of the main prison building, near the death chamber. The barber arrived later that day and shaved their heads and left legs. On their last night Wigger slept soundly but O'Neil and Bruster were restless. The following day all three men asked to be baptized into the Episcopal church, and then communion rites were administered. At 11:15 P.M. Warden John Q. Newell read the death warrants to the three condemned men and told them their time was near.

Wigger had been selected to go first, and he entered the death chamber at 12:06 A.M. Warden Newell asked if he had any last words. Wigger replied, referring to the newsmen among the witnesses, "I ain't got nothing to say to these people. They've done published enough about me. I asked you not to have them here." Wigger then took his seat in the oak chair where his chest and waist, wrists and arms, and ankles were secured with heavy leather straps and he complained, "You are choking me." The copper helmet and leg band, lined with moistened sponge, were secured in place, and a black leather mask was placed over his eyes and forehead and attached to the chair back. As executioner Rich Owen moved toward the switch a few feet behind the prisoner Wigger said, "I hold nothing against you, my boy." At 12:09 the electricity, set at between 600 and 2,300 volts, coursed through Wigger's body for several seconds, and his body stiffened and strained against the straps as Owens, at the "control panel," turned a small wheel to gradually increase the voltage. When the current was switched off Dr. J.A. Munn checked for vital signs and pronounced Wigger dead at 12:12 A.M. Another very brief surge of 2,300 volts was applied for several seconds, as required by regulation to ensure death, and then several black trusties removed the body and hurriedly carried it down the white-washed corridors to a storage room.

Bruster was second, and the same procedures were followed as for Wigger, and when asked if he had any last words he said, "No sir, I haven't." The electricity was applied at 12:15 A.M. but he was not dead so a second jolt of several seconds was applied at 12:18, and he was pronounced dead at 12:21 A.M. O'Neil came last and he entered the chamber at 12:25 A.M. When asked for last words he said, "I wish everybody good luck." The same procedures were followed as for Wigger and Bruster, and the electricity was first applied at 12:28. After a second jolt of several seconds, he was pronounced dead at 12:33 A.M. The three bodies were then sent to a local funeral home to be prepared for burial.

Sources: *Ada Evening News* (OK): March 1, 1925; December 30, 1927; June 29, 1928. *Joplin Globe* (MO): October 25, 1926; October 28, 1926, November 2, 1926. *Morning Herald* (Hagerstown, MD): February 10, 1928. *Oklahoman* (Oklahoma City): June 29, 1928. *Perry Journal* (OK): June 28, 1928. *Salt Lake Tribune* (UT): June 29, 1928. *San Antonio Express* (TX): January 16, 1927.

Forrest, James E.
Guest, Tom
July 17, 1930

At 10:00 A.M. on August 2, 1927, twenty-year-old James E. Forrest, a black man, raped the wife of a white farmer near Comanche in Pottawatomie County, Oklahoma, and fled south. The citizens were outraged and a huge, heavily armed posse soon formed. The men scoured the entire area until ten hours later, just after sunset, when they found the fugitive two and one-half miles south of Comanche and shot him down with several blasts from shotguns. The prisoner was taken to Duncan and lodged in the second-floor jail above the courtrooms, but a large crowd formed and rushed the jail. Sheriff E. R. Young and county attorney Jesse Long intercepted the mob on the first floor of the courthouse and pleaded with them to let the law take its course, and Long promised to bring Forrest to trial as soon as his injuries permitted; only then did the mob disperse.

Forrest recovered from his wounds and was tried in October, found guilty of rape, and on October 12 was sentenced to die in the electric chair. He was immediately taken to the prison while his court-appointed attorney filed an appeal, and the court of criminal appeals, after many months, affirmed the judgment and sentence of the lower court. Forrest's date with the executioner was finally set for Thursday, July 17, 1930, a departure from the usual practice of holding executions on Fridays.

On September 2, 1927, W. J. Whitey drove forty-two-year-old Tom Guest, Robert Marvin "Red" Foster, and Loney Morris from Earlsboro to Asher, Oklahoma. At 2:00 P.M. Guest, Foster and Morris entered the Canadian Valley Bank in that small town and, after announcing it was a hold-up, captured at gunpoint cashier Matt W. Hampton, two clerks and one customer and placed them in the vault. The robbers did not realize that there was a telephone in the vault, and while they were busy gathering up $2,000 Hampton called for help, and a large number of citizens formed a posse and rushed to the bank. One of the first to arrive was druggist Bailey Browder; as he entered Guest shot him, and later he died of his wound. The three men hurried out to the waiting car and escaped.

In the investigation that followed there were nine men thought to be somehow involved, but it was Morris, Foster, and Whitey who would be tried for the robbery, and Guest would be tried for the murder of Browder. Guest and Foster were arrested almost immediately and lodged in a cell at the prison in McAlester. Whitey and Morris were traced to Morris' home in Pecos, Texas, arrested, and extradited to Oklahoma. The four prisoners pled not guilty at their arraignments in November and were scheduled for trial in December. Guest was tried first in the Pottawatomie County court at Tecumseh, and late on the night of December 7 he was aroused from sleep and taken into court to hear the verdict and sentence. The jury, after lengthy deliberations, found him guilty of first-degree murder, and he was sentenced to die in the electric chair in February 1928. After he heard the sentence he told newsmen, "I'm rough enough to stand it. I may have something to tell you much later on, but not now."

The trial of W. J. Whitey, the driver of the getaway car, began at Tecumseh on Tuesday, December 6, immediately after Guest's trial concluded, and the case went to the jury the following afternoon at 3:40 P.M. The jurors found him guilty of robbery with a firearm on Thursday morning, and he was sentenced to serve ten years in prison. The trials of Morris and Foster followed, and they, too, were sentenced to serve terms in prison. The date for Guest's execution had been moved to June 6 when, on February 15, 1928, Guest was pronounced sane, to prevent a delay from a late request for a hearing. However, Guest's attorney filed a series of motions, petitions and appeals which stayed his execution but the court of criminal appeals affirmed the lower court, and after a campaign of more than a year to save Guest's life he was sentenced to die on Thursday, July 17, 1930. Governor W. J. Holloway, when petitioned, refused to intervene.

On Tuesday before the execution the two condemned men were moved from their regular prison cells to the special cells in the basement of the main prison building, near the death chamber. The barber was then admitted, and he shaved the prisoners' heads and left legs. After the witnesses were in the viewing room at 11:00 P.M. Wednesday night Warden J. Q. Newell went to the cells of the condemned men and read their death warrants. At exactly midnight the door to Forrest's cell was swung open and he was escorted into the chamber, where the warden asked, "Boy, have you any last words?" Forrest replied, "I'm prepared to go. It's gonna be a great day when we meet the Father over yonder and I hope to see all of you men over there. God will take care of his chillun (*sic*). I'm going home."

The prisoner took his seat in the oak chair where his chest and waist, wrists and arms, and ankles were secured with heavy leather straps and then the copper helmet and leg band, lined with moistened sponge, were secured in place. A black leather mask was placed over Forrest's eyes and forehead and attached to the chair back. It took only one minute to prepare the condemned man, and at 12:06 executioner Rich Owen flipped the switch and electricity, set between 600 and 2,300 volts, coursed through Forrest's body for several seconds. As the voltage was steadily increased his body stiffened and strained against the straps. The body relaxed when the current was switched off, and Drs. William L. Taylor and J. A. Munn checked vital signs and pronounced him dead at 12:08. Black trusties then removed the body from the chair and quickly carried it down the whitewashed corridor to a storage room while the warden returned to the cell block for Guest.

The second man appeared in two minutes and as soon as he entered he called out, "Howdy! I've been treated very nicely since brought here. The Reverend Ailstock has been very nice to me. I want to say that I'm facing some men out there and I believe that I am better and purer hearted than some of them." While Guest took his seat the Reverend Ailstock announced that Guest had repented an hour earlier. The same preparations as for Forrest were completed, and at 12:13 Rich Owen flipped the switch; two minutes later the doctors pronounced him dead. The bodies were later sent to a local funeral home to be prepared for burial.

Sources: *Ada Weekly News* (OK): November 3, 1927; December 11, 1927; December 14, 1927; August 3, 1928; August 8, 1928. *Anniston Star* (AL): July 17, 1930. *Hutchinson News* (KS): July 17, 1930. *Miami News-Record* (OK): April 27, 1930; July 17, 1930.

Hembree, E. S.
April 17, 1931

On Sunday evening, March 9, 1930, twenty-four-year-old Chad Thurman and twenty-three-year-old Leota Bosely were taking a pleasure drive near Loco, Oklahoma, when they were kidnapped at gunpoint by thirty-nine-year-old E. S. "Choc" Hembree and twenty-three-year-old A. Y. Hembree, Choctaw Indian brothers. The two kidnappers took their captives to an isolated pasture and robbed them, then they raped Bosely. After they took $14 from Thurman they beat him on the head and shoulders with the butt of their pistol, knocking him unconscious, and the elder Hembree tried to shoot Thurman as he lay helpless but missed, and the bullet struck Bosely in her breast. After the Hembrees fled in their distinctive roadster automobile Bosely and Thurman recovered sufficiently to walk out of the pasture to their automobile, and Thurman drove to a place where they could get help. They were rushed to the Duncan hospital where they described their attackers.

On March 11 the Hembree brothers were arrested at their farm fourteen miles northeast of Marlow in Grady County, and the roadster driven by the kidnappers was found there. On March 11 Bosely, escorted by Thurman, was transferred to the Gainesville, Texas, hospital by ambulance where, on the following day, the bullet was removed during a dangerous operation. Bosely had recovered by the time the Hembrees had their preliminary hearing before Judge Scott on April 29, and she positively identified them from among fifteen men. E. S. Hembree was tried during the last week of June, and on June 28 the jurors, after one hour deliberating, found him guilty of "attacking and shooting" Leota Bosely and recommended the death penalty. The trial of A. Y. Hembree followed immediately, and he was found guilty of being an accessory to kidnapping and robbery with a firearm. In July he was sentenced to serve twenty-five years in prison while his brother was sentenced to die in the electric chair. An appeal stayed the death sentence for E. S. Hembree, but the court of criminal appeals affirmed the judgment and sentence of the lower court, and the date for his execution was set for April 17, 1931. Nothing further would arise to delay the proceedings.

On Wednesday morning after breakfast the condemned man was moved from his regular cell to a special death row cell in the basement of the prison's main building, near the electric chair. The barber then arrived and shaved his head and left leg. The prison chaplain had tried to convince Hembree to repent, but he steadfastly refused to confess or discuss the Hereafter. Hembree tried to reconcile with his brother but the request was rejected, so on his last day he wrote a letter to his mother asking her to tell A. Y., "You'll see worse than I got." On Thursday after 11:00 P.M. fourteen witnesses were ushered through the prison yard to the door leading into the basement, and they gathered in the death chamber. Warden Sam Brown had read the death warrant to the prisoner earlier and at the stroke of midnight the cell door was swung open and Hembree was escorted the few steps into the chamber, where he shook hands with everyone present. Warden Brown asked the prisoner if he had any last words and he said, "I appreciate all the favors you have done for me. That is about all."

While the witnesses retired behind the grating between the viewing area and the death chamber, Hembree took his seat in the oak chair where his chest and waist, wrists and arms, and ankles were secured with heavy leather straps. The copper helmet and leg band, lined with moistened sponge, were then secured in place, and a black leather mask was placed over his eyes and forehead and attached to the chair back. At 12:07 A.M. executioner Rich Owen stepped to the control panel behind the prisoner and flipped on the electricity, set between 600 and 2,300 volts, and turned the wheel which gradually increased it to the maximum of 2,300 volts. As the current coursed through Hembree's body he stiffened and strained against the straps, and when the current was switched off his body relaxed. The doctor in attendance pronounced him dead at 12:11 A.M. The body was then removed from the chair by black trusties and carried down the whitewashed corridor to a storage room. Hembree's remains were later sent to a local funeral home to be prepared for burial.

Sources: *Big Springs Daily Herald* (TX): March 11, 1930; April 29, 1930. *Corsicana Sun* (TX): March 12, 1930. *Denton Record Chronicle* (TX): June 28, 1930. *San Antonio Express* (TX): April 17, 1921.

Cole, Paul D.
July 10, 1931

Thirty-one-year-old Paul D. Cole, Tom Woods, Wewoka druggist Ernest Irby, and Tulsa attorney Frank Hunt were involved in a "liquor conspiracy," a federal offense during the prohibition years. The conspiracy was discovered and all four men were charged; Irby agreed to plead guilty and turn state's evidence. Woods was convicted without Irby's testimony but Irby was scheduled to testify against Cole on Monday, April 7, 1930. Irby failed to appear in the Okmulgee federal court, and during the investigation that followed it was determined that Irby had not been seen after March 24. On April 11 Irby's body was discovered at the bottom of the Wewoka city lake, shot twice and weighted down with stones and iron pipes, and in his pocket was a written statement he intended deliver in court. On Saturday, April 12, Cole was arrested at Duncan in Stephens County. His coupe was impounded and searched, blood stains were found, and samples were taken, which proved to be human blood.

Cole and Hunt were charged with Irby's murder. Hunt pled guilty to being an accessory and was sentenced to serve a life term. Cole pled not guilty and was tried during the first week of July, and on July 10 the jurors found him guilty of first-degree murder and recommended the death sentence. Two days later Judge George C. Crump sentenced Cole to die in the electric chair, but his attorney filed a notice of appeal which stayed the execution. The appeal process continued for months before the court of criminal appeals affirmed the judgment and sentence of the lower court, and the date for Cole's execution was set for July 10, 1931, scheduled to die with Bennie Nichols. Petitions were sent to Governor Murray praying for a commutation of sentence or a reprieve, and he granted Nichols a forty-day reprieve but refused to interfere in Cole's case.

On Wednesday, July 8, Cole bid his final farewell to his parents and wife. Later that day the chair was tested and it worked perfectly. While Cole was visiting with his family his attorney was busy filing another appeal, based upon the premise that Frank Hunt had perjured himself and it was Hunt who shot Irby, but the appeal was denied. On Thursday after breakfast Cole was moved from his regular cell to a special death row cell in the basement of the prison's main building, close to the electric chair. Soon after he arrived the barber was brought in, and he shaved Cole's head and left leg. After 11:00 P.M. the witnesses, excluding newsmen at the governor's direction, were ushered through the prison yard to the door to the basement, and they took their places behind the iron grating separating them from the death chamber. Warden Sam Brown had read the death warrant to the prisoner earlier, and at midnight the cell door was swung open and Cole was escorted into the chamber. The warden asked him if he had any last words, and he insisted he was innocent, then took his place in the oak chair where his chest and waist, wrists and arms, and ankles were secured with heavy leather straps. The copper helmet and leg band, lined with moistened sponge, were secured in place, and a black leather mask was placed over his eyes and forehead and attached to the chair back. The electricity, set at the lower end of the range of 600 to 2,300 volts, was switched on and coursed through Cole's body and was gradually increased by the executioner who turned a wheel on the "control panel." Cole's body stiffened as the intensity increased, and he strained against the straps. Once the current was turned off the body relaxed, and then the doctor in attendance checked for vital signs and pronounced Cole dead at 12:10 A.M. The body was removed by several black trusties and carried down the whitewashed corridor to a storage room. Later it was sent to a local funeral home to be prepared for burial, as arranged by his family.

Sources: *Albuquerque Journal* (NM): July 11, 1930. *Circleville Herald* (OH): July 10, 1931. *Miami News-Record* (OK): July 8, 1931. *Morning Avalanche* (Lubbock, TX): April 12, 1930.

Nichols, Bennie
August 21, 1931

On March 27, 1930, John Horton, the night watchman at the Ada Compress, was making his rounds and had punched his time clock for his 3:00 A.M. circuit of the yard when he was confronted by a man and a woman hiding in an alley between cotton bales. The man, thirty-five-year-old Bennie Nichols, beat the old man over the head, crushing his skull, and then he and Bessie Simpson robbed him of $.30 and fled, taking the murder weapon with them. Clues soon led to the arrest of Nichols and Simpson, and the woman quickly confessed to the details of the killing. Both were charged with murder, and Nichols was taken to the prison at McAlester while Simpson was kept in the Ada jail. Nichols was brought back to Ada and tried for murder, with Simpson the primary witness against him, and he was convicted. Nichols was sentenced to die in the electric chair but his court-appointed attorney filed an appeal which stayed the execution. On April 25, 1931, the court of criminal appeals affirmed the judgment and sentence of the lower court, and Nichols' date with the executioner was set for July 10, 1931, scheduled to die with Paul Cole. However, Governor Murray did not feel he had enough time to review the record and granted a reprieve to July 24, then extended it to August 21, 1931. Once the governor reviewed the record and listened to the appeal for clemency, he declined to interfere further.

On Thursday morning after breakfast the prisoner was moved from his regular cell to the special death row cell in the basement of the prison's main building, where he would be close to the electric chair. The barber was then brought in, and he shaved Nichols' head and left leg. After 11:00 P.M. the witnesses were ushered through the prison yard to the door to the basement and they took their places in the viewing area. Warden Sam Brown had read the death warrant earlier, and at midnight the door to the cell was swung open and Nichols was taken into the chamber, where he was asked if he had any last words, but there is no record of a statement. The condemned man took his seat in the oak chair where his chest and waist, wrists and arms, and ankles were secured with heavy leather straps, and the copper helmet and leg band, lined with moistened sponge, were secured in place. A black leather mask was placed over Nichols' eyes and forehead and attached to the chair back to restrain his head. At 12:05 A.M. the electricity, set at the lower end of a range of 600 to 2,300 volts, coursed through Nichols' body and was gradually increased as the executioner turned a wheel on the "control panel." As the current increased toward 2,300 volts the body stiffened and strained against the straps. Once the current was switched off the body relaxed, and then the doctor in attendance checked for vital signs and pronounced Nichols dead at 12:09 A.M. The body was then removed by black trusties and carried down the whitewashed corridor to a storage room, and from there the remains were driven to a local funeral home to be prepared for burial.

Sources: *Miami News-Record* (OK): April 2, 1930. *Moberly Monitor-Index* (MO): March 27, 1930. *Ogden Standard-Examiner* (UT): August 21, 1931.

Lovett, Henry
September 25, 1931

On November 26, 1930, twenty-eight-year-old Dee Foliart, an assistant coach at Geary High School in El Reno, Canadian County, Oklahoma, entered the side door of the First National Bank. There was a robbery in progress, and cashier J. M. Burge had just pulled out his pistol and exchanged shots with thirty-eight-year-old robber Henry Lovett of Chickasha. One of Lovett's bullets struck Foliart in the chest, and Lovett was wounded by at least one shot from Burge's pistol before he fled out the front door of the bank. Lovett ran for a nearby alley, but across the street George Adams, the proprietor of a tire shop, realized that the bank was being robbed and got his pistol, and when Lovett appeared he shot him down with two of four bullets striking Lovett in the chest and head. Foliart and Lovett were taken to the El Reno hospital where neither man was expected to survive; Foliart died that night while Lovett recovered and was charged with his murder.

Lovett's trial began in late January, and he was convicted of first-degree murder with a recommendation for the death penalty. On February 3 Judge Lucius Babcock sentenced Lovett to die in the electric chair on April 17, 1931. The court of criminal appeals quickly affirmed the judgment and sentence of the lower court during the week of July 30, and Lovett's date with the executioner was set for September 25, 1931. A petition was submitted to Governor Murray praying for clemency but on September 24 the governor wired Acting Governor Robert Burns from St. Louis, "I have read all the records. Lovett has been examined as to sanity and found as sane as you or I. (The condemned slayer) should be executed promptly on time."

On Thursday morning after breakfast the condemned man was moved from his regular cell to the special death row cell in the basement of the prison's main building, near the electric chair. After the governor's decision was conveyed to Warden Sam Brown the barber was brought to the cell, and he shaved Lovett's head and left leg. After 11:00 P.M. the witnesses were ushered into the prison, through the yard, to the basement door and down to the viewing area. The death warrant had been read to Lovett earlier, but when it came time to swing open the cell door the guards found the prisoner in a daze. Guards had to carry the prisoner into the death chamber and place him in the oak chair, and when Warden Brown asked him if he had any last words he was not responsive.

Lovett's chest and waist, wrists and arms, and

ankles were secured with heavy leather straps, and then the copper helmet and leg band, lined with moistened sponge, were secured in place. A black leather mask was placed over his eyes and forehead and attached to the chair back to restrain his head. At 12:06 A.M. the electricity, set at the low end of a range of 600 to 2,300 volts, was switched on and coursed through Lovett's body for several seconds, and as the executioner gradually increased the intensity to the maximum, his body stiffened and strained against the straps. When the electricity was switched off the body relaxed, and the doctor in attendance checked for vital signs; he pronounced Lovett dead at 12:09 A.M. Black trusties then removed the body from the chair and carried it down the whitewashed corridor to a storage room, and from there it was delivered to a local funeral home to be prepared for burial.

Sources: *Billings Gazette* (MT): September 26, 1931. *Denton Record-Chronicle* (TX): November 27, 1930. *Moberly Weekly Monitor* (MO): November 27, 1930; September 24, 1931.

Keeney, Martin A.
March 11, 1932

In 1930 forty-five-year-old Martin A. "Badge" Keeney had managed seventy-three-year-old W. H. Folwell's farm, located ten miles north of Britton in Oklahoma County, Oklahoma, for a dozen years. In early September Keeney and Folwell had an angry falling out and Keeney quit, or was fired, from his job. On Sunday evening, September 14, just at dusk Folwell's sixty-eight-year-old wife looked out her back door and saw Keeney standing over her husband, who was on his knees with his arm thrust above his head. Keeney had a shotgun in his hands and was using it as a club to beat his former employer to death. Mrs. Folwell ran to a neighbor's house and they called the authorities.

Before midnight officers captured Keeney when he disembarked from the inter-urban car between El Reno and Oklahoma City, and he was charged with Folwell's murder. Officers then searched the Oklahoma City inter-urban station and found Folwell's spectacles discarded in a trash box. Keeney was arraigned on September 16, he pled not guilty, his preliminary hearing was set for Friday, September 19, and he was "bound-over" for trial. Sheriff Stanley Rogers then took his prisoner to the murder scene, hoping that Keeney might reenact the crime or at least confess or make some admission, but they were met by a mob of thirty angry farmers, neighbors of Folwell, and he had to take his prisoner back to the Oklahoma City jail to prevent a lynching.

Keeney was tried in January 1931, the case based entirely on circumstantial evidence, and the jury deadlocked and was dismissed. Keeney was retried in early February 1931, but this time the evidence was so carefully linked that on February 7 the jurors deliberated less than three hours before convicting Keeney of first-degree murder. On February 14 Judge Sam Hooker sentenced Keeney to die in the electric chair on May 25, 1931, but on May 1 Judge Hooker granted a ten-day reprieve to June 4 so his attorney, Clarence W. Myers, could file an appeal. It was late 1931 before the court of criminal appeals affirmed the judgment and sentence of the lower court, and the date of execution was set for March 11, 1932. On March 8 Governor Murray said he would hear the appeal for clemency from Keeney's attorney, and two days later he refused to interfere.

On Thursday morning, after breakfast, the condemned man was moved from his regular cell to the special death row cell in the basement of the prison's main building, near the electric chair. The barber was brought in, and he shaved the prisoner's head and left leg. During Keeney's last day he seemed resigned to his fate, joked with his death watch guards, ate two chicken dinners, and insisted to the end that he was innocent. After 11:00 P.M. the witnesses were ushered through the prison yard to the door to the basement, and they walked down to take their places in the viewing area. Earlier in the evening the death warrant had been read to the prisoner by Warden Sam Brown, so when midnight arrived the cell door was swung open and Keeney stepped out. He walked into the chamber unassisted and, when asked if he had any last words, told Warden Brown, "Thank you for what you have done for me."

He took his seat in the oak chair where his chest and waist, wrists and arms, and ankles were secured with heavy leather straps. The copper helmet and leg band, lined with moistened sponge, were secured in place, and a black leather mask was placed over his eyes and forehead and attached to the chair back. At 12:06 the first jolt of electricity, set at the lower end of the range of 600 to 2,300 volts, was switched on and gradually increased to the maximum, taking one minute. As the electricity increased Keeney's body stiffened and strained against the straps. When the current was switched off the body relaxed, and the attending physician checked for vital signs and found a heartbeat, so the same procedure was followed for a second one minute jolt, and at 12:13 the doctor pronounced Keeney dead. Black trusties then removed the body from the chair and carried it down the whitewashed corridor to a storage room, and soon after the witnesses departed the body was sent to a local funeral home to be prepared for burial.

Sources: *Big Springs Herald* (TX): September 18, 1930. *Galveston News* (TX): September 16, 1930. *Indian Journal* (Eufaula, OK): March 8, 1932. *Jefferson City Post-Tribune* (MO): March 11, 1932. *Joplin Globe* (MO): February 8, 1931. *Miami News-Record* (OK): March 11, 1932. *Oklahoman* (Oklahoma City): March 11, 1932.

Harris, A. M.
June 17, 1932

Forty-six-year-old A. M. Harris had been separated from his wife for two years but he would not accept the estrangement. On August 18, 1930, his wife was in Oklahoma City's University Hospital, and she had refused to allow her husband to visit. Still, Harris went to the hospital and entered the ward with gun in hand, found his wife's friend sixty-two-year-old Ed Martin sitting at her bedside, and he opened fire without hesitation. In front of thirty-three terrified patients he fired five rounds, the bullets striking Martin in the abdomen, leg and arm. Though severely wounded Martin grappled with Harris for the gun, but he soon collapsed from loss of blood and struck his head on a fan. Doctors and the authorities were summoned and Harris surrendered without resistance, and he told the officers that Martin "was instrumental in breaking up my home," and "I wanted to teach him to keep away from Mrs. Harris."

Harris was lodged in jail while the doctors attended to Martin's wounds, but they proved fatal and Harris was charged with murder. He was tried at the January 1931 term of the district court, convicted of first-degree murder, and sentenced to die in the electric chair. The case was appealed, and it took a year before the court of criminal appeals affirmed the lower court's judgment and sentence and set the date of execution for March 11, 1932. On February 29 Governor Murray granted a reprieve to April 11 and then extended it to June 17 before he refused in interfere further.

On Thursday, June 16, Harris was visited in his cell by his five sons and his mother, but his wife refused to visit him. After they said good-bye for the last time Harris was moved to the special cell in the basement of the main prison building, near the electric chair, and the barber was summoned to shave the prisoner's head and left leg. After 11:00 P.M. the witnesses were ushered through the prison yard to the basement door and down into the viewing area. The death warrant had been read earlier by Warden Sam Brown, so at the stroke of midnight the cell door was swung open and Harris was escorted into the chamber, and he walked directly to the chair and sat down. Warden Brown asked the prisoner if he had any last words and he thanked the warden for his courtesies while in prison, and then handed the warden a letter to deliver to his wife. His chest and waist, wrists and arms, and ankles were secured with heavy leather straps and the copper helmet and leg band, lined with moistened sponge, were secured in place. A black leather mask was placed over his eyes and forehead and attached to the chair back. The executioner moved to the control panel and at 12:11 A.M. switched on the current, set at the lower end of the range of 600 to 2,300 volts, and turning a small wheel gradually increased it to the maximum, taking forty-five seconds before switching it off. Harris' body then relaxed, and the attending physician checked for vital signs and pronounced him dead at 12:12 A.M. The body was removed from the chair by trusties and carried down the whitewashed corridor to a storage room, and from there the remains were sent to a local funeral home to be prepared for burial as arranged by his family.

Sources: *Miami News-Record* (OK): June 17, 1932. *Morning Avalanche* (Lubbock, TX): August 19, 1930.

Alder, Ira J.
Davis, Charles F.
August 19, 1932

On Sunday, September 28, 1930, forty-eight-year-old Ira J. Alder had been drinking during the day, and in the evening he sat down to dinner with his wife, her brother Tom McDonald and his sister-in-law Nora at the McDonald home in Geary, in southern Blaine County, Oklahoma. Pie was served for dessert and Alder felt he had not been given a large enough portion, so he got his gun and shot Tom and Nora to death, then turned the gun on his wife but it misfired. Alder was arrested at the McDonald home shortly after the killings. He confessed to Sheriff Henry J. Law, and he blamed the murders on "family trouble." Alder was lodged in jail at a secret location, as there had been strong talk of lynching, and at his arraignment he pled guilty. On October 3, 1930, he was brought into court, and Judge E. L. Atilchelm sentenced him to die in the electric chair on December 18. Alder's attorney filed an appeal, which stayed the execution, but on June 11, 1932, the court of criminal appeals affirmed the death sentence of the Blaine County district court, and the date of execution was set for August 19. When petitioned for clemency Governor Murray refused to intervene.

On Wednesday night, June 24, a black man later identified as Charles Fillmore Davis was seen siphoning gasoline from the tank of another person's automobile, and the car he was driving was traced to the Dobbin's farm. The following morning, June 25, 1931, Blaine County's thirty-eight-year-old undersheriff Guy M. Jarvis and jailer-deputy George Gender went to the Dobbin's farm northeast of Watonga to arrest forty-five-year-old Davis on a charge of stealing gasoline. They found Davis had barricaded himself in the farmhouse so Jarvis went to the east door and Gender to the west door. Jarvis saw that Davis was armed with a shotgun, and after some negotiating all agreed to lay down their weapons before Davis would surrender. Jarvis and Gender complied with the agreement but Davis, as soon as he stepped out of the house, shot Jarvis to death with a single blast from a shotgun, and he then shot Gender in the leg causing a serious but not fatal wound. Davis stole the officer's automobile and fled, then abandoned it near Cleo Springs, and soon all of Blaine County, but especially the area around Cleo Springs, was being searched by posses of armed, angry men. On June 27 Governor Murray called out troops to help in the search but it was not until July 17 that a Drumright officer arrested Davis, without incident, and lodged him in jail.

After Davis' arrest several people were arrested and charged with a plot to hide the fugitive until they could turn him in for the reward. Davis' trial began with jury selection on the morning of September 21, and by the evening of the following day he was convicted of first-degree murder after two hours of deliberations. His defense was that he had been paid $800 to kill the officer because of Jarvis' success in enforcing liquor laws, but the evidence proved otherwise. Davis was sentenced to die in the electric chair but there was a brief delay while the appeal filed by attorney West Croy was processed. Within months the court of criminal appeals affirmed the judgment and sentence, and Davis' date with the executioner was set for August 19, 1932. Governor Murray, when petitioned, refused to interfere.

Several days before the execution the two condemned men were moved from their regular cells to the special cells in the basement of the main prison building, and the barber was brought in to shave their heads and left legs. On Thursday evening, after supper, the death warrants were read to the prisoners by Warden Sam Brown, and after 11:00 P.M. the witnesses were ushered through the prison yard to the basement door and descended to take their places in the viewing area. Exactly at midnight Alder's cell door was swung open and he was escorted into the death chamber where Warden Brown asked him if he had any last words, and he complained that he had not received a "square deal." He took his seat in the oak chair where his chest and waist, wrists and arms, and ankles were secured with heavy leather straps, and then the copper helmet and leg band, lined with moistened sponge, were secured in place, and a black leather mask was placed over his eyes and forehead and attached to the chair back. At 12:10 A.M. executioner Rich Owen stepped to the control panel and flipped the switch which started the electricity flowing, set at the lower end of the range between 600 and 2,300 volts, but gradually increased the intensity to the maximum intensity before flipping the switch off after forty-five seconds. The doctor in attendance checked for vital signs and pronounced Alder dead at 12:15 A.M. The body was removed from the chair and was just being carried from the room when Warden Brown brought in Davis, who was chewing gum vigorously. The warden asked him for his last words, and the condemned man asked that everyone present forgive him. The same procedures were followed for Davis. The current was turned on at 12:20 A.M. and switched off after fifty seconds, and at 12:27 Davis was pronounced dead. His body was then removed from the chair by prison trusties, who carried the remains down the whitewashed corridor to a storage room. Soon afterward the two bodies were sent to a local funeral home to be prepared for burial.

Sources: *Indian Journal* (OK): September 22, 1931. *Jefferson City Post-Tribune* (MO): June 26, 1931. *Miami News-Record* (OK): August 19, 1932. *Denton Record-Chronicle* (TX): September 30, 1930. *San Antonio Express* (TX): June 28, 1931; July 5, 1931; July 19, 1931; June 12, 1932.

Covington, Ivory
January 27, 1933

In early 1932 twenty-three-year-old Ivory Covington, a black man, worked for Luther Williams at Gay in Choctaw County, Oklahoma, but Covington was fired and he held a grudge. On March 15 Covington found his former employer and murdered him, he was captured, and in early May he pled guilty. On May 12, 1932, Covington appeared in Judge George T. Arnett's Idabel courtroom and was sentenced to die in the electric chair on July 22. The prisoner was delivered to the prison on May 15, and the review of his case took only several months, but the execution was first stayed to October 13, then extended to November 16, and finally after the court of criminal appeals affirmed the death sentence Covington's date with the executioner was set for January 27, 1933. Covington declined to submit a petition requesting clemency so Governor Murray did not even have the opportunity to consider the matter.

On Thursday morning after breakfast Covington was moved from his regular cell and placed in one of the special cells in the basement of the main prison building, near the electric chair. The barber was summoned, and he shaved Covington's head and left leg. Warden Sam Brown read the death warrant during the evening hours, and after 11:00 P.M. the witnesses were ushered through the prison yard to the door into the basement; they descended and took their places in the viewing area. At midnight the cell door was swung open, and the prisoner was brought out and escorted into the death chamber. The warden asked if he had any last words but there is no record of a statement. Covington took his seat in the oak chair where his chest and waist, wrists and arms, and ankles were secured with heavy leather straps, and then the copper helmet and leg band, lined with moistened sponge, were secured in place. A black leather mask was placed over his eyes and forehead and attached to the chair back. At 12:09 A.M. executioner Rich Owen stepped to the control panel just as Covington shouted, "Give me the works!" Owen flipped the switch, and electricity, set at the lower end of a range from 600 to 2,300 volts, coursed through Covington's body and was gradually increased until it reached the maximum and was turned off after forty-seven seconds. When the body relaxed the attending physician checked for vital signs and pronounced the prisoner dead at 12:13:35. The body was then removed by prison trusties and carried down the whitewashed corridor to a storage room, and from there it was transferred to a local funeral home to be prepared for burial.

Sources: *Corsicana Sun* (TX): January 27, 1933. *Miami News-Record* (OK): May 12, 1932.

Rightsell, Nathan
February 24, 1933

In 1931 twenty-four-year-old Nathan Rightsell was serving a prison term in Louisiana when he escaped. He began tramping his way northwest, riding on freight trains, and he arrived in Hugo, Choctaw County, Oklahoma, on December 18. At 9:00 P.M. officers Jason Victor Buchanan and Sterling Jackson were patrolling the railroad yards when they saw three men jumping out of a boxcar, and they approached them for questioning. Without hesitation Rightsell pulled a pistol and shot Buchanan through the body, puncturing both lungs, and he collapsed. Sterling pulled his pistol and exchanged shots with Rightsell, but was wounded in the leg so he could not pursue Rightsell, and he failed to hit the fleeing target. Buchanan was rushed to the hospital in Hugo, and he died the following day. Rightsell fled to Muskogee, and there he was involved in another gunfight with a police officer who tried to arrest him. The officer was wounded but Rightsell was wounded so badly that he could not flee and he was arrested and lodged in jail. He was tried first at Muskogee in late January and convicted of wounding the Muskogee officer, and sentenced to serve a term of ten years in prison.

He was then returned to Hugo, and on February 15 he was lodged in the local jail to await his trial in May, but on April 26 he pled guilty and on May 12 he was sentenced by Judge George T. Arnett to die in the electric chair on July 8. Judge Arnett took enough evidence to provide a record for review, and it included the testimony of a ballistics expert who matched the bullet from Sterling's leg with the gun in Rightsell's possession when arrested. The court of criminal appeals considered the case for several months before affirming the death sentence on November 18, 1932, and Rightsell's date with the executioner was set for January 27, 1933, but he was reprieved to February 24, 1933. Rightsell did not petition Governor Murray for clemency, so nothing delayed the proceedings.

On the Wednesday before his execution Rightsell had several visitors, and he told them, "We all make mistakes. I made mine. I am ready to go and I will go like a man." On Thursday morning, after breakfast, he was moved from his regular cell to a special cell in the basement of the main prison building, near the electric chair. The barber was then brought in, and he shaved the prisoner's head and left leg. The death warrant was read to him by Warden Sam Brown during the afternoon, and after 11:00 P.M. the witnesses were ushered through the prison yard to the door into the basement; they descended and walked to the viewing area. At midnight the cell door was swung open and Rightsell was escorted into the death chamber where the warden asked if he had any last words, and he replied, "All I have to say is, God bless my mother."

He took his seat in the oak chair where his chest and waist, wrists and arms and ankles were secured with heavy leather straps, and then the copper helmet and leg band, lined with moistened sponge, were secured in place. A black leather mask was placed over his eyes and forehead and attached to the chair back. At 12:06 A.M. executioner Rich Owen stepped to the control panel and flipped the switch, and the first jolt of electricity, set at the lower end of the range of 600 to 2,300 volts, coursed through Rightsell's body. Owen turned a wheel which gradually increased the voltage to the maximum, and after forty seconds he flipped the switch to the "off" position. The doctor in attendance then checked for vital signs and at 12:10:50 pronounced the prisoner dead. The body was removed from the chair by trusties, who carried the remains down the whitewashed corridor to a storage room, and later it was delivered to a local funeral home to be prepared for burial.

Sources: *Hutchinson News* (KS): February 24, 1933. *Indian Journal* (OK): February 15, 1932; April 26, 1932; October 13, 1932. *San Antonio Light* (TX): November 18, 1932.

Latimer, Charles
March 24, 1933

On the morning of December 15, 1931, twenty-eight-year-old Charles Latimer, an ex-convict, and his wife were living at Lawton, Oklahoma, when they began arguing, and as was his custom when angry Latimer brutally beat his wife. She fled and while Latimer's father-in-law was summoning officers to arrest Latimer for beating his daughter Latimer got his pistol, accosted his wife on a residential street, and shot his wife to death. He was immediately arrested, lodged in jail, and charged with her murder. He told the officers that the shooting was accidental because the gun went off as his wife tried to wrest the pistol from his grip, but the evidence showed otherwise. Latimer used the same defense when he was tried several months later, but the jurors rejected his version of events and found him guilty of first-degree murder, and he was sentenced to die in the electric chair. His attorney filed an appeal which stayed the execution but the court of criminal appeals, after many months of review, affirmed the judgment and sentence of the district court and set the date of execution at March 24, 1933. The petition sent to Governor William H. Murray, requesting clemency, was denied.

Several days before his execution date, Latimer was moved from his cell in the regular cell block to one of several death row cells in the basement of the main prison building, near the electric chair. The barber was then summoned, and he shaved the prisoner's head and left leg. After 11:00 P.M. on the night before the execution the witnesses were ushered through the prison yard to the door into the basement, and they descended and took their places in the viewing area, except for the prison officials, who gathered in the death chamber. Warden Sam Brown had read the death warrant to Latimer earlier so at midnight the cell door was swung open and the condemned man, unassisted, walked the few steps into the chamber. As he entered he shook hands with Warden Brown and executioner Rich Owen and then with the other officials in the chamber before they retired to the viewing area.

When asked if he had any last words he thanked the prison officials for his kind treatment while in prison, and then he called out, "Good-bye folks," to the witnesses as he took his seat in the oak chair. His chest and waist, wrists and arms, and ankles were bound with leather straps, and then the copper helmet and leg band, lined with moistened sponge, were secured in place. A black leather mask was tied over his eyes and forehead and attached to the chair back. At 12:05 A.M. Owen stepped to the control panel and flipped the switch which applied the electricity, set at the lower range of 600 to 2,300 volts, and then he turned a wheel until the intensity reached the maximum. The electricity was turned off after forty-four seconds, the doctor in attendance checked for vital signs, and he pronounced Latimer dead at 12:09 A.M. Prison trusties removed the body from the chair and carried it down the whitewashed corridor to a storage room, and shortly afterward the remains were delivered to a local funeral parlor to be prepared for burial.

Sources: *Ada Evening News* (OK): March 24, 1933. *Joplin News Herald* (MO): March 24, 1933. *San Antonio Express* (TX): December 17, 1931; March 24, 1933.

Ellis, Albert
Martin, Joe L.
McDonald, Proctor
May 5, 1933

On the evening of August 28, 1932, the Weber family of Fort Worth, Texas—John T., his wife, and three daughters—were forced from their automobile at gunpoint on the old Sulphur Road eighteen miles northeast of Ardmore in Carter County, Oklahoma. They were robbed of money and jewelry, and then the two robbers stole the Weber's automobile and abducted their eighteen-year-old daughter Joanna. The Webers notified authorities, and several hours later a posse found Joanna bound and gagged in the Lone Cedar cemetery, nine miles from the scene of the robbery. She had been raped by one of the men. The automobile was abandoned eight miles south of the cemetery where jewelry and personal items were strewn about the car as the men sorted their loot for valuables. Two men had recently escaped from the state reformatory, and Sheriff Elmer Byrd believed the two robbers were the same men, but soon the police arrested Bud Rowan, a white man living in the black district, and they also arrested a suspected horse thief. None of these suspects proved correct, and officers turned their attention to tenant farmers Albert Ellis and Oscar Brandon. They were quickly arrested and lodged in jail, charged with "robbery with a firearm," and twenty-four-year-old Ellis was also charged with rape. The two men were tried at the fall session of the district court and found guilty on all charges, and Brandon was sentenced to serve a term of ninety years in prison while Ellis was sentenced to die in the electric chair. An appeal stayed the execution, but only briefly, and Ellis was sentenced to die on May 5, 1933. His petition to Governor William H. Murray, pleading for clemency, was denied.

On July 28, 1932, fifty-two-year-old blacksmith Joe L. Martin was traveling through Noble County, Oklahoma, with Dutchman Peter von Nearop when he suddenly pulled out a heavy bolt and crushed his traveling companion's skull. He was arrested and charged with murder, but he claimed that he killed Nearop when the Dutchman "cussed the United States and the American flag." This defense did not work at his trial, and he was convicted of first-degree murder and sentenced to die in the electric chair. The court of criminal appeals disposed of his case expeditiously, and he was sentenced to die on May 5, 1933, with Ellis. His petition for clemency sent to Governor Murray was denied.

On Sunday, October 4, 1931, twenty-one-year-old Proctor McDonald and Carl Higgins tried to hold up druggist M. D. Butler in Oilton near Tulsa in Creek County, Oklahoma, while the Butler family, including Mrs. Butler and their eight-year-old son Raymond, were walking on a residential street. Mrs. Butler carried $3,000 in jewelry in her purse and M. D. had $1,000 in drugstore receipts in his pocket. Butler pulled out a pistol and engaged the robbers in a gun battle and managed to kill Higgins and wound McDonald, but Butler's wife was wounded in her back and Raymond received a fatal wound from stray bullets. Later that day McDonald was arrested in Tulsa and lodged in jail, and he was charged with Raymond's murder. McDonald's trial began on March 21, 1932. He was convicted of first-degree murder after thirty-six hours of deliberations, and he was sentenced to die in the electric chair but his attorney filed an appeal which stayed the execution. The court of criminal appeals had the case under review for a year before the justices finally affirmed the judgment and sentence of the district court, and McDonald's date with the executioner was set for May 5, 1933, to die with Ellis and Martin. McDonald's petition for clemency, sent to Governor Murray, was denied.

On Wednesday Ellis, at his request, was taken into the prison laundry and baptized, and afterward the three condemned men were moved from their cells in the regular cell block to the death row cells in the basement of the main prison building, near the electric chair. The barber was then summoned, and he shaved the prisoners' heads and left legs. On Thursday Ellis spent his time reading his Bible, but Martin and McDonald spent their last hours playing cards, and the only interruption was for supper and the reading of the death warrants by Warden Sam Brown. After 11:00 P.M. on the night before the execution the witnesses were ushered through the prison yard to the door into the basement, and they descended and took their places behind the metal grating in the viewing area.

Martin had been selected to go first so at midnight his cell door was swung open and he was escorted into the chamber. As he entered he broke down but quickly regained his composure, though he talked excitedly and constantly until the electricity was turned on. He was asked if he had any last words, but there is no record that any of his excited utterances were recorded. Martin was seated in the oak chair where his chest and waist, wrists and arms, and ankles were bound with leather straps, and then the copper helmet and leg band, lined with moistened sponge, were secured in place. A black leather mask was tied over his eyes and forehead and attached to the chair back. At 12:05 A.M. the executioner stepped to the control panel and flipped the switch which applied the electricity, set at the lower range of 600 to 2,300 volts, and then he turned a small wheel until the intensity reached the maximum. The electricity was turned off after forty seconds; the doctor in attendance checked for vital signs, and he pronounced Martin dead at 12:09 A.M.

While prison trusties removed the body from the chair and carried it down the whitewashed corridor to storage room, Warden Brown returned to the cells and in a few moments appeared with McDonald. There is no record of a statement and the same procedures were followed as for Martin. The current was switched on at 12:12 A.M., but he required a second shock when it was found his heart was still beating after the first jolt, and he was pronounced dead at 12:18 A.M. Ellis entered the chamber at 12:20, and though there is no record of a statement, he handed the warden a note in which he took full blame for the robbery and rape in an attempt to exonerate Brandon. He took his seat and the current was switched on at 12:21, and he was pronounced dead at 12:25. Soon after his body was removed to the storage room. All three remains were delivered to a local funeral parlor to be prepared for burial.

Sources: *Brownsville Herald* (TX): May 4, 1933. Haddock, Hugh V. *Daring Detective Magazine*, November, 1942, 40–45. *Hutchinson News* (KS): May 5, 1933. *Montana Standard* (Butte): October 5, 1931. *Oakland Tribune* (CA): August 29, 1932. *Port Arthur News* (TX): May 5, 1933. *San Antonio Express* (TX): May 5, 1933. *San Antonio Light* (TX): August 29, 1932.

Nichols, Luke
May 19, 1933

In about 1922 thirty-two-year-old Luke Nichols was involved in a shooting affray at Cushing, Oklahoma, and had part of his chin shot away, and he claimed it happened during a hijacking. Ten years later Nichols, a divorcee for three years with an ex-wife and three children living at Alva, had been dating twenty-six-year-old waitress Harriet Crawford, a widow, since the holiday season of 1930. In April 1932 Crawford refused to see Nichols again, and he was unable to persuade her to reconsider. On April 29 Nichols filled the gas tank of his automobile and parked at the edge of the business district along the route he knew Crawford would take to her home after her shift at a downtown Cherokee restaurant. When she approached his car Nichols jumped out with pistol in hand and spoke a few words before he shot her once, the bullet causing a terrible wound, and she collapsed to the ground helpless. Nichols then stood over her prostrate body and shot her four more times, killing her. He jumped into his car and drove away at a high rate of speed but Cherokee Police Chief Dare Goss, who was a half block away, shot out his tire, and he was captured. He confessed to the shooting and explained as his motive, "She rejected my advances."

He was taken to the Cherokee jail but quickly transferred to the Canadian County jail in El Reno. He was charged with murder on April 30, and when it was determined he was safe from a lynching he was returned to Alfalfa County. When arraigned he pled guilty, but then withdrew the plea and asked for a trial. As his August trial date neared he appeared in Judge J. W. Bird's courtroom in Enid on August 1 and again pled guilty. Judge Bird had the prosecution present evidence to establish a record for review and to assist him in determining the proper sentence. After the prosecution closed the defense declined to make a presentation, and on August 4 Judge Bird sentenced Nichols to die in the electric chair on October 28. The case was appealed, which stayed the execution; the court of criminal appeals had the matter under review for months before affirming the sentence of the district court, and the date of execution was set for May 19, 1933. Governor William H. Murray declined to interfere.

Several days before his execution date Nichols was moved from his cell in the regular cell block to one of several death row cells in the basement of the main prison building, near the electric chair. The barber was then summoned, and he shaved the prisoner's head and left leg. After 11:00 P.M. on the night before the execution forty-four witnesses were ushered through the prison yard to the door into the basement, and they descended and took their places in the viewing area, except for the prison officials, who gathered in the death chamber. Warden Sam Brown had read the death warrant to Nichols earlier so at midnight the cell door was swung open and the condemned man walked calmly the few steps into the chamber. Before being asked for last words Nichols put his arm around Warden Brown and whispered, "I appreciate all you've done for me. I love you dearly and am sorry for myself— sorry that I put the state to all this trouble. I am ready to go."

He then shook hands with the warden and prison officials and waved to the witnesses as he took his seat in the oak chair. His chest and waist, wrists and arms, and ankles were bound with leather straps, and then the copper helmet and leg band, lined with moistened sponge, were secured in place. A black leather mask was tied over his eyes and forehead and attached to the chair back. The executioner stepped to the control panel and flipped the switch, which applied the electricity, set at the lower range of 600 to 2,300 volts, and then he turned a wheel until the intensity reached the maximum. The electricity was turned off after forty-five seconds, and the doctor in attendance checked for vital signs and pronounced Nichols dead several minutes later. Prison trusties removed the body from the chair and carried it down the whitewashed corridor to a storage room, and shortly afterward the remains were delivered to a local funeral parlor to be prepared for burial.

Sources: *Ada Evening News* (OK): May 1, 1932. *El Paso Herald-Post* (TX): May 19, 1933. *Emporia Gazette* (KS): August 1, 1932; May 19, 1933.

Oliver, Claude
Oliver, George
August 25, 1933

Twenty-seven-year-old Claude Oliver, Garvin County farmer, and his seventeen-year-old nephew George conspired to have Claude marry, insure his wife, and then murder her for the insurance money. On August 25, 1932, Claude Oliver married fifteen-year-old Della Ring in Wynnewood, Oklahoma. Immediately after the marriage Claude took out a $5,000 life insurance policy on his bride, and then on September 12 he took out another policy for $393 with a double indemnity clause in case of accidental death. On November 3 Claude and his bride were driving near Davis with George Oliver in the back seat. George took out a heavy file and beat Della into unconsciousness, and then Claude held his bride while George struck the fatal blows with a tire iron. The two men then staged an automobile accident by driving the automobile off a bridge near Davis with Della's body inside, and then they carefully arranged the scene to make it look as if she died in the crash.

During the investigation, and at the autopsy, it was clear that her injuries were not from the crash, and the two men were arrested and charged with her murder. Blair Atkins, a black man, came forward and said the Olivers paid him $25 to claim he was a witness to the crash, but he said he had not been present when the car was driven off the bridge. When the evidence mounted they both confessed, and when they were brought into court at Sulphur in December they changed their plea to guilty. Both men were sentenced to die in the electric chair in early 1933 but they appealed to Governor Murray, who twice granted them reprieves to file appeals with the court of criminal appeals. The governor also reviewed the record to determine if the Olivers should have their sentences commuted, and on August 23 he said, "I'm going to let them go," and he refused to interfere further.

After the two men received word that their last hope was gone they resigned themselves to their fates and slept soundly Wednesday night. The Rev. A. L. James, the prison chaplain, arrived at dawn Thursday, and they spent the morning with the prison chaplain; the six other death row inmates began singing hymns as soon as they finished breakfast and intended to keep singing until midnight. The two condemned men said they hoped relatives would visit them, but none came to the prison. They were moved to the death row cells in the basement of the main prison building, near the electric chair, and the barber was summoned to shave their heads and left legs. After 11:00 P.M. Thursday night two hundred twenty-seven witnesses were ushered through the prison yard to the door into the basement, and they descended and took their places in the viewing area.

Warden Sam Brown had read the death warrants to the Olivers earlier so at midnight the cell door was swung open and George Oliver walked the few steps into the chamber. When asked if he had any last words he said, "I did the crime and I must die for it. I feel like I am going to heaven. Young men — crime does not pay." He then took his seat in the oak chair where his chest and waist, wrists and arms, and ankles were bound with leather straps, and he said, "This is bad." The copper helmet and leg band, lined with moistened sponge, were secured in place, and the black leather mask was tied over his eyes and forehead and attached to the chair back. At 12:08 A.M. the executioner stepped to the control panel and flipped the switch which applied the electricity, set at the lower range of 600 to 2,300 volts, and then he turned a wheel until the intensity reached the maximum. The electricity was turned off after less than a minute. The doctor in attendance checked for vital signs, and he pronounced George dead at 12:12 A.M.

While prison trusties removed the body from the chair George's uncle was brought from his cell, and he declined to speak to the witnesses. The same procedures were followed as for George, and as Claude sat mumbling to himself the switch was thrown at 12:15; he was pronounced dead at 12:19:40 A.M. Prison trusties then removed his body from the chair, carried it down the whitewashed corridor to the storage room where his nephew's remains lay, and shortly afterward the remains were delivered to a local funeral parlor to be prepared for burial.

In September 1934 Della's parents, Mr. and Mrs. T. L. Ring, filed to receive her insurance; by September 24 they had already been paid a $5,000 award, and on that day the Garvin County court awarded them $786.

Sources: *Ada Evening News* (OK): August 24–25, 1933. *Emporia Gazette* (KS): August 24, 1933. *Joplin Globe* (MO): August 24–25, 1933. *Oklahoman* (Oklahoma City): August 25, 1933. *San Antonio Express* (TX): September 25, 1934.

Dumas, Charles
Patton, Ted
October 20, 1933

Charles, or Charley, Dumas was a trusty at the Oklahoma state prison road camp near Coalgate. As a trusty the black man had limited freedom, and on September 10, 1932, he made his way to Atoka where he attacked and raped a fifteen-year-old white girl. He fled back to camp, certain that his imprisonment would direct the investigation away from him. However, his boots were of a peculiar design made and worn only by state prison convicts so the tracks identified him as a current convict, and the direction of the tracks pointed directly to the road camp. He was quickly arrested, confessed, and at his arraignment, pled guilty. On September 14 Judge P. L. Gassoway sentenced Dumas to die in the electric chair on November 18, but the sentence was appealed and set aside, and Dumas' trial began in early March 1933. He was convicted of the rape and on March 15 he was again sentenced to die in the electric chair. His court-appointed attorney filed another appeal, but the court of criminal appeals affirmed the judgment and sentence, and Dumas' date with the executioner was set for October 20, 1933. There would be no further delays from appeals nor from requests to Governor William H. Murray for clemency.

In April 1932 twenty-four-year-old Ted Patton and nineteen-year-old Robert H. Wall, childhood friends, were parked in Wall's automobile in Sequoyah County, Oklahoma, when Patton suddenly pulled out a pistol and shot Wall to death. Patton went through Wall's pockets and took all his valuables, then stole his car and fled into Texas. He was tracked down, and when arrested he was driving Wall's automobile and still had Wall's possessions, and he was extradited to Sequoyah County to be tried for murder. Patton pled not guilty and claimed that he shot Wall in self-defense when he tried to stop Wall from raping his female companion, Vera Frazier. His defense failed when the prosecution proved he had killed Wall to steal his car and rob him. He was convicted of first-degree murder and sentenced to die in the electric chair, but his attorney filed an appeal which stayed the execution. The court of criminal appeals considered the case for many months before the justices affirmed the judgment and sentence, and his date with the executioner was set for October 20, 1933, to die with Dumas. His appeal to Governor Murray, praying for clemency, was denied even though the governor had received petitions with over two thousand signatures asking for a commutation of sentence.

On the morning before the execution, after breakfast, the two condemned men were moved from their death row cells in the cell block to the special cells in the basement of the main prison building, near the electric chair. As they were being taken out Patton called back to the other condemned men, "Keep your heads up — that's what we are going to do." After they were situated the barber was summoned, and he shaved their heads and left legs. After 11:00 P.M. one hundred witnesses, including many police officers, were ushered through the prison yard to the door leading into the basement, and they descended and took their places in the viewing area.

Warden Sam Brown had read the death warrants to the prisoners earlier so at midnight Dumas' cell door was swung open, and he was escorted the few steps into the death chamber and asked if he had any last words. Dumas, in his nervousness, shouted, "I feel fine. I'm ready to go. I got nothing against nobody. Where I'm a-goin' there's no white side and no black side." He shook hands with those in the chamber and took his seat in the oak chair where his chest and waist, wrists and arms, and ankles were secured with heavy leather straps. The copper helmet and leg band, lined with moistened sponge, were secured in place, and a black leather mask was placed over his eyes and forehead and attached to the chair back. The electricity, set at the low end of the range of 600 to 2,300 volts, was switched on a few minutes after midnight, and as the executioner turned the wheel, which increased the intensity, Dumas' body stiffened and strained against the straps. In less than a minute the electricity was switched off, and the attending physician checked for vital signs and pronounced the prisoner dead.

While the prison trusties were still removing Dumas' body from the chair Patton, who persisted in his claim of self-defense, was brought in and he said, "There's the chair," and then to Warden Brown, "If the same thing was to do over again, I'd have to do just what I did." Patton took his seat in the chair, was prepared in the same manner as Dumas, the electricity was switched on, and five minutes after pronouncing Dumas dead the doctor pronounced Patton dead. Patton's body was then removed from the chair by trusties, who carried the remains down the whitewashed corridor to a storage room, and from there the bodies were sent to a local funeral home to be prepared for burial.

Sources: *Ada Evening News* (OK): October 20, 1933. *Denton Record-Chronicle* (TX): October 20, 1933. *Joplin Globe* (MO): October 20, 1933.

Johnson, William
November 10, 1933

On the evening of December 27, 1932, Mary Wolfenberger of Muskogee, Oklahoma, telephoned her eighty-year-old mother and told her she was going to spend the night with a friend. Meanwhile Mrs. C. E. Reams was walking near West High School in Muskogee when a black man suddenly appeared and snatched her purse from her hands and fled, but she had a good look at the purse snatcher. Several minutes later, as Wolfenberger was walking past the high school, the same man tried to snatch her purse but she resisted. The robber pulled out a hammer and crushed her skull, killing the middle-aged seamstress, and then he fled with her purse.

Wolfenberger's body was discovered the following morning, and by the afternoon of December 29 four men had been arrested. Mrs. Reams was able to identify William Johnson as the purse snatcher. Johnson was tried at the spring 1933 term of the district court in Muskogee, convicted of murder in the first degree, and sentenced to die in the electric chair. His court-appointed attorney filed an appeal which stayed the execution, but the court of criminal appeals affirmed the judgment and sentence on September 8, 1933, and his date with the executioner was set for November 10. His petition praying for clemency, sent to Governor William H. Murray, was denied.

On the morning before his execution Johnson was moved from his death row cell to a special cell in the basement of the main prison building, near the electric chair. The barber was summoned, and he shaved the prisoner's head and left leg. After

11:00 P.M. one hundred witnesses were ushered through the prison yard to the door leading into the basement, and they descended and took their places in the viewing area. The warden had read the death warrant to the prisoner earlier so at midnight the cell door was swung open and Johnson walked the few steps into the death chamber. When asked if he had any last words, he insisted he was innocent and declared, "I'm dying for something I never done." He shook hands with the warden and thirteen officials in the chamber and then took his seat in the oak chair, where his chest and waist, wrists and arms, and ankles were secured with heavy leather straps. The copper helmet and leg band, lined with moistened sponge, were secured in place, and a black leather mask was placed over his eyes and forehead and attached to the chair back. The electricity, set at the low end of the range of 600 to 2,300 volts, was switched on at 12:05 A.M. and coursed through Johnson's body for less than a minute, and as the intensity was increased his body stiffened and strained against the straps. When the current was switched off the doctor in attendance checked for vital signs and pronounced Johnson dead at 12:10 A.M. One minute later the body was removed by prison trusties and later sent to a local funeral home to be prepared for burial.

Sources: *Ada Evening News* (OK): November 10, 1933. *Emporia Gazette* (KS): December 29, 1932. *Lethbridge Herald* (Alberta, Canada): December 29, 1932.

Morris, Tom
Quinn, Earl
November 24, 1933

On the morning of November 28, 1932, John Meyers, the McAlester, Oklahoma, sanitation officer, went to the store of seventy-three-year-old Joe House and his sixty-seven-year-old wife Dora but found it closed. Concerned, he went to the House home where he found their milk still on the porch, and when they did not answer his knock he walked to the back of the house and found a window broken out and a blood-stained double-edged ax lying beneath the window. Meyers entered through the broken window and discovered the body of ex–police chief Joe House lying on the bed with a pillow over his head with his skull split open and his wife was seated in a corner with her skull split open as well. He called the authorities, and during the investigation they noted that the shoe prints around the house were of a peculiar design from shoes manufactured at the prison and given to prisoners upon their release; and the shoe prints were clearly visible for two hundred yards in the direction of the prison.

The prison informed the authorities of recent releases with prison shoes, and one of these was thirty-eight-year-old Tom Morris, who had been released on November 23 after serving his sixth term in prison. Morris was arrested on November 30 as he and Blanche Littlejohn, a black woman, were about to board a train, and he had $450 in his pockets. On December 1, when he learned Tom House was already in jail under suspicion, he confessed twice, first claiming he had only waited outside while Tom House murdered his parents, but in his second confession he exonerated Tom House and admitted he alone had killed the couple for their money. Morris was tried at the spring term of the district court in McAlester and convicted of first-degree murder, and Judge Harve L. Melton sentenced him to die in the electric chair. His court-appointed attorney filed an appeal, but the court of criminal appeals quickly disposed of the matter, and Morris' date with the executioner was set for November 24, 1933, less than a year after he "hacked to death" two elderly people.

On the evening of Saturday, December 27, 1930, Jean Quinn, alias Howard, at the insistence of her twenty-six-year-old husband Earl, bought a .32-caliber pistol and ammunition for him at Tonkawa in Kay County, Oklahoma. Earl Quinn then started drinking, and after midnight, as he became increasing drunk, he began brandishing his new pistol and a "gas gun" and threatened to go out on the highway and highjack a bootlegger. He bragged he was going to gas the bootlegger first, then shoot him to death and commandeer his load. Quinn, an ex-convict and "despicable Kansas City rum-runner," then drove up and down the highway south of town terrorizing citizens and motorists for over an hour and a half, but by Sunday afternoon he had disappeared from Tonkawa leaving his wife behind.

At 5:00 Sunday morning twenty-four-year-old Jessie and thirty-four-year-old Zexia Griffith, sisters and school teachers, had left Blackwell, Oklahoma, in their Chevrolet coupe bound for home after a visit with their parents. At 9:00 A.M. C. C. Woods and his sons were hunting when they found the dead bodies of the two girls along the highway, fifteen miles from Blackwell and southwest of the river bridge. The girls had both been shot in the head, and Zexia had also been shot through the body, and their bodies were lying one hundred feet apart. They were taken to Tonkawa for an inquest, and Dr. J. A. Jones determined that Jessie had been raped before being murdered. Their purses, empty of valuables, were found where they had been thrown in the brush, and later Sunday morning the Griffith automobile was found abandoned near the town of Sears, several miles from the murder scene. At noon Virgil Davis contacted the police and told of an encounter with a suspicious man on the highway near the scene of the murders and of seeing the man's black Buick sedan being towed from a ditch at 3:00 A.M. This led the officers to W. S. Winchell, tow truck driver, and he identified the car as belonging to Earl Howard. On Monday afternoon Police Chief Wagner contacted Howard's wife and for the first time learned that Howard's real name was Quinn. Quinn was thought to have escaped in his Buick sedan, and all the evidence, including fingerprints and a vest button found in the Griffiths' automobile, pointed to Quinn as the murderer and rapist.

An intensive manhunt began to find the fugitive. As soon as the double murder was reported in the newspapers a Muskogee woman came forward and told how she had been abducted and raped at gunpoint several weeks earlier and, with a pistol to her head, she submitted to the sexual attack to avoid being killed, but she had been too embarrassed to report the crime. She identified Quinn from a photograph as her attacker. Several months after the murders Quinn's wife contacted the authorities and directed them to a small mound of sand near the murder scene, and they dug up a rusted pistol which ballistics testing proved to be the murder weapon, and the condition suggested it had been buried there about the time of the murders. Mrs. Quinn, who had at first been arrested but then released, was under surveillance when she moved to Kansas City. On Wednesday, May 13, Kansas City detectives George Rayen and William Robeen learned that Mrs. Quinn had bought a train ticket to Omaha, Nebraska, and they drove there overnight on May 14, arriving in time to see her step off the train at 7:00 A.M. They followed Mrs. Quinn to a hotel, and the following afternoon they followed her back to the train station, where she met her husband. As soon as Earl Quinn appeared the detectives captured him without incident, and he said, "I'm glad the chase is over."

The prisoner was taken directly to Kansas City and lodged in jail where he waived extradition on May 19, 1931, and the following day he was returned to Ponca City. Meanwhile, Omaha's chief of police was contemplating filing kidnapping charges against the two Kansas City detectives. Quinn was taken to Newkirk in Kay County. His trial began on September 22 for the murder of Jessie Griffith, and on October 3 he was convicted of first-degree murder, and Judge John S. Burger sentenced him to die in the electric chair. His attorney filed an appeal which stayed the execution, and the conviction was overturned by the court of criminal appeals in November 1932. Quinn's second trial on a change of venue began in late February at Enid in Garfield County, and on March 7, 1933, the jurors convicted him of first-degree murder; he was again sentenced to die in the electric chair. A second appeal failed, and the date for his execution was set for November 24, 1933. On November 23 Governor William H. Murray declined to intervene.

As the hour of execution neared Quinn again claimed he had been convicted in a "frame-up." He argued, "Where is the proof? There ain't none. They've got my wife scared and she don't dare come in and tell the truth." Ignoring all the other incriminating evidence he relied solely on the fact that the murder weapon had never been proven to be the gun his wife had bought for him the night before the murders. The prison chaplain tried numerous times to attend to Morris' spiritual needs, but the hardened ex-convict refused to listen, but Quinn was attended by the Rev. Father John Higgins. On November 23 the two condemned men were moved from their death row cells in the regular cell block to the special cells in the basement of the main prison building, near the electric chair. The barber was then summoned, and he shaved their heads and left legs, and their prison uniforms were exchanged for new clothes. After 11:00 P.M. one hundred witnesses were ushered through the prison yard to the door into the basement, and they descended and took their places in the viewing area.

The death warrants had been read to the prisoners earlier so at midnight Quinn's cell door was swung open and he was escorted into the death chamber. When Warden Sam Brown asked if he had any last words he replied, "If Christ on the cross looked down and said 'Forgive them, for they know not what they do' why should I be better. I don't hold it against all of you folks because you condemned me without a fair trial. You loved them girls. You let your love for revenge overshadow justice." He then took his seat in the oak chair where his chest and waist, wrists and arms, and ankles were secured with heavy leather straps, and the copper helmet and leg band, lined with moistened sponge, were secured in place. A black leather mask was placed over his eyes and forehead and attached to the chair back. The electricity, set at the lower end of a range of 600 to 2,300 volts, was switched on by executioner Rich Owen at 12:07 A.M. for forty-two seconds, and as the intensity was gradually increased to the maximum Quinn's body stiffened and strained against the straps. When the body relaxed Dr. J. A. Munn checked for vital signs and pronounced him dead at 12:08 A.M. The body was then removed to the hallway where Father Higgins administered extreme unction.

Morris was then brought from his cell, and he told the witnesses, "The game is up, that is all." He took his seat and the same procedures were followed as for Quinn, but as the electrodes were secured he fainted and was not conscious when the electricity was switched on for forty seconds, and then he was pronounced dead. Both bodies were carried down the whitewashed corridor to a storage room and later delivered to a local funeral home. Morris' body was returned to the prison and buried in the prison cemetery but Quinn's body was released to his mother Mary to be shipped to Kansas City for burial.

Sources: *Ada Evening News* (OK): November 24, 1933. *Big Springs Herald* (TX): November 29, 1932. *Emporia Gazette* (KS): November 28, 1933; December 1, 1932. *Jefferson City Post-Tribune* (MO): December 31, 1930; May 19, 1931. *Joplin Globe* (MO): November 24, 1933. *Mason City Globe-Gazette* (IA): May 16, 1931. *Master Detective Magazine*: September 1941. *Moberly Monitor-Index* (MO): November 24, 1933. *New Castle News* (PA): November 24, 1933. *Oklahoman* (Oklahoma City): November 24, 1933.

Clark, Frank
October 19, 1934

On February 13, 1934, fifty-eight-year-old Frank Clark, a black tenant farmer, went to the Stiles farm near Idabel in McCurtain County, Oklahoma, to rent a patch of land from neighbor Dan Stiles. He found Dan and his wife Anna working in a field, and Clark tried to make a deal for the land, but Stiles refused to lease it to him. Clark was carrying a rifle and suddenly he raised it and fired a single shot which struck Dan Stiles in the head killing him instantly. He then shot Anna Stiles twice, inflicting fatal wounds, and she died in the Idabel hospital two hours later without regaining consciousness. When the shooting occurred the Stiles' three sons were only a quarter mile away, and they saw the shooting. Clark started for them and fired a single, wild round at them before he fled south toward the Red River bottoms. Twenty-one-year-old Dedrick Stiles positively identified their neighbor as the murderer, and a posse of two hundred armed, angry men began searching the Red River bottoms for the fugitive.

Authorities on the Texas side also formed posses, and they began to search their side of the river. Clark managed to elude capture for three days, even when the National Guard was called out to assist in the hunt, but he was finally captured on the Texas side of the Red River on February 16. He was turned over to Oklahoma authorities, taken directly to McAlester, and lodged in a prison cell. When it was safe he was returned to Idabel for arraignment, where forty-five guardsmen protected him from the angry crowds milling about the courthouse. Clark pled not guilty, and at the spring session of the district court he was tried for killing Anna, convicted of murder in the first degree, and sentenced to die in the electric chair. The court of criminal appeals handled the appeal expeditiously, his date of execution was set for October 19, 1934, and his petition for clemency sent to Governor William H. Murray was quickly denied.

Several days before his execution date Clark was moved from his death row cell to one of several special cells in the basement of the main prison building, near the electric chair. The barber was then summoned, and he shaved the prisoner's head and left leg. After 11:00 P.M. on the night before the execution one hundred sixty-five witnesses were ushered through the prison yard to the door into the basement, and they descended and took their places in the viewing area, while fourteen prison officials gathered in the death chamber. Warden Sam Brown had read the death warrant to Clark after supper so at midnight the cell door was swung open and the condemned man walked the few steps into the chamber.

As he entered the chamber he looked over his shoulder and said to his death watch guard, "Good-bye Captain," then declined to make a further statement. He took his seat in the oak chair where his chest and waist, wrists and arms, and ankles were bound with leather straps, and the copper helmet and leg band, lined with moistened sponge, were secured in place. A black leather mask was tied over his eyes and forehead and attached to the chair back. At 12:07 A.M. the executioner stepped to the control panel and flipped the switch which applied the electricity, set at the lower range of 600 to 2,300 volts, and then he turned a wheel until the intensity reached the maximum. The electricity was turned off after forty-five seconds; the doctor in attendance checked for vital signs, and he pronounced Clark dead at 12:10 A.M. Prison trusties removed the body from the chair and carried it down the whitewashed corridor to a storage room, and shortly afterward the remains were delivered to a local funeral parlor to be prepared for burial.

Sources: *Ada Evening News* (OK): October 19, 1934. *Lubbock Morning Avalanche* (TX): February 14, 1934. *Paris Evening News* (TX): October 19, 1934.

Oglesby, Ernest
January 4, 1935

Cole Oglesby was believed to be a member of "the Newton boys" gang who robbed banks and trains when, on June 12, 1924, they made the biggest haul from a train robbery ever recorded when the gang took $3,000,000 in cash and jewels from a postal train near Rondout, Illinois. Cole later became an associate, or member, of the Charles "Pretty Boy" Floyd gang, and over the next eight years he was believed involved in many bank robberies and murders. Cole was also an accomplished, dedicated car thief, and he taught his younger brother Ernest the trade. On October 17, 1932, Oklahoma City police officer Jerry Campbell arrested Cole Oglesby on suspicion of auto theft. While taking him to the station, with Cole driving the stolen car, the prisoner suddenly pulled a pistol and shot at the officer. Cole missed but Campbell fired back causing four wounds, several of which proved instantly fatal, so Floyd tried to fill the vacancy caused by Cole's death, and Ernest may have been one of several recruits.

During the morning hours of December 3, 1933, Ernest stole a car in Oklahoma City, and he was spotted by Officers Douglas W. Gates and Webb Campbell (no relation to Jerry Campbell) patrolling in a "scout car." They pursued the stolen car, which fled at a high rate of speed, but Oglesby lost control and crashed into a parked car. As the police car pulled up Oglesby jumped out and immediately shot Gates, inflicting a mortal wound. As he ran past the police car Oglesby fired through the back window of the police car and glass shards wounded Webb Campbell in his arm, but the officer pulled his pistol and shot Oglesby in the arm. Oglesby jumped into a passing automobile and made his escape but, though he was only twenty-three years old, he was already well known to the police so within hours he was tracked down and arrested in a home in the company of two women and three men. Meanwhile, Gates had been rushed to the hospital where he lingered for six hours before dying of his wounds, and Oglesby was charged with his murder. Oglesby's arm had not been properly treated for several hours and the wound had festered, and had to be amputated.

Oglesby was tried at the spring term of the district court, and he was convicted of first-degree murder. Judge George A. Henshaw sentenced him to die in the electric chair, and his case was appealed. The court of criminal appeals only took several months before the justices affirmed the judgment and sentence of the lower court and fixed the date of execution at January 4, 1935, and he was scheduled to die with two other condemned murderers. Appeals had been filed with the U.S. Supreme Court for all three men but only Bill Prescott and Joe Bell were granted stays, while the justices refused to consider Oglesby's appeal. Neither appeal nor petition for executive clemency sent to Governor William H. Murray would delay the proceedings.

Several days before his execution date Oglesby was moved from his death row cell to one of several special cells in the basement of the main prison building, near the electric chair. The barber was then summoned, and he shaved the prisoner's head and left leg. After 11:00 P.M. on the night before the execution two hundred twenty-three witnesses, including fifteen Oklahoma City police officers, were ushered through the prison yard to the door into the basement and they descended and took their places in the viewing area. Warden Sam Brown had read the death warrant to Oglesby earlier so at midnight the cell door was swung open and the condemned man walked the few steps into the chamber. As he entered he shook hands with Warden Brown, who asked if he had any last words. Oglesby said, "I hope God will forgive everyone who put me here," and then took his seat in the oak chair.

His chest and waist, wrists and arms, and ankles were bound with leather straps, the copper helmet and leg band lined with moistened sponge were secured in place, and a black leather mask was tied over his eyes and forehead and attached to the chair back. At 12:07 A.M. the executioner stepped to the control panel and flipped the switch which applied the electricity, set at the lower range of 600 to 2,300 volts, and then he turned a wheel until the intensity reached the maximum. The electricity was turned off after forty-five seconds; the doctor in attendance checked for vital signs, and he pronounced Oglesby dead at 12:11 A.M. Prison trusties removed the body from the chair and carried it down the whitewashed corridor to a storage room, and shortly afterward the remains were delivered to a local funeral parlor to be prepared for burial.

Sources: *Ada Weekly News* (OK): January 10, 1935. *Brownsville Herald* (TX): December 4, 1933. *Independent* (Helena, MT): December 4, 1933. *Sandusky Register* (OH): October 18, 1932.

Cargo, Robert
May 24, 1935

In August 1933 elderly Mrs. Luke was killed by a train and her sixty-seven-year-old husband, A. L. Luke, was devastated, but he lived along U.S. Route 66 in the Nazarene settlement of Bethany, Oklahoma, and his friends and his faith helped him brace up. Luke was a well-known and well-liked nurseryman in the settlement, and he often helped out those having difficulties so when he met twenty-year-old Robert Cargo on Wednesday, March 7, 1934, he offered the penniless and homeless youth a job and opened his home to the youngster. C. H. Padgett, Luke's young employee, saw his employer arguing with a stranger (Cargo) at Luke's home Wednesday afternoon but he did not investigate when Luke did not come to work on Thursday. On Friday morning when Luke did not come to work again Padgett became concerned and went to his employer's home, where he found Luke's mutilated body in the back bedroom and the small, bloodstained hatchet that had inflicted three deep gashes on his head lay nearby.

Padgett called the authorities, and they collected the hatchet for testing, and a clear set of fingerprints was lifted. The stranger was described to officers but the best lead was Luke's automobile, which had been stolen. A week later Cargo was arrested driving Luke's automobile near his home in Birmingham, Alabama. Cargo quickly confessed to the killing but claimed self-defense saying the two men fought over the merits of "knee action" on the 1934 Chevrolet Master model automobile. The DuBonnet independent suspension system, also known as "knee action" or "freewheeling," was an innovation but Luke favored the transverse leaf springs on Fords and, according to Cargo, this led to a heated argument, and he had to kill Luke when he was attacked. He could not explain why he had ransacked the house for money and valuables before he fled east driving Luke's car, nor why there was no sign of a struggle in the bedroom where Luke's body was found. He was arraigned, pled not guilty, and was held over for trial. On May 25 Cargo offered to plead guilty but this was rejected by the prosecution so they could seek the death penalty.

The trial began on May 28, and on May 29 the jurors, after deliberating forty minutes, found Cargo guilty of first-degree murder and recommended the death penalty. On May 31 Cargo told reporters, "Somebody will save me. If the courts don't, the governor will." Several days later Cargo was sentenced to die in the electric chair but an appeal stayed the execution until the court of criminal appeals affirmed the judgment and sentence of the district court several months later. On August 29, as Cargo's new date of execution drew near, Governor William H. Murray granted a stay of execution to December 21, 1934, and this was extended to March 15, 1935, when the matter could be taken up by newly elected governor E. W. Marland. Governor Marland then granted a stay of execution to May 24, 1935. On May 21 he heard the plea for clemency from Cargo's attorney Ralph W. Keaby, and then he declined to intervene. The May 23 appeal for a sanity hearing was also denied.

The prison's new warden, W. S. Key, inherited a uniform protocol for conducting executions, and he left it unchanged, including the policy of holding executions on Friday after midnight. Several days before his execution date Cargo was moved from his death row cell to one of several special cells in the basement of the main prison building, near the electric chair. The barber was then summoned, and he shaved the prisoner's head and left leg. After 11:00 P.M. on the night before the execution sixty witnesses were ushered through the prison yard to the door into the basement, and they descended and took their places in the viewing area. Warden Keys had read the death warrant to Cargo earlier so at midnight the cell door was swung open and the condemned man walked the few steps into the chamber. He declined to speak to the witnesses but after he took his seat in the oak chair he whispered to the warden, "I want to thank everybody and all my friends for what they've done for me."

His chest and waist, wrists and arms, and ankles were bound with leather straps, the copper helmet and leg band, lined with moistened sponge, were secured in place, and a black leather mask was tied over his eyes and forehead and attached to the chair back. At 12:09 A.M. the executioner stepped to the control panel and flipped the switch which applied the electricity, set at the lower range of 600 to 2,300 volts, and then he turned a wheel until the intensity reached the maximum. The electricity was turned off in less than a minute, and the doctor in attendance checked for vital signs. He pronounced Cargo dead at 12:13 A.M. Prison trusties removed the body from the chair and carried it down the whitewashed corridor to a storage room, and shortly afterward the remains were delivered to a local funeral parlor to be prepared for burial.

Sources: *Ada Evening News* (OK): May 21, 1935. *Galveston News* (TX): June 1, 1934. *Indian Journal* (OK): August 30, 1934. *Joplin Globe* (MO): December 7, 1934. *Miami News-Record* (OK): May 24, 1935. *Morning Avalanche* (Lubbock, TX): May 24, 1935. *San Antonio Express* (TX): March 10, 1934.

Barrett, Chester
Riley, Bun
Rowan, Alfred
September 20, 1935

Thirty-two-year-old Chester Barrett of Sapulpa, Oklahoma, had been ill and had been out of work for months. On Monday, April 30, 1934, he took a quantity of strychnine he had bought several years earlier to kill rats, which he had stored in a quinine can after the original container broke, and he put it in his family's milk. However, the milk coated their stomachs and the quantity of poison was too weak to cause death, though it made the entire family ill. Barrett resolved to try murder-suicide again on Wednesday but lost his nerve. Several of his eight children had recently recovered from the measles so on Friday he told his wife and children he was going to give them quinine to ward off fever. He administered the poison to himself, his wife, and seven children, excluding only the seven-month-old baby, whom he believed would be taken care of after their deaths. Soon Barrett began to feel the effects of the poison, and he staggered to the home of neighbor Clara Hugo and told her that his family was ill from food poisoning; she called county physician Dr. P. K. Lewis. The doctor immediately recognized the distinctive symptoms of strychnine poisoning and called the police, and they arrested Barrett. The prisoner first claimed that he had intended to give them quinine, and had forgotten that he had switched the poison into the quinine can. However, when he learned that six-year-old Betty Jo, three-year-old Mary Kathryn, and two-year-old Wanda Marie had died, he confessed. Mrs. Barrett and twelve-year-old Cora Lucille, ten-year-old Duane, eight-year-old Mildred, and five-year-old Dorothy recovered.

On May 11, 1934, Barrett was arraigned on three counts of murder and held over for trial at the next term, and he begged Sheriff Willis Strange to remove his handcuffs so he might flee and be shot to death. Barrett was tried and convicted of first-degree murder of one child and was sentenced to die in the electric chair. His court-appointed attorney filed an appeal which stayed the execution, but finally the court of criminal appeals affirmed the judgment and sentence of the district court, and the prisoner was sentenced to die on September 20, 1935.

In May 1934 twenty-six-year-old Bun Riley, twenty-four-year-old William Gann, twenty-seven-year-old Homer Beasley, and twenty-five-year-old Hobart Watkins of Canadian, twenty miles northeast of McAlester, were all somehow involved in a recent store burglary, and Riley believed the other three men might inform on him. On Friday night, June 22, 1934, Riley told Beasley and Watkins that he had put some "Choc beer" in the hills and it was there for the taking. The three men went to the place where a crock of beer was stored, and after they drank a little Riley took a shotgun and shot each man once, then chopped the bodies until he was sure they were dead. The following day he made the same invitation to Gann, but Gann was suspicious. He told fourteen-year-old Pete Coffey, "This isn't right. Something's off about it, but I've got the guts to go." Gann went with Riley, and he was shot once with a shotgun and his body was chopped until Riley was certain he was dead. The murderer then threw down a poorly forged note, supposedly from Gann, naming George Baker, Bill Monroe and Jack Rackley of his murder.

The bodies, the note, and the half-consumed crock of beer were found on Monday, and soon eight men and two women were behind bars and being questioned. All of the men except Riley shouted "Naw, Sir!" and "Don't know nothing like that" when asked about the killings, but Riley told an elaborate story. He told how he barely escaped death when he attended a beer-drinking party at Baker's house on Saturday night, and Baker said he had "put a couple of fellows away and Bill Monroe put his man out of the way too." Riley said that later, as Baker sobered, he felt he had said too much so he marched Riley at the point of a shotgun near the murder scene and was about to shoot him to death, but he lunged at Baker. Failing to wrest the shotgun from Baker's grip he fled, and Baker shot at him twice but missed. As the evidence mounted it pointed directly to Riley as the murderer and refuted the suggestion that several men were involved and that the victims were tortured before being shot.

Riley was charged with three counts of murder, his trial began on September 24, 1934, and two days later he was convicted and sentenced to die in the electric chair. His case was appealed; the court of criminal appeals affirmed the judgment and sentence of the lower court, and Riley was sentenced to die in early 1935. Governor William H. Murray, as he left office, granted stays of execution to a number of men to carry over into newly elected Governor Ernest W. Marland's term, and Riley's execution had been stayed to June 21, 1935. Over the next several months Riley's attorney used every means at his disposal to save the life of his client, but finally Riley's date with the executioner was set for September 20, 1935.

On November 5, 1934, twenty-seven-year-old Alfred Rowan, a black man, was at the farm of twenty-five-year-old Roy D. Gentry, two and one-half miles south of Altus in Jackson County, Oklahoma, when the two men argued. Gentry, according to Rowan, threw a brick at him, so that night just before midnight Rowan returned to the Gentry farmhouse and snuck in through a window. He stabbed and shot Gentry to death. Gentry's wife and eight-year-old boy were awakened by the commotion and saw Rowan as they fled out a window and ran to a neighbor's house. When they returned they found Gentry dead, and Rowan had dropped his pistol before he fled.

On November 7 Rowan was captured in Wichita, Kansas, and he confessed to killing Gentry, told his story of the brick-throwing incident, and was lodged in a cell at the state reformatory at Granite to prevent a lynching. The story of vengeance was weak, and officers believed Rowan was burglarizing the Gentry house, was discovered, and murdered Gentry to avoid being identified. Rowan was tried in early 1935, convicted, and sentenced to die in the electric chair. His attorney filed an appeal which stayed the execution, but the court of criminal appeals affirmed the judgment and sentence of the lower court, and Rowan's date with the executioner was finally set for September 20, 1935.

With three men scheduled to die on the same day Governor Ernest W. Marland was busy with three petitions praying for clemency, but by September 18 he had given each case careful consideration and refused to intervene. As soon as Roy Kenny, acting warden, received word that there would be no further stays or reprieves he had the three men moved from their death row cells to the special cells in the basement of the main prison building, near the electric chair. Barrett then asked to be baptized; after the ceremony was completed he gave his guards a Bible to deliver to his wife, and they found inside an abusive note. The barber was then summoned, and he shaved the prisoners' heads and left legs. The men were then given the opportunity to speak their minds. Barrett insisted he was "framed" and told the officials, "I am the biggest coward in the world. I never did tell the prosecuting attorney I wanted to die. I can't picture any man saying that he would go to the electric chair. I certainly don't want to die." When it was Riley's turn he said, "I'm ready to go. I don't have any kick to make. My conscience is clear. I have no hate for anyone." There is no record of an early statement by Rowan, but he and Riley wrote and left behind religious pleas.

After 11:00 P.M. on the night before the execution the witnesses were ushered through the prison yard to the door into the basement, and they descended and took their places in the viewing area. Warden Kenny had read the death warrants to the condemned men earlier so at midnight Barrett's cell door was swung open and he walked the few steps into the chamber. He was visibly shaken when asked if he had any last words, and after again insisting he was innocent and "framed" he said, "All I want to say is I hope God will forgive everyone for persecuting me." He took his seat in the oak chair where his chest and waist, wrists and arms, and ankles were bound with leather straps, and then the copper helmet and leg band, lined with moistened sponge, were secured in place. A black leather mask was tied over his eyes and forehead and attached to the chair back. At 12:05 A.M. executioner Rich Owen stepped to the control panel and flipped the switch which applied the electricity, set at the lower range of 600 to 2,300 volts, and then he turned a wheel until the intensity reached the maximum. The electricity was turned off in less than one minute. Dr. V. H. Barton checked for vital signs and pronounced Barrett dead at 12:10 A.M.

Prison trusties removed the body from the chair while Riley was being brought in. He too was visibly shaken, with perspiration pouring off his brow, and he declined to speak to the witnesses. He took his seat and was prepared in the same manner as Barrett. Owen flipped the switch at 12:14, and he was pronounced dead at 12:19 A.M. Rowan came last, and, with hands twitching, he nervously told the witnesses, "I want to ask everyone to forgive me for what I've done." He took his seat and was prepared, and at 12:22 A.M. Owen flipped the switch; at 12:26 A.M. he was pronounced dead. The prison trusties removed his body from the chair and, like the two bodies before him, carried him down the whitewashed corridor to a storage room. Shortly afterward the three bodies were delivered to a local funeral parlor to be prepared for burial.

Sources: *Ada Evening News* (OK): June 27, 1934. *Democrat Times* (MS): June 26, 1934. *Joplin Globe* (MO): May 5, 1934; December 7, 1934. *Joplin News Herald* (MO): September 20, 1935. *Mexia Herald* (TX): May 11, 1934. *Miami News-Record* (OK): November 6, 1934. *Morning Avalanche* (Lubbock, TX): December 12, 1934. *Ogden Standard-Examiner* (UT): May 4, 1934. *San Antonio Express* (TX): September 20, 1935.

Guyton, Roy
March 20, 1936

Sixty-year-old E. Lige Bailey was a night watchman at the Oklahoma City dump yard. On August 6, 1934, Bailey was making his rounds when someone snuck up behind him and struck him on the head with a hatchet, killing him. The murderer went through his pockets, taking his money and everything else of value, then stole his pistol. There were no clues to the killer until twenty-five-year-old Roy Guyton pawned the stolen pistol, and he was quickly arrested. He claimed he won the pistol in a dice game but could not provide one corroborating witness. On October 22, 1934, Judge R. P. Hill rejected Guyton's plea of guilty when he told the judge, "Guilty your honor, but I didn't do it," then explained, "Officers told me if I didn't plead guilty they'd kill me for sure with a jury trial."

His trial began right after the plea was rejected, and after the prosecution and defense closed on October 23 the jury deliberated briefly before returning a verdict of guilty of first-degree murder and recommending the death penalty. He was sentenced to die in the electric chair before the end of the year but the case was appealed. In early 1935 the court of criminal appeals affirmed the judgment and sentence of the district court, and he was sentenced to die in March. On March 12 Guyton was granted a stay of execution to July 12, and this was extended several times until all possibilities of judicial relief were exhausted. His date with the executioner was finally set for March 20, 1936. His petition pleading for executive clemency by Governor Ernest W. Marland was denied.

Several days before his execution date Guyton was moved from his death row cell to one of several cells in the basement of the main prison building, near the electric chair. The barber was then summoned, and he shaved the prisoner's head and left leg. After 11:00 P.M. on the night before the execution the small number of witnesses were ushered through the prison yard to the door into the basement, and they descended and took their places in the viewing area. The warden had read the death warrant to Guyton earlier so at midnight the cell door was swung open and the condemned man walked the few steps into the chamber. There is no record of a statement before he took his seat in the oak chair where his chest and waist, wrists and arms, and ankles were bound with leather straps, and the copper helmet and leg band, lined with moistened sponge, were secured in place. A black leather mask was tied over his eyes and forehead and attached to the chair back. At 12:02 A.M. executioner Rich Owen stepped to the control panel and flipped the switch that applied the electricity, set at the lower range of 600 to 2,300 volts, and then Owen turned a wheel until the intensity reached the maximum. As the intensity increased Guyton's body stiffened and strained against the straps. The electricity was turned off in less than a minute, and the doctor in attendance then checked for vital signs and pronounced Guyton dead at 12:06 A.M. Prison trusties removed the body from the chair and carried it down the whitewashed corridor to a storage room, and shortly afterward the remains were delivered to a local funeral parlor to be prepared for burial.

Sources: *Ada Evening News* (OK): March 20, 1936. *Miami News-Record* (OK): August 6, 1934; October 22, 1934. *San Antonio Express* (TX): October 24, 1934.

Hargus, James R.
April 24, 1936

Just before Sunday midnight, July 22, 1934, Tulsa police detectives Lawrence B. Mitchell and W. L. Martin were patrolling in a "scout car" when they received a call of a prowler near a drugstore. When they went to investigate they found twenty-two-year-old James R. Hargus, a Texas ex-convict, acting suspiciously. When they approached Hargus for questioning he pulled a handgun, and the three men engaged in a brief gun battle. Mitchell was killed with a bullet through his heart, but Hargus and Martin were wounded and rushed to the local hospital. Martin was given an even chance to survive the bullet wound in his abdomen but Hargus, who was shot twice in the head and once each in the arm and face, was expected to die. However, both men recovered from their wounds, though Hargus' arm had to be amputated, and he was charged with Mitchell's murder.

As soon as Hargus was able to talk he admitted that he specialized in robbing drugstores and was "casing" a store when approached by the officers. He was tried at the late fall 1934 session of the district court, claimed self-defense, was convicted of first-degree murder, and was sentenced to die in the electric chair in early 1935. His court-appointed attorney filed an appeal, which stayed the execution, and the court of criminal appeals considered the case for months before they affirmed the judgment and sentence of the lower court. The justices set Hargus' date with the executioner for February 7, 1936. On February 5 Governor Ernest W. Marland granted a last-minute reprieve so that Hargus' attorney could file an appeal with the U.S. Supreme Court, and then he granted another reprieve from April 9 to April 24 for a hearing on a new trial scheduled for April 15. All judicial efforts to give Hargus relief failed, and the petition praying for clemency from Governor Marland was quickly denied.

Several days before his execution date Hargus was moved from his death row cell to one of the special cells in the basement of the main prison building, near the electric chair. The barber was summoned, and he shaved the prisoner's head and left leg. On Thursday Hargus told the prison officials that he was being given "a raw deal" as he had only shot in self-defense. After 11:00 P.M. on the night before the execution the witnesses were ushered through the prison yard to the door into the basement, and they descended and took their places in the viewing area. The warden had read the death warrant to the prisoner earlier so at midnight the cell door was swung open, and Hargus, smiling and without assistance, walked the few steps into the chamber. When asked if he had any last words he said, "I just have to wish you good luck and good-bye. I'd like to make you a long talk but the warden says not, so I'll sit down and die while you men watch me."

He then took his seat in the oak chair where his chest and waist, wrists and arms, and ankles were bound with leather straps, and the copper helmet and leg band, lined with moistened sponge, were secured in place. A black leather mask was tied over his eyes and forehead and attached to the chair back. At 12:08 A.M. the executioner stepped to the control panel and flipped the switch that applied the electricity, set at the lower range of 600 to 2,300 volts, and then he turned a wheel until the intensity reached the maximum. The electricity was turned off in less than a minute, and the doctor in attendance checked for vital signs and pronounced Hargus dead at 12:12 A.M. Prison trusties then removed the body from the chair and carried it down the whitewashed corridor to a storage room, and shortly afterward the remains were delivered to a local funeral parlor to be prepared for burial.

Sources: *Ada Evening News* (OK): July 23, 1934; April 24, 1936. *Brownsville Herald* (TX): July 23, 1934.

Gooch, Arthur
June 19, 1936

On October 24, 1934, Ambrose Nix and Arthur Gooch, with two other men and two women prisoners, escaped from a Holdenville, Oklahoma, jail. Nix and Gooch walked across town, stole a car, and managed to avoid arrest for more than a month when, on November 25, they disposed of the stolen car and stole another car with Arkansas license plates in Durant, Texas. They drove this vehicle to Tyler, Texas, where they robbed Q. Mitchell, a lunch stand operator, of $80 in change. After the robbery they drove to Paris, Texas, where they had a flat tire.

During the early morning hours of November 26 police officers R. N. "Newt" Baker and H. R. "Tutt" Marks were on patrol in an unmarked car when they noticed an automobile with Arkansas license plates parked at Clyde Moore's service station on North Main Street in Paris. Attendant M. A. Williams was busy changing the flat tire, and Baker said to Marks, "That looks like a bootlegger's or hijacker's car," as mud splashed on the car suggested it had been driven at high speed through back roads. The two officers went into the service station and found Nix and Gooch, and when questioned Nix claimed ownership and said he had bought the car recently for $675. After more questioning Baker told Marks "to see what he's got," indicating he should pat down Gooch for weapons. Baker drew his pistol but Nix pulled his pistol first, put the barrel near Baker's head and said, "Drop that gun or I'll kill you." Baker dropped his gun but Marks jumped Nix and they struggled, and when Baker tried to retrieve his weapon he was pushed into a glass display case and was cut deeply on his hip. Gooch and Nix overpowered Marks and got the drop on both police officers, then ordered them out to their stolen car. They told them to lower their hands, and Gooch said, "You guys think you're tough? We're going to take you where people are really tough." The tire was fixed but Nix and Gooch decided that the stolen car might again lead to their detection so they moved four shotguns, a rifle, several pistols, clothing and a sack of money from their car to the patrol car. All four men got in, the officers in the back seat, and they headed north into Oklahoma with Nix driving and Gooch holding a sawed-off shotgun on the two officers. Williams, as soon as the four men drove off, ran to another filling station which had a telephone and called the police station.

The officers were kept prisoner all day and allowed a dozen feet away from the robbers one at a time, only when necessary. The two kidnappers dressed the wound on Baker's hip even though one said, "I don't give a damn if you bleed to death," and the officers were not given water or food the entire day. Throughout the day the two kidnappers discussed what they had done, and the ramifications, and considered killing the two officers and making their escape. Several times they warned, "If you make any trouble we'll show you some rough country," but finally they decided against killing the officers. After dark Nix drove to Rattan, Oklahoma, and bought gas, using nickels and dimes from their bag of stolen loot, then drove to Finley where they obtained stale cheese and crackers, but it was too dry to swallow. Doubling back on the highway they drove nine miles past Snow in Pushmataha County, Oklahoma, and turned onto a desolate side road, drove deep into the woods, gave the officers a flashlight, and told them to walk into the woods.

Baker and Marks thought they would be shot in the back but they walked until they were out of sight of the car, then hid in the woods until they heard their car drive off. They walked back into the tiny village of Snow, which had no telephone, and asked W. M. Franks for help but Franks was suspicious of their story and insisted he would only take them to the larger community of Antlers if he could take along an armed man. Marks later said, "We didn't blame him a bit, and I told him I didn't care if he took three guns — all I wanted was to get to a telephone where I could let my folks know where I was." In Antlers the men stopped at a restaurant and telephoned the Paris, Texas, police station, and in a very short time Police Chief Cothran arrived to drive them home.

A week later, on December 3, their police car was found near McAlester, Oklahoma, stripped and burned, but there was no sign of Gooch or Nix. In mid–December two armed and masked men robbed two banks in Okemah, Oklahoma, on the same day, and on December 23 Oklahoma officers tried to arrest Gooch and Nix near Okemah, believing they were the bank robbers. The two fugitives resisted, and during a heated gun battle Nix was shot through the stomach and died, so Gooch surrendered. Gooch was lodged in the jail at Oklahoma City, and on December 26 the prisoner was transferred to the jail at federal headquarters in Muskogee. Gooch was arraigned before U.S. Commissioner R. M. Mountcastle and pled not guilty, had his preliminary hearing on January 26, 1935, and on February 11 was indicted under the new Lindbergh kidnapping law.

Trial was set for the June term at Durant when Judge Robert L. Williams refused to take Gooch's guilty plea, saying life imprisonment, all he would be authorized to give him if he accepted the plea, was too lenient, and he wanted a jury to consider the facts of the case and the possibility of a death sentence. He was tried in mid–June, and the *Durant Democrat* said, after the verdict of guilty was returned, "It was one of the most dramatic court scenes in the history of Durant but came with such suddenness that court fans were unaware of its import. Less than 45 minutes was required for the presentation of testimony and the jury took but two ballots on the verdict, the first standing 11 to 1 for death," and the second ballot was unanimous. On June 19 Judge Williams sentenced Gooch to hang on September 13, 1935, and when the judge asked Gooch if he had anything to say he replied, "I don't see why I should be hanged when no others charged with kidnapping received this sentence." The judge then continued in response, "Just because some juries are spineless and refuse to inflict the capital punishment this is no reason for me to refrain from assessing the death sentence when such a verdict is reached in my court, and I have the courage to assess it. Kidnappers should not be allowed to run loose and roam around the country like mad dogs." Immediately after the sentence of death was pronounced Gooch's attorney, E. M. Frye, gave notice of appeal on five grounds but the process took less than nine months before all avenues of judicial relief were exhausted, and the date for execution was set for June 19, 1936.

After sentencing, the condemned man was taken to the state penitentiary at McAlester and lodged in a death row cell near the electric chair, but Gooch was sentenced to hang under federal law. Gooch, then twenty-seven years old, never lost hope and believed he would be spared at the gallows. On the day before the execution he was visited by his mother and girlfriend, twenty-year-old Marie Lepley, and he said, "I never felt happier in my life. I never had more hope than I have today. I have never been more confident that my life will be full and long. I am sure that I will not hang tomorrow morning, although everyone else interested in me has given up hope." However, after President Franklin D. Roosevelt denied a last-minute stay of execution Gooch said, "I don't want to die but if I do, I will feel better after I am gone than he will." Gooch criticized Roosevelt for his attitude saying, "I don't feel I should die for such a small crime as mine." Gooch's ex-wife also visited him that last day and brought his six-year-old son to visit. After all visitors retired U.S. Deputy Marshal George Hall arrived and read the death warrant.

Gooch spent a restful night and was aroused at an early hour and told to prepare. A crowd of three hundred fifty witnesses, including eight women, came to the penitentiary to watch the execution, and something of a carnival atmosphere developed. They were told that newspaper reporters would be allowed to stand near the gallows but that lay witnesses would have to remain one hundred feet behind, and then at least one hundred lay witnesses pulled out paper and pencils, claimed to be reporters, and were allowed to remain near the gallows. The procession formed with Board of Affairs Chairman L. M. Nichols and deputy warden Jess Dunn leading the way. U.S. Deputy Marshal Hall followed with the handcuffed prisoner, and he escorted Gooch onto the gallows, quietly constructed in the prison yard after prisoners had gone to bed. Just before 5:00 A.M. Gooch took his place on the trapdoor and was asked if he had anything to say, but he just shook his head.

Prison chaplain the Rev. E. S. Priest prayed for his soul as he was prepared by Rich Owen, an executioner experienced in electrocutions, by having the handcuffs removed and re-clasped behind his back; his knees and ankles were bound, the black cap was pulled over his head down to his waist, and the noose was adjusted. The trap was sprung at 5:04 A.M. The noose slipped and his neck was not broken in the fall, but his feet were suspended an inch above the ground. Prison physician Dr. T. H. McCarley, assisted by Drs. W. B. Taylor, B. B. Keys, and O. E. Lovely, stepped beneath the platform and with a stethoscope each man took a turn listening for a heartbeat. At eleven minutes Dr. McCarley announced, "His heart still beats," and in four minutes more they conferred and announced, "He strangled, his neck couldn't have been broken — his heart has stopped." Owen then tried to untie the noose but the coils fouled so guards lifted the body, and Owen climbed atop the beam and untied the rope there. The body was lowered onto a waiting stretcher and carried to an ambulance, which took the body to a McAlester funeral parlor to be prepared for burial later that day. After the execution witnesses rushed to the wooden gallows and cut off pieces for souvenirs, and some were able to cut off pieces of the rope. Then the gallows was dismantled before the prisoners arose.

Sources: *Dallas Morning News* (TX): June 20, 1936. *Denton Record-Chronicle* (TX): December 24, 1934. *Ada Evening News* (OK): June 18–19, 1936. *Galveston Daily News* (TX): December 24, 1934. *Paris News* (TX): August 25, 1936; March 7, 1993. *Tulsa World* (OK): June 20, 1936.

Sands, Charlie
Siler, Leon
June 11, 1937

Seventeen-year-old Charlie Sands and eighteen-year-old Leon Siler, Seminole Indians, had been released from prison less than a week when, shortly before midnight Sunday, May 26, 1935, they drove their black Ford V-8 sedan into Pauls Valley, Oklahoma. Pauls Valley's night policeman George Longacre was talking with a boy named Nelson when the Ford pulled up, and the three armed men inside got the drop on Longacre, took his pistol, and forced Longacre and Nelson to get in their car. They drove a short distance, and just after midnight they saw forty-year-old George Loper, the other night policeman, and ordered him to raise his hands. When he hesitated one of the men fired, the bullet striking Loper in the heart, killing him instantly. Whatever their plan it was abandoned and the three men fled south, but after traveling three miles they ejected Longacre and Nelson from the car. Longacre hailed a passing automobile and returned to Pauls Valley, where he reported the killing and kidnapping, but by 11:00 A.M. the next morning there was no progress on the case.

Four days later, on the morning of May 31, 1935, fifteen-year-old Phyllis Ann Siler with nineteen-year-old Ruby Herring driving, parked their black Ford V-8 sedan in front of the Bank of Elgin in Comanche County, Oklahoma, and, with the engine running, Siler's eighteen-year-old husband Leon and Herring's seventeen-year-old sweetheart Charlie exited. They rushed into the bank and at gunpoint robbed cashier Evelyn Ezell of $600, then ran out, and Herring drove them toward Lawton, but they stopped at the Medrano farm eleven miles outside Elgin. A large posse was quickly formed and tracked the four bank robbers to the farmhouse, where they had taken the family hostage and had barricaded themselves inside the house in anticipation of being discovered. Once the farmhouse was completely surrounded Undersheriff James E. "Pete" Wilson and Elgin Constable R. B. Deeds went in to negotiate the release of the hostages and the surrender of the robbers. Suddenly shooting started, and Wilson died almost immediately with fifteen gunshot wounds riddling his body. Adrian Medrano was killed, and Deeds, Sands, Siler and two posse men were wounded.

Sands and Siler had to surrender, and they were taken to the Granite reformatory for safe keeping, while Phyllis Siler and Ruby Herring, alias Moore, were lodged in the Lawton jail. Officer Longacre then went to the reformatory and identified the two prisoners as two of the three men who had murdered Loper, but the third man was never identified. Sands and Siler were first charged with Wilson's murder. Their trial began at Lawton in September, on September 22 they were convicted of first degree murder, and on September 26 Judge Henry W. Hoel sentenced them to die in the electric chair on December 29, 1935.

Phyllis Siler was convicted of being an accessory to armed robbery and sentenced to serve five years at the State Industrial School for Girls at Tecumseh. She escaped with another girl on November 9 and was recaptured on November 21, 1935, and on February 14, 1936, she was delivered to the state prison to complete her sentence; but then she escaped from the prison on April 27 and was recaptured at Seminole twenty-four hours later. Ruby Herring, the getaway car driver, was convicted of being an accessory to armed robbery and sentenced to serve a ten-year prison sentence, but she died in prison in August 1937. The prisoners, to keep from having Herring buried in the prison cemetery, took up a collection to give her a Christian burial in the McAlester town cemetery.

A notice of appeal for Sands and Siler was filed on October 15, and Governor Ernest W. Marland granted a reprieve of six months. When this reprieve expired on May 1, 1936, the court of criminal appeals granted a stay of execution so the attorneys could perfect their appeals. The appeals were argued on August 22 based upon the premise that the killing of Wilson was in self-defense when the two bank robbers were not given the chance to surrender. This premise was rejected, and on April 9, 1937, the justices affirmed the judgment and sentence of the lower court and set the date of execution at June 11, 1937. Further appeals, motions, writs, and petitions were filed but nothing further would arise to delay the proceedings.

On Wednesday the two condemned men were visited by family and friends, and Sands said, "I have no hard feelings toward anybody. I'm not worrying a bit. The folks and Ruby will be the worst part of it. She sure is a swell kid. No one ever had a sweetheart more true and loyal. I made a mistake and I'd like to tell any young kid who gets started to slow down. It might be different if they had only themselves, but its always their folks that suffer." Siler told his mother, "I hate this because of Phyllis and you folks. I'm not afraid to go now. While there's life there's hope. I may walk out of here yet. I am sorry for the trouble I caused." After the families left Warden Jess Dunn permitted the two women to visit, but refused to allow Sands to marry Herring.

On Thursday morning at 4:30 A.M. Sands and Siler were aroused from a sound sleep and served breakfast, and they changed into their new prison-made pocket-less grey suits. They were then handcuffed and moved from their death row cells to the special cells in the basement of the main prison building, near the electric chair. After they were settled in their cells the barber was summoned, and he shaved the prisoners' heads and left legs. After 11:00 P.M. two hundred thirty-five witnesses were ushered through the prison yard to the door into the basement, and they descended and took their places in the viewing area. Warden Dunn had read the death warrants earlier so at midnight the cell doors were swung open, and both condemned men walked a dozen steps into the chamber. As they entered each man shook hands with Warden Dunn and executioner Rich Owen.

Siler was chosen to go first so he was asked if he had any last words, but there is no record of a statement. He took his seat in the oak chair where his chest and waist, wrists and arms, and ankles were bound with leather straps, and the copper helmet and leg band, lined with moistened sponges, were secured in place. A black leather mask was tied over his eyes and forehead and attached to the chair back. Minutes after midnight Owen stepped to the control panel and flipped the switch that applied the electricity, set at the lower range of 600 to 2,300 volts, and then he turned a wheel until the intensity reached the maximum. As the intensity increased Siler's body strained against the straps, but relaxed when the electricity was turned off in less than a minute. Prison physician Dr. O.E. Lovely, assisted by Drs. F. T. Barthell and William Taylor, checked for vital signs and pronounced Siler dead.

Prison trusties removed the body from the chair and carried it to a storage room while Sands was asked if he had any last words, but there is no record of a statement. He was prepared in the same manner as Siler, the switch was flipped, and within minutes he was pronounced dead. The trusties then removed his body from the chair, carried it down the corridor to the storage room where Siler's remains were stored, and shortly afterward the bodies were delivered to a local funeral parlor to be prepared for burial by their families.

Sources: *Ada Evening News* (OK): May 30, 1935; June 6, 1935; September 22, 1935; May 1, 1936; April 28, 1936; August 23, 1936; April 9, 1937; June 2–3, 1937; August 31, 1937. *Ada Weekly News* (OK): June 17, 1937. *Corsicana Sun* (TX): May 31, 1935. *Miami News-Record* (OK): November 21, 1935; August 18, 1936. *Morning Avalanche* (Lubbock, TX): September 27, 1935. *Oklahoman* (Oklahoma City): June 11, 1937.

Mannon, Roy
March 1, 1940

In November 1938 thirty-seven-year-old Roy Mannon, an ex-convict having completed five prison terms, befriended sixty-seven-year-old Jake Skelly, a Wagoner, Oklahoma, recluse. The two men were seen together between November 12 and 14, and on November 14 they were seen together at a Wagoner filling station as Skelly filled the tank on his automobile, but Skelly was not seen after that time. Mannon was out on bond on a robbery charge, and soon after November 14 he gave his attorney a fine watch as part payment for his defense, and the watch was found to be the property of Skelly. Foul play was still not suspected until Mannon was found driving Skelly's bloodstained automobile, with Skelly's flashlight and personal belongings packed in the car.

Mannon was arrested, lodged in the Muskogee jail, and the search for Skelly's body began, with one group concentrating on the many wells abandoned by sawmills in the Verdigris river bottoms, thirty-five miles from Wagoner. After searching fifteen wells members of the posse were chasing a rabbit when they stumbled upon a partially hidden well, and they discovered Skelly's body at the bottom. He had been shot five times with wounds in his body and head. A search then began for the murder weapon, but it was never found. Mannon claimed that "Clarence" murdered Skelly, as it was Clarence who had given Mannon the car and belongings. Mannon was charged with Skelly's murder and arraigned on November 28.

His trial began in Wagoner in mid–January 1939; on January 27 he was convicted of first-degree murder, and the jurors recommended the death penalty. His continued defense that a man named Clarence was responsible was rejected as a fabrication. On February 11 Judge E. A. Summers sentenced Mannon to die in the electric chair on May 12, but the case was appealed, which stayed the execution. The court of criminal appeals affirmed the judgment and sentence of the lower court on December 27, and the justices set the date of execution for March 1, 1940. The justices wrote, "The evidence reveals that without cause or provocation the defendant took an old and feeble man from his home for the purpose of robbing him of a few hundred dollars of property and shot him and threw his lifeless body into an old and abandoned well." The court of appeals refused to rehear the case, and Governor Leon C. Phillips declined to intervene.

Early Thursday morning Mannon was aroused from a deep sleep, handcuffed, and moved from his death row cell to one of several special cells in the basement of the main prison building, near the electric chair. As soon as breakfast was finished the barber was summoned, and he shaved the prisoner's head and left leg. After 11:00 P.M. Thursday night two hundred witnesses were ushered through the prison yard to the door into the basement, and they descended and took their places in the viewing area. Warden Jess Dunn had read the death warrant to Mannon earlier so at midnight the cell door was swung open and the condemned man walked a dozen steps into the chamber. As he entered he was asked if he had any last words, and he turned to the spectators and shouted, "I want you all to know I am going down for another man." He then shook hands with Warden Dunn and Owen and told his executioner, "Rich, I did my last day's work for you — and now you are going to put the button to me. Do a good job pushing that button."

As Owen smiled, but did not respond, Mannon took his seat in the oak chair where his chest and waist, wrists and arms, and ankles were bound with leather straps, and the copper helmet and leg band, lined with moistened sponges, were secured in place. A black leather mask was tied over his eyes and forehead and attached to the chair back. At 12:14 A.M. Owen stepped to the control panel and flipped the switch that applied the electricity, set at the lower range of 600 to 2,300 volts, and then he turned a wheel until the intensity reached the maximum. The electricity was turned off in less than a minute, and Dr. W. G. Ramsey checked for vital signs and pronounced Mannon dead at 12:17 A.M. Prison trusties removed the body from the chair and carried it down the whitewashed corridor to a storage room, and shortly afterward the remains were delivered to a local funeral parlor to be prepared for burial.

Sources: *Ada Evening News* (OK): February 12, 1939; December 28, 1939; January 7, 1940; March 1, 1940. *Ada Weekly News* (OK): December 1, 1938. *Joplin Globe* (MO): January 28, 1939. *Journal-Times* (Racine, WI): March 1, 1940. *Oklahoman* (Oklahoma City): March 1, 1940. *Pampa News* (TX): March 1, 1940.

Cunningham, Roger
November 15, 1940

In early 1939 thirty-three-year-old Roger and his thirty-year-old wife Eudora Cunningham, socialites in Oklahoma City, had been having marital difficulties for several months, mainly because her husband refused to divulge the amount of his salary, and his wife continually nagged him about the matter. On the evening of March 6 the couple was driving when they began to argue, and at 7:30 P.M. Roger pulled his automobile to the side of the road near an old sewer ditch, where the argument escalated. Roger, frustrated, got out of the car and Eudora followed and said she was going to walk to town, but Roger grabbed at his wife's scarf, pulled it tight, and strangled her to death. The sewer ditch was within thirty feet of several houses but Roger was not discovered as he dug an eight-foot grave at the bottom of the ditch and buried his wife's body. When Eudora was missed Roger told her parents that she had gone to San Francisco, and shortly afterward they received a telegram, purportedly from her, stating, "Don't worry. Everything all right. Eudora." Eudora's mother, however, found that every personal item her daughter would need to take a trip was in its place in her room, and she suspected foul play. When she told the police they arrested Roger on March 12 on suspicion of murder and began questioning him. They discovered that the telegram had been sent from San Francisco by a friend of Roger, at his request, after telling his friend it was meant to be a joke. They also found that Roger had called the school where his wife was the librarian and reported her ill, to excuse her absence. After thirteen days in jail, and just hours before he was to be released on a writ of habeas corpus, he confessed at 1:45 A.M. and drew a crude map to his wife's grave. It was still dark on March 25 as a crew of men, including Assistant County Attorney E. W. Brown, dug at the bottom of the ditch by the light of road flares. At a depth of eight feet Brown uncovered Eudora's head and announced, "I struck her. There she is." Cunningham was then charged with his wife's murder, arraigned, and held over for trial. He was tried at the early fall term of the Oklahoma City district court and convicted of first-degree murder, and Judge R. W. Higgins sentenced him to die in the electric chair before the end of the year. An appeal stayed the execution, and his attorney fought for a year to save his client's life, but the court of criminal appeals finally affirmed the judgment and sentence of the lower court and set the date of execution at November 15, 1940. During the last hours of Cunningham's life Judge Higgins refused to grant writs of habeas corpus and mandamus ordering a sanity hearing, and the justices of the court of criminal appeals also denied the same writs. Governor Leon C. Phillips, when petitioned for clemency, refused to intervene.

During his time in prison Cunningham received religious counseling from Envoy Fred Goddard of the Salvation Army and prison chaplain John D. Seal, and he had in his last hours resigned himself to his fate. Early Thursday morning Cunningham was aroused from sleep, handcuffed, and moved from his death row cell to one of several special cells in the basement of the main prison building, near the electric chair. After he finished his breakfast the barber was summoned, and he shaved the prisoner's head and left leg. After 11:00 P.M. that night eighty witnesses were ushered through the prison yard to the door into the basement, and they descended and took their places in the viewing area. Warden Jess Dunn had read the death warrant to the prisoner earlier so at midnight the cell door was swung open, and four guards escorted the condemned man a dozen steps into the chamber. As he entered at 12:05 A.M. he was asked if he had any last words, but he just shook his head. He took his seat in the oak chair where his chest and waist, wrists and arms, and ankles were bound with leather straps, and then the copper helmet and leg band, lined with moistened sponges, were secured in place. A black leather mask was tied over his eyes and forehead and attached to the chair back. At 12:07 A.M. the executioner stepped to the control panel and flipped the switch that applied the electricity, set at the lower range of 600 to 2,300 volts, and then he turned a wheel until the intensity reached the maximum. The electricity was turned off after thirty seconds, and Dr. W. B. Taylor of Holdenville, assisted by two other doctors, checked for vital signs; when he found a heartbeat, another jolt of electricity was applied for forty seconds, and the prisoner was pronounced dead at 12:13 A.M. Prison trusties removed the body from the chair and carried it down the whitewashed corridor to a storage room, and shortly afterward the remains were delivered to a local funeral parlor to be prepared for burial.

Sources: *Albuquerque Journal* (NM): November 15, 1940. *Joplin Globe* (MO): November 15, 1940. *Oakland Tribune* (CA): March 25, 1939. *Oklahoman* (Oklahoma City): November 15, 1940. *San Antonio Light* (TX): November 15, 1940.

Abby, Warren
August 29, 1941

In 1935 fifty-one-year-old Warren Abby, a divorcee from Oliver, Louisiana, used a matrimonial service to meet his mail-order bride Julia in Cherry Valley, Arkansas. Julia was a seventy-four-year-old widow with a small bank account, and Abby was determined to get his hands on her money. Four years of carefully courting the older woman led to a proposal; Julia agreed to marry him, and after the ceremony the newlyweds started for California on their honeymoon. On Friday, October 6, 1939, when they were near Clinton, Oklahoma, Abby pulled to the side of the road and crushed Julia's skull with an automobile connecting rod, killing her. He drove into Clinton, stopped at a filling station, and reported that his wife had been struck and killed by a hit-and-run driver while they were changing a flat tire. The police were called, and they quickly learned that the car had no flat tire. County Attorney Milton Keen backtracked and found the bloody connecting rod at the murder scene. That night, when confronted with the evidence, Abby confessed but claimed self-defense and explained, "I thought she was going to shoot me. She had a gun and was insanely jealous. She thought I was having affairs with other women and said she meant to have me only for herself. I had stood all I could and was about to take her back home and divorce her when it all happened. She said she would see me dead first and we started to fight. That's all I remember. I just lost my head." Abby was charged with murder, at his arraignment he pled not guilty, and he was held over for trial. Jury selection began in the district court at Clinton on December 11, and the following day his trial began. He pled self-defense and temporary insanity, but when he testified he changed his story saying that the couple had argued over a farm cooperative they planned to start in Cherry Valley. The case went to the jury on December 16, the jurors found him guilty of first-degree murder, and they recommended the death penalty. On December 22 Abby was sentenced to die in the electric chair on March 15, 1940, but his attorney filed an appeal. The court of criminal appeals granted a stay of execution on February 23, 1940, but did not affirm the judgment and sentence of the lower court until June 11, 1941, and the justices set the date of execution for August 29. His attorney continued his campaign to save his client's life, but on July 23, 1941, the court of appeals denied a rehearing on the case. All that remained was a plea to Governor Leon C. Phillips for clemency, but he refused to intervene.

On Thursday morning at 4:30 A.M. Abby was aroused from a sound sleep and served breakfast, and he changed into his new prison-made pocketless death suit. He was then handcuffed and moved from his death row cell to one of several special cells in the basement of the main prison building, near the electric chair. As he was being taken from the regular cell block he called back to the four condemned men he left behind, "Best of luck!" After he was settled in his new cell the barber was summoned, and he shaved the prisoner's head and left leg. During the afternoon the execution team conducted dress rehearsals, with executioner Rich Owen standing in for Abby. After 11:00 P.M. the witnesses were ushered through the prison yard to the door into the basement, and they descended and took their places in the viewing area. Warden Fred Hunt had read the death warrant to Abby earlier so at midnight the cell door was swung open and the condemned man walked a dozen steps into the chamber. As he entered he shook hands with Warden Hunt and executioner Owen and was asked if he had any last words, and he replied, "I am being murdered for an act which was forced on me." He took his seat in the oak chair where his chest and waist, wrists and arms, and ankles were bound with leather straps, the copper helmet and leg band, lined with moistened sponges, were secured in place, and a black leather mask was tied over his eyes and forehead and attached to the chair back. At 12:07 A.M. Owen stepped to the control panel and flipped the switch that applied the electricity, set at the lower range of 600 to 2,300 volts, and then he turned a wheel until the intensity reached the maximum. As the intensity increased Abby's body strained against the straps, but relaxed when the electricity was turned off in less than a minute. The doctor in attendance then checked for vital signs, and he pronounced Abby dead at 12:11 A.M. Prison trusties removed the body from the chair and carried it down the whitewashed corridor to a storage room, and shortly afterward the remains were delivered to a local funeral parlor to be prepared for burial.

Sources: *Ada Evening News* (OK): August 28, 1941. *Billings Gazette* (MT): October 7, 1939. *Joplin News Herald* (MO): December 14, 1939. *Port Arthur News* (TX): August 29, 1941. *Miami News-Record* (OK): August 28, 1941. *San Antonio Express* (TX): December 12, 1939.

Tuggle, J. D.

February 9, 1942

In 1940 nineteen-year-old J. D. Tuggle was living with his aunt and uncle, sixty-seven-year-old D. Wilburn and fifty-eight-year-old Sadie, and his ten-year-old half-sister, Alma Tuggle, near Stratford in Garvin County, Oklahoma. In early May Tuggle attempted to molest Alma, and then he became angry and afraid that he would be discovered and severely punished. During the early morning hours of May 9, 1940, Tuggle took an ax handle and snuck up on the elderly couple while they were asleep. He beat Sadie to death and beat D. Wilburn into unconsciousness, then went to Alma's room and beat her into unconsciousness before he fled, leaving all for dead. When the bodies of D. Wilburn and Alma were discovered they were so badly mutilated it was thought both would die. They were rushed to the hospital, and D. Wilburn died on May 18, while Alma fully recovered.

Tuggle was arrested near Atoka on May 16, lodged in the jail at Pauls Valley, and charged with Sadie's murder, and later a charge of murder was added for killing his uncle. At his arraignment the defendant pled "innocent by reason of insanity" and waived a jury trial, but on May 21 after D. Wilburn died he changed his plea to guilty. On June 2 Judge Ben T. Williams sentenced Tuggle to die in the electric chair on August 26, and as he sat in his jail cell waiting to be taken to his death row cell he told reporters, "If they commute my sentence to life I want them to give me the hardest work in the penitentiary and the roughest, toughest treatment they can devise." On June 15 he was delivered to the prison in McAlester while his attorney was busy filing a notice of appeal, and Tuggle received a stay of execution to December 6. His attorney filed the appeal on November 30, which further stayed the execution. On November 26, 1941, the court of criminal appeals affirmed the sentence given by the district court, and the justices set the date of execution for February 9, 1942. Tuggle had already had a psychiatric examination and had been declared sane when, on January 23, his attorney appealed to Governor Leon C. Phillips for a commutation of sentence or a reprieve, but he was denied three days later, and nothing further would arise to delay the proceedings.

During his last week on death row Tuggle was attended by Father Frank Remus, who was sent for when all judicial and executive relief was exhausted, and the condemned man had resigned himself to his fate. On Saturday his mother, a resident at McAlester, paid a final visit to her son. After she left the prisoner was handcuffed and moved from his death row cell to one of several special cells in the basement of the main prison building, near the electric chair. After he was settled in his new cell the barber was summoned, and he shaved the prisoner's head and left leg; then Tuggle dressed in his prison-made pocket-less suit. After 11:00 P.M. twenty-five witnesses were ushered through the prison yard to the door into the basement, and they descended and took their places in the viewing area. Warden Fred Hunt had read the death warrant to Tuggle earlier so at midnight the cell door was swung open and the condemned man walked a dozen steps into the chamber, accompanied by his priest. As he entered he shook hands with Warden Hunt and executioner Owen and was asked if he had any last words, and he replied, "No, Mr. Hunt, take care of yourself."

He took his seat in the oak chair where his chest and waist, wrists and arms, and ankles were bound with leather straps, the copper helmet and leg band, lined with moistened sponges, were secured in place, and a black leather mask was tied over his eyes and forehead and attached to the chair back. At 12:05 A.M. Owen stepped to the control panel and flipped the switch that applied the electricity, set at the lower range of 600 to 2,300 volts, and then he turned a wheel until the intensity reached the maximum. As the intensity increased Tuggle's body strained against the straps but relaxed when the electricity was turned off in less than a minute. A board of three doctors in attendance then checked for vital signs and pronounced the prisoner dead at 12:10 A.M. Prison trusties removed the body from the chair and carried it down the whitewashed corridor to a storage room, and shortly afterward the remains were delivered to a local funeral parlor to be prepared for burial.

Sources: *Miami News-Record* (OK): May 21, 1940; June 6, 1940; August 28, 1941; December 4, 1941; February 9, 1942. *San Antonio Express* (TX): November 27, 1941.

Porter, Finley
April 16, 1943

In early 1925 twenty-two-year-old Porter Finley, a black man, murdered his wife at Okmulgee, Oklahoma. His motive is not known but it was clear that he believed she had done something unforgivable as he felt the killing was justified. He was tried for her murder and convicted of first-degree

murder, and at his trial he must have presented some mitigating circumstance as he was only sentenced to serve a term of life in prison. He arrived at the prison on March 10, 1925, and served more than nine years before he was paroled on December 31, 1934. After eight months of freedom Porter's parole was revoked and on September 4, 1935, he returned to prison.

In mid–1941 Porter was sharing his cell with L. Z. Beacham, and the two men had a terrible argument. Porter pulled out his crude prison-made dirk and stabbed and slashed Beacham horribly, and guards found the mutilated body. Porter was charged with Beacham's murder, tried in the Pittsburg County district court, convicted of first-degree murder, and sentenced to die in the electric chair. He made no defense to the sentence, except the automatic review by the court of criminal appeals, and the justices affirmed the judgment and sentence and set the date for Porter's execution at April 16, 1943.

Porter's mother visited him on Thursday and they sang hymns together, and after she left he was handcuffed and moved from his death row cell to one of several special cells in the basement of the main prison building, near the electric chair. After he was settled in his new cell the barber was summoned to shave the prisoner's head and left leg, and then he changed into his new prison-made pocket-less death suit. During the afternoon he talked with his guards and insisted that both killings were justified. After 11:00 P.M. the witnesses were ushered through the prison yard to the door into the basement, and they descended and took their places in the viewing area. Warden Fred Hunt had read the death warrant to the condemned man earlier so at midnight the cell door was swung open, and the condemned man, smiling, walked a dozen steps into the chamber. As he entered he shook hands with Warden Hunt and the executioner and was asked if he had any last words, and he replied emphatically, "No, sir!"

Porter took his seat in the oak chair where his chest and waist, wrists and arms, and ankles were bound with leather straps, and the copper helmet and leg band, lined with moistened sponges, were secured in place. A black leather mask was tied over his eyes and forehead and attached to the chair back. Only a few minutes past midnight the executioner stepped to the control panel and flipped the switch that applied the electricity, set at the lower range of 600 to 2,300 volts, and then he turned a wheel until the intensity reached the maximum. As the intensity increased Porter's body strained against the straps, but relaxed when the electricity was turned off in less than a minute. The doctor in attendance quickly checked for vital signs, and about four minutes after the current was first applied the prisoner was pronounced dead. Prison trusties then removed the body from the chair and carried it down the whitewashed corridor to a storage room, and shortly afterward the remains were delivered to a local funeral parlor to be prepared for burial.

Sources: *Joplin Globe* (MO): April 16, 1943. *Reno Evening Gazette* (NV): April 16, 1943. *Waterloo Courier* (IA): April 16, 1943. *Wisconsin State Journal* (Madison): April 16, 1943.

Prather, Hiram
July 14, 1943

On May 11, 1936, twenty-four convicts were eating lunch in the prison brickyard at McAlester, Oklahoma, when they suddenly attacked guards Charles Powell, Tuck Cope, W. W. Gossett, and Victor Conn and, using prison-made dirks, took them hostage. Brickyard foreman Powell tried to run but he was knocked down by a piece of pipe, and then the four guards were used as a shield to approach the nearest guard tower. The prisoners demanded that the two tower guards throw down their guns, and they complied. Now armed, the prisoners forced the four hostages into an automobile parked nearby. Fourteen prisoners climbed in or on the car, and they started driving toward the gate. Other guards then opened fire on the automobile. Powell died of a bullet wound to his head, Cope was wounded in his neck, Gossett was wounded in his stomach, Conn was unharmed, and ten convicts were wounded. Six other convicts were captured with the wounded convicts but eight escaped, and were all captured within weeks. Convicts Roy McGee serving fifteen years for armed robbery, Bill Anderson serving twenty-seven years for armed robbery, and twenty-five-year-old Claude Beavers were among the twenty-four convicts involved in the escape.

On the morning of August 10, 1941, forty-six-year-old Warden Jess Dunn was escorting J. H. Fentriss, an Oklahoma City electrical engineer, through the prison while he designed a new communications system. At 10:45 A.M. thirty-six-year-old McGee and thirty-five-year-old Anderson, with thirty-four-year-old Hiram Prather, serving a life sentence, and Beavers, now serving a life term for Powell's death, hid behind a flight of stairs leading into the hospital and captured Dunn and Fentriss as Dunn went to the hospital to answer a phone call. They used prison-made dirks to march their hostages to the east tower and then ordered the guards to throw down their weapons and open the gate, and they complied. Now armed, the four convicts commandeered an automobile parked in the prison yard. Beavers was driving and the two hostages were put in the front seat while the other three convicts, with the guns, got into the rear seat, and they drove out of the prison.

Meanwhile forty-five-year-old Deputy William E. Alexander, who had been a guard at the prison under Dunn, responded to the call for assistance, and he took along fifty-one-year-old off-duty Deputy William A. "Tab" Ford. Alexander turned his car when three blocks north of the prison so it would choke off the highway, and this forced the fleeing convicts to drive down a dead-end street. The deputies cornered them, and the convicts demanded that Alexander move his police vehicle and let them pass, but Alexander insisted that they would have to let Dunn and Fentriss go free and surrender. Before Alexander left his prison employment he had discussed just such a situation with Dunn, and the warden had told him that if he were taken hostage he might be forced to tell the officers to let them pass or ask them to hold their fire, but they were to ignore his order "and even if I tell you not to shoot, you shoot," and Alexander was determined to follow those instructions. One of the convicts suddenly fired a rifle shot hitting Ford in the head, and he died several hours later. When the shooting began Prather, who had a pistol, shot Dunn in the back of the head twice, killing him, which forced Alexander to open fire on the car.

During the first gun battle Beavers was shot to death, but then McGee managed to drive around the police car, and with Alexander in pursuit they drove a half mile before they became engaged in a second gun battle with Alexander. McGee was killed while Anderson was badly wounded and died two days later, and Prather was wounded and had to surrender. Alexander and Fentriss were unscathed in the hail of bullets.

Prather was returned to prison, and in the fall he was tried in the Pittsburg County district court for Dunn's murder; on October 8 the jurors convicted him of first-degree murder after eight hours ten minutes of deliberations and recommended the death penalty. Prather was then returned to the prison and placed in solitary confinement, but returned to court so Judge R. W. Higgins could formally sentence him to death in the electric chair, as required by Oklahoma law. His court-appointed attorney then filed an appeal which stayed the execution, but on April 29, 1943, the court of criminal appeals affirmed the judgment and sentence of the district court, and the justices set Prather's execution date for July 14, 1943. On July 13 the state Board of Pardons and Paroles reviewed the case and refused to grant clemency, Governor Robert S. Kerr declined to interfere, and nothing further would arise to delay the proceedings.

A small death house had been constructed in the prison yard and the chair had been moved in preparation for the next execution. On Wednesday night, after all the prisoners were asleep, guards went to Prather's cell and took him through the prison yard to the new death house where they placed him in a special cell under close watch, only a dozen steps from the electric chair. In the morning, after breakfast, the barber was summoned, and he shaved Prather's head and left leg. That afternoon the death warrant was read by Warden Fred Hunt, and then the condemned man dressed in his prison-made pocket-less burial suit. After 11:00 P.M. the seventy witnesses were ushered through the prison yard to the death house, and they took their places in the viewing area. At midnight the cell door was swung open and the condemned man walked a dozen steps into the chamber. As he entered he shook hands with Warden Hunt, who asked if he had any last words, and he replied, "No, you've got the best hand."

Prather took his seat in the oak chair where his chest and waist, wrists and arms, and ankles were bound with leather straps, the copper helmet and leg band, lined with moistened sponges, were secured in place, and a black leather mask was tied over his eyes and forehead and attached to the chair back. At 12:04 A.M. the executioner stepped to the control panel and flipped the switch that applied the electricity, set at the lower range of 600 to 2,300 volts, and then he turned a wheel until the intensity reached the maximum. As the intensity increased Prather's body strained against the straps, but relaxed when the electricity was turned off in less than a minute. A board of three doctors was in attendance, and they checked for vital signs and pronounced Prather dead at 12:09 A.M. Prison trusties removed the body from the chair and carried it down the whitewashed corridor to a storage room, and later the remains were delivered to a local funeral parlor to be prepared for burial in the prison cemetery, as no relatives had come forward.

Sources: *Brownsville Herald* (TX): October 8, 1941. *Joplin Globe* (MO): July 14, 1943. *Miami News-Record* (OK): July 12, 1941; October 8, 1941. *Morning Avalanche* (Lubbock, TX): April 30, 1943. *Ogden Standard-Examiner* (UT): August 11, 1941. *Oklahoman* (Oklahoma City): July 14, 1943.

Bever, Harry R.
September 26, 1944

Twenty-six-year-old Harry Ralph Bever was assigned to a parachute battalion at Fort Benning, Georgia, in August 1942, and when he deserted he made his way to Cincinnati, Ohio. There is no record of the crimes he may have committed to support himself while en route to Ohio but on October 31, 1942, he robbed a Cincinnati bank and fled to Excelsior Springs, Missouri. He kidnapped taxicab driver Lawrence W. King and forced him to drive to Kansas City, Kansas, where he was captured and King was rescued unharmed. Bever was returned to the Hamilton County jail in Ohio to be tried for bank robbery, but on February 12, 1943, he escaped with three other prisoners. Bever then fled to Amarillo, Texas, where he found work as a cook in the Lamar Café on Polk Street. On the afternoon of July 22, 1943, his employer, Clinton C. Wood, was shot to death in the driveway of his home, and the police detained anyone who might have played a role in the murder.

One of those arrested was Bever, and when he arrived at the police station he pointed to a poster on the bulletin board and said, "That's what I'm wanted for," meaning the bank robbery and escape. The poster displayed his photograph and fingerprints so it was not long before he was positively identified as Bever, and it was also determined he was a deserter. A strong case was made against him for the murder of Wood, but it was decided to let the military try him for "murder committed during time of war," and he was taken to Fort Sill, Oklahoma, and lodged in the guard house. On October 13, after three days of testimony, the eleven-man court-martial board deliberated for seven hours before returning a verdict of guilty of murder and desertion, and Bever was sentenced to hang. The case was sent to the Eighth Service Command for review, which approved the judgment and sentence and forwarded the case to the Adjutant General's office for review, and then the case was sent to President Franklin D. Roosevelt. The president ordered the execution to proceed and set the date for the hanging at September 26, 1944.

The gallows was built within an empty warehouse at Fort Sill, and early on the final morning Bever was escorted to the scaffold by a guard detachment. He took his place on the trapdoor where his wrists and arms, knees and ankles were bound, the noose was adjusted, and the black hood was pulled over his head. There is no record of the details of the hanging but it was customary to have the fort's chaplain and doctor present, and after the chaplain performed his duties, the trap was sprung and the doctor monitored vital signs until Bever's heart ceased to beat, he was pronounced dead, and the remains were lowered into a coffin. Bever would have been buried in the fort cemetery later that day.

Sources: *Galveston News* (TX): July 24, 1943. *Journal-Times* (Racine, WI): July 25, 1943. *Morning Avalanche* (Lubbock, TX): October 14, 1943. *News-Globe* (Amarillo, TX): July 25, 1943. *News-Herald* (Hutchinson, KS): September 26, 1944. *Sun-News* (Las Cruces, NM): September 26, 1944.

Johnson, Amon
March 23, 1945

On Monday morning, April 3, 1944, twenty-nine-year-old Amon Johnson, a black man, went to the farm of forty-seven-year-old Roy Schat in Cleveland County, Oklahoma. They agreed that Johnson would help load cottonseed meal and cotton hulls onto Schat's truck, and in payment the farmer would drive Johnson to the Cleveland and Oklahoma County line where he could buy whiskey. After the truck was loaded, according to Johnson, the two men began arguing, and Schat went for his knife, but Johnson said, "I got mine and beat him to the draw and cut him with my knife."

Schat bled to death, and Johnson stole his truck and drove to McLeod in Lincoln County near the Gorski farm. He saw several cows grazing and decided to unload the meal and hulls, steal the livestock, and load them onto Schat's truck. Johnson unloaded the truck and was busy loading the cows when thirty-eight-year-old Victoria Gorski, with her three-year-old daughter Martha, confronted him. She asked him what he was doing, and Johnson said he had made a trade with her husband and showed her the meal and hulls in the barn. Gorski said, "No, I wouldn't part with my cows ... it is not right for any man to make a trade without his wife knowing of it." They started arguing, and Johnson claimed Gorski hit him on the hand with a board, and he responded by picking up a one and one-half-foot board from a neck yoke and striking her on the head. Martha then began hitting him in the legs, and he hit both mother and daughter. Gorski then threatened to tell her husband and left, but quickly returned and they started fighting again so Johnson slapped the little girl knocking her to the ground, and then hit her mother with the board again. When Gorski continued to fight Johnson pulled out his knife with a razor-sharp five-inch blade and slashed her throat, and when she collapsed helpless he reached down and slashed Martha's throat. Mother and daughter quickly bled to death, and Johnson left them lying where they fell while he finished loading the cows, drove them into Oklahoma City, and sold them to the American Commission Company.

He abandoned the truck near the South Canadian River, and late Monday night he returned to his home in Oklahoma City. He argued with his common-law wife, Eloise Chandler-Amon, when she saw his blood-soaked clothing, so early on Tuesday morning he built a fire in his yard and burned his bloody clothing, and was seen by his neighbors. He then told Eloise he was going to Vernon, Oklahoma, for Easter, but instead he fled into the thickets along the Northern Canadian River and hid. When the murders were discovered Johnson's wife and her neighbors told of Johnson's bloody clothing, and a large posse was formed from lawmen and Navy men drawn from a nearby base. On Friday they discovered Johnson and pursued him along the river bank until several shots were fired over his head, and he surrendered.

The prisoner was taken to Shawnee in Lincoln County and charged with the Gorski murders. He confessed to the murders, then denied them, and finally confessed again. He pled not guilty, and his trial began in Chandler, Oklahoma, in mid–April. He was convicted of two counts of first-degree murder on April 21, and five days later he was sentenced to die in the electric chair. The case was appealed; the justices affirmed the judgment and sentence within months, and the date for the execution was set for March 23, 1945. Amon's brother Alvin, during the last days, personally pled with Governor Robert S. Kerr to spare his brother's life, but the governor could find no valid reason to intervene.

Shortly before the execution day Johnson was moved from his death row cell to a cell in the small death house in the prison yard, and after breakfast the barber was summoned and shaved Johnson's head and left leg. That afternoon the death warrant was read by the warden, and after supper Johnson dressed in his prison-made pocket-less burial suit. After 11:00 P.M. a small number of witnesses were ushered through the prison yard to the death house, and they took their places in the viewing area. At midnight Johnson's cell door was swung open and the condemned man walked a dozen steps into the chamber. As he entered he was asked if he had any last words, but there is no record of a statement.

He took his seat in the oak chair where his chest and waist, wrists and arms, and ankles were bound with leather straps, the copper helmet and leg band, lined with moistened sponges, were secured in place, and a black leather mask was tied over his eyes and forehead and attached to the chair back. At 12:05 A.M. the executioner stepped to the control panel and flipped the switch that applied the electricity, set at the lower range of 600 to 2,300 volts, and then he turned a wheel until the intensity reached the maximum. As the intensity increased Johnson's body strained against the straps, but relaxed when the electricity was turned off in less than a minute. The doctor in attendance checked for vital signs and pronounced him dead at 12:09 A.M. Prison trusties then removed the body from the chair, and later the remains were delivered to a local funeral parlor to be prepared for burial.

Sources: *Lawton Constitution* (OK): March 23, 1945. *Maryville Forum* (MO): April 8, 1944. *Miami News-Record* (OK): April 10, 1944. *Syracuse Herald-Journal* (NY): April 8, 1944.

Davis, Lee R.
August 14, 1945

Twenty-year-old Private Lee R. Davis, assigned to Company D of the 1324th engineer general service regiment, was "absent without leave"

(AWOL) from Camp Claiborne, Louisiana, between August 2 and September 4, 1944. He returned to the camp on September 4 but left again the following day when he learned he was a wanted man, and he remained AWOL until arrested on September 23. There had been a manhunt for Davis after he broke into the house of Mrs. Gertrude C. Mayoux four miles from camp on August 8 and raped her. Then on August 14 he broke into the home of Mrs. Rose Chevalier, an elderly woman, and attempted to rape her. After he was arrested he was lodged in the guardhouse and faced a court-martial at Camp Claiborne in late October. On October 24 Davis was convicted of rape and attempted rape and sentenced to hang. The prisoner was taken to Fort Sill, Oklahoma, and lodged in the guardhouse while his case was being reviewed. The judgment and sentence were affirmed by the general staff and by the secretary of war before being forwarded to President Harry S Truman, who ordered the execution to proceed and set the date for August 14, 1945.

The gallows, the same on which Harry R. Bever was hanged on September 26, 1944, was assembled in a converted warehouse, and on the morning of August 14, 1945 Davis was taken from his cell and marched under escort to the scaffold. Dressed in his drab military uniform without insignia he climbed the stairs and took his place on the trapdoor, where his wrists and arms, knees and ankles were bound and the noose was adjusted. There is no record of a statement so, after the black hood was pulled over his head and the fort's chaplain concluded his duties, the trap was sprung. An army doctor was in attendance and monitored vital signs until Davis' heart ceased to beat, and then Davis was pronounced dead. The body was cut down, deposited into a coffin, and buried in the Fort Sill cemetery at the request of his mother, Georgia M. Jackson of Saginaw, Michigan.

Sources: *Ada Evening News* (OK): August 14, 1945. *Herald-Post* (El Paso, TX): August 14, 1945. *Lawton Constitution* (OK): August 14, 1945.

Norman, Cliff T.
November 9, 1945

On April 7, 1944, twenty-nine-year-old Cliff Thomas Norman raped a white waitress at Davis, Oklahoma, while her husband was serving overseas. He tied a rag around her neck and strangled her until she was too weak to resist, then raped her. Concerned that she would identify him he stuck a knife in her throat and left it sticking there, but when she still showed signs of life he shoved the barrel of his pistol in her mouth and shot away part of her jaw. She was still alive, but he was certain she would bleed to death, so he went through her belongings and took $46 before he fled. Her mutilated body was discovered, she was rushed to the hospital, and though she never regained the ability to talk she was able to write brief notes describing in detail the attack and her attacker. It took several months for her to recover sufficiently to be released from the hospital, in time to testify against the defendant at his trial.

Based upon the information provided by the victim Norman was soon arrested and lodged in the jail at Sulphur, but when there was talk of lynching he was taken to the state prison at McAlester. He was returned to Murray County in time for his arraignment, and he pled not guilty, but after consulting with John Carruthers, his court-appointed attorney, he changed his plea to guilty. On June 22 Murray County Judge J. I. Goins sentenced Norman to die in the electric chair. His attorney then filed an appeal, and over the next seventeen months the condemned man was granted three stays of execution: first by the court of criminal appeals, which affirmed the sentence in mid–1945; and twice by the state Board of Pardons and Paroles, which both times denied him clemency, the last time on November 2, just a week before his execution date. Governor Robert S. Kerr, though encouraged by the National Association for the Advancement of Colored People (NAACP), declined to intervene.

During his time on death row Norman was attended by the Rev. M. M. Williams, and he asked the clergyman to send his thanks to the NAACP for their efforts to have his sentence commuted. Shortly before the execution day Norman was moved from his death row cell to a cell in the small death house in the prison yard. The barber was summoned, and he shaved Norman's head and left leg. On Thursday afternoon the death warrant was read by the warden, and after supper the prisoner dressed in his prison-made pocket-less burial suit. After 11:00 P.M. a small number of witnesses were ushered through the prison yard to the death house, and they took their places in the viewing area. Before midnight the prisoner's cell door was swung open and the condemned man walked a dozen steps into the chamber. As he entered he was asked if he had any last words and he replied, "No Sir! I have nothing to say."

He took his seat in the oak chair where his chest and waist, wrists and arms, and ankles were bound with leather straps, the copper helmet and leg band, lined with moistened sponges, were secured in place, and a black leather mask was tied over his eyes and forehead and attached to the chair back. At 12:03 A.M. executioner Rich Owen stepped to the control panel and flipped the switch that applied the electricity, set at the lower range of 600 to 2,300 volts, and then he turned a wheel until the intensity reached the maximum. As the intensity increased Norman's body strained against the straps, but relaxed when the electricity was turned off in less than a minute. Dr. A. R. Strough then checked for vital signs and pronounced Norman dead at 12:08 A.M. Prison trusties then removed the body from the chair, and later the remains were delivered to a local funeral parlor to be prepared for burial.

Sources: *Miami News-Record* (OK): November 9, 1945. *Neosho Democrat* (MO): November 8, 1945.

Bingham, Alfred C.
May 31, 1946

Thirty-nine-year-old Alfred Clarence Bingham had been estranged from his thirty-year-old wife Mary for some time, but he kept a close watch on her. On August 8, 1943, Bingham's ten-year-old son Jess saw his father lurking in the front yard of their Tulsa, Oklahoma, home and later said, "I saw daddy standing under a tree in front of mother's house. He had a long bladed [pocket] knife in his hand. I asked him if he was going to hurt mother. He said if he saw her with a man he would hurt her. Then mother came home [alone] and daddy jumped up quick. He looked glary. Daddy jumped toward mother with the knife in his hand. She screamed and he stepped back. Then he stuck the knife in her neck and she fell into the gutter. I grabbed daddy's shirt but he hit me in the chest and ran away." Mary Bingham quickly bled to death, and Bingham was quickly tracked down, arrested, and charged with his wife's murder, and he said, "I must have been dirty drunk."

He pled insanity at his arraignment and at his trial, and when Jess, the principal witness against his father, entered the courtroom in early October he ran to his father and gave him a hug. Jess then took the stand and gave the same testimony as he had previously given to the police. On October 8, 1943, Bingham was convicted of first-degree murder and Judge S. J. Clendinning set October 20 as the date for sentencing; Bingham was sentenced to die in the electric chair. His attorney filed an appeal, and the case was reviewed for more than two years before the court of criminal appeals affirmed the judgment and sentence of the district court. The justices set the date of execution at May 10, 1946. In anticipation of the execution Bingham had a sanity hearing on April 24 and the jurors found him sane, but another request was filed with the Pardons Board pleading for a sanity hearing. On May 2 the members recommended a hearing be held on May 23, and on May 8 the board granted a stay of execution to Friday, May 31. Bingham was examined by experts and found sane, and on May 27 the request that he be sent to the insane asylum, in lieu of execution, was denied. His last hope for relief was a petition pleading for a commutation of sentence, but Governor Robert S. Kerr declined to intervene.

Bingham was moved from his death row cell to a cell in the small death house in the prison yard where the barber was summoned, and he shaved the prisoner's head and left leg. On Thursday afternoon the death warrant was read by Warden R. B. Conner, and after supper the prisoner dressed in his prison-made pocket-less burial suit. At 11:00 P.M. a small number of witnesses were ushered through the prison yard into the death house, and they took their places in the viewing area. Just after midnight the prisoner's cell door was swung open and the condemned man walked a dozen steps into the chamber. As he entered he was asked if he had any last words, and he replied, "I want you folks to look at a guilty sinner," and then over the next four and one-half minutes he asked for God's forgiveness, blamed the murder on his drinking habits, and praised the prison staff for their kind treatment. He shook hands with everyone in the chamber and then began to pray, but halfway through he began sobbing uncontrollably.

He then took his seat in the oak chair where his chest and waist, wrists and arms, and ankles were bound with leather straps, the copper helmet and leg band, lined with moistened sponges, were secured in place, and a black leather mask was tied over his eyes and forehead and attached to the chair back. At 12:09 A.M. the executioner stepped to the control panel and flipped the switch that applied the electricity, set at the lower range of 600 to 2,300 volts, and then he turned a wheel until the intensity reached the maximum. As the intensity increased Bingham's body strained against the straps, but relaxed when the electricity was turned off in thirty-eight seconds. The doctor in attendance then checked for vital signs and pronounced Bingham dead at 12:11 A.M. Prison trusties removed the body from the chair, and later the remains were delivered to a local funeral parlor to be prepared for burial.

Sources: *Ada Evening News* (OK): May 14, 1946; May 31, 1946. *Joplin Globe* (MO): October 9, 1943. *Miami News-Record* (OK): May 31, 1945. *Sheboygan Press* (WI): October 9, 1943.

Johnson, Mose
November 1, 1946

In 1935 Mose Johnson, a black man, was sent to prison for six months for stealing chickens. After he was released he continued to commit increasingly serious crimes until he killed a man, and in 1943 he was serving a sentence of seven years for manslaughter. On December 13, 1943, twenty-eight-year-old Johnson and thirty-one-year-old Stanley Steen, a five-term convict serving fifty years for manslaughter, ganged up on fellow convict L. C. Smalley and robbed him of $40 and his watch. Smalley reported the theft and named the robbers; Chief Sergeant of the Guard W. H. "Pat" Riley notified Warden R. B. Conner, and they went to the power plant to question the two suspects. As Riley questioned them Steen suddenly pulled out a prison-made knife with a fourteen-inch blade, and Johnson grabbed a heavy wrench. They brutally murdered Riley, but did not harm the warden. Before guards could detain them they ran to the prison canteen where Smalley worked, and they stabbed and beat him to death. A large force of guards then overpowered and disarmed the two murderers and lodged them in solitary confinement cells.

The Pittsburg County authorities were summoned, and they questioned the two men, then filed murder charges against them. Johnson obtained a severance of their trials, and Steen was tried first for killing Riley, his trial beginning on February 1 and concluding late February 3, 1944. At 12:30 A.M. the jurors returned a guilty verdict and recommended the death penalty. Johnson's trial for killing Riley followed but the jurors deadlocked during deliberations, so on February 23 Judge R.W. Higgins dismissed the jury and the prisoner was held over to be tried for killing Smalley. Meanwhile Steen was sentenced to die in the electric chair and he was delivered to the prison. Johnson was then tried and convicted of the first-degree murder of Smalley, and he was also sentenced to die in the electric chair. Nearly three years passed as Johnson's attorney used every manipulation of the legal system to save the life of his client, but finally all efforts failed when the U.S. Supreme Court refused to hear the case. Steen had been scheduled to die with Alfred Bingham on May 31, 1946, but on May 30, before being moved to the special cells, Steen used a rusty razor smuggled into his cell and cut his wrists. He was still alive when found but he died in the hospital hours later, leaving Johnson to die alone for the murders of Riley and Smalley. On October 28 the state Board of Pardons and Paroles denied clemency for Johnson, and nothing further would arise to delay the proceedings.

Early Thursday morning Johnson was moved from his death row cell to a special cell in the small death house in the prison yard, and a close death watch guard was placed over him to avoid suicide. At 4:00 A.M., as soon as Johnson was settled in his new surroundings, the barber was summoned, and he shaved the prisoner's head and left leg. That afternoon the death warrant was read by Deputy Warden Raymond Raines, and after supper the prisoner dressed in his prison-made pocket-less burial suit. After Johnson ate a hearty supper, his brother and sister-in-law were allowed a brief final visit, under a very close watch. At 11:00 P.M. a small number of witnesses were ushered through the prison yard into the death house, and they took their places in the viewing area. Just after midnight the prisoner's cell door was swung open and the condemned man walked a dozen steps into the chamber. As he entered he was asked if he had any last words and he replied, "I have no bad feelings and am prepared to go."

He shook hands with those in the chamber and then took his seat in the oak chair where his chest and waist, wrists and arms, and ankles were bound with leather straps, and the copper helmet and leg band, lined with moistened sponges, were secured in place. A black leather mask was then tied over his eyes and forehead and attached to the chair back. At 12:07 A.M. the executioner stepped to the control panel and flipped the switch that applied the electricity, set at the lower range of 600 to 2,300 volts, and then he turned a wheel until the intensity reached the maximum. As the intensity increased Johnson's body strained against the straps, but relaxed when the electricity was turned off in less than a minute. Doctor A. R. Strough then checked for vital signs and pronounced the prisoner dead at 12:08 A.M. Prison trusties removed the body from the chair, and later the remains were delivered to a local funeral parlor to be prepared for burial as arranged by his family.

Sources: *Ada Evening News* (OK): February 4, 1944; May 31, 1946; November 1, 1946. *Miami News-Record* (OK): October 31, 1946. *Joplin Globe* (MO): December 14, 1943.

Broyles, Harlan
January 30, 1947

Twenty-nine-year-old Harlan Broyles escaped from the Missouri State Penitentiary and fled to Seminole in Seminole County, Oklahoma. At 5:00 P.M. on January 10, 1945, Broyles was at a theater at Fourth and Broadway when he tried to cash a forged check, so thirty-five-year-old Seminole County Deputy Sheriff Eric Nicholson was called. Nicholson, who was not armed, arrested Broyles and started walking him to the police station, when the prisoner suddenly pulled out a .32-caliber pistol and shot the deputy twice, once through the heart, killing him instantly.

Broyles fled to Waco, Texas, and on February 2 city police officer A. D. Tennison tried to arrest Broyles. A gun battle followed during which the officer was seriously wounded, and Broyles was slightly wounded in his shoulder and immediately arrested. The Waco authorities filed a charge of assault to murder but they agreed to extradite Broyles to Oklahoma to be tried first for Nicholson's murder.

Broyles was returned to Seminole County on February 7, arraigned, and held over for trial in May. After the case closed on May 23 the jurors deliberated one hour before finding Broyles guilty of first-degree murder, and they recommended the death penalty. On May 27 Broyles was sentenced to die in the electric chair on August 3. Governor Robert S. Kerr then granted several brief stays to allow Broyles' attorney to file an appeal, first to September 29, then to November 23, and finally to December 31, 1945. His attorney filed the appeal, and his execution was then stayed by the court of criminal appeals until the justices affirmed the judgment and sentence in late 1946 and set the date for execution for Thursday, January 30, 1947. Although his attorney tried every means to save his client's life nothing further would arise to delay the proceedings.

During his time on death row Broyles was visited by McAlester Rev. A. R. Vaughn, but the condemned man said, "I can't believe in God or Santa Claus." However, as the hour of his death neared, Broyles embraced the teachings of the Assembly of God Church. On Wednesday morning at an early hour he was handcuffed and moved from his death row cell to the special cell in the small death house in the prison yard. He had been bitter and surly for days and had assaulted several guards, but after he was settled in his new cell he resigned himself to his fate. When his elderly mother and sister visited for the last time on Wednesday afternoon he told his mother, "Mom, I'm saved, and I know now I will meet you some day in heaven. God knows I didn't kill that man. I have committed many crimes but murder is not one of them. I know nothing can stop them now. There is so much torture and persecution in this world, I probably will be better off." As his mother was leaving he shouted after her, "I am going. There is nothing can help me now. I'm going, but nobody wants to be falsely accused of a crime."

The barber was then summoned to shave the prisoner's head and left leg. During the late afternoon hours the death warrant was read by Warden Richard B. Conner, and after supper the prisoner dressed in his prison-made pocket-less burial suit. At 11:00 P.M. a small number of witnesses were ushered through the prison yard into the death house, and they took their places in the viewing area. Just after midnight the prisoner's cell door was swung open and the condemned man walked a dozen steps into the chamber. As he entered at 12:03 A.M. he was asked if he had any last words, and he replied, "I am innocent and pray for these men who have taken my life," and then he spoke for ten minutes. He took his seat in the oak chair where his chest and waist, wrists and arms, and ankles were bound with leather straps, the copper helmet and leg band, lined with moistened sponges, were secured in place, and a black leather mask was tied over his eyes and forehead and attached to the chair back. At 12:14 A.M. the executioner stepped to the control panel and flipped the switch that applied the electricity, set at the lower range of 600 to 2,300 volts, and then he turned a wheel until the intensity reached the maximum. As the intensity increased Broyles' body strained against the straps, but relaxed when the electricity was turned off in one minute. Doctor A. R. Strough then checked for vital signs and pronounced him dead at 12:19 A.M. Prison trusties removed the body from the chair, and later the remains were delivered to a local funeral parlor to be prepared for burial as arranged by his family.

Sources: *Ada Weekly News* (OK): January 30, 1947. *El Paso Herald-Post* (TX): January 30, 1947; *Indian Journal* (OK): January 30, 1947. *Miami News-Record* (OK): December 30, 1943; May 27, 1945. *Pampa News* (TX): February 5, 1945.

Grayson, Lewis
May 25, 1948

In 1945 twenty-eight-year-old Lewis Grayson, a black man, raped a young white girl at Muskogee in Muskogee County, Oklahoma, and he was quickly captured, tried, convicted, and sentenced to die in the electric chair. His attorneys filed a series of appeals and petitions which delayed the execution for three years, but after the court of criminal appeals affirmed the judgment and sentence of the lower court his date with the executioner was finally set for March 26, 1948. On February 25 the state Board of Pardons and Paroles, after a three-day hearing, denied clemency to Grayson. The following day Grayson's attorneys appealed to Governor Roy J. Turner, contending their client was insane, and the governor declared he was going to investigate the matter and granted a reprieve of Grayson's execution from March 26 to May 25. At the sanity hearing evidence indicated that there was insanity in the Grayson family, but when the prisoner had been examined he was found sane, and Governor Turner declined to interfere further. There was a last-minute flurry of appeals, but all were denied, and up to the last hours Grayson held out hope that either the governor or the courts would grant him judicial relief or a commutation of sentence.

Very early Tuesday morning Grayson was aroused from sleep, handcuffed, and moved from his death row cell to a cell in the small death house in the prison yard. After breakfast the barber was summoned, and he shaved the prisoner's head and left leg. During the afternoon he was told that the court had denied his final appeal, the death warrant was read by Warden Clarence P. Burford, and after supper the prisoner dressed in his prison-made pocket-less burial suit. Before 10:00 P.M. sixty-seven witnesses were ushered through the prison yard into the death house, and they took their places in the viewing area. At 10:30 the prisoner's cell door was swung open and the condemned man walked a dozen steps into the chamber. As he entered he was asked if he had any last words, and he replied, "I ask the Lord to forgive me for my sins. I love everyone. I didn't know until this afternoon what the court had done to me. I didn't know they were going to take my life." He then took his seat in the oak chair and turned to executioner M. E. "Big boy" Elliott, who was conducting his first execution since Rich Owen died several months earlier, and asked, "How long is this gonna to be?" but Elliott did not answer. The prisoner's chest and waist, wrists and arms, and ankles were bound with leather straps, the copper helmet and leg band lined with moistened sponges were secured in place, and a black leather mask was tied over his eyes and forehead and attached to the chair back. At 10:40 P.M. Elliott stepped to the control panel and flipped the switch that applied the electricity, set at the lower range of 600 to 2,300 volts, and then he turned a wheel until the intensity reached the maximum. As the intensity increased Grayson's body strained against the straps, but relaxed when the electricity was turned off in forty-five seconds. Dr. Richard A. Harkins of McAlester then checked for vital signs and pronounced Grayson dead at 10:45 P.M. Prison trusties removed the body from the chair, and later the remains were delivered to a local funeral parlor to be prepared for burial.

Sources: *Ada Evening News* (OK): May 26, 1948. *Hutchinson News-Herald* (KS): May 25, 1948. *Lawton Constitution* (OK): February 26, 1948; May 26, 1948. *Northwest Arkansas Times* (Fayetteville): May 25, 1948.

Gould, Ben
September 27, 1948

On Thursday evening, February 5, 1948, thirty-nine-year-old Ben Gould, a black man, went to the feed store in Atoka where fifty-seven-year-old Mary F. Lynn worked as a clerk. Lynn was alone when Gould entered, and he attacked the older woman, strangling and then beating her until she was helpless to resist, then he stabbed her to death with an ice pick. He rifled the cash drawer and took out a little more than $200 before he fled to his Atoka home. He was arrested at home two hours later, confessed to the killing, and showed the officers where he had hidden the money under a rock near his house. The prisoner was taken directly to the prison at McAlester to prevent any thought of lynching, but he was returned to Atoka in time for his arraignment on February 9. He pled guilty to murder for robbery, and on March 15 Judge Sam Sullivan sentenced him to die in the electric chair on May 23. Governor Roy J. Turner granted a sixty-day stay of execution to July 27 while he awaited an opinion from the court of criminal appeals to determine if Gould's constitutional rights had been violated, and on July 22 he extended the stay to September 27. Even though no appeal had been filed by Gould's attorney, the court of criminal appeals, on September 15, affirmed the sentence of the district court and found that his rights had been protected when he pled guilty. The justices left the date for Gould's execution at September 27, 1948, and Governor Turner declined to interfere further.

Early Tuesday morning, the day of execution, Gould was moved from his death row cell to a cell in the small death house in the prison yard. After breakfast the barber was summoned, and he shaved the prisoner's head and left leg. On Tuesday afternoon the death warrant was read by Warden Clarence P. Burford, and after supper the prisoner dressed in his prison-made pocket-less burial suit. Before 10:00 P.M. the small number of witnesses were ushered through the prison yard into the death house, and they took their places in the viewing area. At 10:30 P.M. the prisoner's cell door was swung open and the condemned man walked a dozen steps into the chamber. As he entered he was asked if he had any last words and he replied, "I'm glad to live to see this day. I have nothing against no one and I'm going to die in peace. The warden has been good to me and the inmates have been pretty decent. Anybody here who will pray for me, I'll accept the prayers."

He then took his seat in the oak chair where his chest and waist, wrists and arms, and ankles were bound with leather straps, the copper helmet and leg band, lined with moistened sponges, were secured in place, and a black leather mask was tied over his eyes and forehead and attached to the chair back. At 10:35 P.M. executioner M. E. Elliott stepped to the control panel and flipped the switch that applied the electricity, set at the lower range of 600 to 2,300 volts, and then he turned a wheel until it reached the maximum. As the intensity increased Gould's body strained against the straps, but relaxed when the electricity was turned off in forty-three seconds. The doctor in attendance then checked for vital signs and pronounced Gould dead at 12:09 P.M. Prison trusties removed the body from the chair, and later the remains were delivered to a local funeral home to be prepared for burial.

Sources: *Ada Evening News* (OK): February 9, 1948; September 27, 1948. *Lawton Constitution* (OK): July 22, 1948; September 16, 1948. *Miami News-Record* (OK): September 28, 1948.

Klettke, Max E.
January 4, 1951

In late October 1948 forty-five-year-old Carl E. Beach, a retired railroad worker, drove west from Corfu, New York, on his way to Miami, Arizona to visit his mother. He arrived in Indianapolis, Indiana, on November 1 and offered a ride to hitchhikers eighteen-year-old Harry Riskin and twenty-three-year-old ex-convict Max Eugene Klettke, who were on their way to Galveston, Texas, to work on a fishing boat. They drove west on Highway 66 with Riskin riding in the front passenger seat and Klettke in the rear seat, and the two hitchhikers conspired to kill Beach and steal his car. When they were twenty miles north of Oklahoma City, near Arcadia, Klettke pulled out a concealed .38-caliber pistol and fired at the back of Beach's head but the first shot missed and struck the windshield, and Beach cried out, "What was that?" He slowed the car, and then Klettke fired five more shots, four striking Beach in the back of the head, killing him instantly. Riskin grabbed the steering wheel and guided the car to the side of the road, where they took Beach out and went through his pockets for money, stealing $474, then threw his body in a ravine under a bridge. The body was discovered on Wednesday, November 3, and as soon as Beach was identified the search for his automobile began.

On November 4 the Fort Worth, Texas, police received a tip that two men were driving about town in an automobile with a blood-splattered interior, and they captured the two men as they parked in a downtown parking lot. They were lodged in jail, and the following day both prisoners confessed to murdering Beach and stealing his money but were surprised to learn that $900 in bonds was stored in his luggage in the trunk. They waived extradition, and after Klettke was lodged in the Oklahoma City jail he confessed again and in both cases signed the transcribed confessions.

Klettke's trial began on December 6. He took the stand, admitted that the murder weapon was his, and said that he had shot Beach. The following day, after sixty-five minutes deliberating, the jurors found him guilty of first-degree murder and recommended death, and he was sentenced to die in the electric chair. Riskin was tried the following week and convicted of first-degree murder, but because he did not fire the fatal bullets he was sentenced to serve a life term, and he was paroled in October 1970 with the stipulation that he continue to receive psychiatric care.

On December 15, 1948, Klettke arrived at the prison and was lodged in a death row cell to await the outcome of the appeal filed by attorney Willis Stark. It took nearly two years before the court of criminal appeals affirmed the judgment and sentence of the district court, and the justices set the date of execution for January 4, 1951. Klettke's attorney then filed an appeal with the state Board of Pardons and Paroles asking for a commutation of sentence, but on December 13 they denied clemency. Stark then asked Governor Roy J. Turner for a hearing on the issue of sanity; the governor had Klettke examined by three psychiatrists, and they reported, "he is sane (but) probably never could be a law-abiding citizen." On January 3 the governor denied clemency and declined to interfere further.

During his time on death row Klettke was attended by Father Bernard Collins, and the priest helped him brace up for the ordeal ahead. Early Thursday morning, before the other prisoners were awake, Klettke was handcuffed and moved from his death row cell to a cell in the small death house in the prison yard. After breakfast the barber was summoned, and he shaved the prisoner's head and left leg. That afternoon the death warrant was read by Warden Clarence P. Burford, and after supper the prisoner dressed in his prison-made pocketless burial suit. After 9:00 P.M. one hundred fifty witnesses were ushered through the prison yard into the death house, and they took their places behind the wire mesh screen separating the death chamber from the viewing area. Before 10:00 P.M. the prisoner was taken from his cell by two guards and blindfolded at his request, then guided into the chamber where he knelt and prayed with his priest.

He declined to speak to the witnesses and took his seat in the oak chair where his chest and waist, wrists and arms, and ankles were bound with leather straps. The copper helmet and leg band, lined with moistened sponges, were put in place but the helmet was not properly fitted so executioner M. E. Elliott readjusted it, and the blindfold slipped. As Klettke first saw the witnesses he whispered to Sergeant of the Guards Harlan Brown, "Mr. Brown, why couldn't you have hit me with this when I came in here?" The blindfold was then removed and a black leather mask was tied over his eyes and forehead and attached to the chair back. Elliott signaled Brown to step back, and at 10:03 P.M. the executioner, guard M. E. Elliott, flipped the switch that applied the electricity, set at the lower range of 600 to 2,300 volts. He turned a wheel until the intensity reached the maximum, and as the voltage increased Klettke's body strained against the straps but relaxed when the electricity was turned off in less than a minute. The team of doctors in attendance checked for vital signs and pronounced Klettke dead two minutes later, and prison trusties then removed the body from the chair. The remains were later delivered to a local funeral parlor to be prepared for burial.

Sources: *Abilene Reporter-News* (TX): November 5, 1948. *Ada Evening News* (OK): January 5, 1951. *Amarillo Globe* (TX): November 5, 1948. *Evening Journal* (Lubbock, TX): January 3, 1951. *Joplin Globe* (MO): December 8, 1948. *Lawton Constitution* (OK): October 19, 1970. *Messenger* (Canandaigua, NY): December 13, 1950. *Oklahoman* (Oklahoma City): January 5, 1951. *Record Eagle* (Traverse City, MI): January 3, 1951. *Syracuse Herald-American* (NY): December 31, 1950.

Hathcox, Jearell
July 27, 1951

On Wednesday, February 1, 1950, thirty-seven-year-old Jearell "Bud" Hathcox — eight times an ex-convict — thirty-two-year-old Clay Wallace Ward and thirty-one-year-old Lamon H. Barnett were driving around Oklahoma City and, according to Hathcox, were "looking for a certain spot" but got lost and headed onto a side road which led to the disposal plant. Hathcox said that sixty-eight-year-old night watchman Martin Lyle "Bert" Shaffer, a retired police officer, stepped in front of their car and ordered them out, and they all exited on the driver's side. Hathcox said that Shaffer approached him with his revolver drawn, "made nasty statements," and poked him in the forehead with the gun barrel. Hathcox then pulled a .32-caliber automatic pistol from his pocket and shot at Shaffer seven times, hitting him twice in the chest, once each in the thigh and wrist, and twice in the lower abdomen — killing him. Hathcox claimed that Shaffer managed to fire two shots in return with one bullet going wild and the other hitting Hathcox in the hand, but there was only one expended shell in Shaffer's gun.

Hathcox and Ward fled northwest toward Bethany but they were spotted two hours later, and after a three mile chase they were captured and lodged in the Oklahoma City jail. Barnett was soon captured; he joined the other two men in jail, and all three men were charged with murder. On February 2 they were arraigned and pled not guilty, even though Hathcox had admitted he fired the fatal shots. He claimed self-defense and said, "The old man drew a gun on me first. He jabbed me in the forehead with his pistol, and then I was shot in the gun battle with the night watchman." Hathcox said he was in the custom of carrying a gun because he was in the whiskey-selling business and often had large sums of money on his person.

Hathcox was tried for murder in Oklahoma City beginning on March 20, 1950, and the jurors, after only five hours deliberating, found him guilty of murder in the first-degree after rejecting his claim of self-defense and recommended the death penalty. Hathcox was sentenced to die in the electric chair before the end of the year but the judgment and sentence was appealed and quickly affirmed by the court of criminal appeals. Ward and Barnett were not tried on the murder charge. In late June 1951, as the date of execution neared, Governor Johnston Murray granted a thirty-day stay of execution to July 27, the state Board of Pardons and Paroles then met and denied clemency, and the governor declined to interfere further. On July 24 Hathcox's attorney filed a writ of habeas corpus with Judge W. A. Lackey but on Wednesday morning the judge denied it, and when told of the decision the condemned man said, "Where there is life there is hope," and, "It wasn't cold-blooded murder like many people have been led to believe." Early Thursday morning two ministers appeared before the Board of Pardons and Paroles to plead for a commutation of sentence, but the members refused to grant a stay or clemency. Hathcox's attorney then appealed to the Court of Criminal Appeals for a stay but it was denied late on July 26.

During Hathcox's time on death row he was visited by the Reverend Reed three times a week as the prison chaplain made his regular rounds of the men on death row, but Hathcox "held himself aloof from preachers and religion." For several days he was visited by Charles Rhoades of the *Ada Evening News*, and he related the details of many solved and unsolved crimes during lengthy interviews and related some details of his early life. As the hour of execution approached he persisted in his claim that he was innocent and had been framed by the police, that witnesses including Ward and Barnett had been tampered with, and that his "admission of the shooting" was a fabrication by one detective. Early Thursday morning, before the other prisoners were awake, the condemned man was taken from his death row cell, handcuffed, and moved to one of six special cells near the death chamber. He spent his last hours visiting with his mother, Irene Yarbrough, his brother John, his sister Mrs. Corene Thomas, and four ministers he had invited to see his execution. After his family left the barber was summoned, and he shaved Hathcox's head and left leg. Late in the afternoon the death warrant was read by Warden Jerome J. Waters, Jr., and after supper the prisoner dressed in his prison-made pocket-less burial suit. After 11:00 P.M. twenty-six witnesses were ushered into the death house, and they took their places behind the wire-mesh screen separating the death chamber from the viewing area.

At midnight the prisoner was taken from his cell by two guards and escorted into the chamber, arriving at 12:03 A.M. Warden Waters asked if he had any last words, and Hathcox again claimed that he was innocent and had been framed by Oklahoma City police officers. He took his seat in the oak chair where his chest and waist, wrists and arms, and ankles were bound with leather straps. The copper helmet and leg band, lined with moistened sponges, were secured in place, and a black leather mask was tied over his eyes and forehead and attached to the chair back. Executioner M. E. Elliott flipped the switch at 12:05 A.M., which applied the electricity set at the lower range of 600 to 2,300 volts, and Elliott turned a wheel until the intensity reached the maximum. As the voltage increased Hathcox's body strained against the straps but relaxed when the electricity was turned off in less than a minute. The doctor in attendance then checked for vital signs and pronounced Hathcox dead two minutes later, and prison trusties removed the body from the chair. Hathcox's family had gathered at the main prison gate, and after the execution was complete they claimed the body and had it delivered to a local funeral parlor, to be prepared for shipment to Oklahoma City for burial.

Sources: *Ada Evening News* (OK): July 22, 1951; July 24–27, 1951. *Ada Weekly News* (OK): February 2, 1950. *Fitchburg Sentinel* (MA): July 27, 1951. *Long Beach Press-Telegram* (CA): February 3, 1950.

Mott, Melburn J.
September 20, 1951

The Mott family, living at Sand Springs near Tulsa, Oklahoma, had been having in-law troubles for some time when, on March 8, 1949, thirty-two-year-old Melburn Joseph Mott arrived home late and found the front door locked. His twenty eight-year-old wife Loretta said, "I wouldn't let him in and locked the door. Then he started kicking the door in, and I grabbed as many of the children as I could and ran out the back door." Loretta had taken their eight-year-old twin daughters and five-year-old daughter Melburn Delois, but had left behind their ten-year-old son Charles and six-year-old daughter Mary Frances asleep in the same bed. As soon as Mott was inside the house he took a butcher knife and grabbed Mary Frances, who did not wake up during the commotion, and he cut her throat. He then grabbed Charles but his son cried out, "Daddy, Daddy, don't do it," and struggled to keep the blankets pulled up, so he let the boy go, threw the knife behind the divan, and fled.

Mary Frances had died instantly, and the police were called. Sergeant Frank Parker and deputies Ira Slankard and Joe Edwards gathered details while Sheriff George H. Blaine organized a manhunt, and by morning Mott was found along the highway west of Sand Springs and was captured without resistance. Once he was behind bars Mott confessed to killing his daughter and he was charged with her murder, but at his arraignment on March 9 he pled not guilty "by reason of intoxication" as he claimed to have consumed twenty beers and narcotics during the day. His trial began on April 26 and was given to the jury the following evening, and the jurors found him guilty of first-degree murder and recommended the death penalty. Mott was sentenced to die in the electric chair but his attorney filed an appeal which stayed the execution for more than a year. Finally the court of criminal appeals affirmed the judgment and sentence, and Mott's date with the executioner was set for September 21, 1951. There followed a flurry of appeals, psychiatric examinations and sanity hearings, and petitions praying for clemency, but all efforts failed.

During Mott's time on death row he was attended by a Baptist reverend, and six weeks before the date set for his execution he was baptized. He persisted in asking to see his children, but his wife refused and said, "He didn't need to worry. I've been taking care of them for years. I'll see that they are taken care of," and added, "Let him die. He should die. I hate him for what he did." Early Wednesday morning, before the other prisoners were awake, the condemned man was taken from his death row cell, handcuffed, and moved to one of six special cells near the death chamber. He spent his last hours visiting with his mother, sister and brothers, and with five ministers he had invited to witness his execution. After his family left the barber was summoned, and he shaved Mott's head and left leg. Late in the afternoon the death warrant was read by Warden Jerome J. Waters, Jr., and after supper the prisoner dressed in his prison-made pocket-less burial suit. After 11:00 P.M. thirty witnesses were ushered into the death house, and they took their places behind the wire-mesh screen separating the death chamber from the viewing area. At midnight the prisoner was taken from his cell by two guards and escorted into the chamber where Warden Waters asked if he had any last words. Mott said, "I know you're a man. I want to ask you to see that my children are taken care of. I've asked you this because you are a man of your word." The warden then promised he would look into the matter.

Mott took his seat in the oak chair where his chest and waist, wrists and arms, and ankles were bound with leather straps. The copper helmet and leg band, lined with moistened sponges, were secured in place, and a black leather mask was tied over his eyes and forehead and attached to the chair back. Executioner M. E. Elliott flipped the switch at 12:04 A.M., which applied electricity set at the lower range of 600 to 2,300 volts, and Elliott turned a wheel until the intensity reached the maximum. As the voltage increased Mott's body strained against the straps but relaxed when the electricity was turned off in less than a minute. The doctor in attendance then checked for vital signs and pronounced Mott dead two minutes later, and prison trusties removed the body from the chair. Mott's family had gathered at the main prison gate, and after the execution was completed they claimed the body and had it delivered to a local funeral parlor to be prepared for shipment to Leflore County for burial.

Mrs. Mott and two of her children stayed up late to be certain the execution was completed. She was asked about attending the funeral, and she said that she was concerned that Mott's family "will want the kids to come to the funeral. I'm not going, but I'll let them make up their own minds."

Sources: *Ada Evening News* (OK): September 20, 1951. *Charleston Gazette* (SC): May 10, 1949. *Joplin Globe* (MO): April 27, 1949; September 20, 1951. *Journal* (Salinas, KS): September 20, 1951. *Press-Telegram* (Long Beach, CA): March 10, 1949.

Dewolf, Carl A.
November 17, 1953

On Friday evening, August 30, 1946, a man robbed a grocery store and stole a car. He was spotted by Officers Sandy Hedrick and M. T. Stillwell and, with Hedrick driving, they gave chase through the eastside streets of Tulsa, Oklahoma. After five minutes Traffic Officer Harold Harding tried to flag down the car but he was met with a fusillade of gunshots from a .45-caliber pistol, and he was wounded in his knee; the car continued to flee at a high rate of speed. Stillwell fired numerous shots at the car, which caused the driver to crash into a curb, but the robber jumped out and ran down an alley. Stillwell shot at the fleeing robber and thought one bullet struck him in the shoulder, but the fugitive dodged behind a garage, ran through the backyard of P. R. Erckenbrach while brandishing two pistols to keep the family at bay, jumped a fence, and stole seventeen-year-old Gayle Moreland's coupe.

Twenty-five-year-old detective Jerry St. Clair and Officer Elmer Strotman then took up the chase and exchanged shots in a running gun battle until they reached the corner of First Street and Harvard Avenue, where the robber fired several shots at the police scout car, and one bullet penetrated the windshield, striking St. Clair above the right eye. The robber continued to flee in Moreland's stolen coupe with other police cars following, and the entire chase lasted a half hour. He drove onto the campus of the University of Tulsa and abandoned the coupe, then was seen boarding a bus headed downtown. All buses were halted and searched but the fugitive was not aboard and the trail was lost. Roadblocks were set up on all roads leaving Tulsa but the robber was not found. St. Clair had been rushed to St. John's hospital by Strotman, where he lingered for three days before dying on September 2.

On September 12, 1946, ten days after St. Clair died, Detectives Sylvester R. "Vess" Cormack and Ben Johnston tried to arrest twenty-three-year-old Victor Lloyd Everhart and seventeen-year-old James O. Neely for questioning in the St. Clair murder, in a hit-and-run manslaughter in Vincennes, Indiana, and in the murder of a night watchman in Seneca, Missouri, on September 11. When Everhart and Neely were approached on Tulsa's Frisco Avenue they immediately drew their pistols, shot Cormack to death and wounded Johnston in his chest, damaging his heart, but he was rushed to the hospital and survived. Neely, who was wounded, was quickly captured, lodged in the Tulsa jail, and charged with Cormack's murder. Everhart was quickly tracked to Idaho, arrested, and returned to Tulsa.

On January 3, 1947, Johnston suffered a massive heart attack resulting from the severe damage caused by the bullet wound, he died, and Everhart and Neely were then charged with his murder, as well. On February 2 Everhart, Neely and four other prisoners broke out of the Tulsa jail. Everhart jumped into the back seat of a taxi and at gunpoint captured twenty-nine-year-old cab driver Lester P. Hughes and his twenty-three-year-old wife Lois and told them, "I might as well tell you who I am — I'm Everhart. Speed her up to 50 and keep driving." Just before noon they reached the intersection of State Highway 33 and U.S. Highway 69 near Chouteau, ran a road block, and were pursued. After a mile a tire blew on the taxi, and when Mrs. Hughes got out Everhart grabbed her to use as a shield, but she broke free and ran. Everhart then tried to use the cab driver as a shield but he pushed Everhart away, and officers opened up with sawed-off shotguns and pistols, the fugitive was riddled with bullets and buckshot, and he died instantly.

Neely had been captured soon after the jailbreak and had been returned to his cell, where he confessed to the various crimes committed while he traveled with Everhart, pled guilty to the murder of Cormack, but denied any knowledge of the murder of St. Clair. Everhart's alibi that he was recuperating from a broken collarbone in an Indiana hospital proved true, so he could not have shot St. Clair, and the case went cold again. Judge Eben L. Taylor, on February 21, sentenced Neely to serve a life term in the Oklahoma state prison for Cormack's murder.

In mid–1949 thirty-three-year-old Carl Austin Dewolf tried to rob a liquor store in California, and during a shootout he was badly wounded and captured. Ballistics testing proved that his pistol was the same used to kill Detective St. Clair; he was extradited to Tulsa, Oklahoma, and charged with murder. He pled not guilty at his arraignment. His trial began in late September, and he testified that the gun belonged to Everhart. He claimed he received the murder weapon in a trunk in late September, but prosecution witnesses identified him as the person fleeing from police when St. Clair was murdered. The case went to the jurors on October 1, and after twenty-six minutes in deliberations they found him guilty of first-degree murder and recommended the death penalty. Dewolf was immediately sentenced to die in the electric chair on November 17, 1949, and he was delivered to a death row prison cell on October 5.

Dewolf's attorney filed an appeal which stayed the execution, and over the next four years Governor Johnston Murray granted fifteen stays of executions: one for an investigation by the state legislature; two hearings before the state court of criminal appeals; two hearings before the U.S. Supreme Court; three petitions to the state Board of Pardons and Paroles; and several other motions, appeals, and petitions. A week before the execution date of Tuesday, November 17, 1953, Governor Murray went to McAlester and spoke with Dewolf for nearly two hours, but afterward said, "The situation is status quo." On the day before the execution the Board of Pardons and Paroles heard a third appeal, and Governor Murray said he would grant another stay if one member of the board advised it, but the five members voted unanimously to deny relief.

During his time on death row Dewolf embraced religion and told prison chaplain the Rev. Marcus W. Prather that if his life was spared he wanted to become a minister and dedicate his life to helping young men. He was also attended by the Rev. F. C. Conley who he told, "I'll be in heaven before my heels get cool." On Sunday Dewolf was visited by his brother Elwin, Elwin's wife, and a cousin, and then he was interviewed by representatives from a radio and a television station and "advised all young people to believe in God and join a church." Early Tuesday morning, before the other prisoners were awake, the condemned man was handcuffed, taken from his death row cell, and moved to one of six special cells near the death chamber. The barber was then summoned, and he shaved Dewolf's head and left leg. Before noon the condemned man asked to be baptized and he was taken to the prison chapel for the ceremony. Late in the afternoon the death warrant was read by Assistant Warden H. C. McLeod, standing in for Warden Waters, and after supper the prisoner visited with his brother. After Elwin left Dewolf dressed in his prison-made pocket-less burial suit and then asked to be alone to pen a few personal notes. After 11:00 P.M. thirty-five witnesses were ushered into the death house, and they took their places behind the wire-mesh screen separating the death chamber from the viewing area.

At midnight the prisoner was taken from his cell by two guards and escorted into the chamber, where Assistant Warden McLeod asked him if he had any last words. Dewolf shouted, over the hum of the dynamo, "I never seen Jerry St. Clair. How could I kill a man I've never seen?" He then gestured that the hum was too loud to continue and took his seat in the oak chair. His chest and waist, wrists and arms, and ankles were bound with leather straps, the copper helmet and leg band lined with moistened sponges were secured in place, and a black leather mask was tied over his eyes and forehead and attached to the chair back. Executioner M. E. Elliott stepped to the control panel and flipped the switch that applied the electricity, set at the lower range of 600 to 2,300 volts, and Elliott turned a wheel until the intensity reached the maximum. As the voltage increased Dewolf's body strained against the straps but relaxed when the electricity was turned off in less than a minute. The doctor in attendance then checked for vital signs and pronounced Dewolf dead at 12:14 A.M. Prison trusties removed the body from the chair. Later Dewolf's family claimed the body and had it delivered to a local funeral parlor to be prepared for burial.

Sources: *Ada Evening News* (OK): November 17, 1953. *Atchison Globe* (KS): February 3, 1947. *Baytown Sun* (TX): November 16, 1953. *Corpus Christi Times* (TX): November 17, 1953. *Emporia Gazette* (KS): August 31, 1946. *Miami News-Record* (OK): February 12, 1947; February 21, 1947; September 30, 1949. *Nevada State Journal* (Reno): October 2, 1949. *Reno Evening Gazette* (NV): August 31, 1946. *San Antonio Express* (TX): February 3, 1947.

Fairris, Hurbie F., Jr.
January 18, 1956

During the first half of 1954 there had been a rash of grocery store robberies in Oklahoma City, and on one occasion two market employees were kidnapped but later released unharmed. On Wednesday, July 14, twenty-year-old Hurbie Franklin "Ducky" Fairris, Jr., and nineteen-year-old James Edward Skinner were arrested for second-degree burglary in connection with the robbery of a drugstore, but there was no evidence to suggest they were the supermarket bandits, and they were released on $2,000 bail. On Friday, July 16, Fairris and Skinner kidnapped fifty-three-year-old Amos W. Truman, assistant manager of a supermarket. They tried to force him to give them the combination to the store's safe but he did not have it, so they forced him to drive the very short distance to bookkeeper Fanny Ransom's house. As they drove off Truman yelled out "Boys!" but he was ordered to be silent.

However, this drew the attention of a passerby, and he called the police. At Ransom's house Fairris, Skinner and twenty-three-year-old Raymond Carroll Price bound Truman and three other people, left Skinner to guard them, and took Mrs. Ransom to the store. Detectives Bennie F. Cravatt and Bill Rackley had been sent to the supermarket where they shooed away a gathering crowd, and then Rackley took up a containment position across the street while Cravatt went inside to await the return of the robbers. In less than half an hour Fairris, armed with an automatic pistol, and Price, armed with a .38-caliber revolver, entered the market, and Cravatt tried to arrest Price. Mrs. Ransom was thrown to the floor, out of harm's way, while Price and Cravatt struggled for the detective's gun. Four shots were fired from Cravatt's gun while sixteen shots were fired by Fairris, and one bullet struck Cravatt in the heart, killing him instantly. Price was slightly wounded in the thigh, and he ran to the storage room where he threw away his pistol and hid.

Upon hearing gunfire Rackley ran from his hiding place, and as Fairris ran out of the market Rackley fired at him, critically wounding him before he jumped into a car driven by twenty-year-old year old Peggy Ann Frye, and they sped off. Inside the market Price was discovered in the storage room and arrested by Rackley, and Price's pistol, unfired, was found. When Skinner heard the shots at the market he told the four captives, "I'll be here when you're all dead," and ran out. An hour later Fairris, badly wounded, was thrown from the moving vehicle when near Shawnee. He was identified by Rackley as the robber he had wounded, and he then confessed. Within fifteen hours after they entered the market two of the robbers were behind bars. Price or Fairris, or both, named the third man, and a bulletin was broadcast for the arrest of Skinner. On July 20 Skinner surrendered at Pasadena to Texas Deputy Sheriff Bill Isbell; he was lodged in the Houston jail and extradited to Oklahoma City. All three men were charged with Cravatt's murder, pled not guilty, and were held over for trial, with Fairris being tried separately.

Fairris' trial began in mid–October, and on October 21 he was found guilty of first-degree murder. On October 29 Judge Albert Hunt sentenced Fairris to die on January 28, 1955, and he was delivered to a death row cell. In November Skinner and Price changed their pleas to guilty, and on November 11 they were sentenced to serve life terms. On October 23, 1954, Frye had been arrested in Chicago, Illinois, and she was extradited to Oklahoma City on November 18. She was tried in mid–December, and on December 21 she was cleared of all charges when no witness could place her at the scene of Cravatt's murder. On March 31, 1955, Frye was arrested in Deming, New Mexico, driving a car a stolen from a Fort Worth, Texas, dealer's lot on February 21. She was charged with a violation of the Dyer Act, pled guilty, and was sentenced to serve two and one-half years at a federal prison.

Meanwhile Fairris' attorney filed an appeal which stayed his execution for months, but after the court of criminal appeals affirmed the judgment and sentence of the district court the date of execution was set for October 18, 1955. Price then tried to take the blame for shooting Cravatt, to save Fairris' life, but his confession was dismissed as a fabrication. Governor Raymond D. Gary granted a thirty-day reprieve to November 18 and another sixty-day reprieve to January 18, 1956, but then he declined to interfere further. On January 10, 1956, the case was argued before the state Board of Pardons and Paroles, and Fairris tried to lay the blame on Texas outlaw Tincy Eggleston, deceased, but on January 13 the board members refused to grant clemency. A writ of habeas corpus was then filed with the court of criminal appeals and denied late January 17.

On Wednesday Fairris was visited by his father, out on bond on a Texas burglary charge, but he could not be visited by other family members as all were serving long prison terms for a variety of crimes. During his time on death row Fairris embraced the Catholic religion and was attended by prison chaplain the Rev. John Ellis, the Rev. Harold Morgan and Father Don Kanaly. As his moment of death neared Fairris confessed to killing Cravatt, but had the clergymen, funeral parlor director Paul Smith, and social worker Dan Vinson swear not to release the information until after his death. Early Tuesday morning, before the other prisoners were awake, the condemned man had been handcuffed, taken from his death row cell, and moved to one of six special cells near the death chamber. The barber was then summoned, and he shaved Fairris' head and left leg. During the afternoon hours the death warrant was read by Warden H. C. McLeod. After supper the prisoner asked to be baptized, and this was done by Father Kanaly at 10:00 P.M. in his cell. Afterward he dressed in his prison-made pocket-less burial suit.

After 11:00 P.M. the witnesses were ushered into the death house, and they took their places behind the wire-mesh screen separating the death chamber from the viewing area. At midnight the prisoner was taken from his cell by two guards and escorted into the chamber where Warden McLeod asked if he had any last words, and he grinned, waved, and replied, "It's all for the kicks if that's the way they want it." He then took his seat in the oak chair where his chest and waist, wrists and arms, and ankles were bound with leather straps, the copper helmet and leg band lined with moistened sponges were secured in place, and a black leather mask was tied over his eyes and forehead and attached to the chair back. Executioner M. E. Elliott flipped the switch that applied the electricity, set at the lower range of 600 to 2,300 volts, and then turned a wheel until the intensity reached the maximum. As the voltage increased Fairris' body strained against the straps but relaxed when the electricity was turned off in less than a minute. Dr. John M. Cant checked for vital signs and pronounced Fairris dead at 12:08 A.M. Prison trusties removed the body from the chair, and it was rushed to the hospital, where his cornea and aorta were harvested to give eyesight and life to others. Then the body was delivered to a local funeral parlor to be prepared for shipment to Fort Worth for burial by undertaker Paul Smith.

Sources: *Ada Evening News* (OK): January 18, 1956. *Albuquerque Tribune* (NM): August 29, 1955. *Big Spring Herald* (TX): January 13, 1956; January 17, 1956; January 26, 1956. *Brownsville Herald* (TX): November 18, 1955. *Galveston News* (TX): October 30, 1954. *Brownwood Bulletin* (TX): November 11, 1954. *Corsicana Sun* (TX): October 23, 1954; December 21, 1954. *El Paso Herald-Post* (TX): March 31, 1955. *Evening Journal* (Lubbock, TX): July 20, 1954. *Miami News-Record* (OK): July 18, 1954. *Oklahoman* (Oklahoma City): January 18, 1956.

Loel, Otto A.
January 11, 1957

On January 7, 1954, thirty-one-year-old Elizabeth Jeanne Henderson was in a tavern in Compton, California, when she heard forty-seven-year-old Otto Austin Loel discussing a trip to Syracuse, New York. The Hendersons had known Loel for over a year. Henderson approached Loel and, being homesick to visit her relatives in Newark, Ohio, agreed on a share-the-expenses trip, and Henderson's husband consented. Loel and Henderson left California in his 1947 Buick, and in Barstow, California, they picked up Jerry Cluchta hitchhiking to Toledo, Ohio, and Charles Anderson hitchhiking to McAlester, Oklahoma, and he let them off before they reached Oklahoma City. As the two hitchhikers were being dropped off Henderson asked Cluchta "not to leave the car until we get to Oklahoma City, I'm afraid," but both men left her to continue on to their destinations.

Loel and Henderson reached Oklahoma City late on Sunday, January 10, and rented a motel room to rest before continuing the long drive. On Wednesday, January 13, Henderson's body, dressed only in nightgown and panties, was discovered in the blood-splattered motel room under the bed. She had been beaten, stabbed nineteen times in the neck, breast, and lower torso, and burned with cigarettes. Murder charges were filed against Loel the following day, and the police backtracked the route they followed, identified the hitchhikers, and by January 16 had interviewed both men. Loel had disappeared, and his car was found abandoned in Dallas, Texas, on January 26.

He hitchhiked to Shreveport, Louisiana, where the following day he pawned several personal items, and then the trail was lost. The search for Loel continued for a year, and on May 21 he was placed on the Federal Bureau of Investigation's roster of "Ten Most Wanted." On January 9, 1955, Loel, using the alias Jack McCoy, was arrested for drunkenness in Sanford, Florida, and his fingerprints were collected and sent to Washington, D.C. He was quickly identified as Loel, and on January 17, 1958, he was arrested while walking to his lean-to near a Sanford, Florida, junkyard. When Constable J. Q. Galloway, two Sanford police officers, and two deputy sheriffs confronted him he surrendered without resistance and told them, "I'm glad it's over. I'm ready to go. I'm tired."

He was arraigned before Federal Commissioner James S. Byrd and held on $50,000 bond, and Loel said he would not fight extradition. He was returned to Oklahoma City and, after a sanity hearing determined he was sane, his trial began on October 19 and concluded on October 21, 1955. The jurors, the following day, returned a guilty verdict, and Loel was sentenced to die in the electric chair. He had claimed self-defense as he fought off Henderson's bizarre sexual advances, but the jury rejected his version of the brutal killing. On November 1 Judge A. P. Van Meter sentenced Loel to die on January 24, 1956, and he was delivered to the prison the following day. Harold Witcher, Loel's attorney, immediately filed a notice of appeal, which stayed the execution, but by May 24 he had failed to file the proper briefs with the court of criminal appeals, and the justices criticized Witcher and reviewed the case without the defense position. The justices affirmed the judgment and sentence of the district court, and the date of execution was finally set for January 11, 1957. Witcher then filed a petition with the state Board of Pardons and Paroles pleading for clemency, but by January 4 the appeal had been rejected after the unrepentant Loel insisted he had, at most, committed manslaughter. During Loel's final hours Witcher filed a second petition with the board asking for clemency and a writ of habeas corpus with the court of criminal appeals, but both were denied.

Early Thursday morning, before the other prisoners were awake, the condemned man was handcuffed, taken from his death row cell, and moved to one of six special cells near the death chamber. The barber was then summoned, and he shaved Loel's head and left leg and nicked him several places on his leg. Late in the afternoon the death warrant was read by Warden H. C. McLeod, and then Loel was asked if he was all right; he said, "Sure I'm all right. I give you odds on that. I ain't worried much." After supper the prisoner dressed in his prison-made pocket-less burial suit. At 11:00 P.M. the witnesses were ushered into the death house, and they took their places behind the wire-mesh screen separating the death chamber from the viewing area. At midnight the prisoner was taken from his cell by two guards and escorted into the chamber, where he tossed away a cigarette before he shook hands with Warden McLeod, then asked for a cough drop. No one had a cough drop so he was asked if he had any last words, and he declined to speak to the witnesses.

He took his seat in the oak chair where his chest and waist, wrists and arms, and ankles were bound with leather straps and the copper helmet and leg band lined with moistened sponges were secured in place. He winced as Glover daubed the wounds on his leg with the moistening solution. A black leather mask was tied over his eyes and forehead and attached to the chair back. Executioner B. V. Glover stepped to the control panel and flipped the switch that applied the electricity, set at the lower range of 600 to 2,300 volts, and Glover turned a wheel until the intensity reached the maximum. As the voltage increased Loel's body strained against the straps but relaxed when the electricity was turned off in less than a minute. The doctor in attendance then checked for vital signs and pronounced Loel dead at 12:07 A.M. Prison trusties removed the body from the chair, and later the body was delivered to a local funeral parlor to be prepared for burial.

Sources: *Ada Evening News* (OK): November 2, 1955. *Big Spring Herald* (TX): October 21, 1955. *Lawton Constitution* (OK): January 11, 1957. *Galveston News* (TX): January 18, 1955. *Holland Evening Sentinel* (MI): January 16, 1954. *Syracuse Herald-Journal* (NY): January 19, 1954. *Waterloo Courier* (IA): May 21, 1954.

Hendricks, Robert
February 5, 1957

In 1929 Robert Hendricks and another man murdered phonograph salesman Frank M. Wilson for his money and his demonstration phonograph. They hid the body near Seminole, and when the body was found they were arrested and lodged in the Wewoka jail. They pled not guilty on June 14 but were held over for trial in September. On September 19 Hendricks was convicted of first-degree murder and sentenced to serve a life term, but he was paroled in 1947 after serving eighteen years.

On August 21, 1954, sixty-year-old Hendricks, now a handyman at the stockyards in Vinita, learned that fifty-four-year-old cattle buyer Ream Payton had cashed a check for $2,200 that morning. Payton was not seen after noon that day but on August 26 his body was found in a field, partly decomposed, with the back of his skull shattered and his pockets empty. At first it was believed he had been shot in the back of the head but at the autopsy it was determined he had been bludgeoned several times from behind with a flat object. The place where the body was found did not appear to be the murder scene; an investigation showed Payton had been killed in an old building near the stockyards and carried to the field, and bloodstained furniture from the building was sent to the laboratory for testing. Payton's truck was searched and a bloodstained tire tool was found in the truck bed, and it was also sent for testing and proved to be the murder weapon.

Hendricks was immediately suspected, arrested and lodged in the Vinita jail, and he gave several conflicting stories. It was then discovered that after Payton disappeared the near penniless Hendricks had paid off his automobile mortgage, bought new clothes, and loaned a friend $1,500. On August 31 Hendricks wrote a note containing a partial confession including the statement that "no one else is to blame," then ingested a large dose of narcotics he had hidden on his person and slashed his left wrist and arm with a razor blade he had hidden in his boot. The prisoner was found in his jail cell unconscious, but he had not taken enough narcotic nor lost enough blood to die, so he was rushed to the hospital and placed under guard while he recovered, and later that day murder charges were filed.

Hendricks was arraigned in Justice of the Peace George Zumwalt's courtroom, he waived his preliminary hearing, and was held over for trial in the Craig County district court. On January 28, 1955, Hendricks was found guilty of first-degree murder, and on February 3 Judge Josh J. Evans sentenced him to die in the electric chair. His case was appealed, which stayed the execution, but the court of criminal appeals affirmed the judgment and sentence on February 15, 1956, and he was sentenced to die on May 3. On March 23 he asked for a rehearing and the sentence was stayed to June 4, then extended one day so that preparations for the execution would not have to be made on a Sunday; on May 9 the request for the rehearing was denied. On May 23 the state Board of Pardons and Paroles heard the case and denied clemency, but eight days later the court of criminal appeals asked for a stay so that an appeal could be perfected to the U.S. Supreme Court, and the governor granted a sixty-day stay. The case had not been considered by the U.S. Supreme Court, which was in recess, when on August 1, 1956, the Board of Pardons and Paroles granted a ninety-day stay from August 4 to November 1. On October 29 another sixty-day stay was granted when the U.S. Supreme Court had not acted. The justices then refused to hear the case, but another sixty-day stay had already been granted, which set the final date of execution at February 5, 1957. Pleas for clemency had been before the state Board of Pardons and Paroles four times and denied, but on February 3 the members were polled once more; their recommendations were sent to Governor Raymond Gary the following day, Monday, and he declined to interfere further.

Early Monday morning, before the other prisoners were awake, the condemned man was handcuffed, taken from his death row cell, and moved to one of six special cells near the death chamber. The barber was then summoned, and he shaved Hendricks' head and left leg. During the afternoon hours the death warrant was read by Warden H. C. McLeod. Hendricks was asked what he wanted done with his body, and he replied, "I don't care if the hogs eat me up." After supper the prisoner penned three letters, gave them to Warden McLeod, asked that they be forwarded to Governor Gary, and then dressed in his black prison-made pocket-less burial suit. At 11:00 P.M. the witnesses were ushered into the death house, and they took their places behind the wire-mesh screen separating the death chamber from the viewing area. At midnight the prisoner was taken from his cell by two guards and escorted into the chamber where Warden McLeod asked if he had any last words, and he said, "Be sure the newsboys get those letters."

He then took his seat in the oak chair where his chest and waist, wrists and arms, and ankles were bound with leather straps, the copper helmet and leg band lined with moistened sponges were secured in place, and a black leather mask was tied over his eyes and forehead and attached to the chair back. The executioner flipped the switch that applied the electricity, set at the lower range of 600 to 2,300 volts, and then he turned a wheel until the intensity reached the maximum. As the voltage increased Hendricks' body strained against the straps but relaxed when the electricity was turned off after forty-five seconds. The doctor in attendance checked for vital signs and pronounced Hendricks dead at 12:05 A.M. Prison trusties removed the body from the chair, and later it was delivered to a local funeral parlor to be prepared for burial.

Over the next several days newsmen tried to get possession of the three letters Hendricks had left but the warden had turned them over to Governor Gary, as originally requested by Hendricks. Warden McLeod said that while the letters mentioned the murder of Jack Burris and the Greenlease kidnapping in Kansas they were primarily tirades against state and county officials, and he concluded, "The letters merely displayed the bitterness of a condemned slayer." However, Hendricks had told newsmen they contained information which could solve several prominent crimes, though they contained little that he had not already told the Board of Pardons and Paroles during his several hearings. Governor Gary turned the letters over to the Federal Bureau of Investigation and the State Crime Bureau for their investigation.

Sources: *Ada Evening News* (OK): February 15, 1956; March 23, 1956; May 9, 1956; May 23, 1956; May 31, 1956; October 29, 1956; February 3, 1957. *Hammond Times* (IN): February 5, 1957. *Joplin Globe* (MO): June 14, 1929; September 20, 1929. *Lawton Constitution* (OK): August 2, 1956; February 5, 1957. *Miami News-Record* (OK): August 31, 1954; January 30, 1955; February 16, 1956; February 6, 1957. *Ogden Standard-Examiner* (UT): February 5, 1957.

Williams, Edward L.
July 28, 1960

On Sunday, June 17, 1956, twenty-four-year-old Rev. Tommy Robert Cooke, assistant pastor at the Glenwood Baptist Church in Tulsa, Oklahoma, drove away from the church after the morning service. Meanwhile twenty-seven-year-old Edward Leon "Pete" Williams, an ex- convict, robbed a gas station on South Peoria Avenue near the church and was fleeing when he wrecked his car and started hitchhiking. The Reverend Cooke, who "often picked up hitchhikers and tried to tell them about Jesus Christ," stopped and picked up Williams. When they were near Taft, forty-five miles southeast of Tulsa, Williams pulled out a .38-caliber pistol and took Cooke prisoner, forced him to pull to the side of the road, forced him out of the car, bound him, and then shot him in the head, killing him instantly. Williams drove to Muse, eighteen miles southeast of Talihina, where he abandoned Cooke's automobile.

Williams returned to Tulsa, and that evening he robbed Herman Couzzens and his wife Marie, owners of a Tulsa general store where he had worked for six weeks, of $1,000 and fled to Talihina where he hid in the woods. The Couzzens reported the theft and the search for Williams began, but it was intensified when the police found his fingerprints on the gas-station robbery getaway car, which put Williams in Tulsa when Cooke disappeared. Early on June 19 the searchers were nearing Williams' hiding place so he hijacked a motorist and forced him to drive thirty miles to Wilburton, where he boarded a bus to Poteau. When the motorist reported the hijacking the highway patrol sent a broadcast ahead to Poteau, and Sheriff Jack Craig, Trooper Carl Stevens, and City Marshal Buel Richmond arrested the fugitive after a brief struggle. Williams quickly confessed to shooting Cooke and told Leflore County Undersheriff Orville McCroskey where the body could be found, and later that day he was being brought to the area to help with the search when Cooke's remains were found.

After a "wild escape" he was recaptured and taken to Muskogee where he was charged with murdering Cooke. He pled guilty on February 1, 1957, and was sentenced to serve a life term. He was then taken to Tulsa where he was charged with robbing the gas station and kidnapping Cooke. He pled guilty to both charges and was given a fifty-year sentence for armed robbery, and then Tulsa District Court Judge Leslie Webb sentenced Williams to die in the electric chair on the kidnapping charge. Attorney Whit Pate filed an appeal, based primarily on the theory of double jeopardy, and over the next forty-two months Williams received thirteen stays of execution, but finally his date of execution was set for Thursday, July 28, 1960. On Tuesday, July 26, 1960, Williams told the members of the state Pardon and Parole Board, "If you don't feel I warrant any consideration this time, I don't want any more stays," then read a four-page statement he had prepared. The board denied clemency, and Williams said, "I had a kind of feeling the Board would reject the plea. You know what I mean? You know I could feel when I went in the room I wouldn't get any mercy." Governor J. Howard Edmondson, who was barred by law from granting clemency without a recommendation from the Board, declined to interfere. The final appeal to the U.S. Supreme Court was denied just before 10:00 P.M., only minutes before the prisoner was taken into the death chamber.

On Wednesday night Williams was visited by Purcell's Presbyterian Rev. Kenneth Robinson and Mr. and Mrs. E. Borofsky of Tulsa — Mrs. Borofsky had exchanged letters with her childhood friend for the past three years. Early Thursday morning, before the other prisoners were awake, the condemned man was handcuffed, taken from his death row cell, and moved to one of six special cells near the death chamber, where he was attended by the Reverend Robinson. Newsmen were then admitted, and he said, "When I die tonight it is as it should be. I killed and they are going to kill me — an eye for an eye and a tooth for a tooth." He said he held no malice toward anyone, but "What they do to me tonight won't atone for what I've done, although in our society I can't expect anything else." When asked how he could be so calm he said, "Let's say I've found peace within myself. I've gone through hell down there, so you see, I'm actually relieved that it's almost over."

After the newsmen left the barber was summoned, and he shaved Williams' head and left leg. After supper the prisoner dressed in his dark blue prison-made pocket-less burial suit, white shirt, black tie, and black shoes. After 9:00 P.M. the witnesses were ushered into the death house, and they took their places behind the wire-mesh screen separating the death chamber from the viewing area. As soon as word was received of denial of the final appeal the prisoner was taken from his cell by two guards and escorted into the chamber where Warden Raines read the death warrant, and then Williams shook his hand. The warden asked if Williams had any last words and he shook his head, then spotted *Tulsa World* reporter Jack Kelley among the witnesses, winked, and said only, "Jack." Williams took his seat in the oak chair where his chest and waist, wrists and arms, and ankles were bound with leather straps, the copper helmet and leg band lined with moistened sponges were secured in place, and a black leather mask was tied over his eyes and forehead and attached to the chair back. Executioner Ben V. Glover, a prison guard, flipped the switch that applied the electricity set at the lower range of 600 to 2,300 volts, and then he turned a wheel until the intensity reached the maximum. As the voltage increased Williams' body lurched, his legs strained against the straps, and his hands clenched into tight fists, but he relaxed when the electricity was turned off after less than a minute. Drs. Austin R. Strough and R.A. Harkins of McAlester checked for vital signs and pronounced Williams dead at 10:05 P.M. Prison trusties removed the body from the chair, and later it was delivered to a local funeral parlor to be prepared for burial.

Sources: *Ada Evening News* (OK): July 28–29, 1960. *Lubbock Avalanche-Journal* (TX): July 29, 1960. *Cedar Rapids Gazette* (IA): June 19, 1956. *Lima News* (OH): June 19, 1956. *Oklahoman* (Oklahoma City): July 29, 1960. *Tulsa World* (OK): July 29, 1960.

Spence, James
August 31, 1960

In 1958 twenty-two-year-old Reggie Noel Zimmerman and his nineteen-year-old wife Ruth, with their five-month-old son, lived in a three-room apartment over the Surplus City store in Lawton, Oklahoma, where Reggie worked as assistant manager. At 7:00 P.M. on Monday, March 31, 1958, twenty-nine-year-old James Spence and his twenty-five-year-old brother-in-law Eddie Junior Oxendine, a Cherokee half-breed using the alias Don Locklear, left their wives at their apartment in Lawton and after visiting several taverns found themselves short of money. After 9:00 P.M. they saw Reggie Zimmerman leave the back door of the store and climb the stairs to his apartment, and they were sure he would be able to provide them with cash.

Oxendine went up the stairs and knocked, then told Reggie he had a flat tire and needed a jack to fix it. When the door cracked open Oxendine pushed his way in and pointed his pistol at Reggie and then ordered Ruth, dressed in her nightgown, to come out of the bedroom and join them. In a few minutes Spence, after parking his automobile, joined Oxendine, and the two men brandished their .25-caliber Galesi automatic pistols in a threatening manner. Oxendine, later described as a "Mexican," took Reggie downstairs and made him open the safe while Spence held Mrs. Zimmerman and their baby at gunpoint upstairs. Reggie gave Oxendine $436, including a bag of about $300 in coins, but left $1,000 in the safe and returned to the upstairs apartment. The robbers then used cord and diapers, torn into strips, to bind the couple's wrists and gag them. They threw the couple into the bedroom closet but found they couldn't lock the door. They started to leave but stopped for a whispered conversation and within a minute returned. Oxendine pulled open the closet door while Spence emptied his pistol into the closet, firing seven bullets. Ruth was struck in the breast and right side, and one of those bullets pierced her heart; Reggie was hit twice in the right arm and once in the chest, while two shots missed.

As soon as Spence's gun was empty the two robbers fled, and Reggie rushed out to check the baby. His wife staggered out of the closet behind him and collapsed, so he helped her into the kitchen and removed her bonds, but could not remove the bindings from his wrists. He then staggered across the street to the home of city Police Officer James C. Blackburn and reported the robbery. Reggie was taken to the hospital and rushed into surgery, his life was saved, and the following day he gave the police a good description of the men who had murdered his wife. He described their automobile as a black 1955 or 1956 Pontiac, which he had seen parked in the alley behind the store when he was taken down to open the safe.

The description of the car led to the identification of the two men by their landlord, and items taken from the surplus store were found in the apartment's attic. The officers issued a "pick-up order" including the license number, and the car was located in Albuquerque, New Mexico, by Officers James Bundy and Seth Wyche, parked at an East Central motel near the fairgrounds. On Friday, April 4, Spence and Oxendine were arrested, the two pistols and the coins were found, and Oxendine gave his true name in the hope he would be released as the police were looking for Don Locklear. However, as soon as they were behind bars and it was clear they were the right men, both prisoners confessed to the robbery, and Spence confessed he fired the fatal shots. Their wives, seventeen-year-old Donnie Oxendine and twenty-three-year-old Leacy Spence, were held as witnesses until Saturday night, when the wives were released and the two men were returned to Lawton. The Pontiac was impounded pending repossession by a North Carolina finance company, and another Pontiac bought in Lawton the day following the murder was released to the wives.

Once the two men were back in Oklahoma Oxendine told Deputy Sheriff M. T. McCracken that he and Spence had made a mistake by leaving before they were sure the couple was dead, and said that he would continue to try to escape until he was seated in the electric chair. By Saturday Reggie Zimmerman had recovered sufficiently to attend his wife's funeral, but had to return to the hospital for additional surgery. On April 8 the two prisoners were arraigned before Judge John P. Fullerton, they pled not guilty, and their preliminary hearing was scheduled for Friday, April 11. On May 10 the two men tried to escape from the jail but failed to gain their freedom.

Their joint trial began on May 19 and concluded on the following day, and the jurors deliberated only two hours before finding both men guilty of first-degree murder and recommending the death penalty. On May 25 Comanche County district court Judge Luther B. Eubanks sentenced both men to die in the electric chair on August 16. On May 26 the two men were taken to the state prison, and Oxendine told newsmen, "I stuck with my buddy. We did the robbery together. We did everything together. And I guess we'll die together." Their attorneys filed appeals, and in November the court of criminal appeals overturned both convictions and ordered new trials.

This time the two defendants were tried separately, Oxendine first in April 1959, but the jury deadlocked after two days of deliberations with one juror holding out for a life sentence. A third trial was ordered for Oxendine and began on Wednesday, May 13; the case went to the jury on Friday, and after two ballots they found him guilty of first-degree murder and recommended the death penalty. On May 20 he was sentenced to die July 31, but he received a stay of execution while his case was again appealed.

Spence's trial was scheduled to begin on September 14, after a change of venue to Walters in Cotton County when a jury could not be seated in Comanche County. Judge Eubanks presided, and after the defendant was again convicted of first-degree murder, he was sentenced on September 15 to die, but an appeal stayed his execution, and under Oklahoma law the defense had six months to perfect another appeal. There followed a series of execution dates and stays while appeals were being prepared and filed, and on December 22, 1959, another appeal was filed asking the court of criminal appeals to reduce the sentences to life imprisonment, but it was denied. On May 17, 1960, both condemned men appeared before the state Board of Pardons and Paroles, and Spence testified, "I'm guilty and ready to go, but there's no reason Eddie should go. He harmed nobody. They shouldn't send a man down for hurting nobody." After a few additional comments to exonerate Oxendine he said, "After my execution I would like to have my eyes given to some young woman. That's the least I can do."

The board then set another hearing date for Oxendine June 23 and promised to extend that date if his appeal was still pending, and Oxendine's date with the executioner was extended thirty days from May 24. On June 21 he received another stay, this time for sixty days from his execution date of June 24. However, after a recommendation for clemency from the Board, Governor J. Howard Edmondson granted a thirty- and then a sixty-day stay for Oxendine, and on November 10, 1960, the governor commuted his sentence to life in prison. Spence's date of execution had been set for August 31, 1960, and nothing would arise to delay the proceedings.

Early Wednesday morning, before the other prisoners were awake, the condemned man was handcuffed and moved from his death row cell to one of six special cells near the death chamber. Newsmen were then admitted, and he told them, "I'm guilty of the crime and we have to live by man-made laws or pay. I am bitter at no one." After the reporters left the barber was summoned, and he shaved Spence's head and left leg. During the afternoon hours Spence asked to have a television so he could watch a light-heavyweight boxing match, and one was provided. The death warrant was read by Warden Robert R. Raines before supper was served, and then the prisoner dressed in his prison-made pocket-less burial suit. After 9:00 P.M. twenty-seven witnesses were ushered into the death house, and they took their places behind the wire-mesh screen separating the death chamber from the viewing area.

Shortly before 10:00 P.M. the prisoner was taken from his cell by two guards and escorted into the chamber where Warden Raines asked if he had any last words, but Spence didn't hear him and asked, "What did you say?" When the question was repeated Spence said only "No!" He took his seat in the oak chair where his chest and waist, wrists and arms, and ankles were bound with leather straps, the copper helmet and leg band lined with moistened sponges were secured in place, and a black leather mask was tied over his eyes and forehead and attached to the chair back. Executioner Ben V. Glover flipped the switch that applied the electricity, set at the lower range of 600 to 2,300 volts, and turned a wheel until the intensity reached the maximum. As the voltage increased Spence's body strained against the straps but relaxed when the electricity was turned off in less than a minute. Dr. Austin R. Strough checked for vital signs and pronounced Spence dead at 10:03 A.M. Prison trusties removed the body from the chair, and it was rushed to the hospital, where his corneas were harvested to give eyesight to another. The body was then delivered to a local funeral parlor to be prepared for burial.

Sources: *Ada Evening News* (OK): April 1, 1958; May 25, 1958; April 23, 1959; September 1, 1960. *Albuquerque Journal* (NM): April 6, 1958; April 9, 1958. *Albuquerque Tribune* (NM): April 4, 1958. *Bee* (Danville, VA): August 24, 1960; September 1, 1960. *Big Spring Herald* (TX): May 27, 1958. *Burlington Times-News* (NC): May 15, 1959; September 12, 1959. *Joplin Globe* (MO): September 1, 1960. *Lawton Constitution* (OK): May 19–20, 1958; May 10, 1959; May 20, 1959. *Miami News-Record* (OK): May 17, 1960; November 10, 1960. *Oklahoman* (Oklahoma City): September 1, 1960

Young, Ray A.
December 15, 1960

Thirty-two-year-old Ray Allen Young and his wife Wanda separated and she refused to reconcile, so he conspired with twenty-five-year-old Bernice Scott, an Altus, Oklahoma, prostitute, to kill his wife and to kill Scott's black boyfriend, who refused to move to Oklahoma City with her. On Friday, January 23, 1959, Scott called Eddie Mayfield, an Altus hotel bellhop, and asked him to meet her on a country road three miles west of town. When Mayfield drove up he found Scott and Young standing near a parked car, and the three began arguing. Scott suddenly pulled out her .32-caliber six-shot revolver, and as Mayfield ran across an open field she shot at him six times, emptying her pistol but missing her target. Young then pulled out a .32-caliber automatic pistol and fired several shots at Mayfield, but he also missed.

Thirty-one-year-old highway patrolman John Richard Barter was driving on a main highway nearby, and when he saw two cars parked on the isolated side road he decided to investigate. Barter found his old Marine buddy Young and Scott standing near the cars — Young's and Mayfield's automobiles. Barter asked about the pistol in Young's hand and Young said it was for target practice. Barter then took Scott's empty pistol and said he was going to arrest the couple, and when Barter asked Young to hand over his weapon Young fired a single bullet into Barter's right side, killing him almost instantly. Young and Scott fled, and Barter's body was found later that day in the ditch alongside the country road, where he had fallen.

An hour after shooting Barter, Young and Scott went to the Frederick café where Wanda Young worked as a waitress and fired three shots at her, but again they missed their target. After Mayfield and Wanda Young reported the shootings roadblocks were set up. Ray Young and Scott hired a Frederick taxi driven by Floyd Eugene Gray to take them to Durant, but they were arrested at the roadblock set up near Randlett. They were lodged in the Altus jail, and Young confessed to the murder of Barter and the two attempted murders and said for his written statement, "I just wasn't going to let him or anyone else stand in my way because I had made up my mind to kill my wife." Jackson County Attorney Loys Criswell filed murder charges against Young and Scott on Tuesday, January 27. Gray, who at first was thought to have aided in their flight, was exonerated and released.

On Friday night, February 6, twenty-year-old Robert Boaldin, son of the Altus jailer, took a cup of coffee to Young, and the prisoner pulled out a knife and threatened his life. Young fled down the stairs and into the street where he found the Clayton Tinney family stopped at a traffic light. He jumped into the car and held his knife to the throat of Tinney's two-year-old grandson and said, "Get me out of here fast," and the family surrendered the car to him. Young picked up his wife and they started south into Texas, but near Humphrey they were seen by Highway Patrolman T. G. Byrnes who at times pursued them at speeds in excess of one hundred miles per hour. Young lost his pursuer on a Texas gravel road, but soon he encountered Foard County, Texas, Sheriff Percy Taylor with two deputies eleven miles north of Vernon, and when Young tried to ram them they riddled his car with bullets. Young lost control and the car careened across a field before crashing into a garage. Young and his wife were captured, uninjured but without resistance, and Young was returned to Oklahoma where he was placed in a maximum security cell at the prison. His wife was lodged in the Altus County jail, and it was thought she would be charged with aiding a prisoner to escape, but it was found she had been abducted and was released.

Once Ray Young was at the prison Scott was also moved to a maximum security cell at the prison. Young's trial began at Altus on March 9 but on March 13 the jury, who had agreed on guilt, deadlocked 10–2 for the death penalty, and a mistrial was declared. Scott was then brought in, pled guilty, and was sentenced to serve a life term. Young was retried in mid–April, and on April 15 he was convicted of first-degree murder with a recommendation for the death penalty; on April 25 Judge Weldon Ferris sentenced him to die in the electric chair on July 2. A notice of appeal was filed, which stayed the execution, and the appeal was filed on September 9. The state's Court of Criminal Appeals heard arguments on February 3, 1960, and affirmed the judgment and sentence on May 25, and the justices set Young's date of execution at July 26. On July 24 the Board of Pardons and Paroles heard Young's plea for clemency and granted a stay while the case was under consideration. On September 28 Young's attorney filed another appeal with the state's Court of Criminal Appeals, which was denied on November 2, and Young's date with the executioner was set for Thursday, December 15, 1960. Young's final plea to the Board of Pardons and Paroles was denied on November 23, a request for a rehearing was denied on December 12, and Governor J. Howard Edmondson refused to intervene.

Before Young appeared before the Board for his final plea he had been baptized into the Catholic religion by the Rev. Father Joseph Boucher, and this was presented as a mitigating factor. Young, on December 14, told newsmen, "I've often wondered what would have happened if it hadn't been a patrolman I killed. They say it didn't make any difference, but I bet it did.... I am not afraid to face the electric chair, I would rather die than waste my life away inside these walls." He was attended by Father Boucher during his months on death row, and the priest had helped him resign himself to his fate.

Early Thursday morning, before the other prisoners were awake, the condemned man was handcuffed and moved from his death row cell to one of six special cells near the death chamber. After breakfast the barber was summoned, and he shaved Young's head and left leg. The death warrant was read by Warden Robert R. Raines before supper was served, and then the prisoner dressed in his prison-made pocket-less burial suit. After 9:00 P.M. twenty witnesses were ushered into the death house, and they took their places behind the wire-mesh screen separating the chamber from the viewing area. Young's last thirty minutes were spent in fervent prayer with Father Boucher, and the priest accompanied him into the death chamber. Shortly before 10:00 P.M. the prisoner was taken from his cell by two guards and escorted into the execution room where Warden Raines asked if he had any last words, and Young said, "I wish you all a Merry Christmas and I have no ill feelings toward anyone."

He took his seat in the oak chair where his chest and waist, wrists and arms, and ankles were bound with leather straps, the copper helmet and leg band lined with moistened sponges were secured in place, and a black leather mask was tied over his eyes and forehead and attached to the chair back. As the executioner stepped to the control panel Young winked at Father Boucher and smiled. The executioner flipped the switch that applied the electricity, set at the lower range of 600 to 2,300 volts, and turned a wheel until the intensity reached the maximum. As the voltage increased Young's body strained against the straps but relaxed when the electricity was turned off in less than a minute. Prison physician Dr. Austin R. Strough then checked for vital signs and pronounced Young dead. Prison trusties removed the body from the chair, and it was delivered to a local funeral parlor to be prepared for burial.

Sources: *Abilene Reporter-News* (TX): December 16, 1960. *Ada Evening News* (OK): January 26, 1959; February 8, 1959; March 13, 1959; April 26, 1959; May 26, 1960. *Corpus Christi Times* (TX): December 15, 1960. *Lawton Constitution* (OK): November 23, 1960; December 13, 1960. *Miami News-Record* (OK): November 3, 1960. *Montana Standard* (Butte): January 25, 1959. *Oklahoman* (Oklahoma City): December 16, 1960. *Press-Telegram* (Long Beach, CA): December 16, 1960. *Sheboygan Press* (WI): February 7, 1959.

Doggett, Shelby L.
October 1, 1962

Twenty-one-year-old Shelby Leon Doggett had been discharged from the Navy in March 1960, and in August he was living in Lawton, Oklahoma. Nineteen-year-old Ronald G. Lockwood had been in the Army assigned to Fort Sill but had been recently been discharged when, in August, he was arrested and tried for burglary, and on August 10 he received a suspended sentence. Doggett and Lockwood decided to hitchhike east to Lockwood's hometown of Altoona, Pennsylvania, and at 3:00 A.M. on August 19, 1960, twenty-four-year-old James Lee Lanman, a golf professional at a Lawton, Oklahoma, golf course, picked up the two hitchhikers near Lawton in his 1960 Ford convertible.

Seven miles south of Lawton Lanman stopped at a service station, and while their driver was occupied Doggett and Lockwood conspired to "roll" Lanman for the money he had on him. They continued driving south, and after they had gone a short distance Doggett pulled out a .25-caliber automatic pistol, put it to Lanman's head, and ordered him to turn down an isolated county section-line road. Once the car was stopped Doggett ordered Lanman out and made him strip, but Lanman suddenly ran down the road with Doggett chasing him. Doggett fired a single bullet at Lanman which struck him on the right side of the head, spinning him around. Doggett, then only five feet from Lanman, fired a second bullet which struck Lanman in the chest. Doggett returned to the car where Lockwood was busy searching for valuables and he asked, "Did you kill him?" Doggett told Lockwood he wasn't sure so they returned to the body and found Lanman alive. They carried him to a nearby ditch, and Lockwood said, "Finish him!" and Doggett then fired one bullet into his brain and four more into Lanman's chest.

They returned to the automobile and Lockwood started driving, but when he nearly crashed Doggett took the driver's seat, and they drove to Altoona, Pennsylvania, arriving about August 24. Along the way, and in Altoona, Doggett represented himself as Lanman so he could explain possession of the car and use Lanman's gasoline credit card. For the next week Doggett and Lockwood were involved in various nefarious activities but on August 31 they picked up several girls and, with nineteen-year-old Raymond Sciarrilla driving, crashed the car on East 6th Avenue Road and fled, leaving the girls behind.

While the state troopers were investigating the crash they found evidence that the owner had been involved in recent burglaries of vending machines. At 11:30 A.M. Doggett appeared at the police station posing as Lanman to report the car stolen, and he said Lockwood and Sciarrilla had been driving the car. Lockwood and Sciarrilla were arrested, and Doggett was also held for investigation of the burglaries. Doggett tried to avoid being charged with the burglaries, and he began to make inconsistent statements and admissions; after twenty-four hours behind bars he confessed to murdering Lanman and implicated Lockwood. The car had been towed to Weyandt's garage. It was searched again, and the clothing of Lanman was found, as well as an empty holster. Doggett then admitted he had taken the gun from the car after it was wrecked and hid it in a crevice in a concrete wall at 13th Avenue and 13th Street just before entering the police station, and the murder weapon was found.

On September 1 Altoona officers telephoned the Lawton authorities, and several hours after Doggett confessed they found Lanman's badly decomposed body with seven bullet holes, two in the head and five in the chest. Doggett and Lockwood were returned to Oklahoma on Saturday, September 3, charged with Lanman's murder, and lodged in the maximum security cell on the third-floor jail in the Lawton courthouse. They were arraigned and pled not guilty on November 8, and their trial was set for December 5, 1960, but the trials were separated and then delayed while the prisoners underwent mental testing at the Central State Hospital.

Lockwood was tried first, and on April 17 he was found guilty of first-degree murder, but because he did not fire the fatal bullets he received a sentence of life in prison. Doggett's trial began on May 22. After twenty-six witnesses testified, with only two for the defense on the issue of sanity, the case went to the jurors on the evening of May 24, and they deliberated three and one-half hours before finding the defendant guilty of first-degree murder. Judge Robert S. Landers then sentenced Doggett to die in the electric chair, but his attorney filed an appeal, which stayed the execution. More than a year passed before the state Court of Criminal Appeals affirmed the judgment and sentence of the lower court and Doggett's date of execution was set for Monday, October 1, 1962. The state Board of Pardons and Paroles refused to grant clemency, and Governor J. Howard Edmondson refused to intervene.

During his final days Doggett read two western novels, determined to finish them before Monday night. He was interviewed and told newsmen, "I believe in capital punishment and hold no animosity toward anyone." Early Monday morning, before the other prisoners were awake, the condemned man was handcuffed and moved from his death row cell to one of six special cells near the death chamber, and he told his guards, "I'm ready to go." After breakfast the barber was summoned, and he shaved Doggett's head and left leg. The death warrant was read by the warden before supper was served, and then the prisoner dressed in his prison-made pocket-less burial suit. After 9:00 P.M. the witnesses were ushered into the death house, and they took their places behind the wire-mesh screen separating the chamber from the viewing area.

Shortly before 10:00 P.M. the prisoner was taken from his cell by two guards and escorted into the execution room where he declined to speak to the witnesses. He took his seat in the oak chair where his chest and waist, wrists and arms, and ankles were bound with leather straps, and he asked the guards to make sure the straps were tight. The copper helmet and leg band, lined with moistened sponges, were then secured in place, and he smiled and winked at the prison chaplain just before the black leather mask was tied over his eyes and forehead and attached to the chair back. At 10:00 P.M. the executioner stepped to the control panel and flipped the switch that applied the electricity, set at the lower range of 600 to 2,300 volts, and he turned a wheel until the intensity reached the maximum. As the voltage increased Doggett's body strained against the straps but relaxed when the electricity was turned off in forty seconds. Prison physician Dr. A. R. Strough then checked for vital signs and pronounced Doggett dead at 10:03 P.M.

Prison trusties removed the body from the chair, and it was delivered to a local funeral parlor to be prepared for burial.

Sources: *Abilene Reporter-News* (TX): September 3, 1960. *Altoona Mirror* (PA): September 2, 1960; September 8, 1960; May 24, 1961. *Tyrone Herald* (PA): October 2, 1962.

Dare, Richard H.
June 1, 1963

In early 1960 twenty-seven-year-old Richard Henry Dare and his twenty-four-year-old wife of eight years, Patricia Ann, were having constant arguments about money, and on June 12 Patricia had Richard arrested for assault and battery and soon afterward filed for divorce. After noon on Friday, August 5, 1960, Dare and his wife were alone in the Oklahoma City home of her parents, sixty-year-old Ted Harry Albert and his fifty-eight-year-old wife Virgie, and were discussing reconciliation when they began arguing over a $3 debt. Dare claimed his wife shouted at him that she was pregnant and then struck him, so he beat her to death in a most brutal manner, then tied a cord around her neck to make sure she was dead and dragged her body into a rear bedroom.

He cleaned up the house and went to his sister's home to borrow a rifle, then returned to wait for his mother-in-law. When Virgie returned he told her what had happened, and she became hysterical and started screaming and scratched his face and neck, so Dare pulled down a window cord and strangled her to death. He tied the cord around her neck to be sure she was dead, then dragged her body into the rear bedroom and laid her next to her daughter. Ten minutes later the Albert's seventeen-year-old grandson William McCormick arrived, and Richard, using the borrowed rifle, shot the teenager in the head at close range, killing him instantly. He wrapped a cord around his neck to be certain he could not recover from the gunshot wound and dragged his body into a different rear room. He then hid behind the divan and lay in wait for three and one-half hours until Ted returned home that evening, and he shot him through the temple at close range, killing him instantly, and then took $30 from his wallet. He dragged his father-in-law's body into the rear room and laid him next to his grandson, tied a cord around his neck, and covered all four bodies with bedspreads or sheets.

Dare first went to a tavern, but later fled forty miles south and hid in the woods near the Davis, Oklahoma, farmhouse of Orbie Carter, his brother-in-law. Late Saturday a relative of the Alberts called the police because the Alberts did not answer when he called, and officers entered the house through a window and found the dead bodies. Early Sunday morning Dare went to Carter's farmhouse and told him of the killings, and Carter called McClain County Sheriff Joe Huddleston. The sheriff formed a one hundred-man posse, and they scoured the thirty square mile area near the Carter farm. At 9:30 P.M. Huddleston saw Dare "duck out of the woods and make for the farmhouse." He was captured without resistance, and he handed over his rifle. He said of killing Mrs. Albert, "I just lost my head," and of killing McCormick, "I didn't have much choice," and he said he intended to commit suicide but lost his nerve. His only other comment when arrested was, "I'm hungry."

He was taken to Oklahoma City and lodged in the county jail. On August 8 four murder charges were filed, and when Dare was arraigned he pled not guilty. His trial for the murder of his father-in-law began in early May, and on May 16, 1961, he was convicted of first-degree murder. On July 3 he was sentenced to die in the electric chair on September 7, but his attorney filed an appeal, which stayed the execution. The state Court of Criminal Appeals affirmed the judgment and sentence of the lower court on January 16, 1963, but Dare's attorney used every means to save his client's life. In May 1963 Dare's case came before the state Board of Pardons and Paroles, along with that of Gerald Pate, and the board members recommended commutation to life in prison for both men and sent that recommendation to Governor Henry Bellmon on May 26. On May 29 the governor, after carefully considering the cases, commuted Pate's sentence but refused to interfere with Dare's sentence, saying he had not been shown "any valid fact or reason for such action."

During his time on death row Dare slept about eighteen hours a day, and during the evening hours he and Pate would watch television. Early Saturday morning, before the other prisoners were awake, the condemned man was handcuffed and moved from his death row cell to one of the special basement cells near the death chamber. After breakfast the barber was summoned, and he shaved Dare's head and left leg. The death warrant was read by Warden Ray Page, and then the prisoner dressed in his black prison-made pocket-less burial suit, white shirt, black tie, and black shoes. After 9:00 P.M. the witnesses were ushered in, and they took their places behind the wire-mesh screen separating the chamber from the viewing area.

Dare was then taken from his cell by two guards, and he entered the execution room at 9:57 P.M., carrying his black Bible, which he handed to the Rev. Jack Bybee of Oklahoma City. He was asked if he wanted to make a final statement but only shook his head. He took his seat in the oak chair where his chest and waist, wrists and arms, and ankles were bound with leather straps. The copper helmet and leg band, lined with moistened sponges, were then secured in place, and the black leather mask was tied over his eyes and forehead and attached to the chair back. At 10:00 P.M. the executioner stepped to the control panel and flipped the switch that applied the electricity, set at the lower range of 600 to 2,300 volts, and he turned a wheel until the intensity reached the maximum. As the voltage increased Dare's body strained against the straps but relaxed when the electricity was turned off in less than a minute. Prison physician Dr. Austin R. Strough then checked for vital signs and pronounced Dare dead at 10:03 P.M. Prison trusties removed the body from the chair, and it was delivered to a local funeral parlor to be prepared for burial.

Sources: *Ada Evening News* (OK): May 26, 1963. *Joplin Globe* (MO): June 2, 1963. *Lawton Constitution* (OK): August 8, 1960; June 2, 1963. *Oklahoman* (Oklahoma City): June 2, 1963.

French, James D.
August 10, 1966

In 1956 nineteen-year-old James Donald French was hitchhiking in the Texas Panhandle when he was picked up by Frank Boone. When they reached Stroud, Oklahoma, French murdered Boone, stole his car and money, and dumped the body on the side of the road. He was captured still driving Boone's car, tried and convicted of murder, and sentenced to serve a life term.

In 1961 twenty-six-year-old Eddie Lee Shelton was serving time in prison, and French, his cell mate, ruled the cell and had "unspoken rules of conduct" which Shelton was required to follow. On October 27, 1961, French determined that Shelton had violated his rules and had to be executed, so after Shelton ate his last meal French subdued him in the cell and strangled him to death using a shoe lace. French was tried and convicted of Shelton's murder.

Then he began a vigorous campaign to prevent any delays in his execution, and even wrote to the state and U.S. Supreme Courts, "I am guilty, gentlemen, as guilty as any man or thing has ever been of a crime. Please, gentlemen, please do not reverse this verdict and sentence." However his attorneys, at the urging of his parents, ignored his wishes and managed to get stay after stay, and it took nearly five years before his parents finally relented and withdrew their efforts to save their son. His date with the executioner was set for Wednesday, August 10, 1966. Neither the state Board of Pardons and Paroles nor Governor Henry Bellmon would interfere.

Early Wednesday morning, before the other prisoners were awake, the condemned man was handcuffed and moved from his death row cell to one of the special basement cells near the death chamber. After breakfast the barber was summoned, and he shaved French's head and left leg. The death warrant was read by Warden Ray Page, and then the prisoner dressed in his black prison-made pocket-less burial suit, white shirt, black tie, and black shoes. During an interview on his final night French told reporters, "You can tell the U.S. Supreme Court that it shouldn't hold its breath waiting for me to beg for mercy." He also requested that he be cremated and that a plaque be buried with his ashes with the inscription "Nothing is either good or bad, just thinking makes it so." After 9:00 P.M. the witnesses were ushered in, and they took their places behind the wire-mesh screen separating the chamber from the viewing area.

Shortly before 10:00 P.M. French was taken from his cell by four guards and escorted into the execution room where he announced to the newsmen among the witnesses, "How's this for a headline, 'French Fries?'" He was then asked if he wanted to make a final statement but he replied, "Everything's already been said." He shook hands with the warden and captain of the guards B. E. Mann and took his seat in the oak chair where the four guards strapped his chest and waist, wrists and arms, and ankles. The copper helmet and leg band, lined with moistened sponges, were then secured in place, and the black leather mask was tied over his eyes and forehead and attached to the chair back. At 10:00 P.M. the executioner stepped to the control panel and flipped the switch that applied the electricity, set at the lower range of 600 to 2,300 volts, and he turned a wheel until the intensity reached the maximum. As the voltage increased French's body strained against the straps but relaxed when the electricity was turned off in less than a minute. Prison physician James D. Moore then checked for vital signs and pronounced French dead at 10:02 P.M. Prison trusties removed the body from the chair, and it was delivered to a local funeral parlor to be prepared for burial.

Sources: *Albuquerque Journal* (NM): October 30, 1961. *Charleston Mail* (SC): August 11, 1966. *Joplin Globe* (MO): August 11, 1966. *Morning Herald* (Uniontown, PA): August 11, 1966.

Coleman, Charles T.
September 10, 1990

On February 1, 1979, sixty-eight-year-old John Seward and his sixty two year old wife Roxie were in Muskogee, Oklahoma, visiting John's sister Delthea Warren and her husband Dale. The Sewards walked in on thirty-two-year-old Charles Troy Coleman, an ex-convict who was burglarizing the Warren home, and he took the elderly couple captive using a twenty-eight-gauge shotgun. He herded them into the basement and shot them dead. He then went through their belongings and stole everything of value, and added it to his loot from the Warren home, which he had already stored in his truck.

He fled but several hours later Coleman and his wife were stopped for a traffic violation and the officers found sixty-four pounds of meat marked "Hogle, Not for Sale" and Roxie Seward's wallet in the truck. The couple was arrested and taken to the police station. After they were removed from the police car it was searched, and Mrs. Seward's watch was found under the back seat. Mrs. Coleman would later confess that her husband had given it to her in the police car, and she disposed of it. Lon Hogle was called, and he identified the custom-cut meat he had given to the Warrens, and the bodies of the two victims were found. Neighbors identified Coleman's truck as one seen parked at the Warren home at the time of the killing. It was not long before the odd, rare shotgun was also found and taken for evidence, and Coleman was charged with two counts of murder.

On April 23, 1979, Coleman managed to escape from the Muskogee jail when he was left alone in the visiting area; he broke through the roof, and he was not missed until 7:55 P.M. At 6:00 the next morning a Luther police officer stopped a stolen blue Pontiac, and Coleman stabbed him, then stole his revolver and shotgun, but the wound was not fatal. The fugitive was soon captured and returned to the jail. In October 1979 he was tried for murdering John Seward, convicted on October 12, and sentenced to die by lethal injection. An appeal stayed the execution, and over the next eleven years his attorney used every ploy and legal maneuver to save his client's life, but in 1983 the Court of Criminal Appeals affirmed the judgment and sentence of the lower court, and the following year the U.S. Supreme Court denied certiorari. The case was taken to Oklahoma's Criminal Court of Appeals several times, to the U.S. Tenth Circuit Court of Appeals in Denver, and to the U.S. Supreme Court six times in all, but each time Coleman was denied relief, and finally his date with the executioner was set for Monday, September 10, 1990, the first execution in Oklahoma in twenty-four years. Coleman had his hearing before the state Board of Pardons and Paroles, and they refused to grant clemency. The request for a federal judge to order a rehearing was denied, and two requests for clemency from Governor Henry Bellmon were refused.

Following the reinstatement of the death penalty post-*Furman* in 1976 the Oklahoma legislature enacted a death penalty statute based upon the May 11, 1977, recommendation of Dr. Jay Chapman, the state's medical examiner. Dr. Chapman proposed a drug combination consisting of "an ultra-short acting barbiturate in combination with a chemical paralytic." A three-drug combination was then introduced and approved. The Texas legislature followed suit, and on December 7, 1982, became the first state to use the new method.

During his time on death row Coleman embraced religion and even started his own church within the prison walls, but this did not earn him clemency as he hoped. On Sunday evening the death warrant was read to the condemned man by Warden James Saffle, and at 12:15 A.M. a dozen media witnesses were guided into the viewing room. Coleman had been taken from his cell at 12:02, and when the curtains were drawn open the witnesses found him already lying on a gurney with his chest, waist, and legs secured, his arms strapped to extended supports, and with a sheet covering his torso and legs. A three-person team then inserted an intravenous cannula (IV) into a vein in each arm, the second a backup in case the primary IV failed. Coleman was then asked if he had any last words, and he said, "Just tell everybody I love them and I have a peace[ful] and quiet heart." At 12:25 A.M. the signal was given, and each of the men on the team injected, by hand-held syringes, one of three drugs: first sodium thiopental to cause sleep; second vecuronium bromide to stop respiration; and third potassium chloride to stop Coleman's heart. Once vital signs ceased Coleman was examined, and at 12:35 A.M. he was pronounced dead. The curtains were drawn closed before the body was removed and sent to a local funeral home to be prepared for burial.

Sources: 464 U.S. 1073; 104 S. Ct. 986; 79 L. Ed. 2d 222 (1984); 753 F.2d 832. *Cedar Rapids Gazette* (IA): September 11, 1990. *Coleman v. State*, 668 P.2d 1126 (1983). *Coleman v. State* 693 P.2d 4 (1984). *Galveston News* (TX): September 10, 1990. *Hutchinson News* (KS): September 10, 1990. *Paris News* (TX): April 24, 1979.

Parks, Robyn L.
March 10, 1992

Sometime after midnight on August 17, 1977, twenty-eight-year-old Robyn Leroy Parks, an ex-convict, stopped in the Gulf service station in Oklahoma City and filled his gas tank. He paid for the gas with a stolen credit card but the station attendant, twenty-four-year-old university student Abdullah Ibrahim, became suspicious and wrote his license number—XZ-5710—on a credit card receipt. Parks, who had guns and dynamite in his trunk, was afraid the attendant might call the police so he followed Ibrahim back to the booth. Ibrahim, apparently in his haste to get to the telephone, left the door ajar, and Parks fired a single shot from his .45-caliber revolver, the bullet striking Ibrahim in the chest and killing him. Parks fled.

At 4:30 A.M. another motorist stopped, discovered Ibrahim's dead body, and called the police. Parks had failed to notice the credit card receipt; it was found during the investigation, and the car was traced to Parks. The fugitive was then in California, but the police enlisted the aid of Parks' friend James Clegg, who telephoned Parks on several occasions and authorized the taping of the conversations. In one call Parks confessed "If he don't be around there ain't nothing he can tell them no way," and in another call he told Clegg where he had hidden the murder weapon. The police, guided by Clegg, went to the location and collected a .45-caliber revolver in a holster with additional ammunition, and with one of six bullets in the chambers fired. This pistol proved to be the murder weapon, and Parks was arrested in California and extradited to Oklahoma.

He was tried in 1978, convicted of first-degree murder, and sentenced to die by lethal injection. His defense, that he had been in the station several days earlier and the attendant wrote his license number at that time, and his alibi that he was elsewhere at the time of the murder, was rejected by the jury. His attorney filed an appeal, which stayed the execution, and over the next fourteen years the case was delayed again and again by appeals and stays of execution. In 1982 the Court of Criminal Appeals affirmed the judgment and sentence, and the U.S. Supreme Court denied certiorari in 1983. Next came a writ of habeas corpus filed with the Tenth Circuit Court of Appeals in Denver; the justices granted the writ, but they were overturned by the U.S. Supreme Court. Parks' attorney tried every means to save his client's life but finally the date with the executioner was set for Tuesday, March 10, 1992. On December 2, 1991, Parks had his final hearing before the five-member Pardon and Parole Board, and the members voted four to one to deny clemency. Governor David Walters declined to intervene. The Tenth Circuit Court of Appeals heard oral arguments on Monday, March 9, but declined to grant a stay, and the U.S. Supreme Court refused to hear a last-minute appeal.

During the first months of 1992 Parks was interviewed, and he told reporters, "Death itself is not what I am scared of. I'm more scared of the processes in which man has chosen to end my life." During his final days Parks was visited by his wife Debra, and as she left for the last time he called to her, "I love you." On Monday evening the death warrant was read to the condemned man by Warden James Saffle, and after 1:00 A.M. the witnesses were guided into the viewing room.

Parks had been taken from his cell earlier, and

when the curtains were drawn open the witnesses found him already lying on a gurney with his chest, waist, and legs secured, his arms strapped to extended supports, with a sheet covering his torso and legs. A three-person team then inserted an intravenous cannula (IV) into a vein in each arm, the second a backup in case the primary IV failed. After these preparations Parks must have thought the drugs had been administered because he complained, "I'm still awake." At 1:29 A.M. the signal was given and each of the men on the team injected, by hand-held syringes, one of three drugs: first sodium thiopental to cause sleep; second pancuronium bromide to stop respiration; and third potassium chloride to stop Coleman's heart. After two minutes Parks appeared to suffer an allergic reaction to at least one of the drugs. The muscles in his jaw, neck and abdomen began to spasm, and he started gasping and gagging as if choking, but after forty-five seconds he lay still, and at 1:40 A.M. he was pronounced dead. The curtains were drawn closed before the body was removed and sent to a local funeral home to be prepared for burial.

Sources: 459 U.S. 1155; 103 S. Ct. 800; 74 L. Ed. 2d 1003 (1983). *Paris News* (TX): March 8, 1992. *Parks v. Saffle*, 925 F. 2d 366 (1991). *Parks v. State*, 651 P.2d 686 (1982). *Stars & Stripes* [U.S. Military]: March 11, 1992. *Tulsa World* (OK): March 11, 1992.

Robison, Olan R.
March 13, 1992

In early 1980 forty-two-year-old Mrs. Averil Joan Borque, accompanied by thirty-eight-year-old Julie Sheila Lovejoy of Greenway, England, left her husband and four children in South Wales and traveled to Velma, Oklahoma, to visit friends. On Thursday evening, June 12, 1980, thirty-four-year-old Olan Randle Robison, twenty-eight-year-old Johnny Glen Gillum and twenty-five-year-old William Starr Jordan were at a party at the Healdton home of Robison's girlfriend Sharon Briscoe, and after Robison loaded guns into the trunk he borrowed her white Oldsmobile. The trio drove to the home of forty-one-year-old Robert Leon Swinford four miles east of Velma and ninety miles south of Oklahoma City, intending to rob Borque of a large cache of jewelry.

As soon as the robbers entered the house they encountered Lovejoy, and Robison shot her in the head once with his .380-caliber automatic pistol, killing her instantly. Borque and Swinford were in a bedroom, and when they heard the gunshot they locked the door, but Robison broke in and shot Borque in the head and body, which did not kill her but left her lying helpless on the bed. Swinford then grabbed Robison about the arms and held him tightly, but Robison managed to turn his gun and shoot Swinford through the side, and he collapsed. Swinford would soon have died of the wound but Robison fired another shot into his body, killing him, and then one of the other men murdered Borque with two shots to her forehead. The three murderers ransacked the house, taking everything of value and photographs of Borque and Swinford, but they missed jewelry worth over $6,000 in a purse under a bedspread beneath Borque's body.

The three murderers returned to Briscoe's automobile and started back to her house but soon a car closed in on them, and the driver, Ms. Terry Henderson, got a good look at the car and the front seat passenger — Robison. The three fled from Henderson, and immediately upon their arrival at the Briscoe house, in a nervous state, Robison told everyone to pack for a trip to Wichita Falls, Texas. Robison removed and disposed of his bloodstained shirt and had his niece clean a blood spot from his boot, and while everyone was busy packing Robison displayed photographs of Borque and Swinford and told the details of the killings. The entire group soon left Oklahoma for Texas, where Robison went with Patricia Higdon and threw his murder weapon and a stolen suitcase from a bridge into a river, but the gun was later recovered.

The bodies were found on June 13, the murderers were identified, and flyers were sent out. It was not until early August that Robison was arrested and returned to the Stephens County jail. In mid–August Gillum, an escapee from a prison work-release program in Purcell, was found working on a ranch in Asotin, Washington, and arrested, and he waived extradition on August 21. On December 18 Robison and Gillum were arraigned and their trials were set for late March, with Robison to be tried first. Jordan was arrested at Wichita Falls, Texas, in early March, and on March 5 he was extradited to Oklahoma. Robison's trial began in Stephens County district court Judge George Lindley's courtroom on Monday, March 23, 1981, and on Friday the case went to the jury. After three hours thirty-five minutes deliberating the jurors found him guilty of three counts of first-degree murder and recommended the death penalty. Gillum's trial began on March 30, and on April 4 he was also found guilty of three counts of murder. Formal sentencing was conducted on April 28, and Gillum was sentenced to serve three life terms while Robison was sentenced to die by lethal injection. Jordan had been arraigned on April 13, and at his preliminary hearing on April 17 he was bound over for trial on July 20, but on May 22, 1981, pled guilty to three counts of murder and was sentenced to serve three life terms. Jordan and Gillum are still serving out their sentences as prisoner numbers 114514 and 86391, respectively.

Robison's attorney filed an appeal, which stayed the execution for eleven years. After the state supreme court affirmed the judgment and sentence of the district court Robison's attorney took the case to the federal Tenth Circuit Court of Appeals, but on September 25, 1987, they upheld the previous judgment, and on November 13 the justices denied a rehearing. Robison's attorney then used every means and manipulation at his disposal to save his client's life but finally the date of execution was set for Friday, March 13, 1992. The state Pardons and Paroles Board refused clemency, and Governor David Walters declined to intervene. In a final effort an appeal was filed with the U.S. Supreme Court, but late Thursday night, hours before the execution, the justices refused to hear the case.

During his final days Robison asked that no autopsy be performed as it would be a violation of his body. On Thursday evening the death warrant was read to the condemned man by the warden, and after midnight the witnesses were guided into the viewing room. Robison had been taken from his cell earlier, and when the curtains were drawn open the witnesses found the condemned man already lying on a gurney with his chest, waist, and legs secured, his arms strapped to extended supports, with a sheet covering his torso and legs. A three-person team then inserted an intravenous cannula (IV) into a vein in each arm, the second a backup in case the primary IV failed. As soon as everything was in order the signal was given and each of the men on the team injected one of three drugs: first sodium thiopental to cause sleep; second pancuronium bromide to stop respiration, which would cause death in time; and third potassium chloride to stop Robison's heart. Once his heart stopped the curtains were drawn closed and the body was removed. State officials went to court later that morning to try to obtain a court order to have the body released to medical examiners for an autopsy, without which a death certificate could not be issued.

Sources: 677 P.2d 1085; 829 F.2d 1501 (September 25, 1987). *Chronicle-Telegram* (Elyria, OH): June 15, 1980. March 13, 1992. *Del Rio News-Herald* (TX): March 29, 1981. *Galveston News* (TX): August 21, 1980. *Paris News* (TX): December 21, 1980; April 17, 1981; May 24, 1981.

Grasso, Thomas J.
March 20, 1995

On Christmas Eve 1990 twenty-seven-year-old Thomas J. Grasso, who had a long criminal record, broke into the home of his eighty-seven-year-old Tulsa, Oklahoma, neighbor Hilda Johnson and strangled her with a cord from her electric Christmas tree lights, and when she showed signs of life he bludgeoned her to death with an iron. He ransacked the house but found only $12, so he stole her television and pawned it for $125. He fled to Staten Island, New York, where, on July 3, 1991, he was living in a boardinghouse where eighty-one-year-old Leslie Holtz also lived. He broke into Holtz's room and strangled him to death and then stole everything of value. He was captured two weeks after the murder of Holtz, tried on Staten Island, and on March 31, 1992, was convicted of first-degree murder. Judge Charles A. Kuffner, Jr., sentenced him to serve a twenty years-to-life term in prison, as New York had no death penalty.

Grasso then confessed to Johnson's murder in Tulsa, and he was extradited to Oklahoma where, on September 28, 1992, he pled guilty. Two days later he was sentenced to serve five hundred years in prison for burglary and sentenced to die by lethal injection for first-degree murder. In 1992 Grasso insisted that he wanted to stay in Oklahoma and die, rather than spend the rest of his life in a New York prison. In March 1993 Grasso waived all appeals, and in May 1993, at his request, his parents withdrew from the battle to save their son's life.

On July 15 the waiver of appeals was affirmed, but New York's Governor Mario M. Cuomo filed a suit in August to have Grasso returned to his state. On October 8, 1993, the Tenth Circuit Court of Appeals ruled that New York had priority and that Grasso had to be returned, and rejected his appeal on the judgment on October 27. On October 30 Grasso was transferred back to his East Coast prison cell. Oklahoma and the condemned man then tried every legal maneuver to get his transfer back to Oklahoma for execution, but they failed. In November 1994 Governor George E. Pataki defeated Governor Mario M. Cuomo in the election, and as soon as Pataki took office he and Oklahoma's new Governor Frank Keating reached an agreement to return Grasso to Oklahoma for execution. Grasso arrived at the prison in McAlester, Oklahoma, on January 12, 1995; he was registered as prisoner 209207 and lodged in his fourteen-by-eighteen foot death row cell in H unit. The Criminal Court of Appeals then set his execution date at March 20.

On March 19 the prisoner was moved from his death row cell to the special cell near the lethal injection room. He visited with his lawyers and penned press releases beginning at 3:00 P.M., first stating, "What we call the beginning is often the end, and to make an end is to make a beginning. The end is where we start from." His 8:25 P.M. press release stated, "For most of us, there is only the unattended moment, the moment in and out of time. And right action is freedom from the past and future also." Between the releases he was served a large final meal which included spaghetti, but he became upset when he claimed he had ordered a sixteen-ounce can of "Spaghetti-O's," but he was shown that he had left the "O's" off his order form. At 10:00 P.M. he issued a press release poem:

> As the poison drips into my veins,
> And from my body life does drain,
> I'll know then, one and for all,
> What "last call" means,
> when serving "toxahol."

An hour later he released his final statement, "I did not get my Spaghetti-O's. I want the press to know this."

At 12:49 A.M. Grasso, wearing a new set of prison denims, was removed from his cell and marched twenty-five steps into the injection room where the walls were painted a bright white and the room was barren except for a clock, a gurney, and a black telephone. He took his place on the gurney and his chest, waist, and legs were strapped while his arms were secured to two arm extensions, and then a sheet was pulled over his body. A medical technician carefully inserted one intravenous cannula (IV) into each arm. The executioners were hidden from view in another room, hooded and behind a one-way mirrored window. Warden Ron Ward picked up the telephone and at 1:17 he heard Governor Keating order the execution to proceed, and on his signal the beige curtain was opened and the witnesses, including Grasso's lawyers and twelve newsmen, first saw the condemned man. When he declined to speak to the witnesses the warden announced, "Let the execution begin," and each executioner drained the contents of his syringe into the tube leading to Grasso's arm. The first drug, sodium thiopental, caused unconsciousness; the second drug, pancuronium bromide, caused his respiration to become labored and would have caused death in time; but the third drug, potassium chloride, quickly stopped his heart. His breath rattled at 1:18, his chest heaved at 1:19 and at 1:21 he coughed; his body then relaxed, and at 1:22 A.M. Grasso was pronounced dead.

Sources: *Chronicle-Telegram* (Elyria, OH): May 12, 1993. *New York News* (NY): March 20, 1995. *New York Times* (NY): January 12, 1995; March 21, 1995. *Post-Standard* (Syracuse, NY): October 14, 1993; October 30, 1993; January 12, 1995. *Syracuse Herald-Journal* (NY): October 12, 1993; October 29, 1993; November 25, 1993; November 13, 1994; March 21, 1995.

Stafford, Roger D.
July 1, 1995

In mid-June 1978 a pawn shop was burglarized at Purcell, Oklahoma, and two pistols with ammunition were taken. On June 22, 1978, thirty-eight-year-old Air Force Technical Sergeant Melvin Lorenz and his thirty-one-year-old wife, Staff Sergeant Linda Lorenz, stationed in San Antonio, Texas, with their twelve-year-old son Richard were driving in their pickup truck with camper on Highway 35 north of Purcell on their way to the funeral of Melvin's mother in North Dakota. They saw a stranded automobile and a woman flagged them down, and they stopped to help. As soon as the Lorenz couple stepped out of their car the two Stafford men appeared with their stolen pistols drawn, and Melvin and Linda were taken prisoner by twenty-seven-year-old Roger Dale Stafford, his wife Verna, and his brother Harold. The Staffords set about robbing them, and when Melvin failed to turn over all his money he was shot to death. Linda ran to help her husband but she was knocked to the ground and shot to death, as well.

The Staffords then took the pickup truck and started to drive away when they heard Richard in the camper, so Roger slid open the window and shot the boy. They had only driven a mile when they stopped and pulled out the youngster, who was still alive, and shot him to death. The bodies of Melvin and Linda Lorenz were found in the evening of the day they were killed, and Richard's body was found two days later. On the same day Richard's body was found, the truck was found abandoned at the Will Rogers World Airport.

The case was still being investigated on Sunday, July 16, 1978, when the Staffords went to the Sirloin Stockade at SW 74 and Pennsylvania Avenue in the Southern Hills Shopping Center in Oklahoma City and stayed until closing time at 10:00 P.M. They left but when the employees dimmed the lights they entered through a back door and took hostage six employees: forty-three-year-old assistant manager Louis Zacarias, fifty-six-year-old Isaac Freeman, sixteen-year-old David Salsman, seventeen-year-old Anthony Tew, seventeen-year-old David Lindsay, and fifteen-year-old Terri Horst — and marched them into the large walk-in meat locker in the rear of the restaurant. After they ransacked the restaurant, finding $1,500, they returned to the meat locker and using a small caliber pistol shot each employee in the head and body, with as many as twenty shots fired. When manager Michael J. Click did not receive the required phone call telling him the amount of the day's receipts he returned to the restaurant and found the bodies at 11:00 P.M. Five employees were dead but Terri Horst was still alive and was being rushed to the hospital when she also died, fifteen minutes after midnight, without regaining consciousness. The only clues were fingerprints and a description of an old, green station wagon.

On July 23 Harold Stafford was involved in a collision on his motorcycle and died, and the circumstances suggested it might have been suicide.

The following day, in an unrelated development, investigators began looking for links between the Lorenz murders and the Sirloin Stockade massacre, and ballistic testing of two handguns found in a north Oklahoma City field proved to be that link. By January 2, 1979, the authorities had discovered witnesses and released three sketches of the suspected murderers. The following day a drunken Roger Stafford, after seeing the sketches, called investigators and told them he knew two of the people and named Verna and Harold Stafford.

Based on the lead provided by her estranged husband, Verna was arrested in Chicago in early March, and she named her husband as the murderer; he was arrested in a Chicago YMCA lobby on March 13. Both prisoners were returned to Oklahoma and charged with nine counts of murder, but Verna turned state's evidence. Roger was tried and convicted while Verna was allowed to plead guilty to two counts of second-degree murder in return for her testimony, and she was sentenced to serve a prison term of ten years to life. On October 17 Roger was sentenced to die by lethal injection, and the same day he was delivered to a death row cell in unit H at the state prison at McAlester.

The first of several stays of execution for Roger was granted on December 20, 1979, and the Oklahoma Court of Criminal Appeals then granted a new trial, but on March 7, 1980, he was again convicted and sentenced to die. Further legal delays prevented his execution. On April 2, 1984, just hours before he was to be executed, his appeal to the U.S. Supreme Court was accepted for consideration, and the execution was stayed. Meanwhile Verna's appeal for resentencing was granted, and on August 7, 1989, she was sentenced to serve two consecutive life terms. Stafford exhausted every legal remedy by May 30, 1995, and his date with the executioners was set for July 1. Neither the Board of Pardons and Paroles nor Governor Frank Keating would intervene.

Stafford was moved from his death row cell to the special cell near the death chamber. He spent his last afternoon visiting with his family and ate his final meal for lunch, though he had ice cream in the evening. Just before midnight Stafford, wearing a new set of prison denims, was removed from his cell and marched twenty-five steps into the injection room. He took his place on the gurney, and his chest, waist, and legs were strapped while his arms were secured to two arm extensions, and then a sheet was pulled over his body. A medical technician carefully inserted one intravenous cannula (IV) into the vein of each arm while the executioners were hidden from view in another room, hooded and behind a one-way mirrored window. The warden confirmed by telephone that the execution was to proceed, and on his signal the beige curtains were drawn open and the witnesses, including his third wife Mickey, whom he had married while in prison, first saw the condemned man. When asked for his final words he said, "I'd like to tell the world you're seeing an innocent man murdered. I've got nothing to lose by telling a lie. Somewhere, somehow, some place, somebody, please exonerate me. Seek truth and justice. The truth will set you free, but not me. Give me the peace of giving my name back," and then he proclaimed his love for his wife.

When he concluded at 12:22 A.M. the warden announced, "Let the execution begin," and each executioner drained the contents of his syringe into the tube leading to Stafford's arm. The first drug, sodium thiopental, caused unconsciousness; the second drug, pancuronium bromide, caused his respiration to become labored and would have caused death in time; but the third drug, potassium chloride, quickly stopped his heart, and at 12:30 A.M. he was pronounced dead.

Sources: *Hutchinson News* (KS): July 17, 1978. *Iola Register* (KS): July 17, 1978. *Oklahoman* (OK City): July 16, 2008. *Tyrone Herald* (PA): July 17, 1978.

Brecheen, Robert A.
August 11, 1995

In late February 1983 fifty-nine-year-old Hilton Stubbs, a clothing store owner in Ardmore, Oklahoma, sold a hat to twenty-eight-year-old Robert Allen Brecheen on credit but was never able to collect the debt. In mid–March Brecheen approached Stubbs and asked to borrow $400, but Stubbs refused to loan him the money. On the evening of March 23 Hilton Stubbs retired alone. After a brief period he heard a shot and saw, through the open door to the living room, his fifty-nine-year-old wife, Marie, collapse to the floor. He rolled out of bed and got his pistol from the nightstand just as an intruder appeared at the doorway, and the intruder fired at the empty bed. Stubbs returned gunfire, and after the brief exchange of gunshots the intruder fled. Stubbs found his wife dead and called the police, and within minutes officers found Brecheen two hundred yards from the Stubbses' home, seriously wounded and unable to flee further. He was rushed to the hospital, recovered, and was lodged in jail to await his trial.

Brecheen was tried in the Carter County district court in late September 1983, after the trial judge conducted voir dire of the jurors and then refused to grant a change of venue, and he was convicted of burglary and first-degree murder. Brecheen was sentenced to die by lethal injection, and he was delivered to the prison on October 12. His attorney filed an appeal but the state Court of Criminal Appeals affirmed the judgment and sentence. The next appeal was to the Tenth Circuit Court of Appeals but the federal court could find no reason to overturn the state courts. This was followed by an appeal to the U.S. Supreme Court, which heard the case and decided against Brecheen on February 29, 1988; then in 1993 the justices denied certiorari for a rehearing. The defense team made every effort to save their client's life, but their second appeal to the federal court of appeals failed on October 14, 1994. Brecheen appeared before the state Board of Pardons and Paroles in late July, and clemency was denied; Governor Frank Keating refused to intervene. Nothing further would arise to delay the proceedings, and his date with the executioner remained August 11, 1995.

Early on the morning before his execution Brecheen was moved from his death row cell to a special cell near the death chamber. After his attorneys left at 7:45 P.M. he lay on his bed and appeared to sleep, but at 9:00 P.M. his guards attempted to wake the prisoner so he could prepare for his execution. They found him in a stupor with pupils dilated, breathing heavily, and drifting in and out of consciousness. Oklahoma law required that a condemned man be aware during his execution, so he was rushed to the McAlester Regional Hospital, his stomach was pumped, and it was found he had ingested a large quantity of prison-issued sedatives. During his final weeks the condemned man had been given small quantities of the sedative daily to help him sleep, and by some ploy he had managed to accumulate a large stash, which the guards had not found when he was moved to his new cell. The amount taken, however, was not life-threatening, and as soon as he was stabilized he was returned to the prison.

Just before 2:00 A.M. Brecheen, wearing a new set of prison denims, was marched into the injection room. He took his place on the gurney where his chest, waist, and legs were strapped while his arms were secured to two arm extensions, and then a sheet was pulled over his body. A medical technician carefully inserted one intravenous cannula (IV) into the vein of each arm, while the executioners were hidden from view in another room, hooded and behind a one-way mirrored window. Warden Ron Ward confirmed by telephone that the execution was to proceed and asked if Brecheen had any last words, and he made a brief statement but it was not recorded as the microphone in the death chamber malfunctioned. Witnesses watched on closed-circuit television in a room on the floor below but could not hear the warden announce, "Let the execution begin." Each executioner drained the contents of his syringe into the tube leading to Brecheen's arm: the first drug, sodium thiopental, caused unconsciousness; the second drug, pancuronium bromide, caused his respiration to become labored and would have caused death in time; and the third drug, potassium chloride, stopped his heart. In minutes all sign of life was absent and he was pronounced dead.

Sources: *Brecheen v. State*, 732 P.2d 899. *Brecheen v. State*, 835 P.2d 117, 121 (Okla. Crim. App. 1992). *Brecheen v. Oklahoma*: 485 U.S. 909, 108 S. Ct. 1085, 99 L.Ed.2d 244. 41F.3d 1343 (10th Cir. Ct. of App.; October 14, 1994). *Hutchinson News* (KS): August 12, 1995. *New York Times* (NY): August 12, 1995.

Brewer, Benjamin
April 26, 1996

Twenty-year-old Benjamin Brewer noticed twenty-year-old Karen Joyce Stapleton, a pretty accounting student at the Oklahoma State University at Tulsa, and on August 16, 1978, he followed her to her apartment. He broke in and took her prisoner though she fought hard, but she was overpowered and raped, and then he stabbed her twenty-one times. She was not dead but was unable to move and was bleeding to death, so Brewer sat on her couch and watched her slowly die. The following day her semi-nude body was discovered, and Brewer was suspected and soon arrested.

Brewer, who had a record of "use or threat of violence to a person" when he pled guilty to threatening to cut a woman's throat during a rape in 1976, confessed to the murder of Stapleton, and at his trial in October 1979 he was convicted based upon that confession and overwhelming physical evidence collected at the scene. The defense of insanity was raised by public defender Frank McCarthy and rejected by the jurors. In 1982 the state's Court of Criminal Appeals overturned the conviction and Brewer was retried in 1983, with the same result. The same attorneys and psychiatrist presented the insanity defense but relied on the fact that, though there was no evidence of insanity before or after the crime, the "bizarreness and insaneness of the crime" showed a thought disorder at the time of the murder, but again the jurors rejected the theory. In a separate penalty phase the death penalty was recommended, and he was sentenced to die and delivered to a death row cell on October 28, 1983, but his attorney would not give up. The judgment and sentence were again appealed but the state Court of Criminal Appeals affirmed the lower court in 1986.

In October 1991 Tulsa Judge B. R. Beasley, relying on an eighty-year-old law, ordered Sheriff Stanley Glanz to execute Brewer in his cell but, fifteen minutes before the sheriff arrived at the prison, the state Court of Criminal Appeals issued a stay until all appeals were processed. After all state court remedies were exhausted Brewer's attorney filed the first writ of habeas corpus at the federal Tenth Circuit Court of Appeals in June 1992; it was denied in 1995, and the second writ was denied just four days before his execution. The state Board of Pardons and Parole denied clemency, and Governor Frank Keating refused to intervene.

Early on the morning before his execution Brewer was moved from his death row cell to a special cell near the death chamber. Just before midnight the condemned man, wearing a new set of prison denims, was removed from his cell and marched twenty-five steps into the injection room. He took his place on the gurney where his chest, waist, and legs were strapped while his arms were secured to two arm extensions, and then a sheet was pulled over his body. He kept his eyes closed the entire time. A medical technician carefully inserted one intravenous cannula (IV) into the vein of each arm while the executioners were hidden from view in another room, hooded and behind a one-way mirrored window. Warden Ron Ward confirmed by telephone that the execution was to proceed and asked if Brewer had any last words, but he declined to speak. While members of the victim's family and other witnesses watched on closed-circuit television in a room on the floor below the warden announced, "Let the execution begin," and each executioner drained the contents of his syringe into the tube leading to Brewer's arm. The first drug, sodium thiopental, caused unconsciousness; the second drug, pancuronium bromide, caused his respiration to become labored and would have caused death in time; and the third drug, potassium chloride, was injected to stop his heart. At 12:10 A.M. all signs of life were absent, and he was pronounced dead.

Sources: *Brewer v. Dan Reynolds*, 51 F.3d 1519 (April 5, 1995). *Brewer v. Dan Reynolds*, 83 F. 3d 431 (April 22, 1996). *Brewer v. State*, 650 P.2d 54 (1982). *Brewer v. State*, 718 P2d 354 (1986). *Kokomo Tribune* (IN): April 26, 1996. *Orlando Sentinel* (FL): April 27, 1996. *Stars and Stripes* (U.S. Military): October 28, 1991. *Syracuse Herald* (NY): April 26, 1996.

Hatch, Steven K.
August 9, 1996

When Steven Keith Hatch was eleven years old his mother died and he began to use drugs, steal cars, and forge checks, was determined to be incorrigible, and was sent to the Utah State Industrial School in Ogden. He was released in 1970, when he was seventeen, to join the Marines, and after his discharge in 1973 he met and married Nancy Ake. In 1979 they were living in Oklahoma where twenty-six-year-old Hatch worked in the oil fields with Nancy's twenty-four-year-old brother Glen Burton Ake, and both men were addicted to drugs. Ake began dating Hatch's sister Teresa but on October 10 she celebrated her birthday with another man, and an enraged Ake threatened to kill her. However, Hatch talked him out of murdering his sister, and all seemed normal until three days later when Nancy Hatch left her husband, taking along their three-year-old son Brian.

Ake and Hatch then walked off their jobs at the oil rig outside Enid and headed south, first stopping at Hennessey, Oklahoma. They broke into a home where Dale and Pat Cameron lived with their two young sons and, at gunpoint, stole $1,500. Forty miles south of Hennessey they came upon an isolated ranch house near Okarche, Oklahoma, the home of forty-three-year-old Pastor Dr. Richard Douglass and his family of three. Shortly before 8:00 P.M. on October 15, 1979, as dinner was being prepared, the barking of the family dog disturbed the Douglass family, and twelve-year-old Leslie went out to investigate. In the back yard the beautiful young girl met a stranger, Ake, who asked for a neighbor unfamiliar to her, and then he asked to use the telephone. At the door the stranger was met by Leslie's sixteen-year-old brother, Brooks, who invited him into their home, as his father would have done.

As soon as Ake was inside Hatch burst through the front door and waved his double-barreled shotgun at the family, which included the thirty-six-year-old mother, Marilyn Sue, Leslie, Brooks, and Pastor Douglass. Ake said, "You know what it's all about," as he pulled a .357-magnum pistol from his boot. The family was herded into the living room and forced to lay on the floor face down, then their wrists and ankles were tied with heavy twine. Ake gathered $43, all the money he could find, and then untied Leslie and led her into her bedroom, leaving Hatch to guard the other family members. He ordered her to undress and then he raped her. When Ake finished he changed places with Hatch who then also raped Leslie. When Hatch finished he brought Leslie from the bedroom, laid her on the floor next to her parents, and tied her.

Hatch and Ake next went to the kitchen and leisurely ate the Douglasses' supper, and debated for two hours what they would do with the family. Ake finally settled the matter when he told Hatch, "Go start the car and listen for the sound." After Hatch left Ake went to Brooks and said, "I don't want to have to shoot you, but...," and shot him in the back twice. The second shot Ake fired mortally wounded Marilyn, then Leslie was shot in the back twice, and with his last round Ake shot Dr. Douglass in the back; his wound later proved fatal.

After Ake fled Brooks slid on his belly to his father and, using his teeth, tried to untie the twine but his father told him to untie his mother first, and after he had removed the twine from her wrists he watched her die. Meanwhile Leslie worked her ankles free, got a knife, and cut the twine from her brother's wrists. Brooks then went for help, and while he was gone his father died with Marilyn Sue in his arms. The two children were rushed to the hospital where it was determined that the two bullets shot into Leslie had pierced a lung and a kidney and ripped through her intestines while the shots fired into Brooks had severed his esophagus, collapsed a lung, and punctured the pericardial sac protecting his heart. After three weeks in the hospital they were sent to relatives living in an Oklahoma City missionary house to recuperate.

The murderers fled to New Orleans and after two weeks started west. On November 2 near Lumberton, Texas, Ake and Hatch robbed thirty-five-year-old surveyor Dale Kokenes and his twenty-seven-year-old co-worker, Yerby Land III. Ake ordered

Hatch to do the killing, but later complained, "Steve couldn't do it, no way in hell.... So I went in there and pulled off two rounds." On Nov. 20, 1979, during a blizzard, Ake and Hatch drove Land's car into a snowdrift two hundred yards from the ranch of sixty-four-year-old Michael Pondella in northwest Colorado. When Pondella heard the men approach he opened the door and found a shotgun aimed at his head. Ake ordered Pondella into a bedroom and told him to lie down on his bed, and when Pondella's small dog jumped onto the bed Ake shot it to death with a single blast from his shotgun. Pondella began talking to the two men and they calmed, and as they drank beer together they began telling of the killings. Ake and Hatch soon tired from exhaustion and beer and fell asleep, so Pondella quietly left, drove into the nearest town, and returned with county deputies. The deputies trapped the fugitives while they were trying to escape on foot through the deep snow, and they surrendered without firing a shot.

As soon as they were behind bars Ake confessed and said of Hatch, "Steve can't kill nobody because he don't have no guts to do nothing." In 1980 they were tried and sentenced to die but both judgments were appealed. Ake won a retrial in 1986 and was again convicted of first-degree murder, but he was sentenced to serve a life term. Hatch's many appeals, motions, and petitions failed, and his date of execution was set for August 9, 1996. In late July, at his final clemency hearing, he told the members of the state Board of Pardons and Paroles, "I am not the monster I have been portrayed to be. I am sorry beyond words for the pain I caused the Douglasses." Governor Frank Keating refused to intervene.

As the date of his execution neared Hatch, showing no remorse, became angry that his victims might profit from his death through book and movie deals and issued a statement, "Be stronger than those who sit in judgment and prey upon you, for they are weak with lies and deception.... They will try to use you and profit from you for their own gains. They're evil and barbaric and politicians."

Shortly before the day of his execution Hatch was moved from his death row cell to the special cell near the death chamber. Just before midnight Hatch, wearing a new set of prison denims, was removed from his cell and marched twenty-five steps into the injection room. He took his place on the gurney, and at 12:01 A.M. his chest, waist, and legs were strapped while his arms were secured to two arm extensions, and then a sheet was pulled over his body. A medical technician carefully inserted one intravenous cannula (IV) into the veins of each arm while the executioners were hidden from view in another room, hooded and behind a one-way mirrored window. Warden Ron Ward confirmed by telephone that the execution was to proceed. On his signal the beige curtains were drawn open, and the witnesses, including Brooks and Leslie, first saw the condemned man through the tinted window. When asked if he had any final words he simply told the warden "No!" The warden immediately announced, "Let the execution begin," and each executioner drained the contents of his syringe into the tube leading to Hatch's arm. The first drug, sodium thiopental, caused unconsciousness; the second drug, pancuronium bromide, caused his respiration to become labored and would have caused death in time; and the third drug, potassium chloride, was injected to stop his heart. Hatch began to snore, his face grew pale, and after seven minutes all sign of life was gone and he was pronounced dead.

Sources: *Cedar Rapids Gazette* (IA): August 9, 1996. *Hawkeye,* (Burlington, IA): August 8, 1996. www.people.com/people/archive/article/0,,20142085,00.html.

Carpenter, Scott D.
May 8, 1997

On February 6, 1994, nineteen-year-old Scott Dawn Carpenter pulled his pickup truck up to the gas pumps of the Duchess Creek Bait and Grocery Store near Lake Eufaula in eastern Oklahoma and put $37 worth of gasoline into the tank. He went in to pay for the gas but first selected a sandwich, soft drink and chewing tobacco and placed them on the counter, but this may have been a ruse to distract fifty-six-year-old owner A. J. Kelley, or he may have told Kelley he wanted to buy bait. Carpenter pulled out a knife and stabbed Kelley in the neck. The storekeeper's body was found in the minnow room at the rear of the store.

Carpenter gathered up his snacks just as he was interrupted by two customers, and they pursued him but he made it to his truck and drove off. The two men wrote down the license number, telephoned authorities, and Carpenter was arrested one hour later. Carpenter pled no contest to a charge of first-degree murder and demanded the death penalty, saying he did not want to spend decades in prison. As he had requested he was sentenced to die by lethal injection, and he refused to appeal the judgment and sentence. In January 1997 he wrote to the state Court of Criminal Appeals asking that his date of execution be set, and in response the justices ordered a competency hearing. After Carpenter was pronounced sane his date with the executioner was set for May 8, 1997, and neither the state Board of Pardon and Paroles nor Governor Frank Keating would delay the proceedings.

On the morning before his execution the condemned man was removed from his death row cell to a special cell near the injection room, and shortly before his execution he was allowed to talk with his mother for an hour and a quarter. Just before midnight Carpenter was taken from his cell, marched twenty-five steps into the death chamber, and took his place on the gurney. His chest, waist, and legs were strapped while his arms were secured to two arm extensions, and then a sheet was pulled over his body. A medical technician carefully inserted one intravenous cannula (IV) into the vein of each arm, while the executioners remained hidden from view in another room, hooded and behind a one-way mirrored window. The warden confirmed by telephone that the execution was to proceed and then asked Carpenter if he had any last words, and his final statement was "I tell the young and old, do not stray onto the wrong path in life as I did. I speak from experience when I say it's a long and bumpy road, with a lot of regret and few second chances." He had left behind a letter apologizing to Kelley's family.

The warden then announced, "Let the execution begin," and each executioner drained the contents of his syringe into the tube leading to Carpenter's arm: the first drug, sodium thiopental, caused unconsciousness; the second drug, pancuronium bromide, caused his respiration to become labored and would have caused death in time; and the third drug, potassium chloride, stopped his heart. The drugs began to flow at 12:11 A.M. but at 12:14 A.M. Carpenter experienced seizures in reaction to the drugs. He first made a deep guttural noise and then he experienced eighteen violent spasms of the stomach as his chest heaved, and this was followed by several lesser convulsions. His jaw clenched tightly while his body convulsed for three minutes, but at 12:17 he relaxed. His skin color changed to purple and then to a yellowish gray, and five minutes later, at 12:22 A.M., he was pronounced dead.

Sources: *Journal-Tribune* (Marysville, OH): May 8, 1997. *New York Times,* (NY): April 18, 1998. *Tulsa World* (OK): May 8, 1997.

Long, Michael E.

February 20, 1998

In early 1987 twenty-four-year-old Michael Edward Long was working for a florist in Muskogee, Oklahoma, and he became obsessed with coworker twenty-four-year-old Sheryl Graber. He proposed various relationships but the single mother of a five-year-old boy rejected his advances. On April 7, 1987, Long went to Graber's home and later admitted, "I went there to get it one way or the other." He took along a large knife and a hand gun. He made sexual advances toward Graber, and when he was once again rejected he threw her to the floor and stabbed her. Graber cried out, broke free and made it to the front door, but Long pulled her back into the house. When neighbors came to investigate he believed he had convinced them that she was just drunk. He returned to Graber and stabbed her thirty times so violently that bits of the knife blade broke off against bone, but she was not dead so he shot her in the head and abdomen. He then shot five-year-old Andrew in the head twice, and stabbed him to be sure he was dead.

Meanwhile the suspicious neighbors called the police, and when they arrived they captured Long as he was leaving the murder scene. As soon as he was behind bars he confessed and was charged with two counts of murder. After his trial, conviction on two counts of first-degree murder, and sentencing in October 1987, he arrived on death row on October 16. He had been sentenced to die by lethal injection when his defense of depression, drug and alcohol abuse was rejected by the jurors as a mitigating factor. Over the next ten years he fluctuated from waiving his appeal to filing appeals, but finally the matter was resolved against him, and in 1997 he insisted that no further appeals be filed, so his date of execution was set for February 20, 1998. He had told the justices he would rather die than spend the rest of his life in "a Hell hole."

On the morning of his execution he was moved from his death row cell to a cell near the death chamber. During a late interview for the *Muskogee Phoenix*, Long said, "Tell everybody I just earnestly beg you to repent your sins. Invite Jesus into your heart. Eternity is too long to end up going to the wrong place." He then recounted a parable about a boy who lost his favorite sailboat but discovered that someone had found it and sold it to a pawnshop, so the boy saved his money and bought it back, comparing the recovery of the boat to man's redemption by God. He had previously written a letter to Graber's parents pleading for forgiveness, and they responded, "We bear no malice nor ill will...."

Just before midnight Long was taken from his cell, marched twenty-five steps into the death chamber, and took his place on the gurney. His chest, waist, and legs were strapped while his arms were secured to two arm extensions, and then a sheet was pulled over his body. A medical technician carefully inserted one intravenous cannula (IV) into the vein of each arm, while the executioners remained hidden from view in another room, hooded and behind a one-way mirrored window. The warden confirmed by telephone that the execution was to proceed, the curtains were drawn back for the witnesses, and then Long was asked if he had any last words but he declined to speak.

The warden announced, "Let the execution begin," and each executioner drained the contents of his syringe into the tube leading to Long's arm: the first drug, sodium thiopental, caused unconsciousness; the second drug, pancuronium bromide, caused Long's respiration to become labored and would have caused death in time; and the third drug, potassium chloride, was to stop his heart. As the drugs began to flow he lifted his head and turned toward his attorney, his spiritual adviser, and a woman watching the execution from the witnesses area, and "as his voice grew slow and sluggish" he mouthed the words, "Sissy, I just want to tell you don't be sad because the times of sadness are over." At 12:25 A.M. he was pronounced dead.

Sources: *Journal-Tribune* (Marysville, OH): February 20, 1998. *Sitka Sentinel* (AK): February 20, 1998.

Wood, Stephen E.
August 5, 1998

Presbyterian minister Robert Bruce Brigden was accused of sexually assaulting the daughters of members of his Kansas congregation, but he was not charged, and he moved to a church at Alva in Woods County, Oklahoma. In 1992 fifty-eight-year-old Brigden was accused of twenty counts of sexually assaulting at least eight girls between the ages of four and fourteen, including a "rape by instrumentality" of the seven-year-old daughter of Trish States. He insisted he was innocent and wrote to his wife that the youngest victim was "four going on four hundred years old"; he said she had invited him into her bed and was upset when he refused, concluding, "Hell hath no fury like a woman scorned." The charges and his June trial received extensive, detailed publicity in Oklahoma's newspapers. Brigden was convicted on all twenty counts, sentenced to serve a term of forty to sixty years, and delivered to the Oklahoma State Reformatory at Granite.

On August 25 he arrived at the reformatory and the following morning, as soon as he appeared in the prison yard, he was attacked by other prisoners who were disgusted by his crimes against children. He was classified as a "high potential victim," removed from the general population, and housed in a special protective unit in cell four in the F Unit cell house, which was separated from the rest of the prisoners by a high fence.

After Brigden had been in protective custody for twenty-one months Regional Director James L. Saffle, in an effort to make more efficient use of the F cell house beds in the crowded prison, ordered that the protective custody prisoners be moved to D and E Units. However, Brigden was moved to A Unit and he anticipated problems, so the lieutenant of the guard told him to tell anyone who accosted him that he had been ordered to inform on that prisoner to the lieutenant.

Housed in the same unit as Brigden was thirty-two-year-old Stephen Edward Wood, who was serving a long term for murdering two transients in 1992. At 6:15 P.M. on June 12, 1994, the guard on duty in Unit A was Terry Duane New, and he saw that Brigden's cell door was left open, but when he investigated he was told everything was fine. He sat near the door for a while and then went to the roof to watch the activity in the yard. Just before 7:00 he heard a scream, and as he ran from the roof he heard three more screams and saw a knife, a prison-made "shank," thrown out. When New reached Brigden's cell he found that he had been stabbed numerous times, so he was rushed to the Elkview General Hospital in Hobart where he died. The knife was traced to Wood, and soon prisoner Teddy Graham was implicated and told the details of the killing. Graham said that just before 7:00 he and Wood went to the cell of Brigden, and Wood demanded his watch. Brigden refused and warned that he had been ordered to report Wood to the lieutenant of the guard, so Wood pulled out his "shank" and repeatedly stabbed Brigden in the chest and legs.

Wood was charged with murdering Brigden, and Graham testified against him at his trial in the Greer County district court. Wood tried to gain sympathy by emphasizing the crimes of Brigden and asserting that he had an uncontrollable rage against men who victimized children, but the jurors rejected this as a mitigating factor, and Wood was convicted of first-degree murder and sentenced to die by lethal injection. He was returned to the prison on July 6, 1995, and lodged in a death row cell. He waived his appeals and asked for an early execution date, and after the automatic review required in death penalty cases was completed Wood was sentenced to die on August 5, 1998.

Early on the morning before his execution Wood was moved from his death row cell to a special cell near the death chamber. Just before midnight Wood, wearing a new set of prison denims, was marched into the injection room. He took his place on the gurney where his chest, waist, and legs were strapped while his arms were secured to two arm extensions, and then a sheet was pulled over his body. A medical technician carefully inserted one intravenous cannula (IV) into the vein of each arm, while the executioners were hidden from view in another room, hooded and behind a one-way mirrored window. Warden Cowley confirmed by telephone that the execution was to proceed, had the curtains drawn open, and asked if Wood had any last words but he declined to speak to the witnesses. The warden then announced, "Let the execution begin." Each executioner drained the contents of his syringe into the tube leading to Wood's arm: the first drug, sodium thiopental, caused unconsciousness; the second drug, pancuronium bromide, caused his respiration to become labored and would have caused death in time; and the third drug, potassium chloride, stopped his heart. In minutes all sign of life was absent, and he was pronounced dead.

Sources: *Dallas Morning News* (TX): June 14, 1994. *Oklahoman* (Oklahoma City): June 14, 1992. *Paris News* (TX): August 5, 1998. *Tulsa Tribune* (OK): August 25, 1892. *Tulsa World* (OK): September 3, 1992; June 14, 1994.

Nguyen, Tuan A.
December 10, 1998

As the war in South Vietnam was coming to a close with the "fall of Saigon" sixteen-year-old Tuan Anh Nguyen hitched a ride to America, where he sought asylum as a refugee. In 1982, when Nguyen was twenty-three years old, he was estranged from his twenty-one-year-old wife Donna Nguyen. On May 24, 1982, Nguyen, who used his Americanized name "Tommy Wing," went to the Tulsa, Oklahoma, home of his in-laws where Donna was caring for her three-year-old niece, Amanda Jo White, and six-year-old nephew, Joseph White, and she had custody of the Nguyens' infant son. Nguyen was armed with a knife and he stabbed to death Amanda Jo, Joseph, and Donna but left his infant son unharmed in his crib. The bodies were discovered when Donna's parents returned home. Amanda Jo had been stabbed twenty two times, Joseph had been stabbed seventeen times, and Donna had been stabbed twenty-six times, and all three were dead when discovered.

Nguyen was suspected but he had fled to Arizona and eluded capture for four years, until he fought with the fourteen-year-old girl with whom he was living, the police were called, and he was identified and arrested. Nguyen was extradited to Oklahoma and tried on three counts of murder in late 1986, and he was convicted on all three counts. He was only sentenced to serve a life term in prison for killing his wife but sentenced to die by lethal injection for the murder of the two children. He arrived at the prison on November 21, 1986, as his attorney filed appeals which stayed his execution for a dozen years. Finally all avenues of judicial relief were exhausted, the state Board of Pardons and Parole refused clemency, and Governor Frank Keating declined to intervene so his last date with the executioner remained December 10, 1998.

Sixty days before his execution Nguyen was moved from his H unit death row cell into one of three solitary confinement cells in maximum security, where John Duvall and John Castro were housed. Over the coming two months Nguyen would be isolated from all other prisoners and he and his cell would be searched often, to prevent an occurrence similar to that of Brecheen in August 1996 when he attempted suicide by overdose. On December 8, 1998, Nguyen was moved from his maximum security cell to a special cell near the death chamber. When asked he declined to request any witnesses or have a clergyman present.

Just before midnight December 9 the prisoner, wearing a new set of prison denims, was marched into the injection room. He took his place on the gurney where his chest, waist, and legs were strapped while his arms were secured to two arm extensions, and then a sheet was pulled over his body. A medical technician carefully inserted one intravenous cannula (IV) into the vein of each arm, while the executioners were hidden from view in another room, hooded and behind a one-way mirrored window. The warden confirmed by telephone, with Governor Frank Keating, that the execution was to proceed, had the curtains drawn open, and asked if Nguyen if had any last words but he declined to speak to the witnesses. The warden then announced, "Let the execution begin," and each executioner drained the contents of his syringe into the tube leading to Nguyen's arm: the first drug, sodium thiopental, caused unconsciousness; the second drug, pancuronium bromide, caused his respiration to become labored and would have caused death in time; and the third drug, potassium chloride, stopped his heart. Minutes after midnight all sign of life was absent, and he was pronounced dead.

Sources: *Indiana Gazette* (PA): December 10, 1998. *Nguyen v. Reynolds*: 131 F.3d 1340, 1345 (10th Cir, 1997). *Syracuse Herald-Journal* (NY): December 10, 1998.

Duvall, John W.
December 17, 1998

On September 15, 1986, thirty-seven-year-old John Wayne Duvall received a telephone call from his estranged thirty-year-old wife Karla complaining that he had cancelled her prescription, but she said she had gotten the drugs anyway. That night Duvall, an alcoholic, went to a bar and drank heavily, and at 9:00 P.M. he arranged a ride to his wife's Duncan, Oklahoma, duplex apartment. He stood at the door of the vacant apartment next door until 10:30 P.M. when he got up his nerve and knocked. Karla opened the door and he immediately asked about their son Marcus, and was told he was at his grandmother's home. Duvall then grabbed his wife by the throat as he forced his way into the apartment, threw her to the floor, and dragged her into the kitchen. He took out a meat fork and several knives and stabbed her with the meat fork, but when the prongs of the fork bent he used each knife to stab his wife several times, twenty-four times in all. Karla was not dead and asked her husband to help her shower, so he helped her wash and then laid her on the bed. His wife begged for his help but he replied, "It's just too late for that," and used a pillow to smother her to death.

Duvall fled to the railroad tracks, determined to throw himself in front of the next fast train that passed, but after waiting what seemed a long time and no train appearing he went home. On Thursday, September 18, Duvall went to the courthouse and asked Stephens County commissioner Alvie Chasteen to accompany him to the sheriff's office, where they took seats in a vacant office. Duvall told Chasteen, "I killed my wife Monday night." The commissioner immediately called for Sheriff William Alexander to join them, and after following the proper procedures Duvall provided a detailed confession. He was arrested and lodged in jail while the police went to the Chickasaw Nation Apartment Complex and found Karla's dead body, and the following day the prisoner was charged with murder.

On November 17 the district attorney filed a "Bill of Particulars" seeking the death penalty, and his trial was scheduled for May 1987. Duvall was convicted of first-degree murder, and during the penalty phase the jurors found aggravating circumstances justifying the death penalty. On May 20, 1987, Duvall was sentenced to die by lethal injection, but the execution was stayed by an appeal. On May 28, 1991, the state Court of Criminal Appeals affirmed the judgment and sentence of the district court, and on October 5, 1992, the U.S. Supreme Court denied certiorari. Over the next six years some legal remedy was sought every year, and denied, until all avenues of judicial relief were exhausted, and his date with the executioner was set for December 17, 1998. The state Board of Pardons and Paroles refused to grant clemency, and Governor Frank Keating declined to intervene.

Sixty days before his execution Duvall was moved from his H unit death row cell into one of three solitary confinement cells in maximum security, where John Castro was housed. Over the next two months Duvall would be isolated from all other prisoners, and he and his cell would be searched often, to prevent an occurrence similar to that of Brecheen in August 1996 when he attempted suicide by overdose. On December 15, 1998, Duvall was moved from his maximum security cell to a special cell near the death chamber.

Just before midnight December 16 the prisoner, wearing a new set of prison denims, was marched into the injection room. He took his place on the gurney where his chest, waist, and legs were strapped while his arms were secured to two arm extensions, and then a sheet was pulled over his body. A medical technician carefully inserted one intravenous cannula (IV) into the vein of each arm, while the executioners were hidden from view in another room, hooded and behind a one-way mirrored window. The warden confirmed by telephone, with Governor Keating, that the execution was to proceed, had the curtains drawn open, and asked if Duvall if had any last words, and he asked for forgiveness for his sins. When he concluded the warden announced, "Let the execution begin," and each executioner drained the contents of his syringe into the tube leading to Duvall's arm: the first drug, sodium thiopental, caused unconsciousness; the second drug, pancuronium bromide, caused his respiration to become labored and would have caused death in time; and the third drug, potassium chloride, stopped his heart. Minutes after midnight all sign of life was absent, and he was pronounced dead.

Sources: *Duvall v. Oklahoma*: 506 U.S. 878 (1992). *Duvall v. Reynolds*: 139 F.3d 768 (1998). *Duvall v. State*: 825 P.2d 621 (1991). *Duvall v. State*: 869 P.2d332, 334 (1994). *Duvall v. State*: 871 P.2d 1386 (1994); *Hutchinson News* (KS): December 18, 1998. *Indiana Gazette* (PA): December 17, 1998. *Sitka Sentinel* (AK): December 17, 1998.

Castro, John W.
January 7, 1999

On April 18, 1983, twenty-one-year-old John Walter Castro was hitchhiking near Stillwater, Oklahoma, when he was picked up by thirty-one-year-old Beulah Grace Sissons Cox. Once he was in the car he pulled a pistol and told Cox he would not harm her but wanted her car. After she pulled to the side of the road and got out he shot her in the head twice, killing her instantly. He drove off and later abandoned the car, so there was no clue to the murderer.

Three months later Castro tried to rob the Hobo-T Restaurant in Ponca City, Oklahoma, but twenty-nine-year-old Rhonda Pappan, the owner, grabbed a knife and tried to stop the robbery. Castro overpowered Pappan and took the knife from her, then stabbed her in the neck, back and chest, and she died soon afterward from severe internal injuries and blood loss.

Castro was quickly captured and linked to the murder of Cox. He was charged with two counts of murder and tried in the separate counties where the crimes occurred. He was twice convicted of first-degree murder and sentenced to die by lethal injection. His attorney, Robert Jackson, filed an appeal, which stayed the execution, and Jackson fought for his client's life for the next fifteen years. The Oklahoma Court of Criminal Appeals overturned the death penalty regarding the murder of Pappan but affirmed the death sentence regarding the murder of Cox. Finally all avenues of judicial relief were exhausted. In December 1998 the state Board of Pardons and Parole refused to grant clemency, and Governor Frank Keating declined to intervene, so his last date with the executioner remained January 7, 1999.

Sixty days before his execution Castro was moved from his H unit death row cell into one of three solitary confinement cells in maximum security. Over the next two months Castro would be isolated from all other prisoners, and he and his cell would be searched often, to prevent an occurrence similar to that of Brecheen in August 1996 when he attempted suicide by overdose. During Castro's last days he was interviewed by a newspaper reporter and said, "If I hadn't been caught and stopped, I probably would have killed someone else."

On January 5, 1999, Castro was moved from his maximum security cell to a special cell near the death chamber. Just before midnight January 6 the prisoner, wearing a new set of prison denims, was marched into the injection room. He took his place on the gurney where his chest, waist, and legs were strapped while his arms were secured to two arm extensions, and then a sheet was pulled over his body. A medical technician carefully inserted one intravenous cannula (IV) into the vein of each arm, while the executioners were hidden from view in another room, hooded and behind a one-way mirrored window. The warden confirmed by telephone, with Governor Keating, that the execution was to proceed, had the curtains to the witnesses' area drawn open, and asked if Castro if had any last words. The prisoner turned his head toward the window and said, "I don't know who's behind that one-way glass but whoever is here from the Cox family, I am sorry for what I did. And anybody who is here from the Pappan family, I am sorry. For the people who are here for me, thank you." This last comment was made to his attorney, two federal public defenders, and two women with whom he had been corresponding: Karen Woo and Patricia Peck. His sixteen-year-old son had been denied admittance because of his youth.

When the prisoner concluded the warden announced, "Let the execution begin," and Castro again turned his head toward the witnesses and said, "I love you. Let's do it!" Each executioner drained the contents of his syringe into the tube leading to Castro's arm: the first drug, sodium thiopental, would cause unconsciousness; the second drug, pancuronium bromide, would cause his respiration to become labored and would have caused death in time; but the third drug, potassium chloride, would stop his heart. After a few moments Castro said, "I feel it," and closed his eyes, and in a few minutes, at 12:22 A.M., all sign of life was absent and he was pronounced dead.

Sources: *Oklahoman* (Oklahoma City): January 7, 1999. *Paris News* (TX): January 7, 1999.

Sellers, Sean R.
February 4, 1999

In September 1985 sixteen-year-old Sean Richard Sellers, an avowed Satanist addicted to the game of Dungeons and Dragons, and his teenaged friend Richard Howard discussed breaking the ten commandments and believed they had broken all but "Thou shalt not kill." They decided they must commit a murder and considered several scenarios, finally settling on murdering a convenience-store clerk whom they felt had insulted one of their girlfriends and had refused to sell beer to Sellers. On September 8 Sellers, later claiming to be possessed by the demon "Ezurate," and Howard took a .357-magnum pistol belonging to Howard's grandfather and went to the Circle K convenience store in northwest Oklahoma City where thirty-two-year-old clerk Robert Paul Bower was working.

After they entered the store they talked with Bower until he was at ease, and while Howard distracted him in conversation Sellers pulled out the pistol loaded with hollow point bullets and fired at Bower nearly point blank, but he missed. Bower fled across the store as Sellers fired again, seriously wounding him, but then Howard cut off Bower's retreat while Sellers pursued him from behind. While the clerk lay helpless staring directly in Sellers' eyes the youth shot him to death, and later he admitted that he shot Bower "just to see what it felt like." The two teenagers walked out taking nothing from the store, leaving no clues to the murderers' identities nor a motive. They cleaned and returned the gun and went about their business.

Over the next six months Sellers' relationship with his parents, his thirty-two-year-old mother, Vonda Bellofatto, and forty-three-year-old step-father, Paul "Lee" Bellofatto, deteriorated. On March 5, 1986, while the couple slept, Sellers performed a satanic ritual and then took his step-father's .44-caliber pistol and crept into their bedroom. He stood at the foot of their bed dressed only in his black underwear, so blood would not spatter on his clothing, took careful aim and shot his step-father in the back of the head. He quickly shot his mother in the face, and when she rose up he shot her in the head again. Paul died instantly but the teenager stood and watched his mother's body convulse as her life drained out. Sellers showered and dressed, ransacked the house, and then drove to Howard's house where he convinced his friend and his wife to provide him with an alibi and spent the night. He returned home the next morning to "discover the bodies," and he called the police.

While the murder scene had been arranged to appear as if an intruder had shot the couple the evidence at the scene raised questions. Howard was questioned twice, and the second time he was convinced to tell the truth; this included the details of the killing of Bower and the location of the two murder weapons. Howard was charged as an accessory to murder, he turned state's evidence, and he was sentenced to five years in prison but the sentence was suspended in return for his testimony. Sellers was arrested, lodged in jail and charged as an adult with murdering his parents and Bower, and he claimed amnesia. He was tried in October 1986, and his attorney used the defense that Sellers believed he was possessed when he killed his parents and Bower, and also claimed it was a result of his addiction to the Dungeons and Dragons game, but the jurors rejected the claim, found him guilty of first-degree murder, and declined to recommend clemency.

Sellers was sentenced to die by lethal injection and delivered to the prison on October 16, but his attorney filed an appeal with the Oklahoma Court of Criminal Appeals, which granted him a stay of execution. In 1991 the justices affirmed the judgment and sentence of the lower court. In 1993 Sellers was diagnosed, by a Texas psychiatrist hired by lead defense attorney Steve Presson, with Multiple Personality Disorder (MPD), and the case was appealed at the state level twice more in 1995 and 1999 based upon this new evidence, but relief was again denied. In 1999 his case was appealed to the Tenth Circuit Court of Appeals, claiming he had not received a fair trial as the jurors had not been informed of his MPD, but the justices declined to intervene though they issued a recommendation for clemency. The case was then appealed to the U.S. Supreme Court but that appeal was denied.

The refusal to hear the new evidence may have been decided because Sellers was observed practicing the symptoms of his claimed mental illness and was being coached by his attorneys, and this weighed heavily on the members of the Board of Pardons and Parole when they heard the same claims on January 27, 1999, and denied clemency by a unanimous vote. Sellers' date with the executioner had been set for February 4, 1999, and none of the last minute legal appeals, nor the many national and international appeals to Governor Frank Keating, would delay his execution. His last appeal to the U.S. Supreme Court was denied at 7:00 P.M. on Wednesday, just thirty hours before his execution.

During his time on death row Sellers was attended by the Rev. Bill Mason, he adopted a Christian religion, and even set up his own ministry from prison. He wrote, "It's not some title I put upon myself, or display as a label on my shirt. It is the heart of who I am and all I want to be: Christian — Christlike." However, the prison officials who worked close to him on a daily basis insisted it was all an act — a ploy to manipulate public opinion. Early on the morning before his execution Sellers was moved from his death row cell to a special cell near the death chamber, and he spent the day visiting with ten friends he had made while in prison. He had married in February 1995 while in prison but the marriage was annulled in 1997, and his ex-wife was not among his visitors. He told his step-sister, "All the people who are hating me right now and are here waiting to see me die, when you wake up in the morning, you aren't going to feel any different," but he did not express any remorse for killing their mother, which outraged her and her siblings.

Just before midnight Sellers, wearing a new set of prison denims, was removed from his cell and marched twenty-five steps into the injection room. He took his place on the gurney where his chest, waist, and legs were strapped while his arms were secured to two arm extensions, and then a sheet was pulled over his body. A medical technician carefully inserted one intravenous cannula (IV) into the vein of each arm while the executioners were hidden from view in another room, hooded and behind a one-way mirrored window. Warden Ron Ward confirmed by telephone that the execution was to proceed, and on his signal the beige curtains were drawn open and the witnesses first saw the condemned man through the tinted window. He was asked if he had any last words, and he replied, "Set my spirit free that I might praise Thee. Set my spirit free that I might worship Thee." When he concluded the warden announced, "Let the execution begin," and each executioner drained the contents of his syringe into the tube leading to Seller's arm. The first drug, sodium thiopental, caused unconsciousness; the second drug, pancuronium bromide, caused his respiration to become labored and would have caused death in time; and the third drug, potassium chloride, was injected to stop his heart. At 12:17 A.M. all signs of life were absent and he was pronounced dead.

Sources: *Oklahoman* (Oklahoma City): January 24, 1999; January 27–30, 1999; February 2–5, 1999; May 19, 2000; March 2, 2005; March 5, 2005. *Ponca City News* (OK): February 4, 1999; *Sellers v. State*, 809 P.2d 676 (Okl. Cr., 1991). *Sellers v. State*, 889 P.2d 895 (Okl. Cr., 1995). *Sellers v. State*, 973 P.2d 894 (Okl. Cr. App., 1999).

Moore, Scotty L.
June 3, 1999

In 1978 twenty-one-year-old Scotty Lee Moore was convicted of a robbery in Texas and sentenced to serve a prison term of three and one-half years. After his release he moved in with his aunt and uncle in Umbarger, Texas, where he began courting his cousin Vicki Caster. In late 1983 the couple moved to Oklahoma City where Moore worked as a clerk at the Airline Motel. Moore stole $97 from the motel cash register, and after he was accused by coworker Alex Fernandez the motel owner told Fernandez to fire Moore.

On November 11 Moore and Caster drove to the Dodge City, Kansas, home of Caster's friend June Setzkorn and borrowed $50, then knowing the Setzkorns were leaving town they returned and burglarized the house taking money, guns and ammunition. Next they broke into the Setzkorns' meat-processing business nearby and stole more money and packaged meat. On November 13 Moore tried to sell several of the stolen guns in Oklahoma City, but failed to find a buyer. The couple drove to the Airline Motel intending to rob Alex Fernandez but could not gain entrance, so they left. Moore called to ask if there were rooms available but when Fernandez said no he became angry and planned revenge.

Three days later they checked into the Swank Motel, then the following day they decided once again to rob the Airline Motel, and Moore told Caster to clean out the cash register while he tied and gagged Fernandez. However, after they parked at the rear of the motel and were walking toward the door, Moore said, "Dead people can't talk." Moore brought along one of the stolen .22-caliber rifles, and he sent Caster in first to distract Fernandez, then entered and yelled at Fernandez to look at him, pointed the rifle, and told the clerk to come out from behind the counter. He told Caster how to open the cash register and which drawers would hold "the big money," while he forced Fernandez into the office restroom. Caster was busy wiping her fingerprints from the cash register when she heard five gunshots, and she ran out of the office with Moore close behind.

They drove around for a brief period, returned to the Swank Motel to pack and load their belongings, then called the Airline Motel to see if anyone answered but no one had found the body. After they ate breakfast they drove toward Texas, and during the trip Caster asked Moore if he had killed Fernandez. He replied, "You'd be dead, too, if you had been shot five times in the head." Then he told her how he had ordered Fernandez to lie face down and not move. The clerk complied, expecting to be tied, but Moore shot him to death. He said, "Each time I pulled the trigger there were little red balls of fire that come out. I didn't know it could be so easy to kill someone." The next morning Fernandez's body was discovered by the day shift clerk and other employees, and they called the police.

Moore and Caster arrived at Moore's sister's home in Big Springs, Texas, on November 20, and Moore gave the murder weapon to his brother-in-law as a gift for his nephew, expecting that the rifle could never be traced there. Three days later Caster was driving their automobile through La Mesa, Texas, after sundown without headlights, and they were stopped by a traffic officer. Moore told her, "I will never return to jail. If I have to, I'll take a few of them with me." He reached his left foot across and pressed on the gas pedal, and all Caster could do was steer to avoid crashing. The police pursued them and fired at the car, which had to stop after the front tires were blown. Moore and Caster were arrested and lodged in jail, where Caster confessed and later agreed to cooperate and testify.

Moore's trial began on October 15, 1984, and after five days of testimony and one hour twenty minutes in deliberations, Moore was convicted of first-degree murder. Four aggravating circumstances justifying the death penalty were presented, and Moore was sentenced to die by lethal injection. Moore's attorney filed an appeal, which stayed the execution. In 1987 Oklahoma's Court of Criminal Appeals affirmed the judgment and sentence and denied the petition for a rehearing, and on October 5, 1987, the U.S. Supreme Court denied his writ of certiorari. His applications for post-conviction judicial relief were denied in June 1988, but on the appeal of that denial one of the four aggravating circumstances was struck down by the state Court of Criminal Appeals. However, the justices found that the three remaining aggravating circumstances were sufficient for the jury recommending the death penalty.

In 1992 Moore and other prisoners filed a civil action, and in 1994 the federal court acted by granting the relief requested, but also lifted all stays of execution it had granted previously, and Moore's execution was set for July 12, 1994. A flurry of legal actions followed with appeals and petitions filed over the next four years, followed by a hearing before the state Board of Pardons and Parole which denied clemency and a petition to Governor Frank Keating, who declined to intervene. Moore's date with the executioner was finally set for June 3, 1999. On his final day three requests for stays presented to the U.S. Supreme Court were denied, and nothing would delay the proceedings.

Sixty days before his execution Moore was moved from his H unit death row cell into one of three solitary confinement cells in maximum security. Over the next two months Moore would be isolated from all other prisoners, and he and his cell would be searched often. On June 1, 1999, Moore was moved from his maximum security cell to a special cell near the death chamber. He refused a final meal, and just before midnight June 2 the prisoner, wearing a new set of prison denims, was marched into the injection room. He took his place on the gurney where his chest, waist, and legs were strapped while his arms were secured to two arm extensions, and then a sheet was pulled over his body. A medical technician carefully inserted one intravenous cannula (IV) into the vein of each arm, while the executioners were hidden from view in another room, hooded and behind a one-way mirrored window. The warden confirmed by telephone, with Governor Keating, that the execution was to proceed, had the curtains drawn open, and asked if Moore had any last words, but he declined to speak. The warden announced, "Let the execution begin," and each executioner drained the contents of his syringe into the tube leading to Moore's arm: the first drug, sodium thiopental, caused unconsciousness; the second drug, pancuronium bromide, caused his respiration to become labored and would have caused death in time; and the third drug, potassium chloride, stopped his heart. At 12:14 A.M. all sign of life was absent and he was pronounced dead.

Sources: *Moore v. Oklahoma*: 153 F.3d 1086 (1997). *Moore v. Oklahoma*, 484 U.S. 873, 108 S. Ct. 219 (1987). *Moore v. State*: 736 P.2d 161 (Okla. Crim. App 1987). *Moore v. State*: 809 P.2d 63, 65 (Okla Crim App. 1991). *Syracuse Herald-Journal* (NY): June 3, 1999.

Newsted, Norman L.
July 8, 1999

Thirty-year-old Norman Lee Newsted flew into the Tulsa, Oklahoma, international airport on February 20, 1984, and hired taxicab driver twenty-six-year-old Lawrence Donnell "Larry" Buckley to drive him to his sister's home in west Tulsa. Buckley had only been a cab driver for three months and was having trouble locating the address, so he stopped at a gas station for directions. Newsted bought a beer, and the clerk noticed that Newsted had no money in his wallet. When they still could not locate the address Buckley stopped at the Calvary Temple of God Church for further directions and parked in the northeast corner of the parking lot, not far from a creek bordering the property. Worshipers leaving a service saw Newsted and Buckley standing by the cab with the trunk open before Newsted went into the church and used the telephone to call his sister, and as soon as he returned to the cab two loud reports of gunfire were heard.

Newsted's sister drove to the church to pick him up, and when she arrived her brother approached from the east end of the parking lot and told her that the cab driver had pulled a gun and tried to rob him; then on the way to her home Newsted said he had shot someone. The next morning a minister found Buckley's taxicab partly submerged in the creek, and he notified the police. The car was pulled out, and inside was Buckley's body, with two bullet wounds to the back of his head and his wallet missing. The police went to the home of Newsted's sister and arrested him. They found Buckley's empty wallet, and then Newsted claimed that Buckley had pulled a knife and tried to rob him and he had shot the cab driver in self-defense.

Newsted was charged with murder, tried in July, his claim of self-defense was rejected by the jurors, and he was convicted of first-degree murder. Newsted was sentenced to die by lethal injection, and he arrived at H unit in the state prison on August 3, 1984. His attorney filed an appeal, which stayed the execution. The Oklahoma Court of Criminal Appeals affirmed the judgment and sentence in 1986, and the motion for a rehearing was denied. The matter was then appealed to the U.S. Supreme Court, which denied the writ of certiorari. His subsequent appeal in the state court was denied in 1991, and again the U.S. Supreme Court denied him a hearing. His attorney refiled an appeal for post-conviction relief, and this was denied in 1995. On April 22, 1996, Newsted's attorney filed a writ of habeas corpus in the Tenth Circuit Court of Appeals, but it was denied on October 15, 1998. When all efforts for judicial relief seemed exhausted his date with the executioner was set for July 8, 1999, and a petition for clemency was submitted to the state Board of Pardons and Parole. On June 15, 1999, the members of the board denied clemency, and Governor Frank Keating refused to intervene.

Sixty days before his execution Newsted was moved from his H unit death row cell into one of three solitary confinement cells in maximum security. Over the next two months Newsted would be isolated from all other prisoners, and he and his cell would be searched often to prevent any attempt at suicide. On July 6, 1999, Newsted was moved from his maximum security cell to a special cell near the death chamber. Just before midnight July 7 the prisoner, wearing a new set of prison denims, was marched into the injection room. He took his place on the gurney where his chest, waist, and legs were strapped while his arms were secured to two arm extensions, and then a sheet was pulled over his body. A medical technician carefully inserted one intravenous cannula (IV) into the vein of each arm, while the executioners were hidden from view in another room, hooded and behind a one-way mirrored window. Warden Gary Gibson confirmed by telephone, with Governor Keating, that the execution was to proceed, had the curtains drawn open on the one-way witnesses' window, and asked if Newsted had any last words, but he declined to speak to the witnesses. The warden announced, "Let the execution begin," and each executioner drained the contents of his syringe into the tube leading to Newsted's arm: the first drug, sodium thiopental, caused unconsciousness; the second drug, pancuronium bromide, caused his respiration to become labored and would have caused death in time; and the third drug, potassium chloride, stopped his heart. As the drugs began to flow Newsted turned to the warden and said, "I can taste it." At 12:12 A.M. all sign of life was absent and he was pronounced dead.

Sources: *Indiana Gazette* (PA): July 8, 1999. *Marysville Journal* (OH): July 8, 1999. *Newsted v. Gibson*: 158 F.3d 1085 (10th Cir Ct. Of App, October 15, 1998). *Newsted v. Oklahoma*: 479 U.S. 995, 107 S. Ct. 599 (1986). *Newsted v. Oklahoma*: 501 U.S. 1259, 111 S. Ct. 2913 (1991). *Newsted v. State*: 720 P.2d 734 (Okla. Crim. App., 1986). *Newsted v. State*: 908 P.2d 1388 (Okla. Crim. App. 1995).

Cooks, Cornel
December 2, 1999

In late 1982 twenty-six-year-old Cornel Cooks seemed a good neighbor to his white eighty-seven-year-old disabled neighbor, Jennie Elva Ridling, when he mowed her trailer-home lawn in Lawton, Comanche County, Oklahoma. Before 6:00 P.M. on October 28, 1982, Cooks, with nineteen-year-old Rodney Madson Masters, broke into Ridling's home and beat her on the head, then raped and bound her, wrapping her entire head and mouth with gauze to prevent her from calling out; then the two black men ransacked the house for valuables. At 8:00 P.M. a neighbor, checking on Ridling's welfare, found her dead body and called the police. At 9:00 P.M. Cooks' neighbors saw the two men returning to Cooks' home with a pillow case stuffed with items. Cooks, who had previously been convicted of burglary and rape and served a prison term, was immediately suspected and arrested, his home was searched, and the police found a number of items including Ridling's checkbook. Outside in the trash they found a sock with Ridling's blood on it. The autopsy showed that Ridling had been suffocated and it had taken at least two hours for her to die. Cooks and Masters were charged with her murder and with burglary, and they were tried in March 1983. Both men were convicted of first-degree murder, and Cooks was sentenced to die by lethal injection, while Masters was sentenced to serve a term of life in prison. Cooks was delivered to his death row cell on April 1, 1983, and his attorney filed an appeal, which stayed the execution. The state Court of Criminal Appeals affirmed the judgment and sentence of the district court in 1985, and the U.S. Supreme Court denied certiorari. An application for post-conviction relief was denied in 1987, and a hearing on the denial was refused by the U.S. Supreme Court. A writ of habeas corpus was then denied by the federal circuit court until Cooks exhausted his state remedies. The case was again appealed at the state level, and the judgment and sentence affirmed in 1993. An appeal was then filed in the federal circuit court and denied on December 15, 1998. Yet another year would pass as Cooks' attorney instituted a flurry of legal maneuvers to save his client's life, but to no avail, and his date with the executioner was set for December 2, 1999. In November 1999 Cooks appeared before the state Board of Pardons and Parole but the members refused to grant clemency, and Governor Frank Keating declined to intervene.

Sixty days before his execution Cooks was moved from his H unit death row cell into one of three solitary confinement cells in maximum security. Over the next two months Cooks would be isolated from all other prisoners, and he and his cell would be searched often to prevent any attempt at suicide. On November 30, 1999, Cooks was moved from his maximum security cell to a special cell near the death chamber. Before midnight December 1 the prisoner, wearing a new set of prison denims, was marched into the injection room. He took his place on the gurney where his chest, waist, and legs were strapped while his arms were secured to two arm extensions, and then a sheet was pulled over his body. A medical technician carefully inserted one intravenous cannula (IV) into the vein of each arm, while the executioners were hidden from view in another room, hooded and behind a one-way mirrored window. The warden confirmed by telephone, with Governor Keating, that the execution was to proceed, had the curtains drawn open, and asked if Cooks had any last words, and he said, "It means a lot to me to get a letter from the victim's relatives to say I've been forgiven. A lot of people didn't expect a person like me to change and that's the part they don't understand. Keep peace with your soul, strive to be happy, and keep God in your life." When he concluded the warden announced, "Let the execution begin," and each executioner drained the contents of his syringe into the tube leading to Cooks' arm: the first drug, sodium thiopental, caused unconsciousness; the second drug, pancuronium bromide, caused his respiration to become labored and would have caused death in time; and the third drug, potassium chloride, stopped his heart. At 12:18 A.M. all sign of life was absent and he was pronounced dead.

Sources: *Cooks v. Ward, Warden*: 165 F.3d 1283 (1998). *Cooks v. State*: 699 P.2d 653, 656 (1985). *Cooks v. State*: case PC-86-613 (1987). *Cooks v. State*: case PC-89-131 (1993). *Cooks v. Oklahoma*: 474 U.S. 935 (1985). *Cooks v. Oklahoma*: 510 U.S. 851 (1993).

Ross, Bobby L.
December 9, 1999

Shortly before 2:00 A.M. on Wednesday, January 5, 1983, twenty-five-year-old Bobby Lynn Ross, a black man wearing a black jacket, black pants, and black tennis shoes, and two other black men entered the office of the Los Cuartos Inn, a motel in Elk City, Oklahoma. They captured clerk Debra Jean Sandefur, and Ross, brandishing a Bauer .25-caliber automatic pistol, pushed Sandefur several times and threatened to murder her while his two accomplices cleaned out the cash register. They were leaving the motel when thirty-year-old Police Sergeant Steven Leroy Mahan arrived for a routine security check and noticed that he could not see the clerk while a black man ran from the office. Before he could pursue the man he was captured in the parking lot by the other two robbers, and according to some reports he was shot in the abdomen. Ross took Mahan's Smith & Wesson Model 66 .357-magnum revolver and handcuffs and ordered Mahan to lie on the pavement face down; he handcuffed the officer's wrists behind his back, and then Ross shot him in the back of the head three times at close range with his small caliber Bauer pistol.

The men then drove off toward Clinton, Ross' home, while Sandefur called the police and gave a description of the robbers, but she had not seen the getaway automobile. The wounded officer was rushed to the hospital by Detective James LaFarlette, where Mahan died at 5:30 A.M., and later three .25-caliber bullets were recovered during an autopsy. At 2:30 A.M. the getaway automobile had been stopped by Clinton officers to investigate a broken taillight and windshield, and the robbers were recognized even though Ross had changed clothes. The three men were arrested and searched, and Officer Michael Lumpkin found the murder weapon in Ross' right front pants pocket. The car was searched, and officers found Mahan's .357 revolver, the clothes worn by Ross during the robbery, the bank bags and deposits taken from the motel, and another loaded .25 automatic pistol.

The three men were lodged in jail, and after Mahan died Ross admitted the robbery, but at first denied any part in the killing. He claimed some stranger appeared, grabbed his gun, and shot Mahan. However, he soon weakened and confessed, "Yes, sir, I did it. There wasn't no way of getting around it. I had to live with it on my mind. I couldn't live no longer with it on my mind. Taking another man's life just for some money. Whatever happens to me, I deserve it. I do. I deserve it." All three men were charged with murder, but in a deal his accomplices were permitted to testify at Ross' trial and were charged with second-degree murder, tried in the Roger Mills County district court, convicted, and sentenced to long prison terms.

On October 21 Ross was convicted of the first-degree murder of Mahan and sentenced to die by lethal injection, and he was also sentenced to serve ninety-nine years in prison for robbery. The condemned man was delivered to a death row cell at the prison on November 3 while his attorney, David Autry, filed an appeal, which stayed the execution. In 1986 the state Court of Criminal Appeals affirmed the judgment and sentence of the district court. Ross' attorney then filed a writ of certiorari with the supreme court, and it was granted on June 15, 1987, but on June 22, 1988, the justices affirmed the finding of the state appeals court. Ross' attorney then filed a petition for post-conviction relief at the state level; this was denied on April 6, 1994, and the subsequent petition to the U.S. Supreme Court was denied. This was followed by a petition to the district court on October 24, 1988, and denied on March 24, 1995. The denial was affirmed in the state court of appeals on March 20, 1997, and the petition for a rehearing in the district court was denied on November 17, 1997. Ross' attorney had already filed a writ of habeas corpus in the federal court on December 31, 1996, and on January 12, 1999, the appeal was decided against Ross. There followed a flurry of appeals, petitions, writs, and other legal maneuvers by Autry to save his client's life, but all failed, and Ross' date with the executioner was set for December 9, 1999. The state Board of Pardons and Paroles denied clemency on November 19, 1999, and Governor Frank Keating declined to intervene.

Ross continued to express remorse during his time on death row, and he spent an increasing number of hours with the prison chaplain as his date of execution neared. Sixty days before his execution Ross was moved from his H unit death row cell into one of three solitary confinement cells in maximum security. Over the next two months Ross would be isolated from all other prisoners, and he and his cell would be searched often to prevent any attempt at suicide. On December 7, 1999, Ross was moved from his maximum security cell to a special cell near the death chamber.

Before midnight December 8 the prisoner, wearing a new set of prison denims, was marched into the injection room. He took his place on the gurney where his chest, waist, and legs were strapped while his arms were secured to two arm extensions, and then a sheet was pulled over his body. A medical technician carefully inserted one intravenous cannula (IV) into the vein of each arm, while the executioners were hidden from view in another room, hooded and behind a one-way mirrored window. Warden Ron Ward confirmed by telephone, with Governor Keating, that the execution was to proceed, had the curtains drawn open, and asked if Ross had any last words. He replied, "I'd like to say forgive me to the Mahan family." When he concluded the warden announced, "Let the execution begin," and each executioner drained the contents of his syringe into the tube leading to Ross's arm: the first drug, sodium thiopental, caused unconsciousness; the second drug, pancuronium bromide, caused his respiration to become labored and would have caused death in time; and the third drug, potassium chloride, stopped his heart. After several minutes all sign of life was absent and Ross was pronounced dead.

Sources: *Ross v. Oklahoma*: 487 U.S. 81, 108 S. Ct. 2273 (1988). *Ross v. Oklahoma*: 513 U.S. 970, 115 S.Ct. 441 (1994). *Ross v. State*: 717 P.2d 117 (Okla. Crim. App., 1986). *Ross v. State*: 872 P.2d 940 (Okla. Crim App., 1994). *Ross v. State*: PC-95-294 (Okla. Crim. App., 1997). *Ross v. Ward*: 165 F.3d 793 (10th Cir. Ct. of App., January 12, 1999).

Johnson, Malcolm R.
January 6, 2000

Malcolm Rent Johnson's parents divorced when he was quite young and he remained with his father in Oklahoma City, Oklahoma, while his mother moved to Chicago, Illinois. During his early teen years he ran away from his father to be with his mother, and by the age of fifteen, in 1974, he was arrested on a weapons charge. In 1977 he was arrested and tried for three burglaries and two armed robberies of elderly women, during which he had committed four rapes. He was convicted on two counts of rape and sentenced to serve a prison term. In early 1981 he was released on parole and allowed moved to Oklahoma City.

Though he was living with a girlfriend he continued to stalk elderly women, then attack, brutalize, rob and rape them, and by October 27 he had raped several victims but left no clues to his identity. On October 27 twenty-three-year-old Johnson followed seventy-six-year-old Ura Alma Thompson to her apartment, and he was seen by the building manager. He later broke into her apartment and struck the elderly woman on the jaw and head, then raped her, and during the attack she died of suffocation, either by his weight on her chest or by placing his hand over her mouth and nose. He than ransacked the apartment and stole furs, a typewriter, a watch, keys and key rings, a cigarette case, a hand mirror, rings, a purse, and a variety of other valuables. He fled, and later that evening Thompson's body was discovered by her nephew Frank Thompson, who called the authorities. Meanwhile police officers went to Johnson's apartment to question him on suspicion of a parolee carrying a firearm, and they discovered Ura Thompson's belongings. They arrested Johnson and charged him with burglary, rape, and murder, and the following day police chemist Joyce Gilchrist obtained Johnson's blood and hair samples to match with those collected at the murder scene. DNA testing did not exist in 1982, but Gilchrist reported a match between semen collected in a vaginal smear and Johnson's blood type. When told of the match the accused murderer said, "You couldn't have found my semen in her, I didn't come." He claimed that he had been given the stolen items by his brother, but his brother denied the claim and proved an alibi.

Johnson was tried for murder in March 1982, and after the defense declined to present any witnesses the defendant was found guilty of first-degree murder on March 22. During the penalty phase both sides presented witnesses, but Johnson's presentation was mainly about his early childhood, and he was sentenced to die by lethal injection. He was delivered to a death row cell at the prison on April 7, and his attorney filed the first appeal, which stayed the execution. Over the next eighteen years his attorney tried every means to delay the execution and overturn the conviction, or at least the sentence. The Oklahoma Court of Criminal Appeals affirmed the judgment and sentence of the lower court in 1987 on direct appeal and upheld the decision in 1991 on a post-conviction request for relief. By 1999 the appeals to all state courts had been exhausted, and a writ of habeas corpus was filed in the Tenth Circuit Court of Appeals; in November the U.S. Supreme Court denied certiorari. In December Johnson could have appeared before the state Board of Pardons and Parole but he refused to ask for clemency. Governor Frank Keating declined to intervene, and the date for Johnson's execution remained January 6, 2000.

Sixty days before his execution Johnson was moved from his H unit death row cell into one of three solitary confinement cells in maximum security. Over the next two months Johnson would be isolated from all other prisoners, and he and his cell would be searched often to prevent any attempt at suicide. Johnson was attended by the Rev. Charles Story, and he told the minister, "I'm innocent and I've got peace in my heart, and I'm ready to go home." On January 5, 1999, Johnson was moved from his maximum security cell to a special cell near the death chamber and before midnight the prisoner, wearing a new set of prison denims, was marched into the injection room. He took his place on the gurney where his chest, waist, and legs were strapped while his arms were secured to two arm extensions, and then a sheet was pulled over his body. A medical technician carefully inserted one intravenous cannula (IV) into the vein of each arm, while the executioners were hidden from view in another room, hooded and behind a one-way mirrored window. Warden Gary L. Gibson confirmed by telephone, with Governor Keating, that the execution was to proceed, had the curtains drawn open, and asked if Johnson had any last words. The prisoner replied, "I apologize for everyone I hurt." When he concluded the warden announced, "Let the execution begin," and each executioner drained the contents of his syringe into the tube leading to Johnson's arm: the first drug, sodium thiopental, caused unconsciousness; the second drug, pancuronium bromide, caused his respiration to become labored and would have caused death in time; and the third drug, potassium chloride, stopped his heart. At 12:31 A.M. all sign of life was absent and Johnson was pronounced dead.

Sources: *Johnson v. Gibson*: 169 F.3d 1239 (1999). *Johnson v. Oklahoma*: 484 U.S. 878 (1987). *Johnson v. State*: 731 P.2d 993 (Ok Cr. 1987). *Johnson v. State*: 823 P.2d 370 (1991). *Los Angeles Times* (CA): August 30, 2001. *New York Times* (NY): September 2, 2001.

Walker, Gary A.
January 13, 2000

From the age of fifteen, in 1969, Gary Alan Walker was in trouble with the police, but while he was sentenced to serve brief periods in a reformatory, jail and prison he spent a great deal of his time in mental institutions. Even though he was diagnosed with severe mental problems Walker was paroled from his last commitment on February 7, 1984.

On May 6 thirty-year-old Walker was hitchhiking to Owasso, Oklahoma, when he was picked up by sixty-three-year-old Eddie O. Cash, on his way to visit relatives in Collinsville, Rogers County, and Cash told the young man he lived in Broken Arrow before dropping off his passenger. Walker called telephone directory assistance and was given Cash's address, and he went to Broken Arrow in Tulsa County to burglarize Cash's house, possibly expecting Cash to be in Collinsville. He knocked on the door and was surprised when Cash answered, he was recognized and admitted, and then in the living room he beat Cash on the head with a chimney brick, knocking him senseless. He used the cord from the vacuum cleaner and tied it tightly around Cash's neck, strangling him to death. After he ransacked the house he loaded his plunder into Cash's 1976 Dodge van and fled to Heavener where he sold the vehicle to a salvage yard and hitchhiked to Poteau. On May 8 a neighbor called Cash's daughter, Priscilla Crane, because Eddie had not been seen for two days, and Crane found her father's body and called the police.

Meanwhile, on May 7, Walker went to Henry's Tavern in Poteau where he met thirty-six-year-old Margaret Ann Bell-Lydick, and at closing time she offered him a ride in her white Cadillac. Once they were in the car Walker pulled out a long-bladed knife, kidnapped Lydick and forced her to drive toward Arkansas, and raped and sodomized her at Sharp and again at McCracken. He murdered her before entering Arkansas, where he stopped for snacks and used her credit card to pay. He put her body in the trunk of her car, but after a week the body was decomposing and the stench was becoming unbearable, so he dumped the remains in a haystack in Missouri. Lydick's Cadillac broke down on the highway near Branson, Missouri, and Walker abandoned it, and it was soon found by a state trooper.

There had been reports of Walker trying to kidnap others during that week, but once he was afoot Walker hitchhiked to Vinitia, Oklahoma. On May 14 Walker approached thirty-five-year-old Jane Hillburn, who was working in her garden, and posed as a potential buyer for her home. Hillburn agreed to give him a tour of the house, and as soon as they were inside Walker attacked her, beat her brutally, ripped off her clothing and dragged her to the bedroom, raped her repeatedly, and then strangled her to death. Walker ransacked the house and loaded his plunder into her black Chevrolet Camaro before fleeing to his hometown of Tulsa, Oklahoma.

On May 15 an eighteen-year-old woman, whose name was withheld, was given a ride by a man calling himself Gary Edwards. As soon as she was in the car he pulled out a knife, kidnapped her, and later attempted to rape the woman but she escaped and gave the police a description of her attacker and Hillburn's Camaro.

On May 20 a seventeen-year-old girl, unnamed, was hitchhiking with her boyfriend near Hominy, Oklahoma, and they accepted a ride from Walker, who quickly put the boy out in a remote location and kidnapped the girl at knifepoint. The boy hurried to the nearest telephone and reported the abduction, and a frantic two-day search began for the girl and the Camaro in Hominy, in Skiatook, and in the roads and fields between. Walker had driven the girl to a remote oil property in Osage County where he repeatedly raped the young girl, but he finally fell asleep, and on May 22 she escaped, made her way to the highway, flagged down a truck, and was delivered to the sheriff's office.

When Walker discovered that his captive had fled he abandoned the Camaro, which was found later that day, and he began searching for another car. The following day he saw thirty-two-year-old Janet Jewell, of Beggs, stranded near Fourth and Peoria Streets in Tulsa, her car out of gas. As soon as Walker put gas in the car, and the engine started, he slid into the passenger seat and took Jewell prisoner at knifepoint. He had her drive by a circuitous route to Slick, to a remote oil property, where he tied her hands and raped her several times. The next morning, May 24, Walker was ordered off the private property, but the truck driver did not see Jewell's predicament. They drove through Creek and Okmulgee Counties until Walker found a spot to rape her and then, after tying her, they slept. At dawn, in a frenzy, he raped and sodomized her several times, and for the first time she was afraid he might kill her so she begged, "I'll do whatever you want, only don't kill me for the sake of my three children." He immediately took a piece of cord and strangled her to death, then drove the body to a creek two miles east of Beggs and threw her in.

He eluded capture by avoiding roadblocks, and on the evening of May 24 he drove into the parking lot of the Towne West Shopping Center in Tulsa, where he sat for hours watching for his next victim before abandoning Jewell's Dodge. Twenty-five-year-old Valerie Shaw-Harzell, a popular newscaster for KRAV radio, went into a grocery store for diapers for her baby. When she came out she saw Walker opening the trunk to Jewell's car and paid no attention. As soon as she had the door to her tan pickup truck unlocked Walker put a knife to her back, forced her into the vehicle, and slid into the driver's seat and drove off. He drove her to a bank and tried to cash a personal check for $500, but when that failed he drove to a second bank and succeeded. He drove her to a remote location near Kelleyville and during the night raped and sodomized her, and in the morning, May 25, he raped her twice more in the truck bed. He then had her write a check for $650 and again had to go to two bank drive-up windows to cash it, and then forced Harzell to drive him to Claremore. During the early morning hours of May 26 Walker heard sounds as if men were searching nearby, so he tore a towel into strips, fashioned a garrote, and strangled Harzell to death.

He left the body and drove to Tulsa, where he went on a spree, and then drove to Vinita, where he kidnapped another woman. After two days of repeatedly raping and sodomizing her he dropped her off near her home on May 27, and she immediately telephoned the police. Knowing the police were searching for the truck Walker drove to Heavener and traded it for a .22-caliber revolver.

He next hitchhiked to Van Buren where he attempted to rob a grocery clerk, but another clerk ran out screaming and he fled empty-handed. He returned to his motel and kidnapped a man and woman, forced them into their car, and drove off. When he demanded that they move over for him to drive they managed to escape. He quickly abandoned the car in a field and walked a short distance to an unoccupied mobile home, but the two women who lived there came home and he kidnapped them. He drove them to Claremore, where he pawned the gun for lunch money, and then dropped off the women in Tulsa, keeping their car. On May 28 Walker was identified from his fingerprints lifted from Hillburn's Camaro, his prison photos were sent to the surviving victims, and he was identified.

On May 30 Walker broke into a home in Van Buren, Arkansas, and abducted two girls at knifepoint, taking them on a twenty-minute ride in a stolen car, looking for a remote location, but as soon as they stopped the girls fled and later identified Walker from his photo. On June 2 Walker broke into another home and held the tenants at gunpoint before stealing their car, but did not harm them, and they identified Walker. At 10:45 P.M. Walker was arrested in a Tulsa mobile home in the company of two men as they were planning to break into another home.

As soon as Walker was behind bars he began confessing and complained, "I haven't spent a full year out of jail since I was seventeen years old." He told detectives, regarding the Cash murder, "I knew what I was doing, but I don't know why [because] I know right from wrong. I don't know why I did it, but I know I did do it." He cooperated with the police, and over the next six days he led the police to the missing bodies of Jewell, Harzell and Lydick and returned to Tulsa County where he was arraigned for the murder of Cash and for several other crimes. The following day he was taken to Claremore in Rogers County and arraigned for the murder of Harzell and for several other crimes. In all he was charged with more than thirty-five felonies.

He was first tried in Tulsa County in November, convicted of Cash's murder, sentenced to die, and was delivered to a death row cell on December 5, 1984. In May he was returned to Rogers County where he was tried for Harzell's murder and convicted, and on June 1 he was again sentenced to die. In all he was sentenced to die twice and to serve two centuries behind prison walls. His attorney, Gloyd McCoy, filed an appeal in both death penalty cases and in the other convictions as well. In 1986 the Court of Criminal Appeals affirmed the judgment and sentence in Cash's murder case, and in two post-conviction appeals Walker was denied relief. In 1990 the justices decided the appeal for Harzell's murder in favor of Walker and ordered a new trial, and he was retried in 1991 with the same outcome regarding the conviction but he was sentenced to serve a sixth life term and five hundred years in prison, bringing his total prison time to seven hundred years. Over the next nine years McCoy used every legal maneuver to save his client's life but by November 1999 he had exhausted all state and federal appeals, and the justices of the Court of Criminal Appeals, on November 24, set the date for his execution at January 13, 2000. He declined to appeal to the state Board of Pardons and Parole.

Sixty days before his execution Walker was moved from his H unit death row cell into one of three solitary confinement cells in maximum security. Over the next two months Walker would be isolated from all other prisoners, and he and his cell would be searched often to prevent any attempt at suicide. On January 12 Walker was moved from his maximum security cell to a special cell near the death chamber, and before midnight the prisoner, wearing a new set of prison denims, was marched into the injection room. He took his place on the gurney where his chest, waist, and legs were strapped while his arms were secured to two arm extensions, and then a sheet was pulled over his body. A medical technician carefully inserted one intravenous cannula (IV) into the vein of each arm, while the executioners were hidden from view in another room, hooded and behind a one-way mirrored window.

Warden Gary L. Gibson confirmed by telephone, with Governor Frank Keating, that the execution was to proceed, had the curtains drawn open, and asked if Walker had any last words for the dozen witnesses in the witness area, including his cousin and sister and ten members of the Cash family, and the thirty witnesses watching on closed-circuit television from a room below. The prisoner replied, "I'm sorry for what I've done. I hope when I go to the hate you have, and it's natural for you to hate me, that you would let it go with me." When he concluded the warden announced, "Let the execution begin," and at 12:16 A.M. each executioner drained the contents of his syringe into the tube leading to Walker's arm: the first drug, sodium thiopental, caused unconsciousness; the second drug, pancuronium bromide, caused his respiration to become labored and would have caused death in time; and the third drug, potassium chloride, stopped his heart. At 12:20 A.M. all sign of life was absent and Walker was pronounced dead.

Sources: Rogers County case CRF-84–108. Tulsa County case CRF-84–2088. *Tulsa World* (OK): November 24, 1999; January 13, 2000; *Walker v. State*: 723 P.2d 273 (1986). *Walker v. State*: 795 P.2d 1064 (1990). *Walker v. State*: 826 P.2d 1002 (1992). *Walker v. State*: 940 P.2d 509 (1997).

Roberts, Michael D.
February 10, 2000

In 1968 eleven-year-old Michael D. Roberts was driven from his home in Oklahoma City by an abusive step-father, and he turned to a life of crime to support himself. In 1987 two black burglars, thirty-year-old Roberts and a juvenile, were terrorizing the elderly in northwest Oklahoma City. The two men had broken into nineteen homes to steal property, and Roberts had committed a sexual assault on one victim. The burglars were brazen and had been seen by witnesses and victims, and yet they were not identified during the year.

Roberts had lived three houses from eighty-year-old Lula Mae Brooks for several years, and they knew each other. On Saturday evening, January 16, 1988, Roberts, without his youthful partner, broke into Brooks' home, and he was seen at the Brooks house by a neighbor. Brooks discovered Roberts in her living room and tried to defend herself with a knife, and Roberts took out the knife he always carried and stabbed her once each in the head and neck, threw her to the floor, placed a covering over her mouth to suppress her screams, and slit her throat. Brooks died by drowning in her own blood while Roberts ransacked the house and stole everything of value he could carry. Brooks' body was discovered that night, and the police recovered a knife, the one Brooks had used to defend herself, photographed a diamond-patterned shoe print, and documented the evidence of the break-in.

The murder intensified efforts to find the two burglars and the juvenile was quickly arrested, and as soon as he was behind bars he informed on Roberts. Soon afterward, during a routine traffic stop, Roberts was recognized riding in the passenger seat of the automobile. He was arrested on outstanding traffic warrants and lodged in the Oklahoma County jail. A knife was found in his pocket and his shoes were taken, and though human blood was found on the knife blade it could not be matched to Brooks, but his shoe soles matched perfectly the print on the living room floor.

When Roberts was interviewed he confessed three times, and his story evolved as he learned more about what the police knew. First he said that he entered the house the day after the murder, to explain the shoe print, and saw that the house had been ransacked and a chalk line had been drawn around Brooks' body, but the detectives had not drawn a chalk line. When confronted with this inconsistency he said he was walking by the house when he heard a noise inside Brooks' house, entered and found her on the floor with blood gushing from her neck wound, then fled to avoid getting blood on his jeans. In his third version he said he burglarized Brooks' house when he found her door partially open, and she came at him with a knife saying she had been robbed before and wouldn't allow it to happen again. He said he grabbed her hand wielding the knife as he drew his own knife and stabbed her in the neck, then helped her to the bathroom to wash the wound. He said he returned to the living room and found two purses, but just then Brooks came at him from behind so he threw her to the floor, covered her face, and slit her throat when she pleaded, "Finish the job, finish the job."

During the confessions he also admitted to the nineteen previously unsolved burglaries and one sexual assault. Roberts was charged with Brooks' murder and he was tried in July 1988. He recanted his confessions but, though there was no physical evidence tying him to the murder scene, he was convicted of first-degree murder and sentenced to die. Roberts was delivered to a death row cell on July 18, and his attorney, Gary Chubbuck, filed an appeal, which stayed the execution. Over the next twelve years Chubbuck would do everything he could to save his client's life. In 1994 the direct appeal was denied when the justices of the state Court of Criminal Appeals affirmed the judgment and sentence of the district court, and the U.S. Supreme Court denied certiorari. Chubbuck filed for post-conviction relief, and this was denied in 1996. There was a flurry of efforts over the next four years but the state Court of Criminal Appeals finally set the date of execution at February 10, 2000. The state Board of Pardons and Parole heard the plea for clemency on January 25, 2000, and denied relief, and Governor Frank Keating declined to intervene. The last-minute appeal to the federal Tenth Circuit Court of Appeals was denied, and the appeal to the U.S. Supreme Court was denied late on Roberts' final day.

Sixty days before his execution Roberts was moved from his H unit death row cell into one of three solitary confinement cells in maximum security. Over the next two months Roberts would be isolated from all other prisoners, and he and his cell would be searched often to prevent any attempt at suicide. On February 9 Roberts was moved from his maximum security cell to a special cell near the death chamber, and before midnight the prisoner was marched into the injection room. He took his place on the gurney where his chest, waist, and legs were strapped while his arms were secured to two arm extensions, and then a sheet was pulled over his body. A medical technician carefully inserted one intravenous cannula (IV) into the vein of each arm while the executioners were hidden from view in another room, hooded and behind a one-way mirrored window.

Warden Gary E. Gibson confirmed by telephone, with Governor Keating, that the execution was to proceed. Gibson had the curtains drawn open, and asked if Roberts had any last words for the dozen witnesses in the witness area, including six witnesses for Roberts and six others, but none for Brooks, and additional witnesses watching on closed-circuit television from a room below. The prisoner said, "What y'all are seeing here today is wrong. This is supposed to be a Christian state. You've got to ask the Lord to forgive them." When he concluded the warden announced, "Let the execution begin," and each executioner drained the contents of his syringe into the tube leading to Roberts' arm: the first drug, sodium thiopental, caused unconsciousness; the second drug, pancuronium bromide, caused his respiration to become labored and would have caused death in time; and the third drug, potassium chloride, would stop his heart. As the drugs began to flow he turned his head to the witnesses and said, "I love all of y'all and thank the good Lord for bringing you into my life," and then made a kissing gesture toward them. He quickly lapsed into unconsciousness and had several labored breaths before he lay still, and at 12:21 A.M. all sign of life was absent and Roberts was pronounced dead.

Sources: Oklahoma criminal case CRF-88-677. *Oklahoman* (Oklahoma City): February 10, 2000. *Roberts v. Oklahoma*: 115 S. Ct. 158 (1994). *Roberts v. State*: 868 P.2d 712 (1994). *Roberts v. State*: 910 P.2d 1071 (1996).

Rogers, Kelly L.
March 23, 2000

In 1986 eighteen-year-old Kelly Lamont Rogers was arrested, tried, and convicted of robbery but he was free by 1988 when he was charged with forgery. While in jail on this new charge he attempted to escape and was charged with that offense as well, convicted and sent to prison. He was released in mid–November 1990, about the same time that Oklahoma State University student twenty-one-year-old Karen Marie Lauffenburger started delivering pizza for the Buy 'n Bye Pizza Parlor in Stillwell, Oklahoma, using her 1984 Toyota Tercel to make the deliveries.

On December 19 Rogers announced to his girlfriend, Audra Lynn Taylor, that he planned to rob a pizza delivery person and had her order a pizza to be delivered to her Stillwell apartment. Lauffenburger delivered the pizza at 7:00 P.M., and as she left Rogers captured her at knifepoint, stole her $40 pizza bank, and forced her to drive to her apartment where he raped her. He then forced her to drive to an ATM machine and, after checking her account at 7:52 A.M., made her draw out the balance of $175. They returned to her apartment where he stabbed her in the chest, neck and abdomen nine times and then raped her again as she was dead or dying. He fled using her automobile and abandoned it near Taylor's apartment; the Toyota was found with the keys and her identification inside at 5:15 A.M. the next morning. When Lauffenburger did not return to the pizza parlor her employer, Eric Zanotelli, retraced her route and spoke with Rogers and Taylor, her last scheduled delivery, and they insisted she had delivered the pizza and left. Zanotelli then telephoned Lauffenburger's fiancée Peter Gilmartin, and he went to her apartment where he discovered her nude, dead body at 10:15 P.M. and called the police.

Rogers and Taylor were arrested, and the swabs taken from Lauffenburger were matched with Rogers' sperm, but he insisted they had consensual sex even though the autopsy proved injuries consistent with a peri-mortem and post-mortem, brutal rape. Rogers and Taylor were charged with murder on December 20, 1990, and on January 29, 1991, Rogers was charged with rape, two counts of robbery, and theft of a motor vehicle. Taylor made a deal to turn state's evidence, and her charge was reduced to second-degree murder and accomplice to the robbery, but she was convicted of robbery only and sentenced to serve a term of ten years in prison.

Rogers' trial in the Payne County District Court began on December 9, 1991, and on December 17, after only eighty minutes in deliberations, the jurors found him guilty of first-degree murder and recommended the death penalty, and also found him guilty on all other charges as well. He was sentenced to die for the murder and to serve three hundred twenty-five years on the other counts, and on January 21, 1992, Rogers arrived at the prison to begin serving his time on death row. Meanwhile his attorney, Jack S. Bowyer, filed an appeal, which stayed the execution. The direct appeal concluded in 1995 when the justices of the state Court of Criminal Appeals affirmed the judgment and sentence of the district court, and the U.S. Supreme Court denied certiorari on October 10. Legal maneuvers continued to delay the proceedings. By early 1999 all state judicial relief was exhausted, and Bowyer filed a writ of habeas corpus with the federal Tenth Circuit Court of Appeals, but it was denied in April, and the state Court of Criminal Appeals finally set his execution date for March 23, 2000. No last-minute appeals were filed to stop the execution. On March 1, 2000, the state Board of Pardon and Parole held a hearing and voted unanimously to deny clemency, and Governor Frank Keating declined to intervene.

Sixty days before his execution Rogers was moved from his H unit death row cell into one of three solitary confinement cells in maximum security. Over the next two months Rogers would be isolated from all other prisoners, and he and his cell would be searched often to prevent any attempt at suicide. On March 22 Rogers was moved from his maximum security cell to a special cell near the death chamber, and during his final hours Rogers confessed to killing Lauffenburger. Shortly before midnight the prisoner was escorted into the injection room where he took his place on the gurney, and his chest, waist, and legs were strapped while his arms were secured to two arm extensions and a sheet was pulled over his body. A medical technician carefully inserted one intravenous cannula (IV) into the vein of each arm while the executioners were hidden from view in another room, hooded and behind a one-way mirrored window.

Warden Gary E. Gibson confirmed by telephone, with Governor Keating, that the execution was to proceed, had the curtains drawn open, and asked if Rogers had any last words for the dozen witnesses seated in the witness area, including Lauffenburger's parents and several other relatives and members of Rogers' family, while additional witnesses watched on closed-circuit television from a room below. The prisoner turned toward the window, smiled, told his family he loved them, and then said, "To the Lauffenburger family, I just pray you guys will find peace and in time that God will heal you from the inside and out. And for those that might not know Jesus, I just ask that you know him, trust him as your Lord and Savior. He will get you through, just give him a chance." When he concluded the warden announced, "Let the execution begin," and at 12:23 A.M. each executioner drained the contents of his syringe into the tube leading to Rogers' arm: the first drug, sodium thiopental, caused unconsciousness; the second drug, pancuronium bromide, caused his respiration to become labored and would have caused death in time; and the third drug, potassium chloride, would stop his heart. A minister began reading from his Bible as Rogers puffed his cheeks twice and then lay motionless for two minutes before his chest heaved a dozen times. At 12:27 A.M. all sign of life was absent and Rogers was pronounced dead.

Sources: *Oklahoma v. Rogers* cases CRF-90–412; CRF-91–26; CRF-91–27; CRF-91–28; CRF-91–29 (Payne County). *Rogers v. Gibson*: 173 F.3d 1278 (1999). *Rogers v. State*: 890 P.2d 959 (1995). *Rogers v. State*: 934 P.2d 1093 (1997). *Tulsa World* (OK): March 23, 2000.

Boyd, Ronald K.
April 27, 2000

Twenty-nine-year-old Ronald Keith Boyd had just been released from jail when, on the evening of January 7, 1986, he was riding around Oklahoma City in the van of twenty-nine-year-old Byron Demetrius Gibbs, with twenty-three-year-old Joe Cornelius Jackson and twenty-nine-year-old Lenora Denise Dunn as additional passengers. Just before 9:00 P.M. Boyd asked Gibbs to stop at Tom's Market, a convenience store at 1000 N.E. 36th Street. Gibbs pulled into the parking lot, and Jackson, Boyd and Dunn got out of the van, but Jackson went to use the pay phone while Dunn talked with Boyd about robbing the store. Boyd handed Dunn a .38-caliber revolver from his coat pocket, and Dunn went into the market. Dunn robbed clerk Dorothy Trimble and immediately ran out carrying the gun and a fistful of money.

As soon as Dunn left the market Trimble called the police and provided a description of the robber and their green getaway van. Dunn returned the pistol to Boyd and he put it back in his coat pocket while Gibbs drove east on 36th Street toward Interstate 35. Boyd told Gibbs to pull into the parking area of a Phillips 66 gasoline station so that he could make a phone call, so Gibbs stopped the van near the pay phones, and Boyd got out.

Thirty-two-year-old veteran Oklahoma City Police Officer Richard Oldham Riggs and rookie Officer Craig Gravel had responded to Tom's Market and were informed that the suspect was a black female who fled the area in a green van, and the officers drove in the direction the van had fled. Minutes after 9:00 P.M. the officers noticed a green van parked at a gasoline station, and Riggs stopped his police car behind the van to investigate. Riggs was standing beside his patrol car while Gravel approached the rear of the van and reported that the vehicle was occupied by a female and two males. Riggs walked several steps toward Boyd, who was still talking on the telephone, and twice ordered him to hang up the phone and walk toward him. Boyd dropped the receiver and approached Riggs with his hands concealed in his coat pockets, and when Riggs ordered him to take his hands out of his pockets he shot Riggs in the abdomen without drawing out the weapon. Riggs staggered backwards, fell against the patrol car in a sitting position and returned fire wildly until his pistol was empty, and then Boyd placed the muzzle of his pistol against Riggs' chest and fired a second shot.

Boyd next went for Gravel, who took cover behind the gas pumps, and he was shot at several times as he ran. Meanwhile Boyd took cover behind the front of the van as it moved slowly forward out of the parking lot, so Gravel ran to Riggs, who had reloaded, and both men shot in the direction of the van. The van rolled across 36th Street and crashed into a fence where Gibbs, Jackson and Dunn were arrested for robbery, and Jackson identified Boyd as the shooter. Riggs died of his wounds before midnight, and the search for his murderer intensified.

When the van crashed Boyd had fled on foot to the house he shared with Fred Tubbs, but fled again when a police helicopter and patrol cars arrived. The next morning Boyd went to the home of Reginald Walker, told him he had to leave town, and confessed that he had shot a police officer. Boyd told Walker he had panicked when the officer approached him, he had "blanked out," and the gun just went off. Boyd was arrested at Walker's home nineteen hours after the shooting, when the police received a tip providing his location.

Boyd was taken to the hospital where his hands were swabbed for gunpowder residue — particles of antimony, barium, and lead — and examined under a microscope but there was no residue present. Gunshot residue is significantly reduced in about three hours, and wiping or washing the hands can remove all the residue, but Boyd would later rely upon the absence of residue to "prove his innocence." Boyd told the officers that as they fled from the robbery they stopped to pick up a hitchhiker, then stopped again so he could use the telephone, and he left his knapsack in the van. When approached by the officers the unknown hitchhiker took his pistol from the knapsack and shot the officer before fleeing afoot. However, a passing motorist saw Boyd fire the fatal shots, all the occupants of the van were arrested, and no one except Boyd had fled afoot.

On January 10 Boyd's pistol was found in a ravine at the Twin Hills Country Club, not far from the murder scene. On January 11 all four prisoners were charged with Riggs' murder but the charges were dropped for Jackson and Gibbs. Dunn, after making a deal, pled guilty to robbery and was sentenced to serve forty years in prison.

Boyd was tried in September 1986 and convicted of first degree murder. Judge James L. Gullett sentenced him to die, and he arrived on death row on September 29. His attorney, Robert H. Macy, filed an appeal, which stayed the execution but in 1992 the state Court of Criminal Appeals affirmed the judgment and sentence of the district court. His appeal for post-conviction relief was denied in 1996, and his writ of habeas corpus, filed with the federal Tenth Circuit Court of Appeals, was denied in 1999. The justices of the Court of Criminal Appeals finally set his execution date at April 27, 2000. At his hearing before the state Board of Pardons and Parole in March he reiterated his claim of innocence without offering any new evidence, and the board members voted unanimously to deny clemency. Governor Frank Keating declined to intervene.

Sixty days before his execution Boyd was moved from his H unit death row cell into one of three solitary confinement cells in maximum security. Over the next two months Boyd would be isolated from all other prisoners, and he and his cell would be searched often to prevent any attempt at suicide. On April 26 Boyd was moved from his maximum security cell to a special cell near the death chamber, and he persisted to the end in his claim of innocence. Shortly before midnight the prisoner was escorted into the injection room where he took his place on the gurney and his chest, waist, and legs were strapped while his arms were secured to two arm extensions, and a sheet was pulled over his body. A medical technician carefully inserted one intravenous cannula (IV) into the vein of each arm while the executioners were hidden from view in another room, hooded and behind a one-way mirrored window.

Warden Ward confirmed by telephone, with Governor Keating, that the execution was to proceed, had the curtains drawn open and asked if Boyd had any last words for the dozen witnesses seated in the witness area, including his brother, uncle, two nephews, a cousin and two clergymen, along with five members of Riggs' family. Additional witnesses watched on closed-circuit television from a room below. The prisoner turned toward the window, smiled and told his family he loved them, and then said, "I'm all right. I'm at peace with God. I'm fine. Don't worry about me. I'm OK y'all." When he concluded the warden announced, "Let the execution begin," and at 12:17 A.M. each executioner drained the contents of his syringe into the tube leading to Boyd's arm: the first drug, sodium thiopental, caused unconsciousness; the second drug, pancuronium bromide, caused his respiration to become labored and would have caused death in time; and the third drug, potassium chloride, would stop his heart. Boyd breathed deeply several times, closed his eyes halfway, and at 12:21 A.M. all sign of life was absent and Boyd was pronounced dead.

Sources: *Ardmoreite* (OK): April 27, 2000. *Boyd v. State*: 839 P.2d 1363 (1992). *Boyd v. State*: 915 P.2d 922 (1996). *Boyd v. Ward*: 179 F.3d 904 (1999). *State v. Boyd* case CRF-86–218.

Foster, Charles A.
May 25, 2000

Charles Adrian Foster had twice been convicted of felony crimes involving the use or threat of force. On the evening of April 1, 1983, Eula Mae Foster, a black woman, telephoned the Weddles neighborhood grocery store in Muskogee, Oklahoma, and placed an order to be delivered by store owner seventy-four-year-old Claude Wiley. Wiley had operated the store for decades and insisted on making deliveries to the poor, disabled and elderly using his El Camino pickup truck. When Wiley arrived after 6:00 P.M. Eula Mae invited him into the living room while she went for the money to pay him but her husband, thirty-four-year-old Foster, was waiting behind the door with a Louisville Slugger baseball bat. Foster stepped out and accused Wiley of "trying to mess with my wife," then struck him on the head several times with the baseball bat knocking him unconscious. Wiley suffered blunt-force trauma to his ear, the orbit of the right eye, and the crown of his skull, which was so badly fractured it caused internal hemorrhaging to the brain. Wiley was still alive so Foster wrapped him in a blanket and drove him in the El Camino a mile to a remote wooded area near an abandoned house, pulled out his body, and then, seeing Wiley was still alive, stabbed him in the chest three times.

Foster returned home after forty-five minutes, but a quarter-hour later he drove to Wiley's home and broke in, ransacked the house, and stole a number of items. Foster returned home after 9:00 P.M. and packed up their belongings in Wiley's truck, and the couple fled to the home of Eula's mother in Texas. Once they arrived Foster disposed of the truck, pawned a number of Wiley's belongings, and bought a Cadillac with the money he had taken from Wiley's pockets, home, and hocked items.

When Wiley was missed a search began, and in checking the location of his last delivery — the Foster home — investigators found blood on the walls and ceiling and bits of Wiley's teeth spread about the floor. Wiley's body was discovered several days after he was murdered, and the search for the Fosters intensified, and they were quickly found and arrested in Texas.

After they were extradited to Muskogee, Foster said that his wife had sent him to Weddles (Wiley's) grocery store to buy several items, and he arrived at 6:20 P.M., but it was raining so he stood outside until 7:50 P.M. when his wife arrived driving Wiley's El Camino pickup truck. He said she told him she had borrowed it for a trip to Texas, and said he had pawned Wiley's belongings at his wife's request.

Foster's two-day trial began in November, he was convicted of first-degree murder, robbery, burglary and auto theft. His wife testified against him, and Jody Lynch — a former cell-mate — testified that Foster had confessed to murdering Wiley, but Foster took the stand and told the same story of his wife arriving at the store in Wiley's El Camino. On November 28 Foster was sentenced to death for the first-degree murder of Wiley and sentenced to serve ninety years for the other crimes, and he arrived at his death row cell on December 12, 1983. Eula Mae had her charges reduced to accessory after-the-fact. She was sentenced to serve three concurrent five-year prison terms and was released in nine months.

Foster's attorney filed an appeal, which stayed the execution, and over the next seventeen years he would use every means at his disposal to delay the execution. In 1986 the state Court of Criminal Appeals affirmed the judgment and sentence of the Muskogee County district court, and the U.S. Supreme Court denied certiorari. In 1988 his appeal for post-conviction relief was denied, but other appeals followed. It was not until 1999, however, that his writ for habeas corpus was denied by the federal Tenth Circuit Court of Appeals and the case was remanded back to the state Court of Criminal Appeals, where the justices set the date of execution for May 25, 2000. Foster appeared before the state Board of Pardons and Parole on April 26, 2000, and insisted he was innocent but his appeal for clemency was denied, and Governor Frank Keating declined to intervene. His last hope, an appeal for a stay from the U.S. Supreme Court, was denied during his final hours.

On May 24 Foster was moved from his death row cell in H unit to a special cell near the death chamber, and he persisted to the end in his claim of innocence. Shortly before midnight the prisoner was escorted into the injection room where he took his place on the gurney and his chest, waist, and legs were strapped while his arms were secured to two arm extensions, and a sheet was pulled over his body. A medical technician carefully inserted one intravenous cannula (IV) into the vein of each arm while the executioners were hidden from view in another room, hooded and behind a one-way mirrored window.

Warden Ronald Ward confirmed by telephone, with Governor Keating, that the execution was to proceed, had the curtains drawn open and asked if Foster had any last words, but Foster said, "No sir, I don't," and declined to speak further to the dozen witnesses in the witnesses room and the additional witnesses watching on closed-circuit television from a room below. As his spiritual adviser read scripture it posed the question, "Do you believe in God?" and Foster responded, "Yes!" When the minister concluded the warden announced, "Let the execution begin," and at 12:12 A.M. each executioner drained the contents of his syringe into the tube leading to Foster's arm: the first drug, sodium thiopental, caused unconsciousness; the second drug, pancuronium bromide, caused his respiration to become labored and would have caused death in time; and the third drug, potassium chloride, would stop his heart. Foster gasped deeply three times and lay still, and at 12:16 A.M. all sign of life was absent and Foster was pronounced dead.

Sources: *Ardmoreite* (OK): May 25, 2000. *Foster v. Oklahoma*: PC 87–729 (1988). *Foster v. Oklahoma*: PC 93–1020 (1995). *Foster v. Oklahoma*: 479 U.S. 873 (1986). *Foster v. Oklahoma*: 497 U.S. 1032 (1990). *Foster v. Oklahoma*: 488 U.S. 884 (1988). *Foster v. Oklahoma*: 714 P.2d 1031 (1986). *Foster v. Oklahoma*: 779 P.2d 591 (1989). *Foster v. Ward*: 182 F.3d 1177 (1999).

Robedeaux, James G.
June 1, 2000

In March 1978 twenty-seven-year-old James Glenn Robedeaux, a habitual wife-abuser, strangled to death his wife Linda Sue, but he was allowed to plead guilty to second-degree murder. He was sentenced to serve twenty-five years in prison with fifteen years suspended, received an additional year for escape when he failed to return to the Oklahoma City Treatment Center, and was released in September 1984. Between his release from prison and July 1985 Robedeaux met and married Doris M. Robedeaux, but they were soon separated because of his frequent abuse.

In early July 1985 Robedeaux met thirty-seven-year-old Nancy Rose Lee McKinney. By early August McKinney had rented apartment 204 in an Oklahoma City complex, and Robedeaux moved in with her and her four children. McKinney worked at a nearby hospital but she began missing work and was soon fired, and her four children were taken away when there were allegations that Robedeaux was abusing them and had strangled her thirteen-year-old daughter into unconsciousness. The couple had numerous loud, violent fights, and these were heard by Bobby and Barbara Jones, who lived beneath them.

On September 15 during one fight Barbara heard McKinney plead, "Don't hit me anymore." Barbara last saw McKinney at 10:00 A.M. on September 22, but at 10:00 P.M. the Jones couple heard loud noises coming from the apartment above them, as if something was crashing to the floor, and it was so violent it shook their apartment. The sounds decreased in frequency and violence until 1:00 A.M. before the sounds ceased. Barbara said she could distinguish between the footsteps of her two upstairs neighbors and never heard McKinney's footsteps after that night. The following morning Barbara saw Robedeaux drive away in McKinney's blue Ford Fairmont, and after noon the following day Robedeaux was seen by Bobby removing two dark trash bags from the apartment, and he paused to apologize for the noise.

On September 27 Robedeaux went with JoAnn Robinson to retrieve tapes pawned by McKinney and had Robinson sign McKinney's name, and then they rented a carpet-cleaning machine which they took to apartment 204. Robedeaux cleaned the bloodstains and was seen by the Jones couple again on September 28 as he loaded the rug-cleaning machine into a pickup truck.

Allen Savill, a maintenance man at the apartment building, had gone into apartment 204 on September 23 and noticed a dark stain on the carpet at the door to the bedroom closet, but it had been cleaned when he returned on September 28, though he noticed three bloodstained towels hanging in the bathroom. On September 25 Carmen McKinney visited apartment 204 to look for her daughter, who had always called her several times a week, and she left a note on the door. That same day the Ford Fairmont was repossessed, and Robedeaux at first denied then admitted knowing McKinney. Carmen returned on September 28 and saw the rug-cleaning machine and soon afterward, when she still had not heard from her daughter, she reported her missing.

On October 1 landlord A. D. Smedley accompanied Savill and Roy Aber into apartment 204 and noticed several dark spots resembling blood stains on the carpet and a blood smear on the wall. Smedley locked the apartment and had the locks changed, but allowed Robedeaux entrance on October 11 to retrieve his clothes, and Robedeaux took two boxes of trash to the trash dumpster before he left. Savill went to the dumpster and retrieved the three stained towels from Robedeaux's trash, and these were eventually given to the police. When Savill returned to the apartment he noticed that the blood smear on the wall had been wiped cleaned.

When suspicion grew Smedley called the police and they arrived on October 15, and when they entered the apartment there was the distinctive odor of rotting flesh. The police took parts of the carpet and pad for testing and found that it was type A human blood, then returned nine days later and took the entire bedroom carpet and pieces of pad. The following day, October 25, the carpet was replaced, and the carpet layer found the disgusting odor overwhelming, but he also noted blood stains in the hallway.

On September 28 Robedeaux had met Patricia Avery at Marie's Club and they lived together for two weeks. On October 18, 1985 Robedeaux met Lisa Gail Austin and they moved in together, and over the next month he told Austin about McKinney, saying he had killed her, dismembered the body, and buried her. He was still living with Austin when he was questioned by detectives on November 14, and the following day he was arrested. Robedeaux told detectives that McKinney had left him about the beginning of September to stay with her parents in Red Rock, the stain in the apartment was red Kool-aid he had spilled, the stain in the hallway was oil from lubricating door hinges, and that some tenant prior to him may have bled on the carpet. When accused of killing McKinney he denied the charge.

Sometime between September 23 and November 15 Robedeaux had arranged to meet his estranged wife Doris; he beat her so badly that he broke her nose and eye socket, and he strangled but did not kill her. On November 19, 1985, after Robedeaux was behind bars, Doris filed a complaint, and Robedeaux was charged with trying to murder her.

In early December Robedeaux was charged with murdering McKinney, though no body had been found. On December 28 Charles Dewayne Stokes and another boy were playing near the Deep Fork River outside Wellston, and Stokes noticed a dog chewing on a human leg and called the authorities. On February 3, 1986, David Habben, who lived in South Logan County near Coon Creek, found a human skull in the front yard of his ranch house, and it was sent to the coroner. McKinney's brother joined in the search of the Coon Creek area and found an arm with hand attached in the Coon Creek streambed. The body parts were examined by medical examiner Dr. Larry Balding and forensic anthropologist Dr. Clyde Snow and were confirmed to be the remains of McKinney, but the cause of death could not be determined. However, it was evident that the body had been dismembered using a thin-bladed saw and a knife or machete, and it was estimated that dismemberment took four to five hours to accomplish.

Robedeaux was tried in June 1986, convicted of first-degree murder after the jurors deliberated only ninety minutes, and sentenced to die. He was delivered to a death row cell at the prison on July 8, 1986, while his attorney filed an appeal, which stayed the execution. The state Court of Criminal Appeals affirmed the judgment and sentence of the district court in 1993 and denied his 1995 appeal for post-conviction relief. The Court of Criminal Appeals set the date for the execution at June 1, 2000, and further efforts on his behalf failed. On May 23, 2000, Robedeaux appeared before the state Board of Pardons and Parole, but the members voted unanimously to deny clemency, and Governor Frank Keating declined to intervene.

On May 31 Robedeaux was moved from his death row cell in H unit to a special cell near the death chamber. Shortly before midnight the prisoner was escorted into the injection room where he took his place on the gurney and his chest, waist, and legs were strapped while his arms were secured to two arm extensions, and a white sheet was pulled over his body. A medical technician carefully inserted one intravenous cannula (IV) into the vein of each arm while the executioners were hidden from view in another room, hooded and behind a one-way mirrored window.

Warden Gary Gibson confirmed by telephone, with Governor Keating, that the execution was to proceed, had the curtains drawn open and asked if Robedeaux had any last words, and he said, "Dad, I just want you to know I love you. Tell Mother I love her. Tell sister I love her. Tell the kids I love them." He then said that he had found salvation and told his father to trust in Christ before he added, "I'll see you again." He next addressed the dozen members of the McKinney family present to witness the execution and told them, "God bless you all. I'm going to be all right. I love you." There were a dozen witnesses seated in the witness room and additional witnesses watched on closed-circuit television from a room below. When Robedeaux concluded his remarks Warden Gibson announced, "Let the execution begin!" Each executioner in turn drained the contents of his syringe into the tube leading to Robedeaux's arm: the first drug, sodium thiopental, caused unconsciousness; the second drug, pancuronium bromide, caused his respiration to become labored and would have caused death in time; and the third drug, potassium chloride, stopped his heart. Robedeaux closed his eyes at 12:28 A.M. as the first drug began to flow, and at 12:34 A.M. all sign of life was absent and Robedeaux was pronounced dead.

Sources: *Amarillo Globe-News* (TX): June 2, 2000. *Robedeaux v. State*: 866 P.2d 417 (1993). *Robedeaux v. State*: 908 P.2d 804 (1995).

Berget, Roger J.
June 8, 2000

In 1971, when Roger James Berget was ten years old, his stepfather drove him out of the house, and he took refuge in an abandoned house nearby. His mother began sneaking food to her young son but when his stepfather found out he beat her and the boy, and then he burned down the vacant house. Berget turned to crime and by October 1985, at the age of twenty-four, Berget had a long record of arrests and convictions.

Late on the evening of October 19 Berget and twenty-year-old Mikell Patrick Smith were on the prowl for a car to steal, and they spotted thirty-three-year-old Richard Lee "Rick" Patterson in an Oklahoma City supermarket parking lot. When Patterson, a much-loved math teacher at Moore Central Mid-High School, unlocked the car door Berget pointed a shotgun at him and forced him to slide over to the passenger seat, then passed the shotgun to Smith in the backseat and he took the driver's seat. Berget drove them to a remote area of the town where they took Patterson out of the automobile, secured his wrists behind, and gagged him before putting their captive in the trunk. They drove to an isolated woods near Rockwell, arriving after midnight, and when they opened the trunk they found that Patterson had freed his wrists, so they tied him again and stood him against a tree. Smith fired the first blast from a 12-gauge shotgun; this was immediately followed by a second blast fired by Berget so both would be equally implicated, and both blasts were fired in such a brief period it could not be determined which was the fatal shot.

On October 21 two hunters found Patterson's body and called the police. The investigation dragged on for ten months even though both men had bragged of the murder, and during that time Smith was arrested for forgery, convicted and sentenced to serve a prison term. In early August 1986 Berget was arrested with twenty-two-year-old Scott M. Thornton and charged with several robberies and burglaries in Midwest cities.

Berget was linked to the murder of Patterson and charged, and on August 13 he confessed that he helped Smith kidnap Patterson, drove them to the wooded area where the body was found, and insisted that Smith had shot Patterson twice. Smith was also charged with the murder but he told of each man shooting Patterson once, and this was corroborated by Donald Gene Wheeler who later would testify for the prosecution. Berget was also charged with four burglaries and with "a felon carrying a firearm."

Berget agreed to testify against Smith in return for life sentences on six charges. Berget and Smith met while awaiting trial and made some arrangement; Smith pled not guilty, and at his trial Berget testified that Smith had not been present at the murder scene. However, the jurors disbelieved Berget and Smith was convicted of first-degree murder and sentenced to die, and his attorney filed an appeal, which stayed his execution.

On January 23, 1987, Berget pled guilty to all charges before Oklahoma County district court Judge John Amick, and on March 12 the judge sentenced him to die, and also to serve a number of years in prison on the other charges. He was delivered to his death row cell on March 18. Berget tried to withdraw his guilty plea after sentencing, recanted his confession, and claimed Smith alone had murdered Patterson but the motion was denied. Then Berget confessed to killing forty-four-year-old James Meadows during a robbery at Holdenville in April 1986. Berget's attorney, James Rowan, filed an appeal, which stayed his execution.

Thornton, in a plea deal on the robbery and burglary charges, had testified against Smith and Berget and received a twenty-five-year prison sentence to be served outside Oklahoma. In 1992 the Court of Criminal Appeals granted Smith a new trial, and in 1995, as his trial date neared, he pled guilty to first-degree murder, and Judge Nancy L. Coates sentenced him to a life sentence without the possibility of parole. While in prison Smith murdered two fellow convicts in separate incidents and attempted to murder a prison guard, and he was tried, convicted, and sentenced to serve three additional life sentences.

The Court of Criminal Appeals affirmed the judgment and sentence against Berget in 1991, and over the next nine years Rowan used every legal maneuver at his disposal to save his client's life, but all failed. Berget's date with the executioner was set for June 8, 2000, and at his hearing before the state Board of Pardons and Parole on May 30, 2000, he was denied clemency on a three to one vote. Governor Frank Keating refused to intervene.

On June 7 Berget was moved from his death row cell in H unit to a special cell near the death chamber. Shortly before midnight the prisoner was escorted into the injection room where he took his place on the gurney and his chest, waist, and legs were strapped while his arms were secured to two arm extensions, and a sheet was pulled over his body. A medical technician carefully inserted one intravenous cannula (IV) into the vein of each arm while the executioners were hidden from view in another room, behind a one-way mirrored window. The warden confirmed by telephone, with Governor Keating, that the execution was to proceed and had the curtains drawn open. At 12:08 A.M. Berget was asked if had any last words, but the condemned man almost in a whisper said, "No sir," and then he declined to speak further to the dozen witnesses in the witness room and the additional witnesses watching on closed-circuit television from a room below.

The warden announced, "Let the execution begin," and each executioner drained the contents of his syringe into the tube leading to Berget's arm: the first drug, sodium thiopental, caused unconsciousness; the second drug, pancuronium bromide, caused his respiration to become labored and would have caused death in time; and the third drug, potassium chloride, would stop his heart. Berget exhaled several gasping breaths and lay still, and at 12:12 A.M. all sign of life was absent and Berget was pronounced dead.

Sources: *Berget v. Oklahoma*: 824 P.2d 364 (1991). Oklahoma County District Court case numbers: CRF 86–1536; CRF 86–4264; CRF 86–4475; CRF 86–4476; CRF 86–4478; CRF 86–4533. *Oklahoman* (Oklahoma City): May 29, 2000. *Shawnee News-Star* (OK): June 8–9, 2000.

Bryson, William C., Jr.
June 15, 2000

Plantz, Marilyn K.
May 1, 2000

In 1988 thirty-three-year-old James Earl Plantz and his twenty-seven-year-old wife Marilyn Kay, whites, had been married eleven years and appeared to have a good marriage. However, in early 1987 Marilyn met sixteen year old William Clifford Bryson, Jr., a black man, and the two began having sexual relations. When Bryson turned eighteen Marilyn decided to have her boyfriend kill James for his two life insurance policies, which had recently been increased to $319,000, and they recruited nineteen-year-old Clinton Eugene McKimble by offering him $45,000 for his help. The plan was for the two young men to steal a car, watch for James on the highway when he got off work at 4:00 A.M., bump the rear of his Nissan pickup truck so he would stop, then shoot him or beat him to death. Marilyn provided Bryson and McKimble with baseball bats but, after they lay in wait along the highway in their stolen automobile, they pursued James but lost him.

Marilyn then obtained a pistol and gave it to Bryson but he pawned it for drug money. On August 24 Bryson hired Roderick Farris to carry out the plan, and they all gathered at the Plantz home, but that night someone else came to the home, and after being seen they postponed the murder. Soon afterward Farris was arrested on an unrelated charge and held in jail, so he was no longer available to murder James. Two days later, on Friday, August 26, 1988, Bryson and McKimble were at the Plantz house, and the Plantz children, nine-year-old Trina and six-year-old Christopher, were asleep when James returned home shortly before 5:00 A.M., his usual time. Bryson and McKimble hid in the dark on each side of the door with Christopher's baseball bats in hand, and as soon as James stepped into the living room Bryson struck James in the head. James cried out for Marilyn as he fell, but Bryson immediately hit him again as McKimble joined in the beating. They struck James repeatedly because "he would not stay down," but finally he collapsed. He was helpless but moaning as they carried him out to his truck, and Marilyn came out and gave them the keys. She told them, "His head is busted open. It is not going to look much like an accident," and then she instructed them to "burn him."

They cleaned out his pockets before they put him in the bed of his truck, and Bryson drove to a remote location along James' route from work in northeast Oklahoma City while McKimble followed in Marilyn's Chevrolet Camaro. Bryson and McKimble carefully positioned James behind the steering wheel, and McKimble used a rag as a wick to try to ignite the fuel tank, but this failed. They next poured gasoline in the cab and over the body, lit it and drove off, but when they stopped to look back they saw James rise up amidst the flames and attempt to exit before he collapsed back into the burning truck.

When Bryson and McKimble reached the Plantz house Marilyn was busy cleaning up the blood on the living room carpet so they changed into James' clothes, put their bloody clothing in a sack, and threw it into the river. They next went to a convenience store and ate, using the money they had stolen from James' pockets. McKimble said he could still smell blood so he went home to bathe while Bryson went to the home of his friend Michael Kendrick. Bryson told Kendrick of the murder, and Kendrick would later say he saw the spots of blood on Bryson's shoes and hands, and when McKimble arrived he and Bryson talked and laughed over the details of the killing. McKimble returned to his home, and soon afterward Bryson got a ride to McKimble's house from Terry Norman, and Bryson bragged to him of the killing.

At 6:30 A.M., only ninety minutes after the time her husband was due to arrive home, Marilyn telephoned the police to report that her husband was missing, and the police discovered that she had made no effort to contact his employer or friends. At about the same time Marilyn was calling the police a passing motorist noticed the burned truck and called police, and James' body was discovered. There was no evidence of a crash at the scene, and during the autopsy it was discovered that James' skull had been fractured and his arms were broken as if defending himself from an attack, and the coroner concluded he was alive when burned. The police, at the Plantz home, noticed a new rug in the living room and learned Marilyn had bought it at 9:00 A.M. on the day her husband was reported missing. They then learned of her affair with Bryson and numerous other infidelities.

Marilyn was arrested on Monday, August 29, and Bryson and McKimble were arrested the following day. McKimble quickly confessed, and when Bryson learned of this development he tried to hang himself using his shoelaces. He was rushed to the hospital where he recovered and then was returned to a special cell under a close watch, so when he tried to drown himself in his toilet he was stopped. On Wednesday all three prisoners were charged with murder, and prosecutors announced they would seek the death penalty. Marilyn had first insisted she had a perfect marriage and knew nothing of the murder of her husband, but finally all three prisoners confessed to their various roles in James' murder. Bryson told investigators, "I didn't have no specific reason why I killed him. All I was thinking while I was beating him was all the times she came up to me with a black eye and crying. I didn't like that." He said that James had threatened to kill Marilyn and himself if she divorced him, and Bryson insisted he loved Marilyn.

On October 20 McKimble negotiated an agreement in which he would testify, plead guilty, and receive a life sentence. A motion was filed with Oklahoma County District Judge Charles Owens requesting separate trials for Bryson and Plantz, and this was denied. Following their trial the jurors spent only three hours finding both defendants guilty of first-degree murder on March 22, 1989. The next day the jurors spent only five hours deliberating before recommending the death penalty, and they were also sentenced to serve one hundred years for hiring others to commit murder, ten years for conspiracy to murder, and fifteen years for arson of the truck.

On April 3, 1989, Bryson and Plantz arrived on death row while their attorneys filed appeals. In 1994 the justices of the Oklahoma Court of Criminal Appeals affirmed the judgment and sentence of the district court in Bryson's case, and the following year the justices denied the appeal for post-conviction relief. In 1999 the writ for habeas corpus, filed with the federal Tenth Circuit Court of Appeals, was denied. The justices of the state Court of Criminal Appeals set the date of execution at June 15, 2000. At Bryson's June 6 hearing before the state Pardon and Parole Board four members voted to deny clemency, with one member abstaining, and Governor Frank Keating declined to interfere.

On June 14 Bryson was moved from his death row cell to a special cell near the death chamber. Shortly before midnight the prisoner was escorted into the injection room where he took his place on the gurney and his chest, waist, and legs were strapped while his arms were secured to two arm extensions, and a sheet was pulled over his body. A medical technician carefully inserted one intravenous cannula (IV) into the vein of each arm while the executioners were hidden from view in another room, behind a one-way mirrored window. Warden

Ronald Ward confirmed by telephone, with Governor Keating, that the execution was to proceed and then had the curtains drawn open. Bryson was asked if he had any last words but there is no record of a statement to the witnesses, including thirteen members of the Plantz family, a few among the dozen in the witness room and the remainder with the additional witnesses watching on closed-circuit television from a room below. The warden announced, "Let the execution begin," and each executioner drained the contents of his syringe into the tube leading to Bryson's arm: the first drug, sodium thiopental, caused unconsciousness; the second drug, pancuronium bromide, caused his respiration to become labored and would have caused death in time; and the third drug, potassium chloride, would stop his heart. Minutes after the first drug was administered all sign of life was absent and Bryson was pronounced dead at 12:14 A.M.

The fight to save Marilyn Plantz's life continued; the same week that Bryson had his board hearing her writ of habeas corpus was denied by the federal Tenth Circuit Court of Appeals. Her final appeal to the U.S. Supreme Court was denied on February 26, and the state Court of Criminal Appeals, on March 8, 2001, set her date with the executioner for May 1. At her hearing before the state Board of Pardons and Parole she was denied clemency, and Governor Keating refused to intervene. On April 30 Plantz was moved from her death row cell to a special cell near the death chamber.

Shortly before 9:00 P.M. the prisoner was escorted into the injection room where she lay down on the gurney, and her chest, waist, and legs were strapped while her arms were secured to two arm extensions and a sheet was pulled over her body. A medical technician carefully inserted one intravenous cannula (IV) into the vein of each arm while the executioners were hidden from view in another room, behind a one-way mirrored window. Warden Massie confirmed by telephone, with Governor Keating, that the execution was to proceed and then had the curtains drawn open.

Plantz was asked if she had any last words but there is no record of a statement to the witnesses including twelve members of the Plantz family, a few among the dozen in the witness room and the remainder among the additional witnesses watching on closed-circuit television from a room below. As Plantz prayed the warden announced, "Let the execution begin," and each executioner drained the contents of his syringe into the tube leading to Plantz's arm: the first drug, sodium thiopental, caused unconsciousness; the second drug, pancuronium bromide, caused her respiration to become labored and would have caused death in time; and the third drug, potassium chloride, would stop her heart. Minutes after the first drug was administered all sign of life was absent and Plantz was pronounced dead at 9:11 P.M.

Sources: *Bryson v. Oklahoma*: 513 U.S. 1090 (1995). *Bryson v. Oklahoma*: 517 U.S. 1144 (1996). *Bryson v. State*: 876 P.2d 240 (1994). *Bryson v. State*: 903 P.2d 333 (1995). *Bryson v. Ward*: 187 F.3d 1193 (1999). *Herald* (Tyrone, PA): May 2, 2001. *Lethbridge Herald* (Alberta, Canada): November 3, 1996. *Oklahoman* (Oklahoma City): May 2, 2001. *Plantz v. Massie*: 216 F.3d 1088 (2000). *Plantz v. Oklahoma*: 513 U.S. 1163 (1995). *Plantz v. State*: 876 P.2d 268 (1994). *Plantz v. State*: 936 P.2d 339 (1997). *Sitka Sentinel* (AK): June 15, 2000. *Tecumseh Countywide News* (OK): June 20, 2000.

Braun, Gregg F.
July 20, 2000

On July 19, 1989, twenty-eight-year-old Gregg Francis Braun, a college graduate with a degree in criminal justice, was in Garden City, Kansas, where his father was a prominent attorney, when he decided to rob two convenience stores at opposite sides of the city to support his drug habit. He first captured twenty-seven-year-old clerk Barbara Kochendorfer and cleaned out the cash register before he took his captive to a remote location, where he shot her in the back of the head with his .25-caliber automatic pistol. He then went to the second convenience store and captured twenty-eight-year-old clerk Mary Raines, and after he cleaned out the cash register he took her to a remote location and shot her in the back of the head. Both bodies were found three miles apart in ditches along the same rural roadway.

Braun fled to Pampa, Texas, and the following day he went into the One Hour Photo development store and captured fifty-four-year-old E. P. "Pete" Spurrier, cleaned out the cash register, had him lie face down on the floor and shot him in the back of the head, even though Spurrier did not resist.

Braun then drove to Ardmore, Oklahoma, where, on July 21, he entered Dodson's Flower Shop and took thirty-one-year-old clerk Gwendolyn Sue Miller, female bookkeeper JoAnn Beane, and female customer Mary Mannings prisoner and herded them into the stockroom. He had them lie face down on the floor and then shot each woman in the back of the head before he took $600 from Mannings' purse and $80 from the cash register, but only Miller died from her wound.

Braun fled to Springer, New Mexico, where, on July 23, he robbed a gasoline station and shot forty-eight-year-old Geraldine Valdez in the back of the head twice, killing her. Forty minutes after the murder the police captured Braun driving on the highway and recovered the murder weapon from his car, and he told them, "You guys must be proud. You don't know what kind of famous criminal you caught." While being taken to jail he told a deputy, "I shot some women in a flower shop. It wasn't as good as shooting craps in Vegas, but it was all right."

In April 1990 Braun pled guilty in New Mexico, and in September 1991 he was sentenced to serve life in prison. Braun was then extradited to Kansas where he pled guilty and was sentenced to serve four life terms for the murders and kidnappings and two fifteen-years-to-life terms for the two robberies. Braun was then extradited to Oklahoma where, on August 17, 1993, he waived the assistance of counsel and pled nolo contendere in the Carter County district court. On August 23 Judge Thomas Walker sentenced Braun to die for the murder of Miller and also sentenced him to serve two life sentences for the other two shootings — Beane and Mannings — and to twenty-five years for each of two counts of robbery — Mannings and the flower shop's cash register.

He was delivered to his death row cell on August 25, 1993, and on August 27 his appointed attorney moved to withdraw his nolo contendere plea, but the motion was denied after a hearing on September 21. Jim Rowan, his appointed trial attorney, then filed appeals, which stayed the execution but in 1995 the state Court of Criminal Appeals affirmed the judgment and sentence of the district court, and two years later the justices denied him post-conviction relief. His writ of habeas corpus filed with the federal Tenth Circuit Court of Appeals was denied on September 10, 1999, and the state Criminal Court of Appeals then set his execution date at July 20, 2000. On June 27 Braun appeared before the state Board of Pardons and Parole and the members denied clemency, and Governor Frank Keating declined to intervene.

On July 19 Braun was moved from his death row cell to a special cell near the death chamber. Shortly before midnight the prisoner was escorted into the injection room where he took his place on the gurney and his chest, waist, and legs were strapped while his arms were secured to two arm extensions, and a sheet was pulled over his body. A medical technician carefully inserted one intravenous cannula (IV) into the vein of each arm while the executioners were hidden from view in another room, behind a one-way mirrored window.

Warden Ronald Ward confirmed by telephone, with Governor Keating, that the execution was to proceed and had the curtains drawn open before he asked Braun if he had any last words. Braun then named each of his victims in the order he murdered them and said, "I'm sorry. I'm sorry I murdered you. I'm sorry I took your lives. I pray for our Lord Jesus Christ to bless your lives and to save you. I'm so sorry I killed you." His entire slurred and rambling speech lasted three minutes as he apologized to each of his victims' family members saying, "What I did was unforgivable, but I ask you to forgive me." He also asked to be forgiven by each person he hurt while on his crime spree. Thirty-nine family members had come to witness the execution, eleven in the witness room and twenty-eight by closed-circuit television from a room below the death chamber. Catholic Father Chi Peter Phung, Braun's only witness, was also in the witness room. When Braun concluded the warden announced, "Let the execution begin," and at 12:11 A.M. each executioner drained the contents of his syringe into the tube leading to Braun's arm: the first drug, sodium thiopental, caused unconsciousness; the second drug, pancuronium bromide, caused his respiration to become labored and would have caused death in time; and the third drug, potassium chloride, would stop his heart. Braun just seemed to go to sleep, and at 12:17 A.M. all sign of life was absent and Braun was pronounced dead.

Sources: *Ardmoreite* (OK): July 19, 2000. *Braun v. Oklahoma*: 909 P.2d 783 (1995). *Braun v. Oklahoma*: 937 P.2d 505 (1997). *Braun v. Ward*: 190 F.3d 1181 (1999). *Salina Journal* (KS): July 21, 2000.

Wallace, George K.
August 10, 2000

On July 30, 1976, thirty-five-year-old George Kent Wallace, a truck driver, abducted fourteen-year-old Jeffrey Lee Foster from Winston-Salem,

North Carolina, and took him to a remote wooded area near Bethania where he stabbed the youngster to death. On August 24 the Forsyth County coroner announced that a skull found by two boys cutting grass, and parts of a skeleton found afterward, were the remains of Foster, but the case remained unsolved. In 1982 Thomas Stewart Reed met a similar fate, and that case also remained unsolved.

In 1986 Wallace moved from Forsyth County, North Carolina, to Fort Smith, Arkansas, perhaps fearing he might be discovered. On February 17, 1987, Wallace, then forty-six years old, kidnapped fifteen-year-old William von Eric Domer near Fort Smith, Arkansas, by posing as a police officer and telling the boy he was under arrest. Wallace, dressed in dark clothing to resemble a uniform and flashing a fake badge, handcuffed Domer and applied ankle shackles before placing him in the rear seat of his rented car, and he drove Domer to remote Leard Pond near Pocola in Leflore County, Oklahoma. Wallace pulled down Domer's trousers and underwear and tried to spank him with a paddle but when he resisted Wallace pulled up his underwear and trousers and then shot him twice in the back of his head with a .25-caliber pistol. He dragged his body to the edge of the pond where he removed the handcuffs and leg shackles and threw the body into the water. On February 22 Domer's body was discovered floating in the pond.

On November 11, 1990, fourteen-year-old Mark Anthony McLaughlin was abducted at Van Buren, Arkansas, when Wallace, again posing as a police officer, "arrested" and handcuffed him, shackled his ankles, and put him in the back seat of his rented car, and then drove him to the same pond near Pocola, Oklahoma. When they arrived Wallace got into the back seat and took down McLaughlin's trousers and underwear and spanked him with a plunger handle, took him out of the car and pulled up his underwear and trousers and then shot him in the back of his head once with a .22-caliber pistol. The next day McLaughlin's body was discovered floating in Leard Pond.

Between November 12 and December 8 Wallace tried to abduct nineteen-year-old Isidro Hernandez but the youth talked his way out of being "arrested." He abducted eighteen-year-old James Branson but released him when the youth persisted in kicking and screaming. On November 24, 1990, Wallace abducted twelve-year-old Alonzo Don Cade after he left the Westark Community College campus, and his body was found on December 20 in a gas-well pit near Fort Chaffee, federal property east of Fort Smith, Arkansas.

On December 9, 1990, Wallace used the same ruse to "arrest" eighteen-year-old Ross Alan Ferguson in a grocery store parking lot in Van Buren, Arkansas. Wallace told Ferguson he was suspected of a recent, nearby robbery, applied handcuffs and ankle shackles, and put him in the back seat of his rented car. Wallace drove his captive to a remote area along a country road near a farm pond east of Greenwood and then climbed into the back seat, pulled down Ferguson's trousers and underwear, and beat him with a rod. He got Ferguson out of the car, pulled up his trousers and underwear and walked him toward the pond, but when Ferguson asked if Wallace was going to shoot him he replied "No!" and immediately stabbed him five times in the back and once in the arm. Ferguson collapsed to the ground and played dead so Wallace dragged his limp body to the edge of the pond and removed the handcuffs and ankle shackles. As soon as he was free Ferguson sprang up, knocked Wallace to the ground, and ran to Wallace's car with his abductor in close pursuit. He locked the car doors and then drove to a nearby house for help.

Deputy Sheriff Frank Atkinson found Wallace walking in a ditch along the roadway and arrested him. He was questioned, and after he confessed he led officers to a pasture near Seminole where he had buried the .22-caliber pistol with which he had murdered McLaughlin. He was first tried in Arkansas and convicted of abducting four boys and the attempted murder of Ferguson; he was sentenced to serve three life terms and sixty years. He waived extradition and was delivered to Leflore County, Oklahoma, where in 1991 he pled guilty to murdering Domer and McLaughlin and told Judge Michael Lee he wanted to die as quickly as possible.

On April 12 he was twice sentenced to die and was transferred to his death row cell the same day. He waived his appeals, excepting for the automatic appeal in all capital cases, and on March 27, 1995, the state Court of Criminal Appeals affirmed the judgment and sentence of the district court and set the date of execution at May 26. The U.S. Supreme Court stayed the execution to give Wallace's attorney time to file an appeal, but the petition was denied on October 2, and on the 29th the state justices set the date of execution for

December 1, 1995. On November 21 the state Court of Criminal Appeals granted a stay of execution when Wallace withdrew his waiver of appeals, and his attorney filed his application for post-conviction relief on June 9, 1996, and his revised application on July 9. In 1996 Wallace also, finally, confessed to the murders of Foster and Reed in North Carolina, and was still suspected in the abduction and murder of Cade. Wallace's application was denied on March 18, 1997, and with his state remedies exhausted he filed a writ of habeas corpus with the federal Tenth Circuit Court of Appeals, which was rejected on September 10, 1999. On June 9, 2000, the justices of the state Court of Criminal Appeals set the execution date for August 10, and Wallace then waived his clemency hearing.

On August 9 Wallace was moved from his death row cell to a special cell near the death chamber. Shortly before 9:00 P.M. the prisoner was escorted into the injection room where he took his place on the gurney and his chest, waist, and legs were strapped while his arms were secured to two arm extensions, and a sheet was pulled over his body. A medical technician carefully inserted one intravenous cannula (IV) into the vein of each arm while the executioners were hidden from view in another room, behind a one-way mirrored window. Warden Ronald Ward confirmed by telephone, with Governor Keating, that the execution was to proceed and had the curtains drawn open before he asked Wallace if he had any last words. Wallace declined to speak but mouthed the words "I love you!" Nine members from the McLaughlin and Domer families came to witness the execution from the witness room, and the other witnesses watched by closed-circuit television from a room below the death chamber.

When Wallace concluded the warden announced, "Let the execution begin," and at 9:24 P.M. each executioner drained the contents of his syringe into the tube leading to Wallace's arm: the first drug, sodium thiopental, caused unconsciousness; the second drug, pancuronium bromide, caused his respiration to become labored and would have caused death in time; and the third drug, potassium chloride, would stop his heart. Wallace peacefully went to sleep, and at 9:27 P.M. all sign of life was absent, and Wallace was pronounced dead.

Sources: *High Point Enterprise* (NC): August 24, 1976. *Tulsa World* (OK): August 10, 2000. *Wallace v. Oklahoma*: 516 U.S. 888 (1995). *Wallace v. State*: 521 U.S. 1108 (1997). *Wallace v. State*: 893 P.2d 504 (1995). *Wallace v. State*: 935 P.2d 366 (1997). *Wallace v. Ward*: 191 F.3d 1235 (1999).

Trice, Eddie L.
January 9, 2001

Thirty-four-year-old Eddie Leroy Trice, who had been convicted of a previous violent felony, dated Geraldine Jones but they had ended their relationship. On February 13, 1987, Trice spent most of the day drinking with roommate Archie Landon, and after they returned home Landon went to sleep on the couch. Trice then took a pair of nunchakus, a martial arts weapon consisting of two sticks tied together with rope or chain, and after midnight he arrived at 1613 NE 24th Street in Oklahoma City — the home of eighty-four-year-old Earnestine Jones, who was his ex-girlfriend's mother. He entered the home through the northwest bedroom window and was discovered by Earnestine, so Trice beat her severely breaking an eye socket, her upper and lower jaw, injuring her neck, crushing her rib cage which caused bruising to her heart and lungs, and breaking two fingers, and the attack was so violent the nunchukas broke. Earnestine's sixty-three-year-old retarded son, Emanuel, came to her aid but Trice took a hammer and beat him severely, puncturing his right eye and breaking his right cheekbone and right forearm, and after Emanuel was disabled and helpless Trice raped Earnestine causing bruising in her vaginal area and scratches in the vaginal canal and on her cervix. He then ransacked the house, stole $500 from Emanuel, and threatened to return and kill him if he reported the attack. Earnestine lived for several hours before she died from internal injuries, and the next morning her body was discovered by Geraldine, who urged Emanuel to tell the police the details of the attack.

At 1:00 A.M. Trice had returned home, and Landon was told, after he saw the blood on Trice's clothing, "I tore up my nunchukas on some homosexual's head." They unwrapped and counted the money, which was in several packages, and then Trice wrapped his bloody clothing in his blood-splattered coat and hid then in a nearby abandoned house. When he returned he and Landon went to Landon's brother's house where they spent the rest of the night drinking. After Trice fled Landon called the police and told them where they could find the bloody clothing.

Four days later Trice was arrested, he confessed, and he was charged with murder, rape, burglary, and assault with a deadly weapon. The district attorney announced that the prosecution would seek the death penalty. His trial started before Judge William Burkett on June 8, and he was convicted on June 11. During the trial his attorney conceded that his client was "guilty on all of the counts in the information," and during the penalty phase he told the jurors that "I can think of a lot of things that could be said in support of giving Mr. Trice death." The jurors found four of five aggravating circumstances and recommended the death penalty, and on June 13 Judge Burkett sentenced Trice to die for the murder of Earnestine and to three consecutive sentences of 999 years each for rape, robbery, and the beating of Emanuel.

Trice arrived on death row on June 25, and his attorney filed an appeal, which stayed the execution. The initial appeal was decided on April 15, 1993, when the justices of the state Court of Criminal Appeals affirmed the judgment and sentence of the district court, and on December 11 the U.S. Supreme Court denied certiorari. Trice's attorney then filed for post-conviction relief, which was denied on November 18, 1994, and on February 29, 1996, the U.S. Supreme Court again denied certiorari. With state remedies exhausted Trice's attorney filed a writ of habeas corpus with the federal Tenth Circuit Court of Appeals, but this was denied on November 15, 1999, and the case was remanded to the state Court of Criminal Appeals. The justices set the execution date for January 9, 2001, leaving only the state Board of Pardons and Parole and the governor to grant clemency. On November 2, 2000, Trice had his hearing before the board, and after hearing about his mental issues the members denied clemency in a unanimous vote. Governor Frank Keating declined to intervene.

Early on January 9 Trice was moved from his death row cell to a special cell near the death chamber. Shortly before 9:00 P.M. the prisoner was escorted into the injection room where he took his place on the gurney and his chest, waist, and legs were strapped while his arms were secured to two arm extensions, and a sheet was pulled over his body. A medical technician carefully inserted one intravenous cannula (IV) into the vein of each arm while the executioners were hidden from view in another room, behind a one-way mirrored window.

Warden Ronald Ward confirmed by telephone, with Governor Keating, that the execution was to proceed and had the curtains drawn open before he asked Trice if he had any last words. Trice thanked his family and apologized to the Jones family, who were seated in the witness room, while the other witnesses watched by closed-circuit television from a room below the death chamber. When Trice concluded the warden announced, "Let the execution begin," and each executioner drained the contents of his syringe into the tube leading to Trice's arm: the first drug, sodium thiopental, caused unconsciousness; the second drug, pancuronium bromide, caused his respiration to become labored and would have caused death in time; and the third drug, potassium chloride, would stop his heart. At 9:15 P.M. all sign of life was absent and Trice was pronounced dead.

Sources: *Oklahoman* (Oklahoma City): January 9, 2001. *Trice v. Oklahoma*: 510 U.S. 1025 (1993). *Trice v. State*: 853 P.2d 203 (1993). *Trice v. State*: 912 P.2d 349 (1996). *Trice v. Ward*: 196 F.3d 1151 (1999). *Tulsa World* (OK): September 24, 2000; January 8, 2001.

Allen, Wanda J.
January 11, 2001

On June 29, 1981, twenty-two-year-old Wanda Jean Allen, during a particularly heated argument with the boyfriend of her childhood friend Detra Pettus at an Oklahoma City motel, pulled a pistol from beneath her clothing and pistol-whipped Pettus, then shot her point-blank. When Pettus died Allen, contradicting the forensic evidence, claimed her friend had been shot by accident when she exchanged gunfire with Pettus' boyfriend, but later when confronted with the inconsistency she insisted she did not know how the gun was discharged. Allen was charged with murder but in a plea deal she was allowed to plead guilty to manslaughter and was sentenced to serve four years in prison.

In 1982, while in prison, Allen met twenty-four-year-old Gloria Jean Leathers, a lesbian mother of three, when Leathers was serving a prison term not related to the killing of her lesbian lover. Leathers had stabbed to death Sheila Marie Barker at a Tulsa disco in 1979, but that killing was later proved to be self-defense.

Allen was released on parole after serving two years. When Leathers was released in 1985 she called Allen for help, and the two shared a house in Oklahoma City, but their relationship over the next three years was turbulent and sometimes violent. Late on December 1, 1988, Allen and Leathers had another violent confrontation in a grocery store, and Leathers picked up a rake and struck Allen in the face. A police officer responded and escorted the two women to their shared home so Leathers could gather her belongings, and Leathers' mother Ruby Wilson arrived to pick her up. The officer was called away so Leathers and her mother started for the village police station to file a complaint against Allen for stealing some of her clothes. Allen followed closely behind, and as Leathers stepped out of her car in front of the police station the two women exchanged words. As Leathers reached back into the car for her purse Allen pulled a .38-caliber pistol from beneath her sweat shirt, stuck the barrel against Leathers' ribs and fired once as she shouted, "If I can't have you, nobody can!" After shooting Leathers in the abdomen Allen fled to her home and discarded the pistol nearby before she fled to Duncan, Oklahoma. Leathers collapsed into the car and was rushed to a hospital where she identified Allen as the shooter before she died on December 5, and the same day Allen was captured in Duncan.

The following day Allen, who was still on parole, was charged with murder, and she confessed to shooting Leathers, but again claimed she did not know how the gun was discharged. Allen's trial began in April 1989, and she claimed self-defense but could not provide a single witness to corroborate her claim; Leathers had no weapon, and Leathers' mother was an eyewitness to the murder. A letter was introduced into evidence, which read: "You're not only in my prayers, you're also in most of my confessions. You're everything I ever wanted. I'm very happy with your love. You're my everything. P.S. I'm the type of person who will hunt someone down I love and kill them. Do I make myself clear, Gloria?" Allen was convicted of first-degree murder on April 19, and jurors deliberated only two hours before recommending the death penalty.

On April 27 Allen was sentenced to die and delivered to her death row cell the same day. An appeal was filed, and the state Court of Criminal Appeals affirmed the judgment and sentence of the district court on February 15, 1994. Certiorari was denied, and the application for post-conviction relief was denied in 1995. There were a number of mental issues raised at various times, and in each case resolved against Allen. In all there were eleven appeals, with three in 2000 and two in 2001, but all were denied. On December 15, 2000, the state Board of Pardons and Parole held a hearing and voted three to one to deny clemency. On Allen's final day the federal Circuit Court of Appeals rejected her appeal; forty-five minutes later Governor Frank Keating rejected her application for a thirty-day stay of execution; and at 7:30 P.M. Allen's last hope ended when the U.S. Supreme Court declined to intervene.

During her time in prison Allen became a born-again Christian and renounced lesbianism, under the guidance of her spiritual adviser the Rev. Robin Meyers. Early on her final day Allen was taken from her cell in the Mabel Basset Correctional Center in Oklahoma City to the special cell near the death chamber at the state prison in McAlester. Shortly before 9:00 P.M. the prisoner was escorted into the injection room where she took her place on the gurney and her chest, waist, and legs were strapped while her arms were secured to two arm extensions, and a sheet was pulled over her body. A medical technician carefully inserted one intravenous cannula (IV) into the vein of each arm while the executioners were hidden from view in another room, behind a one-way mirrored window.

The warden confirmed by telephone, with Governor Keating, that the execution was to proceed and had the curtains drawn open before he asked Allen if she had any last words. Allen said, "Father forgive them. They know not what they do," and then playfully stuck out her tongue at her appeal attorney Steve Presson. Twenty-four members of the Pettus and Leathers families, a dozen media witnesses and seven others chosen by Allen, including the Revs. Vernon Burris, Walter Little, and Robin Meyers, witnessed the execution. Most were gathered in a room behind clear glass directly across from the official witness room where a dozen witnesses, mostly family members of the victims, were seated behind a one-way glass window.

When Allen concluded the warden announced, "Let the execution begin," and each executioner drained the contents of his syringe into the tube leading to Allen's arm: the first drug, sodium thiopental, caused unconsciousness; the second drug, pancuronium bromide, caused her respiration to become labored and would have caused death in time; and the third drug, potassium chloride, would stop her heart. At 9:21 P.M. all sign of life was absent, and Allen was pronounced dead. Presson later said, "She was dancing on the mattress while they tried to kill her."

Sources: *Advocate* (San Francisco, CA): February 27, 2001. *Allen v. Massie*: 202 F.3d 281 (2000). *Allen v. Massie*: 121 S. Ct. 244 (2000). *Allen v. Massie*: 121 S. Ct. 616 (2000). *Allen v. Massie*: 236 F.3d 1243 (2001). *Allen v. Oklahoma*: 513 U.S. 952 (1994). *Allen v. Oklahoma Pardon and Parole Board*: 121 S. Ct. 848 (2001). *Allen v. State*: 871 P.2d 79 (1994). *Allen v. State*: 909 P.2d 836 (1995). *Hays News* (KS): January 12, 2001. *Oklahoman* (Oklahoma City): January 11, 2001.

Medlock, Floyd A.
January 16, 2001

In January 1990 Gina Ford and her seven-year-old daughter Katherine Ann Busch moved from one-bedroom apartment number 406 in the Woodoaks Apartment complex in Yukon, Oklahoma, to a two-bedroom unit in the same complex. Apartment 406 was then rented to twenty-year-old Floyd Allen Medlock, and he moved in during the first week of February.

During the afternoon of February 19 Katherine was riding her bicycle in the complex when she became hungry, and perhaps confused, and went to apartment 406 and tried to open the door. Medlock had been watching cartoons on television when he heard the doorknob rattle and when he opened the door Katherine walked past him into his apartment. He began to chastise her for "barging into my apartment" but she told him she used to live there and she was hungry. While Katherine watched cartoons Medlock prepared macaroni and cheese and served it to Katherine with potato chips. According to Medlock he suddenly grabbed Katherine, and when she pulled away and screamed he grabbed her again and put his hand over her mouth and nose and held her until she was unconscious. When she revived he carried her into the bathroom and submerged her head in the water in the toilet bowl, but she fought back and pulled her head out of the water and gasped for breath. Medlock then took a steak knife and stabbed her in the back of her neck and in her eye, but the knife broke so he went into his bedroom where he kept a "hunting knife," more a dagger than a cutting instrument.

He later said he stabbed Katherine to death while holding her over the toilet bowl so no blood would spill on the floor, and then stripped off her clothing to wash her in his bathtub. He claimed that after seeing her naked he tried to molest the lifeless body before he wrapped her in a blanket and packed her bloody clothing and body in the cardboard box that had held his television. Later that night he carried the box and her bicycle three blocks to a drug store, threw her remains in the trash dumpster at the rear of the store, and propped her bicycle against the trash bin.

Katherine's mother called the police at 7:00 P.M. to report her daughter missing, but Katherine had wandered off before to feed the ducks at a nearby pond or to visit a local school playground. When Katherine hadn't returned home by 10:00 P.M. the police mobilized a search, and at about 4:30 A.M. an officer spotted her bicycle leaning against the trash dumpster. Detective Major James McDaniel, the lead detective, rushed to the scene and searched the trash bin, and he found her body. The family was notified but they did not learn the details until they listened to the 6:00 A.M. news reports on television.

Medlock returned to his restaurant job the following day but when he heard coworkers say that the murderer would kill again he left his job and telephoned the police from a nearby pay phone. The officers responded and found him standing near the phone, he confessed, and he handed them the dagger. In contradiction to Medlock's claims the medical examiner determined that Katherine had been beaten, raped and sodomized while still alive, and in examining her clothing it was found that her panties had been ripped to shreds during the brutal attack.

Medlock was examined by psychiatrists who diagnosed him as a schizophrenic, and they claimed that it was his twelve-year-old, enraged alter-ego who had murdered Katherine.

Medlock was charged with Katherine's murder but on the day that jury selection was scheduled to begin he pled guilty without making any agreement with the prosecutors. The judge held a hearing to create a record for the appellate court detailing the murder, Katherine's injuries, and Medlock's mental state. During testimony it was revealed that in 1987 Medlock had planned but failed to rape, and possibly murder, a ten-year-old neighbor girl, and when he could not find her in her house he set it afire. Medlock testified that in May 1990 he had moved out of the Fresno, California, home of his sister because he was driven to rape and murder her two young daughters.

On March 28, 1991, Canadian County Judge Edward Cunningham sentenced Medlock to die by lethal injection, and he was immediately delivered to a death row cell at the state prison in McAlester. The case was appealed, and in 1994 the Court of Criminal Appeals affirmed the sentence and denied a rehearing on the case in 1995 and 1996. In June 1997 Medlock's attorneys filed a writ of habeas corpus; in 2000 the federal Tenth Circuit Court of Appeals denied relief, and finally Medlock's date with the executioner was set for January 16, 2001. Medlock declined to petition the state Board of Pardons and Parole for clemency and refused to have any last minute appeals filed.

Early on January 16 Medlock was moved from his death row cell to a special cell near the death chamber. Shortly before 9:00 P.M. the prisoner was escorted into the injection room where he took his place on the gurney and his chest, waist, and legs were strapped while his arms were secured to two arm extensions, and a sheet was pulled over his body. A medical technician carefully inserted one intravenous cannula (IV) into the vein of each arm while the executioners were hidden from view in another room, behind a one-way mirrored window.

Warden Ronald Ward confirmed by telephone, with Governor Frank Keating, that the execution was to proceed and had the curtains to the witness room drawn open before he asked Medlock if he had any last words, and Medlock replied, "Y'all take it easy!" When it was clear that Medlock had concluded the warden announced, "Let the execution begin," and each executioner drained the contents of his syringe into the tube leading to Medlock's arm: the first drug, sodium thiopental, caused unconsciousness; the second drug, pancuronium bromide, caused his respiration to become labored and would have caused death in time; and the third drug, potassium chloride, would stop his heart. At 9:20 P.M. all sign of life was absent and Medlock was pronounced dead.

Sources: *Medlock v. Oklahoma*: 516 U.S. 918 (1995). *Medlock v. State*: 887 P.2d 1333 (1994). *Medlock v. State*: 889 P.2d 344 (1995). *Medlock v. State*: 927 P.2d 1069 (1996). *Medlock v. Ward*: 200 F.3d 1314 (2000).

Smallwood, Dion A.
January 18, 2001

Terri Jo Frederick and twenty-two-year-old Dion Athanasius Smallwood had been dating since January 1991, and they began living together in an Oklahoma City apartment. Smallwood became controlling and abusive, and he threatened to kill his girlfriend and her family if she ever tried to leave him. Once he pushed the barrel of a pistol into Terri Jo's mouth, breaking a tooth, to emphasize his determination, but Terri Jo's mother still demanded that she leave him. Terri Jo had left him several times for brief periods but she returned, perhaps out of fear for herself and her family. In January 1992 Terri Jo finally moved out, told Smallwood she would not return, filed a protective order, and moved back to the home of her adoptive mother, sixty-eight-year-old Lois Frederick.

On February 5, 1992, Smallwood arrived at the Frederick home at 4:00 P.M. and entered without knocking. He was there to find Terri Jo but she was not home, and Lois ordered him out of her home and took his arm to guide him out but Smallwood pushed her away, and she fell to the floor. Lois then told Smallwood she would "make him pay" and tried to call the police, but Smallwood yanked the phone from her hand and smashed it. He then took hold of Lois' arm and dragged her from room to room looking for Terri Jo, and when she resisted he struck her in the nose, bloodying it and knocking her to the ground once again. The blow was with such force that her dentures flew out of her mouth and landed across the room. In one of the bedrooms Smallwood allowed Lois to enter the bathroom and clean off the blood, but when she came out, he later claimed, she kicked him in the shin. Smallwood grabbed a croquet mallet that lay nearby and he struck her on the head and she collapsed. Lois did not move but Smallwood said later he heard her choking as he left the room, but claimed he thought he had killed her. He then went through the house cleaning up the evidence of his attacks, wrapped Lois in bed sheets, carried her to her car, and locked her in the trunk.

Lois' biological daughter, Mone Moody, called the police at 6:30 P.M. and reported that Smallwood had threatened to kill her mother and that she believed he was at her mother's home. She met the officer at the door, and they knocked but received no answer, and then they looked in the windows but saw no one nor any evidence of a struggle or crime. Smallwood had just finished cleaning and rearranging the house when the officer arrived, and he hid in a storage cabinet, then after Lois' daughter and the officer left he went out to Lois' car and drove around for several hours, bought a can of gasoline, and parked in an isolated location. He took Lois' body from the trunk and found that she was alive but still unconscious. He placed her body in the passenger seat and doused her and the car with gasoline before he set it afire. Lois died in the blaze, and her body was so badly burned that the coroner could not determine the injuries that had occurred prior to her cremation.

Smallwood was arrested and charged with one count of murder and the related crimes committed during the attack and abduction. He was tried in May 1993 and convicted of first-degree murder when the jurors rejected his claim of self-defense, saying Lois had attacked him with a knife before he beat her with the mallet, and on May 26 he was sentenced to die by lethal injection and delivered to a death row cell at the state prison in McAlester. His attorneys filed an appeal, which stayed the execution but in 1995 the state Court of Criminal Appeals affirmed the judgment and sentence of the lower court. After the U.S. Supreme Court denied certiorari in 1996 he filed for post-conviction relief, which was denied in 1997. A writ of habeas corpus was then filed in the federal Tenth Circuit Court of Appeals and denied on September 10, 1999. The case was remanded to the state court where, on October 4, 2000, Smallwood's execution date was set for Thursday, January 18, 2001. As the date neared Smallwood appeared before the state Board of Pardons and Parole, and on December 4, 2000, they denied clemency. On the afternoon of the day of execution Lieutenant Governor Mary Fallin and the U.S. Supreme Court denied a last minute request for a stay of execution.

Early on January 18 Smallwood was moved from his death row cell to a special cell near the death chamber. Shortly before 9:00 P.M. the prisoner was escorted into the injection room where he took his place on the gurney and his chest, waist, and legs were strapped while his arms were secured to two arm extensions, and a sheet was pulled over his body. A medical technician carefully inserted one intravenous cannula (IV) into the vein of each arm while the executioners were hidden from view in another room, behind a one-way mirrored window. Warden Gibson confirmed by telephone, with Governor Frank Keating, that the execution was to proceed and had the curtains to the witness room drawn open before he asked Smallwood if he had any last words. Smallwood replied, "To the victims of this case, if you didn't hear me before, hear me now, I'm sorry. This doesn't change anything. It just creates more victims. I am truly sorry," and then told the members of his family in the witness room, "I'll be waiting for y'all on the other side."

When it was clear that Smallwood had concluded the warden announced, "Let the execution begin," and each executioner drained the contents of his syringe into the tube leading to Smallwood's arm: the first drug, sodium thiopental, caused unconsciousness; the second drug, pancuronium bromide, caused his respiration to become labored and would have caused death in time; and the third drug, potassium chloride, would stop his heart. At 9:09 P.M. all sign of life was absent and Smallwood was pronounced dead.

Sources: *Progress* (Clearfield, PA): January 19, 2001. *Smallwood v. Gibson*: 191 F.3d 1257 (1999). *Smallwood v. Oklahoma*: 519 U.S. 980 (1996). *Smallwood v. State*: 907 P.2d 217 (1995). *Smallwood v. State*: 937 P.2d 111 (1997).

Fowler, Mark A.
January 23, 2001

Fox, Billy R.
January 25, 2001

In January 1985 nineteen-year-old Billy Ray Fox was fired from his job at Wynn's IGA supermarket in Edmond, Oklahoma, but he kept the keys to the store, the cash register, and the safe. On July 1, 1985, Fox and twenty-year-old Mark Andrew Fowler began planning a robbery of the store. Two days later they put their plan into action, and they took two shotguns belonging to their roommates. During the early morning hours of July 3 Fowler and Fox, armed with the shotguns and at least one knife, entered the store, captured overnight employees thirty-three-year-old night manager Rick Cast, twenty-seven-year-old John Barrier, and forty-four-year-old Chumpion Chaowasin and forced them into a rear room of the store. They forced the three men to kneel, and then they bludgeoned all three men with a shotgun before Cast and Chaowasin were shot in the back of the head with a single shotgun blast, execution-style, killing them instantly. Barrier, who may have been helpless from the beating, was stabbed nine times with wounds to his neck, chest, back and side, and he quickly bled to death. Fowler and Fox then leisurely shopped through the store taking steaks and other food items for a party before they rifled the store's cash register and safe, taking $1,200 in cash and $1,500 in checks.

Later a sixteen-year-old employee arrived for work, and when she could not find the other employees she searched, found the bodies lying next to each other in a huge pool of blood, and called the police. The following day Fox paid off several debts and then had a party for his friends, and Fowler went to a nearby mall and bought clothes and jewelry. Fox was quickly suspected, and on the evening of July 4 both men were arrested and lodged in jail. They were charged with three counts of murder; each pointed to the other as the murderer, but it was clear the work could not have been done by one man. They were tried together in the Oklahoma County district court. They snickered and passed notes throughout their trial. On May 15, 1986, the jurors found them guilty of first-degree murder and recommended the death penalty. On June 20 both men were sentenced to die by lethal injection and delivered to death row cells at the state prison in McAlester.

Fowler's attorneys filed appeals, and in 1989 the state's Court of Criminal Appeals affirmed the judgment and sentence of the court and denied post-conviction relief in 1994 and 1995. A writ of habeas corpus was filed after all state judicial relief was exhausted, the federal Tenth Circuit Court of Appeals denied relief in 2000, and the U.S. Supreme Court denied certiorari. On October 10 Oklahoma's Attorney General Drew Edmondson asked for an execution date to be set, and the Court of Criminal Appeals fixed Fowler's death at Tuesday, January 23, 2001.

Fox's attorneys had also filed appeals; his judgment and sentence were affirmed in 1989, and post-conviction relief was denied in 1994. In 2000 the federal Tenth Circuit Court of Appeals denied his writ of habeas corpus, the U.S. Supreme Court denied certiorari, and his date of execution was then set for Thursday, January 25, 2001.

Edmondson had asked for a single execution date for both men, to accommodate the victims' families, but the court set separate dates. Fox refused to ask for a clemency hearing but Fowler appeared before the state Board of Pardons and Parole on January 3, 2001, and he was denied clemency.

During his time on death row Fowler was attended by his uncle, Friar Gregory Gier, and by Archbishop Eusebius J. Beltran. Early on January 23 Fowler was moved from his death row cell to a special cell near the death chamber. Shortly before 9:00 P.M. the prisoner was escorted into the injection room where he took his place on the gurney and his chest, waist, and legs were strapped while his arms were secured to two arm extensions, and a sheet was pulled over his body. A medical technician carefully inserted one intravenous cannula (IV) into the vein of each arm while the executioners were hidden from view in another room, behind a one-way mirrored window. Warden Ron Ward confirmed by telephone, with Governor Frank Keating, that the execution was to proceed and had the curtains to the witness room drawn open before he asked Fowler if he had any last words. Fowler began reciting a "Hail Mary" prayer and his family members, who were among the witnesses, joined in, led by Friar Gier, "Hail Mary, full of grace, the Lord is with thee. Blessed are thou amongst women and blessed is the fruit of thy womb, Jesus. Holy Mary, mother of God, pray for us sinners now and at the hour of our death. Amen."

When it was clear that Fowler had concluded the warden announced, "Let the execution begin," and each executioner drained the contents of his syringe into the tube leading to Fowler's arm: the first drug, sodium thiopental, caused unconsciousness; the second drug, pancuronium bromide, caused his respiration to become labored and would have caused death in time; and the third drug, potassium chloride, would stop his heart. At 9:07 P.M. all sign of life was absent and Fowler was pronounced dead.

Early on January 25 Fox was moved from his death row cell to a special cell near the death chamber. Shortly before 9:00 P.M. the prisoner was escorted into the injection room where he took his place on the gurney and his chest, waist, and legs were strapped while his arms were secured to two arm extensions, and a sheet was pulled over his body. A medical technician carefully inserted one intravenous cannula (IV) into the vein of each arm while the executioners were hidden from view in another room, behind a one-way mirrored window.

Warden Ron Ward confirmed by telephone, with Governor Frank Keating, that the execution was to proceed and had the curtains to the witness room drawn open before he asked Fox if had any last words. Fox replied, "No!" and turned his head to smile at his family behind the one-way mirrored glass window. The warden announced, "Let the execution begin," and each executioner drained the contents of his syringe into the tube leading to Fox's arm: the first drug, sodium thiopental, caused unconsciousness; the second drug, pancuronium bromide, caused his respiration to become labored and would have caused death in time; and the third drug, potassium chloride, would stop his heart. At 9:06 P.M. all sign of life was absent and Fox was pronounced dead.

Sources: *Fowler v. State*: 779 P.2d 580 (1989). *Fowler v. State*: 873 P.2d 1053 (1994). *Fowler v. State*: 896 P.2d 566 (1995). *Fowler v. Ward*: 200 F.3d 1302 (2000). *Fox v. State*: 779 P.2d 562 (1989). *Fox v. State*: 880 P.2d 383 (1994). *Fox v. Ward*: 200 F.3d 1286 (2000). *National Catholic Register*: January 3, 2001.

Lafevers, Loyd W.
January 30, 2001
Cannon, Randall E.
July 23, 2002

During the first half of 1985 nineteen-year-old Loyd Winford Lafevers and twenty-five-year-old Randall Eugene Cannon had brutally attacked three women on separate occasions in south Oklahoma City. Late on the evening of June 24, 1985, they were driving around a northwest Oklahoma City neighborhood when Lafevers' car broke down. They decided to steal a car, looked for a likely house to invade, and chose the home of eighty-four-year-old Addie Mae Hawley. At 10:00 P.M. they broke in and took Hawley prisoner before they ransacked the house and stole $8 from her purse, the garage door opener, and the keys to her car. They took their prisoner and put her in the front seat between them, but after Cannon drove a mile they locked Hawley in the trunk. They drove to a nearby convenience store and bought a two-liter bottle of orange soda; after drinking some they poured out the remainder and filled the bottle with gasoline. Just before midnight Lafevers told Cannon to drive to a secluded area two miles north of Hawley's home, and once they arrived they took Hawley from the trunk, beat, raped and sodomized her, and then poured gasoline on her and set her afire. She squirmed and writhed in pain and managed to move fifteen feet from the place she was set ablaze. Lafevers and Cannon drove the car a short distance away and set it afire as well.

The flames were seen, and the fire department and rescue vehicles were called. When the rescuers arrived they found Hawley burned over sixty-five percent of her body, and she had been bludgeoned on the forehead, resulting in two black eyes, and had multiple cuts and bruises, but she was still alive. She was rushed to the Baptist Hospital where she died at 5:25 A.M. Lafevers and Cannon were soon arrested and charged with her murder, and each pointed to the other and claimed to have only been a lookout. In April 1986 the two men were tried together, convicted of first-degree murder, and sentenced to die.

Appeals were filed, which stayed the executions, and in 1991 the state Court of Criminal Appeals overturned the convictions and ordered the two men retried separately. Lafevers was tried first in late June 1993 and was found guilty, and on July 7 he was again sentenced to die. Cannon then had his second trial, was convicted, and on August 5 he was sentenced to die. Both condemned men were returned to their death row cells at the state prison in McAlester while their teams of attorneys prepared new appeals. The state Court of Criminal Appeals affirmed the judgment and sentence for Lafevers in 1995, and this was followed by three appeals to the federal Tenth Circuit Court of Appeals, which failed in 1999, 2000, and early 2001. The state's Attorney General, before Lafevers' third federal appeal, asked for an execution date and Tuesday, January 30, 2001, was set. His attorneys then filed for a clemency hearing; it was conducted on January 29, and clemency was denied. Cannon's appeal on his second conviction was affirmed in 1995, and in 1997 post-conviction relief was denied. Federal appeals followed, and on August 7, 2001, the Tenth circuit Court of Appeals denied his writ of habeas corpus. After additional brief delays, his date with the executioner was set for Tuesday, July 23, 2002. His last-minute appeal to the U.S. Supreme Court was also denied.

As the time neared for his execution Lafevers was moved from his death row cell to a special cell near the death chamber, and shortly before 9:00 P.M. the prisoner was escorted into the injection room. He took his place on the gurney where his chest, waist, and legs were strapped while his arms were secured to two arm extensions, and a sheet was pulled over his body. A medical technician carefully inserted one intravenous cannula (IV) into the vein of each arm while the executioners were hidden from view in another room, behind a one-way mirrored window. Warden Gary Gibson confirmed by telephone, with Governor Frank Keating, that the execution was to proceed and had the curtains to the witness room drawn open before he asked Lafevers if he had any last words. The warden then announced, "Let the execution begin," and each executioner drained the contents of his syringe into the tube leading to Lafevers' arm: the first drug, sodium thiopental, caused unconsciousness; the second drug, pancuronium bromide, caused his respiration to become labored and would have caused death in time; and the third drug, potassium chloride, would stop his heart. At 9:19 P.M. all sign of life was absent and Lafevers was pronounced dead.

When his date with the executioner arrived Cannon was escorted into the injection room shortly before 6:00 P.M., where he took his place on the gurney and his chest, waist, and legs were strapped while his arms were secured to two arm extensions, and a sheet was pulled over his body. A medical technician carefully inserted one intravenous cannula (IV) into the vein of each arm while the executioners were hidden from view in another room, behind a one-way mirrored window. Warden Gary Gibson confirmed by telephone, with Governor Frank Keating, that the execution was to proceed and had the curtains to the witness room drawn open before he asked Cannon if he had any last words, but Cannon declined to speak. The warden then announced, "Let the execution begin," and each executioner drained the contents of his syringe into the tube leading to Cannon's arm: the first drug, sodium thiopental, caused unconsciousness; the second drug, pancuronium bromide, caused his respiration to become labored and would have caused death in time; and the third drug, potassium chloride, would stop his heart. At 6:05 P.M. all sign of life was absent and Cannon was pronounced dead.

Sources: *Cannon v. Gibson*: 259 F.3d 1253 (2001). *Cannon v. State*: 827 P.2d 1339 (1992). *Cannon v. State*: 904 P.2d 89 (1995). *Cannon v. State*: 933 P.2d 926 (1997). *Denver Post* (CO): June 25, 2002. *Lafevers v. State*: 819 P.2d 1362 (1991). *Lafevers v. State*: 897 P.2d 292 (1995)*Lafevers v. Gibson*: 182 F.3d 705 (1999). 208 F.3d 226 (2000); 238 F.3d 1263 (2001).

Jones, Dorsie L.
February 1, 2001

Early on Wednesday evening, March 14, 1979, thirty-nine-year-old Dorsie Leslie "Wayne" Jones met forty-year-old Betty Jean Strain in a bar in Lawton, Oklahoma, but when Jones stepped away to use the telephone Strain slipped out. Jones later went to the Wichita Lounge and found Strain seated at the bar, and he took the seat next to her and resumed their conversation. Royce Linker, the barmaid, noticed the butt of a revolver protruding from Jones' boot and asked him to pull his pant leg down to cover it. Instead Jones pulled the pistol, pointed it at the barmaid, and threatened, "Shut your mouth or I'll blow your head off." Linker crawled to a hiding place behind the bar as he turned the gun on Strain and shot her under the right breast, but she was able to walk to a nearby bar and ask for help, and she survived after having her spleen removed.

Meanwhile Jones threatened to shoot everyone in the bar; he approached forty-eight-year-old Stanley Eugene Buck, Sr., who was shooting pool and eating chicken with his nineteen-year-old son, Stanley Jr., and Jones asked, "What are you doing?" Buck Jr. replied, "I just came down to play some pool with my dad." Jones immediately shot him and the bullet tore through his throat. Jones immediately turned on Buck Sr. and shot him once in the head, and he collapsed to the floor. Jones stood over Buck Sr. and mimicked the sounds he was making, then asked, "Aren't you dead? You're dead!" and shot him in the head a second time killing him instantly. He then turned back to Buck Jr. and said, "If I let you live you'll tell the cops, won't you?" and without further hesitation he shot Buck Jr. again. Jones looked around the bar and said, "Now that I've killed every son-of-a-bitch here, I guess I'll get me another beer," but instead he fled.

After Jones left Buck Jr. staggered to a nearby fruit stand and, though he could not talk, made it clear he wanted the proprietor to call the police. A tracheotomy saved the life of Buck Jr., but he was permanently paralyzed on his left side. The police arrived, Jones was identified, and a short time later detectives arrested Jones without resistance as he parked his pickup truck in his driveway, with the revolver lying on the seat next to him.

Jones was lodged in jail and charged with the

murder of Buck Sr. and the attempted murders of Strain and Buck Jr., among other lesser and included crimes. He was tried in the Comanche County District Court, and on April 12, 1980, he was convicted of first-degree murder when the jurors rejected his plea of insanity and his explanation that a prescription drug in combination with alcohol made him unconscious of his actions. On June 9, 1980, Jones was sentenced to die, and he was delivered to a death row cell at the state prison in McAlester four days later.

His attorneys filed an appeal, which stayed the execution. In July 1982 the state Court of Criminal Appeals affirmed the judgment and sentence of the district court, the U.S. Supreme Court denied certiorari in 1983, and his appeal for post-conviction relief was denied in 1985. His attorneys prolonged the appeals process for an additional fifteen years until 2000 when the federal Tenth Circuit Court of Appeals denied the writ of habeas corpus. On November 13, 2000, Attorney General Drew Edmondson requested that a date be set for Jones' execution, and the justices of the Court of Criminal Appeals set Thursday, February 1, 2001. On January 23 Jones' attorneys appeared before the state Board of Pardons and Parole, but the members denied Jones clemency after viewing a videotaped interview during which he said, "Saying I'm sorry is the understatement of a lifetime."

Before the time of execution Jones was moved from his death row cell to a special cell near the death chamber. He ordered chicken as his last meal, the same meal the Bucks were eating when shot, and Buck Jr. said he felt it was Jones' way of saying, "I remember, but I don't want anyone to know." Shortly before 9:00 P.M. the prisoner was escorted into the injection room where he took his place on the gurney and his chest, waist, and legs were strapped while his arms were secured to two arm extensions, and a sheet was pulled over his body. A medical technician carefully inserted one intravenous cannula (IV) into the vein of each arm while the executioners were hidden from view in another room, behind a one-way mirrored window.

Warden Gary Gibson confirmed by telephone, with Governor Frank Keating, that the execution was to proceed and had the curtains to the witness room drawn open before he asked Jones if he had any last words. Jones replied, "Well, I guess I'm going to get out of here before something bad happens. So long, I guess that's it, so long!" When it was clear he had concluded the warden announced, "Let the execution begin," and each executioner drained the contents of his syringe into the tube leading to Jones' arm: the first drug, sodium thiopental, caused unconsciousness; the second drug, pancuronium bromide, caused his respiration to become labored and would have caused death in time; and the third drug, potassium chloride, would stop his heart. He breathed deeply several times as the drugs began to flow and then lay still, and at 9:16 P.M. all sign of life was absent and Jones was pronounced dead.

Sources: *Jones v. Gibson*: 206 F.3d 946 (2000). *Jones v. Oklahoma*: 459 U.S. 1155 (1983). *Jones v. State*: 648 P.2d 1251 (1982). *Jones v. State*: 704 P.2d 1138 (1985).

Clayton, Robert W.
March 1, 2001

Before 1985 Robert William "Eagle" Clayton had been implicated in a Texas robbery and a Mississippi rape, but there was not enough evidence to charge him with either crime, so he moved to Tulsa, Oklahoma, and was hired as a groundskeeper at an apartment complex. At noon on June 25, 1985, twenty-four-year-old Clayton came upon nineteen-year-old Rhonda Kay Timmons, who was sunbathing outside her Tulsa apartment. Clayton beat Timmons on her forehead, fracturing her skull, and on the back of her head, causing severe bruising. Timmons fled into her apartment while Clayton followed, stabbing her twelve times in the chest, neck, side and arms, and as she reached the crib of her infant son Clayton used her bikini top to strangle her to death.

At 12:30 P.M. Timmons' husband William returned home for lunch and found his wife's dead body lying near the crib of their infant son and the apartment splattered with blood, and he called the police. Clayton was immediately suspected, and when the police went to his home they found a bloody sock lying next to the washing machine; inside the machine was a recently washed pair of overalls, and in the backyard they found a bloody knife. These were taken for evidence, tested, and the blood type matched Timmons' blood.

Clayton was arrested and lodged in jail, charged with murder, and his trial was conducted in the Tulsa County District Court in early 1986. He pled insanity and retardation but he was convicted of first-degree murder, sentenced to die by lethal injection, and delivered to his death row cell at the state prison in McAlester on March 12.

His attorneys filed an appeal, which stayed the execution, but the state Court of Criminal Appeals affirmed the judgment and sentence in 1992, and the U.S. Supreme Court denied certiorari in 1993. The attorneys then appealed for post-conviction relief, and this was denied in 1995. When all state appeals were exhausted Clayton's attorney's filed for a writ of habeas corpus, but the federal Tenth Circuit Court of Appeals denied the request in 1999. This was followed by brief delays until the attorney general requested a date for his execution, and the justices of the state Criminal Court of Appeals set the date at January 3, 2001. Lieutenant Governor Mary Fallin, acting for Governor Frank Keating, granted Clayton a thirty-day reprieve from January 3 when misplaced evidence from his trial was discovered. The bloody sock and knife were then examined for DNA but the results only confirmed Clayton's guilt, and therefore did not change the governor's position on denying clemency. On February 7, 2001, the state Court of Criminal Appeals set Clayton's date for execution at March 1.

Before the time of execution Clayton was moved from his death row cell to a special cell near the death chamber. Shortly before 9:00 P.M. the prisoner was escorted into the injection room where he took his place on the gurney and his chest, waist, and legs were strapped while his arms were secured to two arm extensions, and a sheet was pulled over his body. A medical technician carefully inserted one intravenous cannula (IV) into the vein of each arm while the executioners were hidden from view in another room, behind a one-way mirrored window. Warden Gary Gibson confirmed by telephone, with Governor Frank Keating, that the execution was to proceed and had the curtains to the witness room drawn open for Clayton's two sisters, a cousin, a brother-in-law, and one of his attorneys and for Timmons' mother and step-father, as well as five other witnesses.

Warden Gibson then asked Clayton if he had any last words, and he replied, "I want to say I'm glad I'm leaving this place and I'm going to a better place. I love my family and I'm sorry for this other lady that was killed. You're still killing an innocent man. May God have mercy on my soul." When it was clear Clayton had concluded the warden announced, "Let the execution begin," and each executioner drained the contents of his syringe into the tube leading to Clayton's arm: the first drug, sodium thiopental, caused unconsciousness; the second drug, pancuronium bromide, caused his respiration to become labored and would have caused death in time; and the third drug, potassium chloride, would stop his heart. The drugs began to flow at 9:07 P.M. Clayton quickly lapsed into unconsciousness, and he was pronounced dead at 9:10 P.M.

Sources: *Clayton v. Gibson*: 199 F.3d 1162 (1999). *Clayton v. Oklahoma*: 507 U.S. 1008 (1993). *Clayton v. State*: 840 P.2d 18 (1992). *Clayton v. State*: 892 P.2d 646 (1995). *Oklahoman* (Oklahoma City): March 1, 2001.

Fluke, Ronald D.
March 27, 2001

Forty-eight-year-old Ronald Dunaway Fluke, a self-employed safety consultant, had been a compulsive gambler with poor luck and worse skills for nearly three decades, and his business had failed. By October 1997 he was deeply in debt with no means to repay the many loans he had taken from every source he could find, and he was three years behind in his taxes. He decided upon murdering his wife of nineteen years, forty-four-year-old Ginger Lou, and his two daughters, thirteen-year-old Susanne Michelle and eleven-year-old Kathryn Lee to spare them the embarrassment of bankruptcy and his suicide.

At 1:30 A.M. on October 17 he took his .380-caliber automatic pistol and a large hatchet and crept up on his wife, who was sleeping on the living room couch in their Tulsa, Oklahoma, house at South 69 East Avenue because of marital difficulties. He struck his wife on the back of her head with the hatchet but she awoke and started to scream, so he struck her seven more times on the back of her head, neck, and shoulder. When she had not died of the hatchet wounds he shot her in the head once, killing her instantly. The odd sounds awoke his two daughters, who were sleeping in separate bedrooms upstairs, and Fluke then went to each of their bedrooms. When he pointed the gun at Susanne Michelle it jammed, and she thought he was joking with her, but he cleared the jammed round and killed her with a single shot to her head; he next went to the bedroom of Kathryn Lee and killed her with a single gunshot to her head.

After murdering his family he made a feeble attempt at suicide, but changed his mind when it occurred to him that suicide would prevent him from seeing them again in heaven. At 8:00 A.M. he appeared at the police station and told detectives of the murders and said, "I'm the sorriest individual on the face of the Earth right now, and I deserve to die. I believe I killed the flesh, but I believe their souls are in heaven now." Detectives went to the Fluke home and found the bodies, and Fluke was charged with three counts of murder.

He was at first represented by public defender Pete Silva but after several days of jury selection he asked to represent himself and was found competent at a hearing. He then withdrew his "not guilty" plea and pled guilty, and on October 12, 1998, Tulsa County District Court Judge Gillert sentenced him to die by lethal injection on November 16. Fluke said, "I don't have a death wish, but I did a terrible thing and I feel sorry for what I did and I'm ready to pay the price." He waived all but the automatic appeal and the state Court of Criminal Appeals affirmed the sentence before the end of the year, but delays followed as the time for filing state and federal appeals ran out. Then on February 21, 2001, Attorney General W. A. Drew Edmondson asked the Court of Criminal Appeals to set an execution date, and the justices chose Tuesday, March 27. Fluke declined to petition the state Board of Pardons and Parole for a clemency hearing, saying, "I feel I will receive my just punishment for my crimes," and he refused to write the governor for consideration.

During his time on death row Fluke slept a great deal of the time, and said of his imprisonment, "Days seem long at times, but the weeks and months fly by. I've told people it's kind of like a retirement home with really good security. Being locked down twenty-three hours a day isn't a bad thing. You don't have to deal with people who are struggling with a lot of issues. I am sorry for what I did. I would take it all back. I can't, so the only thing I can do is to take my just punishment."

Before the time of execution Fluke was moved from his death row cell to a special cell near the death chamber, where he had his last supper of grape juice and a cracker. Shortly before 9:00 P.M. the prisoner was escorted into the injection room where he took his place on the gurney and his chest, waist, and legs were strapped while his arms were secured to two arm extensions, and a sheet was pulled over his body. A medical technician carefully inserted one intravenous cannula (IV) into the vein of each arm while the executioners were hidden from view in another room, behind a one-way mirrored window. The warden confirmed by telephone, with Governor Frank Keating, that the execution was to proceed and had the curtains to the witness room drawn open for Fluke's two witnesses and ten witnesses of the Fluke family, with others watching on closed-circuit television from a room below the execution chamber. The warden asked Fluke if he had any last words, and he replied, "I've done a terrible thing, I'm sorry. I wish I could take it back. I've been through a fiery trial that has increased my faith and made my heart purer. I'm a Christian saved by the blood of Jesus," and he asked for prayers for his wife's family.

When it was clear Fluke had concluded the warden announced, "Let the execution begin," and each executioner drained the contents of his syringe into the tube leading to Fluke's arm: the first drug, sodium thiopental, caused unconsciousness; the second drug, pancuronium bromide, caused his respiration to become labored and would have caused death in time; and the third drug, potassium chloride, would stop his heart. As the drugs began to flow he turned his head to the one-way glass window of the witnesses room and mouthed the words "I love you" to his friend Phyliss Neu, who attended with his minister, and she mouthed the words back though he could not see her. Before the execution he had asked Neu to contact his sisters and his son, who had not been home when the murders occurred, and Neu replied, "Thank you for being my friend." Fluke quickly lapsed into unconsciousness and was pronounced dead at 9:34 P.M.

Sources: *Fluke v. State*: 14 P.2d 29 (1998). *Oklahoman* (Oklahoma City): March 27–28, 2001.

James, Terrance A.
May 22, 2001

In early 1983 twenty-two-year-old Terrance Anthony James, Dennis Earl Brown, and twenty-five-year-old Mark Allen Berry were arrested and charged with theft of federal government property, and they were lodged in the Muskogee County jail. James and Brown felt certain that Berry had informed on them, which had resulted in their arrests. James and Brown pled guilty and were sentenced to serve five years in prison while Berry pled not guilty and was awaiting trial. On February 5 James and Brown were discussing murdering Berry when fellow prisoner Samuel Raymond Van Woundenberg, in jail on a federal charge of kidnapping, offered to assist them and suggested a method.

Van Woundenberg had been serving a life sentence for a 1972 murder but he escaped from prison. During the month he was free he committed the kidnapping, and after he was recaptured he was lodged in the Muskogee jail where he met James and Brown. Van Woundenberg proposed to James and Brown that he would unwind a wire from a broom used to sweep the cells, and they could use that wire to strangle Berry and then hang him in the shower to simulate a suicide. They tore strips from towels to use for the "suicide hanging," and then Van Woundenberg unwound the wire from the broom and gave it to James.

During the early morning hours of February 6, 1983, Van Woundenberg slipped a piece of paper over the lens of the surveillance camera and quickly returned to his cell to act as a lookout. Brown then invited Berry to play cards, and at 4:30 A.M. while Berry was distracted by the game James snuck up behind and began strangling him. Brown held Berry's feet and, to prevent him from calling out, put his hand over Berry's mouth. When Van Woundenberg said he heard someone coming James and Brown dragged Berry into Van Woundenberg's cell and finished strangling him to death. The three men carried Berry's body into the shower and hung him in a shower stall, using the strips torn from towels.

The body was discovered the next morning, and the circumstances and the autopsy revealed that he had been murdered by strangulation with a wire before being hung by towel strips. When James and Brown were suspected Brown turned state's evidence and testified against James and Van Woundenberg, and for his cooperation he was allowed to plead guilty to second-degree murder and was sentenced to serve thirty-five years in prison. James and Van Woundenberg were tried together and convicted of first-degree murder. In early October 1985 both men were sentenced to die by lethal injection, and on October 4 they were delivered to death row cells at the state prison in McAlester.

The cases were appealed; James' direct appeal was argued on March 22, 1987, and the judgment and sentence were affirmed by the state Court of Criminal Appeals. The U.S. Supreme Court denied certiorari the same year, and the state court of appeals denied post-conviction relief in 1991. James' attorneys continued to file every petition, appeal and motion they could manage and in 2000 the federal Tenth Circuit Court of Appeals denied the writ of habeas corpus. The case was returned to the state, and on January 22, 2001 Attorney General W. A. Drew Edmondson requested an execution date for James; the justices of the Court of Criminal Appeals set the date at May 22, 2001.

Before the time of execution James was moved from his death row cell to a special cell near the death chamber. Shortly before 9:00 P.M. the prisoner was escorted into the injection room where he took his place on the gurney and his chest, waist, and legs were strapped while his arms were secured to two arm extensions, and a sheet was pulled over his body. A medical technician carefully inserted one intravenous cannula (IV) into the vein of each arm while the executioners were hidden from view in another room, behind a one-way mirrored window. Warden Gary Gibson confirmed by telephone, with Governor Frank Keating, that the execution was to proceed and had the curtains to the witness room drawn open for the dozen witnesses, while other witnesses watched on closed-circuit television from a room below the execution chamber. The warden asked James if he had any last words but none are recorded. The warden announced, "Let the execution begin," and each executioner drained the contents of his syringe into the tube leading to James' arm: the first drug, sodium thiopental, caused unconsciousness; the second drug, pancuronium bromide, caused his respiration to become labored and would have caused death in time; and the third drug, potassium chloride, would stop his heart. James quickly lapsed into unconsciousness and was pronounced dead at 9:06 P.M.

Sources: *James v. Gibson*: 211 F.3d 543 (2000). *James v. Oklahoma*: 484 U.S. 970 (1987). *James v. State*: 736 P.2d 541 (1987). *James v. State*: 818 P.2d 918 (1991). *James v. State*: 14 P.2d 29 (1998). Muskogee County case CRF 83–64. *Oklahoman* (Oklahoma City): March 23, 2001; March 27–28, 2001. *Van Woundenberg v. Gibson*: 98–7167 (2000). *Van Woundenberg v. Oklahoma*: 479 U.S. 956 (1986). *Van Woundenberg v. Oklahoma*: 484 U.S. 1036 (1988). *Van Woundenberg v. Oklahoma*: 503 U.S. 993 (1992). *Van*

Woundenberg v. State: 720 P.2d 328 (1986). *Van Woundenberg v. State*: PC-87-633 (1987). *Van Woundenberg v. State*: 818 P.2d 913 (1991). *Van Woundenberg v. State*: 942 P.2d 224 (1997).

Johnson, Vincent A.
May 29, 2001

Theodore "Ted" Holt had lived with forty-four-year-old Shirley A. Mooneyham in her rural Lona Valley home in eastern Pittsburg County, Oklahoma, but they had some difficulty and separated. In January 1991 thirty-two-year-old Vincent Allen Johnson, a recent parolee, and his wife of one month, Deborah Elaine, were staying at the home of John Crain in Lona Valley, Pittsburg County, Oklahoma. Crain was ill and the Johnsons agreed to care for him and his horses, and Crain introduced the couple to Holt. Crain and Holt were both angry at Mooneyham, and they knew that Johnson had been sentenced on November 7, 1979, to serve a fifteen-year term for a manslaughter conviction, so they offered Johnson $100,000 to murder Mooneyham.

Johnson, with a .38-caliber pistol in his pocket, went to Mooneyham's home on February 8. Mooneyham knew Johnson and invited him in, and they smoked marijuana together. Mooneyham, fearing some retaliation by Holt, kept her pistol close at hand, and Johnson saw it lying on the kitchen table. Johnson suddenly pulled the pistol from his pocket, grabbed Mooneyham's .38-caliber pistol from the kitchen table, and opened fire with both guns, shooting Mooneyham six times in the head and chest, killing her.

Her body was found later that day by fourteen-year-old Robin Dawn Jackson, Holt's niece, and she called the police. The Oklahoma State Bureau of Investigations (OSBI) was then having one of their informants audiotape incriminating conversations, and he taped a telephone conversation in which Johnson admitted murdering Mooneyham, stating he was angry at Holt for not paying the $100,000 he had been promised. In May 1991 Johnson was arrested for driving while drunk, and when he was confronted with the conversation he confessed; he confessed twice more, and he implicated Holt and Crain in the murder-for-hire plot. The police then searched his belongings and found the murder weapons.

Crain and Holt were arrested, and all three men were charged with Mooneyham's murder, but charges against Crain were dropped and Holt was acquitted at his trial. Johnson pled not guilty, and his trial began in the Pittsburg County District Court in September 1991. He was convicted of first-degree murder and sentenced to die by lethal injection, and on September 24 he was delivered to his death row cell at the state prison in McAlester.

His attorneys filed an appeal, which stayed the execution, but the state Court of Criminal Appeals affirmed the judgment and sentence of the district court in 1995, and the U.S. Supreme Court denied certiorari the following year. In 1998 Johnson's appeal for post-conviction relief was denied by the state appeals court, and after all state remedies were exhausted his attorney filed a writ of habeas corpus in the federal Tenth Circuit Court of Appeals, which was denied in 2000. After the time expired for further federal and state appeals Oklahoma's Attorney General Drew Edmondson, on March 26, 2001, requested a date for Johnson's execution, and the justices of the Court of Criminal Appeals chose Tuesday, May 29, 2001. Neither the state Board of Pardons and Parole nor the Governor would grant clemency.

Before the time of execution Johnson was moved from his death row cell to a special cell near the death chamber. Shortly before 9:00 P.M. the prisoner was escorted into the injection room where he took his place on the gurney and his chest, waist, and legs were strapped while his arms were secured to two arm extensions, and a sheet was pulled over his body. A medical technician carefully inserted one intravenous cannula (IV) into the vein of each arm while the executioners were hidden from view in another room, behind a one-way mirrored window. Warden Gary Gibson confirmed by telephone, with Governor Frank Keating, that the execution was to proceed and had the curtains to the witness room drawn open for the dozen witnesses, while other witnesses watched on closed-circuit television from a room below the execution chamber.

The warden asked Johnson if he had any last words, but he replied only, "No sir, I don't." The warden announced, "Let the execution begin," and at 9:05 P.M. each executioner drained the contents of his syringe into the tube leading to Johnson's arm: the first drug, sodium thiopental, caused unconsciousness; the second drug, pancuronium bromide, caused his respiration to become labored and would have caused death in time; and the third drug, potassium chloride, would stop his heart. Johnson quickly lapsed into unconsciousness and was pronounced dead at 9:07 P.M.

Sources: *Johnson v. Gibson*: 229 F.3d 1163 (2000), *Johnson v. Oklahoma*: 519 U.S. 839 (1996). *Johnson v. State*: 911 P.2d 918 (1995). *Johnson v. State*: 952 P.2d 1003 (1998), *Oklahoman* (Oklahoma City): March 26, 2001; May 29, 2001.

Walker, Jack D.
August 28, 2001

Twenty-one-year-old Jack Dale Walker dated sixteen-year-old Shelly Deann Ellison, and in January 1988 she became pregnant. In late September she gave birth to their son Joshua, but Ellison and Walker had separated before the birth, and Ellison was living with her grandmother, Juanita Epperson.

Early on December 30, 1988, Ellison's thirty-year-old uncle Donald Gary Epperson, his wife Linda, and their four children were visiting Donald's mother Juanita at her mobile home in Bixby, Tulsa County, Oklahoma. Walker, who was being driven to work by Hansel Norton, asked him to stop at the Epperson trailer, and they arrived before 8:00 A.M. Soon after Walker entered he began arguing with Ellison over custody of their son, and he tried to convince her to leave with him.

The argument became heated, and Walker attacked Ellison with a hunting knife he had brought with him. Her uncle rushed from the bedroom, and he and Walker began fighting. Donald was stabbed eleven times, and when Juanita came to help him by hitting Walker with a pipe wrench, he took the wrench away and broke her arm before stabbing her, and she collapsed. Walker then went into the kitchen and returned with an ice pick, but Ellison had managed to pull herself to the telephone and told the police dispatcher, "I need help. He's stabbing me. I'm dead. Please." The attack lasted twenty minutes; Ellison had been cut and stabbed a total of thirty-two times, including several wounds from the ice pick, and she was already dead before the police arrived. Walker went into the kitchen and tried to commit suicide by stabbing himself in the throat with a paring knife, but it broke, so he cut his wrist and staggered onto the porch, where he lapsed into unconsciousness.

When the police arrived he was arrested, rushed to the hospital for treatment, and then lodged in the county jail. Linda Epperson and the four young children were present but could do nothing to stop the brutal attack, and when Linda and her son Brian were threatened they fled from the trailer. Donald and Juanita were rushed to the hospital where Donald died but Juanita recovered. At the jail Walker told the police he went to the Epperson home with the intention "of either taking the baby or murdering her or whoever got in the way." Walker was charged with two counts of murder and was tried in the Tulsa County District Court in May 1989. On May 19 he was convicted of two counts of murder and received two death sentences, plus forty years for three counts of assault with a deadly weapon against Juanita, Linda and Brian.

He was sentenced to die by lethal injection and delivered to a death row cell at the state prison in McAlester, but his attorneys filed an appeal, which stayed the execution. Oklahoma's Court of Criminal Appeals affirmed the judgment and sentence in 1994, and the following year the U.S. Supreme Court denied certiorari. His appeal for post-conviction relief was denied in 1997, and certiorari was denied the same year. His attorneys then filed a writ of habeas corpus with the federal Tenth Circuit Court of Appeals, and it was denied in 2000, with the U.S. Supreme Court denying certiorari the following year. The state Attorney General then asked the Court of Criminal Appeals to set a date of execution, and the justices chose August 28, 2001. Walker's attorneys then tried to gain clemency for their client and at his clemency hearing, before the state Board of Pardons and Parole, he said he was sorry "for all the pain I've caused them and for this whole ordeal that has been tragic for a lot of people." His thirteen-year-old son, who had been adopted by his maternal grandparents, wrote to the board supporting his father's execution, and the board members voted to deny clemency. Governor Frank Keating declined to intervene.

A week before the execution Walker granted an interview with a *Tulsa World* reporter and told him that as a Jehovah's Witness he believed death to be merely unconsciousness, and said, "God has forgiven me of my sins, not mankind." Shortly before the time of execution Walker was moved from his death row cell to a special cell near the death chamber. Just before 9:00 P.M. the prisoner was escorted into the injection room where he took his place on the gurney and his chest, waist, and legs were strapped while his arms were secured to two arm extensions, and a sheet was pulled over his body. A medical technician carefully inserted one intravenous cannula (IV) into the vein of each arm while the executioners were hidden from view in another room, behind a one-way mirrored window. The warden confirmed by telephone, with Governor Keating, that the execution was to proceed and had the curtains drawn open for the witnesses, including seven witnesses invited by Walker, and he grinned broadly and nodded to them. Seventeen relatives of Ellison and the Eppersons witnessed the execution, twelve in the witnesses' room behind a one-way glass while five relatives, with other witnesses, watched on closed-circuit television from a room below the execution chamber.

The warden asked Walker if had any last words and he replied, "I'd just like to tell my family and friends good-bye," then turned his head toward the clear glass window opposite the one-way glass to the regular witness room, focused on two women who were racked with sobbing, and said, "I love you and I hope to see you soon. Take care." When Walker concluded the warden announced, "Let the execution begin," and at 9:07 P.M. each executioner drained the contents of his syringe into the tube leading to Walker's arm: the first drug, sodium thiopental, caused unconsciousness; the second drug, pancuronium bromide, caused his respiration to become labored and would have caused death in time; and the third drug, potassium chloride, would stop his heart. Walker quickly lapsed into unconsciousness, and at 9:09 P.M. all sign of life was absent and he was pronounced dead.

Sources: *McAlester News-Capital & Democrat* (OK): August 30, 2001. *Oklahoman* (Oklahoma City): August 28, 2001. *Tulsa World* (OK): August 22, 2001. *Walker v. Gibson*: 228 F.3d 1217 (2000); 521 S. Ct 2560 (2001). *Walker v. Oklahoma*: 516 S. Ct. 166 (1995); 117 S. Ct. 2524 (1997). *Walker v. State*: 887 P.2d 301 (1994); 933 P.2d 327 (1997).

Hale, Alvie J., Jr.
October 18, 2001

Twenty-four-year-old William Jeffrey Perry, his parents and his sister Ronnye owned the Farmers' and Merchants' Bank in Tecumseh in Pottawatomie County, Oklahoma. On Monday, October 10, 1983, Perry did not report to the bank so his sister went to his Tecumseh home to check on his welfare, but he was not there. Soon after Perry went missing the Perrys began receiving telephone calls demanding payment of $350,000 for his return and making arrangements for the drop of the ransom on October 12 at a site in Oklahoma City. The Perrys called in the Federal Bureau of Investigation (FBI), and they traced the phone call and were watching when Mrs. Perry dropped off the money. Before she could return to her vehicle thirty-five-year-old Alvie James Hale, Jr., a former Shawnee bakery shop owner, appeared and gathered up the ransom and ran to his pickup truck.

FBI agents pursued Hale at high speeds until he hit a drainage ditch and went airborne, and then an FBI automobile collided with him head-on, stopping his truck. The agents captured Hale and recovered the ransom, and as soon as Hale was arrested and identified the agents went to his father's home in Shawnee and were given permission to search the property. Two hours after Hale's arrest Perry's body was found wrapped in a trampoline tarp in a metal storage shed. He had been shot five times with a .38-caliber handgun. As the search continued the agents found a .38-caliber revolver in a kitchen cabinet, and this proved to be the murder weapon. A bloodstained towel and hair matching Perry's were found in Hale's cream-colored station wagon parked at his father's home. Hale insisted he knew nothing of the disappearance of Perry, and later tried to implicate Nicky Johnson and Mayo Bates in a scheme he claimed was concocted by Perry to stage his kidnapping to extort money from his parents. He claimed that when Perry tried to withdraw from the conspiracy Johnson killed Perry and hid the body on the Hale property.

In 1983 Hale was tried in the federal Circuit Court, the jurors rejected his defense, he was convicted of kidnapping and murder, and he was sentenced to serve twenty years in prison. In October 1984 Hale was denied a change of venue, and he was tried in the Pottawatomie County District Court for the kidnapping and murder of Perry, convicted and sentenced to die by lethal injection. He was delivered to a death row cell at the prison in McAlester on October 26.

His attorneys filed appeals of the federal and state convictions. The federal judgment and sentence was affirmed in 1992, post-conviction relief was denied in 1993, 1996, and 2000, and the U.S. Supreme Court denied certiorari in 2001. The state conviction and sentence was affirmed in 1988, post-conviction relief was denied in 1991 and 1997, and certiorari was denied by the U.S. Supreme Court in each instance. Hale's attorneys then filed a writ of habeas corpus with the federal Tenth Circuit Court of Appeals, and this was denied in 2000; the U.S. Supreme Court again denied certiorari. Oklahoma's Attorney General Jennifer Miller requested an execution date, and on July 13, 2001, the state Court of Criminal Appeals set the date for Hale's execution at September 4, 2001. At Hale's August 13 hearing before the state Board of Pardons and Parole he was denied clemency, but then the Tenth Circuit Court of Appeals granted a stay of execution. The U.S. Supreme Court quickly vacated the order, and on October 2 the state Court of Criminal Appeals reset Hale's date with the executioner for October 18, 2001. Governor Frank Keating declined to intervene.

As the time of execution neared Hale was moved from his death row cell to a special cell near the death chamber, and shortly before 9:00 P.M. the prisoner was escorted into the injection room. He took his place on the gurney and his chest, waist, and legs were strapped while his arms were secured to two arm extensions, and a sheet was pulled over his body. A medical technician carefully inserted one intravenous cannula (IV) into the vein of each arm while the executioners were hidden from view in another room, behind a one-way mirrored window. Warden Gary Gibson confirmed by telephone, with Governor Keating, that the execution was to proceed and had the curtains drawn open for the witnesses, including the victim's sister. The warden asked Hale if he had any last words, and he replied, "Watch what you see here. Remember it and go tell somebody."

When he concluded the warden announced, "Let the execution begin," and at 9:21 P.M. each executioner drained the contents of his syringe into the tube leading to Hale's arm: the first drug, sodium thiopental, caused unconsciousness; the second drug, pancuronium bromide, caused his respiration to become labored and would have caused death in time; and the third drug, potassium chloride, would stop his heart. Hale quickly lapsed into unconsciousness, and at 9:24 P.M. all sign of life was absent and he was pronounced dead.

Sources: *In re Hale*: 122 S. Ct. 418 (2001). *Hale v. Gibson*: 227 F.3d 1298 (2000); 121 S. Ct. 2608 (2001). *Hale v. Oklahoma*: 109 S. Ct. 195 (1988); 112 S. Ct. 280 (1991). *Hale v. State*: 750 P.2d 130 (1988); 807 P.2d 264 (1991); 934 P.2d 1100 (1997). *Hale v. U.S. Dept. of Justice*: 973 F. 2d 894 (1992); 2 F.3d 1055 (1993); 99 F.3d 1025 (1996); 113 S. Ct. 3029 (1993); 226 F.3d 1200 (2000); 122 S. Ct. 18 (2001). *Shawnee News-Star* (OK): July 31, 2001, August 31, 2001; October 19, 2001. *Tulsa World* (OK): February 27, 2007.

Harjo, Jerald W.
November 17, 2001

Jerald Wayne Harjo, a Seminole Indian, had served a prison term for burglary and in 1988, when he was twenty-six years old, he received a suspended sentence for auto theft. On January 16, 1988, Harjo was riding a bicycle to his brother's home in Wewoka, and because it was a stormy night he was noticed near Sasakwa, Seminole County, Oklahoma, by a state trooper. When it began to rain Harjo threw the bicycle into a ditch near the rural home of sixty-four-year-old Ruth Marie Harris-Porter, a World War II veteran and then secretary at the Sasakwa Elementary School, and Harjo decided to steal her car. Porter had cared for her husband John after he was paralyzed in an automobile accident in 1960 but John was in the Veteran's Hospital in Memphis, Tennessee, so Ruth was home alone.

Harjo tried to hot-wire the ignition to Porter's van but when that failed he went to the window of a vacant rear bedroom of the Porter house and stacked two cinder blocks to help him crawl through the window. He took a pillow case from the bed and tore two eye holes before pulling it over his head, and then he crept into Porter's bedroom to search for her van keys. Porter awoke and she and Harjo struggled, but he overpowered her and placed a pillow case over her head before he strangled her to death with his hands, at least according to Harjo. However, during the struggle Porter was bruised and scratched on her face, chest, arms and in her vaginal area — indicating that at least an attempt was made to rape her — and her pubic hair had been singed with a lighter. The strangulation crushed her windpipe and had been so violent that her lower dentures were displaced. After Porter was dead Harjo found the keys and stole her van.

On Sunday morning, January 17, 1988, Porter's daughter Mary Branscum and her husband went to her mother's home, found Porter's body with her nightgown pulled up to her neck and a pillow over her face, and she called the police. During the investigation the officers documented muddy tennis-shoe prints on the floor of Porter's house, and when they realized her van was missing they began to search for it. Acting on a hunch from a Wewoka police officer the police found Porter's van parked at the Wewoka home of Harjo's brother, and in Sasakwa they found the bicycle Harjo had used to peddle to the Porter home.

Harjo was arrested, and after questioning he confessed to the murder. He was charged with Porter's murder, pled not guilty, and was tried in September 1988. He claimed that he was too drunk to premeditate at the time of the murder, but he was convicted when the jurors rejected his defense, and on September 29 he was sentenced to die by lethal injection.

His attorneys filed an appeal, which stayed the execution, but the state's Court of Criminal Appeals affirmed the judgment and sentence in 1994, and the U.S. Supreme Court denied certiorari. Over the next seven years his attorneys filed various appeals and motions but all failed. Finally the U.S. Supreme Court denied his final appeal on May 14, 2001, and the following day the state's Attorney General Drew Edmondson requested that a date be set for Harjo's execution. The justices of Oklahoma's Court of Criminal Appeals then sentenced Harjo to die Tuesday, November 17, 2001. The flurry of last-minute appeals at all levels were denied, he was denied clemency by the state's Board of Pardons and Parole, and Governor Frank Keating declined to intervene.

Before the time of execution Harjo was moved from his death row cell to a special cell near the death chamber, and during his last hours he visited with his attorney and a friend before being served his final meal. Shortly before 9:00 P.M. the prisoner was escorted into the injection room where he took his place on the gurney and his chest, waist, and legs were strapped while his arms were secured to two arm extensions, and a sheet was pulled over his body. A medical technician carefully inserted one intravenous cannula (IV) into the vein of each arm while the executioners were hidden from view in another room, behind a one-way mirrored window. The warden confirmed by telephone, with Governor Frank Keating, that the execution was to proceed and had the curtains to the witness room drawn open for the witnesses, including Porter's daughter and seven other relatives, while other witnesses watched on closed-circuit television from a room below the execution chamber, but Harjo had requested that his family not attend.

The warden asked Harjo if he had any last words and he replied only, "Uh, no." The warden then announced, "Let the execution begin," and at 9:08 P.M. each executioner drained the contents of his syringe into the tube leading to Harjo's arm: the first drug, sodium thiopental, caused unconsciousness; the second drug, pancuronium bromide, caused his respiration to become labored and would have caused death in time; and the third drug, potassium chloride, would stop his heart. Harjo's feet knocked together beneath the sheet and his eyes fluttered before he closed them, he took one deep breath and began to snore, and at 9:10 P.M. all sign of life was absent and he was pronounced dead.

Sources: *Harjo v. State*: 882 P.2d 1067 (1994). *Oklahoman* (Oklahoma City): July 16–18, 2001.

Smith, Lois N.
December 4, 2001

During the first half of 1982 James "Greg" Smith dated twenty-one-year-old Cindy Baillee but the relationship ended badly in June. After Greg and Cindy separated Greg's mother, forty-one-year-old Lois Nadean Smith, heard rumors that Baillee had threatened to report her son's use of illegal drugs to law enforcement officers, and also that she had made arrangements for the murder of her son. On July 4, 1982, Lois, Greg, and Teresa Baker picked up Baillee at a Tahlequah, Oklahoma, motel and drove toward the home of James Smith, Lois' ex-husband and father of Greg, in Gans, Sequoyah County, Oklahoma. Lois confronted Baillee with the rumors, but Baillee denied soliciting Greg's murder or threatening to report him to the police. Lois strangled Baillee, and when she was helpless she took a knife from Baillee's purse, stabbed her in the throat, and twisted the knife to widen the wound.

When they arrived at James Smith's home Lois forced Cindy into the house and made her sit in a recliner chair, where Lois taunted her by brandishing a pistol in a threatening manner and fired one shot into the chair near her head. Lois then fired three shots at Baillee with one bullet striking her in the chest and one in her back as she collapsed to the floor. Lois, laughing, stomped on

Baillee's neck while Greg reloaded the pistol, and then Lois shot Baillee six times, with four bullets striking her in the chest and two bullets striking her in the back of her head, killing her instantly. At the autopsy it was determined that five of the gunshot wounds and the knife wound were fatal. James Smith was a witness to the murder but his current wife, Robyn, had left as soon as Lois arrived. Lois then made arrangements to dispose of some of the evidence and concocted an alibi for all those present.

Lois Smith and her son were soon arrested and charged with the murder of Baillee, and their Sequoyah County trials were separated. Lois claimed, in her defense, that Teresa Baker had shot Baillee out of jealousy over Greg's attentions. Greg was convicted of first-degree murder and sentenced to serve a life term in prison, and the Court of Criminal Appeals affirmed the judgment and sentence in 1988. Lois was tried in December 1982, and on December 29 Judge Bill E. Rogers sentenced her to die when the jurors found the murder to be "especially heinous, atrocious and cruel" and that Smith had been "wholly indifferent to the pain inflicted."

Over the next nineteen years her attorneys used every maneuver to save their client's life. On her direct appeal, the Court of Criminal Appeals affirmed the lower court in 1986; the U.S. Supreme Court denied certiorari on June 26, 1987; her petition for post-conviction relief was denied on August 1, 1994; and a writ of habeas corpus was denied in 2000. By mid–2001 all judicial relief had been denied, her date with the executioner was set for December 4, 2001, and in November she appeared before the state Board of Pardons and Parole and was denied clemency. Her execution would clear the women's section of death row, as she had been preceded by Wanda Jean Allen and Marilyn K. Plantz earlier that year.

Early on her final day Smith was taken from her death row cell in the Mabel Basset Correctional Center in Oklahoma City to the special cell near the death chamber at the state prison in McAlester. Shortly before 9:00 P.M. the prisoner was escorted into the injection room where she took her place on the gurney and her chest, waist, and legs were strapped while her arms were secured to two arm extensions, and a sheet was pulled over her body. A medical technician carefully inserted one intravenous cannula (IV) into the vein of each arm while the executioners were hidden from view in another room, behind a one-way mirrored window. The warden confirmed by telephone, with Governor Frank Keating, that the execution was to proceed and had the curtains drawn open before he asked Smith if she had any last words. Smith thanked her attorney for all his efforts, sent her love to her children, then said, "To the families, I want to say I'm sorry for the pain and loss I've caused you. I ask that you forgive me. You must forgive to be forgiven." In the witness room, behind a one-way glass, were four members of the Baillee family who sat with Smith's witnesses, including four attorneys, her spiritual adviser, and her investigator.

When Smith concluded the warden announced, "Let the execution begin," and at 9:11 P.M. each executioner drained the contents of his syringe into the tube leading to Smith's arm: the first drug, sodium thiopental, caused unconsciousness; the second drug, pancuronium bromide, caused her respiration to become labored and would have caused death in time; and the third drug, potassium chloride, would stop her heart. At 9:13 P.M. all sign of life was absent and Smith was pronounced dead. Her body was released to her family, which had arranged for her burial in the Tahlequah City cemetery.

Sources: *Galveston News* (TX): December 5, 2001. *Oklahoman* (Oklahoma City): April 12, 2001; December 4, 2001. *Paris News* (TX): December 5, 2001. Sequoyah County case CRF 82–104. *Smith v. Massie*: 235 F.3d 1259 (2000). *Smith v. Oklahoma*: 483 U.S. 1033 (1987). *Smith v. State*: 727 P.2d 1366 (1986). *Smith v. State*: 766 P.2d 1007 (1988). *Smith v. State*: 915 P.2d 927 (1996).

Al-Mosawi, Sahib L.
December 6, 2001

In May 1991 forty-three-year-old Sahib Lateef Al-Mosawi, after the abduction and murder of his son in Iraq, fled from his home to a refugee camp in Saudi Arabia. There he met twenty-five-year-old Inaam Al-Nashi, also an Iraqi refugee, and Al-Mosawi had their marriage arranged. In July 1992 the Al-Mosawis and the Al-Nashis moved to the United States under a sponsorship and settled in Oklahoma City, Oklahoma. The couple had marital difficulties, and soon Al-Nashi, who was pregnant, left her husband and moved into the apartment of her uncle Mohammed Al-Nashi in the same complex.

Before they separated the couple had agreed that

they would name their baby after Al-Mosawi's father, but after Al-Nashi gave birth to their son on November 11, 1992, she reneged. A dispute arose at the Deaconess Hospital over the baby's name, and Police Officer Karen Maule was called but Josephine Warden, Director of the Oklahoma Refugee Settlement Program, resolved the matter when she told Al-Nashi that state law allowed the mother to name her child. Al-Mosawi had been at the hospital and had threatened to kill his wife and her entire family, but after Officer Maule gave him a faked "gift birth certificate" with the name he had demanded he left without taking any action.

The following day Al-Nashi obtained a temporary protective order. It was made permanent on November 20, with Al-Mosawi present at the hearing, but the following day Al-Mosawi and their sponsor were at the Al-Nashi apartment. Warden tried to intervene, but sponsor Dr. Albahadily became angry and said the order meant nothing. The sponsor then left with the couple and their son.

On the evening of November 28 Warden invited the Al-Nashis to a dinner party at the home of recent refugee arrivals, and told Fatima to be at her house at 6:45 P.M. At 6:38 Warden heard a knock on her door and found Fatima bleeding from a stab wounds to her stomach, hand and left side, and she said, "Inaam, Mohammed, Al-Mosawi." Fatima then told Warden that Inaam had asked Al-Mosawi if she could go to the dinner party, and he became angry, went to his apartment, and when he returned called Inaam and Fatima derogatory names. Mohammed ordered him to leave but Al-Mosawi pulled a knife from his jacket and stabbed Mohammed in the chest. When Inaam tried to help her uncle Al-Mosawi stabbed her in the stomach, and when Mohammed told Fatima to help Inaam she was stabbed and she staggered out to Warden's apartment to ask for help.

Meanwhile Al-Mosawi dragged Inaam outside and into a back alley, with Mohammed pursuing them, and when she screamed two men from a nearby garage went to help her. They saw, over a fence, Al-Mosawi hitting his wife on the head and shoulders, but they did not see him cut her throat as they ran around a building. However, another witness saw Al-Mosawi put his left arm around Inaam's neck and draw his knife across her throat with his right hand, and when Inaam collapsed Al-Mosawi fled south with Mohammed in pursuit. Mike Walker, one of the garage men, stayed with Inaam's dead body until Al-Mosawi returned within view, and then Walker followed him to his car. Mohammed had also died, and when Al-Mosawi returned to his apartment he was arrested and charged with two counts of murder and one count of attempted murder, as Fatima survived her wounds.

Al-Mosawi told the police that he had returned to the Al-Nashi apartment to drop off Inaam's and the baby's clothes when he was attacked with knives by Fatima and Mohammed. Inaam stepped between them just as Mohammed thrust the knife and Mohammed stabbed Inaam, but he did not know how Fatima was stabbed, nor how Mohammed was stabbed to death, and he claimed self-defense. Al-Mosawi was tried in April 1994. The jurors rejected his defense and found him guilty of two counts of first-degree murder, and on April 15 he was sentenced to die by lethal injection.

On April 26 he arrived at his death row cell in the state prison at McAlester, while his attorneys filed an appeal, which stayed the execution. The state Court of Criminal Appeals affirmed the judgment and sentence of the Oklahoma County District Court in 1996, and his appeal for post-conviction relief was denied in 1998. Once his state remedies were exhausted his attorneys filed a writ of habeas corpus with the federal Tenth Circuit Court of Appeals, but it was denied in 2000. After the period lapsed to file further appeals the state's attorney general asked the Court of Criminal Appeals to set a date for Al-Mosawi's execution, and they chose December 6, 2001. Al-Mosawi did not request a clemency hearing.

As the time of execution neared Al-Mosawi was moved from his death row cell to a special cell near the death chamber, and shortly before 9:00 P.M. the prisoner was escorted into the injection room. He took his place on the gurney and his chest, waist, and legs were strapped while his arms were secured to two arm extensions, and a sheet was pulled over his body. A medical technician carefully inserted one intravenous cannula (IV) into the vein of each arm while the executioners were hidden from view in another room, behind a one-way mirrored window. Warden Gary Gibson confirmed by telephone, with Governor Keating, that the execution was to proceed and had the curtains drawn open for the witnesses. The warden asked Al-Mosawi if he had any last words, but none are recorded.

The warden announced, "Let the execution begin," and each executioner drained the contents of his syringe into the tube leading to Al-Mosawi's arm: the first drug, sodium thiopental, caused unconsciousness; the second drug, pancuronium bromide, caused his respiration to become labored and would have caused death in time; and the third drug, potassium chloride, would stop his heart. Al-Mosawi quickly lapsed into unconsciousness, and when all sign of life was absent he was pronounced dead.

Sources: *Al-Mosawi v. Gibson*: 242 F.3d 387 (2000). *Al-Mosawi v. State*: 929 P.2d 270 (1996); 956 P.2d 906 (1998). *Oklahoman* (Oklahoma City): December 6, 2001.

Romano, John J.
January 29, 2002
Woodruff, David W.
January 31, 2002

In 1985 fifty-two-year-old Roger Joel Sarfaty was making his living by selling jewelry out of his apartment and his pocket, primarily at the Celebrity Club near his home in Oklahoma City, Oklahoma. Sarfaty went to the club nearly every night; he was there on the evening of Friday, October 11, and left for his apartment at 2:00 A.M. Sarfaty was acquainted with twenty-seven-year-old John Joseph Romano, who had recently stolen his girlfriend's rings and sold them to Sarfaty, but when she discovered the theft and threatened to make a report Romano promised to get the rings back. Romano was then serving a prison sentence on a weekend release program, and Romano knew that Sarfaty kept a great deal of jewelry and money in his apartment, including six large containers of quarters. In late September Romano, who said he needed money, asked Tracy Greggs to help him rob Sarfaty but Greggs declined.

Romano was released from prison on Friday evening, October 11, as usual. On Saturday, October 12, 1985, Romano rendezvoused with twenty-five-year-old David Wayne Woodruff, and they went to Sarfaty's apartment. Between the hours of 2:00 A.M. and 2:00 P.M. they captured Sarfaty and bound his wrists and ankles, beat him on the head, stabbed him five times with at least one wound in his heart, and then strangled him to death. They ransacked the apartment and took everything of value, including the rings from each finger of Sarfaty and the containers of quarters, but missed a bag of seventeen diamonds in a jacket pocket in his closet, and they dropped a diamond on the living room floor near Sarfaty.

On Saturday afternoon Romano and Woodruff tried to buy a television at a mall store using a large number of quarters, but both men were intoxicated and taken into custody by mall security. The security guards recorded that Romano had a "lock-blade folding knife" and was wearing a gold necklace, and Woodruff had an injured hand and blood on his jeans. The following day Woodruff's girlfriend noticed that her boyfriend had a large quantity of new jewelry he could not have afforded to buy. At 11:00 P.M. on October 15 a friend stopped by Sarfaty's apartment and discovered the body, and he called the police. Evidence was collected but there was no clue to the murderers, so the case went cold for ten months.

On July 19, 1986, sixty-three-year-old Lloyd Thompson, another acquaintance of Romano, was robbed and murdered, and this led to the arrest of Woodruff. After Woodruff was arrested he telephoned his girlfriend and told her to "clear the house," and she removed a pair of gloves, a watch, and several pieces of rope including one fashioned into a garrote. The police later collected this evidence, which led to a charge of murdering Sarfaty, and Romano was implicated in both murders and arrested.

Romano and Woodruff were first tried together for the murder of Lloyd Thompson; they were convicted of first-degree murder, and on January 30, 1987, they were sentenced to die. The case was appealed, and in 1992 the state Court of Criminal Appeals overturned the convictions and required that the two men be tried separately. They were retried and found guilty of the first-degree murder of Thompson, but Woodruff's jury recommended life in prison while Romano's jury recommended death, and they were sentenced accordingly.

In June 1987 the two men were tried together for the murder of Sarfaty and were convicted of first-degree murder when their efforts to shift the blame onto T. R. "Tippy" Ballard, Kathy Ford and Susan Babbitt failed. The jurors recommended death and both men were sentenced to die, and each was also sentenced to serve one thousand years in prison for robbery. The Sarfaty conviction was appealed, and in 1993 the Court of Criminal Appeals affirmed the judgment and sentence of the Oklahoma County District Court. The U.S. Supreme Court denied certiorari to Woodruff in 1993 and to Romano in 1994.Their post-conviction appeals were denied in 1996; after the period for further appeals lapsed their attorneys filed a writ of habeas corpus with the federal Tenth Circuit Court of Appeals, and this was denied on February 13, 2001. On November 27, 2001, the state's Attorney General, Drew Edmondson, asked the Court of Criminal Appeals to set a date for the executions, and the justices chose Tuesday, January 29, 2002, for Romano and Thursday, January 31 for Woodruff. A week before Romano's execution the U.S. Supreme Court denied a stay of execution to allow time for DNA testing of evidence, and the day before his execution the Tenth Circuit Court of Appeals refused to intervene. Neither the state's Board of Pardons and Paroles nor Governor Frank Keating would grant clemency to either prisoner.

As the date for Romano's execution neared he was removed from his death row cell to a cell near the injection room. Shortly before 9:00 P.M. the condemned man was escorted into the death chamber where he took his place on the gurney. He was strapped down, his arms were strapped to arm extensions, and a sheet was pulled over his body. A medical technician carefully inserted one intravenous cannula (IV) into the vein of each arm while the executioners were hidden from view behind a one-way mirrored window. The warden confirmed by telephone, with Governor Frank Keating, that the execution was to proceed, and the curtains to the witness area were then drawn open. Romano was asked if he had any last words, and he replied, "For whoever I've wronged, I'd like for them to forgive me. I'd like to tell my family and friends I love you. Thanks for your love and support." When Romano concluded the warden announced, "Let the execution begin," and the executioners emptied their syringes into the tube leading to Romano's arm: first sodium thiopental, a strong sedative; second pancuronium bromide to stop his respiration; and finally potassium chloride to stop his heart. All sign of life was absent at 9:12 P.M. and Romano was pronounced dead.

As the date for Woodruff's execution neared he was removed from his death row cell to a cell near the injection room. Shortly before 9:00 P.M. the condemned man was escorted into the death chamber where he took his place on the gurney. He was strapped down, his arms were strapped to arm extensions, and a sheet was pulled over his body. A medical technician carefully inserted one intravenous cannula (IV) into the vein of each arm while the executioners were hidden behind a one-way mirrored window. The warden confirmed by telephone, with Governor Frank Keating, that the execution was to proceed, and the curtains to the witness area were then drawn open. Woodruff was asked if he had any last words, and he replied, "We're not here for a social event, we're here for a killing. Name's David Wayne Woodruff. Let's get this show on the road." The warden then announced, "Let the execution begin," and the executioners emptied their syringes into the tube leading to Woodruff's arm: first sodium thiopental, a strong sedative; second pancuronium bromide to stop his respiration; and finally potassium chloride to stop his heart. All sign of life was absent at 9:12 P.M. and Woodruff was pronounced dead.

Sources: *Oklahoman* (Oklahoma City): January 29, 2002; January 31, 2002. *Romano v. Gibson*: 239 F.3d 1156 (2001). *Romano v. Oklahoma*: 512 U.S. 1 (1994). *Romano v. State*: 827 P.2d 1335 (1992); 847 P.2d 368 (1993); 909 P.2d 92(1995); 917 P.2d 12 (1996). *Woodruff v. Oklahoma*: 114 S. Ct. 349 (1993); 510 U.S. 934 (1993). *Woodruff v. State*: 825 P.2d 273 (1992); 846 P.2d 1124 (1993); 910 P.2d 348 (1996).

Frederick, Earl A., Sr.
July 30, 2002

Forty-one-year-old Bradford Lee Beck had served in Vietnam two decades earlier, and on November 6, 1989 the partially paralyzed veteran allowed thirty-eight-year-old Earl Alexander Frederick to move into his Spencer, Oklahoma, home. Beck's friends and acquantances questioned his benevolence, and wanted to know more about the recipient. Beck explained his charity by claiming Frederick was an old Vietnam buddy and said that they had spent time together in the veteran's hospital. Frederick, Beck claimed, had, at one time, been the assistant chief of police at Noble, Oklahoma. On November 11 Frederick beat Beck over the head with some blunt instrument, killing him, then ransacked his house for valuables and stole Beck's pickup truck. He put the body into the bed of the truck and took it to a field in the 8700 block of N.E.

23rd Street. He dumped the body and then fled to Dallas, Texas, his hometown.

Within a week Frederick tried to rob seventy-seven-year-old Shirley C. Fox in Texline, Texas, beat him on the head with a hammer and finally killed him with a shotgun blast in his mouth. Officer's found Beck's pickup truck parked near the scene of Fox's murder. Oklahoma authorities related that Beck was missing under suspicious circumstances, and the Texas police began searching for Frederick. The fugitive was arrested in an Amarillo, Texas, tavern on November 19, 1989, and charged with Fox's murder, but when he was lodged in jail it was found he was wearing Beck's clothing. Frederick then confessed to murdering Beck but claimed to be schizophrenic, with at least four personalities, and claimed his alternate personality named Jeff had murdered Beck. Texas authorities decided, since Oklahoma was seeking the death penalty, to let them try Frederick first, and he was extradited to Oklahoma County, Oklahoma. On January 15, 1990, the badly decomposed body of Beck was found, and the coroner determined the cause of death to be "undetermined head trauma."

Frederick was tried for Beck's murder in November 1992, and after the jurors deliberated three and one-half hours they found the defendant guilty of first-degree murder; in the penalty phase they recommended the death penalty. On November 19 the judge sentenced Frederick to die by lethal injection, and he was delivered to his death row cell at the state prison in McAlester while his attorneys filed appeals. The state Court of Criminal Appeals overturned the judgment and sentence and remanded the case to the district court for retrial. Frederick was tried again in February 1998 and convicted of first-degree murder with the death penalty recommended, and on March 6 the judge sentence him to die by lethal injection.

On March 30 the twice-condemned man was returned to his death row cell. After sentencing he said, "I certainly feel the conviction and sentence I received the first time was justified, just as it was the second time also." His attorneys then tried various ways to save their client's life but in February 2001 Frederick wrote to the assistant state's Attorney General Sandy Howard, "Mere words cannot begin to express the sorrow I feel over my actions. I am guilty of the crime, let there be no doubt of that," waived his right to further appeals, and insisted he wanted the death sentence carried out. On June 7, 2002, after the time lapsed for filing further appeals, Attorney General Drew Edmondson requested that the justices of the state Court of Criminal Appeals set an execution date, and they chose Tuesday, July 30.

As the date for Frederick's execution neared he was removed from his death row cell to a cell near the injection room. Shortly before 6:00 P.M. the condemned man was escorted into the death chamber where he took his place on the gurney. He was strapped down, his arms were strapped to arm extensions, and a sheet was pulled over his body. A medical technician carefully inserted one intravenous cannula (IV) into the vein of each arm while the executioners were hidden from view behind a one-way mirrored window. The warden confirmed by telephone, with Governor Frank Keating, that the execution was to proceed, and the curtains to the witness area were then drawn open. Frederick was asked if he had any last words, and he replied, "I'm sorry it's taken so long to have justice served for y'all, but it's being served now." When Frederick concluded the warden announced, "Let the execution begin," and the executioners emptied their syringes into the tube leading to Frederick's arm: first sodium thiopental, a strong sedative; second pancuronium bromide to stop his respiration; and finally potassium chloride to stop his heart. All sign of life was absent at 6:19 P.M. and Frederick was pronounced dead.

Sources: *Amarillo Globe-News* (TX): November 19, 1992. *Oklahoman* (Oklahoma City): March 6, 1998; June 7, 2002; July 30, 2002.

McCracken, Jerry L.
December 10, 2002

In 1989 twenty-two-year-old Jerry Lynn McCracken began serving a brief prison term for three counts of "assault with a deadly weapon" when he stabbed three people in a Lawton, Oklahoma, bar, but in July 1990 he was freed to a half-way house on a pre-parole release program. On the evening of a October 13 McCracken armed himself with a .22-caliber pistol and, with David Keith Lawrence, went to the New Ferndale Lounge at 1216 West Archer Street in Tulsa, arriving just after 7:00 P.M. They ordered drinks until, between 12:40 and 12:55 A.M., they decided to rob the bar and became boisterous saying, "We aren't afraid to fight nobody," and "We aren't afraid to shoot somebody."

They had waited until only three customers remained before McCracken pulled his pistol and took twenty-seven-year-old Tyrell Lee Boyd, thirty-four-year-old Steve Allen Smith, thirty-seven-year-old Timothy Edward Sheets, and the forty-one-year-old bartender Carole Ann McDaniels prisoner. After the pair had taken $350 from the cash register, two beer pitchers, and four beer mugs, McCracken shot each person in the head once. Ten minutes later, at 1:05 A.M., another patron entered and found one of the men lying on the floor in a pool of blood, and he ran across the street to a convenience store and summoned three police officers. They found Boyd and Smith dead while Sheets and McDaniels were seriously wounded, and the last two were rushed to the hospital where they soon died.

McCracken and Lawrence were immediately suspected as lounge owner Patricia Harrington had seen them in the bar earlier. They were arrested and lodged in jail, charged with four counts of murder, and each confessed and pointed to the other as the shooter. Lawrence was believed and he turned state's evidence, and after he testified against McCracken he pled guilty and was sentenced to a life term for the murders plus twenty years for robbery.

McCracken was tried in September 1991, and he testified that Lawrence asked to see his pistol, and said, "I am not the one who pulled the trigger. I am sorry I gave Dave the gun. If I had known he would do this, I would have never given him that gun." McCracken was convicted of first-degree murder with a recommendation for the death penalty, and on October 15 he was sentenced to die by lethal injection. He was delivered to his death row cell in the state prison at McAlester seven days later while his attorneys filed an appeal. His execution was stayed but the state's Court of Criminal Appeals affirmed the judgment and sentence in 1994, the U.S. Supreme Court denied certiorari in 1995, and his appeal for post-conviction relief was denied in 1997. After all state remedies were exhausted his attorneys filed a writ of habeas corpus and on October 10, 2001, the justices of the federal Tenth Circuit Court of Appeals denied the writ. Once the time for additional appeals lapsed the state's Attorney General Drew Edmondson, on October 17, 2002, requested that the Court of Criminal Appeals set an execution date, and the justices chose Tuesday, December 10. Neither the Board of Pardons and Parole nor Governor Frank Keating would intervene.

During his years on death row McCracken spent his time watching television, sketching, going to church services, and reading his Bible. He had "discovered religion" in 1991 just weeks before his trial. In late 2001, as the appeals process neared an end, he finally admitted in an interview, "I am guilty. I have no excuse." As the moment of McCracken's execution neared he was removed from his death row cell to a cell near the injection room. Shortly before 6:00 P.M. the condemned man was escorted into the death chamber where he took his place on the gurney. He was strapped down, his arms were strapped to arm extensions, and a sheet was pulled over his body. A medical technician carefully inserted one intravenous cannula (IV) into the vein of each arm while the executioners were hidden from view behind a one-way mirrored window. Warden Gary Gibson confirmed by telephone, with Governor Frank Keating, that the execution was to proceed, and the curtains to the witness area were then drawn open.

McCracken was asked if he had any last words as his mother said, "We're proud of you," and when told of her words he responded "I'll see you in heaven." He then made a lengthy statement including greetings to each witness, he recited a prayer, and then he began leading a hymn. The warden announced, "Let the execution begin," and the executioners emptied their syringes into the tube leading to McCracken's arm: first sodium thiopental, a strong sedative; second pancuronium bromide to stop his respiration; and finally potassium chloride to stop his heart. As McCracken sang he slowly lapsed into unconsciousness, and when all sign of life was absent, at 6:06 P.M., a doctor pronounced him dead. His mother then said, "Thank you, Jesus, for taking my boy home," and continued to softly sing the hymn to its conclusion.

Sources: *McCracken v. Gibson*: 268 F.3d 970 (2001). *McCracken v. Oklahoma*: 516 U.S. 859 (1995). *McCracken v. State*: 887 P.2d 323 (1994); 946 P.2d 672 (1997). *Oklahoman* (Oklahoma City): October 17, 2002; December 10, 2002.

Neill, Jay W.
December 12, 2002

In the summer of 1984 nineteen-year-old Jay Wesley Neill had been discharged from the Army for being a homosexual, and he moved into a

Lawton, Oklahoma, apartment with twenty-one-year-old Robert Grady Johnson, whom he had met in February. It was not long before the couple was having serious financial problems, and they made a pact to rob a bank and then commit suicide when the money ran out. On December 12 the two men learned they needed a gun permit to buy a pistol, and the applicant had to be at least twenty-one years old, so on December 13 Johnson applied for and was issued the gun permit. Meanwhile Neill contacted a travel agent to arrange airline tickets to San Francisco, California, as well as hotel accommodations and limousine service. They next bought two hunting knives at a discount store where they learned the guns in the store were not real firearms. At 10:00 A.M. Friday, December 14, the two men went to a pawn shop and bought a five-shot .32-caliber revolver they had previously examined. Neill received a tutorial on loading and shooting, and they were told where to buy ammunition.

At 1:00 P.M. Neill went to the First Bank of Chattanooga in Geronimo, a small temporary-type structure lacking any security measures, where they had a joint checking account and a delinquent loan. Forty-two-year-old bank manager Kay Bruno saw Neill when he entered and took out his bank file and laid it on her desk, in anticipation of another talk about the loan delinquency. At gunpoint Neill took the three employees hostage: Bruno, nineteen-year-old teller Jerri Annette Bowles, and twenty-five-year-old teller Joyce Marie Tanner-Mullenix, who was six months pregnant. He herded them into a back room where he forced the three women to lie face down and then used his hunting knife to stab them to death, driving the knife in so deeply that he severed ribs. Mullenix was stabbed twenty-seven times, Bruno was stabbed thirty-three times, and Bowles was stabbed fifteen times, and Neill then cut the throat of each woman so viciously that Mullenix and Bruno were nearly decapitated.

Fifteen-year-old Bellen Robles entered the bank but finding no employees went out and told her twenty-year-old husband Ruben that she thought the bank was being robbed. Ruben, carrying their fourteen-month-old daughter, went in to investigate, with his wife and thirty-three-year-old Ralph Zeller following. Neill took the three adults and the child hostage and secured them in the back room, and then he captured twenty-four-year-old Marilyn Roach as she entered the bank, and she joined the others. Once again Neill ordered them to lie on the floor face down and he shot Roach in the head twice and Zeller and the Robles adults in the back of their head once each, but his pistol clicked on an expended bullet when he tried to shoot the fourteen-month-old girl. Before being shot Roach said she heard Neill talking with another man, and it was supposed this was Johnson though he was not seen by any of the victims. Zeller died of his wound but the Robles couple and Roach survived to testify against Neill.

When Neill fled he took $17,000 with him, and he and Johnson boarded a plane for San Francisco at 2:30 P.M. At 1:25 P.M. Pam Matthews entered the bank and found no employees, but heard the baby crying. She followed the sound and found the victims, and she rushed across the street to a diner and called the police. Before Neill left his apartment he wrote a note to his other roommates saying he and Johnson were going to Georgia, and on Saturday and Sunday he called friends in Lawton several times to learn of any news on the robbery and to convince them he was in Georgia, but he gave one friend the telephone number of his San Francisco hotel. His friend told him that there was a composite sketch of the murderer and it matched Neill exactly.

Neill and Johnson were captured on Monday, December 17, and only $3,700 of the marked, stolen bills was recovered. Both men were extradited to Oklahoma County, and in June 1985 they were tried together for four counts of murder. They were convicted, and on July 2 both men were sentenced to die by lethal injection on each count. Their attorneys filed appeals, which stayed the execution, and the Court of Criminal Appeals overturned their conviction and ordered that they be tried separately.

In September 1992 each had his retrial with Neill again sentenced to death but Johnson sentenced to serve four life terms in prison. Neill's second conviction was appealed by his attorney, James Hankins, and the state Court of Criminal Appeals affirmed the judgment and sentence in 1994. The U.S. Supreme Court denied certiorari in 1996, and Neill's application for post-conviction relief was denied in 1997. After all avenues of state relief were exhausted his attorneys filed a writ of habeas corpus with the federal Tenth Circuit Court of Appeals, but this was denied in 2001. On October 7 his final appeal to the U.S. Supreme Court was denied; the state's Attorney General Drew Edmondson immediately requested that the Court of

Criminal Appeals fix the date of execution, and on October 14, 2002, the justices chose December 12. Neither the state's Board of Pardons and Parole nor Governor Frank Keating would intervene.

While on death row Neill converted to Christianity and then to Buddhism. As the moment of Neill's execution neared he was removed from his death row cell to a cell near the injection room. Shortly before 6:00 P.M. the condemned man was escorted into the death chamber where he took his place on the gurney. He was strapped down, his arms were strapped to arm extensions, and a sheet was pulled over his body. A medical technician carefully inserted one intravenous cannula (IV) into the vein of each arm while the executioners were hidden from view behind a one-way mirrored window. Warden Gary Gibson confirmed by telephone, with Governor Keating, that the execution was to proceed, and the curtains to the witness room were then drawn open for a dozen members of the victims' families in the room and eleven more family members watching on closed-circuit television from a room below the chamber.

Neill was asked if he had any last words and he replied, "I want everyone to know I'm really sorry for what I did to you. I'm not sorry for dying here today. I'm not sorry because I'm lying here. I'm sorry for the horrible, horrible thing I did. I hope you find some comfort in that, please forgive me." The warden, when Neill concluded, announced, "Let the execution begin," and as the drugs began to flow at 6:15 P.M. Neill said, "Robert Johnson wasn't in that bank. I know some of you think he was, but he wasn't." The executioners emptied their syringes into the tube leading to Neill's arm: first sodium thiopental, a strong sedative; second pancuronium bromide to stop his respiration; and finally potassium chloride to stop his heart. In a minute Neill became dizzy and asked, "Are they starting?" and then he prayed until he lapsed into unconsciousness. At 6:18 P.M. all sign of life was absent and Neill was pronounced dead.

Sources: *Neill v. Gibson*: 263 F.3d 1184 (2001). *Neill v. Oklahoma*: 516 U.S. 1080 (1996). *Neill v. State*: 896 P.2d 537 (1994); 943 P.2d 145 (1997). Oklahoma County case CRF 84-597. *Oklahoman* (Oklahoma City): December 13, 2002.

Carter, Earnest M., Jr.
December 17, 2002

In 1989 Frederick Jenkins was murdered by being burned to death, and twenty-two-year-old Earnest Marvin Carter, Jr., was charged with his murder, but he was acquitted at his trial and released. He was hired by the Oklahoma Auto Auction near I-35 and Wilshire in Oklahoma City and County, Oklahoma, but he was fired for sleeping on the job, and he decided to break in and steal a tow truck. He had borrowed a .38-caliber automatic pistol several months earlier, and he took the gun with him when, late on the evening of January 27, 1990, he went to the home of Charles L. Summers in Chandler. He told Summers he needed a ride to the Auto Auction lot, and Summers' girlfriend, Tammy Lewis, drove Carter and her boyfriend to the Auto Auction lot where Carter got out, while Summers and his girlfriend returned home.

After midnight Carter cut a hole in the chain-link fence with bolt cutters, climbed through, and cut the electrical wires to the guard shack where thirty-five-year-old security guard Eugene Mankowski was on duty. Carter crept up on Mankowski and shot him in the head with his .38-caliber handgun, killing him instantly, and then he stole the tow truck. After 2:00 A.M. Carter returned to Summers' home and told them he had killed a man and stolen the tow truck, but it had broken down. Summers then went with Carter and they towed the truck to Summers' auto body shop, later painted it to disguise its appearance, and when they thought it might lead to their arrest they burned it.

The body of Mankowski was discovered the morning of his death, and investigators documented muddy boot prints and a .38-caliber shell found in the guard shack. Carter was eventually suspected, and during the investigation officers found .38-caliber bullets, matching the shell in the guard shack, in the trunk of Carter's automobile, and they matched his boots to the muddy prints. They also interviewed Leonard "Lenny" Denson, a mechanic at Summers' body shop, who told them Carter told him he had "offed" a man to steal the tow truck. Carter was lodged in jail, and he professed his innocence to the end, but he was tried in February 1991, convicted of first-degree murder, and on February 22 was sentenced to die by lethal injection.

He was delivered to a death row cell at the state prison in McAlester three days later while his attorney, Gary Chubbuck, filed an appeal, which stayed the execution. Summers was tried and convicted of being an accessory to murder for knowing of the plan to steal the tow truck and helping Carter tow and paint the tow truck after he learned of Mankowski's murder, and he was sentenced to serve a term of life in prison. The state Court of Criminal Appeals affirmed Carter's judgment and sentence in 1994, and then Carter's attorney used every legal means to save his client's life. At the November 2002 hearing of the state Board of Pardons and Parole Chubbuck convinced the members to vote 4–0 to recommend clemency, but Governor Frank Keating had investigators interview Denson again, and after hearing how Carter had been remorseless after the killing, denied clemency.

As the moment of Carter's execution neared he was removed from his death row cell to a cell near the injection room. He ate what would be his last meal at noon, and at 3:00 P.M. he learned that his final appeal had been denied. Just after 5:30 P.M. the one hundred five prisoners on death row began a demonstration, banging on their cell doors and hollering. Shortly before 6:00 P.M. the condemned man was escorted into the death chamber where he took his place on the gurney and was strapped down, and then his arms were strapped to arm extensions and a sheet was pulled over his body. A medical technician carefully inserted one intravenous cannula (IV) into the vein of each arm while the executioners were hidden from view behind a one-way mirrored window. The warden confirmed by telephone, with Governor Keating, that the execution was to proceed, and the curtains to the witness room were drawn open for ten members of the Mankowski family seated behind a one-way mirrored window; and in the opposite room behind clear glass were Carter's mother and sister and his religious advisers, while other witnesses watched on closed-circuit television in a room beneath the chamber.

Carter was asked if he had any last words, and he thanked his attorneys and said, "I'll be with y'all on the other side. I'm going home now," then told his mother he loved her and said, "God bless you sweetheart." The warden announced, "Let the execution begin," and the executioners emptied their syringes into the tube leading to Carter's arm: first sodium thiopental, a strong sedative; second pancuronium bromide to stop his respiration; and finally potassium chloride to stop his heart. As Carter lapsed into unconsciousness his mother said, "Thank you, Jesus. Thank you for my child. Please God, don't let this happen to no one else's child." At 6:14 P.M. all sign of life was absent and Carter was pronounced dead.

Sources: *Carter v. State*: 879 P.2d 1234 (1994). *Oklahoman* (Oklahoma City): October 14, 2002; December 17–18, 2002.

Revilla, Daniel J.
January 16, 2003

When Michelle McElmurry was in her mid-teens she had a relationship with Juan Gomez that led to a pregnancy. They separated, and in December 1985 McElmurry gave birth to a son, Mark Gomez. By December 1986 McElmurry, still in her teens, and one-year-old Mark Gomez were living at Altus in Jackson County, Oklahoma, and near the end of the month eighteen-year-old Daniel Juan Revilla, a local farmhand, moved in with her. Revilla despised Mark because the baby was not his, and he abused the boy terribly over the next month. On one occasion Revilla put the baby in a kitchen drawer and closed him in; on another occasion he folded him up into a hide-a-bed; he once dunked the baby in freezing cold water, and on another occasion hung him by his ankles with duct tape. He often refused to allow the toddler to go to his mother, and he maliciously deprived him of toys and sleep, and these were only the abuses that McElmurry and several friends knew about.

On January 26, 1987, Revilla took McElmurry to the Jackson County Health Department for a check-up, leaving thirteen-month-old Mark home alone, and Revilla left her there while he returned home. Revilla began abusing the boy by punching him in the abdomen, then placed him in the bathtub and ran scalding water over him. He next struck him in the head, and then dropped him onto a concrete floor and crushed him, possibly by falling on top of him. Forty minutes after he left McElmurry he rushed into the lobby of the county hospital yelling that the boy had swallowed his tongue and had stopped breathing. Upon examination the doctors found that the baby had bruises on his back, blisters on his chest, skin peeling from his chest and groin area, burns on his thighs and ears, and lacerations on his thighs and arms.

The baby was dead on arrival, and during the autopsy the medical examiner discovered that

Mark had been beaten so severely that he had swelling and bleeding on the brain and his liver had been completely severed. When questioned by the police Revilla explained that when he returned home he had found the boy lying on the floor lifeless, tried to revive him by hitting him in the abdomen, then put him in the bathtub and in his panic turned on the hot water, then as he left the house he struck the boy's head on the door frame, causing Revilla to trip and fall on top of the baby on a concrete floor. This explanation did not explain most of the injuries, however, and Revilla was arrested and charged with murder by child abuse.

In mid–September Revilla was tried for the murder of Mark Gomez, and the jury rejected his explanation of the injuries when doctors testified that Mark was "certainly a battered child who was literally beaten to a pulp," and sustained injuries "we only see in beatings." Revilla was found guilty and the jurors recommended the death penalty. In October, during the time Revilla was to appear for sentencing, he escaped from the Jackson County jail, met his new girlfriend, and they went to Wellington, Texas, where he eluded capture and the couple fled into Mexico. A few days after his escape Revilla was captured by Mexican authorities in Acapulco and returned to Jackson County.

Revilla had been sentenced to death in absentia but on December 4, 1987, he was brought into court and the Jackson County District Court judge sentenced him to die by lethal injection; he arrived at his death row cell the same day. His attorneys filed appeals, which stayed the execution, and in 1994 the state Court of Criminal Appeals affirmed the judgment and sentence. His petition for post-conviction relief was denied in 1997. In 1996 he claimed that he wanted to stop the appeals process, but two years later he withdrew that statement and his attorneys, in January 1998, filed a writ of habeas corpus with the federal Tenth Circuit Court of Appeals. The federal justices denied him relief in 2002. His case was appealed to the U.S. Supreme Court and denied on November 12, 2002, and Attorney General Drew Edmondson then requested that the Court of Criminal Appeals set a date for his execution. The justices set the date at January 2, 2003, but on December 19 the justices adjusted it to Thursday, January 16 to allow a full sixty days from the denial of his final appeal. Neither the state Board of Paroles and Pardons nor Governor Brad Henry would intervene by granting clemency. A last-minute appeal to the U.S. Supreme Court was denied hours before the execution.

During his final days Revilla was interviewed by a reporter from the *Tulsa World* newspaper, and he continued to insist he was innocent. As the moment of Revilla's execution neared he was removed from his death row cell to a cell near the injection room, where he was served his last meal and then spent his final hours visiting with his brother and godmother. They were escorted out, and shortly after 6:00 P.M. the condemned man was marched into the death chamber where he took his place on the gurney and was strapped down. His arms were strapped to arm extensions, and a sheet was pulled over his body. A medical technician carefully inserted one intravenous cannula (IV) into the vein of each arm while the executioners were hidden from view behind a one-way mirrored window. The warden confirmed by telephone, with Governor Henry, that the execution was to proceed, and the blinds in the witness room were drawn for four members of the Gomez family, including Mark's father, and other witnesses seated behind a one-way mirrored window. Revilla was asked if he had any last words, and he turned his head away from the witnesses, shook his head and said, "No!" Warden Mike Mullin announced, "Let the execution begin," and the executioners emptied their syringes into the tube leading to Revilla's arm: first sodium thiopental, a strong sedative; second pancuronium bromide to stop his respiration; and finally potassium chloride to stop his heart. As the drugs began to flow a chaplain read scripture, and Revilla turned his face to the ceiling, closed his eyes, and exhaled one deep breath before he lay still. At 6:12 P.M. all sign of life was absent and Revilla was pronounced dead.

Sources: *Oklahoman* (Oklahoma City): December 20, 2002; January 17, 2003. *Revilla v. Gibson*: 283 F.3d 1203 (2002). *Revilla v. Oklahoma*: 123 S. Ct 963 (2003). *Revilla v. State*: 877 P.2d 1143 (1994); 946 P.2d 262 (1997). *Tulsa World* (OK): January 2003; February 27, 2007.

Fields, Bobby J.
February 13, 2003

In 1986 twenty-two-year-old Bobby Joe Fields, a drug addict, snatched a purse from a fifty-eight-year-old woman in a parking lot; he was chased and caught by her daughter, and he threw the young woman to the ground. He was captured, tried and convicted of robbery, and he served a term in prison.

On March 1, 1993, ex-convict Fields, then twenty-nine years old, was invited to a party with his girlfriend Shirley Masterson, her two daughters and her daughters' friend at Masterson's Oklahoma City home at 1312 N. Indiana Avenue. The party continued to noon the following day when Fields walked down two doors to 1324 Indiana Avenue, the home of seventy-seven-year-old Louise J. Schem, and he asked her if he could do yard work for her. Later Fields offered to sell a television set and VCR for $70 to Masterson's upstairs neighbor Albert Anuario, planning on stealing it from Schem, but Anuario did not have the $70 demanded.

At 5:00 P.M., when Fields thought that Schem had left, he returned to her home and opened the screen door, pushed open the front door, entered the living room and walked to the television set which he knew he could pawn for drug money. As he reached down to unplug the television Schem came up behind Fields with a .25-caliber semiautomatic pistol in her hand, and Fields struggled with her. The fight for control of the gun continued from the living room out the front door, down the steps, and onto the sidewalk in front of Schem's home. Robert Vallejo was just driving by when he heard Schem cry out, "Help! Help!" just as Fields took the gun from Schem, and then Fields, with the gun barrel less than twelve inches from his victim's head, shot the elderly woman in the neck just below her left ear, and she collapsed to the sidewalk. The bullet passed through Schem's spinal cord, through the back of her throat, and exited from her mouth, damaging two teeth and killing her. Vallejo drove a short distance before he made a U-turn and returned to the murder scene, but Fields had fled taking the murder weapon with him.

Fields returned to Masterson's home forty minutes later but as the nervous murderer entered the gun went off. Thirty minutes later Fields sold Schem's pistol to Anuario for $40, and then Masterson's daughter Dia Russell drove Fields and her mother to the home of Geraldine Banks — Fields' sister. On the way Fields remarked, as Russell would later report, "He didn't have any kind of remorse or guilt; he (said he) wouldn't lose any sleep because white people deserve what they got," and he had "thought about being on television's Most Wanted program." Soon after the murder another black man was arrested but he proved an alibi and the police began looking for Fields, and he was arrested two days after the murder. He confessed to the officers that he had fought with Schem in self-defense, and he insisted the gun went off accidentally.

Fields was charged with Schem's murder, and on May 7, 1993, the prosecution served notice they would seek the death penalty. Trial had been set for October but was continued to February 7, 1994. Fields' attorney, Catherine Burton, thought she had reached a life-in-prison agreement with trial Judge James L. Gullet so on February 7, 1994, Fields entered a "blind plea" of "guilty." The sentencing hearing took place on March 28 and 29; on April 7 Judge Gullet sentenced Fields to die by lethal injection, and he arrived at his death row cell five days later.

The motion to withdraw the guilty plea was filed on April 15 and denied on May 3, and the petition for a writ of certiorari to the U.S. Supreme Court was filed on November 14, 1994, and denied pending the outcome of the appeal at the state level. The automatic appeal in death sentence cases had stayed the execution but in 1996 the state's Court of Criminal Appeals affirmed the sentence, and Fields' appeal for post-conviction relief was denied the following year. When all state judicial relief was exhausted his attorneys filed a writ of habeas corpus with the federal Tenth Circuit Court of Appeals, and on January 17, 2002, this appeal was denied. When the time to file additional appeals lapsed on November 14, 2002, Attorney General Drew Edmondson asked the state Court of Criminal Appeals to set a date for Fields' execution, and the justices chose January 14, 2003. However, this date was adjusted to February 13 when outgoing Governor Frank Keating granted a stay of thirty days. On January 6 the state's Board of Pardons and Parole recommended clemency in a three-to-one vote but on Monday, February 10, newly inaugurated Governor Brad Henry denied clemency.

As the time neared for Fields' execution he was moved from his death row cell to a cell near the injection room. Shortly before 6:00 P.M. the condemned man was escorted into the death chamber where he took his place on the gurney and was strapped down, and then his arms were strapped to arm extensions and a sheet was pulled over his body. A medical technician carefully inserted one intravenous cannula (IV) into the vein of each arm while the executioners were hidden from view behind a one-way mirrored window. Warden Mike Mullin confirmed by telephone with Governor Henry that the execution was to proceed, and the blinds were drawn open for the witnesses seated behind a one-way mirrored window, including members of Fields' family, but no one from the Schem family was present.

Fields was asked if he had any last words and he told his attorneys, "Stay strong. You all keep fighting," then he asked his cousins to take care of his son and said to his sister, "Baby girl, stay strong and hold the family together. I love you all. Let's get this out of the way." When he concluded the warden announced, "Let the execution begin," and at 6:02 P.M. the executioners emptied their syringes into the tube leading to Fields' arm: first sodium thiopental, a strong sedative; second pancuronium bromide to stop his respiration; and finally potassium chloride to stop his heart. Fields slowly closed his eyes, his head jerked, he lay still, and at 6:05 P.M. all sign of life was absent and Fields was pronounced dead.

Sources: *Fields v. Gibson*: 277 F.3d 1203 (2002). *Fields v. State*: 923 P.2d 624 (1996); 946 P.2d 266 (1997). Oklahoma County case CF 93-1352. *Oklahoman* (Oklahoma City): November 14, 2002; February 14, 2003.

Robinson, Walanzo D.
March 18, 2003

In 1989 eighteen-year-old Walanzo Deon Robinson, nicknamed "Bandit," was a member of the violent Van-Ness Gangster Bloods street gang located east and west between Western Avenue and 3rd Avenue and north to south between 52nd and 57th Streets in the southwest part of south central Los Angeles, California. They took their name from one of the main streets that ran through their territory, and the members usually congregated at the heart of their territory on the corner of Van Ness and 54th Street. The gang made a large part of their money from the sale of crack cocaine, but they often engaged in murders and drive-by shootings.

In 1989 Robinson went to Oklahoma City to stay with friends, and he quickly claimed a drug sale location on a street corner in northeast Oklahoma City near a popular bar, where twenty-six year old Dennis Eugene Hill had already established his cocaine drug sale location. Earlier on May 19 Robinson had argued with another man over the drug sale location, and he had brandished a .38-caliber revolver, but did not shoot at the man. At 1:30 A.M. Robinson confronted Hill and they argued over the territory and drug sale money, and Robinson again pulled his pistol and fired into the ground between Hill's feet. Hill turned and ran and Robinson shot him in the back twice. Hill ran a short distance before he collapsed in the street with Robinson following, and as Hill lay helpless and crying out for someone to call for an ambulance Robinson shot Hill twice more, once in the arm and once in the chest, killing him. Robinson was identified by four eyewitnesses, some who knew him only as "Bandit."

Robinson fled to Los Angeles, and on September 7 he was arrested and extradited to Oklahoma City. Robinson was charged with Hill's murder, tried in early 1990, and convicted, and on June 19 Judge Bana B. Blasdel sentenced Robinson to die by lethal injection. His attorneys filed a notice of appeal, which stayed the execution, but in 1995 the state Court of Criminal Appeals affirmed the judgment and sentence of the District Court, and in 1997 the justices denied post-conviction relief. His attorneys then filed a writ of habeas corpus but in January 2002 the justices of the federal Tenth Circuit Court of Appeals denied him relief. After the time passed for additional appeals Attorney General Drew Edmondson, on January 15, 2003, requested that the justices of the Court of Criminal Appeals set a date, and on February 5 they set the date for Robinson's execution at March 18. The newly appointed Board of Pardons and Parole met on March 12 and in a vote of three to zero, one member abstaining and another recusing herself, denied clemency on March 12, 2003. Governor Brad Henry refused to intervene.

During his time on death row Robinson converted to the Muslim faith, claimed to have become a minister, and changed his name to Shabaka. As the time neared for Robinson's execution he was moved from his death row cell to a cell near the injection room. Shortly before 6:00 P.M. the condemned man was escorted into the death chamber where he took his place on the gurney and was strapped down, and then his arms were strapped to arm extensions and a sheet was pulled over his body. A medical technician carefully inserted one intravenous cannula (IV) into the vein of each arm while the executioners were hidden from view behind a one-way mirrored window. Warden Mike Mullin confirmed by telephone with Governor Henry that the execution was to proceed, and the blinds were drawn open for the witnesses seated behind a one-way mirrored window. Robinson was asked if he had any last words and he talked for two minutes, but the microphone system malfunctioned and his words were not heard by the witnesses and newspaper reporters. The staff later said that Robinson persisted in his claim of innocence and said "It's all the state of Oklahoma's fault" that an innocent man was being executed. When he concluded Warden Mullin announced, "Let the execution begin," and at 6:07 P.M. the executioners emptied their syringes into the tube leading to Robinson's arm: first sodium thiopental, a strong sedative; second pancuronium bromide to stop his respiration; and finally potassium chloride to stop his heart. At 6:10 P.M. all sign of life was absent and Robinson was pronounced dead.

Sources: *Kansas City Star* (MO): March 18, 2003. Oklahoma County case CRF 89–4791. *Robinson v. Gibson* (unpub. opinion): 99–6438 (2002). *Robinson v. State*: 900 P.2d 389 (1995); 937 P.2d 101 (1997). *Tulsa World* (OK): September 24, 2003.

Hooker, John M.
March 25, 2003

In 1971 seventeen-year-old John Michael Hooker attended a party where he argued with the hostess and twice brandished a handgun, the second time firing two bullets. One bullet wounded the hostess and the second killed his friend. Hooker was convicted of manslaughter and he served a prison term. In 1980 ex-convict Hooker, then twenty-six, met twenty-year-old Sylvia Stokes, and over the next eight years they had a turbulent relationship, marked by violence and periods of separation; during that time they had three children. In October 1987 Hooker and Stokes separated again, amidst the customary threats of violence and murder against her and her family, which prompted Stokes to obtain a protective order. Still Hooker and Stokes reconciled when he agreed to marry her in February 1988, but he reneged on this promise. On March 20 they argued and she left him, then moved in with her mother, fifty-three-year-old Drucilla Morgan, who had an apartment in the same Oklahoma City complex — the Providence Apartments.

On Sunday, March 27, Hooker went to the Morgan apartment several times to convince Stokes to return to their apartment, but she refused. Later that afternoon Stokes, with her mother, returned to her apartment to get clean clothes and food for the children, and neighbors saw Hooker return to the apartment after 4:00 P.M. Stokes and Morgan were not seen the rest of that day so the following day Cynthia and Crystal Stokes, Sylvia's sisters, went to the Hooker apartment to find their sister and mother. Cynthia had difficulty opening the door but finally pushed it far enough to see her mother lying on the floor in a pool of blood, and she called the police. The investigation determined that Morgan had been stabbed twelve times while Stokes had been stabbed eight times, and the stab wounds were so deep that they bled to death internally without being able to rise from the places they first collapsed. The neighbors in the apartment beneath the Hooker apartment heard the scuffling, but no voices, and believed that the couple was just having another violent argument. Hooker had left the apartment through a bedroom window, and a bloody butcher's knife with an eight-inch blade was found on the floor beneath the window. There was a bloody footprint and later this would be matched with Hooker's tennis shoes, and neighbors saw Hooker with blood on his clothing as he left the complex.

The search for Hooker continued for a week before he was captured, lodged in the Oklahoma County jail, and charged with two counts of murder. Blood spots found on Hooker's pants were matched to the blood of Stokes and Morgan; then in 2001 after police chemist Joyce Gilchrist was discredited, the blood was tested and again proved to be Stokes' and Morgan's blood. Hooker's trial began on October 24, 1988, and ended four days later, he was convicted of first-degree murder, and on November 9 Judge Leamon Freeman sentenced him to die by lethal injection. His attorneys filed an appeal, which stayed the execution but in 1994 the state Court of Criminal Appeals affirmed the lower court's judgment and sentence. The U.S. Supreme Court denied certiorari the following year, and in 1997 the state appeals court denied post-conviction relief. A writ of habeas corpus was filed with the federal Tenth Circuit Court of

Appeals and denied in 2002. When the time passed for further appeals state Attorney General Drew Edmondson, on January 21, 2003, requested the justices of the Court of Criminal Appeals to set a date for Hooker's execution, and on January 22 they set the date at March 25. The state Board of Pardons and Parole denied clemency on March 12, 2003, and Governor Brad Henry declined to intervene. The U.S. Supreme Court late Tuesday, March 25, denied a writ of habeas corpus and a request for a last-minute stay of execution.

As the time neared for Hooker's execution he was moved from his death row cell to a cell near the injection room. Shortly before 6:00 P.M. the condemned man was escorted into the death chamber where he took his place on the gurney and was strapped down, and then his arms were strapped to arm extensions and a sheet was pulled over his body. A medical technician carefully inserted one intravenous cannula (IV) into the vein of each arm while the executioners were hidden from view behind a one-way mirrored window. Warden Mike Mullin confirmed by telephone with Governor Henry that the execution was to proceed, and the blinds were drawn open for the witnesses seated behind a one-way mirrored window, including nine members of Morgan's and Stokes' family. Across the room behind clear glass sat Hooker's daughter, sister, brother, two spiritual advisers and his attorney. Hooker was asked if he had any last words, and he lifted his shaved head, looked toward his family and said, "To all my family and friends, what's up guys? I'm all hooked up. I can't even move my hands, or none of that. But that's all right, I'm at peace. I'm good, Y'all are good. Y'all stay up. I'm out!" He made no statement to the victims' family. When he concluded Warden Mullin announced, "Let the execution begin," and at 6:05 P.M. the executioners emptied their syringes into the tube leading to Hooker's arm: first sodium thiopental, a strong sedative; second pancuronium bromide to stop his respiration; and finally potassium chloride to stop his heart. Hooker made several snoring sounds, his head and feet twitched, and then he lay still. At 6:07 P.M. all sign of life was absent and Hooker was pronounced dead.

Sources: *Hooker v. Mullin*: 293 F.3d 1232 (2002). *Hooker v. Oklahoma*: 516 U.S. 858 (1995). *Hooker v. State*: 887 P.2d 1351 (1994); 934 P.2d 352 (1997). *McAlester News-Capital and Democrat* (OK): March 26, 2003. *Oklahoman* (Oklahoma City): March 24, 2003; March 26, 2003. *Tulsa World* (OK): February 27, 2007.

Hain, Scott A.
April 3, 2003

In early 1984 thirteen-year-old Scott Allen Hain committed grand larceny, and in May, a month before his fourteenth birthday, he was arrested and charged with theft and with concealing the stolen property. Because of his youth he was handled by the Oklahoma juvenile justice system and he was placed on probation. Over the next eighteen months Hain was in and out of juvenile court for minor offenses, and he was placed in several juvenile institutions, but he always walked away. In October 1985 Hain was sent to the Rader Treatment Center in Sand Springs near Tulsa but he walked away in February 1987. Hain joined his father, and the pair committed a burglary; he was arrested, but the charges were dropped when he was returned to the treatment center. A month later he fled again but was quickly captured, and it took three months before he found an opportunity to escape a third and last time. He met his father and they went to Kansas where Hain took a job in a warehouse so he could steal items his father could sell. When the police questioned them about the stolen property they fled back to Tulsa, Oklahoma.

Without a source of income seventeen-year-old Hain had to live on the streets where he met twenty-one-year-old Robert Wayne Lambert. During the early morning hours of October 6, 1987, Hain and Lambert were in the parking lot of a Tulsa tavern waiting to burglarize a nearby house when they saw twenty-seven-year-old Michael William Houghton and twenty-two-year-old Laura Lee Sanders sitting in Sanders' automobile talking. They approached and with knife in hand forced their way into Sanders' car and then drove a short distance before Hain robbed Houghton at gunpoint and took his truck keys before he made him climb into Sanders' car trunk. They drove a short distance further but again stopped and put Sanders in the trunk as well, and from the two they stole $565. They returned to the parking lot, and Lambert drove Houghton's pickup truck while Hain drove Sanders' car toward Sand Springs, but they turned down an isolated country road along the way. They stripped the car of Sanders' belongings and put them in the truck before they put a blanket under the gas tank and cut the gas line. After the blanket was soaked with gasoline they lit a newspaper and set the car afire. Later Hain and Lambert would say that they stood there while the car became engulfed in flames, and they listened to Houghton and Sanders banging on the trunk lid and begging to be saved. When the yelling stopped Hain and Lambert drove away, but they soon returned to be sure the car was still burning, and then they drove to Jennings where they left some of Sanders' belongings in a friend's garage.

They drove Houghton's truck to Wichita, Kansas, where they spent the stolen money, and on October 9 they returned to Tulsa and were arrested. Lambert was tried in 1988 and retried in 1996, he had four competency hearings, was declared retarded, and was sentenced to serve life terms without parole. On October 13, 1987, Hain was charged in the District Court of Creek County with two counts of murder, two counts of kidnapping, two counts of robbery with a firearm, one count of arson, and two counts of theft of an automobile. Later three aggravating factors were presented when the district attorney filed a bill of particulars seeking the death penalty: these were the rape of Phyliss Comstock in her Kansas home, the kidnap and rape of a Wichita woman, and the kidnapping and beating with a claw hammer of a Tulsa man and the robbery of the man and his wife and her beating and rape, all during the four months preceding the two murders. Hain was tried in May 1988 and he was found guilty on all counts, and on June 14 he was sentenced to die by lethal injection on each count of murder and to serve two hundred fifty-five years in prison on the other counts.

His attorneys filed an appeal, which stayed the execution, and in 1993 the state Court of Criminal Appeals affirmed the judgment but reversed the sentencing for the two murder convictions and ordered Hain to be resentenced. His hearing began on September 22, and on October 26 he was again twice sentenced to die by lethal injection. His attorneys again filed appeals but in 1996 the Court of Criminal Appeals affirmed the sentence of the district court, and the justices denied post-conviction relief in 1998. When the time for further state appeals lapsed his attorneys filed a writ of habeas corpus with the federal Tenth Circuit Court of Appeals, but on February 20, 2002, the federal justices denied him relief. Hain's attorneys then filed an appeal with the U.S. Supreme Court but the justices denied certiorari on January 27, 2003, and Oklahoma's Attorney General Drew Edmondson then asked the Court of Criminal Appeals to set an execution date. On Friday, January 31, 2003, the state justices set the date of execution for April 3. On April 1 the state Board of Pardons and Parole unanimously denied clemency after Hain tried to shift the blame onto Lambert, and Governor Brad Henry declined to intervene. Hain's attorneys had filed several last-minute appeals, and on Wednesday, April 2 the Tenth Circuit Court of Appeals granted a stay of execution pending a May 6 hearing but it was quickly vacated by the U.S. Supreme Court, and the execution had to be delayed for two hours.

As the time neared for Hain's execution he was moved from his death row cell to a cell near the injection room. Shortly after 8:00 P.M. the condemned man was escorted into the death chamber where he took his place on the gurney and was strapped down, and then his arms were strapped to arm extensions and a sheet was pulled over his body. A medical technician carefully inserted one intravenous cannula (IV) into the vein of each arm while the executioners were hidden from view behind a one-way mirrored window. Warden Mike Mullin confirmed by telephone with Governor Henry that the execution was to proceed, and the blinds were drawn open for the witnesses seated behind a one-way mirrored window. Hain was asked if he had any last words, but he declined to make a statement. Warden Mullin then announced, "Let the execution begin," and at 8:31 P.M. the executioners emptied their syringes into the tube leading to Hain's arm: first sodium thiopental, a strong sedative; second pancuronium bromide to stop his respiration; and finally potassium chloride to stop his heart. At 8:35 P.M. all sign of life was absent and Hain was pronounced dead.

Sources: Creek County case CRF 87–240. *Hain v. Gibson*: 01–5014 (2002). *Hain v. Mullin*: 327 F.3d 1177 (2003). *Hain v. State*: 852 P.2d 744 (1993); 919 P.2d 1130 (1996); 962 P.2d 649 (1998). *Oklahoman* (Oklahoma City): April 2, 2003; April 4, 2003; December 8, 2005.

Hawkins, Don W., Jr.
April 8, 2003

In early 1985 twenty-five-year-old Don Wilson Hawkins, Jr., was living with his girlfriend Shirley Pitts in a trailer near Denver. He became angry at his employer and took several shots at his car, and he was fired. In July Hawkins had some disagreement with David Coupez in Denver, Colorado, and he robbed him and then hanged him until he was dead.

Shirley Pitts had moved to a large house on 50th Street and Bryant in Oklahoma City and was living with her fifteen-year-old nephew Chris Lovell and Hawkins' cousin Dale Shelton when Hawkins joined her there. In August 1985 Hawkins and Shelton began making plans to "kidnap a rich woman and hold her for ransom," and on the morning of August 19 Hawkins went to the Ace Pawn Shop and bought a set of handcuffs and six .38-caliber bullets for his revolver. That evening they drove to the Shepherd Shopping mall and staked out the free-standing postal station and had selected a woman to kidnap when a mall security officer drove by and they postponed their plan. The next customer at the postal station was twenty-nine-year-old Linda Ann Thompson who had daughters, four-year-old Lori and eighteen-month-old Katie in the car with her. While Shelton stood lookout Hawkins, armed with his revolver, forced his way into Thompson's 1983 Toyota Tercel and took her and her two daughters prisoner, handcuffed Thompson and drove them to Pitts' home, with Shelton following in Hawkins' car.

He separated the mother from her children, which prevented resistance, and guarded her in the house until after dark. During the hours before sunset Hawkins and Shelton stole the few dollars Thompson had in her purse and discussed how they could collect a ransom, but realized that they had not kidnapped a woman for whom a ransom would be paid so they made no telephone calls. They had Thompson change into Hawkins' clothes before Hawkins and Shelton "dog chained" Thompson's ankle and took her to a barn several hundred yards from the house, and there they chained her in the loft. The children were kept locked in a bedroom and left in the care of Pitts and Lovell. During the night Shelton unchained Thompson, raped her, then forced her to perform "oral sodomy." Soon afterward Lovell went to the loft and raped Thompson again. In the morning Shelton raped Thompson once more before she was taken to the house to change into her own clothes and then she yelled good-bye to her daughters as she was being taken to her car.

Hawkins and Shelton told Thompson they were going to drive her to Arkansas and release her, and they started driving east until they neared Sportsman's Lake near Seminole. They turned off the highway, and Hawkins forced Thompson to walk to the lakeshore where he hog-tied her. Hawkins threw her in and jumped in after her, and he held her under water until she drowned. After Thompson was dead Hawkins and Shelton dragged her body to a ravine, covered it with brush, and drove to a project's area in northeast Oklahoma City where they wiped the car clean of fingerprints, left the car doors unlocked and the keys in the ignition, and started for Pitts' home, but a resident saw them and called the police.

Meanwhile Pitts and Lovell had taken the two children to the neighborhood of their babysitter and dropped them off, and they were seen by two boys. The boys took the two little girls to their babysitter, and she called the police. The boys knew Lovell and directed the police to his house; Pitts and Lovell were arrested, and they told what they knew. In searching the outside of the house the officers found Thompson's purse where it had been discarded in a crate. While the police were at Pitts' home, Hawkins and Shelton arrived and, seeing the officers, fled to San Diego, California.

Over the next two months Hawkins and Shelton kidnapped, raped and sodomized two teenaged girls and the next day kidnapped and robbed two women, one of whom Shelton raped and sodomized. They then fled to Sacramento, California. In mid–October Hawkins was trying to steal a battery from a car when he was arrested, and the police found he had a sawed-off shotgun, falsified identification, and stolen credit cards. He told the officers where Shelton could be found, and his accomplice was arrested at a nearby motel; he also had falsified identification. As soon as both men were behind bars they began confessing to their crimes.

Hawkins was first taken to Denver where he pled guilty to the murder of Coupez and was sentenced to a life term in prison. He was then extradited to Oklahoma and tried with Shelton for the murder of Thompson. He had confessed several times, once on video tape, but at his trial in the Oklahoma County District Court he testified that he left Thompson hog-tied at the shoreline and started to walk away when he heard the "shriek of a supernatural creature" and rushed back, dove in the water, and tried to save Thompson. The jury rejected his defense and found him guilty of first-degree murder, recommended the death penalty, and on June 24, 1986, the District Court judge sentenced him to die by lethal injection. Shelton was found guilty of first-degree murder, two counts of kidnapping for ransom, rape, and forced oral sodomy, and he was sentenced to serve five consecutive life terms without parole.

Their attorneys filed appeals, and the state Court of Criminal Appeals affirmed Shelton's judgment and sentences in 1990. The Court of Criminal Appeals affirmed the judgment and sentence in Hawkins' case in 1994, and the U.S. Supreme Court denied certiorari the following year. Hawkins' appeal for post-conviction relief was denied in an unpublished opinion. After the time had lapsed for further state appeals his attorneys filed a writ of habeas corpus with the federal Tenth Circuit Court of Appeals, which was denied on May 22, 2002. On February 13, 2003, after the U.S. Supreme Court denied Hawkins' final appeal, the state's Attorney General Drew Edmondson asked the Court of Criminal Appeals to set a date for Hawkins' execution, and the justices chose April 8. The state Board of Pardons and Parole met on April 1 and denied clemency, and Governor Brad Henry declined to intervene.

In 2002 Hawkins was interviewed by a reporter from the *McAlester News-Capital and Democrat*, and he said, "I know what I did was terrible; but at least I don't have that particular crime (rape) on my conscience." During the week before the execution he told an *Oklahoman* reporter that he was ready to die, and "It's time to move on."

As the time neared for Hawkins' execution he was moved from his death row cell to a cell near the injection room. Shortly before 6:00 P.M. the condemned man was escorted into the death chamber where he took his place on the gurney and was strapped down, and then his arms were strapped to arm extensions and a sheet was pulled over his body. A medical technician carefully inserted one intravenous cannula (IV) into the vein of each arm while the executioners were hidden from view behind a one-way mirrored window. Warden Mike Mullin confirmed by telephone with Governor Henry that the execution was to proceed, and at 6:04 P.M. the blinds were raised for the witnesses seated behind a one-way mirrored window.

Hawkins was asked if he had any last words, and as he raised his head he saw his wife Joelle, whom he married while on death row, through the clear glass of the other witness area and said, "I love you," and continued addressing his attorney and investigator, "You guys keep fighting." He next told his two religious advisers, "Carry the torch," and then said, "I've got peace. The state needs vengeance for the crime I've done. They're going to punish my body, but Jesus has forgiven me. I'm truly sorry I got everyone into this. I'm ready to go." He was smiling when Warden Mullin announced, "Let the execution begin," and at 6:05 P.M. the executioners emptied their syringes into the tube leading to Hawkins' arm: first sodium thiopental, a strong sedative; second pancuronium bromide to stop his respiration; and finally potassium chloride to stop his heart. His eyes closed, then opened slightly, and at 6:07 P.M. all sign of life was absent and Hawkins was pronounced dead.

Sources: *Hawkins v. Mullin*: 291 F.3d 658 (2002). *Hawkins v. Oklahoma*: 516 U.S. 977 (1995). *Hawkins v. State*: 891 P.2d 586 (1994). *Oklahoman* (Oklahoma City): February 13, 2003; April 9, 2003. *Shelton v. State*: 793 P.2d 866 (1990).

Jackson, Larry K.
April 17, 2003

In 1985 twenty-two-year-old Larry Kenneth Jackson was living with Freda Laverne Washington when they became embroiled in a heated argument and Jackson shot his common-law wife to death. He was charged with her murder and scheduled to be tried in 1986, but his attorneys reached a plea deal in which he pled guilty to second-degree murder. Jackson was sentenced to serve thirty years in prison, where he met twenty-nine-year-old Wendy Cade and a relationship developed. Jackson was moved to the minimum security Joseph Harp Correctional Institution in Oklahoma City and placed on a work crew, and Cade visited him at the facility on Sundays and twice at work locations, where Jackson would sneak away for a sexual encounter. Jackson believed that when he was released he and Cade would be married and that she would help him get an earlier parole.

On September 6, 1994, Jackson was on a work crew assembling furniture for Oklahoma State Industries in the Jim Thorpe Building in Oklahoma City. He was issued tools to do the job, including a utility knife, or box cutter, and when he walked away at 10:00 A.M. he took the tools with him. He met Wendy Cade and the couple left in her Jeep

Cherokee. Jackson's absence was soon discovered and he was reported as an escapee. The couple drove to a convenience store where Jackson bought beer and cigarettes while Cade went across the street to a liquor store and bought a fifth of liquor. Cade then drove to Martha Gulley's, her mother's, home and they dropped off Cade's four-year-old daughter. At noon the couple stopped to buy food and then went to the Motel 6 at N.E. 122nd Street and I-35 (the Turner Turnpike) in north Oklahoma City where Cade rented a room.

After the couple ate and drank they had sex, and while they were in the bathroom Cade told Jackson that she was engaged to and living with Victor Dizer, they were going to be married, and her relationship with Jackson was ended and she would be unable to assist him in getting his early parole. Jackson flew into a rage, and using the utility knife, he stabbed and slashed Cade thirty times, with two deep gashes to her neck severing her jugular veins. Cade bled to death so quickly that she never made it out of the bathroom, and she had bled out so completely that when Jackson dragged her to the bed she left only a little blood on the carpet and hardly any on her body. Jackson propped her against the bed, wrapped the knife in a washrag and put it between the mattress and box spring, and then he took her watch, jewelry and Jeep keys and fled.

He drove a short distance to the I-35 on-ramp but lost control of the Jeep and crashed, and the Jeep was disabled so he abandoned it. The Jeep was found by a state trooper at 3:30 P.M. and Cade's mother was notified. Jackson said that he later awoke in a field and contacted Dorothy Leffette's brother, who gave him a ride to the Ambassador Court Apartments at 1634 South Phillips, where Jackson's sister worked and Leffette's sister lived. However, Jackson's sister was not there so Leffette allowed Jackson to stay overnight at her apartment. At 9:00 A.M. Dizer and Gulley went to the on-ramp of the I-35 to recover her daughter's Jeep, and they noticed the Motel 6 nearby. They checked and found that Cade had checked in the previous afternoon, and they called the police. Officers entered the room and found Cade's body, the bathroom splattered with her blood, and the utility knife where it was hidden. By noon officers had traced Jackson to the Ambassador Court Apartments; he was arrested, and he told them, "If Wendy is dead, I killed her."

He was lodged in the Oklahoma County jail and charged with Cade's murder. He was tried in the Oklahoma County District Court in late 1995 and convicted of first-degree murder. The jurors recommended the death penalty, and on December 22, 1995, Judge Daniel L. Owens sentenced Jackson to die by lethal injection. His attorneys filed an appeal, which stayed the execution, but in 1998 the state Court of Criminal Appeals affirmed the judgment and sentence of the District Court. The justices denied post-conviction relief on November 20, 1998, and the U.S. Supreme Court denied certiorari the following year. After all state judicial relief was exhausted, and the time had lapsed for further state appeals, Jackson's attorneys filed a writ of habeas corpus with the federal Tenth Circuit Court of Appeals, but on September 16, 2002, the justices denied relief, and the appeal to the U.S. Supreme Court was also denied. On January 15, 2003, Oklahoma's Attorney General Drew Edmondson requested that the state Court of Criminal Appeals set a date for Jackson's execution, and on February 13 the justices chose Thursday, April 17, 2003. The state Board of Pardons and Parole met on April 7 and denied clemency, and Governor Brad Henry declined to intervene.

As the time neared for Jackson's execution he was moved from his death row cell to a cell near the injection room. Shortly before 6:00 P.M. the condemned man was escorted into the death chamber where he took his place on the gurney and was strapped down, and then his arms were strapped to arm extensions and a sheet was pulled over his body. A medical technician carefully inserted one intravenous cannula (IV) into the vein of each arm while the executioners were hidden from view behind a one-way mirrored window. Warden Mike Mullin confirmed by telephone with Governor Henry that the execution was to proceed, and the blinds were raised for the witnesses seated behind a one-way mirrored window, including eight relatives of Wendy Cade and four relatives of Freda Washington.

Jackson was asked if he had any last words. He raised his head and looked at his family members behind the opposite clear-glass window and said, "Take care of my mama," then turned to the one-way mirrored window of the witness room and said, "I want to ask for forgiveness from Martha Cade. I'm sorry for everything I brought upon her.

I'm sorry for the pain, sorrow I brought on her and her family and kids." He turned again to his family and continued, "I'm sorry to all of you for the same thing. I guess I'm going to go now, 'Bye y'all." When he concluded at 6:05 P.M. the warden announced, "Let the execution begin," the executioners emptied their syringes into the tube leading to Jackson's arm: first sodium thiopental, a strong sedative; second pancuronium bromide to stop his respiration; and finally potassium chloride to stop his heart. At 6:08 P.M. all sign of life was absent and Jackson was pronounced dead.

Sources: *Jackson v. Oklahoma*: 526 U.S. 1008 (1999). *Jackson v. State*: 964 P.2d 875 (1998); PC-97-1349. *Kansas City Star* (MO): April 18, 2003. *McAlester News-Capital and Democrat* (OK): April 18, 2003. Oklahoma County case: CF 94-6070. *Oklahoman* (Oklahoma City): February 13. 2003.

Knighton, Robert W.
May 27, 2003

In 1968 twenty-six-year-old Robert Wesley Knighton committed a robbery and was arrested, tried, and convicted. Knighton was sentenced to serve a prison term, and he was convinced that Coffier Day had informed on him though Day never testified at his trial. He was released, and on September 15, 1973, Knighton went to the Springfield, Missouri, home of Coffier Day and his father Claude. Shortly after Knighton left the Day home he shot at the Days with a pistol, wounded Claude in the neck, and killed Coffier.

He ran two blocks to the home of Charles Jarrett and tried to steal an old car parked in the driveway which was posted "for sale," but the battery had been removed. No one was home so he broke in and hid in a bedroom to await the return of the family. At 4:00 P.M. Charles and his six-year-old daughter Traci returned in a pickup truck and as they entered the house Knighton took them prisoner at gunpoint. He threatened Charles and Traci, saying, "I've killed four people in the last two weeks. I just killed two." Mrs. Jarrett arrived soon afterward, and he told them he needed to get away and if they tried to run "or do anything" he would kill them and "Traci would be the first to die." As he spoke he placed his hand on Traci's head and pointed the pistol at the back of her head, and asked, "Have you ever seen what one of these (a pistol) will do? I can get any of you faster than you can run." He had the radio and television turned on and monitored the progress in the investigation of the Day shootings, and when he heard one Day had not died he said he should go back for the other, but when he heard it was Coffier who had died he said he was satisfied.

Knighton had Mrs. Jarrett call her employment and say she would not be in at 5:00 P.M., and he had Mr. Jarrett turn away several customers for the automobile he had for sale. After 6:00 P.M. he changed into Charles' clothes and donned a short wig belonging to Mrs. Jarrett, then had Charles swallow a quantity of pills which made him groggy. They all got into the Jarretts' automobile with Knighton driving, and Charles had to lie down on the back seat. They stopped and filled the gas tank and then made several stops before arriving at Marshfield, and he kept the Jarretts in line with threats against Traci as well as against her parents. Knighton was on his way to the farmhouse of "Francis," and when they arrived they met Francis and a man called "Big J." In the farmhouse was a police scanner, and they kept track of the search for Knighton, but after several hours Knighton took another pistol and a shotgun, had the family get into their car, and drove to a café in Rolla. Knighton took the Jarretts in with him while Traci slept in the back seat, and Mrs. Jarrett managed to signal the waitress of their situation, then attacked Knighton with a steak knife. During the struggle male customers overpowered Knighton, disarmed him, and held him for the police.

Knighton made a deal to plead guilty to manslaughter in the killing of Coffier Day, but he was also charged with three counts of kidnapping, and Judge James H. Keet, Jr., sentenced him to serve three consecutive prison terms of ten years; these convictions and sentences were affirmed on appeal. In 1989 Knighton, after serving seventeen years, was continuing his prison time at a halfway house in Kansas City, Missouri, where he met seventeen-year-old Lawrence Brittain. The younger man was at the halfway house on probation for stealing an automobile, but in December he learned that he was about to be moved into a more restrictive prison setting. Knighton, then forty-eight years old, told Brittain that they would escape together, with his twenty-year-old girlfriend Ruth Renee Williams. They left the halfway house on January 6, 1990, stole a van, and drove to the Springfield home of Knighton's mother.

The next day they drove to Clinton, Missouri,

to the home of Brittain's friend Frank Merrifield, and they found Merrifield drinking with Ray Donahue and joined them. Merrifield and Donahue had been taking practice shots with their pistols, and Merrifield showed Knighton his pearl-handled .22-caliber pistol and encouraged him to take a few practice shots. Knighton shot Merrifield in the back of the head, killing him, and then he shot Donahue to death. They ransacked the house; searched the dead men's pockets for money, and stole the .22-caliber pistol and Donahue's .38-caliber pistol. They drove the stolen van in the direction of Tonkawa in Noble County, Oklahoma. When the gas tank was nearly empty they began looking for another vehicle to steal and pulled into the driveway of the Denney farmhouse.

Sixty-two-year-old Richard Denney came out as Knighton exited the van and asked directions to Bristow, and Denney started for his pickup truck to get a map. Knighton had told Brittain that he was to make the next kill, but the youngster froze and could not pull out the .22-caliber pistol so Knighton pulled the .38-caliber pistol, held it to Richard's head, and took him into the house. Richard's wife, sixty-four-year old Virginia, was seated at the kitchen table, and Richard sat with her. Knighton demanded beer but all they had was milk, and as the minutes passed Knighton said several times that he did not want to kill the Denneys, and Richard told him there was no need, they could have anything they wanted, and the Denneys could not report them as they had no telephone. Finally Knighton offered Brittain one more chance to shoot Richard, but he declined, so Knighton shot Richard in the chest once, then shot Virginia in the chest once, and thinking Richard might still be alive he shot him again, killing the couple. They stole $61 and started to leave, but Knighton sent Brittain back for the keys to Denney's pickup truck, and they drove into Texas.

When they reached Canadian they became concerned that the truck might be on a wanted list so they began driving slowly around a neighborhood looking for another to steal. Debbie Clark saw their suspicious actions, and after returning home and watching them pass her house for a third time, she called the sheriff's office. Hemphill County deputy sheriff Tennant stopped the truck, and when he was joined by Sheriff Billy Bowen they ordered the three occupants to step out. Sheriff Bowen then saw the .22-caliber pistol lying on the floorboard of the truck, and upon closer examination he found the .38-caliber pistol partially concealed on the seat, and the three were arrested. When he checked the registration on the truck and found the owner lived in Noble County, he called officers to investigate further, and the bodies of Richard and Virginia Denney were discovered.

The three prisoners were extradited to Oklahoma where Knighton and Brittain were charged with two counts of murder and Williams was charged as an accessory-after- the-fact. Brittain and Williams turned state's evidence and testified against Knighton. After pleading guilty Brittain received two concurrent sentences of life in prison without parole while Williams received two concurrent sentences of fifteen years. Knighton was tried in late 1990 and found guilty on two counts of first-degree murder, the jurors recommended the death penalty, and on December 17 trial judge Neal Beekman sentenced him to die by lethal injection.

His attorneys filed an appeal, which stayed the execution, but in 1996 the state Court of Criminal Appeals affirmed the judgment and sentence, and the U.S. Supreme Court denied certiorari. Knighton was denied post-conviction relief, and then his attorneys filed a writ of habeas corpus in the federal Tenth Circuit Court of Appeals, which was denied on June 14, 2003. On March 24, 2003, when the time had lapsed for further appeals, the state's Attorney General Drew Edmondson asked the Court of Criminal Appeals to set a date for Knighton's execution, and on April 11 the justices set the date at Tuesday, May 27. The state Board of Pardons and Parole met on May 20 and unanimously (voting 4–0) denied clemency, and Governor Brad Henry declined to intervene.

As the time neared for Knighton's execution he was moved from his death row cell to a cell near the injection room. Shortly after 6:00 P.M. the condemned man was escorted into the death chamber where he took his place on the gurney and was strapped down, and then his arms were strapped to arm extensions and a sheet was pulled over his body. A medical technician carefully inserted one intravenous cannula (IV) into the vein of each arm while the executioners were hidden from view behind a one-way mirrored window. Warden Mike Mullin confirmed by telephone with Governor Henry that the execution was to proceed, and the blinds were drawn open for the witnesses seated behind a one-way mirrored window. Knighton was asked if he had any last words, and he could hardly be heard when he thanked his attorneys and apologized for what he had done. He spoke to Sue Norton, the adopted daughter of the Denneys who had befriended him while in prison, and he told her, "I'll see you again, someday. God bless you." When Knighton concluded the warden announced, "Let the execution begin," and at 6:25 P.M. the executioners emptied their syringes into the tube leading to Knighton's arm: first sodium thiopental, a strong sedative; second pancuronium bromide to stop his respiration; and finally potassium chloride to stop his heart. Knighton became unconscious within seconds; his stomach heaved, his body shook and his face reddened as he snored several times, then he stopped breathing. At 6:32 P.M. he was pronounced dead.

Sources: *Knighton v. Gibson*: 293 F.3d 1165 (2002). *Knighton v. Oklahoma*: 519 U.S. 841 (1996). *Knighton v. State*: 912 P.2d 878 (1996). Noble County case CRF 90–1. *Oklahoman* (Oklahoma City): April 11, 2003. *Shawnee News-Star* (OK): May 28, 2003. *State* (MO) *v. Knighton*: 518 S.W.2d 674 (1975).

Charm, Kenneth C.
June 5, 2003

Michael Hill and his wife divorced in 1981, and his wife, who lived in Michigan, retained custody of their daughter while Hill moved to Lawton in Comanche County, Oklahoma. During the summer of 1993 fourteen-year-old Brandy Crystian Hill traveled to Lawton to spend several weeks with her father. On July 20 Hill's drinking buddy twenty-seven-year-old Kenneth Chad Charm, with his sixteen-year-old cousin Ronald Jessie, visited Michael. As Charm, an ex-convict with nine prior non-violent felony convictions, and Jessie were driving away they spotted Brandy walking along the street, and because she had met them previously they were able to lure her into their car under the ruse of taking her home.

They tied a rag around her neck to control her and drove to an isolated country road one mile west of Lawton, where they stopped and dragged Brandy into a pasture. Brandy begged them repeatedly to take her home and not hurt her, but each man raped her twice, and afterward Jessie asked Charm what they were going to do with Brandy. Jessie then tried to strangle her to death with the rag but he was not able to kill the girl so Charm took over, but he also failed to strangle Brandy to death. Jessie said he thought someone was coming so Charm continued to restrain Brandy while Jessie ran to the car and took out a sledgehammer. Brandy lay helpless when Jessie struck her on the head twice, but she was still moving. Charm said, "We're going to go to jail," grabbed the sledgehammer, and struck two more blows to her head, killing her, but any of these wounds would have proven fatal in time.

They fled, leaving Brandy where she died, and returned to the Hill home, hoping this would serve as an alibi. Two days later Brandy's body was discovered. It was not long before Charm and Jessie were arrested, and then Charm told the detectives that he had raped and murdered Brandy because he thought Michael had "snitched" on him and sent him to jail. He gave a full confession on a videotape, and then during a hearing on pre-trial motions he again admitted his guilt in court. He also admitted to robbing a convenience store several days after the murder, and during interrogations he threatened to kill his wife and said he had previously threatened to kill his former employer.

In late 1994 Charm was tried for the rape and murder of Brandy Hill. His defense was that he was too drunk to form the specific intent, but he was convicted on all counts, and the jurors recommended the death penalty. On October 6 Comanche County District Court Judge Roy D. Moore sentenced Charm to die by lethal injection for the murder, to serve fifty-four years imprisonment for kidnapping, and to serve one hundred twenty years imprisonment for rape, and eleven days later he was delivered to his death row cell. Jessie, probably because of his youth and cooperation, was sentenced to serve a life term without the possibilty of parole.

Charm's attorneys filed an appeal, which stayed the execution, but the Court of Criminal Appeals affirmed the judgment and sentence in 1996, and the following year the U.S. Supreme Court denied certiorari. His attorneys then filed an appeal for post-conviction relief, and it was denied in 1998. The attorneys next filed a writ of habeas corpus, but it was also denied. On April 1, 2003, after the U.S. Supreme Court denied Charm's final appeal, the state's Attorney General Drew Edmondson requested that the Court of Criminal Appeals set a date for Charm's execution, and ten days later the justices set the date at June 5. The state Board of Pardons and Parole met on May 22 and denied clemency, and Governor Brad Henry declined to intervene. The U.S. Supreme Court denied the last-minute appeals, based on Charm's low Intelligence Quotient (I.Q.), hours before the execution.

During his time on death row Charm was an uncooperative prisoner and was cited several times for fighting with other inmates and fashioning weapons. As the time neared for Charm's execution he was moved from his death row cell to a cell near the injection room. Shortly before 6:00 P.M. the condemned man was escorted into the death chamber where he took his place on the gurney and was strapped down, and then his arms were strapped to arm extensions and a sheet was pulled over his body. A medical technician carefully inserted one intravenous cannula (IV) into the vein of each arm while the executioners were hidden from view behind a one-way mirrored window. Warden Mike Mullin confirmed by telephone with Governor Henry that the execution was to proceed, and the blinds were opened for the witnesses seated behind a one-way mirrored window. Charm's witnesses included his spiritual adviser, his attorney and an investigator but none of his family attended. Brandy's father and her father's stepson witnessed the execution as well. Charm was asked if he had any last words and he said, "I want to apologize to the victim's family and to my family and ask their forgiveness." When he concluded Warden Mullin announced, "Let the execution begin," and the executioners emptied their syringes into the tube leading to Charm's arm: first sodium thiopental, a strong sedative; second pancuronium bromide to stop his respiration; and finally potassium chloride to stop his heart. Charm grimaced, closed his eyes, exhaled several deep breaths, and lay still. He was pronounced dead at 6:05 P.M.

Sources: *Charm v. Oklahoma*: 520 U.S. 1200 (1997). *Charm v. State*: 924 P.2d 754 (1996); 953 P.2d 47 (1998). Comanche County case CRF 93-259. *McAlester News—Capital and Democrat* (OK): April 10, 2003; May 23, 2003. *Tulsa World* (OK): September 24, 2000.

Gilbert, Lewis E.
July 1, 2003

In 1992 twenty-year-old Lewis Eugene Gilbert of Newcomerstown, Ohio, was sentenced to a prison term for child abuse after biting and bruising his three-month-old baby. He was released from prison in early August 1994, and when he returned home his wife slammed the door in his face.

On August 29 Gilbert, then twenty-two years old, and sixteen-year-old Eric Elliott were in Port Washington, Ohio. Elliott had stolen a .22-caliber pistol from his father, and they used that gun to kidnap seventy-nine-year-old Ruth Lucille Loader. The pair had entered her home through a side door, captured the elderly woman at gunpoint and rifled her purse and stole $40 before they threw it onto the kitchen table, jerked the phone cord from the wall, and left one dusty shoe print on the doorstep. They bound Loader, put her in the trunk of her car, and drove her to a secluded wooded area. Gilbert shot her in the head, killing her, and her body was never found.

They drove Loader's car to a rural area near Kingdom City in Callaway County, Missouri, and abandoned it near the farmhouse of eighty-six-year-old William and seventy-six-year-old Flossie Brewer when it became mired in mud. They went to the farmhouse, knocked on the door and asked to use the telephone to call a wrecker. They talked with the couple for a half hour before they decided to kill them and steal their car, so they captured the elderly couple at gunpoint, again using the .22-caliber pistol, bound their wrists with a telephone cord, and marched them to the wood storage room in the basement. Elliott then shot each of them in the head three times, killing them. They stole the Brewers' money, rifles, and car and drove toward Norman, Oklahoma. The bodies of the Brewers were discovered by relatives, and the search for their murderers and their car began.

On September 3, 1994, thirty-seven-year-old Roxanne Lynn Ruddell, who worked as a security guard in Norman in Cleveland County, Oklahoma, was fishing at Point 6 of Stanley Draper Lake not far from the city when she was seen by Gilbert and Elliott, who had abandoned the Brewers' car nearby. They captured Ruddell at gunpoint and marched her into a secluded wooded area where they had her sit against a tree. They went through her purse and took $3 and the keys to her pickup truck. Ruddell promised that she would not call the police if they did not hurt her, but this only made Gilbert mad. Elliott tied her wrists behind her back and then Gilbert shot her in the head three times and once in the back of her neck, killing her almost instantly. They drove Ruddell's truck into New Mexico and parked it off the road near Sante Fe, then walked a mile away to sleep.

Three days after Ruddell was murdered her truck was found abandoned near a culvert, the trail of the two murderers was followed, and they were surrounded and captured while still asleep. As soon as the two men were in jail they began confessing to their crime spree. They were indicted but never tried in Ohio. They were then extradited to Oklahoma and indicted on kidnapping, robbery, and murder charges. Elliott was convicted on all charges, and because of his youth, he was sentenced to serve a term of life in prison without parole. Gilbert was tried, and the jurors convicted him of all charges and recommended the death penalty. They were then tried in Missouri in June 1995, and after the jurors deliberated only five hours they were convicted of first-degree murder, and Gilbert was twice sentenced to die, but he was returned to Oklahoma where on January 9, 1996, District Court Judge Thomas A. Lucas sentenced him to die by lethal injection.

His Oklahoma attorneys filed an appeal, which stayed his execution until 1997 when the state Court of Criminal Appeals affirmed the judgment and sentence of the District Court and then denied post-conviction relief in 1998. The U.S. Supreme Court denied certiorari in both instances, and his attorneys then filed a writ of habeas corpus, but on September 3, 2002, the federal Tenth Circuit Court of Appeals denied him relief. Gilbert's final appeal to the U.S. Supreme Court was quickly denied so on April 28, 2003, Oklahoma's Attorney General Drew Edmondson requested the justices of the Court of Criminal Appeals to set a date for Gilbert's execution, and on May 8, 2003, they set the date for July 1. The state Board of Pardons and Parole held a hearing and denied clemency, and Governor Brad Henry declined to intervene. Last-minute, desperate appeals delayed the execution for only one hour.

As the time neared for Gilbert's execution he was moved from his death row cell to a cell near the injection room. Shortly before 7:00 P.M. the condemned man was escorted into the death chamber where he took his place on the gurney and was strapped down, and then his arms were strapped to arm extensions and a sheet was pulled over his body. A medical technician carefully inserted one intravenous cannula (IV) into the vein of each arm while the executioners were hidden from view behind a one-way mirrored window. Warden Mike Mullin confirmed by telephone with Governor Henry that the execution was to proceed, and the blinds were drawn open for the witnesses seated behind a one-way mirrored window, including members of the Ruddell and Brewer families. Gilbert was asked if he had any last words, and most of his statement was inaudible, but he said, "This is weird, but I'm actually looking forward to seeing God. I'm going home. Thank you, God." When he concluded Warden Mullin announced, "Let the execution begin," and the executioners emptied their syringes into the tube leading to Gilbert's arm: first sodium thiopental, a strong sedative; second pancuronium bromide to stop his respiration; and finally potassium chloride to stop his heart. At 7:11 P.M. all sign of life was absent and Gilbert was pronounced dead.

Sources: *Dayton News* (OH): July 1, 2003. Cleveland County case CF 94–1125. *Gilbert v. Mullin*: 3021 F.3d 1166 (2002). *Gilbert v. State*: 951 P.2d 98 (1997); 955 P.2d 727 (1998). *Kansas City Star* (MO): July 1, 2003. *Norman Transcript* (OK): July 2, 2003. *Oklahoman* (Oklahoma City): May 8, 2003.

Duckett, Robert D.
July 8, 2003

In 1982 eighteen-year-old Robert Don Duckett severely beat an eighty-five-year-old man during a robbery, but the man could not describe his attacker, and the case went cold. The following year Duckett beat and robbed a fifty-six-year-old man while robbing him, and this time he was arrested. He was charged with the robbery, he confessed to the earlier beating and robbery to prevent additional prosecutions, he was tried and convicted, and he was sentenced to serve ten years in the Oklahoma State prison at McAlester. His attorneys filed an appeal and the state Court of Criminal Appeals affirmed the judgment and sentence in 1985, and Duckett began to look for an opportunity to escape. In October 1987 the opportunity finally materialized and Duckett fled from the prison.

In early October 1988 Duckett was hitchhiking on an Oklahoma Interstate when he was picked up by fifty-three-year-old John E. Howard, who lived in an apartment in Oklahoma City. Howard had recently come to Oklahoma from New York to help his son run his convenience-store businesses, and he allowed Duckett to move in with him. Howard first got Duckett a job at the Oklahoma County fairgrounds but then hired him to work in one of his son's stores. On October 18 Howard told Duckett it was time for him to move out, so Duckett subdued Howard and tied his wrists and ankles with wire and then, first using the wooden stand from an ashtray and then a fireplace poker, he bludgeoned Howard to death. The curtains were open when he started beating Howard, but he stopped to close them and then continued to beat Howard. He stole $200 and took the keys to Howard's car and fled west. Howard's body was found, and there was blood splattered all over the room where he died, and there were smears on the floor as if he tried to crawl before he died or had been dragged through the blood.

When it was determined that his car had been stolen the police started searching for Duckett and for Howard's automobile. Two weeks later Duckett was arrested in Clear Creek, Arizona, still driving Howard's automobile, but he had switched the license plates with another car parked in Howard's apartment complex. In the car were found Duckett's bloody jeans, a bloody jacket, and a bank bag from the convenience store. Duckett told investigators that Howard had made homosexual advances toward him, they had exchanged blows, and that Howard was "on his feet and breathing" when he left. He said he had bound Howard's ankles and wrists only to keep Howard from assaulting him again. However, the autopsy found that Howard's ankle was broken, his skull had been fractured, his left eye had been ruptured, and he was left bound, which proved he had not "been on his feet and breathing" when Duckett left.

Duckett was extradited to Oklahoma County, tried in the district court in June 1989, and convicted of first-degree murder, and the jurors recommended the death penalty. On July 6 Judge James B. Blevins sentenced Duckett to die by lethal injection, and he arrived at his death row cell the following day. His attorneys filed an appeal, which stayed the execution, but in 1995 the state Court of Criminal Appeals affirmed the judgment and sentence of the District Court, and the following year the justices denied a rehearing. After Duckett's attorneys had exhausted state remedies they filed a writ of habeas corpus, but this was denied on September 4, 2002. After the U.S. Supreme Court denied Duckett's final appeal on April 28, 2003, Oklahoma's Attorney General Drew Edmondson requested that a date be set for the execution, and on May 30, 2003, the justices set the date at Tuesday, July 8. The Board of Pardons and Parole met in June and denied clemency, Governor Brad Henry declined to intervene, and Duckett instructed his attorneys not to file the usual last-minute flurry of appeals.

As the time neared for Duckett's execution he was moved from his death row cell to a cell near the injection room. Shortly after 6:00 P.M. the condemned man was escorted into the death chamber where he took his place on the gurney and was strapped down, and then his arms were strapped to arm extensions and a sheet was pulled over his body. A medical technician carefully inserted one intravenous cannula (IV) into the vein of each arm while the executioners were hidden from view behind a one-way mirrored window. Warden Mike Mullin confirmed by telephone with Governor Henry that the execution was to proceed, and the blinds were drawn open for the witnesses seated behind a one-way mirrored window, including four members of the Howard family. Duckett was asked if he had any last words and he said, "I just want to apologize and hope my family forgives me. I love them very much, and I hope they never forget that. Let's go!" When he concluded the warden announced, "Let the execution begin," and at 6:14 P.M. the executioners emptied their syringes into the tube leading to Duckett's arm: first sodium thiopental, a strong sedative; second pancuronium bromide to stop his respiration; and finally potassium chloride to stop his heart. At 6:16 P.M. all sign of life was absent and Duckett was pronounced dead.

Sources: *Duckett v. Mullin*: 306 F.3d 982 (2002). *Duckett v. State*: 711 P.2d 944 (1985); 919 P.2d 7 (1995); 922 P.2d 631 (1996). *Kansas City Star* (MO): July 9, 2003. Oklahoma County case CRF 88-6248. *Oklahoman* (Oklahoma City): May 30, 2003.

Toles, Bryan A.
July 22, 2003

Late on July 15, 1993, twenty-one-year-old Bryan Anthony Toles, sixteen-year-old David Flowers and teenager Casey Young got into a fight near the Honeymooners Bar in Lawton in Comanche County, Oklahoma, and fled on foot. They started walking to the house of their friend Herbie Foster, but it was a long distance and they tired. Shortly after midnight they reached the Franceschi home and decided to steal the Ford Mustang 5.0 parked in the driveway, but no one knew how to hot-wire a car so they decided they had to get the car keys. Young had an unloaded .22-caliber pistol with him, but he also had the ammunition, so he loaded the pistol and gave it to Toles. Young and Flowers hid around the corner and donned handkerchiefs over their faces while Toles knocked on the door. Fifteen-year-old Lonnie Franceschi answered the door, and Toles forced his way in at gunpoint, ordered Lonnie to "Get down and shut up," and began beating and kicking the youngster who was lying on the floor facedown with his hands behind his back.

Young and Flowers entered and started down the hallway toward the bedrooms where they were met by Lonnie's very petite mother Norma, who came out when she heard the commotion. Norma screamed for her thirty-nine-year-old husband Juan, and she continued toward her son. Juan met Young and Flowers in the hallway and they had a brief struggle before he joined his wife in the front room, and Toles then shot Juan in the arm. The couple retreated toward their bedroom with Toles following, and he pointed the pistol at Juan's head, but Norma grabbed his arm before he could fire. Toles broke free and Norma fled to the bedroom of their daughter, who was not home, while Toles shot Juan in the chest. Even though he was mortally wounded Juan struggled with Toles, smearing his blood all over Toles' clothes, but this gave Norma the chance to hide; she first tried the closet but then curled into the drawer beneath her daughter's water bed. After Juan collapsed Toles looked for Norma, but he never checked the drawer as it seemed too small to hold a person. As the three men left the home Toles stopped where Lonnie still lay facedown with his hands behind his back, placed the muzzle of the pistol six inches from the back of Lonnie's head, and shot him.

The three men then walked two blocks to another friend's house and got a ride to Foster's home. After they left the Franceschi home, Norma came out of hiding and heard her son in his bedroom crying and gasping for breath. She tried to telephone for help but the phone had been disabled, so she went to a neighbor's house and called for the police and paramedics. Juan died while being treated at the scene but the paramedics put Lonnie on life support and rushed him to the hospital. Later that day Lonnie was pronounced brain-dead, he was taken off life support, and he was allowed to die.

Toles gave his bloody clothes to a homeless girl and told her to burn them, called a family friend and told him he had shot two people, and then spent the night at the home of another friend. That afternoon he went to the corner of 17th Street and Gore and called his mother on the pay phone, where he was recognized and arrested. During his first interrogation he admitted being at the murder scene but tried to shift the blame to Young, but in three subsequent interrogations he confessed on videotape to being the shooter. David Flowers was also charged with the murders, convicted, and sentenced to serve two terms of life in prison. Casey Young was tried, convicted, and punished as a juvenile.

Toles was tried in the Comanche County District Court in September 1994, and he continued to shift the blame onto Young, but he was convicted of two counts of murder, conspiracy, and use of a firearm. On October 27 Judge Mark R. Smith sentenced him to die by lethal injection for the murder, and to twenty and ten years respectively on the other two charges. Four days later he was delivered to his death row cell while his attorneys filed an appeal, which stayed the execution. In 1997 the state Court of Criminal Appeals denied him relief, and the following year the U.S. Supreme Court denied certiorari. After his appeal for post-conviction relief was denied his attorneys filed a writ of habeas corpus, which was denied on October 26, 2001. When his final appeal to the U.S. Supreme Court was denied the state's Attorney General Drew Edmondson requested that the Court of Criminal Appeals set a date for the execution, and on June 2, 2003, the justices set the date for July 22, 2003. The state Board of Pardons and Parole denied clemency, and Governor Brad Henry declined to intervene.

As the time neared for Toles' execution he was moved from his death row cell to a cell near the injection room. At 5:45 P.M. the prisoners on death row began a protest and "send-off" by banging on their cell doors, and the noise was so loud it was difficult to hear Toles when he spoke his last words.

Shortly before 6:00 P.M. the condemned man was escorted into the death chamber where he took his place on the gurney and he was strapped down, and then his arms were strapped to arm extensions and a sheet was pulled over his body. A medical technician carefully inserted one intravenous cannula (IV) into the vein of each arm while the executioners were hidden from view behind a one-way mirrored window. Warden Mike Mullin confirmed by telephone with Governor Henry that the execution was to proceed, and the blinds were drawn open for the witnesses seated behind a one-way mirrored window, including Norma and other members of the Franceschi family, and across the injection room behind the clear glass window were the members of the Toles family and his spiritual adviser. Toles was asked if he had any last words, and he said, "I'd like to apologize to the victim's family and ask them for their forgiveness," and then to his family he said, "I love all y'all, thanks for coming. Take care of my mother. I'll see y'all later. We're all right." When he concluded Warden Mullin announced, "Let the execution begin," and the executioners emptied their syringes into the tube leading to Toles' arm: first sodium thiopental, a strong sedative; second pancuronium bromide to stop his respiration; and finally potassium chloride to stop his heart. Toles' eyelids began to flutter and he said, "I'm fixing to pass out, I think." At 6:10 P.M. all sign of life was absent and Toles was pronounced dead.

Comanche County case CRF 93-241. *Oklahoman* (Oklahoma City): June 2, 2003. *Toles v. Gibson*: 269 F.3d 1167 (2001). *Toles v. Oklahoma*: 524 U.S. 958 (1998). *Toles v. State*: 947 P.2d 180 (1997).

Willingham, Jackie L. July 24, 2003

On December 20, 1994, twenty-five-year-old Jackie Lee Willingham was working as a door-to-door perfume salesman when he stopped at a downtown Lawton, Oklahoma, office building and began working his way through the offices. When he came to the Arts for All, Inc., office of sixty-two-year-old Jayne Ellen Van Wey she refused to buy his perfume, but following his company's policy of "three 'Nos!'" he continued to pressure her. Van Wey became rude, both parties became vulgar, and Van Wey ordered Willingham to leave.

He continued on to other offices but soon noticed Van Wey entering a hallway restroom near her office. Still angry over her manner in rebuffing him, Willingham went into her office and took several credit cards from her purse, to make the attack he planned look like a robbery, and then he followed Van Wey into the restroom. He pulled her out of the stall and struck her in her face several times, and when she fought back Willingham struck her head against the wall. Van Wey collapsed to the floor and as she got to her hands and knees to rise he kicked her in the face with his boot "breaking her nose and busting her mouth," which knocked her unconscious onto her back, and then he fled. Van Wey was bleeding into her throat and she soon drowned in her own blood.

When her body was discovered the police were called, and they traced one of Willingham's brochures to his company and learned that one salesman, Kevin Longenecker, fit the description of their suspect. Detective John Whittington attended the afternoon sales meeting at a local restaurant and learned that Longenecker was not present, but Willingham was acting strangely and had a fresh scratch on his neck. When Willingham offered a ridiculous explanation for the scratch all of the salesmen were asked to go to the police station to investigate an attack on a woman, but no mention was made of murder. At the police station Willingham at first denied any knowledge of the attack on Van Wey, but after the blood on his boots was pointed out to him he confessed. He walked through the scene describing the attack, and when two of Van Wey's credit cards were found in the restaurant where Willingham was first confronted he told how he had taken them.

Willingham was charged with Van Wey's murder and tried in the Comanche County District Court in 1995, and his defense was limited to intent, which determined whether the killing was first- or second-degree murder. He was convicted of first-degree murder and on September 6 was sentenced to die by lethal injection, and on September 25 he was delivered to his death row cell.

His attorney filed an appeal, which stayed the execution. In 1997 the Oklahoma Court of Criminal Appeals affirmed the judgment and sentence, and denied him post-conviction relief in 1998; in both instances the U.S. Supreme Court denied certiorari. When all state judicial relief was exhausted his attorney filed a writ of habeas corpus with the federal Tenth Circuit Court of Appeals, and on June 17, 2002, the justices denied him relief. When the time had lapsed for further appeals the state's Attorney General Drew Edmondson requested the Court of Criminal Appeals to set a date for Willingham's execution, and on May 19 the justices set the date for July 24. The state Board of Pardons and Parole met on June 25 and voted three to two to recommend clemency and notified Governor Brad Henry, but on July 19 the governor declined to grant clemency. His attorney then filed an appeal with the U.S. Supreme Court requesting a stay of execution but on the morning of July 24 the U.S. Supreme Court justices refused to grant the stay.

As the time neared for Willingham's execution he was moved from his death row cell to a cell near the injection room. At 6:00 P.M. the condemned man was escorted into the death chamber where he took his place on the gurney and was strapped down, and then his arms were strapped to arm extensions and a sheet was pulled over his body. A medical technician carefully inserted one intravenous cannula (IV) into the vein of each arm while the executioners were hidden from view behind a one-way mirrored window. Warden Mike Mullin confirmed by telephone with Governor Henry that the execution was to proceed, and the blinds were drawn open for the victim's witnesses seated behind a one-way mirrored window and Willingham's witnesses in an opposite room behind clear glass. Willingham was asked if he had any last words and he said, "I want to apologize to the Van Wey family. I'm so sorry for the pain I've caused you. I hope by my death you find some closure and one day forgive me. For my family, I'm so sorry for this. I love you. OK, I'm ready." When he concluded the warden announced, "Let the execution begin," and at 6:07 P.M. the executioners emptied their syringes into the tube leading to Willingham's arm: first sodium thiopental, a strong sedative; second pancuronium bromide to stop his respiration; and finally potassium chloride to stop his heart. Willingham exhaled several deep breaths and closed his eyes, but as he felt the drugs entering his system he opened his eyes slightly. At 6:09 P.M. all sign of life was absent and Willingham was pronounced dead.

Sources: *Oklahoman* (Oklahoma City): June 2, 2003. *Willingham v. Mullin*: 296 F.3d 917 (2002). *Willingham v. State*: 947 P.2d 1074 (1997); PC 97-389 (1998).

McElmurry, Harold L., III
July 29, 2003

In mid–July 1999 eighty-year-old Robert Pendley, a paraplegic confined to a wheelchair, and his seventy-five-year-old wife, Rosa Vivien Pendley, hired a handyman to clear some the land west of their home, ten miles west of Eufaula in McIntosh County, Oklahoma, so they could have a better view of the sunset. When it was time to do the work the man brought along twenty-nine-year-old Harold Loyd McElmurry III, an ex-convict, and his wife Vickie, and the Pendleys put them to work doing yard work and odd jobs.

Two weeks later McElmurry thought he was about to be returned to prison for a probation violation, he had lost his job and was broke, and he was not able to register a car he had bought recently, but he was certain the Pendleys had money and he knew they had a car. The McElmurrys walked for two days to get to the Pendley home, traveling through the woods most of the time so they would not be seen, and they arrived on August 2. They visited with the Pendleys, and McElmurry stole a pair of scissors before they retired to the nearby woods to "shoot up on drugs." They discussed whether they should just rob or rob and kill the Pendleys and two hours later, after they made their decision, they returned to the Pendley home.

They found the couple in their garage, and Vickie lured Rosa into the backyard away from her husband. As soon as they were alone McElmurry stabbed Robert in the chest seven times with the scissors, and when the old man did not die he beat him over the head three times with a garden hoe, but the handle broke. Pendley had fallen out of his wheel chair and lay facedown on the floor so McElmurry took a garden rake and struck him on the back several times. Rosa began to run but Vickie grabbed her and choked her until her husband could join them, and he stabbed Rosa with the scissors and dragged her limp body into the garage. He saw that Robert was still alive so he picked up a three foot length of pipe and crushed his skull, killing him, and then he checked Rosa and found she was also still alive so he crushed her skull, killing her as well. The McElmurrys ransacked the house and stole $70, two pistols, some costume jewelry, and the Pendleys' twelve-year-old Oldsmobile and fled to Houston, Texas, and later that day drove into Mexico.

On August 5 the McElmurrys tried to cross back into the United States and were arrested at the Laredo, Texas, border crossing, and the following day McElmurry confessed in writing. They were extradited to Oklahoma and charged with two counts of murder. Harold's trial was scheduled to begin on June 12, 2000, but at 10:15 P.M. on June 11 he managed to slip between the bars on the window to his cell and drop twelve feet to the ground. During the early morning hours he was spotted in front of the Eufaula City Hall and arrested by Police Chief Randy Johnson, so his trial was not delayed. McElmurry was convicted of two counts of murder, and on June 16 McIntosh County District Court Judge Steven W. Taylor sentenced him to die by lethal injection; ten days later he was delivered to his death row cell at the prison in McAlester. Vickie McElmurry was tried separately because of their adversarial defenses, but she was convicted and sentenced to serve two life terms in prison.

On June 16, 2002, McElmurry wrote to Attorney General Drew Edmondson asking for an execution date and said, "There is no question as to my guilt and I feel competent to make this decision." His attorneys argued on his behalf during the automatic appeal process, a requirement in all death sentence cases, but on December 2, 2002, the Oklahoma Court of Criminal Appeals affirmed the judgment and sentence of the District Court. The rehearing was conducted on February 28, 2003, and McElmurry again waived further appeals and would not allow his attorneys to file a writ of certiorari with the U.S. Supreme Court nor a writ of habeas corpus with the federal Tenth Circuit Court of Appeals. On May 29, when the time had passed for McElmurry to recant his waiver and file an appeal, Attorney General Edmondson requested the Court of Criminal Appeals to set a date for his execution, and on June 2, 2003, the justices set the date for July 29. The state Board of Pardons and Parole and the governor did not intervene.

As the time neared for McElmurry's execution he was moved from his death row cell to a cell near the injection room. Shortly before 6:00 P.M. the condemned man was escorted into the death chamber where he took his place on the gurney and was strapped down, and then his arms were strapped to arm extensions and a sheet was pulled over his body. A medical technician carefully inserted one intravenous cannula (IV) into the vein of each arm while the executioners were hidden from view behind a one-way mirrored window. Warden Mike Mullin confirmed by telephone with Governor Henry that the execution was to proceed, and the blinds were raised for the victim's witnesses seated behind a one-way mirrored window. Four news reporters sat in an opposite room behind clear glass. McElmurry glanced at the reporters and then stared at the ceiling as he was asked if he had any last words, and he said, "I'd like to say I'm sorry to the Pendleys. I hope they can forgive me." When he concluded the warden announced, "Let the execution begin," and at 6:04 P.M. the executioners emptied their syringes into the tube leading to McElmurry's arm: first sodium thiopental, a strong sedative; second pancuronium bromide to stop his respiration; and finally potassium chloride to stop his heart. At 6:06 P.M. all sign of life was absent and McElmurry was pronounced dead.

Sources: *Ardmoreite* (OK): June 12, 2000. *McElmurry v. State*: 60 P.3d 4 (2002). McIntosh County case CF 99–153. *Oklahoman* (Oklahoma City): June 2, 2003. *Tri-City Herald* (Kennewick, WA): July 29, 2003.

Darks, Tyrone P.
January 13, 2004

Tyrone Peter Darks and Sherry Goodlow were married in February 1992, separated in July 1992, and a divorce followed. Over the six months of marriage and the two years that followed Darks abused Goodlow often, and he had a police record of domestic abuse arrests. The couple had a son, Scott, and it was then that the nature and frequency of the abuse increased. In the divorce decree the court awarded Goodlow custody of Scott while Darks had been granted visitation privileges, but by early August 1994 Darks' visitation privileges had been revoked and protection orders had been filed by both parties. Twenty-nine-year-old Darks telephoned Goodlow's father and told him that his daughter should "get her insurance papers up to date because I'm going to put a cap in her," meaning he was going to shoot his twenty-six-year-old ex-wife.

On the afternoon of August 7 Goodlow and her two-year-old son went to church with friends and after 2:00 P.M. they went shopping, but Goodlow declined an invitation to dinner saying she just wanted to go home. At 2:52 P.M. Goodlow made a frantic call to the police saying Darks had just taken their son by force. The dispatcher told her to go to Darks' home and an officer would meet her there to reclaim Scott, but seventeen minutes later Goodlow called the police again and was told the officer had been delayed. When Sergeant Ken Davis arrived at 3:27 P.M. Darks' mother said neither Goodlow nor her son nor Scott had been at the house.

While Davis was at Darks' home Jamey Harrison, living at S.E. 89th and Westminister Road east of Lake Stanley Draper, saw Goodlow's white Ford Mustang stop at a stop sign, and Darks' car pulled into his driveway and then backed out quickly to follow Goodlow's car. Ten minutes later he heard gunshots, which he thought might be firecrackers exploding near Lake Stanley Draper. Mark Folks was working on his pickup truck in the driveway of his home at 97th and Westminister Road when he heard dogs barking and went to investigate, and he found Goodlow's white Mustang parked in his driveway, but as he approached she backed out and sped away while screaming. Folks followed in his pickup truck, found tire tracks in the grass leading off the road at Westminister and Stanley Draper Drive, and found the Mustang in the heavy brush with the engine running and the emergency flasher lights activated. He returned home, and at 3:55 P.M. he called the police, but he then returned near the Mustang and called out but got no response. He left to make another call for help, and then with his neighbor Mrs. Heinken, wife of a police officer, he returned to the Mustang and found the dead body of Goodlow still wearing her seatbelt and bloodied, lying across the seat.

The police arrived quickly, and after they confirmed that Goodlow was dead they began their murder investigation. After 5:30 P.M. they dispatched officers to Darks' home and found him and Scott there. Darks told the officers that he had picked up his son at 2:30 at his ex-wife's insistence, then gave her money at 4:00 P.M. when she came to his home, she left and he did not see her again. He said that he and Scott went to the mall to shop and then went to his girlfriend's home, and he agreed to go to the police station for further questioning. At the police station he told the officers the same story, but added that Goodlow "got what she deserved" and that they could never place him at the murder scene because they had no gun and no fingerprints. Darks was arrested, and while in a cell with Richard Maytubby and other inmates he bragged about killing Goodlow, describing how he had taken his son from her after she left the church. He said Goodlow had followed him to Stanley Draper Lake to reclaim their son, where he had shot her through the open window of her car "twice in the head and three or four times in the back" with his .38-caliber pistol, and the car rolled off the road. The autopsy showed that Goodlow had been shot twice in the head, once in the back and once in the arm with a .38-caliber handgun, and three spent bullets were recovered from her body and one from the car's interior.

Darks was charged with murdering Goodlow, tried in October 1995, and convicted of first degree murder, and the jurors recommended the death penalty. On November 20, 1995, Cleveland County District Court Judge William C. Hetherington sentenced Darks to die by lethal injection, and he was delivered to his death row cell on December 4. Darks' attorneys filed an appeal, which stayed the execution, and while the appeal was pending they filed a writ of habeas corpus which was denied on June 24, 1997. The state Court of Criminal Appeals affirmed the judgment and sentence of the District Court in 1998 and denied post-conviction relief the same year. A federal judge overturned the conviction in early 2001 but the Tenth Circuit Court of Appeals reversed that decision in April 2001. Another writ of habeas corpus was filed. On April 12, 2003, the federal Tenth Circuit Court of Appeals denied relief, and the U.S. Supreme Court denied certiorari. After the final appeal was denied by the U.S. Supreme Court in October 2003 the state's Attorney General Drew Edmondson, on October 20, requested the Court of Criminal Appeals to set a date for Darks' execution, and the justices set the date at January 13, 2004. The state Board of Pardons and Parole met on December 12 and denied clemency, and Governor Brad Henry declined to intervene. A last-minute appeal to the Tenth Circuit Court of Appeals resulted in a stay of execution, but this order was vacated by the U.S. Supreme Court so expeditiously that there was no delay in the execution protocol.

In 2001 Darks had forged letters to look like a sworn affidavit from a recently executed death row inmate claiming to be Goodlow's murderer, and he sent them to the *Daily Oklahoman* newspaper, but they were easily discredited. While Darks sat on death row he tried to claim up to one million dollars from the compensation fund for the victims of the September 11, 2001, catastrophe, asserting that his wife was a businesswoman earning over four million dollars a year and that she had disappeared after the World Trade Center towers collapsed. He was charged with fraud in January 2003, tried and convicted in a federal court, and sentenced to serve one year in prison and two years of supervised release.

On Tuesday morning, the day of his execution, Darks was moved from his death row cell to a holding cell in H Unit near the injection room. Shortly before 6:00 P.M. the condemned man was escorted into the death chamber where he took his place on the gurney and was strapped down, and then his arms were strapped to arm extensions and a sheet was pulled over his body. A medical technician carefully inserted one intravenous cannula (IV) into the vein of each arm while the executioners were hidden from view behind a one-way mirrored window. Warden Mike Mullin confirmed by telephone with Governor Henry that the execution was to proceed, and the blinds were raised for the Goodlow family witnesses seated behind a one-way mirrored window. Darks, with tears running from his eyes down the side of his head, was asked if he had any last words, and he lifted his head and looked to his family behind the clear glass of the opposite witness room and said, "Y'all take care of yourselves. Do what you can for Scott. I'll see y'all later. This is it. It's over. Praise the Lord. Praise God. Whooo!" but made no remarks to the Goodlow family. When he concluded the warden announced, "Let the execution begin," and at 6:06 P.M. the executioners emptied their syringes into the tube leading to Darks' arm: first sodium thiopental, a strong sedative; second pancuronium bromide to stop his respiration; and finally potassium chloride to stop his heart. At 6:08 P.M. all sign of life was absent and Darks was pronounced dead.

Sources: *Ardmoreite* (OK): January 17, 2003. Cleveland County case CF 94–1024. *Darks v. Mullin*: 327 F.3d 1001 (2003); 124 S. Ct. 433 (2003). *Darks v. State*: 954 P.2d 152 (1998); 954 P.2d 169 (1998). *Darks v. Ward*: 116 F.3d 489 (1997). *McAlester News-Capital and Democrat* (OK): January 14, 2004. *Oklahoman* (Oklahoma City): November 4, 2003.

Cleary, Norman R.
February 17, 2004

Norman Richard Cleary had been convicted of several first-degree burglaries, and he spent a term in prison for assault and battery with a dangerous weapon, robbery, and burglary when he broke into the home of an eighty-seven-year-old woman and attacked her, but he was released on parole in 1991.

On December 6 twenty-five-year-old Cleary and Kenneth "KC" Chandler were driving around Tulsa, Oklahoma, when they decided to burglarize a house. Their passenger, Jack Bell, refused to take part and was dropped off. They began scouting the upper-class neighborhood of Maple Ridge in Tulsa, Tulsa County, Oklahoma, for a home to burglarize and had knocked on several doors, but they did not find the opportunity they wanted. When forty-four-year-old Wanda Neafus, a housekeeper, answered the knock, a gun fell from Chandler's jacket pocket, so the two men decided they would have to take her prisoner and rob this home. Cleary led Neafus around the house, and they ended in the basement where Cleary found a safe. When Neafus insisted she did not know the combination he pushed her into a chair and shot her five times in the face, neck and head, killing her; several of the shots were point-blank. Chandler fled as soon as he realized that Cleary was going to shoot Neafus, and as Cleary followed he took Neafus' purse and a distinctive cane her employer had purchased from the Smithsonian Institution.

Neafus' dead body was found later that day, the police were called, and the homicide investigation began. Meanwhile, Cleary confessed to his girlfriend it was he who had killed the housekeeper, and later she would testify against him. Cleary and Chandler were arrested, lodged in the Tulsa jail, and charged with the murder of Neafus and with burglary. They were tried separately in the Tulsa County District Court. Chandler was convicted and sentenced to serve a term of life in prison. Cleary was tried in early 1993 and convicted of first-degree murder, and the jurors recommended the death penalty, so on February 26 District Court Judge B. R. Beasley sentenced Cleary to die by lethal injection.

His attorneys filed an appeal at the state level, which stayed the execution, and while it was pending they filed an appeal with the federal Tenth Circuit Court of Appeals, but the justices denied him relief in an unpublished opinion on January 18, 1995. The state Court of Criminal Appeals affirmed the judgment and sentence of the District Court in 1997, and the U.S. Supreme Court denied certiorari in 1998. The federal Tenth Circuit Court of Appeals denied a writ of habeas corpus in 2003, and the U.S. Supreme Court denied certiorari the same year. After the U.S. Supreme Court denied Cleary's final appeal, state's Attorney General Drew Edmondson, on December 1, 2003, requested that the Court of Criminal Appeals set a date for his execution, and on January 5, 2004, the justices set the date at February 17. The state Board of Pardons and Parole met on February 13 and denied clemency, and Governor Brad Henry declined to intervene.

Cleary was a troublesome inmate while in prison, and on one occasion he stabbed a fellow convict, but the man recovered. On the morning of his execution Cleary was moved from his death row cell to a holding cell in H Unit near the injection room. Shortly before 6:00 P.M. the condemned man was escorted into the death chamber where he took his place on the gurney and was strapped down, and then his arms were strapped to arm extensions and a sheet was pulled over his body. A medical technician carefully inserted one intravenous cannula (IV) into the vein of each arm while the executioners were hidden from view behind a one-way mirrored window. Warden Mike Mullin confirmed by telephone with Governor Henry that the execution was to proceed, and the blinds were raised for the victim's witnesses seated behind a one-way mirrored window. Across the room in another witness room behind clear glass sat Cleary's parents, sister, two friends and his two spiritual advisers.

Cleary was asked if he had any last words, and he first looked at the mirrored window and said, "Again, I'd like to apologize to my victim's family, to tell them how sorry I am for the pain I've caused them. I hope that someday they can forgive me." He then turned to look at the clear glass window and said, "For my family, just thank you for loving me. Thank you and God bless you," and each responded, "I love you." When the exchange concluded the warden announced, "Let the execution begin," and at 6:11 P.M. the executioners emptied their syringes into the tube leading to Cleary's arm: first sodium thiopental, a strong sedative; second pancuronium bromide to stop his respiration; and finally potassium chloride to stop his heart. At 6:14 P.M. all sign of life was absent and Cleary was pronounced dead.

Sources: *Cleary v. Mullin*: F-92-1234 (1995); 62 Fed. Appx. 243 (2003); 124 S. Ct 825 (2003). *Cleary v. Oklahoma*: 118 S. Ct 1528 (1998). *Cleary v. State*: 942 P.2d 736 (1997). *McAlester News-Capital and Democrat* (OK): February 13, 2004; February 17, 2004. Tulsa County case CF 91-5395.

Brown, David J.
March 9, 2004

In 1983 twenty-eight-year-old David Jay Brown married Lee Ann McGuire but it lasted only six months before they divorced, and then over the next three years Brown repeatedly harassed the McGuire family with threats of violence. In 1983 Brown was shot by Lee Ann's father Eldon Lee McGuire, a captain of the Chickasha Fire Department, during one particularly threatening confrontation, but Brown recovered and McGuire was not charged.

In 1986 Brown armed himself with a rifle and went to the Chickasha, Oklahoma, beauty salon owned by his ex-wife — The Clipper Ship — and took twelve people hostage, including employees and customers. He made threats and brandished the rifle in a threatening manner before finally firing it into an empty chair. He was arrested and charged with twelve counts of kidnapping and four other felony counts and faced the possibility of one hundred fifty years in prison, but he made bail and fled to Louisville, Kentucky, where he hid for a year.

He returned in 1987 and again began harassing the McGuire family, but this time he also demanded that they drop the charges still pending against him, which Brown believed were concocted by Lee Ann's father. He proved, during a telephone call, that he had been stalking the family in their Norge, Oklahoma, home, and he left an obscene note in their woodpile. In January Brown called the McGuire house and told Eldon, "You all's time is up and you will pay for what you did to me."

Still they refused to drop the charges so late on the evening of February 19, 1988, Brown went to the McGuire home and confronted Lee Ann's father. Brown brought a 9-mm automatic pistol with eighteen rounds in the magazine, and he shot at McGuire until the gun was empty. McGuire was hit eight times, including once in the index, middle and ring fingers of the left hand, making it impossible for him to use the lever action of his rifle, and twice in the head, and one of these was a "hard contact wound" meaning the barrel of the pistol was pressed hard against the back of his skull. Brown returned to his El Reno motel room for his belongings and then fled to Louisville, Kentucky.

The following day, when McGuire did not answer his telephone, Lee Ann and McGuire's mother went to the home, forced entry, and found McGuire's body lying in the south end of the living room. The police were called, and they found 9-mm shell casings scattered around the living room and a lever-action rifle lying on the floor, which had been fired once, and the lever was partially pulled. The police began looking for Brown, and on March 3 he was arrested in Kentucky. A 9-mm pistol was found in his possession and later proved to be the murder weapon, and he was extradited to Oklahoma where he was charged with murdering McGuire. He claimed that he had gone to the McGuire home and had been invited in, but McGuire hit him from behind knocking him down, kicked him, and threatened to kill him. Brown said as he ran to the front door McGuire fired a shotgun at him, so he pulled his pistol and fired back, killing McGuire in self-defense. He was tried in the Grady County District Court in late 1988, the jurors rejected his claim of self-defense, he was convicted of first-degree murder, and the jurors recommended the death penalty. On January 3, 1989, District Court Judge James R. Winchester sentenced Brown to die by lethal injection, and he was delivered to his death row cell the same day.

His attorneys filed an appeal, which stayed the execution but the state's Court of Criminal Appeals affirmed the judgment and sentence of the district court in 1994, and the U.S. Supreme Court denied certiorari the same year. His appeal for post conviction relief was denied in 1997, his first writ of habeas corpus filed with the federal Tenth Circuit Court of Appeals was denied in 2001, and on December 3, 2001, the U.S. Supreme Court denied certiorari. On January 8, 2002, his date of execution was set for February 5, but when Brown asked to allow his attorneys to withdraw, his request was granted and a stay was issued. Brown's new attorney then filed a new writ of habeas corpus petition, which was denied on April 23, 2002. A date of execution was requested, and on May 6 it was set for June 25. The state Board of Pardons and Parole met on June 11 and recommended clemency to Governor Frank Keating, but on June 18 the governor denied clemency. Brown then filed a request for a stay of execution, and it was granted on July 17, 2002. On March 26 the following year the Oklahoma Court of Criminal Appeals granted his request for an evidentiary hearing and remanded the case to the Grady County District Court, where the judge found no error and sent the case back to the appeals court. On January 6, 2004, the Oklahoma Court of Criminal Appeals set the date for Brown's execution at March 9. Governor Brad Henry declined to grant clemency, and Brown's final emergency appeal to the U.S. Supreme Court was denied at 5:43 P.M. on the day of his execution.

On the morning of his execution Brown was moved from his death row cell to a holding cell in H Unit near the injection room. Shortly before 6:00 P.M. the condemned man was escorted into the death chamber where he took his place on the gurney and was strapped down, and then his arms were strapped to arm extensions and a sheet was pulled over his body. A medical technician carefully inserted one intravenous cannula (IV) into the vein of each arm while the executioners were hidden from view behind a one-way mirrored window. Warden Mike Mullin confirmed by telephone with Governor Henry that the execution was to proceed, and the accordion blinds were raised for the victim's witnesses seated behind a one-way mirrored window, including two of McGuire's cousins.

Brown was asked if he had any last words and he said, "All I want to know is ... I want to tell y'all people that the state and federal courts that works on our cases, specifically on our appeals, are nothing but a bunch of morons. Specifically, the Oklahoma Court of Criminal Appeals and the U.S. Court of Appeals for the Tenth Circuit. My records prove this. That's it. Let's go." The warden then announced, "Let the execution begin," and at 6:04 P.M. the executioners emptied their syringes into the tube leading to Brown's arm: first sodium thiopental, a strong sedative; second pancuronium bromide to stop his respiration; and finally potassium chloride to stop his heart. At 6:07 P.M. all sign of life was absent and Brown was pronounced dead.

Sources: *Brown v. Gibson*: 7 Fed. Appx. 894 (2001); 122 S. Ct. 650 (2001). *Brown v. Oklahoma*: 115 S. Ct. 517 (1994).*Brown v. State*: 871 P.2d 56 (1994); 933 P.2d 316 (1997). *In Re: Brown*: 122 S. Ct. 2652 (2002). Grady County case CRF 88–45. *McAlester News-Capital and Democrat* (OK): January 6, 2004; March 9, 2004.

Le, Hung T.
March 23, 2004

During the fall of Saigon in early 1975 Hung Thanh Le and Hong Hai Nguyen fled from Vietnam and first met while living in a Thailand refugee camp. In the mid-1980s Le emigrated to the United States and settled in Cleveland, Ohio, where he worked as a machinist, while Nguyen emigrated to Oklahoma City, Oklahoma, where he and his wife, Thuy Tiffany Nguyen, operated a beauty salon. On July 4, 1992, twenty-five-year-old Le flew to Oklahoma City to visit the Nguyens, and then returned to Cleveland where his family joined him in September 1992.

After Le lost his job in October he returned to Oklahoma City, and on November 2 he visited the Nguyens and told them he was then returning to Cleveland to prepare for a move to Texas, where he had a new job. Le visited again on November 9, and the Nguyens invited him to stay with them when he claimed he had lost his wallet. The following day Le accompanied the Nguyens on a shopping trip, and Hong Hai gave Le $200. On November 11 Le went with the couple to their beauty salon, borrowed their car and returned to their home. Using the house key on the car's key ring he entered and stole a stereo and karaoke equipment which he packaged and mailed to himself in Cleveland, and he returned the car that afternoon. The Nguyens noticed the missing equipment and searched the house, but Le denied any knowledge of the theft and said he was also missing an expensive bag, but there was no sign of forced entry and the Nguyens were suspicious.

Early on November 12, 1992, Le snuck up behind thirty-four-year-old Hong Hai Nguyen while he sat on his couch watching television and struck him on the head with an eighteen-inch metal bar from a weightlifting set. Nguyen called to his wife, who was still in bed, that Le was killing him, and after she called the police she rushed into the living room. Le dropped the steel bar but Nguyen picked it up and swung at Le, striking Le on the forearm, and when Thuy said she had called the police Nguyen dropped the bar. Le then went into the kitchen and returned with a butcher knife with a thirteen-inch blade and a meat cleaver with a seven-inch blade, and he closed in on Nguyen while telling him, "Don't make me do it," but without hesitation Le stabbed Nguyen with the butcher knife. Thuy begged Le to stop so he next attacked her with the butcher knife, inflicting wounds to her head and defensive wounds to her hands. Le told Thuy she should not have called the police, he was going to kill her, and that he was being paid $20,000 to kill them both. He then offered to stop if she would write him a check for $20,000. Nguyen had collapsed onto the coffee table, and when Thuy hesitated and said they did not have that much money, Le began to hack and slash at the back of Hong Hai's neck and head with the meat cleaver. Thuy ran out the back door and met the ambulance as it arrived, and she pleaded with the paramedics to hurry inside and save her husband.

While the paramedics were treating Thuy's wounds, and waiting for the police to arrive, Le stole Nguyen's car keys and the key to his safety deposit box and drove off in the Nguyens' automobile. One paramedic, with two police officers who had just arrived, went in to treat Nguyen and found him writhing on the floor and crying out, "Help me! Help me! I'm dying. I'm dying." Nguyen had wounds to his chest, neck, head, abdomen, and arms, and he lapsed into shock while en route to the hospital, where he soon went into full cardiac arrest and died from a massive loss of blood.

After Le fled he drove south to a farm pond and washed off the blood, then changed clothes and drove to the bank. He used the stolen key to open the Nguyens' safety deposit box and stole $36,000 in cash and a diamond ring. He abandoned the stolen car in the bank parking lot, with the Nguyens' blood and Le's fingerprints inside, and took a taxicab downtown where he shopped for clothes and bought a first-class airline ticket to Cleveland in the name of Paul Koring, and then he spent the night in Oklahoma City. The following day Le went to the Remington Park horse-racing track and made a few bets, then went to the Will Rogers World Airport to fly home, but he was recognized by a police officer and arrested. He claimed to be Paul Koring, but the officers found in his possession Nguyen's wallet and brief case, safety deposit box key, car keys, and $34,966.37. Le was taken to the police station, and his interrogation was videotaped. He admitted attacking Nguyen but said he did not intend to kill him but only knock him unconscious to steal the safety deposit box key. He insisted he only got the knife and cleaver to defend himself from Nguyen when his victim picked up the bar with which Le had first struck him. Le was charged with murder, and on October 18, 1993, he entered a "blind plea" of guilty and was scheduled to be sentenced on December 27, but he hired new attorneys, which postponed sentencing, and on their advice he withdrew his plea on October 28, 1994.

His trial began in September 1995, and the defendant claimed that he lent Nguyen $10,000 in July 1992 to start up a joint business venture — a machine shop — and that Nguyen did not start the business and refused to refund the money, but the victim's wife, Thuy Tiffany Nguyen, testified that Le had never loaned money to her husband and there was never an agreement to start a joint business. Police investigators testified that Le had never mentioned a loan nor the machine shop business during interviews, but had said he knew Nguyen had $10,000 and he had come to Oklahoma City with the intention of robbing the Nguyens. The jury convicted Le of first-degree murder and during the penalty phase recommended the death sentence. On November 21 Oklahoma County Judge Nancy L. Coates sentenced Le to die by lethal injection, and he was delivered to his death row cell on December 4.

His attorneys filed an appeal, which stayed the execution, but in 1997 the state Court of Criminal Appeals affirmed the judgment and sentence of the District Court, and the justices denied post-conviction relief the following year. When all state judicial relief was exhausted his attorneys filed a writ of habeas corpus with the federal Tenth Circuit Court of Appeals, but in 2002 the justices denied him relief. The U.S. Supreme Court denied Le's final appeal on October 6, 2003, and Le's execution was scheduled for January 6, but Governor Brad Henry granted a thirty-day stay, and when the state Court of Criminal Appeals met on February 6, 2004, the justices set Le's execution date at February 26. Governor Brad Henry then granted another thirty-day reprieve to March 23 when the Vietnamese government requested that the governor review the case again and grant clemency. On December 9 the state Board of Pardons and Parole had voted unanimously to recommend commutation of Le's death sentence to life in prison, but on January 28 Governor Henry had denied clemency, and after further review and consideration he declined to intervene.

On the morning of his execution Le was moved from his death row cell to a holding cell in H Unit near the injection room. Shortly before 6:00 P.M. the condemned man was escorted into the death chamber where he took his place on the gurney and was strapped down, and then his arms were strapped to arm extensions and a sheet was pulled over his body. A medical technician carefully inserted one intravenous cannula (IV) into the vein of each arm while the executioners were hidden from view behind a one-way mirrored window. Warden Mike Mullin confirmed by telephone with Governor Henry that the execution was to proceed, and at 6:01 P.M. the accordion blinds were raised for the witnesses seated behind a one-way mirrored window, but none of Nguyen's family attended. Le was asked if he had any last words and he said,

> Thank you all for being here today. I would like to apologize to both families. I can't take back what happened. I hope my death will help replace the hatred for each other. Instead of hatred, love each other. Life is short. If you see a stranger on the street and he needs help, please help him with a smile. I wish I could take back the things I have done, but it's impossible. We all make mistakes in our lives. To my parents, tell them I love them very much. I'll be home soon. I'll see you in Heaven when you get there. I will be there first. If you see a stranger on the street and he needs help, help him. I wish I could take back the thing I had done, but it's impossible. We all make mistakes in our lives.

When Le concluded the warden announced, "Let the execution begin," and at 6:02 P.M. the executioners emptied their syringes into the tube leading to Le's arm: first sodium thiopental, a strong sedative; second pancuronium bromide to stop his respiration; and finally potassium chloride to stop his heart. Le closed his eyes, exhaled deeply, the color drained from his face, and at 6:04 P.M. all sign of life was absent and Le was pronounced dead.

Sources: *Le v. Mullin*: 311 F.3d 1002 (2002). *Le v. State*: 947 P.2d 535 (1997); 953 P.2d 52 (1998). *McAlester News-Capital and Democrat* (OK): February 6, 2004; March 24, 2004. Oklahoma County case CF 92-6838.

Bryan, Robert L.
June 8, 2004

In early 1989 forty-nine-year-old Robert Leroy Bryan solicited an undercover police officer to kidnap an Elk City banker. Bryan planned to force the banker to sign a number of fraudulent documents and promissory notes, and then the undercover officer was supposed to murder him and dump the body in a stand of trees one quarter-mile from Bryan's home. Bryan was arrested but he was found incompetent to stand trial, and in March 1989 he was sent to the Eastern State Hospital for evaluation and treatment, declared competent in 1990, and released.

On September 6, 1993, Bryan, then fifty-two years old, arranged to rent a 1986 Lincoln Town Car "because it had a large trunk," and he picked it up two days later. Early on Saturday, September 11, a neighbor helped Robert change a tire on his rented car and noticed a .22-caliber rifle in the trunk. Later Robert stopped at the Elk City Homeland grocery store and bought a lavender chrysanthemum plant. That evening Robert drove to the home of his sixty-nine-year-old aunt, Mildred Inabell Bryan, known by all as Inabell, near Sweetwater in Roger Mills County, Oklahoma, and he put her at ease by bringing her a plant.

Inabell's daughter Linda Daley tried to telephone her mother on September 12 and 13, and when Inabell did not answer Daley called her mother's neighbor, Don Walker. On the evening of September 13 Walker made two welfare checks, taking his wife along on the second visit, and they found rugs disturbed, the living room curtains open, the bed unmade, Inabell's diary lying next to her chair, and tire tracks later determined to be from a Lincoln automobile, but after they checked everywhere on the property they could find no sign of Inabell. When Walker returned the next day he noticed Inabell's suitcase and a small overnight case containing her medicines, and the police were notified. Family and friends joined the officers in several searches of the area, and during one search Linda Daley noticed the fresh lavender chrysanthemum plant at her home.

On September 16 the search area was widened to include the Bryan property and adjoining properties near Elk City in Beckham County, twenty-five miles from Inabell's home, and Inabell's dead body was found lying near a combine in a stand of trees one quarter-mile from the Bryan home. Her head was covered with a pillowcase and duct tape was wrapped loosely around her neck, and she had been shot in the forehead once with a .22-caliber bullet. The area was checked for evidence, and officers found more duct tape and what appeared to be a contrived duct-tape-and-cloth gag. They also found a Homeland grocery store receipt for a plant and a large crushed mushroom with a clear tire imprint, which later proved to match the right rear tire of the rental car.

After the body was found officers asked to search the Bryan house and they were given permission, and a .22-caliber rifle and boxes of ammunition were found along with several expended shells. A pair of Robert's overalls with a spent shell casing in the pocket was discovered, and a roll of duct tape matching the tape at the murder scene was found in his bedroom. Officers also found several blank checks and five checks from Inabell's personal bank account with her signature on four and her forged signature on the fifth, made payable to Robert, and Robert had many handwritten documents from Inabell conveying property to Robert or agreeing to pay him millions of dollars as the result of an investment in his failed businesses. Inabell's checkbook was found burned in a can outside the Bryan home. Robert had returned the car on September 13 but he did not have the cash to pay for the car rental, so he showed a check for $1680 payable to him from his aunt Inabell. The police traced the car he had rented, and when they searched it they found a hair in the trunk matching the victim, a .22-caliber shell casing under the seat, and grass and weeds lodged in the undercarriage matching those at the murder scene. Fibers on the murder victim's clothing matched fibers from the car's trunk.

Robert Bryan was arrested and charged with murdering his aunt; he had his first competency hearing on December 30, 1993, and Dr. Richard Kahoe found him competent to stand trial. He was tried in January 1995 and found guilty of first-degree murder, the jurors recommended the death penalty, and Beckham County District Court Judge Charles L. Goodwin sentenced Bryan to die by lethal injection. His attorneys filed an appeal but the state Court of Criminal Appeals affirmed the judgment and sentence in 1997 and denied post-conviction relief the same year, and the U.S. Supreme Court denied certiorari. Bryan had been found competent again in late 1994 and in 1996. When all state judicial relief was exhausted his attorneys filed a writ of habeas corpus, but on December 27, 2001, the justices of the federal Tenth Circuit Court of Criminal Appeals denied relief. His attorneys then filed another writ of habeas corpus but it was denied in 2003. On April 6, 2004, after the U.S. Supreme Court denied Bryan's final appeal, the state's Attorney General Drew Edmondson requested an execution date from the Court of Criminal Appeals, and on April 14 the justices set the date for Tuesday, June 8. The state Board of Pardons and Parole met on May 10, and on May 20 they voted to deny clemency; Governor Brad Henry followed their recommendation. Bryan's attorneys filed last-minute, emergency appeals asking for a stay of execution but the federal court of appeals denied the stay, and Bryan's last chance was an appeal to the U.S. Supreme Court, which was denied at 6:30 P.M. and delayed the execution for one hour.

On Monday Wilma Wykoffe visited her brother for three hours, and the parting was touching. On the morning of his execution Bryan was moved from his death row cell to a holding cell in H Unit near the injection room. Shortly after 7:00 P.M. the condemned man was escorted into the death chamber where he took his place on the gurney and was strapped down, and then his arms were strapped to arm extensions and a sheet was pulled over his body. A medical technician carefully inserted one intravenous cannula (IV) into the vein of each arm while the executioners were hidden from view behind a one-way mirrored window. Warden Mike Mullin confirmed by telephone with Governor Henry that the execution was to proceed, and then the accordion blinds were raised for Inabell's family witnesses seated behind a one-way mirrored window, while across the room behind clear glass sat the fourteen witnesses for the condemned man, including members of his family and four reporters. Bryan was asked if he had any last words, and he said to his family, "I have been on death row for some time. I've made peace with my Maker. I'll be leaving here shortly. I hope I'll see you on the other side. Until then, so long." He had no words for Inabell's family so the warden announced, "Let the execution begin," and at 7:21 P.M. the executioners emptied their syringes into the tube leading to Bryan's arm: first sodium thiopental, a strong sedative; second pancuronium bromide to stop his respiration; and finally potassium chloride to stop his heart. Bryan's abdomen rose and he gave one loud snort before he lay still, and at 7:24 P.M. all sign of life was absent and Bryan was pronounced dead.

Beckham County case: CF 93-61. *Bryan v. Mullin*: 276 F.3d 1163 (2001); 335 F.3d 1207 (2003). *Bryan v. Oklahoma*: 522 U.S. 957 (1997). *Bryan v. State*: 935 P.2d 338 (1997); 948 P.2d 1230 (1997). *McAlester News-Capital and Democrat* (OK): June 9, 2004. *Oklahoman* (Norman): June 9, 2004.

Workman, Windel R.
August 26, 2004

Rebecca Holman, the live-in girlfriend of twenty-nine-year-old Windel Ray Workman, left her twenty-eight-month-old daughter, Amanda, in the care of her boyfriend from January 8 through January 10, 1987. At 10:30 A.M. on January 10 Workman and Rebecca Holman rushed into the emergency room of the children's section of the South Community Hospital in Oklahoma City carrying the limp body of Amanda, and Workman told the hospital staff that she was not breathing. He told the medical staff that she had fallen backwards out of bed the night before, trying to explain the many bruises on Amanda's face, chest, back and buttocks, and that she had started vomiting the night of January 9. He later admitted to the police that he had spanked Amanda quite hard and had played with the little girl by throwing her into air and catching her, trying to further explain the bruises to her arms, chest and buttocks. Amanda could not be resuscitated and was pronounced dead.

Workman was lodged in the Oklahoma County jail to await trial, and he was charged with murdering Amanda by child abuse. The medical examiner determined that the injuries were not caused as described, that Amanda would not bruise easily, the cause of death was blunt-force trauma to her head causing a subdural hemorrhage, and there were three distinct head injuries, any of which would have killed her. It was determined that a fall of between ten feet and twenty feet would have been necessary for each of the head injuries, but could have been caused by a brutal beating. At his trial several months later Workman tried to expand on the cause of Amanda's many injuries and claimed that Amanda had fallen out of bed on January 8, may have struck her head on a dresser and then complained of a stomach ache afterwards. He admitted spanking Amanda, and said that the following day Amanda slipped and fell in the bathtub, and she had slipped and fallen out of her bed again, striking her head on the floor. His effort to explain the three separate head injuries was rejected by the jurors, he was found guilty of first-degree murder for beating the little girl to death, and the jury recommended the death penalty. On June 3, 1987, Oklahoma County District Court Judge John M. Amick sentenced Workman to die by lethal injection, and he was delivered to his death row cell the same day.

His attorneys filed an appeal, which stayed the execution, but the state Court of Criminal Appeals affirmed the judgment and sentence in 1991. His attorneys then used every manipulation to save their client's life, and when all state judicial relief was exhausted they filed a writ of habeas corpus with the federal Tenth Circuit Court of Appeals. In 2003 the writ was denied. After Workman's final appeal to the U.S. Supreme Court was denied on June 24, 2004, Oklahoma's Attorney General Drew Edmondson requested the Court of Criminal Appeals to set a date for the execution, and the date was set for August 19 but later changed to August 26 when conflicts arose. The state Board of Pardons and Parole met on August 5 and denied clemency, and Governor Brad Henry followed their recommendation. His attorneys filed last-minute emergency appeals, but the state Court of Criminal Appeals and the Tenth Circuit Court denied relief on Workman's final day.

On the morning of his execution Workman had been moved from his death row cell to a holding cell in H Unit near the injection room, where he received notification that his appeals were denied. Shortly before 6:00 P.M. the condemned man was escorted into the death chamber where he took his place on the gurney and was strapped down, and then his arms were strapped to arm extensions and a sheet was pulled over his body. A medical technician carefully inserted one intravenous cannula (IV) into the vein of each arm while the executioners were hidden from view behind a one-way mirrored window. Warden Mike Mullin confirmed by telephone with Governor Henry that the execution was to proceed, and the accordion blinds were raised for the victim's witnesses seated behind a one-way mirrored window and for Workman's witnesses behind clear glass in an opposite room. Workman was asked if he had any last words, and he said to his witnesses, including his attorneys, "Thanks for everything you've done. I appreciate it. Keep up the good fight. Understand what I'm saying? OK, let's go!" The warden then announced, "Let the execution begin," and at 6:05 P.M. the executioners emptied their syringes into the tube leading to Workman's arm: first sodium thiopental, a strong sedative; second pancuronium bromide to stop his respiration; and finally potassium chloride to stop his heart. At 6:08 P.M. all sign of life was absent and Workman was pronounced dead.

Sources: *Denton Record-Chronicle* (TX): August 26, 2004. *McAlester News-Capital and Democrat* (OK): June 24, 2004; August 25, 2004. Oklahoma County case: CRF 87-254. *Workman v. Mullin*: 342 F.3d 1100 (2003). *Workman v. State*: 824 P.2d 378 (1991).

Slaughter, Jimmie R.
March 15, 2005

Jimmie Ray Slaughter, a psychiatric nurse and Army Reserve officer, and Melody Sue Wuertz had a relationship that resulted in the birth of a daughter, Jessica Rae Wuertz, on July 7, 1990, and on July 17 Slaughter signed an affidavit admitting paternity. Slaughter was called to active duty in the fall of 1990 and stationed at Fort Riley, Kansas, and the payments to Wuertz stopped. Slaughter, who did not want his wife to learn of his infidelities, had paid Wuertz child support money irregularly and was angry at Wuertz's incessant demands for support of his daughter.

After Slaughter was served with a Department of Human Services child-support order in mid-1991 Slaughter told several people that he was thinking of killing Wuertz and their daughter, and mentioned how easy it would be to place items about the murder scene to incriminate someone else, or at least misdirect the investigation. He had Cecilia Johnson, a young woman whom he had under his influence since he had worked with her at the Veteran's Administration Health Center in Oklahoma City, collect and mail him specimens from a black patient for this purpose.

Wuertz had told several people she was afraid of Slaughter and planned to change the locks on her home, but she had not done so. During the early morning hours of July 2, 1991, forty-four-year-old Slaughter drove from Fort Riley, Kansas, to the Edmond home of his former girlfriend, a four hour trip. Slaughter was armed with a small-caliber pistol and a knife, and he still had a key to Wuertz's house so there was no need for forced entry. Just before noon Slaughter crept into the home, found twenty-nine-year-old Melody in her bathroom preparing for work at the Veteran's Hospital, and shot her in the cervical spine leaving her conscious but paralyzed. Slaughter then went into the hallway where he found Jessica and shot her twice in the head, killing her. Slaughter returned to Melody and dragged her body into the bedroom before he shot her in the head, killing her, and then he stabbed her in the chest and genitalia and slashed her breasts and abdomen many times in the form of symbols, including the letter "R" carved on her abdomen.

After he planted a pair of undershorts and hairs from the Oklahoma City patient, he drove back to Topeka in time to meet his wife and two daughters at a store, but the clerks later only remembered seeing Nicki Slaughter and the two daughters but not Jimmie Ray. At noon on the day of the murders, a neighbor of Wuertz, Ginger Neal's dog panicked and ran into the house, and she checked her back yard but saw nothing. A few minutes later she heard a sound she later believed to be the single gunshot which killed Melody. The police began their investigation with ten suspects but quickly narrowed their investigation to Slaughter, whom they found had a history of befriending young women, manipulating them into sexual liaisons, and then controlling them in various ways. One of these liaisons was a doctor who, over a ten-year period, had seven abortions, but Melody had refused when ordered by Slaughter to terminate her pregnancy.

Slaughter claimed that at the time of the murders he was in Topeka, Kansas, shopping with his family but when his alibi could not be proved he was arrested and charged with two counts of murder. He was tried in late August and early September 1994. He still insisted he was in Topeka at the time of the murders and also tried to implicate Cecilia Johnson as the murderer, but he was convicted on two counts of first-degree murder with malice aforethought, and the jurors recommended the death penalty. On December 9, 1994, Oklahoma County District Court Judge Thomas C. Smith sentenced Slaughter to die by lethal injection, and he was delivered to his death row cell three days later.

His attorneys filed an appeal, which stayed the execution, but in 1997 the Oklahoma Court of Criminal Appeals affirmed the sentence and judgment of the lower court and on February 3, 1998, denied a rehearing, and twice in 2005 they denied post-conviction relief. The U.S. Supreme Court denied certiorari in 1998 and in 2004. His attorneys filed a petition for a writ of habeas corpus with the federal Tenth Circuit Court of Appeals but they had denied him relief in 2003. On January 19, 2005, the state Court of Criminal Appeals set Slaughter's execution date at March 15. The state Board of Pardons and Parole voted unanimously to deny clemency, and Governor Brad Henry followed their recommendation. On March 10 the state Court of Criminal Appeals denied him a stay, and the Tenth Circuit Court of Appeals and the U.S. Supreme Court followed with denials on March 14 and 15, respectively.

On the morning of his execution Slaughter was moved from his death row cell to a holding cell in H Unit near the injection room. There was no prisoner demonstration on death row, which was somewhat unusual, and shortly after 6:00 P.M. the condemned man was escorted into the death chamber where he took his place on the gurney and was strapped down. His arms were strapped to arm extensions, and a sheet was pulled over his body. A medical technician carefully inserted one intravenous cannula (IV) into the vein of each arm while the executioners were hidden from view behind a one-way mirrored window. Warden Mike Mullin confirmed by telephone with Governor Henry that the execution was to proceed, and then the accordion blinds were raised for the witnesses seated behind a one-way mirrored window, while across the room behind clear glass sat the witnesses for the condemned man.

Slaughter was asked if he had any last words, and he said to his family, "I've been accused of murder and it's not true. It was a lie from the beginning. God knows it's true, my children who were with me know it's true, and you people will know it's true someday. May God have mercy on your souls." When he concluded the warden announced, "Let the execution begin," and the executioners emptied their syringes into the tube leading to Slaughter's arm: first sodium thiopental, a strong sedative; second pancuronium bromide to stop his respiration; and finally potassium chloride to stop his heart. Slaughter kept his head raised for a full minute as he told his three daughters by a previous marriage, "It's OK! It's OK! I love you! I'll be seeing you soon," then he lowered his head and sighed heavily as the drugs began to take effect, and his face drained of all color. His mouth and eyes were slightly open when all sign of life was absent, and at 6:19 P.M. he was pronounced dead.

Sources: *Lexington Herald Leader* (KY): March 15, 2005.

McAlester News-Capital and Democrat (OK): January 19, 2005; March 16, 2005. Oklahoma County case: CF 1992–82; F-1994–1312. *Slaughter v. Mullin*: 68 Fed. Appx. 141 (2003). *Slaughter v. Oklahoma*: 525 U.S. 886 (1998); 541 U.S. 947 (2004). *Slaughter v. State*: 950 P.2d 839 (1997); 969 P.2d 990 (1998); 105 P.2d 832 (2005); 2005 WL 562759 (2005).

Miller, George J., Jr.
May 12, 2005

During the last two weeks of August 1994, twenty-seven-year-old George James Miller, Jr., an ex-convict with two felony convictions working under the alias Jay Elkins, was hired as a maintenance man at the Central Plaza Hotel located at the I-40 and Martin Luther King Drive in Oklahoma City in Oklahoma County, Oklahoma, but he was fired. On September 16 Miller was broke and still unemployed when he tried to borrow money from several people, including one person living at the hotel, but everyone turned him down. At 10:00 P.M. Miller, with Chris Carriger and Jeremy Collman, went to the Central Plaza Hotel and tried to cash Carriger's check payable to Miller, but it could not be cashed so Miller returned home.

Later that night Miller took the keys to his wife's car from her hiding place under the mattress and left home. At 3:15 A.M. on September 17, 1994, twenty-five-year-old Gary Kent Dodd, who worked as the night clerk at the hotel and knew Miller only as Jay Elkins, registered Miller as a guest. Minutes later Miller attacked Dodd with a knife, stabbing him repeatedly, then beat him on the head with hedge shears and a paint can, and finally poured muriatic acid over his body and down his throat. The attack took place in various parts of the hotel lobby but ended in the unused restaurant section of the hotel, and Miller then robbed the cash register of $122 before he fled. The clerk started each shift with $250, and later a one-hundred-dollar bill was found hidden in the drawer with an entry which accounted for $28.

Dodd managed to scrawl "Jay" and "J" on the double doors of the restaurant and the floor, using his own blood, before he was found. A hotel housekeeper arrived for her shift at 5:45 A.M., saw that Dodd was not at the counter, and heard what sounded like animal groans, and after she discovered Dodd's body she ran to a nearby restaurant and called the police. The acid had burned Dodd's throat so the officers could not understand most of what he tried to tell them, but he did manage to say he was attacked by a black man wearing grey trousers, and there were bloody footprints at the scene from the murderer's sandals. Dodd was rushed to the hospital but he died later that day; the cause of death was blunt-force trauma caused by the garden shears.

The morning after the murder Miller gave his wife $120, and later told a friend that the motive could not have been robbery as there was only $150 in the cash drawer. When the investigation focused on Miller he told the police interviewer that he had cashed a paycheck and given the money to his wife, then denied giving his wife any money when reminded he had no job. A drop of blood consistent with Dodd's blood type was found on his sandals, and the bloody footprints were matched to the sandals but not exclusively, as there were no distinguishing marks on the soles. While the investigation continued Miller moved to Sherman, Texas, where he lived with his mother, but he committed several federal crimes and was in prison when he was extradited to Oklahoma and charged with Dodd's murder. Miller was tried in late 1996, and Miller's ex-wife, who had divorced him while he was in Texas, refuted his alibi that he was at home. She testified that she found sand in her car the next day, and that certain articles of Miller's clothing disappeared the following day and two buttons found at the crime scene were consistent with those from Miller's missing shirt. The jurors found the defendant guilty of first-degree murder and recommended the death penalty. On October 31, 1996, Oklahoma County District Court Judge Charles L. Owens sentenced Miller to die by lethal injection, and on January 27, 1997, he was delivered to his death row cell.

Miller's attorneys filed an appeal but the state Court of Criminal Appeals affirmed the judgment and sentence in 1998 and denied post-conviction relief. When all state judicial relief was exhausted his attorneys filed a petition for a writ of habeas corpus, but the federal Tenth Circuit Court of Appeals denied the petition on January 21, 2004. When Miller's final appeal was denied by the U.S. Supreme Court the state's Attorney General Drew Edmondson, on February 22, 2005, requested the Court of Criminal Appeals to set a date for his execution; on March 7 the justices set the date at May 12. Neither the state Board of Pardons and

Parole nor Governor Brad Henry granted clemency, and all last-minute emergency appeals failed.

On the morning of his execution Miller was moved from his death row cell to a holding cell in H Unit near the injection room. Shortly after 6:00 P.M. the condemned man was escorted into the death chamber where he took his place on the gurney and he was strapped down. His arms were strapped to arm extensions, and a sheet was pulled over his body. A medical technician carefully inserted one intravenous cannula (IV) into the vein of each arm while the executioners were hidden from view behind a one-way mirrored window. Warden Mike Mullin confirmed by telephone with Governor Henry that the execution was to proceed, and then the accordion blinds were raised for the witnesses seated behind a one-way mirrored window, while across the room behind clear glass sat the witnesses for the condemned man. Miller was asked if he had any last words, and he turned his head toward the clear glass window, nodded to his mother, other family members, and his attorney and said, "I love you." The warden then announced, "Let the execution begin," and the executioners emptied their syringes into the tube leading to Miller's arm: first sodium thiopental, a strong sedative; second pancuronium bromide to stop his respiration; and finally potassium chloride to stop his heart. Miller caught his breath suddenly, then exhaled deeply as the drugs began to take effect. At 6:14 P.M. all sign of life was absent, and at 6:19 P.M. Miller was pronounced dead.

Sources: *Miller v. Mullin*: 354 F.3d 1288 (2004). *Miller v. State*: 977 P.2d 1099 (1998). *McAlester News-Capital and Democrat* (OK): March 7, 2005. Oklahoma County case: CF 94-8859.

Pennington, Michael L.
July 19, 2005

In late October 1991 twenty-three-year-old Michael Lannier Pennington, a soldier stationed at Fort Sill near Lawton, Oklahoma, awaiting his discharge, went to the local K-Mart store and bought a Maverick 12-gauge shotgun and sawed off the barrel. At 5:00 A.M. on October 21 he went into the Lawton 7–11 convenience store at Fort Sill Boulevard and Rogers Lane armed with the shotgun and demanded money. He fired several rounds, and one struck twenty-year-old clerk Bradley Thomas Grooms in the chest. Twelve pellets were later removed from his left back area, and one pellet had exited the back of his neck on the right. Another blast struck a cooler and four blasts struck the cash register, but he could not pry it open and left empty-handed.

Another clerk, James Principi, had been busy stocking shelves when he first saw Pennington enter to use the bathroom, then leave and return in a minute wearing a trench coat and a black baseball cap, and when he heard the first blast from the shotgun he hid in the bathroom and locked the door. While Pennington, alone in the store and without the trench coat, was standing behind the counter customer Lynn Renee Smith entered and was given a cup for ice. She knew Pennington, and she identified the murderer for the police. Smith drove to her sister's home nearby and watched as Pennington came out of the store and drove away in his automobile, alone.

Pennington returned to the barracks to change clothes and then went to the airport and flew to Dallas, Texas, where he caught a connecting flight to Akron, Ohio. The following day he was traced to the home of his wife in Akron and arrested by Ohio authorities. He told the officers where he had put the shotgun and shells, and they found them in the basement of his wife's house and matched them to the murder weapon. The officers searched the next day and found the trench coat and the black baseball cap he had worn during the robbery. Pennington, a body builder and weight-lifter, claimed that a notorious gang member known to him only as "T" was with him and committed the murder, but later changed his defense to steroid rage. However, during questioning he had admitted that he had not taken any steroids since April 1991. He was extradited to Comanche County, identified by Principi, and tried for Grooms' murder in late 1993. He was convicted of first-degree murder and the jurors recommended the death penalty, so on September 17 Judge Peter Clinton Moore sentenced Pennington to die by lethal injection, and four days later he was delivered to his death row cell.

His attorneys filed an appeal but the state Court of Criminal Appeals affirmed the judgment and sentence of the District Court in 1995. The U.S. Supreme Court denied certiorari early the following year, his petition for a rehearing was denied on April 26, 1996, and the state appeals court denied post-conviction relief in 1997. Between the time of his first appeal and his post-conviction appeal on January 15, 1997, Pennington converted to the Muslim religion and adopted the name Sharieff Imani Sallahdin. When all state judicial appeals were exhausted Pennington's attorneys filed a petition for a writ of habeas corpus with the federal Tenth Circuit Court of Appeals, but it was denied in 2002, and a second petition was denied in 2004. When the U.S. Supreme Court turned down Pennington's final appeal the state's Attorney General Drew Edmondson requested the Court of Criminal Appeals set a date for his execution, and the justices set the date at Tuesday, July 19, 2005. His attorneys filed last-minute emergency appeals but a week before his execution date the federal court of appeals and the U.S. Supreme Court turned down stays of execution. The Board of Pardons and Parole and Governor Brad Henry denied clemency.

On the morning of his execution Pennington was moved from his death row cell to a holding cell in H Unit near the injection room. At 6:00 P.M. the condemned man was escorted into the death chamber where he took his place on the gurney and was strapped down. His arms were strapped to arm extensions, and a sheet was pulled over his body. A medical technician carefully inserted one intravenous cannula (IV) into the vein of each arm while the executioners were hidden from view behind a one-way mirrored window. Warden Mike Mullin confirmed by telephone with Governor Henry that the execution was to proceed, and then the accordion blinds were raised on the clear glass window for the witnesses of the condemned man, but there were no witnesses from the victim's family. Pennington was asked if he had any last words but he replied, "No statement," and the warden then announced, "Let the execution begin." The executioners first flushed the two tubes leading to his arms with a saline solution, and then they emptied their syringes into the tube leading to Pennington's arm: first sodium thiopental, a strong sedative; second pancuronium bromide to stop his respiration; and finally potassium chloride to stop his heart. As the drugs began to flow Pennington turned his head toward his family and mouthed the words, "I love you." When all sign of life was absent at 6:10 P.M. he was pronounced dead.

Sources: Comanche County case: CRF 91–386. *Lawton Constitution* (OK): July 20, 2005. *McAlester News-Capital and Democrat* (OK): June 6, 2005. *Pennington v. State*: 913 P.2d 1356 (1995). *Pennington v. Oklahoma*: 519 U.S. 841 (1996). *Sallahdin v. Gibson*: 275 F.3d 1211 (2002); *Sallahdin v. Mullin*: 380 F.3d 1242 (2004). *Sallahdin v. State*: 947 P.2d 559 (1997). *Washington Post* (D.C.): July 19, 2005.

Turrentine, Kenneth E.
August 11, 2005

Kenneth Eugene Turrentine was married to Catherine but they had marital difficulties, separated, and eventually divorced. In early March 1994 Turrentine, then forty-one years old, was living with thirty-nine-year-old Anita Louise Richardson, her blind and mentally disabled twenty-two-year-old daughter, Tina L. Pennington, and her thirteen-year-old son, Martise D. Richardson, at 2518 South 121st East Avenue in Tulsa, Oklahoma. Turrentine and Richardson were having trouble so Turrentine moved out, and he moved in with his forty-eight-year-old sister Avon Stevenson at her Tulsa home located at 8130 East 12th Street. Richardson and Stevenson had become close friends, and by late May Turrentine believed that Richardson was having affairs with two men, that his sister and his girlfriend conspired to keep the affairs a secret, and that they had also cheated him out of money to support their drug habits.

Late on June 3 Turrentine called his ex-wife and said he was "at Anita's house and things are about to come to a head." He asked Catherine to return the .22-caliber pistol he had left with her when he moved out of their home, but she refused to give it to him. The next morning Turrentine went to his ex-wife's home, asked again for the pistol, and she gave it to him, fully loaded. Turrentine drove immediately to his sister's home and confronted her with allegations against her and Richardson, but she laughed at him and called him a "punk." Without hesitation Turrentine pulled the pistol, pressed it against his sister's head, and shot her through the brain, and she soon died of the wound. Turrentine then drove to his girlfriend's home and confronted her with the allegations of infidelity and theft, and they began to argue. They moved from the front to the back bedroom where the arguing escalated to a struggle, and Turrentine shot Richardson in the head, killing her. He next shot and killed Richardson's daughter and son with a single shot to each of their heads, and then called the police emergency dispatcher. He said, "I just shot my old lady, her kids, and my sister," and then went outside to wait for the police.

When they arrived he surrendered and, after hearing his rights read to him, he confessed again. The police found that Richardson and her two children were dead, and they found the dead body of Stevenson when they checked at her home. Turrentine was charged with four counts of murder. He was tried in late 1995 and convicted on four counts of first-degree murder with three recommendations for the death penalty. On October 4 Tulsa County District Court Judge B. R. Beasley sentenced Turrentine to one term of life in prison without parole for killing his sister and to three sentences of death for the murders of Richardson and her children, and the condemned man was delivered to his death row cell on October 16.

His attorneys filed a notice of appeal, which stayed the execution, but in early 1998 Oklahoma's Court of Criminal Appeals affirmed the judgment and sentences of the District Court and denied post-conviction relief in July 1998. In December 1998 the U.S. Supreme Court denied certiorari. When all state judicial relief was exhausted Turrentine's attorneys filed a petition for a writ of habeas corpus, and in 2004 the federal Tenth Circuit Court of Appeals found technical errors in sentencing and threw out the death sentences for the murders of Tina and Martise, but upheld the death sentence for the murder of their mother. The affirmation was then appealed to the U.S. Supreme Court but the justices denied relief, so on June 6, 2005, the state's Attorney General Drew Edmondson requested that the Court of Criminal Appeals set a date of execution. On June 15 the justices set the date for Turrentine's execution at August 11. The state Board of Pardons and Parole met on August 5 and denied clemency, and Governor Brad Henry followed their recommendation. The last-minute emergency appeals failed, the last when the U.S. Supreme Court denied a stay at 5:00 P.M. on August 11.

On the morning of his execution Turrentine was moved from his death row cell to a holding cell in H Unit near the injection room. Shortly before 6:00 P.M. the condemned man was escorted into the death chamber where he took his place on the gurney and was strapped down. His arms were strapped to arm extensions and a sheet was pulled over his body. A medical technician carefully inserted one intravenous cannula (IV) into the vein of each arm while the executioners were hidden from view behind a one-way mirrored window. Warden Mike Mullin confirmed by telephone with Governor Henry that the execution was to proceed, and then the accordion blinds were raised for the witnesses, the victim's witnesses seated behind a one-way mirrored window while across the room behind clear glass sat the witnesses for the condemned man, including Turrentine's mother and father.

Turrentine was asked if he had any last words and he said, "I've always maintained I've been innocent of (the) crimes charged. This is a violation of my 14th Amendment rights. It's not over. With that being said, Mom, Dad, I love you all. Be strong." When he concluded the warden announced, "Let the execution begin," and following a saline flush of the tubes the executioners, at 6:07 P.M., emptied their syringes into the tube leading to Turrentine's arm: first sodium thiopental, a strong sedative; second pancuronium bromide to stop his respiration; and finally potassium chloride to stop his heart. Turrentine's eyes flickered and he took five deep breaths before he lay still. At 6:10 P.M. all sign of life was absent and Turrentine was pronounced dead.

Sources: *McAlester News-Capital and Democrat* (OK): June 15, 2005; August 12, 2005. *Pryor Times* (WA): August 12, 2005. Tulsa County case: CF 94–2784. *Turrentine v. Mullin*: 390 F.3d 1181 (2004). *Turrentine v. Oklahoma*: 525 U.S. 1057 (1998). *Turrentine v. State*: 965 P.2d 955 (1998); 965 P.2d 985 (1998).

Thornburg, Richard A.
April 18, 2006

On September 23, 1996, thirty-one-year-old Richard Alford Thornburg, a drug dealer in Alex, Grady County, Oklahoma, asked Jimmy Scott to repay $60 dollars he had loaned him. Moments later Thornburg was shot and slightly wounded and, though he did not see his assailant, he suspected customers Smith, Marvin Matheson and fifty-one-year-old James Donald Poteet. When deputy sheriff Terry Alexander investigated the shooting Thornburg told him, "Don't worry about it, I'll take care of it."

On the evening of September 27 Thornburg asked to borrow a police scanner from Julie Maxon, but she refused. Later Thornburg went to a bar with a small party of friends, including Glenn Anderson and Roger Embrey. They left the bar at

2:00 A.M. and made a few stops before the three men, all armed with pistols, drove to the trailer home of Matheson before 4:00 A.M. and captured him. Thornburg accused Matheson of shooting him, and when he denied it they drove their prisoner to the home of Poteet, telling Matheson not to lock his trailer as he was not coming back.

At the Poteet house Thornburg and Embrey went in while Anderson covered Matheson with his pistol in the car, and when they heard several gunshots they followed. Once inside the Poteet residence they found thirty-nine-year-old Terry Shepard sitting in a chair in the front room and saw Poteet sitting on the bed in the back bedroom. Thornburg had shot him in the left big toe and struck him on the forehead, causing a bloody cut and bruising. Thornburg again shot at Poteet's feet, trying to scare him into saying who had shot him, but he missed on purpose. Anderson then told Thornburg to take Matheson to the rear rental unit where Jimmy Scott lived and bring him back, but when they arrived they found that Jimmy was away so they captured his brother Donald "Donnie" Brent Scott. Twenty-four-year-old Keith Alan Smith arrived at that moment to pickup his girlfriend's purse, which had been left at the Scott residence, and Thornburg took all three men back to Poteet's house at gunpoint.

Anderson and Embrey took control of the four prisoners and put them in the kitchen while Thornburg returned to the back bedroom and argued with Poteet over drugs and money. Anderson and Embrey then herded everyone into the back bedroom where Matheson and Poteet were injected with drugs "to OD them," and Anderson and Thornburg also injected themselves with a lesser dose. Thornburg continued to argue with Poteet over who had shot him, and said he was going to shoot Poteet but then said, "Better yet, I ain't gonna shoot you." He instructed Matheson to shoot Poteet while Anderson and Embrey pointed their pistols at Matheson, and they threatened to shoot him if he did not fire, but Matheson refused. Thornburg then shot Poteet in the side and told Matheson, "You are going to shoot somebody, or you will not leave this house alive."

The men took Scott into the bathroom and gave Matheson a gun, and he tried to shoot Scott in the head but the gun was not loaded. Anderson took the gun into the hallway and loaded it, returned it to Matheson, and he shot Scott in the chest. At that point Embrey gave his gun to Anderson and said he wanted no part in the shooting, and Embrey took Matheson back to the car. Thornburg took Smith and Shepard into the northeast bedroom and shot them to death. In all, four more shots were fired while Matheson sat in the car. Embrey left Matheson and took a bag of empty beer bottles from the trunk and siphoned gasoline from the tank, and when Anderson and Thornburg came out the three men fashioned four Molotov cocktails, lit the fuses, and threw the four bottles through the northeast bedroom window. Once the house was afire they drove off, but Thornburg soon stopped to let Anderson and Embrey hide their guns, and Thornburg continued on a short distance with Matheson. Thornburg stopped again and ordered Matheson out of the car and warned him to hide and keep his mouth shut, or they would blame him for the murders.

Meanwhile Scott tried to help Poteet crawl out of the house, but with Poteet's wound and the drugs he only got as far as the hallway and could not continue, so Scott crawled out before the house became completely engulfed in flames, and he tried to crawl to the neighbor's house. Loyd Keagans and his son drove by the Poteet house at 5:30 A.M., and while Loyd went to the burning house his son started for the neighbor's house, and he found Scott. They drove Scott to a local convenience store and called the police, and Scott described the four men.

On September 30 Matheson, who learned the police were looking for him, surrendered to Alex Police Chief Jeff Franklin, and after his family was under police protection he told his story, which was corroborated by Scott. The search for Thornburg, Anderson and Embrey began in earnest. That same night Thornburg was drinking at a local bar and talking to himself when Teresa Burgess, who had just arrived in town, was sitting next to Thornburg and overheard him say to himself, "Three died last night and three more will die tomorrow." Thornburg was arrested at the bar, and soon Anderson and Embrey joined him behind bars; they were charged with three counts of murder and other related charges. Anderson was convicted of three counts of murder and sentenced to die on each count, while Embrey was convicted of three counts of murder and sentenced to serve one term of life and two terms of life without parole at the state prison. Thornburg was tried in April

1997; his defense, that he was drunk and passed out in his car, was rejected, and he was convicted on all counts. On May 12 he was sentenced to three death sentences by Grady County District Court Judge James R. Winchester, and the judge also sentenced him to serve three consecutive life sentences for shooting with intent to kill, thirty-five years in prison for first-degree arson, and two terms of ten years in prison for kidnapping.

His attorneys filed an appeal but in early 1999 the state Court of Criminal Appeals affirmed the judgment and sentence of the District Court. On November 9, 1999, the justices denied post-conviction relief, and on May 15, 2000, the U.S. Supreme Court denied certiorari. When all state judicial relief was exhausted his attorneys filed a petition for a writ of habeas corpus with the federal Tenth Circuit Court of Appeals, but this was denied on September 7, 2005. On March 27, 2006, after the U.S. Supreme Court denied Thornburg's final appeal, state Attorney General Drew Edmondson requested the Court of Criminal Appeals to set a date for the execution, and the following day the justices set the date at April 18. Thornburg waived a clemency hearing, Governor Brad Henry declined to intervene, and all last-minute emergency appeals failed.

On the morning of his execution Thornburg was moved from his death row cell to a holding cell in H Unit near the injection room. At 6:00 P.M. the condemned man was escorted into the death chamber where he took his place on the gurney and was strapped down. His arms were strapped to arm extensions and a sheet was pulled over his body. A medical technician carefully inserted one intravenous cannula (IV) into the vein of each arm while the executioners were hidden from view behind a one-way mirrored window. Warden Mike Mullin confirmed by telephone with Governor Henry that the execution was to proceed, and then the accordion blinds were raised on the windows to the witness rooms, where members of the victim's family sat behind a one-way mirrored window while Thornburg's wife, sister, and two brothers-in-law and one other witness watched the execution through a clear glass window.

Thornburg was asked if he had any last words and he replied, "I just want to say I'm sorry for all the pain I've caused. I'm truly ashamed of my actions. I wish I could take it back." Warden Mullin then announced, "Let the execution begin." The executioners first flushed the two tubes leading to his arms with a saline solution, and then at 6:16 P.M. they emptied their syringes into the tube leading to Thornburg's arm: first sodium thiopental, a strong sedative; second pancuronium bromide to stop his respiration; and finally potassium chloride to stop his heart. As the drugs began to flow Thornburg strained to lift his head to look at his family, then relaxed, and when all signs of life were absent at 6:20 P.M. he was pronounced dead. Thornburg's body was shipped to the Callaway-Smith-Cobb Funeral Home in Marlow, Oklahoma, and prepared for burial in the Bradley Cemetery on April 20.

Sources: Grady County case: CF 96–240. *Thornburg v. Mullin*: 422 F.3d 1133 (2005). *Thornburg v. State*: 985 P.2d 1234 (1999); P. C. 99–490 (1999). *U.S.A. Today*: April 19, 2006.

Boltz, John A.
June 1, 2006

On April 18, 1984, Patricia "Pat" Kirby-Boltz left her job in Shawnee, Pottawatomie County, Oklahoma, and drove to Stroud to meet her friend and former employer Duane Morrison. Her husband, fifty-two-year-old John Albert Boltz, wearing camouflage fatigues and dark glasses, followed her because he believed that his wife was having an affair with Morrison, and when he saw her meeting with Morrison he flew into a rage. He began swearing at Morrison and threatening to cut off his head, and he yelled that he had killed men, women and children during the Korean conflict and "killing doesn't faze me. I have cut off people's heads in the war for less serious infractions." When he left he went to the VFW hall and began drinking while Mrs. Boltz returned to the trailer home they shared in Shawnee, wrote a note saying their marriage was over, called her twenty-three-year-old son Doug Kirby to help her move her clothes and some of her belongings, and moved to her mother's home.

Boltz was intoxicated when he returned home and found the note. He drove to his mother-in-law's house, and at 9:30 P.M. he broke in and told his wife's mother terrible things about her daughter. When Mrs. Boltz threatened to call the police her husband left and returned to their trailer home. She called the police, but when she later learned that her husband had not been arrested she decided to go to the home of her son. Soon after she arrived Boltz called Doug twice and they talked for several minutes, and apparently Boltz made the same disparaging accusations, but Doug was not upset when he left to talk with Boltz. While he was en route Boltz called again and talked to his wife saying, "I'm going to cut your loving little boy's head off," and he also threatened to kill his wife within the hour. Mrs. Boltz called the police and reported the threats.

When Doug arrived he went toward the Boltz trailer but he met Boltz outside and they exchanged loud and angry words, which brought neighbor Vita Witt to her window. She saw Boltz standing over a man lying on the ground "motionless as a rag doll," and he was yelling obscenities and beating Doug. Boltz pulled a shiny object from his belt and attacked Doug, inflicting eight stab wounds to his neck, chest and abdomen and three slashes to his throat. One neck wound was so deep it nearly severed Doug's spine, slashes had cut both carotid arteries and his voice box and esophagus were severed, and several stab wounds had cut the major arteries in his heart. A bloody trail led to the trailer and then back to the passenger door of Doug's car, and a .22-caliber revolver was found lying on the passenger seat of the car, but the gun had no blood on it even though blood had spattered into the car and all over the seat, so it was supposed the gun had been planted by Boltz to bolster a claim of self-defense.

Doug was dead when the police arrived but Boltz had fled, and during the early morning hours of the next day he broke into Doug's house looking for his wife. Later that next day he went to the American Legion Hall in Midwest City, started drinking, and told a friend he had killed his stepson so the friend called the police and Boltz was arrested. Boltz claimed that Doug had threatened his life earlier that evening, kicked in his front door and reached for a gun, and he had stabbed and slashed the boy in self-defense. Boltz was arrested and charged with murder, and after he refused to plead guilty to voluntary manslaughter he was tried in late 1984 and convicted of murder in the first-degree; the jurors recommended the death penalty. On November 21, 1984, Pottawatomie County District Court Judge Glenn Dale Carter sentenced Boltz to die by lethal injection, and he was delivered to his death row cell later that day.

His attorneys filed an appeal, which stayed the execution, but in 1991 Oklahoma's Court of Criminal Appeals affirmed the judgment and sentence of the District Court, and the justices denied post-conviction relief on July 2, 1992. After all state judicial relief was exhausted his attorneys filed a petition for a writ of habeas corpus on September 9, 1999, but it was denied on March 25, 2004. This was followed by an application for a "certificate of appealability" which was granted, and on July 27, 2005, the matter was decided against Boltz. When the final appeal was denied by the U.S. Supreme Court, Attorney General Drew Edmondson requested an execution date, and it was set for April 18, 2006, but following more delays the justices of the Court of Criminal Appeals reset the date for June 1. The state Board of Pardons and Parole met the previous week and denied clemency, and Governor Brad Henry followed their recommendation. A federal judge granted a stay of execution on the Thursday prior to June 1, but it was lifted in two hours by the justices of the Tenth Circuit Court of Appeals. Last-minute appeals were denied in time to keep the execution on schedule, the last two appeals to the U.S. Supreme Court decided at 5:00 P.M.

On the morning of his execution Boltz was moved from his death row cell to a holding cell in H Unit near the injection room. At 6:00 P.M. the condemned man was escorted into the death chamber where he took his place on the gurney and was strapped down. His arms were strapped to arm extensions and a sheet was pulled over his body. It took the medical technician an hour to find suitable veins, and then the technician carefully inserted one intravenous cannula (IV) into the vein of each arm while the executioners were hidden from view behind a one-way mirrored window. Warden Mike Mullin confirmed by telephone with Governor Henry that the execution was to proceed, and then the accordion blinds were raised on the window to the witness room, where members of the victim's family sat behind a one-way mirrored glass.

Boltz was asked if he had any last words and at 7:13 P.M. he said, "This is a time of gladness for me and a time of sadness. It's a time of gladness because I know I'm going to a better place. It's a time of sadness because I think of all the people involved who got me here and what's in store for them." Boltz then referred to several passages from the Bible and continued, "They need to read this portion of the Bible and see what's down the road for them. I've seen so much pain for all these years, and now it's come down to this." When it was clear that he had concluded Warden Mullin announced, "Let the execution begin." The executioners first flushed the two tubes leading to his arms with a saline solution, and then at 7:15 P.M. they emptied their syringes into the tube leading to his arm: first sodium thiopental, a strong sedative; second pancuronium bromide to stop his respiration; and finally potassium chloride to stop his heart. As the drugs began to flow Boltz took several deep breaths, sighed deeply, closed his eyes, his color turned ashen and then a purple hue, and at 7:22 P.M. he was pronounced dead.

Sources: *Amarillo Globe* (TX): June 2, 2006. *Boltz v. Mullin*: 415 F.3d 1215 (2005). *Boltz v. State*: 806 P.2d 1117 (1991). *Oklahoman* (Oklahoma City): June 2, 2006. Pottawatomie County case: CRF 84–97. *Tulsa World* (OK): June 2, 2006.

Patton, Eric A.
August 29, 2006

Eric Allen Patton had an extensive prison record for burglaries in Oklahoma and California, and he was on parole from a California felony conviction when he returned to Oklahoma City. Thirty-seven-year-old Patton, a brick mason by trade but an all-around handyman, had done some painting in the northeast Oklahoma City home of Les and Charlene Elizabeth Kauer earlier in 1994, and he had worked with them at the Dial American Marketing Company.

On December 16 he was working on an Edmond, Oklahoma, job site when he left to buy electrical boxes. He borrowed Chris William's car, a coworker on that job site, and he drove to the Kauer home expecting the couple to be at work, which would allow him to burglarize their house. However, when he knocked on the door Charlene answered, as she had taken the day off from her job to do her Christmas shopping. When she opened the door Patton asked to borrow money, and she gave him ten dollars. As soon as she handed him the money he pushed his way into the house and grabbed Charlene by the throat, then dragged her from room to room as he searched for money and valuables. During the search he took Charlene to her bedroom and stabbed her several times. He dragged her to the kitchen and tore off her clothes, to make it look like an attempted rape, and then using a variety of kitchen knives he stabbed her repeatedly with such force that he broke several blades. He next stabbed her in the throat and chest with a pair of scissors and with a barbeque fork and left both imbedded in her chest. When it appeared she might still be alive he kicked her in the head with his steel-toed boot, causing a subgaleal hematoma to a bone in her head, which resulted in extensive hemorrhaging on the brain, and she died of a combination of these mortal wounds.

Her husband found her nude, bloody body in the kitchen later that day and called the police, and they compiled a list of possible suspects. Patton, after leaving the Kauer home, washed and changed into a pair of overalls he found in William's car, then discarded his bloody clothes in a field in northwest Oklahoma City. He had been gone from the job site for four hours when he returned without the electrical boxes. Over the next thirteen days officers worked through their list of suspects, and on December 29, after matching fingerprints from the bloody barbeque fork with Patton's fingerprints and matching blood at the scene with Patton's blood, he was arrested and charged with murdering Charlene Kauer.

He first denied any involvement but then, once his minister was summoned, he said that he had been driving by the Kauer home when he saw a strange automobile parked at the Kauer home and stopped to investigate, and he suggested that Charlene's husband had to be involved since the murderer had to control the Kauer dogs. He explained his injuries, a scratch on his lip and cuts on his hands, as an accident while changing a tire. When that alibi failed he tried to implicate Chris Williams, whose car he had borrowed, then recanted and claimed that a female family member who was "a strawberry"—a woman who exchanged sex for drugs—had killed Charlene while he fought with a dog, and the dog caused his cuts and scratches. He refused to give her name to protect her. He finally resorted to a claim that he had been possessed by demonic forces and had observed himself committing the murder during an out-of-body experience, and he added that he was under the influence of drugs and believed that Kauer was a demon. He took the officers to the field where he had discarded his bloody clothes, and they were recovered for evidence, and he pointed out several convenience stores he had robbed. He complained,

"I only got a lousy $14 and the woman didn't even put up a fight."

He was tried in November 1996, and the defense presented expert testimony that he was in a "drug delirium" and unable to form the intent to murder, but his behavior after the murders and testimony from his coworker and his girlfriend proved he was quite normal that day. The defense was rejected by the jurors, and they found him guilty of first-degree murder and first-degree burglary and recommended the death penalty on the murder count. On December 2 Oklahoma County District Court Judge Leamon Freeman sentenced Patton to die for the murder and to one thousand one hundred twenty years in prison for the burglary, and he was delivered to his death row cell the same day.

His attorneys filed an appeal, which stayed the execution, but in early 1998 the state Court of Criminal Appeals affirmed the judgment and sentence of the district court. On March 13, 1998, the appeal for post-conviction relief was filed, heard on July 28, and denied the following year. When all state remedies were exhausted Patton's attorneys filed a petition for a writ of habeas corpus, but the federal Tenth Circuit Court of Appeals denied relief in 2005. After the final appeal to the U.S. Supreme Court was denied the state's attorney general asked the Court of Criminal Appeals to set a date of execution, and they set the date for Tuesday, August 29, 2006. Patton's last-minute emergency appeal to the U.S. Supreme Court was denied early on the day of his execution, and neither the state Board of Pardons and Parole nor Governor Brad Henry would intervene.

On the morning of his execution Patton was moved from his death row cell to a holding cell in H Unit near the injection room. Shortly before 6:00 P.M. the condemned man was escorted into the death chamber where he took his place on the gurney and was strapped down. His arms were strapped to arm extensions and a sheet was pulled over his body. A medical technician carefully inserted one intravenous cannula (IV) into the vein of each arm while the executioners were hidden from view behind a one-way mirrored window. Warden Mike Mullin confirmed by telephone with Governor Henry that the execution was to proceed and then the accordion blinds were raised for the witnesses. Patton's witnesses included four members of his legal team and a Catholic priest, but no members of the Kauer nor the Patton family attended.

Patton was asked if he had any last words, and he thanked his legal team and his family, and then said, "I want to thank the guards here on death row who have been like a family to me and their lives have been a blessing to me. I've had a good life here on Earth. It's been a blessing. It's been a blast. I want to thank my Savior Jesus Christ for all he's done for me. I look forward to being with him now and for eternity." When he concluded the warden announced, "Let the execution begin," and following a saline flush of the tubes the executioners, at 6:03 P.M., emptied their syringes into the tube leading to Patton's arm: first sodium thiopental, a strong sedative; second pancuronium bromide to stop his respiration; and finally potassium chloride to stop his heart. Patton had challenged the dosage of the first drug in the three-drug combination but a federal judge rejected his argument; however the prison officials changed their protocol and doubled the anesthetic portion of the three drugs. As the drugs began to flow Patton exhaled deeply, then stopped breathing, and at 6:10 P.M. all sign of life was absent and he was pronounced dead.

Sources: Oklahoma County case: CF 95–55. *Oklahoman* (Oklahoma City): August 29, 2006. *Patton v. Mullin*: 425 F.3d 788 (2005). *Patton v. State*: 973 P.2d 270 (1998); 989 P.2d 983 (1999). *Shawnee News-Star* (OK): August 30, 2006. *Tulsa World* (OK): August 30, 2006.

Malicoat, James P.
August 31, 2006

Twenty-one-year-old James Patrick Malicoat met and dated Mary Ann Leadford, and on February 2, 1997, he moved into her Chickasha, Grady County, home. Malicoat worked the night shift on an oil rig, and during the day he watched Leadford's thirteen-month-old daughter Tessa while Leadford was at work. Over the next nineteen days Malicoat violently abused Tessa, but her mother did nothing to stop the abuse nor to protect her daughter.

Late on February 21 Mary returned home and found her daughter in her crib, covered with a blanket and dead. At 8:25 P.M. she and Malicoat rushed Tessa into the hospital emergency room of the local hospital where the doctors found that the little girl had broken ribs, three human bite marks, and extensive bruising on her face and body. The police were called, and Malicoat admitted that he had struck her head on a dresser two days earlier and had punched her in the stomach twice at 12:30 P.M. that day, which had caused her to stop breathing. He said he revived Tessa and then they laid down for a nap. He said that when he awoke Tessa was dead so he placed her in her crib and covered her. The hospital staff determined Tessa had been dead several hours.

Officers went to the Leadford home and found the floor littered with dog feces, and there was little food for humans and none for the baby. The autopsy determined that Tessa had died of two subdural hematomas and abdominal hemorrhaging from a torn mesentery, she had seven broken ribs from "thrusts to her abdomen," her liver, lungs and one kidney were ruptured, and her head had a soft spot just above her right eye where her skull had been crushed, causing one of the hematomas and bleeding into the brain. Malicoat and Leadford were arrested and charged with murder by child abuse. They were tried in 1997, and Leadford was found guilty of first-degree murder and sentenced to serve a life term in prison. Malicoat was tried twice and, after a mistrial was declared, he was found guilty of first-degree murder by child abuse at his second trial in 1998, after only one-half hour in deliberations; the jurors recommended the death penalty. On March 2, 1998, the Grady County District Court judge sentenced Malicoat to die, and he was delivered to his death row cell the same day.

His attorneys filed an appeal, which stayed the execution, but the Oklahoma Court of Criminal Appeals affirmed the judgment and sentence in 2000. The U.S. Supreme Court denied certiorari the same year, and in 2006 the justices denied post-conviction relief. His attorneys had filed a petition for a writ of habeas corpus but it was denied on October 11, 2005. After the U.S. Supreme Court denied Malicoat's final appeal state Attorney General Drew Edmondson, on June 5, 2006, requested that the justices of the state Court of Criminal Appeals set a date for Malicoat's execution, and they set the date for August 22, but then moved it to Thursday, August 31. On August 1 the state Board of Pardons and Parole met and unanimously denied clemency, and Governor Brad Henry followed their recommendation. All last-minute emergency appeals failed, and were handled so expeditiously that there were no delays.

On the morning of his execution Malicoat was moved from his death row cell to a holding cell in H Unit near the injection room. Shortly before 6:00 P.M. the condemned man, wearing glasses, was escorted into the death chamber where he took his place on the gurney and was strapped down. His arms were strapped to arm extensions and a sheet was pulled over his body. A medical technician carefully inserted one intravenous cannula (IV) into the vein of each arm while the executioners were hidden from view behind a one-way mirrored window. Warden Mike Mullin confirmed by telephone with Governor Henry that the execution was to proceed, and then the accordion blinds were raised for the witnesses, the victim's witnesses seated behind a one-way mirrored window while across the room behind clear glass sat the witnesses for the condemned man.

No members of the Leadford family were in attendance. Malicoat's witnesses included two spiritual advisers, three of his attorneys, and two acquaintances. Malicoat was asked if he had any last words, and he turned his head to face his witnesses, smiled and gave a small wave before he said, "I just want everybody to know how sorry I am this thing had to happen, any of it. I am sorry I caused the death of another human being. There is nothing I can do to change it. Contrary to what some people believe I spent many years going over it in my head. It's never left me. I hope someday people involved in it will move on." He then thanked his witnesses for supporting him and turned his head to stare at the ceiling as he said, "That's just about it." When he concluded the warden announced, "Let the execution begin," and following a saline flush of the tubes the executioners emptied their syringes into the tube leading to Malicoat's arm: first sodium thiopental, a strong sedative; second pancuronium bromide to stop his respiration; and finally potassium chloride to stop his heart. Malicoat was the second condemned man to have a double dose of the sedative portion of the three-drug combination. He took two deep breaths and closed his eyes, and in a few moments his breathing stopped. When all sign of life was absent at 6:09 P.M. he was pronounced dead.

Sources: *Chickasha Express-Star* (OK): August 19, 2006; August 26, 2006; September 1, 2006. *Malicoat v. Mullin*: 426 F.3d 1241 (2005). *Malicoat v. Oklahoma*: 531 U.S. 888 (2000). *Malicoat v. State*: 992 P.2d 383 (2000); 137 P.3d 1234 (2006). *Oklahoman* (Oklahoma City): June 5, 2006; August 31, 2006. *Shawnee News-Star* (OK): September 1, 2006. *Tulsa World* (OK): September 1, 2006.

Hamilton, Corey D.
January 9, 2007

Twenty-three-year-old Corey Duane Hamilton and twenty-one-year-old Donnie Daniels had worked at the Lee's Famous Recipe Chicken restaurant on South Sheridan Road in east Tulsa, Oklahoma. On the afternoon of August 17, 1992, Donnie Daniels and twenty-two-year-old Tyrone Johnson borrowed a .38-caliber revolver from one of Johnson's relatives, and that evening they went to the home of Denicsha Gunter to play cards with Corey Hamilton and his twenty-year-old brother William Hamilton, who was visiting from Detroit. The four men discussed robbing the restaurant and left the Gunter home before 9:45 P.M., to allow time to change clothes before arriving at the restaurant at the closing time of 10:00 P.M., but they made no effort to don disguises even though they knew Corey and Daniels would be recognized. Using Daniels' blue Chevrolet they drove up and down 9th Street near the restaurant and stopped to retrieve a shotgun they had previously hidden in a ditch. They parked Daniels' automobile behind the restaurant, and the four men got out of the car: William Hamilton wearing black shorts and a black shirt with a gold "7" on it and carrying a bag and the shotgun; Daniels wearing a dark shirt and white "fleece" shorts; the clothes of Corey Hamilton were not later described by witnesses, but Johnson was dressed all in black, and he went behind the restaurant and did not return.

The Hamiltons and Daniels went into the restaurant where they were met by nineteen-year-old employee Theodore "Ted" Kinley, and at gunpoint they ordered him to lock the doors. They captured the other three employees — seventeen-year-old Joseph "Joey" Gooch, twenty-four-year-old Stephen Williams, and twenty-seven-year-old Senaida "Sandy" Lara — and ordered them into the rear walk-in cooler. Corey kept Kinley in the restaurant and used the .38-caliber revolver to force him to open the safe, while William Hamilton guarded the cooler door with the shotgun. After Kinley handed Corey a little more than $2,000 from the safe he was taken into the cooler where Corey, using the .38-caliber revolver, forced them to kneel, and then he systematically murdered each with a single point-blank shot to the back of their heads.

Later that night Gaylon Frazier found the dead bodies and called the police, and after speaking with witnesses Lisa Frazier and John Andrew Waltrip the police began looking for the blue Chevrolet. Daniels had walked away from the restaurant, leaving his car for the Hamiltons, but they met later to divide the money, and Corey told Daniels he had shot "Ted and Sandy and them." The Hamiltons, after leaving the restaurant, had driven Daniels' car to his apartment complex and parked it, where it was soon found. Daniels was arrested, and Johnson soon joined him in the Tulsa County jail. The Hamiltons had fled to Detroit, and when Corey heard there was a warrant for his arrest he surrendered to the police, and he and his brother were extradited to Oklahoma. After the Hamiltons were identified as the robbers, and Corey as the murderer, the area around Corey's apartment was searched and the murder weapon was recovered hidden in a field.

Daniels was tried first on four counts of first-degree murder and convicted, and on September 28, 1993, he was sentenced to serve four prison terms of life without parole and one term of life for the robbery with a firearm. The Hamiltons and Johnson were tried together and convicted of first-degree murder, but after Daniels testified that it was Corey who had murdered the four employees William Hamilton was sentenced to serve four terms of life without parole and one life term for robbery with a firearm, and Johnson was sentenced to serve four life terms. On December 9, 1993, Corey Hamilton faced Tulsa County District Court Judge Jay D. Dalton and was sentenced to four death penalties and to serve life in prison for robbery with a firearm, and five days later he was delivered to his death row cell.

His attorneys filed an appeal, which stayed the execution but in 1997 Oklahoma's Court of Criminal Appeals affirmed the judgment and sentence of the District Court. The U.S. Supreme Court denied certiorari in 1998, and the state justices denied post-conviction relief in an unpublished opinion. After all state judicial relief was exhausted his attorneys filed a petition for a writ of habeas corpus, but the federal Tenth Circuit Court of Appeals denied relief in 2006. After the U.S. Supreme Court denied Hamilton's final appeal Oklahoma's Attorney General Drew Edmondson, on November 6, 2006, requested the Court of Criminal Appeals to set a date for his execution, and on December 7, 2006, the justices set the date for Tuesday,

January 9, 2007. Oklahoma's Board of Pardons and Parole met on December 27 and recommended denial of clemency, and Governor Brad Henry followed their recommendation. The Tenth Circuit Court of Appeals denied an appeal on Thursday, January 4, because it had not been filed in a timely fashion, but the justices observed that he would not have won on the merits, and the U.S. Supreme Court denied Hamilton's last-minute emergency appeal on the day before his execution Tuesday.

On the morning of his execution Hamilton was moved from his death row cell to a holding cell in H Unit near the injection room. At 6:00 P.M. the condemned man was escorted into the death chamber where he took his place on the gurney and was strapped down. His arms were strapped to arm extensions and a sheet was pulled over his body. A medical technician carefully inserted one intravenous cannula (IV) into the vein of each arm while the executioners were hidden from view behind a one-way mirrored window. Warden Mike Mullin confirmed by telephone with Governor Henry that the execution was to proceed, and then the accordion blinds were raised on the windows to the witness rooms, where the victim's witnesses sat behind a one-way mirrored glass and across the room Hamilton's witnesses watched through a clear glass window.

Hamilton was asked if he had any last words and he said, "I wish everyone could experience the love of God the way I have experienced it. I love everybody and hope to see you on the other side. To the victims' families, I pray that you have peace and all that you are in need of." When Hamilton concluded the warden announced, "Let the execution begin." The executioners first flushed the two tubes leading to his arms with a saline solution, and then they emptied their syringes into the tube leading to his arm: first sodium thiopental, a strong sedative; second pancuronium bromide to stop his respiration; and finally potassium chloride to stop his heart. As the drugs began to flow into his system at 6:08 P.M. Hamilton said, "Into thy hands I commit my spirit, Oh Lord," and as the first drug took effect Hamilton prayed, mouthing several incoherent words with "Jesus" being the only word understood. Six times he made a gurgling sound through his open mouth, and he died with his mouth still open. He stopped breathing at 6:10 P.M., and he was pronounced dead at 6:14 P.M.

Sources: *Hamilton v. Mullin*: 436 F.3d 1181 (2006). *Hamilton v. Oklahoma*: 522 U.S. 1059 (1998). *Hamilton v. State*: 937 P.2d 1001 (1997). *Oklahoman* (Oklahoma City): December 7, 2006; January 9–10, 2007. *Shawnee News-Star* (OK): January 11, 2007. Tulsa County case: CF 92-3584. *Tulsa World* (OK): January 10, 2007.

Bland, Jimmy D.
June 26, 2007

The parents of Jimmy Dale Bland had lived near Frederick, Oklahoma, but divorced, and Bland lived with his mother in California. As soon as he was old enough he joined the army and was stationed at Fort Sill, not far from Frederick.

On Saturday evening, March 1, 1975, seventeen-year-old Bland knocked on the door to the Prentice home in Granfield, near Frederick, and asked for the Johnsons, but he was told they did not live there. He returned on Monday evening, March 3, and again knocked, getting twenty-four-year-old Raymond Prentice and his wife Brenda out of bed, but when the men stepped outside to talk Brenda returned to their bed. Brenda soon heard several gunshots, and then Bland appeared in her bedroom and ordered her to dress and get her three-year-old son, Ronnie Dale, ready to leave. When Brenda's brother arrived she begged Bland to spare his life so he sent Harold McCammon away, and McCammon called the police. Bland then ushered them through the living room. Brenda saw that Bland had dragged her dead husband into the room by his boots, and she yelled for him to cover the bloody body so her son would not see it.

Bland kidnapped Brenda and Ronnie Dale, put them in the family car, and drove off. The police arrived in time to chase them at high speeds until, in Frederick, he turned down a dead-end street. He fired several shots at the officers to keep them away, but they did not return fire for fear of harming the hostages. Bland told Brenda, "I guess if I went to sleep they'd probably get me," and then he dozed. The officers rushed the vehicle, removed the hostages unharmed, and arrested Bland without further resistance. The next day he was sent to the Western State Hospital for psychiatric observation, where he was found sane and able to stand trial as an adult.

He was tried on a charge of first-degree manslaughter and two counts of kidnapping, convicted on August 28, 1975, and sentenced to serve a prison term of sixty years. Bland escaped from the prison in 1987, was recaptured and tried, and was convicted of escape on February 3 and sentenced to serve one year in prison and one year on probation, concurrent with his current sentence.

On August 10, 1995, Bland was released from prison, and he settled in Manitou, Oklahoma. Bland was befriended by the sixty-two-year-old ex-mayor Doyle Windle Rains of Manitou in Tillman County, Oklahoma, and the ex-convict was put to work doing construction jobs and general handyman chores. On November 14, 1996, Bland borrowed Rains' Cadillac and drove to Oklahoma City to visit his girlfriend, but when he returned the car the two men began arguing. Bland got a .22-caliber rifle and shot Rains in the back of his head, killing him, and then took the body from the garage to a nearby creek and hid it under a pile of logs. He fled in Rains' automobile but was stopped for drunk driving two days later, and when questioned about the owner of the car he confessed to murdering Rains and told where his body could be found. He said he had killed Rains after they argued over money Rains owed him.

Bland was charged with murder and tried in early 1998; his defense of voluntary intoxication was rejected, and he was convicted of first-degree murder. On February 6 Bland was sentenced to die, and he was delivered to his death row cell seventeen days later. His attorneys filed an appeal, which stayed the execution but in early 2000 the state Court of Criminal Appeals affirmed the judgment and sentence of the District Court. On June 26, 2000, the justices denied post-conviction relief, and on January 8, 2001, the U.S. Supreme Court denied certiorari. After all state appeals were exhausted his attorneys filed a petition for a writ of habeas corpus on November 26, 2001, which was denied by the federal Tenth Circuit Court of Appeals in 2006, at about the time he was diagnosed with terminal lung cancer. Over the months that followed he received radiation and chemotherapy, but it was expected he would die of the disease before the end of 2007 after the cancer spread to his brain and hip. The issue of executing a terminally ill murderer then became a cause célèbre for death penalty opponents.

When the U.S. Supreme Court denied his final appeal the state's Attorney General Drew Edmondson, on April 23, requested the Court of Criminal Appeals to set a date for Bland's execution, and on May 15 they set the date at Tuesday, June 26, 2007. Bland's hearing before the state Board of Pardons and Parole was held in early June and the members voted unanimously to deny clemency, and Governor Brad Henry followed their recommendation. Late on Tuesday the U.S. Supreme Court denied his last-minute emergency appeal, clearing the way for the execution to proceed.

On the morning of his execution Bland was moved from his death row cell to a holding cell in H Unit near the injection room. At 6:00 P.M. the condemned man was escorted into the death chamber where he took his place on the gurney and was strapped down. His arms were strapped to arm extensions and a sheet was pulled over his body. A medical technician carefully inserted one intravenous cannula (IV) into the vein of each arm while the executioners were hidden from view behind a one-way mirrored window. Warden Marty Sirmons confirmed by telephone with Governor Henry that the execution was to proceed, and then the accordion blinds were raised on the windows to the witness rooms, where the witnesses for the Rains and Prentice families sat behind a one-way mirrored glass and across the room behind a clear glass window sat the condemned man's mother, two sisters, brother, and spiritual adviser. Bland was asked if he had any last words. Most of what he said was inaudible because of a defect in the sound system, but he was heard to say "I'm sorry for what happened," and to his family "I love you all. I love you all." He then turned to the prison staff and said, "I'm ready," and the warden announced, "Let the execution begin." The executioners first flushed the two tubes leading to his arms with a saline solution and then emptied their syringes into the tube leading to his left arm: first sodium thiopental, a strong sedative; second pancuronium bromide to stop his respiration; and finally potassium chloride to stop his heart. The drugs began to flow at 6:12 P.M., and he closed his eyes, he breathed heavily for several seconds, and his color turned ashen. At 6:19 P.M. all sign of life was absent and he was pronounced dead.

Sources: *Bland v. Oklahoma*: 531 U.S. 1099 (2001). *Bland v. Sirmons*: 459 F.3d 999 (2006). *Bland v. State*: 4 P.3d 702 (2000); PCD 99–1200 (2000). *Joplin Globe* (MO): June 27, 2007. *Lawton Constitution* (OK): March 4, 1975. *Oklahoman* (Oklahoma City): May 16, 2007; June 27, 2007. *Paris News* (TX): March 3, 1975. *Tulsa World* (OK): June 27, 2007.

Welch, Frank D.
August 21, 2007

In December 1986 twenty-five-year-old Frank Duane Welch, a repairman for Norman Cablevision, made a service call at the home of the Coopers in Norman. In early 1987 Welch was fired from his job when he was charged with forging checks and embezzlement, but did not turn in his uniform. On February 25, 1987, Welch appeared at the front door of the Cooper home in Norman, Cleveland County, Oklahoma, dressed in his cablevision uniform, and twenty-nine-year-old Jo Talley Cooper, who was four months pregnant, locked the dogs in the garage and let him enter. He took Cooper prisoner and tied her wrists and neck with leather straps and duct-taped her mouth, and as she strangled to death he raped and sodomized her and then inserted a plastic toy pylon into her vagina. He left her lying in the living room nude, face-up, and spread-eagled, where her husband found her body at 1:00 P.M. and called the police. The Coopers' seven-month-old son lay in his crib unharmed, and drawers had been opened and rifled suggesting a burglary-gone-wrong, but nothing was taken. Welch fled and left no clues to the identity of the rapist, though sperm was recovered from a kitchen towel and held as evidence, and the case went cold.

Welch and his wife Bonnie were friends of the Stevens family and lived on property next to the Stevens home near Tuttle in Grady County. On May 6, 1987, the day after Welch appeared in court on criminal charges, he gained entrance to the home of Debra Anne Stevens, and after she locked the dogs in her sister's bedroom Welch took her captive and forced her into her bedroom, tied a thin rope around her neck and bound her wrists with similar rope, stuffed a wad of toilet paper in her mouth, laid her face up on the bed spread-eagled, and raped her as she died of strangulation. Her daughter, Stacie Stromberg, found her body later that day and called the police. During the autopsy the medical examiner Larry Balding recovered swabs of sperm from Stevens' vagina, and later these were tested for DNA, but the case went cold.

In 1989 Welch was imprisoned on charges of grand larceny but he was released on July 18, 1994. On May 5, 1995, Welch was convicted of kidnapping, possession of a stolen vehicle, and assault and battery with a deadly weapon, and he was sentenced to serve forty-five years in prison for each of the first two counts and a life term for the third offense. He was serving his time when a blood sample was taken, his DNA was entered into the database, and it was matched with the DNA recovered in the Stevens murder. In October 1996 Ed Briggs of the Oklahoma State Bureau of Investigation telephoned Norman detective Steven Lucas and suggested that they look at Welch as a suspect in the Cooper murder, because of similarities in the cases. Lucas obtained a blood sample from Welch, and the DNA from the blood matched the DNA of the sperm recovered at the Cooper murder scene.

On February 25, 1997, Welch was charged with murdering Cooper, and on July 10 a bill of particulars was filed showing aggravating circumstances justifying the death penalty. Welch's trial for murdering Cooper began on March 23, 1998, and he claimed he and Cooper had been having an affair and the killing of Cooper was an accident when, at his suggestion following anal sex at her request, they tried sexual asphyxiation and were having vaginal sex from behind when he discovered she was dead. He said he then altered the scene to look like an attack because he was an ex-felon. He also told the jury that he and Stevens were having an affair and said he killed her during an argument over her threats to expose him for the Cooper murder, when she demanded $10,000. The jury rejected his defense, and he was convicted of first-degree murder with a recommendation for the death penalty. On April 3 District Court Judge Thomas A. Lucas sentenced Welch to die by lethal injection. He was then taken to Grady County and tried for the murder of Stevens, and on December 1, 1998, he was sentenced to serve a term of life in prison without parole, and he was delivered to his death row cell that day.

His attorneys filed an appeal in the Cooper conviction, which stayed the execution, but on April 10, 2000, the state Court of Criminal Appeals affirmed the judgment and sentence of the lower court, post-conviction relief was denied on May 25, and the U.S. Supreme Court denied certiorari the same year. Once all state relief was exhausted his attorneys filed a petition for a writ of habeas corpus but it was denied by the federal Tenth Circuit Court of Appeals in 2006. After the U.S. Supreme Court denied Welch's final appeal the state Attorney General Drew Edmondson, on June 18, 2007, requested that an execution date be set by the Court of Criminal Appeals, and the justices set the date for Tuesday, August 21. The state Board of Pardons and Parole met in July and denied clemency, and Governor Brad Henry followed their recommendation. No last-minute emergency appeals were filed or pending on the day set for the execution.

On the morning of his execution Welch was moved from his death row cell to a holding cell in H Unit near the injection room. At 6:00 P.M. the condemned man was escorted into the death chamber where he took his place on the gurney and was strapped down. His arms were strapped to arm extensions and a sheet was pulled over his body. A medical technician carefully inserted one intravenous cannula (IV) into the vein of each arm while the executioners were hidden from view behind a one-way mirrored window. Warden Marty Sirmons confirmed by telephone with Governor Henry that the execution was to proceed, and then the accordion blinds were raised on the windows to the witness rooms, where the witnesses for the victims' families sat behind a one-way mirrored glass and across the room behind a clear glass window sat the condemned man's witnesses.

Welch was asked if he had any last words, and he looked at the mirrored window as he said, "There's nothing that can change the horrible thing I've done. There is nothing that can change that. I take full responsibility for what I've done. I am truly, truly sorry for all the hurt and pain I've caused you. There's no excuse for it — there never was. It was just me." He then turned to his witnesses and said, "I love y'all. God bless y'all," and to the warden he said, "I'm ready," and the warden announced, "Let the execution begin." The executioners first flushed the two tubes leading to his arms with a saline solution and then emptied their syringes into the tube leading to his left arm: first sodium thiopental, a strong sedative; second pancuronium bromide to stop his respiration; and finally potassium chloride to stop his heart. As the drugs began to flow Welch's brother, among his witnesses, began having breathing difficulties and collapsed. He was attended by prison medical staff and refused to be taken by ambulance to a hospital. At 6:21 P.M. all sign of life was absent and Welch was pronounced dead.

Sources: Cleveland County case: CF 97–247. *Oklahoman* (Oklahoma City): August 22, 2007. *Shawnee News-Star* (OK): August 22, 2007. *Tulsa World* (OK): August 22, 2007. *Welch v. Oklahoma*: 531 U.S. 1056 (2000). *Welch v. Sirmons*: 451 F.3d 675 (2006). *Welch v. State*: 2 P.3d 356 (2000); PCD 2000–86 (2000).

Short, Terry L.
June 17, 2008

Thirty-four-year-old Terry Lyn Short, an ex-convict who had spent a year in prison in 1987 and four years in prison between 1988 and 1991, and Brenda Gardner had been living together since early 1994, but Short was abusive and several times had threatened to "burn Brenda and her family up," so Gardner finally ended the relationship. Short then trashed their apartment, threw rocks at the car of Gardner's mother, and tried to run Gardner's mother off the road. Once he pulled his car next to her mother's car, and when Gardner refused to talk with him he said, "I'll just get some gas and pour it on your mother and set her on fire." Short had previously shown Brenda that he knew how to make a fire bomb using gasoline, wax, and a towel wick in a glass bottle.

By December 26, 1994, Short was living at the Melrose Motel, and Gardner had moved in with her sister Tammy and Tammy's two young children in apartment 127 at the Royal Chateau Apartments in south Oklahoma City, but Gardner saw Short nearly every day. Between December 28 and January 4 Short and Gardner were arrested for shoplifting, and when they went to court Short insisted that Gardner "take the rap for it. She'd better or else," and for the first time he threatened Robert Hines, the father of one of Tammy's children.

On January 8, 1995, at 3:00 A.M. Brenda heard loud noises at their front door and called out. The noises quickly ended but thirty minutes later Hines arrived and found the front door jammed shut from the outside, and he had to go around to the patio door to enter. After he awoke the family Hines repaired the front door and remained to visit. At 5:00 A.M. Brenda saw Short, wearing a red coat, standing in the parking lot near Hines' pickup truck, and Hines moved to the patio door to see what Short was doing. At that moment Short turned his back to Hines and seemed to be lighting a cigarette, but when he turned back he immediately threw a firebomb through the patio door, and it set the apartment on fire. Hines was burned seriously but everybody in apartment 127 escaped through the front door.

Upstairs in apartment 227 lived twenty-two-year-old Ken Yamamoto, a Japanese exchange student, who was asleep. The intense fire spread quickly and the ceiling collapsed, so that Yamamoto fell down into the inferno beneath and was badly burned over 95 percent of his body. He regained consciousness as the paramedics tried to save his life, and he was rushed to the Oklahoma City Hospital, but he died in several hours.

That evening Short called his cousin David Davis and asked him to bring a change of clothes and then accompany him to the police station to surrender, and he surrendered later that evening. Short's red coat was found in Davis' car and, along with his sneakers, tested positive for gasoline. Detectives also found a handwritten journal with an entry saying he had lost Brenda and, "I need her to go on in my life. She is all I got." While in jail Short told cellmate Jay Brown that he had started the fire, "because I found Brenda and Hines having sex," and he had scratched derogatory comments about Gardner into the cell wall.

Short was tried in the Oklahoma County District Court and convicted of five counts of attempted murder and one count of first degree murder. On April 21, 1997, Judge Charles L. Owens sentenced Short to die by lethal injection and to serve two consecutive terms of two hundred years and three consecutive terms of one hundred years, and a week later he was delivered to his death row cell. His attorneys filed an appeal but in 1999 the state Court of Criminal Appeals affirmed the judgment and sentence of the district court, and the motion for post-conviction relief was denied. When all state judicial remedies were exhausted Short's attorneys filed a petition for a writ of habeas corpus, and this was denied in 2006. In 2008, after the U.S. Supreme Court ruled that lethal injection was a constitutional method of execution, the state's Attorney General Drew Edmondson on April 16 requested an execution date from the Court of Criminal Appeals, and on April 29, 2008, the justices set the date for June 17. The state Board of Pardons and Parole met in May and denied clemency, and Governor Brad Henry followed their recommendation.

On the morning of his execution Short was moved from his death row cell to a holding cell in H Unit near the injection room. At 6:00 P.M. the condemned man was escorted into the death chamber where he took his place on the gurney and was strapped down. His arms were strapped to arm extensions and a sheet was pulled over his body. A medical technician carefully inserted one intravenous cannula (IV) into the vein of each arm while the executioners were hidden from view behind a one-way mirrored window. Warden Marty Sirmons confirmed by telephone with Governor Henry that the execution was to proceed, and then the accordion blinds were raised on the windows to the witness rooms, where a dozen witnesses waited. Short was asked if he had any last words and, as tears streamed down his cheeks, he said, "I have nothing to say." The warden announced, "Let the execution begin," and the executioners first flushed the two tubes leading to his arms with a saline solution and then emptied their syringes into one of the tubes leading to his arm: first sodium thiopental, a strong sedative; second pancuronium bromide to stop his respiration; and finally potassium chloride to stop his heart. Short appeared to stop breathing and the color drained from his face as the drugs began to flow. At 6:08 P.M. all sign of life was absent, and he was pronounced dead.

Sorces: Oklahoma County case: CF 95–216. *Oklahoman* (Oklahoma City): April 29, 2008. *Short v. Sirmons*: 472 F.3d 1177 (2006). *Short v. State*: 980 P.2d 1081 (1999). *Tulsa World* (OK): June 18, 2008.

Cummings, Jessie J.
September 25, 2008

In 1987 thirty-one-year-old Jessie James Cummings married a girl named Sherry Marie Mitchell (Cummings), and then without divorcing her he married her sister Juanita Marie Lewis (Cummings) in 1989. In 1991 Cummings was living in a polygamous relationship with his two wives, Sherry's daughter Debra by her husband, Juanita's son Robbie by her husband's father, and Cummings' cancer-stricken father, Jessie Samuel Cummings, in Phillips, Coal County, Oklahoma. Jessie maintained tight control over his family through threats and violence, rape and incest. His forty-two-year-old half-sister, Judy Ann Moody-Mayo, and his eleven-year-old niece, Melissa Marie Moody, lived in nearby Tushka, and Cummings became determined to have sexual relations with his niece.

On September 4 he told Juanita to take Judy Ann to look for houses, and when they came to a vacant house she was to shoot his half-sister to death with his .38-caliber revolver. The next morning Jessie left to take his father to Oklahoma City for cancer treatment, and while he was gone Judy Ann and Melissa, with Sherry, drove around the Phillips area in Judy Ann's pickup truck looking at houses, but Sherry could not kill Judy Ann with Melissa present.

They returned to the Cummings' house and sent the children out to play, and while Sherry was in the bathroom she heard five gunshots and returned to find Judy Ann slumped over on the couch dead, with five bullet wounds in her head and neck. The two women called in the children and covered their eyes as they took them through the living room into a rear bedroom and locked them in, then they dragged the dead body outside and into a cellar. They returned, handcuffed Melissa to the bed, and sent their two children outside to play while they cleaned up the blood on the couch, floor and wall.

Jessie returned a little after midnight, and when they showed him the body he wrapped it in a quilt and mattress pad, and the three carried the body to the bed of Judy Ann's pickup truck. Jessie drove Judy Ann's pickup truck while Sherry followed in the family car, and when they were near Atoka Lake Jessie stopped and carried Judy Ann's body to a small pond near the lake and threw it in. He then parked Judy Ann's truck along the road, lifted the hood, and had Sherry drive him to the opposite side of Atoka Lake where he washed and threw away his boots, and along the road back to their house he threw out his overalls. Once at the house they loaded the couch into the bed of their pickup, took it to a bridge near Centrahoma and threw it over the side, so there would be no chance of finding Judy Ann's blood on it.

They returned to the house again, and Jessie had Juanita bring Melissa out of the bedroom and ordered her and Sherry to get into the family car, took along the keys to their car and truck, told Juanita to stay inside the house, and they started driving toward Choctaw County. When they reached a remote location near the bridge over the Clear Boggy River, Jessie parked and, leaving Sherry in the car, had Melissa climb over a rail. He took her into a field where he molested her and then stabbed her to death.

On September 8 Jessie went to the police to report his half-sister and niece missing, and he gave them photographs and said friends had seen Judy Ann's truck disabled and abandoned near Highway 43 at Atoka Lake. On September 9, 1991, the body of Judy Ann was discovered, but Melissa was still missing. On October 16 Melissa's skeletal remains were found in Choctaw County, and later it was determined she had been stabbed to death.

During the next three years the Cummings family moved to Lehigh, and Juanita began working for the Rev. Edward Fields. When she felt comfortable with the pastor she confessed, and the reverend encouraged her to confess to the police. There had been no clue to the murderers of Judy Ann and her daughter until July 1994 when Juanita Cummings confessed to killing Moody-Mayo, and claimed that she only murdered her to save the life of her son when her husband threatened to kill him if she did not comply. Cummings was arrested on July 28 and on August 1 charges were filed against the three prisoners, but Jessie would profess his innocence to the end, and he tried to shift the blame onto his wives. Juanita was charged with second-degree murder, convicted, and sentenced to serve a life term while Sherry, through a plea deal, was tried and convicted of being an accessory to murder and sentenced to serve a term of thirty-five years in prison. Juanita testified against Cummings when it was shown her marriage was null and void by the prior marriage to Sherry.

At his trial in early 1996 Cummings was convicted of both murders, and on May 30, 1996, he was twice sentenced to die by lethal injection. He was delivered to his death row cell on June 3, and his attorneys filed an appeal. In 1998 the state Court of Criminal Appeals overturned the death sentence in the murder of Judy Ann, because only the testimony of his accomplice tied him to the crime, but the justices affirmed the judgment and sentence regarding the rape and murder of his niece. His attorneys filed a motion for post-conviction relief but it was denied in 1998. When all state judicial relief was exhausted Cummings' attorneys filed a petition for a writ of habeas corpus, but the federal Tenth Circuit Court of Appeals denied relief in 2007. After the U.S. Supreme Court denied Cummings' final appeal Oklahoma's Attorney General Drew Edmondson, on June 16, 2008, requested that a date be set for Cummings' execution, and on June 27 the justice of the Court of Criminal Appeals set the execution for Thursday, September 25. The state Board of Pardons and Parole met in August and denied clemency, and Governor Brad Henry followed their recommendation.

On the morning of his execution Cummings was moved from his death row cell to a holding cell in H Unit near the injection room. At 6:00 P.M. the condemned man was escorted into the death chamber where he took his place on the gurney and was strapped down. His arms were strapped to arm extensions and a sheet was pulled over his body. A medical technician carefully inserted one intravenous cannula (IV) into the vein of each arm while the executioners were hidden from view behind a one-way mirrored window. Warden Marty Sirmons confirmed by telephone with Governor Henry that the execution was to proceed, and then the accordion blinds were raised on the windows to the witness rooms, where Cummings' witnesses seated behind clear glass included a female friend, his defense attorney Chris Eulberg, and two spiritual advisers. Across the room behind a one-way mirrored window sat Atoka County Sheriff Gary McCool and four members of the Moody-Mayo family.

Cummings was asked if he had any last words and he said, "I love my family. I love my children. I love my gorgeous angel. The justice system let me down on this case. It turned a blind eye to the truth in this. You came here today to see an innocent man die." The warden then announced, "Let the execution begin." The executioners first flushed the two tubes leading to his arms with a saline solution and then emptied their syringes into the tube leading to his arm: first sodium thiopental, a strong sedative; second pancuronium bromide to stop his respiration; and finally potassium chloride to stop his heart. When the drugs began to flow Cummings took two deep breaths and said, "I forgive everybody involved in this," and then lapsed into unconsciousness as the color drained from his face. At 6:11 P.M. all sign of life was absent and he was pronounced dead.

Sources: Coal County Case: CF 94-32. *Cummings v. Sirmons*: 506 F.3d 1211 (2007). *Cummings v. State*: 968 P.2d 821; 970 P.2d 188. *Oklahoman* (Oklahoma City): June 27, 2008. *Tulsa World* (OK): September 26, 2008.

Brown, Darwin D.
January 22, 2009

Nineteen-year-old Michael L. Wilson was employed at the QuikTrip convenience store at 215 North Garnett Road in Tulsa, Oklahoma. During the early morning hours of February 26, 1995, Wilson, with eighteen-year-old Darwin Demond Brown, twenty-three-year-old Billy D. Alverson, and seventeen-year-old Richard J. Harjo, went into the QuikTrip store and waited for the opportunity to capture thirty-year-old clerk Richard K. Yost. When Yost finished cleaning the windows to the walk-in refrigerator and started walking through the passageway to the rear, they surrounded him, handcuffed their prisoner, and dragged him into the cooler. After Yost's ankles were duct-taped, Alverson returned to the store area and tidied up the items knocked from the shelf during the brief struggle, then he kept watch.

Brown and Wilson remained with Yost while Harjo joined Alverson. They left the store and Yost, thinking a customer had entered, began calling for help but in a few moments the two men returned, and Harjo carried a black aluminum baseball bat into the cooler. One of the men began beating Yost; he was struck fifty-four times in a little over two minutes, and each blow could be heard on the audio monitor of the store's surveillance system. Yost threw up his hands in a defensive posture, and the handcuffs were broken by the blows, and one cuff was knocked off his wrist. As the beating was taking place Wilson walked from the back room, donned Yost's QuikTrip jacket, went behind the counter, and tried to remove the safe. When he failed Wilson cleaned out the cash drawer and the currency change machine. While Wilson was behind the counter several customers came in and Wilson served them, then went to the video machine, turned it off, and removed the tape. The men came out, removed two safes and loaded them into Wilson's car, using the store dolly.

Customer Larry Wiseman stopped at the store at 6:00 A.M. and, finding no one to serve him, investigated and found Yost's dead body lying in a pool of blood, milk and beer. The police were called, and they determined that Wilson had been in the store between 4:00 and 6:00 A.M., but he did not show up for his shift at 3:00 P.M. The police quickly set up surveillance on his house, and an hour later Wilson got into a gray car with three other men. The car was stopped, and all four men were arrested. The police found an unusually large number of five-dollar bills in Harjo's pockets, and at the police station money was recovered from Brown and Alverson. Officers searched Alverson's home and found the drop safe, the store's dolly, money tubes and the surveillance tape. They found nothing at Wilson's home, but the next day his mother called and the police found, on her front porch, the baseball bat, a bloody QuikTrip jacket with Yost's name embroidered on it, the Nike jacket Wilson had worn into the store, and the cuff broken from the set on Yost's wrists.

In early 1997 Brown was tried with co-defendant Wilson after separate juries were seated, and both were found guilty of first-degree murder and robbery. On April 9 a Tulsa County District Court Judge sentenced both men to die by lethal injection for the murder and to life in prison for the robbery. The trials of Alverson and Harjo followed, and on July 11 Alverson was sentenced to death while Harjo, because he was only seventeen years of age at the time of the crime, was sentenced to life in prison without parole. Brown's attorneys filed an appeal, which stayed the execution, but the Oklahoma Court of Criminal Appeals affirmed the judgment and death sentence in 1998 and denied a rehearing on the issues on February 22, 1999. The U.S. Supreme Court denied certiorari. Brown's attorneys then filed a motion for post-conviction relief, and this was denied on November 9, 1999. When all state judicial relief was exhausted a petition for a writ of habeas corpus was filed with the federal Tenth Circuit Court of Appeals on February 2, 2000, and denied in 2006. The U.S. Supreme Court denied Brown's final appeal on October 14, 2008, and the state's Attorney General Drew Edmondson immediately asked the Court of Criminal Appeals to set a date for his execution; the justices set the date for January 22, 2009. On January 7, 2009, the state Board of Pardons and Parole met and denied clemency, and Governor Brad Henry followed their recommendation.

On the morning of his execution Brown was moved from his death row cell to a holding cell in H Unit near the injection room. Just before the time for Brown's execution the death row inmates staged a demonstration, beating on their cell doors and the building's pipes. Just before 6:00 P.M. the condemned man was escorted into the death chamber where he took his place on the gurney and was strapped down. His arms were strapped to arm extensions and a sheet was pulled over his body. A medical technician carefully inserted one intravenous cannula (IV) into the vein of each arm while the executioners were hidden from view behind a one-way mirrored window. Warden Marty Sirmons confirmed by telephone with Governor Henry that the execution was to proceed, and then the accordion blinds were raised on the windows to the witness rooms, where the witnesses for victim's families sat behind a one-way mirrored glass and across the room behind a clear glass window sat the condemned man's witnesses.

Brown was asked if he had any last words and he said, "I apologize for anybody I hurt. I'm sorry to everybody." He looked at his father and two uncles and said, "I'd like to thank all of my family for the support that they've given me," and then he mouthed the words, "I love you." The warden announced, "Let the execution begin," and after the executioners flushed the two tubes leading to his arms with a saline solution at 6:05 P.M. they emptied their syringes into the tube leading to his arm: first sodium thiopental, a strong sedative; second pancuronium bromide to stop his respiration; and finally potassium chloride to stop his heart. As the drugs began to flow Brown's eyes rolled back and his mouth opened slightly, he rose up slightly straining against the leather straps as he coughed several times and gasped heavily, the color drained from his face and then he lay still, with his eyes and mouth half-open. At 6:11 P.M. all sign of life was absent and he was pronounced dead.

Sources: *Brown v. Sirmons*: 415 F. Supp. 2d 1268 (2006). *Brown v. State*: 989 P.2d 913 (1998); F 97-493 (1999); PC 98-1251 (1999). Tulsa County case: CRF 95-1024. *Tulsa World* (OK): October 14, 2008; January 22, 2009.

Gilson, Donald L.
May 14, 2009

During the fall of 1994 the Cleveland County Sheriff's Department received a complaint that the six children of thirty-eight-year-old Bertha Jean Coffman were being neglected and one child was being sexually abused by her live-in boyfriend. Deputies investigated Coffman's rented mobile home in Newalla, Oklahoma, and, upon finding the living conditions deplorable and the children in need of medical attention, the deputies removed twelve-year-old Jeremy, eleven-year-old Isaac, ten-year-old Tranny, nine-year-old Tia, seven-year-old Shane, and six-year-old Crystal.

Coffman was at the time employed as a janitor at the Little Axe School, and she worked with fellow-janitor thirty-four-year-old Donald Lee

Gilson. Coffman's boyfriend left, and Gilson helped Coffman refurbish her trailer so she could get the children back. Once the children were home Gilson began spending an increasing amount of time with the family and was given permission to discipline them. However, Gilson's treatment was so harsh that in June 1995 Jeremy, then thirteen, ran away.

The following month Coffman, with her five remaining children, walked to Gilson's mobile home and moved in. Gilson's trailer had only two bedrooms and he and Coffman shared one, while the second bedroom was reserved for Gilson's leather materials and tools, so the children had to sleep on the living room floor on blankets. Gilson required the children to remain indoors at all times, they were removed from school on the ruse they were being home-schooled, and they could no longer attend church services on Sundays. When the children misbehaved, in Gilson's opinion, either he or their mother would discipline them, and this took the form of standing at the wall or sitting in an empty or filled bathtub for hours, or by beatings with a bamboo stick, belt, paddle board, wooden or metal ruler, or a bull whip, and food was often withheld, especially from Tia and Isaac.

On the evening of August 16 Shane wet his bed and the following day he was punished. Shane was beaten, causing a fracture to the right side of his jawbone, and a tooth was knocked out, and there was another fracture to the left side of his head, each injury from a separate blow. By the end of the day Shane had also received fractures to his collarbone, both shoulder blades, numerous ribs, both legs, and several vertebrae. Several of these injuries could have proven fatal, but the accumulation of injuries killed eight-year-old Shane. Gilson took Shane's body back to the Coffman trailer, stored it in an abandoned freezer, and later filled the freezer with dirt.

On February 9, 1996, the skeletal remains of Shane Coffman were discovered and the sheriff's department was called. At 5:00 P.M. deputy sheriff Cliff Winkler arrived, looked into a deep freezer, and confirmed they were remains of a human child, and a search of the vacant mobile home where the freezer was located turned up a photograph of Gilson. Two days later deputies met with Gilson, and the four remaining children were taken to the Children's Hospital in Oklahoma City and examined. Tranny and Crystal had a few scars but were in reasonable health, but Isaac and Tia were malnourished, and Tia's feet were swollen, making it difficult for her to stand or walk. Tia had gangrenous tissue on her right foot and an oozing ulcer on her right buttocks. Still, it was Isaac who was in the worst condition, with numerous injuries in various stages of healing.

Meanwhile deputies questioned Gilson and Coffman, and they denied any knowledge of Shane's death, claiming he had run away in early November, they had found him lying dead among the weeds near Coffman's old home, and they had put his body in the freezer. In later interviews, however, they began to make inconsistent statements, indicating they knew more than they had originally disclosed, and finally recanted their original story. When the children were questioned Tranny and Isaac told the officers that on August 17 Shane had wet his bed and was stood against the wall where Gilson hit him with a board, and then he took Shane into the bathroom. All the children were ushered in to see Shane sitting in the bathtub and were required to chastise him "for being such a bad boy." After some time Shane was allowed to come out and join the other children watching television, but he got into more trouble, and Coffman and Gilson took Shane outside. Tranny heard him screaming. When Shane was carried back into Gilson's trailer he had swollen arms, he was "breathing weird," and he had a soft spot on his head, but the other children were not permitted to speak with him. Shane was put in the bathtub again, and Tranny heard banging and more screaming. When the sounds ceased the children were put to bed, but they were awakened a short time later and told Shane had run away. Coffman and Gilson then left "to look for Shane."

After his arrest Gilson tried to shift the blame onto Coffman, claiming he was asleep when she came to him and said Shane was dead, and he took him from the tub and laid him on the floor. Shane's lips were blue and he was not breathing so Gilson performed CPR for over an hour, and then they decided to dispose of the body so the Department of Human Services would not take away the other children. They decided to place him in the freezer because, "even though he wasn't alive he would still be part of the family being on her property," and they could concrete over the freezer and "make a flower bed out of it."

Gilson and Coffman were charged with murder by child abuse, and on August 20, 1997, Coffman entered an Alford plea — a plea whereby the defendant does not admit the crime but agrees that the charge could be proved at trial — and she was held in the local jail until Gilson was tried. On May 28 she was sentenced to serve prison terms of five and ten years, five life terms, and one life term without parole, and she was delivered to her cell at the Mabel Bassett Correctional Center in McCloud on June 12, 1998.

Gilson was tried in early May 1998, and on May 20 he was convicted of first-degree murder and four other counts and was sentenced to serve prison terms of five and ten years in prison, two life terms, and death by lethal injection. He was delivered to his death row cell on May 26, 1998, and his attorneys filed an appeal, which stayed the execution. The state Court of Criminal Appeals affirmed the judgment and sentence of the district court in 2000, denied post-conviction relief, and then denied a rehearing. When all state judicial remedies were exhausted Gilson's attorneys filed a petition for a writ of habeas corpus, and the federal Tenth Circuit Court of Appeals denied the petition in 2008. After the U.S. Supreme Court denied Gilson's final appeal on February 23, 2009, the state Attorney General Drew Edmondson requested the Court of Criminal Appeals to set a date for his execution, and on February 27 they set the date for May 5, but it was later moved to May 14. The state Board of Pardons and Parole met on April 14, 2009, and denied clemency, and Governor Brad Henry followed their recommendation.

On the morning of his execution Gilson was moved from his death row cell to a holding cell in H Unit near the injection room. At 6:00 P.M. the condemned man was escorted into the death chamber where he took his place on the gurney and was strapped down. His arms were strapped to arm extensions and a sheet was pulled over his body. A medical technician carefully inserted one intravenous cannula (IV) into the vein of each arm while the executioners were hidden from view behind a one-way mirrored window. Warden Marty Sirmons confirmed by telephone with Governor Henry that the execution was to proceed, and then the accordion blinds were raised on the windows to the witness rooms. Gilson's parents and sister, a friend, and his religious adviser sat behind a clear glass window, and across the room a dozen members of the victim's family sat behind the one-way mirrored window, while below in a room with closed-circuit television several others watched the execution. Gilson was asked if he had any last words and he said, "I'm an innocent man, but I get to go to heaven, and I'll see Shane tonight. It's God's will that this take place." The warden then announced, "Let the execution begin." The executioners first flushed the two tubes leading to Gilson's arms with a saline solution and then emptied their syringes into the tube leading to one arm: first sodium thiopental, a strong sedative; second pancuronium bromide to stop his respiration; and finally potassium chloride to stop his heart. He lifted his head and smiled at his family as the drugs began to flow at 6:14 P.M., and at 6:19 P.M. all sign of life was absent and he was pronounced dead.

Sources: Cleveland County case: CRF 96-245, 96-247, 96-256. *Gilson v. Sirmons*: 520 F.3d 1196 (2008). *Gilson v. State*: 8 P.3d 883 (2000). *Tulsa World* (OK): February 27, 2009; May 15, 2009. *U.S. v. Alford*: 400 U.S. 25 (1970).

DeLozier, Michael P.
July 9, 2009

In September 1995 fifty-four-year-old Paul Steven Morgan and sixty-year-old Orville Lewis Bullard were camping along the Glover River in northern McCurtain County, Oklahoma. Six hundred yards from Bullard's converted step-van, nineteen-year-old Michael Paul DeLozier, eighteen-year-old Glenney Dale Madison and seventeen-year-old Nathaniel Brandon Madison, brothers, with several others were camping in a bus belonging to Damon and Michelle Tate. During the evening hours, while the young men were riding four-wheelers along the river, they came upon the campsite of Morgan and Bullard, and while they talked DeLozier noticed their generator which he thought would be worth at least $700.

Once they returned to their campsite Delozier proposed killing the two men and stealing the generator, the matter was discussed and later that night DeLozier, carrying a single-shot shotgun, Glenney Madison carrying a Birchfield .22-caliber rifle, and his brother snuck into the campsite of Morgan and Bullard. DeLozier stepped into the van and immediately fired his shotgun, and the blast struck Bullard; then Glenney stepped in and fired a single round from the rifle which also struck

Bullard. They both stepped out and Glenney fired several rounds into the front of the camper while DeLozier was reloading the shotgun, and then Nathaniel called out to the two men to come out, and he promised that nothing would happen to them. Morgan stepped out and immediately DeLozier fired a shotgun blast into his chest, and he collapsed to the ground, face-up with his pants in his hand. DeLozier then took the rifle and point-blank fired a round into Morgan's face.

The three men ransacked the campsite, loading the generator and other items of value into Morgan's pickup truck, and took it to the Tate bus, requiring several trips to transport everything of value. They burned Morgan's body where it lay and set the step-van on fire, and it had burned out by the time they made their final return trip to their campsite, but they saw headlights coming at them so they abandoned the truck and ran. George Vance managed to drive around Morgan's truck and into the Morgan-Bullard campsite, but as soon as he saw Morgan's body lying on the ground he turned around and drove off. When he came to Morgan's truck he could not get around it so he got out of his truck, moved Morgan's truck, and at the first place with a phone he called the police. After Vance left, DeLozier and the Madisons returned and set Morgan's truck on fire.

All three men were arrested. DeLozier confessed to carrying the shotgun, the murder weapon in both killings, and while in jail he admitted to inmate Rodney Broades that he had killed two men. On May 26, 1996, Nathaniel pled guilty to a charge of conspiracy-to-murder and agreed to testify against DeLozier. He was sentenced to serve ten years in prison and arrived on June 4, 1996, and he was released on December 11, 2000. Glenney Madison was tried and convicted of two counts of first-degree murder on June 3, 1996, and he was sentenced to serve two life terms in prison. Delozier was the last to be tried, in early June. He testified that at the time of the murders felony charges were pending on two counts of fighting with police dogs, killing one and injuring another, and on March 13, 1996, he had pled guilty and was twice sentenced to serve two-year terms. His trial for murder ended with a conviction on two counts of murder in the first degree, and on June 18 he was twice sentenced to die by lethal injection and was delivered to his death row cell the following day.

His attorneys filed an appeal but in 1998 the Court of Criminal Appeals affirmed the judgment and sentence of the McCurtain County District Court and denied post-conviction relief on April 28, 1999. The U.S. Supreme Court denied certiorari. When all state judicial remedies were exhausted his attorneys filed a petition for a writ of habeas corpus, but the federal Tenth Circuit Court of Appeals denied the petition in 2008. On April 27, 2009, the U.S. Supreme Court denied DeLozier's final appeal. Two days later Attorney General Drew Edmondson requested a date for his execution, and on May 14 the justices of Oklahoma Court of Criminal Appeals set the date of execution for July 9. The state Board of Pardons and Parole met on June 29 and unanimously denied clemency, and Governor Brad Henry followed their recommendation. On the morning of the execution the state Court of Criminal Appeals denied a last-minute emergency appeal claiming new evidence that methamphetamines had affected DeLozier's brain on the day of the murders.

Before the execution DeLozier's attorney released his statement saying, "I cannot wait to finish paying this debt I owe so I can apologize to the souls of Mr. Morgan and Mr. Bullard, and ask them to forgive me for my taking their lives. To the families of my victims all I can say is, I'm sorry for the pain I've caused you. I hope my death will bring you some peace." On the morning of his execution DeLozier was moved from his death row cell to a holding cell in H Unit near the injection room. At 6:00 P.M. the condemned man, wearing glasses and a full beard, was escorted into the death chamber where he took his place on the gurney and was strapped down. His arms were strapped to arm extensions and a sheet was pulled over his body. A medical technician carefully inserted one intravenous cannula (IV) into the vein of each arm while the executioners were hidden from view behind a one-way mirrored window. Warden Marty Sirmons confirmed by telephone with Governor Henry that the execution was to proceed, and then the accordion blinds were raised on the windows to the witness rooms.

DeLozier's witnesses included two of his attorneys, his Dutch wife whom he had married while on death row, and two sisters-in-law, who watched the execution through a clear glass window, and across the room fourteen members of the victim's family witnessed the execution from behind the one-way mirrored window. DeLozier was asked if he had any last words but he declined to speak, and Warden Sirmons then announce, "Let the execution begin." The executioners first flushed the two tubes leading to his arms with a saline solution and then emptied their syringes into one of the tubes leading to his arm: first sodium thiopental, a strong sedative; second pancuronium bromide to stop his respiration; and finally potassium chloride to stop his heart. As he felt the drugs DeLozier nodded to his witnesses and then laid his head back on the gurney, his breath hitched once, and the color drained from his face. At 6:10 P.M. all sign of life was absent and he was pronounced dead.

Sources: *DeLozier v. Oklahoma*: 528 U.S. 1023 (1999). *DeLozier v. Sirmons*: 531 F.3d 1306 (2008). *DeLozier v. State*: 991 P.2d 22 (1998); PC 98–517 (1999). McCurtain County case: 95–150; 95–258. *Tulsa World* (OK): April 29, 2009; May 14, 2009; July 10, 2009.

Young, Julius R.
January 14, 2010

Forty-four-year-old Julius Ricardo Young, a former Boynton preacher, had an intimate relationship with twenty-year-old Joyland Morgan, and he had a key to her apartment at 115 East 16th Street in Tulsa, Oklahoma, where she lived with her six-year-old son Kewan. On September 30, 1993, Morgan told Young she wanted to end their relationship and asked him to return the key to her apartment, but he refused. Each night Joyland locked two locks on her front door and attached a security chain, but at about 3:30 A.M. the next day, October 1, Young used his key to open both locks and broke through the security chain, and Morgan heard the commotion and confronted him in the living room. Young attacked Joyland with a baseball bat, and she was struck thirteen heavy blows to her face and head, which broke her jaw, tore open her scalp, and fractured her skull, killing her as she collapsed against the living room wall. The intruder then went into the bedroom where Kewan lay asleep and struck two heavy blows to his head, crushing his skull and killing him. Young stopped to pickup the security chain from the door and took along the murder weapon.

That morning Young arrived early at the home of Morgan's mother, about 4:15 A.M., because he drove Joyslon Edwards to work, and when she asked him for change for the vending machines she saw a piece of the security chain among the change in his pocket. After the bodies were discovered the police were called, and Edwards was among the first to be interviewed. She reported seeing the chain in Young's pocket and described her daughter's security measures. She told the police that she had seen a baseball bat in the trunk of Young's car the night before her daughter and grandson were murdered, but the day afterward it was gone, and the murder weapon was never found. A search warrant was issued for Young's residence, his mother's home, and a spot of blood was found on his shoes that tested positive for human blood consistent with the Morgans. They also found a shirt that had been recently washed, but it still tested positive for blood when exposed to luminal.

On February 22, 1994, Young was charged with two counts of murder and one count of burglary, and on May 5 the prosecution announced they would seek the death penalty. A motion for a psychological evaluation was entered on June 17, 1994, but Young was found sane, and his trial began on September 5, 1995. On September 20 Young was convicted on all counts, and on October 16 he was twice sentenced to die by lethal injection and to serve a fifty-year prison term for the burglary; he was delivered to his death row cell the same day.

His attorneys filed an appeal but on November 6, 1998, the Oklahoma Court of Criminal Appeals affirmed the judgment and sentence of the district court and denied post-conviction relief in 1999. The U.S. Supreme Court denied certiorari on October 4, 1999. When all state judicial relief was exhausted his attorney filed a petition for a writ of habeas corpus, but the federal Tenth Circuit Court of Appeals denied the petition in 2008. On October 5, 2009, the U.S. Supreme Court denied Young's final appeal. State Attorney General Drew Edmondson asked the Court of Criminal Appeals to set the date for his execution, and on October 21 the justices set the date for Thursday, January 14, 2010. The state Board of Pardons and Parole met on December 8, 2009, and Young told them, "I cannot confess to something I did not do." The members voted four to one to deny clemency, and Governor Brad Henry followed their recommendation.

On the morning of his execution Young was moved from his death row cell to a holding cell in H Unit near the injection room. At 6:00 P.M. the condemned man was escorted into the death chamber where he took his place on the gurney and was strapped down. His arms were strapped to arm extensions and a sheet was pulled over his body. A medical technician carefully inserted one intravenous cannula (IV) into the vein of each arm while the executioners were hidden from view behind a one-way mirrored window. Warden Marty Sirmons confirmed by telephone with Governor Henry that the execution was to proceed, and then the accordion blinds were raised on the windows to the witness rooms, where the sixteen members of the Morgan family sat behind a one-way mirrored window, and across the room behind a clear glass window sat Young's family. Young was asked if he had any last words and he said, "I am an innocent man. This is a miscarriage of justice. I didn't take the lives of Joyland Morgan and her son Kewan. My attorney failed me. It's a tragedy. I'm an innocent man. To my family, I love you all." Warden Sirmons then announced, "Let the execution begin." The executioners first flushed the two tubes leading to his arms with a saline solution and then emptied their syringes into the tube leading to his left arm: first sodium thiopental, a strong sedative; second pancuronium bromide to stop his respiration; and finally potassium chloride to stop his heart. The drugs began to flow at 6:21 P.M., and he took several gasps of air before he lapsed into unconsciousness; at 6:27 P.M. all sign of life was absent and he was pronounced dead.

Sources: *Norman Transcript* (OK): December 8, 2009. Tulsa County case: 94–937. *Tulsa World* (OK): October 21, 2009; January 15, 2010. *Young v. Sirmons*: 551 F.3d 942 (2008). *Young v. State*: 992 P.2d 332 (1998). *Young v. Oklahoma*: 528 U.S. 837 (1999).

Wackerly, Donald R., II
October 14, 2010

On the evening of September 6, 1996, Donald Ray Wackerly II told his wife Michelle that they needed money and he was going to do whatever it took to get it. He wore gloves as he loaded his .22-caliber rifle, careful to wipe any fingerprints from the shell casings. The next morning the couple left their Muldrow apartment and began searching for someone to rob, and they drove to the remote area of Lock and Dam 14 on the Arkansas River near Muldrow in Sequoyah County, Oklahoma. They spotted a lone pickup truck parked near the levy, and Wackerly parked his jeep nearby, then had Michelle walk down to the water's edge to confirm that the fisherman was alone. She returned in a few minutes and said he was alone, so they waited.

Forty-five minutes later fifty-five-year-old Pan Sayakhoummane, a Laotian immigrant, walked back to his truck, his hands filled with his fishing gear, and Wackerly raised the hood of his jeep and asked Sayakhoummane for a jump-start. Michelle hid behind their jeep as her husband shot Sayakhoummane eight times in the face and chest, and she heard him fall to the ground. Wackerly then began gathering up all the fishing gear and other valuables. He put Sayakhoummane's body into the bed of his pickup truck, and Michelle saw he was still breathing. Wackerly drove Sayakhoummane's truck down a dirt road and stopped, while his wife followed in their jeep. Wackerly removed the reels from the rods and threw away the rods, went through the truck and Sayakhoummane's pockets, and put the tackle box in the jeep. He drove the truck into the river but the bumper caught on the embankment and the truck was only partly submerged.

The couple drove to a nearby Sonic Drive-in Restaurant and, using their new found wealth, bought dinner. That night Wackerly went through Sayakhoummane's belongings and destroyed and disposed of any identification cards, then stored the other property in a spare room, and several weeks later he sold the reels to Rocky's Pawn Shop in Roland for $60. On September 8 a passerby saw the truck and found Sayakhoummane's body, and he called the police. At the autopsy it was determined he had died of the gunshot wounds before entering the water.

On September 16 Wackerly, wearing a mask and wielding a pistol, robbed a convenience store in Webber Falls, Oklahoma, after forcing his wife to stand watch outside. He demanded money, and when the clerk refused he placed the barrel of his pistol inches from the clerk's forehead and gave the same order, and the clerk cleaned out the register and handed the cash to Wackerly. As he was leaving the store Wackerly heard a noise at the back of the store and, thinking it was another employee, turned and pointed the pistol at the clerk. He said, "I'll kill both of you," then ran out without shooting anyone.

Meanwhile the police were making little progress in the murder case, but after the robbery the Wackerlys separated, and in December Michelle went to the police and told them the details of the murder. Investigators found the fishing poles where they had been discarded, and they also found the reels at the pawn shop where the owner identified Wackerly as the man who sold them. They obtained a warrant to search Wackerly's residence and found Sayakhoummane's tackle box, latex gloves, the .22-caliber rifle, and a box of ammunition with bullets missing. Ballistics testing proved the rifle and bullets consistent with those used to kill Sayakhoummane. Wackerly was arrested and charged with one count of murder and robbery, and Michelle Wackerly was granted immunity for her testimony against her husband.

Wackerly was tried in May 1998, and on May 11 he was convicted of murder and robbery and sentenced to life imprisonment for "robbery with a deadly weapon" and to death by lethal injection for first degree murder, and he arrived at his death row cell on May 18. His attorneys filed an appeal but the state Court of Criminal Appeals affirmed the judgment and sentence in 2000 and denied post-conviction relief. After all state judicial remedies were exhausted his attorneys filed a petition for a writ of habeas corpus, but the federal Tenth Circuit Court of Appeals denied the petition in 2009. After the U.S. Supreme Court denied Wackerly's final appeal the state's Attorney General Drew Edmondson, on June 7, 2010, asked the Court of Criminal Appeals to set a date for his execution, and on August 12 the justices set the date at October 14, 2010. Wackerly had joined with another prisoner to appeal the use of a substitute for sodium thiopental, but the federal court ruled that pentobarbital was acceptable in the three-drug combination.

In 2007 Wackerly converted to the Buddhist religion, and several monks tended to his spiritual needs. On the morning of his execution the prisoner was moved from his death row cell to a holding cell in H Unit near the injection room. At 6:00 P.M. the condemned man was escorted into the death chamber where he took his place on the gurney and was strapped down. His arms were strapped to arm extensions and a sheet was pulled over his body. A medical technician carefully inserted one intravenous cannula (IV) into the vein of each arm while the executioners were hidden from view behind a one-way mirrored window. Warden Randy Workman confirmed by telephone with Governor Henry that the execution was to proceed, and then the accordion blinds were raised on the windows to the witness rooms, where the witnesses for the victim sat behind a one-way mirrored glass and across the room behind a clear glass window sat the condemned man's witnesses.

Warden Workman asked Wackerly if he wanted to make a final statement. His last words were a Buddhist mantra of compassion, "Om mani padme hum," and two monks and his attorneys joined him. They were still chanting when the warden announced, "Let the execution begin." The executioners first flushed the two tubes leading to his arms with a saline solution and then emptied their syringes into the tube leading to his left arm: first pentobarbital, a strong sedative; second pancuronium bromide to stop his respiration; and finally potassium chloride to stop his heart. The drugs began to flow at 6:06 P.M., and Wackerly exhaled deeply, and then lay still. At 6:12 P.M. all sign of life was absent and he was pronounced dead. Immediately following the execution the Buddhist monks were allowed access to the body, as agreed during the previous week.

Sources: *Fort Smith Times-Record* (AR): October 15, 2010. Sequoyah County case: 96–349. *Sequoyah County Times* (OK): October 15, 2010. *Tulsa World* (OK): August 12, 2010; October 15, 2010. *Wackerly v. State*: 12 P.3d 1 (2000). *Wackerly v. Workman*: 580 F.3d 1171 (2009).

Duty, John D.
December 16, 2010

In early 1978 twenty-six-year-old John David Duty was living in Altus, Jackson County, Oklahoma, when he decided to rob a convenience store. He took the female clerk prisoner at gunpoint, found $7.66 in the cash register, and took some beer. He kidnapped the clerk and drove her to a remote location in Tillman County where he raped her, hit her in the head with a metal pipe, and then shot her in the head three times. Duty left her for dead but she regained consciousness and managed to walk some distance to a house and ask for help. She survived and testified against Duty, and on July 18, 1978, he was convicted in Tillman County of rape and shooting-with-intent-to-kill and sentenced to serve two concurrent life terms. In Jackson County he was convicted of robbery-with-a-firearm and kidnapping, and he was sentenced to serve a third concurrent life term as well as twenty years for kidnapping.

After Duty arrived at the prison in August 1978

he proved to be a dangerous prisoner and several times took hostages. In 1979 he was charged with assault-with-a-dangerous-weapon, and on April 18, 1980, he was sentenced to serve a concurrent five-year term in prison. In 1986 Duty had been transferred to the Dick Conner Correctional Center in Hominy, Oklahoma, which had opened in 1979 as a minimum security facility. He escaped but was soon captured, returned to prison, and on February 27, 1987, he was convicted of escaping from a penal institution and sentenced to serve a two-year prison term concurrent with his other sentences.

On Friday, December 14, 2001, twenty-two-year-old Curtis J. Wise, Jr., had been convicted in Grady County of burglarizing an automobile and on March 31, 1999, he was sentenced to serve five years, and was moved into a cell with Duty. On the evening of December 19 Duty convinced Wise to let him tie his ankles and his wrists behind his back using bed sheets and pretend to be his hostage in exchange for cigarettes, which Duty would obtain while in administrative segregation. After Wise was bound with bed sheets Duty used a shoe lace to strangle him to death. He then wrote a letter to Wise's mother saying, "Mary Wise. Well, by the time you get this letter you will already know that your son is dead. I know now because I just killed him an hour ago. Gee, you'd think I'd be feeling some remorse, but I'm not. I've been planning since the day he moved in last Friday. Tonight I finally pulled it off.... Its not like the movies, it took a while. But I really did him a favor as he was too stupid to live.... I've been in 24 years, wish someone would have done me the same favor back then.... Well I'll close for now, and I'll tell the police in the morning about Curtis." Curtis' body was discovered the next morning, the letter was confiscated, and Duty confessed to murdering his cellmate.

Following competency evaluations at the Carl Albert Community Mental Health Center and the Eastern State Hospital, Duty was declared competent, and he appeared at his October 28, 2002, hearing before District Court Judge Steven Taylor. Mary Wise was one of the two witnesses who had been called during the hearing, and she begged for Duty to be given a life without parole sentence, telling the judge he should not have the choice and, "I think he ought to sit in that cell and face those walls and think about what he did for the rest of his natural-born life. And I pray to God that you live to be 110 years old...." However, Duty had demanded a death penalty in a plea deal and at his hearing he waived presentation of mitigating factors, and Judge Taylor sentenced him to die by lethal injection. His attorneys, at his insistence, did not file a motion to withdraw his plea so he was entitled only to the mandatory review provided in death penalty cases, and in 2004 the Oklahoma Court of Criminal Appeals affirmed the sentence.

As the months passed Duty decided to fight the death penalty and had his attorneys file a petition for a writ of habeas corpus on January 13, 2005, then stopped the appeal on April 25, and on July 7 he had another competency hearing. When he was found competent again the petition for the writ was renewed, but denied first in the district court in 2007, and in early 2010 the federal Tenth Circuit Court of Appeals denied the petition. Duty then joined with two other death row prisoners in appealing the substitution of pentobarbital for sodium thiopental as the first drug in the three-drug combination, but on October 4, 2010, the U.S. Supreme Court denied his appeal and found pentobarbital a proper substitute. The state's Attorney General Drew Edmondson asked the Court of Criminal Appeals to set a date for Duty's execution, and the justices set the date at December 16, 2010.

On the morning of his execution Duty was moved from his death row cell to a holding cell in H Unit near the injection room. After his final meal he was visited by the prison chaplain, who had attended to his spiritual needs while on death row, and his family and attorneys, and they were taken to the witness room before 6:00 P.M. The condemned man was then escorted into the death chamber where he took his place on the gurney and was strapped down. His arms were strapped to arm extensions and a sheet was pulled over his body. A medical technician carefully inserted one intravenous cannula (IV) into the vein of each arm while the executioners were hidden from view behind a one-way mirrored window. Warden Randy Workman confirmed by telephone with Governor Henry that the execution was to proceed, and then the accordion blinds were raised on the windows to the witness rooms, but none of the Wise family members were present behind the one-way mirrored glass. Across the room behind a clear glass window sat Duty's witnesses, including three media representatives, three attorneys from his defense team, and his brother and sister-in-law.

Duty was asked if he had any last words and he said, "Um, yes! To the family of Curtis Wise, I'd like to make my apology. I hope one day you'll be able to forgive me, not for my sake but for your own. My family and friends are here, too. Thank you. You've all been a blessing. Thank you, Lord Jesus. I'm ready to go home," and he repeated "Thank you, Lord!" several times as the execution began. As soon as Duty concluded his remarks to the witnesses the execution director announced, "Let the execution begin." The executioners first flushed the two tubes leading to his arms with a saline solution and then emptied their syringes into the tube leading to his left arm: first five grams of pentobarbital, a strong sedative; second pancuronium bromide to stop his respiration; and finally potassium chloride to stop his heart. The drugs began to enter his system at 6:12 P.M., and in one minute his breathing became labored. At 6:15 he stopped breathing and the color drained from his face. At 6:18 P.M. all sign of life was absent and he was pronounced dead.

Sources: *Duty v. State*: 89 P.3d 1158 (2004). *Duty v. Workman*: 366 Fed. Appx. 863 (2010). Grady County case: CRF 99–177. Jackson County case: CRF 78–75; 78–76. Osage County case: CRF 86–118. Pittsburg County case: CRF 79–278; CRF 2002–243. Tillman County case: CRF 78–12; 78–13. *Tulsa World* (OK): December 17, 2010.

Bibliography

Books, Magazines, Reports, and Web Sites

Adjutant General's Report, 1885. List of U.S. Soldiers Executed by United States Military Authorities during the Late War.

Alotta, Robert I. *Civil War Justice: Union Army Executions Under Lincoln.* Shippensburg, PA: White Mane, 1989.

Andreas' History of the State of Nebraska; Douglas Co., Omaha; Section 4.

Andreas' History of the State of Nebraska; Otoe Co.; Part 5.

Bang, Roy T. *Heroes Without Medals: A Pioneer History of Kearney County Nebraska.* Minden, NE: Warp, 1952.

Dale, Edward E., and Gaston Litton. *Cherokee Cavaliers.* Norman: University of Oklahoma Press, 1939.

Fort Worth Historical Society. "German POW Execution." www.ftlvnhistsoc.org/German_POW_execu tion.htm.

Gray, P. L. *Gray's Doniphan County History: A Record of the Happenings of Half a Hundred Years.* Bendena, KS: The Roycroft Press, 1905.

Haddock, Hugh V. *Daring Detective Magazine,* November 1942, 40–45.

Johnson, Edward C., Gail R. Johnson and Melissa Johnson Williams. *All Were Not Heroes: A Study of U.S. Soldiers Executed by U.S. Military Authorities During the Late War.* Chicago, IL: E. C. Johnson, 1997.

Master Detective Magazine, September 1941.

Payne, John H. *Indian Justice: A Cherokee Murder Trial at Tahlequah in 1840.* Norman: University of Oklahoma Press, 2002.

Ressler, Robert K., and Tom Shachtman. *Whoever Fights Monsters: My Twenty Years Hunting Serial Killers for the FBI.* New York: St. Martin's, 1992.

RG 153: Records of the Judge Advocate General's Office, Entry 15: Court-Martial Case Files (Army), 1809–1894; 7E3:14/5/02; Box # 1514; File # NN-105.

Sorenson, Alfred. *History of Omaha from the Pioneer Days to the Present Time.* Omaha, NE: Gibson, Miller & Richardson, printers, 1889.

Walker, William. *Journal of William Walker.* Lincoln: Nebraska State Historical Society, 1899.

Court Cases

Allen v. Massie: 202 F.3d 281 (2000); 121 S. Ct. 244 (2000); 121 S. Ct. 616 (2000); 236 F.3d 1243 (2001).

Allen v. Oklahoma: 513 U.S. 952 (1994).

Allen v. Oklahoma Pardon and Parole Board: 121 S. Ct. 848 (2001). *Allen v. State*: 871 P.2d 79 (1994); 909 P.2d 836 (1995).

Al-Mosawi v. Gibson: 242 F.3d 387 (2000).

Al-Mosawi v. State: 929 P.2d 270 (1996); 956 P.2d 906 (1998).

Beckham County case CRF 93-61.

Berget v. Gibson: 98-6381.

Berget v. State: 824 P.2d 364 (1991).

Binyon v. United States: 1903 IT 15; 76 S. W. 265.

Bland v. Oklahoma: 531 U.S. 1099 (2001).

Bland v. Sirmons: 459 F.3d 999 (2006).

Bland v. State: 4 P.3d 702 (2000); PCD 99-1200 (2000).

Boltz v. Mullin: 415 F.3d 1215 (2005).

Boltz v. State: 806 P.2d 1117 (1991).

Boyd v. State: 839 P.2d 1363 (1992); 915 P.2d 922 (1996).

Boyd v. Ward: 179 F.3d 904 (1999).

Braun v. Oklahoma: 909 P.2d 783 (1995); 937 P.2d 505 (1997).

Braun v. Ward: 190 F.3d 1181 (1999).

Brecheen v. Oklahoma: 485 U.S. 909 (1988).

Brecheen v. Reynolds: 41 F.3d 1343 (1994).

Brecheen v. State: 732 P.2d 899 (1988); 835 P.2d 117 (1992).

Brewer v. Reynolds: 51 F.3d 1519 (1995); 83 F. 3d 431 (1996).

Brewer v. State: 650 P.2d 54 (1982); 718 P.2d 354 (1986).

Brown v. Gibson: 7 Fed. Appx. 894 (2001); 122 S. Ct. 650 (2001).

Brown v. Sirmons: 415 F. Supp. 2d 1268 (2006).

Brown v. Oklahoma: 115 S. Ct. 517 (1994).

Brown v. State: 871 P.2d 56 (1994); 933 P.2d 316 (1997).

Brown v. State: 989 P.2d 913 (1998); F 97-493 (1999); PC 98-1251 (1999).

Bryan v. Mullin: 276 F.3d 1163 (2001); 335 F.3d 1207 (2003).

Bryan v. Oklahoma: 522 U.S. 957 (1997).

Bryan v. State: 935 P.2d 338 (1997); 948 P.2d 1230 (1997).

Bryson v. Oklahoma: 513 U.S. 1090 (1995); 517 U.S. 1144 (1996).

Bryson v. State: 876 P.2d 240 (1994); 903 P.2d 333 (1995).
Bryson v. Ward: 187 F.3d 1193 (1999).
Canadian County cases CRF 79–302, 303, 304, 305; 90–89.
Cannon v. Gibson: 259 F.3d 1253 (2001).
Cannon v. State: 827 P.2d 1339 (1992); 904 P.2d 89 (1995); 933 P.2d 926 (1997).
Carter County cases CRF 83–127; 89–332.
Carter v. State: 879 P.2d 1234 (1994).
Castro v. Oklahoma: 485 U.S. 978 (1988); 114 S. Ct. 135 (1993).
Castro v. Reynolds: 71 F.3d 1502 (1995).
Castro v. State: 745 P.2d 394 (1987); 749 P.2d 1146 (1987); 844 P.2d 159 (1992); 880 P.2d 387 (1994).
Charm v. Oklahoma: 520 U.S. 1200 (1997).
Charm v. State: 924 P.2d 754 (1996); 953 P.2d 47 (1998).
Clayton v. Gibson: 199 F.3d 1162 (1999).
Clayton v. Oklahoma: 507 U.S. 1008 (1993).
Clayton v. State: 840 P.2d 18 (1992); 892 P.2d 646 (1995).
Cleary v. Mullin: F-92-1234 (1995); 62 Fed. Appx. 243 (2003); 124 S. Ct 825 (2003).
Cleary v. Oklahoma: 118 S. Ct 1528 (1998).
Cleary v. State: 942 P.2d 736 (1997).
Cleveland County cases CRF 94–1024; 94–1125; 96–245, 96–247, 96–256; 97–247.
Coal County Case CRF 94–32.
Coleman v. Brown: 753 F.2d 832 (1985).
Coleman v. Oklahoma: 464 U.S. 1073 (1984).
Coleman v. State: 668 P.2d 1126 (1983); 693 P.2d 4 (1984).
Comanche County cases CRF 79–372; 82–812; 85–365; 89–76; 91–386; 93–241; 93–259; 94–499.
Cooks v. Oklahoma: 474 U.S. 935 (1985); 510 U.S. 851 (1993).
Cooks v. State: 699 P.2d 653, 656 (1985); PC 86–613 (1987); PC 89–131 (1993).
Cooks v. Ward: 165 F.3d 1283 (1998).
Creek County cases CRF 87–240; 88–30; 94–324.
Cummings v. Sirmons: 506 F.3d 1211 (2007).
Cummings v. State: 968 P.2d 821; 970 P.2d 188.
Darks v. Mullin: 327 F.3d 1001 (2003); 124 S. Ct. 433 (2003).
Darks v. State: 954 P.2d 152 (1998); 954 P.2d 169 (1998).
Darks v. Ward: 116 F.3d 489 (1997).
DeLozier v. Oklahoma: 528 U.S. 1023 (1999).
DeLozier v. Sirmons: 531 F.3d 1306 (2008).
DeLozier v. State: 991 P.2d 22 (1998); PC 98–517 (1999).
Duckett v. Mullin: 306 F.3d 982 (2002).
Duckett v. State: 711 P.2d 944 (1985); 919 P.2d 7 (1995); 922 P.2d 631 (1996).
Duty v. State: 89 P.3d 1158 (2004).
Duty v. Workman: 366 Fed. Appx. 863 (2010).
Duvall v. Oklahoma: 506 U.S. 878 (1992).
Duvall v. Reynolds: 139 F.3d 768 (1998).
Duvall v. State: 825 P.2d 621 (1991); 869 P.2d 332 (1994); 871 P.2d 1386 (1994).
Fields v. Gibson: 277 F.3d 1203 (2002).
Fields v. State: 923 P.2d 624 (1996); 946 P.2d 266 (1997).
Fluke v. State: 14 P.2d 29 (1998).
Foster v. Oklahoma: 479 U.S. 873 (1986); 488 U.S. 884 (1988); 497 U.S. 1032 (1990).
Foster v. State: 714 P.2d 1031 (1986); PC 87–729 (1988); 779 P.2d 591 (1989); PC 93–1020 (1995).
Foster v. Ward: 182 F.3d 1177 (1999); 200 F.3d 1302 (2000).
Fowler v. State: 779 P.2d 580 (1989); 873 P.2d 1053 (1994); 896 P.2d 566 (1995).
Fox v. State: 779 P.2d 562 (1989); 880 P.2d 383 (1994).
Fox v. Ward: 200 F.3d 1286 (2000).
General Order No. 55, Headquarters 2d Kansas Cavalry: July 9, 1862. Court-Martial case file KK-151.
Gilbert v. Mullin: 3021 F.3d 1166 (2002).
Gilbert v. State: 951 P.2d 98 (1997); 955 P.2d 727 (1998).
Gilson v. Sirmons: 520 F.3d 1196 (2008).
Gilson v. State: 8 P.3d 883 (2000).
Grady County cases CRF 88–45; 96–240; 97–59; 99–177.
Greer County case CRF 95–3.
Hain v. Gibson: 01–5014 (2002).
Hain v. Mullin: 327 F.3d 1177 (2003).
Hain v. State: 852 P.2d 744 (1993); 919 P.2d 1130 (1996); 962 P.2d 649 (1998).
Hale v. Gibson: 227 F.3d 1298 (2000); 121 S. Ct. 2608 (2001).
Hale v. Oklahoma: 109 S. Ct. 195 (1988); 112 S. Ct. 280 (1991).
Hale v. State: 750 P.2d 130 (1988); 807 P.2d 264 (1991); 934 P.2d 1100 (1997).
Hale v. U.S. Dept. of Justice: 973 F. 2d 894 (1992); 2 F.3d 1055 (1993); 99 F.3d 1025 (1996); 113 S. Ct. 3029 (1993); 226 F.3d 1200 (2000); 122 S. Ct. 18 (2001).
Hamilton v. Mullin: 436 F.3d 1181 (2006).
Hamilton v. Oklahoma: 522 U.S. 1059 (1998).
Hamilton v. State: 937 P.2d 1001 (1997).
Harjo v. State: 882 P.2d 1067 (1994).
Hatch v. Oklahoma: 116 S. Ct. 1881 (1996).
Hatch v. Reynolds: 76 F.3d 392 (1996).
Hatch v. State: 835 P.2d 880 (1992); 58 F.3d 1447 (1995); 92 F.3d 1012 (1996).
Hawkins v. Mullin: 291 F.3d 658 (2002).
Hawkins v. Oklahoma: 516 U.S. 977 (1995).
Hawkins v. State: 891 P.2d 586 (1994).
Hooker v. Mullin: 293 F.3d 1232 (2002).
Hooker v. Oklahoma: 516 U.S. 858 (1995).
Hooker v. State: 887 P.2d 1351 (1994); 934 P.2d 352 (1997).
In Re: Brown: 122 S. Ct. 2652 (2002).
In Re: Hale: 122 S. Ct. 418 (2001).
Jackson County cases CRF 78–75, 76; 87–18.
Jackson v. Oklahoma: 526 U.S. 1008 (1999).
Jackson v. State: 964 P.2d 875 (1998); PC-97–1349.
James v. Gibson: 211 F.3d 543 (2000).
James v. Oklahoma: 484 U.S. 970 (1987).
James v. State: 736 P.2d 541 (1987); 818 P.2d 918 (1991); 14 P.2d 29 (1998).
Johnson v. Gibson: 169 F.3d 1239 (1999); 229 F.3d 1163 (2000).
Johnson v. Oklahoma: 484 U.S. 878 (1987); 519 U.S. 839 (1996).
Johnson v. State: 731 P.2d 993 (1987); 823 P.2d 370 (1991); 911 P.2d 918 (1995); 952 P.2d 1003 (1998).
Jones v. Gibson: 206 F.3d 946 (2000).
Jones v. Oklahoma: 459 U.S. 1155 (1983).

Jones v. State: 648 P.2d 1251 (1982); 704 P.2d 1138 (1985).
Kay County case CRF 83–130.
Knighton v. Gibson: 293 F.3d 1165 (2002).
Knighton v. Oklahoma: 519 U.S. 841 (1996).
Knighton v. State: 912 P.2d 878 (1996).
Lafevers v. Gibson: 182 F.3d 705 (1999); 208 F.3d 226 (2000); 238 F.3d 1263 (2001).
Lafevers v. State: 819 P.2d 1362 (1991); 897 P.2d 292 (1995).
Le v. Mullin: 311 F.3d 1002 (2002).
Le v. State: 947 P.2d 535 (1997); 953 P.2d 52 (1998).
Leflore County case: CRF 91–1, 2.
Lincoln County case CRF 92–156.
Malicoat v. Mullin: 426 F.3d 1241 (2005).
Malicoat v. Oklahoma: 531 U.S. 888 (2000).
Malicoat v. State: 992 P.2d 383 (2000); 137 P.3d 1234 (2006).
Marion v. Nebraska: 16 Neb. 349 (1884); 20 Neb. 233 (1886).
McClain County case 79–83.
McCracken v. Gibson: 268 F.3d 970 (2001).
McCracken v. Oklahoma: 516 U.S. 859 (1995).
McCracken v. State: 887 P.2d 323 (1994); 946 P.2d 672 (1997).
McCurtain County cases CRF 95–150; 95–258.
McElmurry v. State: 60 P.3d 4 (2002).
McIntosh County cases CRF 94–18; 99–153, 154.
Medlock v. Oklahoma: 516 U.S. 918 (1995).
Medlock v. State: 887 P.2d 1333 (1994); 889 P.2d 344 (1995); 927 P.2d 1069 (1996).
Medlock v. Ward: 200 F.3d 1314 (2000).
Miller v. Mullin: 354 F.3d 1288 (2004).
Miller v. State: 977 P.2d 1099 (1998).
Moore v. Oklahoma: 484 U.S. 873, 108 S.Ct. 219 (1987); 502 U.S. 913 (1991).
Moore v. Reynolds: 153 F.3d 1086 (1998).
Moore v. State: 736 P.2d 161 (1987), 809 P.2d 63 (1991).
Muskogee County cases CRF 79–102; 83–64; 87–161.
Neill v. Gibson: 263 F.3d 1184 (2001). Neill v. Oklahoma: 516 U.S. 1080 (1996).
Neill v. State: 896 P.2d 537 (1994); 943 P.2d 145 (1997).
Newsted v. Gibson: 158 F.3d 1085 (1998).
Newsted v. Oklahoma: 479 U.S. 995 (1986); 501 U.S. 1259 (1991). *Newsted v. State*: 720 P.2d 734 (1986); 908 P.2d 1388 (1995).
Nguyen v. Oklahoma: 509 U.S. 908 (1993).
Nguyen v. Reynolds: 131 F.3d 1340 (1997).
Nguyen v. State: 844 P.2d 176 (1992); 879 P.2d 148 (1994).
Noble County case CRF 90–1.
Oklahoma County cases CRF 77–3159; 79–926; 84–500; 84–597; 84–3236; 84–3511 85–3254; 85–3343; 85–6156; 85–6362; 86–218; 86–1231, 1232; 86–1502; 86–1536; 86–3920; 86–4264; 86–4475; 86–4476; 86–4478; 86–4533; 87–254; 87–397; 87–878; 88–677; 88–1939; 88–6248; 88–6621; 89–4791; 90–734; 90–1012; 92–82; 92–6838; 92–7217; 93–1352;94–1312; 94–6070; 94–8859; 95–55; 95–216.
Osage County cases CRF 84–26; 86–118.
Parks v. Oklahoma: 459 U.S. 1155 (1983).
Parks v. Saffle: 925 F. 2d 366 (1991).
Parks v. State: 651 P.2d 686 (1982).
Patton v. Mullin: 425 F.3d 788 (2005).
Patton v. State: 973 P.2d 270 (1998); 989 P.2d 983 (1999).
Payne County cases CRF 90–412; 91–26, 27, 28, 29.
Pennington v. Oklahoma: 519 U.S. 841 (1996).
Pennington v. State: 913 P.2d 1356 (1995).
Pittsburg County cases CRF 79–278; 91–114; 2002–243.
Plantz v. Massie: 216 F.3d 1088 (2000).
Plantz v. Oklahoma: 513 U.S. 1163 (1995).
Plantz v. State: 876 P.2d 268 (1994); 936 P.2d 339 (1997).
Pottawatomie County cases CRF 83–348; 84–97.
Revilla v. Gibson: 283 F.3d 1203 (2002).
Revilla v. Oklahoma: 123 S. Ct 963 (2003).
Revilla v. State: 877 P.2d 1143 (1994); 946 P.2d 262 (1997).
Robedeaux v. Gibson: 99–7954.
Robedeaux v. State: 866 P.2d 417 (1993); 908 P.2d 804 (1995).
Roberts v. Oklahoma: 115 S. Ct. 158 (1994).
Roberts v. State: 868 P.2d 712 (1994); 910 P.2d 1071 (1996).
Robinson v. Gibson (unpub. opinion): 99–6438 (2002).
Robison v. Maynard: 829 F.2d 1501 (1987).
Robinson v. State: 677 P.2d 1085 (1984); 900 P.2d 389 (1995); 937 P.2d 101 (1997).
Roger Mills County case 83–27.
Rogers County case CRF-84–108.
Rogers v. Gibson: 173 F.3d 1278 (1999).
Rogers v. State: 890 P.2d 959 (1995); 934 P.2d 1093 (1997).
Romano v. Gibson: 239 F.3d 1156 (2001).
Romano v. Oklahoma: 512 U.S. 1 (1994).
Romano v. State: 827 P.2d 1335 (1992); 847 P.2d 368 (1993); 909 P.2d 92(1995); 917 P.2d 12 (1996).
Ross v. Oklahoma: 487 U.S. 81 (1988); 513 U.S. 970 (1994).
Ross v. State: 717 P.2d 117 (1986); 872 P.2d 940 (1994); PC-95–294 (1997).
Ross v. Ward: 165 F.3d 793 (1999).
Sallahdin v. Gibson: 275 F.3d 1211 (2002).
Sallahdin v. Mullin: 380 F.3d 1242 (2004).
Sallahdin v. State: 947 P.2d 559 (1997).
Sellers v. State: 809 P.2d 676 (1991); 889 P.2d 895 (1995); 973 P.2d 894 (1999).
Sellers v. Ward: 135 F.3d 1333 (1998).
Seminole County cases CRF 85–116, 88–7.
Sequoyah County cases CRF 82–104; 96–349.
Shelton v. State: 793 P.2d 866 (1990).
Short v. Sirmons: 472 F.3d 1177 (2006).
Short v. State: 980 P.2d 1081 (1999).
Slaughter v. Mullin: 68 Fed. Appx. 141 (2003).
Slaughter v. Oklahoma: 525 U.S. 886 (1998); 541 U.S. 947 (2004). *Slaughter v. State*: 950 P.2d 839 (1997); 969 P.2d 990 (1998); 105 P.2d 832 (2005); 2005 WL 562759 (2005).
Smallwood v. Gibson: 191 F.3d 1257 (1999).
Smallwood v. Oklahoma: 519 U.S. 980 (1996).
Smallwood v. State: 907 P.2d 217 (1995); 937 P.2d 111 (1997).
Smith v. Massie: 235 F.3d 1259 (2000).
Smith v. Oklahoma: 483 U.S. 1033 (1987).
Smith v. State: 727 P.2d 1366 (1986); 766 P.2d 1007 (1988); 915 P.2d 927 (1996).
State (MO) *v. Knighton*: 518 S.W.2d 674 (1975).
Stephens County cases CRF 80–165; 86–251.

Thornburg v. Mullin: 422 F.3d 1133 (2005).
Thornburg v. State: 985 P.2d 1234 (1999); P. C. 99–490 (1999).
Tillman County cases CRF 75–19, 78–12, 13; 96–90.
Toles v. Gibson: 269 F.3d 1167 (2001).
Toles v. Oklahoma: 524 U.S. 958 (1998).
Toles v. State: 947 P.2d 180 (1997).
Trice v. Oklahoma: 510 U.S. 1025 (1993).
Trice v. State: 853 P.2d 203 (1993); 912 P.2d 349 (1996).
Trice v. Ward: 196 F.3d 1151 (1999).
Tulsa County case: CRF 73–0701; 78–2137; 82–1986; 84–2088; 85–2501; 87–4730; 89–18; 90–4347; 91–3404; 91–5395; 92–3584; 94–937; 94–2784; 95–1024; 97–4924.
Turrentine v. Mullin: 390 F.3d 1181 (2004).
Turrentine v. Oklahoma: 525 U.S. 1057 (1998).
Turrentine v. State: 965 P.2d 955 (1998); 965 P.2d 985 (1998).
U.S. Army Court Martial Case #264081.
U.S. v. Alford: 400 U.S. 25 (1970).
Van Woundenberg v. Gibson: 98–7167 (2000).
Van Woundenberg v. Oklahoma: 479 U.S. 956 (1986); 484 U.S. 1036 (1988); 503 U.S. 993 (1992).
Van Woundenberg v. State: 720 P.2d 328 (1986); PC-87–633 (1987); 818 P.2d 913 (1991); 942 P.2d 224 (1997).
Wackerly v. State: 12 P.3d 1 (2000).
Wackerly v. Workman: 580 F.3d 1171 (2009).
Walker v. Gibson: 228 F.3d 1217 (2000); 521 S. Ct 2560 (2001).
Walker v. Jones: 10 F.3d 1569 (1994).
Walker v. Oklahoma: 516 S. Ct. 166 (1995); 117 S. Ct. 2524 (1997).
Walker v. State: 723 P.2d 273 (1986); 795 P.2d 1064 (1990); 826 P.2d 1002 (1992); 887 P.2d 301 (1994); 933 P.2d 327 (1997); 940 P.2d 509 (1997).
Walker v. Ward: 934 F. Supp. 1286 (1996); 167 F.3d 1339 (1999).
Wallace v. Oklahoma: 516 U.S. 888 (1995); 521 U.S. 1108 (1997). *Wallace v. State*: 893 P.2d 504 (1995); 935 P.2d 366 (1997).
Wallace v. Ward: 191 F.3d 1235 (1999).
Welch v. Oklahoma: 531 U.S. 1056 (2000).
Welch v. Sirmons: 451 F.3d 675 (2006).
Welch v. State: 2 P.3d 356 (2000); PCD 2000–86 (2000).
Willingham v. Mullin: 296 F.3d 917 (2002).
Willingham v. State: 947 P.2d 1074 (1997); PC 97–389 (1998).
Woodruff v. Oklahoma: 114 S. Ct. 349 (1993); 510 U.S. 934 (1993). *Woodruff v. State*: 825 P.2d 273 (1992); 846 P.2d 1124 (1993); 910 P.2d 348 (1996).
Workman v. Mullin: 342 F.3d 1100 (2003).
Workman v. State: 824 P.2d 378 (1991).
Young v. Oklahoma: 528 U.S. 837 (1999).
Young v. Sirmons: 551 F.3d 942 (2008).
Young v. State: 992 P.2d 332 (1998).

Newspapers

Abilene Reporter-News (TX)
Ada Evening News (OK)
Ada Weekly News (OK)
Advocate (Newark, NJ)
Advocate (San Francisco, CA)
Advocate (Victoria, TX)
Alaska Citizen (Fairbanks)
Albuquerque Journal (NM)
Albuquerque Tribune (NM)
Alton Evening Telegraph (IL)
Altoona Mirror (PA)
Amarillo Globe (TX)
Anniston Star (AL)
Appleton Post-Crescent (WI)
Ardmoreite (OK)
Arizona Republican (Phoenix)
Arizona Silver Belt (Globe)
Arkansas Gazette (Little Rock)
Atchison Daily Champion (KS)
Atchison Daily Globe (KS)
Baytown Sun (TX)
Beacon (Wichita, KS)
Beatrice Express (NE)
Beatrice Republican (NE)
Beatrice Sun (NE)
Bee (Danville, VA)
Belleville Telescope (KS)
Big Springs Herald (TX)
Billings Gazette (MT)
Border Sentinel (Mound City, KS)
Brainerd Daily Dispatch (MN)
Brownsville Herald (TX)
Brownwood Bulletin (TX)
Burlington Times-News (NC)
Capital News (Jefferson City, MO)
Cedar Rapids Gazette (IA)
Cedar Rapids Tribune (WI)
Charleston Daily Mail (SC)
Charleston Gazette (SC)
Checotah Times (OK)
Cherokee Advocate (Tahlequah, I.T.)
Chester Times (PA)
Chicago Evening American (IL)
Chicago Tribune (IL)
Chickasha Express-Star (OK)
Chillicothe Constitution (MO)
Chillicothe Constitution-Tribune (MO)
Chronicle-Telegram (Elyria, OH)
Circleville Herald (OH)
Citizen (Iowa City, IA)
Columbus Daily Telegram (NE)
Columbus Enquirer (KS)
Conservative (Leavenworth, KS)
Corpus Christi Caller Times (TX)
Corpus Christi Times (TX)
Corsicana Sun (TX)
Council Bluffs Nonpareil (IA)
Courier (Connellsville, PA)
Courier and Reporter (Waterloo, IA)
Cumberland Evening Times (MD)
Dallas Morning News (TX)
Davenport Leader (IA)

Dayton News (OH)
Decatur Republican (IL)
Del Rio News-Herald (TX)
Democrat Times (MS)
Denton Record Chronicle (TX)
Denver Post (CO)
Dubuque Herald (IA)
Duluth News Tribune (MN)
Edgefield Advertiser (SC)
El Paso Herald-Post (TX)
Elgin Echo (IA)
Emporia Gazette (KS)
Emporia News (KS)
Eufaula Democrat (OK)
Evening Gazette (Cedar Rapids, IA)
Evening Journal (Lubbock, TX)
Evening News (Lincoln, NE)
Evening Standard (Ogden, UT)
Evening Times (Monroe, WI)
Fitchburg Sentinel (MA)
Fort Gibson Gazette (OK)
Fort Gibson Post (I.T.)
Fort Smith Times-Record (AR)
Fort Wayne Gazette (IN)
Fort Wayne News (IN)
Fresno Bee (CA)
Galveston News (TX)
Galveston Times (TX)
Garden City Telegram (KS)
Gazette (Janesville, WI)
Globe Gazette (Mason City, IA)
Great Bend Daily Tribune (KS)
Greeley Tribune (CO)
Guymon Herald (OK)
Hammond Times (IN)
Haskell News (OK)
Hawarden Independent (IA)
Hawk-eye (Burlington, IA)
Hays News (KS)
Hearne Democrat (TX)
Herald (Tyrone, PA)
Herald (Utah County, UT)
Herald-Post (El Paso, TX)
High Point Enterprise (NC)
Holdenville Times (OK)
Holland Evening Sentinel (MI)
Hope Star (AK)
Huronite (Huron, SD)
Huronite (Dakota Territory)
Hutchinson News (KS)
Hutchinson News-Herald (KS)
Independent (Helena, MT)
Independent-Record (Helena, MT)
Independent (Long Beach, CA)
Indian Journal (Eufaula, OK)
Indian Journal (Muskogee, I.T.)
Indiana Democrat (PA)
Indiana Gazette (PA)
Indiana Progress (PA)
Iola Register (KS)
Iowa State Reporter (Waterloo)
Janesville Gazette (WI)
Jefferson City Post-Tribune (MO)
Joplin Globe (MO)
Joplin News Herald (MO)
Journal (Logansport, IN)
Journal (Salinas, KS)
Journal Gazette (Matoon, IL)
Journal of Commerce (Kansas City, MO)
Journal-Times (Racine, WI)
Journal-Tribune (Marysville, OH)
Kane Weekly Blade (PA)
Kansas City Star (MO)
Kansas City Times (KS)
Kansas Patriot (Burlington)
Kansas Tribune (Lawrence)
Kearney County Gazette (NE)
Kokomo Tribune (IN)
Las Vegas Optic (NM)
Lawton Constitution (OK)
Lawton Constitution-Democrat (OK)
Leavenworth Daily Commercial (KS)
Leavenworth Evening Bulletin (KS)
Leavenworth Times (KS)
Leavenworth Times and Conservative (KS)
Lebanon Daily News (PA)
Lethbridge Herald (Alberta, Canada)
Lexington Herald Leader (KY)
Lima News (OH)
Lincoln Evening News (NE)
Lincoln Star (NE)
Lincoln State Journal (NE)
Lincoln Sunday Journal and Star (NE)
Logansport Journal (IN)
Logansport Pharos (IN)
Logansport Pharos-Tribune (IN)
Logansport Press (IN)
Logansport Reporter (IN)
Long Beach Press-Telegram (CA)
Los Angeles Times (CA)
Lowell Sun (MA)
Lubbock Journal (TX)
Madison County Courier (Edwardsville, IL)
Manhattan Express (KS)
Marysville Journal (OH)
Maryville Forum (MO)
Mason City Globe-Gazette (IA)
McAlester News-Capital and Democrat (OK)
Messenger (Canandaigua, NY)
Mexia Daily News (TX)
Mexia Herald (TX)
Mexia Journal (TX)
Miami News-Record (OK)
Miami Record-Herald (OK)
Middleton Argus (NY)
Milwaukee News (WI)
Minnetonka News (MN)
Moberly Monitor (MO)
Moberly Monitor-Index (MO)
Monessen Independent (PA)

Montana Standard (Butte)
Morning Avalanche (Lubbock, TX)
Morning Eagle (Wichita, KS)
Morning Herald (Hagerstown, MD)
Morning Herald (Uniontown, PA)
Muldrow Sun (OK)
Muscatine Journal (IA)
Muskogee County Democrat (OK)
Muskogee Phoenix (I.T.)
Muskogee Pioneer (I.T.)
Muskogee Times-Democrat (OK)
Nashua Reporter (IA)
National Catholic Register
Nebraska State Journal (Lincoln)
Neosho Times (MO)
Neosho Democrat (MO)
Nevada State Journal (Reno)
New Castle News (PA)
New Era (Humeston, IA)
New Orleans Picayune (LA)
New State Tribune (Muskogee, OK)
New York Times (NY)
Newark Daily Advocate (OH)
Newport News (RI)
News (Fredericksburg, MD)
News (Greensburg, IN)
News (Huntingdon, PA)
News-Globe (Amarillo, TX)
News-Herald (Hutchinson, KS)
News-Journal (Mansfield, OH)
News-Palladium (Benton Harbor, MI)
Norman Transcript (OK)
Northwest Arkansas Times (Fayetteville)
Northwestern (Oshkosh, WI)
Oakland Tribune (CA)
Oelwein Register (IA)
Ogden Standard (UT)
Ogden Standard-Examiner (UT)
Oklahoma City Times (OK)
Oklahoman (Oklahoma City)
Omaha Nebraskian
Omaha World (NE)
Orlando Sentinel (FL)
Osceola Record (NE)
Ottawa County Beacon (OK)
Pampa News (TX)
Paris News (TX)
Perry Journal (OK)
Piqua Daily Call (OH)
Pittsburgh Press (PA)
Ponca City News (OK)
Port Arthur News (TX)
Post-Standard (Syracuse, NY)
Post-Tribune (Jefferson City, MO)
Press Telegram (Long Beach, CA)
Progress (Clearfield, PA)
Pryor Times (WA)
Racine Journal-Times (WI)
Record Eagle (Traverse City, MI)
Reno Gazette (NV)
Republic (Mitchell, SD)
Republican (Oscatur, IL)
Republican Compiler (Gettysburg, PA)
Review (Decatur, IL)
Richmond Gazette (OH)
Salina Journal (KS)
Salt Lake Tribune (UT)
San Antonio Evening News (TX)
San Antonio Express (TX)
San Antonio Light (TX)
Sandusky Register (OH)
Savannah Morning News (GA)
Sentinel (Fort Wayne, IN)
Sequoyah County Democrat (OK)
Sequoyah County Times (OK)
Shawnee News-Star (OK)
Sheboygan Press (WI)
Sioux City Journal (IA)
Sitka Sentinel (AK)
Star Gazette (Sallisaw, OK)
Stars and Stripes (U.S. Military)
State Journal (Lawrence, KS)
Statesman (Boise ID)
Statesville Record (NC)
Stillwell Democrat-Journal (OK)
Sun-News (Las Cruces, NM)
Sunday World (Tulsa, OK)
Syracuse Herald (NY)
Syracuse Herald-American (NY)
Syracuse Herald-Journal (NY)
Syracuse Morning Standard (NY)
Tecumseh Countywide News (OK)
Telegram (Columbus, Nebraska)
Times (Kansas City, MO)
Times-News (Burlington, NC)
Tishomingo News (I.T.)
Topeka Leader (KS)
Tri-City Herald (Kennewick, WA)
Tribune (Chillicothe, MO)
Tribune (Lawrence, KS)
Troy Record (NY)
Tucson Daily Citizen (AZ)
Tulsa Tribune (OK)
Tulsa World (OK)
Tyrone Herald (PA)
U.S.A. Today
Union-Bulletin (Walla Walla, WA)
Van Buren Intelligencer (AR)
Victoria Advocate (TX)
Washington Post (D.C.)
Waterloo Courier (IA)
Waterloo Sunday Courier (IA)
Waukesha Freeman (WI)
Western Kansas Press (Great Bend)
Whig (Beaver Dam, WI)
Wichita Times (KS)
Wisconsin (Milwaukee)
Wisconsin Rapids Tribune (WI)
Wisconsin State Journal (Madison)
Xenia Daily Gazette (OH)

Index

www.ingramcontent.com/pod-product-compliance
Ingram Content Group UK Ltd.
Pitfield, Milton Keynes, MK11 3LW, UK
UKHW051929100926
8556IPUK00022B/1451

9 780786 466511